# BIOGRAPHICAL MEMOIRS
# OF FELLOWS
# OF THE ROYAL SOCIETY

VOLUME 25

Royal Society of London

# BIOGRAPHICAL MEMOIRS OF FELLOWS OF THE ROYAL SOCIETY

1979
VOLUME 25

Published by The Royal Society
6 Carlton House Terrace
London SW1Y 5AG

Published November 1979

PRINTED BY

JOHN WRIGHT & SONS LTD

BRISTOL, ENGLAND

ISBN 0 85403 119 7

# CONTENTS



A photograph of the subject is printed with each memoir

# EDGAR DOUGLAS ADRIAN, BARON ADRIAN OF CAMBRIDGE

30 November 1889 — 4 August 1977

Elected F.R.S. 1923

By Sir Alan Hodgkin, O.M., F.R.S.

Contents

## I. Ancestry and family

On his father's side E. D. Adrian was descended from a Huguenot refugee, Richard Adrian, who fled to England from France or Flanders after the massacre of St Bartholomew in 1572. There had been Adrians living in England since the thirteenth century and it seems possible that Richard Adrian was attracted to England for that reason. This suggestion was made by E. D. Adrian's father, Alfred Douglas Adrian, in a private history written for his family. The genealogical tree reproduced on the opposite page summarizes what is known about E. D. Adrian's ancestry on the paternal side.

In the eighteenth, nineteenth and early twentieth centuries the Adrians lived in London, moving their home progressively westwards, as might be expected from a reasonably prosperous family. E. D. Adrian's father, grandfather and great-grandfather were civil servants; the last, named William Obadiah, was an official at the Treasury whose work involved him in appearance at the House of Commons.

Two points of general interest stand out from A. D. Adrian's writings about his family. First, it seems reasonably certain that the Bartholomew Adrian who was at Trinity College in 1581 became a surgeon and was one of those who attended Sir Philip Sidney in 1586 after the Battle of Zutphen, when he received the wound from which he eventually died. The strongest evidence for this conclusion is that Bartholomew Adrian had studied medicine at Leiden and that a surgeon named Adrian is mentioned with three others in Sidney's will and was left the sum of ten pounds by Sidney.

The other point of particular interest in the Adrian chronicle is why E. D. Adrian's grandfather, who was born in the year 1809, in the middle of the Peninsular War, should have been given the name Emperor, apparently after the Emperor Napoleon. According to A. D. Adrian's account,[1] the cause of 'this distinctly troublesome name' was as follows.

> 'William Obadiah Adrian had at the Treasury a colleague named Dwight. Each looked forward to fruition of the joys and burdens of fatherhood at an early date. And each was an interested observer of the progress of French arms upon the continent. For reasons which seem to have been always obscure the pair entered into an agreement binding each, on the birth of a son, to name the boy so that the two children should, in combination, perpetuate the title of the ambitious disturber of the peace of Europe.
>
> 'The two sons were born in due course, and Emperor Adrian and Napoleon Dwight lived to testify to a strange and inconvenient outcome of their parents' friendship.
>
> 'The story in itself exhibits the two Treasury men in a distinctly unfavourable light; and without knowledge of the ancestry or birth of Dwight, it is now perhaps impossible to frame an excuse for Adrian.'

A. D. Adrian goes on to say: 'There is apparently no ground for the supposition that Adrian and Dwight were, at heart, admirers of the military genius, then fresh from the overthrow of the Austrian armies.' But admiration of

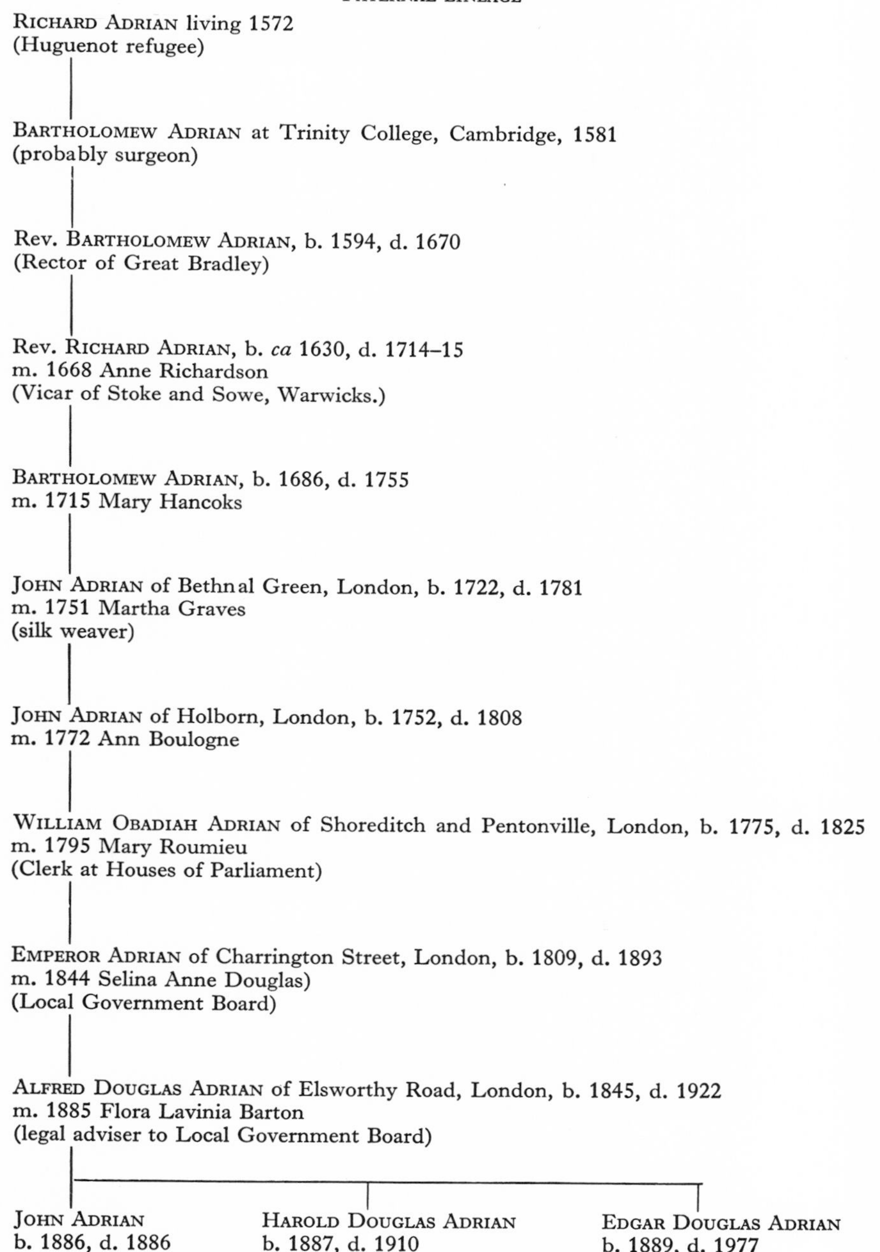

PATERNAL LINEAGE

RICHARD ADRIAN living 1572
(Huguenot refugee)

BARTHOLOMEW ADRIAN at Trinity College, Cambridge, 1581
(probably surgeon)

Rev. BARTHOLOMEW ADRIAN, b. 1594, d. 1670
(Rector of Great Bradley)

Rev. RICHARD ADRIAN, b. *ca* 1630, d. 1714–15
m. 1668 Anne Richardson
(Vicar of Stoke and Sowe, Warwicks.)

BARTHOLOMEW ADRIAN, b. 1686, d. 1755
m. 1715 Mary Hancoks

JOHN ADRIAN of Bethnal Green, London, b. 1722, d. 1781
m. 1751 Martha Graves
(silk weaver)

JOHN ADRIAN of Holborn, London, b. 1752, d. 1808
m. 1772 Ann Boulogne

WILLIAM OBADIAH ADRIAN of Shoreditch and Pentonville, London, b. 1775, d. 1825
m. 1795 Mary Roumieu
(Clerk at Houses of Parliament)

EMPEROR ADRIAN of Charrington Street, London, b. 1809, d. 1893
m. 1844 Selina Anne Douglas)
(Local Government Board)

ALFRED DOUGLAS ADRIAN of Elsworthy Road, London, b. 1845, d. 1922
m. 1885 Flora Lavinia Barton
(legal adviser to Local Government Board)

| JOHN ADRIAN | HAROLD DOUGLAS ADRIAN | EDGAR DOUGLAS ADRIAN |
|---|---|---|
| b. 1886, d. 1886 | b. 1887, d. 1910 | b. 1889, d. 1977 |

(From Burke's *Peerage and Baronetage* and the family history written by A. D. Adrian.)

Napoleon does in fact seem to be the only plausible explanation, even for two Treasury officials, and is not as improbable as it seems now. Thus Hazlitt openly admired Napoleon during and after the war and gave up alcohol in 1815 after a long drinking bout intended to drown the memory of Napoleon's defeat at Waterloo.[2] The present Lord Adrian thinks that Dwight and William Obadiah Adrian must have admired Napoleon and that his grandfather has been excessively loyal to the family in the sentence quoted above.

Less is known about E. D. Adrian's ancestry on the other side of the family. His mother, Flora Lavinia, who married Alfred Douglas Adrian in 1885, was the daughter of Charles Howard Barton, a scholar and graduate of Trinity College, Cambridge, who taught mathematics at the Royal Military College, Sandhurst, from 1840 until the 1860s when he moved to South Australia where relations of the family still flourish. These are the descendants of Flora Barton's eldest sister who married C. W. Babbage, a grandson of Charles Babbage, F.R.S. In appearance E. D. Adrian resembled C. H. Barton, who had fine sharp features and plentiful white hair, much more than his father.

## II. Childhood and school

In contrast to the wealth of detail available about E. D. Adrian's ancestors on his father's side, information about his own early life is sketchy and it is difficult to form more than a shadowy impression of him as a child or schoolboy. His parents had three sons: John, who died a few days after birth in 1886, Harold Douglas, who was born in 1887 and who died in 1910, and Edgar Douglas, who was born on 30 November 1889. Harold, who was educated at Westminster and Christ Church, was an exceptionally gifted classical scholar and although it is now hard to believe, it is possible that E. D. Adrian was somewhat overshadowed by his elder brother's brilliance.[3] At all events, as Adrian always seemed diffident about his own talents, in spite of his extraordinarily successful academic career, it does not seem altogether fanciful to suppose that a memory of a much cleverer elder brother remained with him all his life as a sort of unattainable standard.

In the brief autobiographical notes which Adrian left for the Royal Society he records that, until he went to Cambridge in 1908, his life was spent in London, with holidays at the seaside and that he saw little of the countryside except from the windows of a train. Much care was evidently devoted to the choice of a suitable holiday resort as can be seen from the following reminiscence written by Adrian in 1956.[4]

> 'As a Local Government Board inspector in the 'eighties my father had to conduct inquiries into the proposals of local authorities for new schemes of water supply and drainage. He must have been an impartial chairman, for he had no knowledge of engineering or bacteriology, but he was a good lawyer and was in close touch with Dr. Thorne, who had succeeded Dr. Buchanan as chief medical officer of the Board. He had ceased holding inquiries and had become legal adviser to the board when I was still a small boy, but considerations of public health made a deep impression on

my mind because my father's inside knowledge gave him decided views on the seaside places where we could stay in safety for the summer holidays. Many had to be ruled out. He knew that X was in trouble with its sewage disposal and that there had been cases of typhoid at Y. The families of my school friends could go where they pleased, and I used to envy their freedom and wonder whether I ought to warn them of the risks they were running. But those were the days when one could not take the water supply for granted even in a considerable town and when no one would dream of drinking water in any of the capitals of Europe unless it came in an expensive bottle with the magic label of a famous spa.'

The note of envy in this quotation makes one feel that perhaps Adrian's adventurous disposition, which showed itself in his love of rock-climbing, mountaineering and driving at a dangerously high speed, may have been a reaction against his father's cautious nature and the circumscribed character of his early days.

The Adrian family lived at 40 Elsworthy Road, N.W.3, opposite the entrance to Primrose Hill and Adrian records that they often visited the Zoo or the Botanical Society's Garden in the Inner Circle of Regent's Park. At his preparatory school (Heddon Court) Adrian writes that he was interested in photography and aeroplanes (then just beginning); it is also evident that a ride in one of the earliest Benz cars made a deep impression on him.[5]

In 1903 Adrian went as a day boy and King's Scholar to Westminster. He started in classics, but read books on science and moved to the modern side in 1906, two years before leaving the school. John Sargeant, the master of the VIth form at Westminster, who taught classics and literature, had a considerable influence on Adrian's education as he had on that of many Westminster boys. Adrian says that he counted himself very lucky to have spent a year in Sargeant's form before going on to the modern side. As Adrian spent two years on the modern side it is evident that he must have reached the VIth form at a remarkably early age. But his knowledge of Latin and Greek remained with him all his life, as the writer realized when someone at Trinity High Table quoted a line from a Greek play which Adrian was able to continue for a dozen lines or more.

Although Adrian does not mention it in his brief notes, another important influence on his early life was H. R. Robertson, the father of Adrian's Westminster and Trinity friend Donald Robertson (later Regius Professor of Greek) and of the distinguished botanist (and artist) Agnes Arber, F.R.S. Adrian studied drawing with H. R. Robertson and it is reasonable to suppose that this helped him to produce the very spirited sketches with which some of his later papers are illustrated (see figures 3 and 4). Adrian remained interested in drawing and painting all his life and regarded a certain amount of skill in drawing as one of the important things that a would-be medical student should acquire at school. Although he rarely fell into the trap of running down the younger generation, the writer remembers him complaining quite sharply in the late

1940s about the total failure of the average medical student to convey anything by means of a drawing or diagram.

## III. Cambridge, 1908–14

Adrian entered Trinity College, Cambridge, as a Major Scholar in Natural Science in 1908. In those days the Cambridge curriculum in science was surprisingly similar to that existing today. The able men read three or four subjects in Part I of the Natural Sciences Tripos, which took nearly two years, and then specialized in a Part II which occupied the last year. Adrian read five subjects in Part I: physics, chemistry, physiology, anatomy and botany, and obtained a first class in 1910. It is said that he never went to a lecture in botany, but managed all the same to get a first class in that subject. The remarkably high standard of his overall performance is borne out by a letter from his tutor, Walter Morley Fletcher, to his former headmaster at Westminster, Dr. James Gow:

22 June 1910

Dear Dr. Gow,

No doubt you have noticed that E. D. Adrian has passed the Natural Sciences Tripos in the First Class. I think you will like to know that his performance was exceptionally brilliant, as I have privately learnt from the Head Examiner. Most men take three subjects in the Tripos, many take four, scoring low marks in their fourth subject. Adrian took five subjects and in his fifth and worst subject, which he has read for a year, he gained more marks than any one else in the University in the same subject. He would have been placed in the First Class if the marks of only his three worst subjects had been counted, and the papers in his two best subjects torn up. Altogether he obtained something like 30% more than the previous maximum marks given in the Tripos within recent memory.

Adrian has done this without anything that might be called cramming. He has worked steadily of course, but has had time enough to take an interest in many outside subjects and occupations. I now find it most embarrassing to know in what direction to advise him to steer, seeing that he has first-rate ability in so many different directions. If he has original powers at all comparable with his powers of reception, he ought to do magnificent work in scientific medicine.

Believe me,

Yours sincerely,

(signed) W. M. Fletcher

We know less about Adrian's performance in Part II in which he read physiology, but, as everyone must have expected, he obtained another first class in 1911 and received the awards which enabled him to do post-graduate research.

In his biographical notes Adrian mentions classwork (i.e. tutorials) with Keith Lucas as being particularly important and determining his career (see p. 10). He also refers to his contacts with G. I. Taylor who taught him in physics for a short time and showed him that the textbook way of solving a problem was not always the best.

Adrian became a member of the Natural Science Club at the end of his first year in Cambridge. This is a small society which has flourished for more than a hundred years and remains active today. In Adrian's time the club met every Saturday evening in term; its members were all undergraduates or B.A.s and although the numbers of members in residence rarely exceeded 15 the club could claim a long list of Fellows of the Royal Society among its past members. Some of those who overlapped with Adrian and were or subsequently became his friends or colleagues are listed below.[6]

*Some Members of Cambridge Natural Science Club who read papers between* 1909 *and* 1914

Sir Geoffrey L. Keynes, M.D., F.R.C.P., F.R.C.S.
Sir Geoffrey I. Taylor, O.M., F.R.S.
T. L. Eckersley, F.R.S., M.I.E.E.
W. H. C. Romanis, F.R.C.S.
E. Hindle, F.R.S.
Sir W. Lawrence Bragg, F.R.S.
A. W. R. Don, B.A. (obiit 1916)
Sir James Gray, C.B.E., F.R.S.
Sir Rudolph A. Peters, M.C., F.R.C.P., F.R.S.
Sir Alan N. Drury, C.B.E., F.R.S.
Sir George P. Thomson, F.R.S.
N. K. Adam, F.R.S.

In the preface to *The mechanism of nervous action* (1932a) Adrian tells us that a few weeks before Keith Lucas's death in 1916, Lucas had talked to him about the great possibilities which might lie in the use of thermionic valves for amplifying nerve action currents. As Adrian probably attended the papers read by T. L. Eckersley on 'Electrons' (6 May 1911) and 'Wireless telegraphy' (24 February 1912) it seems possible that he may have considered the idea at an even earlier date.

Adrian helped to get the club going again after the 1914–18 war and probably remained an ordinary member until June 1919 and an Honorary Member thereafter. His papers to the club (listed below) during the period before and

*Papers to Cambridge University Natural Science Club*, 1909–21[7]

Heliotropism in animals (6 November 1909)
The investigation of muscle and nerve (11 March 1911)
Over-eating (28 October 1911)
Balloons (11 May 1912)
The structure of protoplasm (17 May 1913)
The nervous impulse (31 January 1914)
Freud without tears (31 May 1919)
Fits (30 April 1921)

immediately after the war, give a good idea of the width of his knowledge as well as the nature of his specialized interest.

Adrian's friendship with C. D. Broad, which was to last all his life, brought him into contact with philosophy, and helps to explain the knowledgeable, if cautious, way in which he later approached problems involving the mind and the brain. In an article on 'The mental and physical origin of behaviour', which was published in 1946,[8] Adrian tells us that he had two friends both of whom were killed in the war, who were particularly interested in disorders of the mind. Adrian writes that he and his friends dabbled in hypnotism, which was then fashionable and read papers by Ernest Jones on psycho-analysis. These extracurricular activities were to play an important part in Adrian's scientific and medical career later on.

Adrian did many other things besides work. He was known for his skill in roof-climbing and obtained a half-blue in fencing, a sport which may have been responsible for the rapid darting movements that characterized his work in the laboratory or (according to his family) for his general method of preparing meals in the kitchen at home. In the days before the First World War practical jokes were in fashion and Adrian and his friend, Archie Don, gained some notoriety from the contributions that they made to the successful hoax which took off the exhibition of post-impressionist painters at the Grafton Galleries in 1913. Their exhibition in Cambridge, which was successful in that it fooled a number of critics, was described by Adrian[9] in a book about Don who died on active service in the Salonika campaign in 1916. From Adrian's account of the exhibition it is evident that while he and Don started in a spirit of mockery they came away feeling that the post-impressionists were not as bad as they were painted. This remark is characteristic of Adrian's attitude to many things. I remember a conversation with him in the 1950s when we were discussing a friend who had given up physiology for social sciences. 'I can't think why he should do that', said Adrian, and then at once, 'Oh, but I mustn't say that as I am speaking at the British Association next week and am supposed to give sociology a puff.' The reason for this kind of inconsistency was, I think, that Adrian regarded most human activities as both odd and interesting, so it was perfectly possible for him to laugh at something with which he really had a good deal of sympathy, without being in any way insincere.

While at Trinity, Adrian began to enjoy hill-walking and mountaineering. This interest remained with him throughout his life and it may have developed through his membership of the Trinity Lake Hunt, another institution like the Natural Science Club which still flourishes. The Lake Hunt was an offshoot of the much more energetic Trevelyan man hunt, a game invented by George Trevelyan[10] and Geoffrey Winthrop Young, which involved chasing people at high speed over the hills and valleys of the Lake District. Adrian says about it: 'At the end of the May term a party of fifteen or sixteen, mainly from Trinity, went up to the Lakes for a week for the annual Lake Hunt. Every year such a party would stay a week at Mrs Pepper's farm at Seatoller, and spend its days in an extended game of hide-and-seek over the fells between Wastdale, Ennerdale and Buttermere.'

One of the features of the Trinity Lake Hunt was that it was attended by both senior and junior members of the College and Adrian continued going to it occasionally until the mid thirties. The writer remembers his first sight of Adrian in 1933 as a figure in a mackintosh cape running downhill at high speed, emerging briefly from the mist and then disappearing again as another cloud swirled up the Ennerdale Valley. This tableau encapsulates several of Adrian's characteristics, not least his elusive quality.

Adrian became a Fellow of Trinity College in 1913, a position which he held throughout his life except for the 14 years when he was Master. As will soon appear he left Cambridge in 1914 and did not return until 1919. But he evidently kept in touch with the College for he attended a controversial College meeting in January 1916 and later in the same year was one of the 22 Fellows who signed a letter protesting against the dismissal of Bertrand Russell as a College lecturer, after Russell had been convicted of an offence committed in the course of his activities as a pacifist.[11]

Adrian was deeply attached to Trinity and in later years seemed more at home there than anywhere else. People who knew him only in College were surprised to learn that he could occasionally be sharp or unapproachable or that his colleagues in the laboratory found him difficult to consult. The reason why he should have felt so much at ease in College is not obvious. It is no explanation to say that Trinity was then in its second golden age and that Adrian's generation and the one immediately preceding it include names as famous as almost any in its long history: Whitehead, Russell, Housman, Trevelyan, G. H. Hardy, G. I. Taylor, J. J. Thomson, Hopkins, Rutherford and W. L. Bragg, to choose only a few. The company of great scholars may be inspiring and is sometimes stimulating but it is not necessarily relaxing, and the fact is that Adrian relaxed in College in a way that was unusual unless he was on holiday or with his family.

One explanation may be that Adrian very much disliked being got at and he could feel reasonably secure in College where there was a tradition between the wars that you did not raise items of business at lunch or dinner. There may be something in this, but I believe that a more important factor was that Adrian's life as a boy at home was somewhat narrow and serious, almost gloomy in fact, and that coming to Trinity, a large and tolerant college, opened up all sorts of enjoyable opportunities, as well as intellectually stimulating ones. So he came to think of the College and its beautiful buildings as a place where he expected to be free and happy, and this feeling remained with him all his life. The same sensation had been expressed a hundred years earlier in a more exuberant way than Adrian would have done by Lord Byron when he said about Trinity: 'I am allowed 500 a year, a servant and horse, so feel as independent as a German Prince who coins his own cash, or a Cherokee Chief who coins no cash at all, but enjoys what is more precious, Liberty.'[12]

## IV. The collaboration with Keith Lucas and Adrian's early researches, 1911–14

Throughout his life Adrian was anxious to make plain the debt that he owed to Keith Lucas, who was his Director of Studies in Trinity, and with whom he started experiments in 1911. As few people except physiologists have heard of Lucas, who was killed in an aeroplane accident in 1916, something should be said about his scientific contribution. This is best done by quoting Adrian's own account, written in 1934 and published in a biography of Lucas written by friends and colleagues.[13]

> 'The whole of Keith Lucas' research work in physiology dealt with the properties of nerve and muscle. He discovered one fact of quite fundamental importance, and established a method of theoretical analysis which brought fresh life into the subject. There were, of course, a number of minor results, important in their place and at the time they were obtained; they would have amply justified his election to the Royal Society and his recognition as one of the leading physiologists in this particular field. But many scientists are eminent in their day, make useful contributions to their subject and are then forgotten. For permanent recognition something more is needed and this was supplied by the whole spirit of his work as much as by the particular discoveries which he made.
>
> 'For 100 years physiologists had been engaged in the study of muscle and nerve. What kind of change takes place in our muscles to make them contract and what signals are sent down through the nerve fibres from the brain to order the contraction of the muscles ? A great deal was already known and there is still a great deal to find out. Nothing would be gained by summarizing the thirty papers which are Keith Lucas' contribution to muscle and nerve physiology, but it is worth describing the research which seems, twenty-nine years later, to contain his most important discovery—that dealing with the "all-or-none" law in skeletal muscle.'

Adrian then goes on to describe the famous experiment published by Lucas in 1905, which showed that the single fibres of skeletal muscle obeyed the 'all-or-none' law which Bowditch had established for heart muscle in 1871. This was done by cutting down a small muscle until there were only a few fibres left in it and showing that as the electrical stimulus was made stronger the force of contraction increased in a series of distinct steps, the number of which were no greater than the number of muscle fibres. Clearly the individual muscle fibres obeyed the all-or-none law: that is, in a single fibre if the stimulus is strong enough it produces a full-sized mechanical twitch, but below a threshold it gives nothing at all. Four years later Lucas carried out a similar type of experiment in which a small muscle was stimulated through a nerve containing only a few motor nerve fibres, each of which innervated about 20 muscle fibres. His finding that there were four or five relatively large steps in the response of the muscle is very strong evidence that nerve fibres as well as muscle fibres, obey the 'all-or-none' law, but Lucas was careful to express a reservation which does not at first occur to the modern reader. In referring to these two experiments Adrian continues:

> 'The proof of the all-or-none law for muscle fibre was soon followed by a mass of evidence which showed that it was true for nerve fibre as well. The impulses which make up a nervous message are of fixed size in each nerve fibre. Each is a brief explosive wave involving the entire resources of the nerve fibre and all the nervous signalling which takes place in the body is carried out by such unvarying units. The consequences are endless, both in regard to the working of the nervous system and to the nature of the mechanism which produces the waves of activity in muscle and nerve.'

This paragraph summarizes not only Keith Lucas's own experiments but also the work which Adrian and Zotterman carried out in 1925 with valve amplifiers. Until that time it was not possible to measure the electrical activity of a single nerve fibre and all evidence about the 'all-or-none' nature of the nerve impulse was necessarily somewhat indirect. The final demonstration of discrete electrical impulses in single nerve fibres must be regarded as one of Adrian's principal contributions.

Arthur Koestler says that 'We can add to our knowledge but we cannot subtract from it'.[14] By this he means that it is impossible, or at any rate extraordinarily difficult, to put ourselves in the position of our scientific ancestors who did not accept some scientific law or principle of nature that we now regard as self-evident. It is important to recognize this difficulty if we are to understand the value of Adrian's own work, as well as that of Keith Lucas.

Nowadays, a student of the history of electrophysiology might be forgiven for thinking that Bernstein's or Overton's picture of the mechanism of nerve conduction was pretty much the same as the one we hold today. Perhaps it was; but it is also true that, until the work of Lucas and Adrian, no one was clear that the nerve impulse was an 'all-or-none' event in which the energy for propagation came from the nerve and not from the stimulus. The whole subject was in a muddle, occasionally illuminated by important experiments and hypotheses, such as those of Overton and Bernstein, but full of conflicting evidence and without any generally accepted principles based on solid experimental evidence. In the chapter about Lucas from which I have already quoted, Adrian describes the position better than I can. He remarks that the problem Lucas solved was straightforward enough and asks why his solution should be regarded as a particularly brilliant piece of work.

> 'The answer is that the problem had never been thoroughly formulated until he took it up. Gotch had discussed it in a paper on nerve three years before, but Gotch's paper had not attracted much attention, as it contained a suggestion rather than a proof. The idea was difficult to grasp because the whole subject was in confusion. It was almost the oldest branch of physiology and it had attracted countless workers. It is dangerously easy to make experiments with the classical preparation of a frog's nerve and muscle, but the vast majority of the experiments which

were published from year to year did little but add to the confusion. Words such as "stimulus", "excitation", "conductivity", etc., were used in the same argument with several different meanings, and a nerve or a muscle was thought of as a single unit and not as a collection of fibres. To this confusion of thought there was added a traditional technique, the gastrocnemius–sciatic preparation of the frog as the object of study, the du Bois Reymond coil for stimulating and the smoked-paper drum for recording muscular contractions. All these were good enough in their way and there had been many innovations, but few physiologists had enough knowledge of physics and of instrument design to enable them to dispense with the time-honoured methods, and if they had, their interest centred in the technique and not in the physiological problem.'

A little further on Adrian continues:

'It is sometimes held that the English are best at those branches of science which deal with relatively simple ideas not far removed from the experimental facts. Keith Lucas dealt mainly with such ideas and his more abstract speculations were rarely allowed to appear in print. This gives all his papers a feeling of solid achievement, of a definite step towards a definite end. The feeling is enhanced by the quality of the figures which illustrate the text, particularly the drawings of apparatus. They are given in clear, bold outlines, with nothing indeterminate and no unnecessary detail. No one who sees them could doubt the quality of the experiments which they illustrate or of the thoughts which shaped the experiments.'

So much for the theoretical background: it is time to consider the material conditions in the laboratory when Adrian started work with Keith Lucas in 1911. Here again I cannot do better than use Adrian's own words.[15]

'In those days the Cambridge School of Physiology was at the height of its fame. It was housed deplorably, judged by modern standards, and run so economically that there was no mechanic and no common stock of tools or apparatus. The research rooms were barely rooms at all. Keith Lucas was lucky to have a small cellar all to himself. It was approached through a larger cellar which housed A. V. Hill and many cages of rats on which Hopkins was carrying out his classical work on the vitamins. A side door led to a dark chamber in which all the frogs were kept and beyond this was the centrifuge driven by a large gas engine of obsolete design which shook the building and added the smell of warm oil and half-burnt gas to that of frog and rat: upstairs worked Barcroft, Mines, [W. B.] Hardy, Anderson, Fletcher, Langley, to name only those who were in permanent occupation, and their accommodation was little better. This state of affairs was only brought to an end by the gift of the Drapers' Company which provided the new laboratory in 1914. For Keith Lucas the lack of workshop and apparatus did not matter very much, since he had a small workshop of his own at his house: for those of us who had no workshop training it was probably a good thing to be thrown on our own resources and made to improvise apparatus out of the scrap heap.

But research work involves some expense and the laboratory would provide very little besides the animals and the room. There were a few special funds for apparatus like the Government Grant fund administered by the Royal Society, but the total sum available in those days was far smaller than it is now.'

Another well-known point about the cellar in which Keith Lucas and his colleagues worked was that it filled with water after rain so that people had to walk about on duckboards in wet weather. For those who know Cambridge, it should be said that the cellar was situated in a position coinciding roughly with the foundations of the Babbage Lecture Theatre. This was the pit in which Adrian dug the beginnings of his scientific reputation.

Adrian's first paper with Keith Lucas had the well-defined objective of finding out why, when two like stimuli are sent into an excitable tissue, the first may often have no visible effect whereas the second will produce an obvious response.[16] This phenomenon was of interest both for its own sake and because the temporal summation or facilitation that it illustrated is an important property of the central nervous system. Adrian and Lucas showed that there are two kinds of summation (a) that in which the first stimulus is not strong enough to set up impulses but leaves behind a local excitatory effect which can sum with the second stimulus, and (b) that in which the first stimulus sets up a volley of nerve impulses whose propagation is blocked in a region of weakened conductivity, but which leaves behind it a state of enhanced conductivity that enables the second volley to get through. The second type of summation might occur either at a neuromuscular junction or in a region in which conductivity was impaired by a narcotic. The paper describes a wide variety of experiments, one of which was to provide a figure found in textbooks for the next 30 to 40 years. This is the classical picture showing the recovery of excitability (i.e. sensitivity to an electric shock) after one impulse, or set of impulses, has been started. Under certain experimental conditions, which were defined in a later paper by Adrian, excitability does not return monotonically but with an overshoot in which the excitability is greater than normal, instead of subnormal as in the relative refractory period, or zero as in the absolute refractory period; the period of enhanced excitability is called the supernormal phase. Adrian and Lucas considered that the supernormal phase of excitability would be associated with a similar phase of increased conductivity so that the second impulse would have a better chance of getting through a blocked region than the first. This was supported by the observation that the time course of the facilitation of conductivity was similar to that of the supernormal phase. The paper is logical and beautifully written with many controls and ingenious experiments, but anyone reading it today is bound to part company with the authors at several points.

Adrian and Lucas had adopted the working hypothesis that there might be nothing very special about synapses and the neuromuscular junction and that a region where conductivity was impaired might, in modern terms, be a good model for synapses and junctions. They were therefore very interested in studying processes like facilitation or Wedensky inhibition and thought that the explanation which they found appropriate for a blocked region of nerve might be transferred directly to the neuromuscular junction or synapse. Today we know that impulses get across neuromuscular junctions and synapses by chemical transmission, and would seek an explanation of neuromuscular facilitation either in terms of the cumulative effects of successive releases of acetylcholine, or, conceivably, in terms of a potentiating effect of the first impulse on the release of acetylcholine by the nerve terminal. But virtually nothing was known of chemical transmission in 1912 and the authors can be forgiven for preferring an explanation closer to their own experience. The same fate has overtaken their interest in Wedensky inhibition, which no longer seems a good model of central inhibition, since we know that there are inhibitory nerves and inhibitory transmitters which have the opposite effect to excitatory ones. But again one can understand why Lucas and Adrian should have preferred their idea to that of McDougall and von Uexkull who accounted for inhibition by 'postulating a process unknown to the student of nervous conduction, namely the passage along nervous paths of a something which can stay and accumulate in one part or another of the nervous system'.[17]

Another objection which applies rather generally to Adrian's early work and to Lucas's posthumous book (which Adrian edited and completed for publication in 1917) comes from their views about conduction with a decrement in narcotized nerve. This subject provided the basis for a fierce controversy in the 1920s which Adrian managed to avoid, partly by opening up another major field and partly by following his invariable practice of refusing to be drawn into anything like a polemic. The outcome of the work of Kato[18] in Japan and Davis[19] and his colleagues in Harvard was that by 1926 Lucas and Adrian's idea of a continuous decrement in narcotized nerve was abandoned and was replaced by the concept that, after undergoing a short transitional decrement, the impulse was conducted at a reduced but constant amplitude in narcotized nerve.

Perhaps the most ambitious of Adrian's pre-war publications were two papers[20] in which he attempted to prove that the intensity of the impulse at any point in a normal nerve is independent of the strength of the stimulus, or of changes in intensity which may have occurred elsewhere. These papers were later criticized by Davis *et al.*[21] in their work on conduction in narcotized nerve. Adrian's method of measuring the intensity was to set the impulse to face a region of decrement and to see how far it travelled before being extinguished. If there were no decrement, or only a transitional one, Adrian's proof is weakened, although the lengths he used may just have been short enough for the method to be valid. Yet, although the evidence is certainly not as watertight as Adrian originally hoped, these early experiments do provide general support for the idea that conduction of a nerve impulse is like the burning of a fuse of gunpowder, in which the energy for propagation comes from the fuse, and is unlike the propagation of a sound wave in which the energy comes from the source. Thus Adrian showed (a) that at a given level of narcosis a volley of nerve impulses could not pass a 9 mm length of narcotized nerve, but could pass two widely separated regions each of length 4.5 mm, (b) that the level of narcosis needed to extinguish the volley was no greater with two widely separated narcotized regions, each 4.5 mm long, than it was with a single 4.5 mm region. From this Adrian rightly concluded that after being reduced in intensity in the first narcotized region the impulse recovers its full size in the stretch of normal nerve before entering the second narcotized region. Such behaviour would not be expected if the energy for propagation came from the stimulus because in that case the impulse would not recover after emerging from the first narcotized region, and the effect of the two regions would be additive, whether they were separated or not.

A paper on Wedensky inhibition[22] which Adrian published in 1913 is interesting because it reveals some of the difficulties, now quite forgotten, which made people reluctant to accept the all-or-nothing principle. Adrian's preamble gives the background in his usual elegant style.

> 'Only one serious objection has been brought against the all-or-none principle from an experimental standpoint. This objection is based on the phenomena described as Wedensky inhibition. Wedensky found that at a certain stage in the fatigue or narcosis of a muscle nerve preparation, a series of strong or rapidly recurring stimuli may produce a small initial contraction only (*Anfangszuckung*), whereas a series of weak or slowly recurring stimuli produce a continued tetanus. At present we are concerned only with the results of an alteration in the strength of the stimuli when their frequency remains unchanged. Since a series of very strong stimuli have an effect on the preparation entirely different to that given by a series of weak stimuli the alteration in the strength of the stimuli must have produced some alteration in the propagated disturbances set up in the nerve. How then can it be maintained that the size of the disturbance is unaffected by the strength of the stimulus? Both Max Cremer and F. Hofmann have used this argument in favour of the view that the size of the propagated disturbance depends on the strength of the stimulus.'

Adrian's explanation, for which he provided much evidence, is to be found in the observations that the impulse set up by a second strong stimulus, which comes too early to get through to the muscle, leaves a refractory period which inhibits a third stimulus following soon after the second. 'Wedensky's observation that a series of strong stimuli may produce inhibition whilst a series of weak stimuli of the same frequency produces a continued tetanus is to be explained by the fact that a strong stimulus can excite the nerve at an early stage of recovery before a summated contraction can be produced. The disturbance set up in the nerve will be followed by a refractory period which will cut down the size of a succeeding disturbance. Thus a series of strong stimuli will set up a series of small disturbances none of which will reach the muscle. A weak stimulus has no effect on the nerve until a more advanced stage of recovery has been reached and then the stimulus cannot avoid affecting the muscle as well as the nerve. Thus a series of weak stimuli cannot produce inhibition.'

One other early paper[23] will be mentioned because it gave a result which Adrian did not expect and which was very difficult to reconcile with the idea of a continuous decrement. Adrian found that although the conduction velocity of a nerve treated with alcohol vapour might be well below normal the velocity was constant over several centimetres of narcotized nerve. As Adrian believed in a continuous decrement in narcotized nerve, his observation forced him to conclude that the velocity did not vary with the size of the impulse. The correct explanation, which was proposed later by Davis *et al.*,[24] was that after passing through a short transitional region the impulse is conducted without decrement but at a reduced amplitude over the whole of the narcotized region; this is consistent with a reduced but constant velocity.

Although it was not a pre-war publication, Adrian's work in completing the monograph by Keith Lucas in 1917[25] should be considered with his early papers. In the spring of 1914 Keith Lucas delivered a course of lectures at University College London; the lectures were founded in memory of the neurologist Page May, and Lucas chose conduction in nerve as his subject. By July 1914 he had finished a draft of 11 out of the 13 chapters of the book. At the beginning of the war Keith Lucas 'volunteered' and was sent to the Royal Aircraft Factory at Farnborough. From that time, until his death on 5 October 1916, he was concerned solely with the problems of flying, and the manuscript of his book was as he had left it in 1914. Although he must have been intensely busy with his important neurological work, Adrian was able to complete Lucas's book in time for it to be published as one of the Monographs on Physiology in 1917. This involved editing the whole manuscript and writing most of chapter VI and the whole of chapter XIII along lines of which Adrian thought Keith Lucas would have approved.

## V. The war years, 1914–19

Some time before the war Adrian had decided to abandon research for a few years in order to complete his medical degree. On 16 May 1914 he wrote to Alexander Forbes declining an invitation to work at Harvard in the following terms:[26] 'I wish I could come over for a term or so and I feel that it is a great honour to have been asked, but I don't see how I can possibly manage it—for the next two years at any rate. Unfortunately I haven't got a medical degree yet and I shall have to spend the next two years remedying this defect. Most of the younger physiologists in Cambridge are not medical, but this is all the more reason why I should be, if I want a job here. So I shall have to stop research for two years, and after that I don't quite know what I shall be doing.'

There is some doubt about the exact date on which Adrian went to St Bartholomew's Hospital to complete his clinical training on which he had made a start at Addenbrooke's Hospital, Cambridge. According to his autobiographical notes he worked at Bart's from July 1914 to August 1915 and acquired the Cambridge M.B. in the autumn of 1915. His application form indicates that he should have been formally admitted at Bart's on 1 October 1914, but it seems possible that he worked there informally from July onwards. In either case the fact that he qualified after only about a year's clinical work must be something of a record. When he had acquired his medical degree he worked on nerve injuries and shell shock, first at Queen Square and later at the Connaught Military Hospital in Aldershot, where he remained until the end of the war in spite of strenuous efforts to get to France. Adrian writes that he owed his continued interest in clinical neurology to Sir Francis Walshe, F.R.S., who taught him to examine cases at Queen Square in 1915, and to Sir Adolph Abrahams, who gave him general clinical interest at the Connaught Hospital in 1916–17. Another major influence must have been Dr L. R. Yealland of Queen Square with whom he wrote a paper in 1917.

During the two years that Adrian was working in Aldershot he lived at 'Chudleigh' with various members of the scientific staff at the Royal Aircraft Factory, Farnborough. These included Aston, Lindemann, G. I. Taylor, Farren, Glauert and Melvill Jones.[27]

Adrian wrote three papers on certain aspects of his clinical work during the war but the cases described there were naturally only a small fraction of those which he saw in hospital. The first two papers[28] are concerned with the electric excitation of normal and denervated muscle, a subject of obvious clinical interest in wartime. Adrian showed that with normal muscle the time factor in excitation known as the chronaxie was very short and that it increased by a factor of 100 in denervated muscle after the nerve endings had degenerated. When the muscle was in process of recovery, the slow strength–duration curve of denervated muscle did not pass gradually into the rapid curve of healthy muscle; instead, the first sign of recovery was marked by a double curve with a discontinuity between a fast curve characteristic of nerve and a slow one characteristic of muscle. This fitted well with the conclusions reached by Keith Lucas[29] on the basis of his studies of strength–duration curves. It did not agree with Lapicque's[30] doctrine of isochronism which was strongly attacked by Rushton[31] 15 years later. Nowadays, no one would question the correctness of the conclusion that the chronaxie of muscle and nerve are widely different and today Adrian's paper seems to be a straightforward clinical application of a standard electrophysiological result.

The third paper with L. R. Yealland[32] deals with the treatment of some common war neuroses and is of considerable interest, both for its own sake and for the light which it sheds on the strange mixture of sympathy and cynicism with which Adrian regarded the weaknesses of human nature. The article is also remarkable for its understanding of psychoanalysis, which Adrian had studied in his undergraduate days. Cases of hysterical paralysis, deafness and mutism seem to have been more frequent in the First World War than in the Second. This was partly because soldiers were more carefully screened for battle in the last war, and partly because, except in the battles in the U.S.S.R., nothing facing the soldier quite approached the horrors of the Somme, nor was he so clearly faced with the possible alternatives of a very unpleasant death on the one hand or being shot for desertion[33] or cowardice on the other.

In their paper Adrian and Yealland describe a method which they applied with at least 95% success to more than 250 cases including all the common hysterical disorders such as mutism, deafness, paralysis of limbs and so on. No great orginality was claimed for the technique which was based on the work of French neurologists such as Vincent, Babinsky and Frument. However, it is evident that Yealland and Adrian applied the method, which depended on suggestion, re-education and discipline, with much ingenuity and understanding. The method is best explained in their own words. To begin with 'the patient must be convinced that the physician understands his case and is able to cure him and this idea should be fostered as soon as the patient enters the ward. The case is investigated as briefly as possible and each physical sign is accepted as perfectly normal in the circumstances, and not as in any way interesting or obscure. . . . The barest statement [about previous treatment] should suffice and the patient should be silenced at once if he attempts to air his own views on the subject.'

The suggestive treatment might take any form but it was essential that the patient should be convinced that it would produce an immediate recovery. For instance, cases of mutism could be cured by tickling the back of the mouth so as to induce a reflex phonation. The patient was then compelled to make a noise, and the fact that he had done so would convince him that the treatment would be effective. In the same way a strong electric stimulation produced a sensation and motion in a limb that was supposed to be anaesthetized and paralysed; this helped to convince the patient that he was on the road to recovery. As the authors say, 'The therapeutic uses of electricity are still mysterious enough to the layman, and nearly every patient will accept the suggestion that some form of electricity will cure him.'

What is meant by re-education and discipline is clarified by another quotation 'As soon as the least sign of recovery has appeared the re-education is begun. The patient is given no time to collect his thoughts, but is hurried along by a mixture of persuasion and command until the disordered function has completely recovered. The patient is never allowed any say in the matter. He is not asked whether he can raise his paralysed arm or not; he is ordered to raise it, and told that he can do it perfectly if he tries. Rapidity and an authoritative manner are the chief factors in the re-education process and in every case an effort should be made to produce complete recovery before the patient goes back to the ward.'

In some cases, often where the pitch had been queered by incompetent handling of electrical stimulation, these relatively simple methods failed and the authors then resorted to more complicated methods, for example suggesting that stimulation of the motor cortex through the scalp would restore movement to a limb.

Adrian and Yealland state that they had no direct experience of hysterical blindness in both eyes in military cases. However, later on in the war Adrian did see one case, which he cured, of genuine hysterical blindness. This was mentioned in the Doyne Memorial Lecture at the Oxford Ophthalmological Congress in 1943.[34] The interesting point was that the patient who was perfectly genuine, i.e. not malingering, complained of extreme photophobia and wore dark glasses or screwed up his eyes. That behaviour was in sharp contrast to the hysterically deaf who can shut out sounds from consciousness without plugging up their ears. The implication is that in man, vision makes a special claim on attention and visual signals are the most difficult to dissociate from consciousness.[35]

Adrian and Yealland were careful to point out that their method might remove hysterical symptoms but not the underlying neurasthenia which might have been treatable by psychoanalysis. The reason that they did not use psychoanalysis was not because they disapproved of the method, but simply that there would have been no time to apply it to a large number of cases under wartime conditions. In an unpublished lecture 'Freud without tears'[36] Adrian describes one case of a neurasthenic with a bad stammer whom he questioned in a 'hypnoidal state'. The man was an regular soldier who had been in France for two years, and remembered nothing of a series of traumatic experiences which took place between a shell burst and his 'coming round in hospital'. The case proceeded along classic lines. In a series of interviews Adrian uncovered experiences that even by the standards of the First World War seem particularly horrifying, as well as suppressed childhood memories of an incident that led to stammering. When all these memories were brought back to the patient's mind he had a considerable emotional discharge but in a day or two he began to improve and soon became an absolutely different man. Adrian concluded that those who have tried this method of treatment become convinced of two things: (a) that the patient does seem quite honestly to forget a series of events of very great emotional significance, which one would have supposed him to remember to his dying day, and (b) that his neurasthenic symptoms often disappear very rapidly after he has recalled these events.

## VI. Life in Cambridge, 1919–37

The first thing to be said about Adrian in the immediate post-war years—and it is not something he ever said himself—is that he must have been intensely busy. He was appointed a College Lecturer in Natural Science at Trinity College, Cambridge, on 31 January 1919, with leave of absence till demobilization. At about the same time he became a University Demonstrator in the Physiological Laboratory and was appointed to a University Lectureship in 1920. He seems to have returned to Cambridge in June or July of 1919.

Adrian's post at Trinity involved him in looking after all the medical students, as well as a few natural scientists reading physiology. Today, this college work would probably be divided between two or three people, but Adrian's position was in fact a good deal worse than that comparison might imply, for he inherited a post-war bulge of undergraduates. From records left in an enormous ledger, started by Keith Lucas, it is evident that he had to direct the studies of about 40 new entrants in 1919. The numbers drop off after that but between 1920 and 1922 he seems to have been looking after nearly 80 undergraduates single-handed. This must have involved him in a weekly total of about 10 hours of tutorial and advisory work. In addition a few hours each day were probably devoted to lecturing and running practical classes in the Physiological Laboratory. He is remembered as a very successful Part II lecturer by several eminent biologists: Wigglesworth, Needham, Rushton, and Bryan and Rachel Matthews; his Trinity pupils include a number of distinguished names such as: F. J. W. Roughton, L. E. Bayliss, E. J. M. Bowlby, J. H. Gaddum and R. J. Lythgoe. From 1920 to 1924 he was a member of the College Council which took him away from the laboratory for a morning every week.

Adrian was Secretary of the Physiological Society from 1923 to 1926, a member of its Committee from 1927 to 1934 and a member of the Editorial Board of the *Journal of Physiology* from 1926 to 1936; the letter quoted on p. 21 indicates that after Langley's death he acted as temporary editor in 1925. From this it is evident that with the other members of the first Editorial Board, A. V. Hill, J. B. Leathes and Sir Charles Sherrington, he must have played a major role in setting the *Journal* on the very successful course that it has followed during the last 53 years. The *Journal* was started in 1877 by Michael Foster, Burdon-Sanderson, Bowditch and others; it was run by a committee of British and American physiologists until J. N. Langley bought it in 1894 and became joint editor with Michael Foster. In the early 1920s Langley was in sole command and his dominance was occasionally resented; thus we find Forbes writing to Adrian in May 1922 about the 'Langleyized' version of their joint paper. The *Journal* had always been closely associated with the Physiological Society and in 1925 the Society bought it from Langley's estate for £1000, not without some tricky negotiations.[37] Since that time it has continued to flourish both scientifically and financially, a fact which gave Adrian a good deal of satisfaction.

An extract from a letter to Alexander Forbes written in July 1920 summarizes Adrian's activities at that time:

> 'I have so much to learn from you that I shall look forward very eagerly to your visit and I have a very good room in the new lab. which is not over-crowded. The best time for working here is July and August. In the October term I have a good deal of teaching and College work to do but I manage to get in a fair number of hours research work—at least I did last year and if you could put up with rather irregular attendance on my part I think we should have no difficulty in getting something done. We could start something at the beginning of July and come back to it in October.'[38]

As a counterweight to his intense activities in term time Adrian usually managed a number of enterprising holidays each year, skiing in Switzerland in January and climbing in Skye or the Alps in the summer, or occasionally sailing with G. I. Taylor in the Hebrides.[39] But by 1925, in spite of holidays, the strain of trying to do too much in term time was beginning to tell, as one can see from the letters written by Yngve Zotterman to Professor Johansson in 1925–26,[40] of which a few extracts are given below.

(22 November 1925) 'Adrian has a mass of lectures, etc., so that we can't manage more than three or four experiments a week.'

(16 December 1925) 'Adrian has an unheard of capacity for work. All the time he has had two lectures a day, besides a mass of private teaching in the College and he has also been temporary editor of the Journal of Physiology. He now gives the impression of being somewhat exhausted so that it has been a little difficult to work with him this last week as he can become beside himself if one merely leaves a tap dripping. However, he is very pleased with the result of our work.'

A holiday clearly has a beneficial effect because Zotterman wrote in January:

(13 January 1926) 'I had a letter yesterday from Adrian, who is in Switzerland. He sounds rested and active again.'

And on 21 February 1926:

'Adrian who has a very volatile disposition is now very happy again and the work has become very much more pleasant.'

Early in the 1920s Adrian began to be recognized internationally as a neurophysiologist of great distinction, and strenuous efforts were made to tempt him to major chairs in America, such as those at Johns Hopkins University, Baltimore, or the University of Rochester. In connection with the second possibility, Alexander Forbes[41] wrote in 1923 to N. W. Faxon at Rochester saying that he considered Adrian to be one of the foremost physiologists in the world, and added that he had a very attractive personality and sense of humour. He also said that Adrian had declined the chair at Johns Hopkins and preferred to remain in Cambridge where he has excellent facilities for research. However, he adds that Adrian is to be married next month which may change his views about remaining in Cambridge as his Trinity Fellowship provides more benefit to a bachelor than to a married man. Fortunately, for British physiology, Adrian resisted all such temptations and remained firmly based in Cambridge, although making frequent visits abroad.

The following extract from a letter from Forbes to Adrian illustrates the American publicity that Adrian was receiving in 1926.[42]

'In my last letter I forgot to say what I had in mind about your newspaper publicity. Perhaps I was prevented by a suppressed complex. The fact is that I got mixed up in the same thing. The New York papers had a dispatch about your experiment and one day while I was very much occupied with another problem far from physiology I received a long distance call from the New York "World" asking if I had done the same thing that you were reported to have done; namely isolate a single nerve fiber and record its response. The obvious impossibility of dissecting out a single nerve fiber without destroying it rose at once in my mind, and with characteristic indiscretion precipitated by a long distance telephone call I replied that I did not believe that anyone had done that. The unfortunate result was that I was rather conspicuously quoted as doubting the reports of your experiments. Immediately afterwards I received the Journal of Physiology and saw what you had done. I therefore wrote to the "World" explaining to them the difference between mechanical isolation of a nerve fiber and what you had actually done. They very decently referred my letter to their Bureau of Accuracy and Fair Play and published my letter. They then asked for a Sunday Feature story on the subject, and since they seemed to want to get the truth I got a second year student to write an article on the physiology of the nervous system with special reference to these recent developments. It appeared last Sunday. One result of this is that I received a letter from a paranoia case asking me how to break a mesmerized man away from a mesmerizer who controls him with a machine.'

Adrian was elected to the Royal Society early in 1923 at just about the time that he became engaged to Hester Pinsent. On 1 March he informed Forbes about both events and mentioned the consequent 'incapacity for serious thought about the nervous impulse'.[43] He became a Foulerton Research Professor of the Royal Society in 1929, a post which he held for eight years, and the substantial reduction in teaching which came with this must have been a great relief to him.

Adrian shared the Nobel Prize for Physiology and Medicine with Sir Charles Sherrington in 1932, an award which came as a surprise to him. In his autobiographical notes Adrian said that he greatly enjoyed the visit to Stockholm with Hester and that the aeroplane trip home from Malmö was his first experience of long-distance flying. Adrian replied for the guests at the dinner in the great banqueting room in the City Hall and, according to Hester, this was the first time that she or anyone else realized that Adrian was a superb after-dinner speaker. Perhaps fortunately for Adrian this did not become widely known until the late 1940s.

The Nobel Prize was followed 10 years later by the award of the Order of Merit and by many other honours which testified to the esteem in which Adrian was held throughout the world.

### *Marriage to Hester Pinsent*

On 14 June 1923 Adrian married Hester Agnes Pinsent whom he had first met in Cambridge at 'The Orchard', the hospitable home of Horace Darwin, one of the great clan described in Gwen Raverat's *Period piece*.[44] Hester came of a distinguished intellectual family, being related on her father's side to the philosopher David Hume and on her mother's to Lord Parker of Waddington, a law-lord who died in 1918. Her mother, Dame Ellen Frances Pinsent, was a pioneer in problems connected with mental health, an interest which Hester later shared.

It was a very happy marriage and Adrian depended greatly on Hester's calmness and wisdom, qualities which helped her to make an important, if indirect, contribution to his scientific achievements. In a brief autobiographical note written in 1969 Adrian says:

> 'I hope later to write a short account of our life together: here I will only say that our feelings for one another remained unchanged from 1923 until her death in 1966 and that I relied on her enterprise and great ability at every stage of our married life.'

Hester was a distinguished person in her own right and, like her mother, became famous for her work on mental health; she was made a D.B.E. in 1965. She and Adrian had many tastes in common and spent holidays skiing, mountaineering or sailing long distances with G. I. Taylor and his wife. To begin with they lived at 'Glebelands' in Grange Road but later moved to a larger house, 'St Chad's', in the same road. They had three children, Anne (now The Hon. Mrs R. D. Keynes), Jennet (The Hon. Mrs P. Campbell) and Richard Hume Adrian, F.R.S., who succeeded to his father's title.

In the summer of 1942 while on a short holiday in the Lake District with Adrian, Hester was seriously injured in a climbing accident on Great Gable. She had a compound fracture of the right leg, which had to be amputated above the knee. But she did not allow this to interfere with her many private and public activities, and although not able to walk long distances she was often to be seen bicycling around Cambridge. The accident meant that the Adrians had to have less energetic holidays than previously but they enjoyed a great deal of travelling together including a visit to the Brazilian jungle arranged by Professor Chagas. They also spent much time at 'Umgeni', their cottage near Cley on the Norfolk coast, where Adrian could write or relax if he felt so inclined.

Hester died suddenly of a coronary thrombosis in 1966 to Adrian's lasting distress and the sorrow of a wide circle of friends.

## VII. Research in the early post-war period, 1919–24

During the spring of 1919 Adrian continued his clinical work on patients with nerve injuries after having been moved from Aldershot to a hospital in Woolwich. But he was hoping to get back to Cambridge within a few months and his thoughts were returning to neurophysiology, as can be seen from the following extract from a letter written on 21 March 1919 to Alexander Forbes.[45]

> 'I don't know when I shall get back to Cambridge; probably not for some months. When I get there I shall have to look round for some ideas—at present my mind is a complete blank as regards physiology proper.
>
> 'I saw a paper of Lillie's in 1915 or 1916 on nerve conduction and I liked the look of it very much although I have forgotten most of it. It seemed that he was on the way to a theory which could be tested experimentally. I must look up the American Journal to see if he has any later papers on it.
>
> 'I suppose you haven't got a reprint of your paper on inhibition? If so I should very much like a copy.

'The valve idea for magnifying the electric response sounds an excellent idea; if you don't make it work we shall have to breed a new kind of frog with a large electric response.

'I saw A. V. Hill the other day in Cambridge, he is still working at artillery but he is going to start physiology again before long. Barcroft is going strong already as they have finished researching on poison gases.'

By mid-July Adrian was back in Cambridge and was enquiring from Forbes about the latter's wireless valve string galvanometer (see p. 25). He must have got down to work with his usual speed because we find the following remark in a further letter to Forbes written on 19 October 1919: 'I enclose a reprint of a thing I have just written. It is so inconclusive that I am sorry I published it but I was so glad to get back to physiology that I was rather uncritical at the time.'

The paper in question must be the one dealing with the chronaxie of human sensory nerves which was published in September 1919,[46] Although it reaches no very definite conclusion the paper needs to be considered briefly as it skirmishes with a subject that was to become a major interest of Adrian's later on. In the introduction Adrian points out that on the theory of Head and Rivers,[47] sensory nerves from the skin are divisible into two distinct systems, known as protopathic and epicritic, which are functionally and anatomically separable. This theory is no longer held, but it was running strongly in 1920, and there seemed to be a possibility that pain, a protopathic sensation, was carried in non-medullated nerve fibres, which were believed to have a long chronaxie. Adrian's experiments gave no support to this suggestion for he found short chronaxies in all the sensory nerves examined irrespective of the sensation carried. Thus when the glans penis was stimulated electrically the sensation was always painful yet the chronaxie was no longer than in the hand where one obtains a mixture of sensations from electrical stimulations.

This short article was followed by two papers of major importance dealing with the recovery process of excitability in nerve and muscle.[48] These experiments were begun in the autumn of 1919[49] and probably occupied him until early in 1921. In the first paper Adrian obtained convincing evidence of the now generally accepted fact that a supernormal phase of recovery is present when the external pH is more acid than pH 7 and is absent when it is more alkaline than pH 7.4. The same was true for heart muscle (frog's ventricle) and Adrian also showed that when a supernormal phase is present the second contraction was greater than the first. So far as I know, no one has attempted to explain this interesting correlation in terms of modern theories of excitation–contraction coupling in heart muscle.

The second paper of the series, which was published in 1921, dealt with the relation between the time course of the electric change and the recovery of excitability. The tissues included the frog's ventricle where the electric response lasts 1–2 s and the frog's sciatic nerve where it lasts about 2 ms at 13 °C;[50] in both cases the duration of the absolute refractory period was about the same as that of the electric change. Modern work has confirmed this correlation and indicates that it probably holds for skeletal muscle which Adrian thought might be an exception, at any rate at room temperature. The correlation in nerve and heart muscle was important because Tait and others had suggested that the absolute refractory period coincided with the rising phase and the relative refractory period with the descending phase of the electric response. This paper and its predecessor are more biophysical than any other of Adrian's researches and contain interesting speculations about the way in which one might 'explain' the refractory period in terms of the membrane theory of Bernstein, Brünnings and Lillie. However, perhaps the most remarkable feature of the papers is that Adrian was able to get such accurate corrected curves for the nerve action potential by analysing capillary electrometer records with the machine designed by Keith Lucas.[51] Adrian tested out the method by taking records of condenser discharges and comparing his corrected records with a calculated curve; the results indicate an error less than about 0.2 ms, which is quite an achievement considering that the time constant of the electrometer was 10–20 ms and his photographic plate moved at 0.8 mm/ms.[52]

The next two publications to appear are relatively short articles dealing with the electrical properties of muscle. The first with D. R. Owen on denervated muscle shoots down a hypothesis proposed by Henriques and Lindhard in which it was suggested that the electrical change in stimulated muscle arises wholly at the end plate. Adrian was strangely diffident about the next publication. In a letter to Forbes dated 22 May 1922[53] Adrian wrote that he had just finished a silly little research on the electrical response of a single muscle fibre with a Pratt electrode for localized stimulation. He got the expected steps in the electrical response but did not regard the result as very exciting, presumably because it was a foregone conclusion from Keith Lucas's 1905 and 1909 papers. Nevertheless, in spite of Adrian's depreciatory remarks, the paper must be regarded as something of a milestone for it contained the first direct evidence that the electrical response of muscle obeys the all-or-nothing law.[54] As Adrian concluded, the result also suggests that in muscle the all-or-nothing relation intervenes at an early stage in the chain of processes which lead up to contraction.

From the middle of 1920 Adrian and Alexander Forbes of Harvard had been corresponding about the possibility of Forbes coming to work in Cambridge. After a certain amount of worry on Adrian's part about finding a suitable house, Forbes arrived in England on 21 May 1921 and stayed till the end of October. Apart from a fortnight's holiday and visits to scientific meetings or other laboratories, Forbes spent most of his time working in Adrian's laboratory. At Adrian's suggestion he brought some wireless valves with him and set up a one-stage amplifier to go with the string galvanometer. When he went back to America Forbes left this, or a similar amplifier, set up in Cambridge.[55] However, as they do not mention the amplifier in their 1922 paper, it does not appear that they used it very much and it probably burnt the gold off the quartz string too frequently for Adrian's liking.[56] Both Forbes and

Adrian clearly enjoyed the collaboration very much; in subsequent correspondence each refers to the benefit he has derived from the visit.[57] They had many interests in common, often went on holidays together and remained close friends until Forbes's death in 1965. They were an impressive pair in old age, both with white hair, both bronzed by sun and wind, but with Adrian looking like Erasmus and Forbes more like an explorer or sea captain, as indeed he was—he frequently sailed long distances and made an aerial map of Labrador, largely on his own.

The experimental question which Adrian and Forbes wished to answer was whether sensory nerves obeyed the all-or-nothing law. As the evidence that motor nerves were all-or-nothing was strong, one may wonder why they felt it worthwhile to make a major effort on this problem. The explanation lay in the widespread belief that the extreme gradation of certain sensations and certain reflex responses made it necessary to assume that sensory nerve fibres differed from motor nerve fibres in possessing some means of varying their response, apart from changes in frequency. In contrast to their expectations, Adrian and Forbes[58] found that mammalian sensory nerves obeyed the all-or-nothing law, and there was no evidence of decremental conduction either in normal nerve or in a narcotized region. (Much greater lengths were used than in Adrian's earlier experiments with frog nerve.) They concluded that the response of a sensory nerve to a single momentary stimulus varied in two ways: (a) a strong stimulus excited more nerve fibres than a weak one, and (b) a stimulus which is more than strong enough to excite all the fibres may set up two or more impulses in each fibre.

Anyone who has the curiosity to read Adrian's papers in chronological order will feel, as he approaches the mid-1920s, an almost irresistible temptation to skip a few years to the time when Adrian started to use valve amplifiers to record impulses in single nerve fibres. This is probably what Adrian would have wished the reader to do as he refers later to getting bogged down in a series of very unprofitable experiments carried out at about this time (p. 28) Another reason for skipping is that the papers published with Sybil Cooper in 1923 are best regarded as forerunners of the important experiments carried out with Bronk four or five years later.

## VIII. Research from 1925 to 1933

### (i) *Recording nerve impulses with valve amplifiers*

The successful recording of trains of nerve impulses travelling in single sensory or motor nerve fibres, which Adrian and his colleagues carried out between 1925 and 1935, marks a turning point in the history of physiology. In an article published in 1954, for a series entitled 'Memorable experiences in research'[59], Adrian described how these experiments began:

> 'It was in the early 20's I had taken up electrophysiological research on the central nervous system and had spent a great deal of time making string galvanometer records of action currents in the hope of being able

to find out exactly what was coming down the nerve fibres when the muscle contracted. We knew then that nerves sent down nerve impulses as signals, but we didn't know anything about the way in which the impulses would follow one another. We didn't know whether they came at a high frequency, or at a steady frequency. We didn't know whether the frequency varied or not. In fact, we didn't know at all how the nervous signals were controlled. Alexander Forbes had been working with me in Cambridge and I had learned a great deal from him about string galvanometers and about mammalian preparations, but the experiments I had started became more and more unprofitable. You know the sort of thing that happens—they became more and more complicated and the evidence more indirect, and after a time it was quite clear that I was getting nowhere at all. But it was fairly clear at that time that the valve amplifier was going to make it very much easier to record action potentials, particularly very small ones, and there had been various descriptions of valve amplifying arrangements. In particular, Gasser and Newcomer had used a three-stage one to record action potentials in the phrenic nerve. I had rigged up a single valve one, but it wasn't much good, so having decided that I was getting nowhere, I wrote to Gasser for the details of the arrangement he was using for the phrenic. He was then beginning his studies with the cathode-ray oscillograph on the action potentials of nerve fibres of different sizes, but he gave me a full description of the amplifier that he and Newcomer had used, and I built one to much the same pattern. I knew very little about it and was rather afraid of all the complications in it. When it was ready, I decided to test it using the capillary electrometer which was in the laboratory, built by Keith Lucas about fifteen years before. I used the capillary electrometer because, although it wasn't as sensitive as the string galvanometer, it had the great advantage of being more foolproof in that it wasn't so easy to break the string if you overloaded it. The amplifier had to be treated with great respect, as in those days the valves were terribly microphonic. The arrangement I had gave a magnification of about 2000, so I set up a pair of non-polarizable electrodes in a shielded chamber, and put the normal accompaniment of physiological research, the frog's nerve-muscle preparation, on the electrodes, to see whether I could get a steady base line. Well, I was distressed, but not very greatly surprised, to find that the base line wasn't a bit steady. It was oscillating rapidly all the time. As soon as the circuit was open there was this constant rapid oscillation going on and I naturally suspected that I was picking up an artifact from somewhere and that I should have to pull the whole apparatus down and stick it all together again and go on for another month or so, getting no results.

'I began re-adjusting the apparatus, and then I found that sometimes the oscillation was there (it was a fine, rapid affair) and sometimes the base line was quite steady. There was a ray of hope, and after trying various arrangements, I found that this little oscillation was only there when the muscle was hanging down quite freely, from the knee joint of the frog's nerve-muscle preparation. If the muscle was supported on a glass plate there was no oscillation at all and the base line was quite steady. The explanation suddenly dawned on me, and that was a time when I was very pleased indeed. A stretched muscle, a muscle hanging under its own weight, ought, if you come to think of it, to be sending sensory impulses up the nerves coming from the muscle spindles, signalling the stretch on the muscle. When you relax the stretched muscle, when you support it, those impulses ought to cease.

'I don't think it took more than an hour or so to show that that was what the little oscillations were. I was able to make photographic records of them, and within about a week I was nearly certain that many of these oscillations were action potentials coming up sensory fibres in the nerve, and what was more, that many of them came from single nerve fibres and that by some extension of the technique it ought to be possible to find out exactly what was happening in single nerve fibres when the sense organs attached to them were stimulated.

'That particular day's work, I think, had all the elements that one could wish for. The new apparatus seemed to be misbehaving very badly indeed, and I suddenly found that it was behaving so well that it was opening up an entire new range of data. I'd been bogged down in a series of very unprofitable experiments and here suddenly was the prospect of getting direct evidence instead of indirect, and direct evidence about all sorts of problems which I had set aside as outside the range of the techniques that one could use. The other point about it was that, as I said, it didn't involve any particular hard work, or any particular intelligence on my part. It was one of those things which sometimes just happens in a laboratory if you stick apparatus together and see what results you get.'

These entertaining reminiscences set Adrian's biographer a number of questions, of which the most obvious is 'What is meant by "It was in the early 20's" '. The answer (for which I am indebted for much helpful discussion with Mr R. Frank) is: probably somewhere between September 1924 and July 1925. This may seem inconsistent with 'early 20's' but Adrian, in spite of his excellent memory, was not always reliable about dates and, as is well known, it is usually difficult to be sure of the date of something that happened 30 years ago, even though the experience itself is vividly remembered.

The reason for placing the experiments after the autumn of 1924 is that, on 7 September 1924, Adrian wrote to Forbes saying that he liked Forbes's 'leg-puller' results. This is clearly a reference to the paper by Forbes, Campbell and Williams[60] in which the authors used a string galvanometer aided by electron-tube amplification to demonstrate the passage of sensory impulses travelling towards the central nervous system when a muscle is stretched. If Adrian had detected such impulses before September 1924 he would almost certainly have mentioned this in the letter written on 7 September.

No correspondence between Gasser and Adrian survives, but, from a study of the Adrian–Forbes letters, Mr R. Frank concludes that it was probably early in 1925 that Adrian wrote to Gasser asking for the details of the three-stage amplifier which he and Newcomer had used in their 1921 paper and subsequently improved for Gasser's work with Erlanger[61] in recording with the cathode-ray oscillograph. In the first full paper of the series Adrian[62] acknowledges his debt to Gasser and to the staff of Messrs W. G. Pye and Co. of Cambridge, who redesigned an instrument on the same general lines and planned the very compact and well-shielded layout of the apparatus.

Adrian and Sybil Cooper gave a preliminary report of the detection of action currents in sensory nerve fibres recorded with the Gasser type amplifier and capillary electrometer at the Physiological Society meeting in Oxford on 4 July 1925.[63] This date sets the later limit to Adrian's initial amplifier experiments, but it seems likely that he must have been working with the amplifier for at least a month before that because in Adrian (1926a) he describes experiments on the vagus and cardiac depressor nerve as well as those on stretch receptors. We know that the experiments on the vagus were done before the autumn of 1925 and probably earlier because Adrian talked about them to the Physiological Society on 17 October 1925.[64] All this suggests that the critical experiment referred to in 'Memorable experiences' was done during the first half of 1925.

Mr R. Frank,[65] who has studied the history of electrophysiology during this period, raised the question of why there was a gap of three or four years between Adrian's initial interest in the valve amplifiers which Forbes was developing and the successful development of Adrian's three-stage amplifier and capillary electrometer. He suggested that a possible reason might have been that Forbes's one-stage amplifier was not powerful enough for use with the capillary electrometer, and that Adrian had insufficient funds to pay for all the blown strings that using an amplifier with a string galvanometer would involve. There may be something in this, but the main reason was probably psychological rather than financial. Adrian was intensely busy at this period of his life and, as long as things were going reasonably well, he preferred to use such time as he had doing experiments that worked, as opposed to developing apparatus for which he saw no obvious function. It was only when he felt himself becoming bogged down in unprofitable experiments that Adrian took time off to consult Gasser and W. G. Pye and Co., and then built the three-stage amplifier which he used with a capillary electrometer. He became really enthusiastic in the summer of 1925 and on 30 August wrote from Switzerland to Forbes saying that he had been having a fine time with an amplifier and the capillary electrometer and could hardly bring himself to go off on a holiday.

### (ii) *Collaboration with Yngve Zotterman*

Adrian's early work on impulses produced by sensory endings is described in a series of four papers; the first and last of which are by Adrian alone and the middle two are with Zotterman.[66] In the first paper, in which the valuable help of Sybil Cooper (Mrs Creed) is acknowledged, Adrian describes the new technique and gives records from several kinds of sensory ending in which one can see oscillations that Adrian thought (correctly) represented action currents travelling in single nerve fibres. However, all the records were made from nerve trunks containing many afferent nerve fibres and it was impossible to tell with certainty what was happening in each fibre, what was the frequency of the response, how it varied with the stimulus and so on.

After the arrival of Yngve Zotterman on 22 September 1925[67] the deficiency was remedied by isolating one end-organ and studying trains of impulses in a single sensory nerve fibre. The end-organ chosen was one of the stretch-sensitive receptors in the sternocutaneous muscle of the frog which could be isolated by cutting the muscle into strips. When only one end-organ was left, stretch caused a regular discharge of impulses, all of the same size but with frequency varying with the intensity of the stimulus.

The third paper of the series was concerned with impulses set up by touch and pressure and the fourth, which will be considered later, with pain. The general conclusion which now seems rather obvious can be stated in a few words. In a single nerve fibre the electrical impulse is invariant and does not change with the nature or strength of the stimulus; the intensity of a sensation is controlled by the frequency of the discharge and the number of fibres in action, whereas the quality depends on the central connections of the type of nerve fibre that is being stimulated. Another very important point which came out of Adrian's work in the mid-1920s is that adaptation to a steady stimulus takes place peripherally, and that some sense organs, like those concerned with touch, are rapidly adapting, whereas others, like muscle spindles, are slowly adapting, or may not adapt at all. To illustrate this last point in lay terms: the reason we do not feel our clothes all the time is not that the brain gets used to a steady stream of impulses, but that the touch endings in the skin are rapidly adapting and fire off impulses only when the local pressure or contact changes.

Adrian summarized the position at the end of his first book *The basis of sensation*[68] in the following way:

> 'The sequence of events between the stimulus and the mind can be seen most clearly in a diagram [figure 1]. The stimulus is represented as appearing suddenly and remaining at a constant value. The excitatory process in the receptor declines gradually, and as it declines the intervals between the impulses in the sensory fibre become longer and longer. The impulses are integrated by some central process, and the rise and decline of the sensation is a fairly close copy of the rise and decline of the excitatory process in the receptor. The quality of the sensation seems to depend on the path which the impulses must travel, for apart from this there is little to distinguish the message from different receptors.
>
> 'Figure 1 makes a fitting conclusion to this book, for it summarizes all that has been said so far about the action of the sense organs. A diagram of this kind is bound to be crude and it is not meant to imply any

particular psycho-physical doctrine. It does not bridge the gap between stimulus and sensation, but at least it shows that the gap is a little narrower than it was before.'

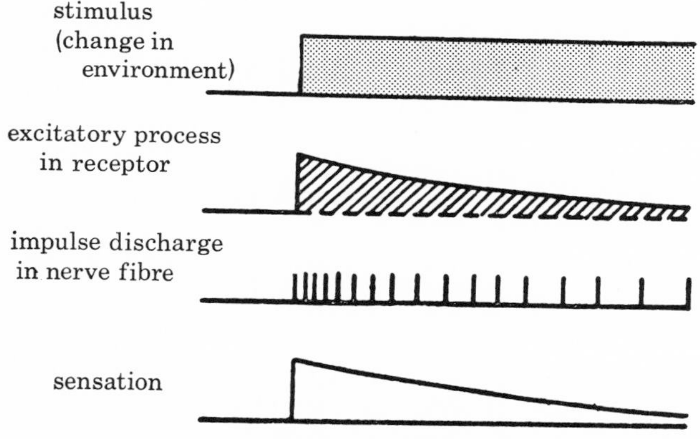


FIGURE 1. Relation between stimulus, sensory message and sensation. (From Adrian 1928a.)

### (iii) *Collaboration with Rachel Matthews*

Zotterman left Cambridge in April 1926 and although Adrian had three longish papers to write up, as well as doing his usual massive amount of teaching, he seems to have forged straight ahead with a new paper on pain; he also started experiments on the action of light on the frog's eye.[69] In the autumn he took up the subject of vision again in an extended investigation with Rachel Eckhard (later Matthews) to whom he gave the job of finding a suitable cold-blooded vertebrate with a long optic nerve. After looking at plaice as well as fresh-water and conger eels, they chose congers, a supply of which was laid on by Rachel Eckhard. The new work involved substantial changes in technique, partly because, as Adrian and Rachel Matthews said, the recording of optic nerve impulses was a more difficult undertaking than the recording of impulses from peripheral sense organs. A capillary electrometer was still employed, but the gain of the amplifier was increased and four, rather than three, stages were sometimes employed. The research involved building much new optical equipment for stimulating the eye, and photographic films rather than plates were employed; a note at the end of the first paper thanks the Royal Society for financing the research in which 4000 feet [1300 m] of film was used.

The electroretinogram had been studied since the time of Holmgren[70] but no one before Adrian and Matthews had looked at the impulses in the optic nerves of vertebrates, although Fröhlich[71] had carried out this experiment on cephalopod eyes. Adrian and Rachel Matthews were then opening up a field which has grown in magnitude until it is almost an industry. A rough estimate is that some 1000 papers are now published annually on the electrophysiology of vision. Nevertheless, if someone who considers himself reasonably well up in the modern literature takes time off to re-read Adrian and

Matthews on the eye, he will find himself making mental comments such as 'I had forgotten that' or 'I wonder why that is?' or 'that would be a good question for a research student to look at'.

The final account of the research was divided into three parts.[72] The first deals with the discharge of impulses in the optic nerve; the second with the relation of the optic nerve discharge to the retinal current, and the third with the interaction of retinal neurons. The main findings were that the action currents in optic nerve fibres did not differ appreciably in time relation or groupings from those in other sensory nerve fibres, and again that the size of the action current was not affected by the strength of the stimulus. When the eye was illuminated the discharge of impulses rose rapidly to a maximum frequency and then declined almost to zero; hence the eye, like other sense organs which give information that reaches consciousness in man, exhibits the phenomena of adaptation and responds mainly to alterations of intensity. An unexpected feature of the response of the optic nerve was the off discharge. Thus if the illumination was maintained for more than a second there was a renewed outburst of impulses when the light was switched off. Owing to the relatively high sensitivity to changes in illumination, movements of light and shadow in the visual field were a much more effective pattern than steady illumination. These general conclusions have been confirmed repeatedly; the only major point which Adrian and Matthews missed and which was not discovered for 20–25 years was the phenomenon of lateral inhibition and the existence of an inhibitory surround.

In commenting on adaptation in the eye in *The basis of sensation*, Adrian anticipates modern work on the stabilized retinal image which indicates that we constantly regenerate the visual scene by making small, involuntary, saccadic movements of the eye as well as larger conscious movements. Thus he says:[73]

> 'An uncritical examination of our own visual impressions would lead us to suppose that there is no such adaptation in the human eye, that a light of moderate intensity appears equally bright as long as we look at it. But it has been known for a long time that the brightness of an image does, in fact, decline fairly quickly provided that the eye is not moved. It is easy to satisfy oneself of this by looking at something which is faintly visible in a darkened room with one eye closed and the other kept from moving by light pressure with the finger on the lower lid. In twenty seconds or less the object will have disappeared and the whole field will be uniformly dark (not black however). As soon as the eye is moved the object reappears. The eye is a much more important sense organ in man than in the eel, but evidently the rapid adaptation of the eel's retina is shared to some extent by our own.'

Another important finding was that provided a flash of light covered an area less than about 1 $mm^2$ and did not exceed a critical duration of about 0·05 s, then the initial part of the optic nerve discharge obeyed both Riccó's law and the Bunsen–Roscoe law, as had previously been proposed on the basis of psychophysical experiments.[74] Quantitatively, if $I$ is the light intensity, $T$ the duration of the flash and $A$ the area illuminated, then all stimuli for which $ITA$ = constant gave discharges in the optic nerve with the same latency and maximum frequency, provided $T < 0{\cdot}05$ s and $A < 1$ mm$^2$. From these and other experiments the conclusion was that there is a primary change coinciding with the flash of light which forms a product proportional to the quantity of light received and a secondary change outlasting the flash which leads ultimately to the excitation of nervous structures. The rate of the secondary change is a linear function of the amount of 'light product' or light 'effect' formed in the primary change. In order to explain the effects of area it was necessary to suppose that the secondary effect must be diffused widely over the retina or concentrated into a small number of nervous paths with overlapping fields.

The third paper which deals with neural interactions in the retina contains two interesting observations on the action of strychnine. In the first place the authors found that strychnine caused a marked increase in the range over which spatial summation occurred, from which they concluded that many of their area effects were due to nervous summation in the synaptic layers of the retina. A related observation, which brings up a subject that was to become one of Adrian's recurrent interests, is that strychnine strongly promotes the tendency of the optic nerve to give synchronized rhythmic discharges at a frequency of 5–15Hz, in response to steady light.

Adrian could easily have worked on the retina for the rest of his life but by the autumn of 1927 he was anxious for a change and wrote to Forbes[75] saying that the eye was 'beastly complex' and that he wanted to get on to something easier. So when Detlev Bronk arrived in 1927 Adrian was ready to switch from the sensory to the motor side and to reinvestigate one of the subjects in which he had felt himself getting bogged down in 1923–24.

### (iv) *Impulses in motor nerve fibres: the collaboration with Detlev Bronk*

The two papers published by Adrian and Bronk in 1928 and 1929 deal with efferent impulses in the phrenic nerve to the diaphragm, and with similar impulses evoked by reflex action or volition in a variety of nerves supplying voluntary muscle. The authors introduced two technical procedures which have been widely used ever since. The first[76] was to listen to nerve impulses on a loudspeaker, as well as to record them electrically, and the second was to isolate all but two or three fibres by cutting through practically all the nerve trunk in a region central to the recording electrodes. Both papers reach similar conclusions, which now seem absurdly simple and straightforward. In order to understand their significance we must go back a long way in time.

It had been known since the end of the eighteenth century that application of brief electric shocks to a nerve-muscle preparation caused the muscle to give a brief twitch and that a succession of shocks gave a series of incompletely fused twitches, unless the frequency was high enough to give a fused response of maximal force. The twitch-like movements evoked by electrical stimulation were similar to certain voluntary movements or to a rapid reflex response such as a knee jerk, but seemed quite unlike the slow, graded contractions involved in maintaining posture. The matter was complicated by the fact that a strong voluntary movement was accompanied by a fairly regular rhythmic electric response, of frequency about 50/s, known as the Piper rhythm, whereas very small irregular waves of no definite frequency were all that could be seen in a weak voluntary contraction.

These observations led to a good deal of theorizing of which Adrian gave the following account in a review written in 1918:[77]

> 'Many attempts have been made to show that voluntary muscle contains two distinct contractile mechanisms for the twitch and for the tonic contraction supplied by two sets of nerves, medullated and non-medullated, or by two forms of nervous impulse. If this is so it is clear that the production (and inhibition) of tone must be due to a mechanism quite distinct from that studied in the muscle-nerve preparation. The theory owes most of its development to Bottazzi, who identifies the two contractile mechanisms with the sarcostyles and sarcoplasm of the muscle; it certainly offers an easy way out of the many difficulties which arise when we attempt to compare the twitch and the tetanus of the frog's gastrocnemius with the nicely adjusted movements of the living body, but it does so by postulating a mechanism of which we have as yet no direct proof and of a nature sufficiently vague to make disproof very difficult.'

Adrian and Bronk's[78] observations show that such complicated theories were incorrect as well as unnecessary. There is only one kind of impulse in a motor nerve fibre, as well as in a sensory one, and the force of contraction, like the intensity of a sensation, is graded by varying the frequency of nerve impulses and the number of nerve fibres in action. A smooth graded contraction is obtained at low levels of stimulation because the response of the nerve fibres is not synchronized, so the muscle as a whole gives a smooth response even though the response of the individual motor units may be very jerky. At high levels of stimulation the different nerve fibres may work more in unison, but they can do so 'without prejudice to the smoothness of the contraction for there will be a nearer approach to a complete tetanus in each unit'.[79]

By using concentric needle electrodes inserted into their own muscles (one of Adrian's favourite demonstrations to students), Adrian and Bronk[80] showed that the results which they had obtained on cats applied equally to man. As Adrian says, 'with the best will in the world it is impossible to send a regular succession of impulses into one's triceps at a frequency lower than 5–10/s, but above this the regularity is very good; the upper limit seems to be in the region of 45–50/s, but usually so many units are in action that their rhythms cannot be distinguished'.[81]

This seems the right place to consider some little-known but interesting experiments carried out with Bronk and Phillips[82] on post-ganglionic sympathetic nerve fibres which are very small, 2 μm or less, and unmyelinated. The electrical impulses recorded looked like single fibre action potentials but were much larger than those expected from 1 or 2 μm axons. Adrian and his colleagues suggested that as one preganglionic fibre supplies about 30 post-ganglionic ones, the post-ganglionic fibres are synchronized into groups like the responses of muscle fibres in a motor unit.[83] The discharge of impulse is rather less regular than in nerves supplying skeletal muscle, but apart from these minor differences the general features of sympathetic motor control are similar to those in the somatic system.

### (v) *Collaboration with Bryan Matthews: advances in instrumentation*

Adrian and B. H. C. Matthews's first joint paper appeared in 1933 but they had been working together for five or six years before that in the sense that each had a strong influence on the other's research. Adrian was Matthews's research supervisor and provided the initial inspiration for the beautiful work on amphibian and mammalian muscle spindles which Matthews carried out between 1928 and 1933. But Matthews's contributions to instrumentation had an equally important effect on Adrian's own research, as well as on the activities of the small team of visitors who worked with them in the period 1928–38.

Until Matthews joined his group all Adrian's experiments were done with an amplifier and capillary electrometer. Although records obtained in this way could be corrected by a machine devised by Keith Lucas,[84] this was a laborious procedure and not practicable when impulses followed one another in rapid succession. The alternatives were the string galvanometer, whose string was easily broken and which had other disadvantages, a Duddell type oscilloscope, which would have required enormous amplification,[85] and the cathode-ray oscillograph, which now seems the obvious instrument. However, until the early 1930s the cathode-ray tubes available had such low actinic power that many traces had to be superposed in order to obtain a clear photographic record. This could be done when a nerve was stimulated electrically but was clearly impossible when impulses followed one another at varying intervals, as in all Adrian's work. The Matthews oscilloscope, a simple, robust and relatively cheap instrument, proved ideal for recording naturally occurring nerve impulses. It was essentially similar to a loudspeaker but with modifications to give it a flat frequency response, and with a mirror fixed to an iron tongue that could be deflected electromagnetically. This instrument was responsible for the many elegant pictures taken by Adrian, B. H. C. Matthews, Bronk, Hartline and others, which are still widely reproduced in textbooks. It is singularly fortunate that at a time when the work of Adrian and his colleagues was in full swing they should have been able to use an instrument that produced such aesthetically satisfying records as the Matthews oscilloscope.

Matthews also developed one of the earliest 'push–pull' amplifiers as well as a multichannel inkwriter. Both these innovations were important for the work that Adrian and Matthews did together on cortical waves in the early 1930s.

### (vi) *The mechanism of nervous actions*

A good deal of the work done by Adrian and his colleagues in the period 1927–32 is described in *The mechanism of nervous action*, a book, based on the Eldridge Reeves Johnson Lectures, which was published in 1932.[86] The first two chapters go over much the same ground as *The basis of sensation*, but show that the principles established in the earlier book have a general application. The range of adaptation rates is broadened; at one extreme there are certain very rapidly adapting touch receptors and, at the other, the stretch receptors supplying vagal nerve fibres, which signal the degree of inflation of the lungs with virtually no adaptation at all. Adrian describes an interesting analogy between the injury discharge of a nerve depolarized at one end and the rather similar discharge of a sense organ, with a discussion which foreshadows modern ideas about the generator potential of sense organs.

Adrian also looked at impulses in the auditory nerve, a short thick nerve trunk which is very difficult to isolate from the surrounding tissue and therefore poor material for electrical investigation. In 1930 Wever and Bray had connected the nerve to an amplifier and telephones and obtained a result at variance with the Helmholtz theory of pitch discrimination (the place theory). For they found that any sound reaching the ear was reproduced in the telephone: speech could be understood and a voice identified, as if the cochlea was translating sound waves into electrical vibrations which were then transmitted up the auditory nerve. Adrian was initially sceptical about these results.[87] and later says, rather handsomely,[88] 'I have to confess that I thought they were mistaken (Adrian 1931c) and as it turns out I was mistaken myself (Adrian, Bronk & Phillips 1931). The fact is that very large potential changes are generated within the cochlea and these confuse the issue'. This is not the place to discuss the difficult subject of hearing, but a modern verdict might be that Adrian was being rather hard both on himself and on Helmholtz's theory when he says:[89] 'It is, I think, an open question whether there will be much left of the resonance hypothesis of the cochlea when Wever and Bray have finished their investigations; the structure of the cochlea is the main argument for the resonance hypothesis, but it is clear that we might expect to obtain something like the Wever and Bray effect in any preparation of tactile receptors thrown into rapid vibration.' Characteristically, Adrian goes on to hedge his bets by pointing out how difficult it would be for the auditory centres in the brain to distinguish one composite[90] high frequency from another, and concludes 'But it will be time to discuss these knotty problems of central activity when we are more certain of the peripheral events'.

Several years later Adrian[91] collaborated with Craik and Sturdy in an interesting series of experiments on the ears of tortoises, terrapins and alligators, animals which have since proved to be particularly favourable for auditory studies. Their paper makes entertaining reading because the authors first obtained a general idea of the response to sound by speaking, singing or humming to the animals and comparing the electrical response of the auditory nerve with that of a microphone. The reader is then shown records of the response of a tortoise to phrases like 'Good morning', or 'How do you do'. Later the experiments were moved to the Psychological Laboratory where Rawdon Smith had arranged a high class sound-proof room fitted with sound generators of advanced design. The upshot was that the electric response of the auditory nerve followed the response to sound up to frequencies of 200–300/s, but that the upper limit was greatly influenced by temperature. The results emphasized the value of a constant high temperature for the nervous mechanism of the ear, and for any group of receptors signalling frequencies of vibration.

The third chapter of *Nervous action* deals with the problem of pain, a subject of great medical as well as physiological importance. As Adrian said:[92] 'We have come to realise nowadays that, although pain may be a valuable danger signal, it may be better to have no signal at all than to have one that makes life a burden.' In his 1926e paper Adrian thought it possible that a momentary stimulation of a pain receptor might evoke a sensation that was not painful. This may be true, but as Adrian pointed out in *Nervous action* it does not follow from the evidence he obtained in 1926 because he made 'the beginner's mistake of assuming that the method was perfect'[93]—i.e. that all impulses would be recorded. On reinvestigating the subject he concluded that in frogs at 16 °C, tactile impulses travel at 15–18 m/s, heat impulses at 6–9 m/s and those due to injury at 0·5 to 5 m/s and probably at even slower velocities. From this Adrian concluded that pain reactions are produced mainly by impulses carried in small nerve fibres, often unmyelinated, which have slow conduction rates.

In an important paper with McKeen Cattell and Hudson Hoagland,[94] Adrian was able to exclude the possibility that a high frequency of impulses in any sensory nerve fibre might cause pain. For he and his colleagues found that an air blast interrupted at 150/s, or higher, gave a discharge of the same frequency in the nerve fibres from tactile endings in the frog's skin. Yet when the same intermittent air blast was directed on the skin of an intact frog the animal frequently paid no attention, or made only small movements, quite different from those elicited by a pin prick.

Adrian returned to the subject of pain in his last book *The physical background of perception*, which was based on the Waynflete Lectures given in Oxford in 1946.[95] Some of his tentative conclusions are best conveyed by direct quotations from that book which will, incidentally, give the reader some idea of Adrian's style as a lecturer.

(P. 27) 'In the nerves from the teeth,[96] for instance, the usual streams of potential waves are set up by the slightest touch on the intact tooth, but the exposure and laceration of the pulp, the mere thought of which is painful, produces no more than a slight irregularity of the electrical record—something which we should never take to be of any significance at all if we had never been to a dentist and did not know what urgent messages must be passing up the nerve fibres and what pain they would cause if they were allowed to reach an unanaesthetized brain.'

And as to why pain has to be so painful:

(p. 29) 'It [pain] must be a sensation to which we cannot manage to remain inattentive and one which we feel compelled to bring to an end as soon as possible. If it were not so painful there is the danger that we should disregard it and damage ourselves still more.'

And as to the absence or paucity of the representation of pain in the cortex:

(p. 30) 'At all events, as far as the brain is concerned pain signals may cause profound changes in general activity but seem to have no clear place in the map of events which is found there. We do not think in terms of pain as we do in terms of sight and sound. That, no doubt, is related to the fact that the signalling mechanism for pain is less elaborate and depends on such small and obscure nerve-fibres. It is disappointing to the electro-physiologist that they are not larger and more numerous, but it is probably a good thing for our comfort.'

## IX. Experimental work on the brain, 1933–46

### *Electrical oscillations and the Berger rhythm*

During the early 1930s, Adrian was becoming increasingly interested in the ways in which the nervous system might generate rhythmic electrical activity. He and his colleagues had studied electrical oscillations in preparations of increasing complexity: single muscle fibres[97] treated with 0·6% NaCl, the optic ganglion[98] of the water beetle *Dytiscus*, the isolated brain stem[99] of the goldfish and the cortex[100] of anaesthetized rabbits or cats. This work led to the famous papers with B. H. C. Matthews[101] and Yamagiwa[102] which consolidated the initial work of Berger[103] and helped to found the important clinical subject of electroencephalography.

In 1929 Hans Berger of Jena reported that under certain conditions an electrical oscillation of frequency about 10/s could be recorded from the surface of the human head. This rhythm appeared when the eyes were closed and disappeared when they were opened. Berger supposed that the whole cortex gave rise to the rhythm and that it disappeared when the eyes were opened because activity of the visual centres was associated with inhibition of the rest of the brain. In the middle 1930s Adrian, Matthews and Yamagiwa confirmed Berger's main findings, but showed that the rhythm was developed in the occipital and parietal regions, the large areas between the receiving stations for vision and touch.[104] Adrian and his colleagues confirmed Berger in showing that the rhythm disappeared in deep sleep, or if the subject is anaesthetized. In conscious subjects the easiest way of turning it on or off is by closing or opening the eyes (figure 2). However, as Adrian helped to show, the overriding condition is that the subject should be inattentive visually. Thus the rhythm can often be abolished in the dark, or when the eyes are closed if the subject makes strenuous attempts to see; and it may develop with the eyes open in the light if the visual scene is blurred and the subject's attention to it is distracted by an auditory stimulus. Adrian and Matthews[105] found, as Berger had done, that when the eyes are closed the rhythm can usually be abolished if the subject tries to solve a problem or to answer a question involving mental arithmetic. Adrian and Matthews demonstrated this effect to the Physiological Society at the Cambridge meeting in May 1934 with Adrian as

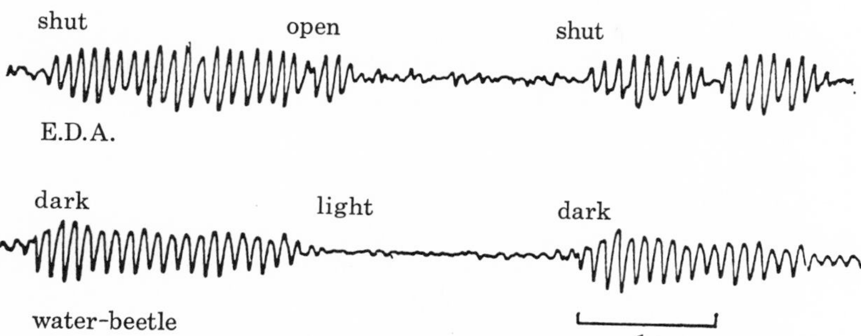


FIGURE 2. The electroencephalogram of a human subject (E. D. A.), recorded with electrodes on the scalp, showing the prominent α rhythm at about 10 Hz with the eyes shut, and its disappearance when the eyes are open.

The lower record shows the very similar rhythm obtained by leading from the optic ganglion of a water beetle in the dark, which again is blocked by allowing light to enter the eye. (Adrian and Matthews, *Brain*, **57**, 355, 1934.)

subject. Everything worked according to plan until the questioner pushed too hard and asked something too difficult, such as the cube root of 343, at which point Adrian made no real effort and his Berger rhythm continued undisturbed.

The extent to which subjects are able to influence their Berger rhythm by mental activity, or by switching their attention to or away from vision, varies considerably between different people, and it is interesting that Adrian's own rhythm was unusually responsive, though it is an open question whether this had anything to do with his powerful, darting, intelligence.

Soon after Adrian and his colleagues had established that the Berger rhythm came from the occipital part of the cortex, the field of human electroencephalography (e.e.g.) was taken up enthusiastically by clinicians and physiologists and has continued to grow until the subject has its own societies, journals and international congresses. The e.e.g. is used to diagnose certain conditions, for example *petit mal*, *grand mal* and several kinds of encephalitis. It is also helpful in a more general context and no large hospital is likely to be without its electroencephalograph. Thus if a subject who has had a motor accident thought to be caused by a blackout has a normal electroencephalogram (e.e.g.) it is unlikely that he is an epileptic; a normal e.e.g. helps to eliminate several unpleasant neurological complaints and an abnormal one to confirm a diagnosis made on other grounds.

Adrian's own ideas about internally generated cortical rhythm, as opposed to rhythms generated by flickering lights, which he also studied, was that cells in the cortex tended to beat in unison when they were not engaged in detailed activity of a kind which might come to consciousness. This fitted with several lines of evidence which he had accumulated on animals and with the fact that major epileptic fits (*grand mal*) are associated with very large electrical oscillations. But as he said:[106]

> '. . . it is clear that for consciousness it is not necessary that the whole of the cortex should be capable of differential activity. Electrical records show that in some epileptics considerable regions may be involved in an abnormal rhythmical activity for some time before or after the attack where consciousness is lost. No doubt Dostoievsky's hero, Prince Muishkin, would have shown abnormal waves throughout the periods of mental stress which preceded his fits. That the mind can still function with abnormal waves in much of the cortex is not more remarkable than that it can still function when half the cortex is giving the regular beat of the $\alpha$ rhythm, or when a large part is removed by the neuro-surgeon. What seems to be necessary is that some part of the cortex should still be free to react to the incoming messages from the sense organs and to those handed on from other parts of the brain, that there should be differential rather than uniform activity in some part of the cortical area, though not necessarily in a very large part.'

### *Studies on the motor cortex*

As might be expected from his interest in sensation and perception Adrian did far more work on the areas of the cortex concerned with sensation than those concerned with voluntary movement. In a paper published in 1936[107] he showed that both sensory and motor cortex exhibited a particular kind of facilitation on repeated stimulation in that the electrical response was at first confined to the superficial layers but later spread to the deeper layers. In the case of the motor cortex Adrian found that movement of the limb occurred only when the response had spread to the deeper layers. This interesting finding was followed up in a later paper with G. Moruzzi[108] in which the authors were able to record trains of impulses from the nerve fibres in the pyramidal tract which runs from the motor cortex to the appropriate part of the spinal cord. This paper established that spinal motoneurons have a definite threshold and do not fire until the discharge in the pyramidal tract reaches a certain intensity in terms of the frequency in each fibre and the number of fibres in action. The paper contains several interesting observations but it is difficult to do justice to them here without becoming too technical.

### *Experiments on the cerebellum*

The general functions of the cerebellum had been made clear by clinical studies particularly those of Gordon Holmes[109] in the First World War which showed that the cerebellum played a major part in maintaining posture as well as in helping man to carry out voluntary movements in a smooth, semi-automatic manner. But in 1940 nothing was known of the intimate working of the cerebellum, a subject to which Adrian was able to make a major contribution.[110]

By using what by then were standard electrical methods and barbiturates as an anaesthetic he mapped out both the representation of the body and the input from the motor cortex on the surface of the cerebellum of cats and monkeys. He also showed that a characteristic electrical rhythm of relatively high frequency, 150–250Hz, could be recorded from the surface of the cerebellum.

Once again these studies opened up a large field of which an admirable account was written by Adrian's pupil Moruzzi[111] in 1950. Since then the subject has continued to expand and to attract outstanding scientists from many disciplines, as can be seen from the book by Eccles, Ito and Szentágothai[112] or the writings of D. Marr.[113] But the student or non-specialist who wants to get a general idea of what is going on in the cerebellum cannot do better than read the few pages devoted to cerebellar functions in Adrian's last book,[114] from which the following passage is taken:

> 'There is one other folded sheet of nerve-cells, the cerebellum, which protrudes behind the cerebrum. It looks like a smaller version of the cerebrum and has a structure resembling it though with finer folding of the surface and different types of nerve-cell. In spite of its resemblance to the cerebrum the cerebellum has nothing to do with our mental activity. Conscious experience seems to depend entirely on what goes on above it in the cerebral cortex and its central cell masses. The cerebellum has the more immediate and quite unconscious task of keeping the body balanced whatever the limbs are doing and of ensuring that the limbs do what is required of them. Its action shows what complex things can be done by the mechanism of the nervous system in carrying out the decisions of the mind. If I decide to raise my arm a message is dispatched from the motor area of one cerebral hemisphere to the spinal cord and a duplicate of the message goes to the cerebellum. There, as a result of interactions with other sensory impulses, supplementary orders are sent out to the spinal cord so that the right muscles come in at the exact moment when they are needed, both to raise the arm and to keep the body from falling over. The cerebellum has access to all the information from the muscle-spindles and pressure organs and so can put in the staff-work needed to prevent traffic jams and bad coordination. If it is injured the timing breaks down, muscles come in too early or too late and with the wrong force. The staff-work needs to be elaborate, particularly when the body has to be balanced on two legs and uses its arms for all manner of movement, but it is done by the machinery of the nervous system after the mind has given its orders. The cerebellum has nothing to do with formulating the general plan of campaign. Its removal would not affect what we feel or think, apart from the fact that we should be aware that our limbs were not under full control and should have to plan our activities accordingly.'

### *Work on the sensory cortex*, 1940–46

In 1937 Marshall, Woolsey & Bard[115] showed that when an animal is deeply anaesthetized with one of the barbiturates, stimulation of cutaneous receptors produces a localized activity in an area which seems to depend on fixed anatomical connections. Adrian[116] found the same fixed localization when he studied afferent impulses instead of the slower electrical changes, and he used this method to map out the representation of tactile and pressure receptors in a number of different animals: rabbit, cat, dog and monkey in 1941, sheep, goat, pig and Shetland pony in 1943, and again Shetland pony in 1946. The experiments must have been physically demanding. After 1938 Adrian worked alone, his custom being to dispense with the help of his faithful assistant, Leslie Hatton, as soon as the animal was anaesthetized and a single pair of hands could cope.

The general results fitted in with what was known from the earlier work of Dusser de Barenne[117] and the contemporary work of several American groups.[118] The body is represented by a crude cortical map upside down and on the opposite side in the somatic receiving area. However, there are great differences between animals. In man and monkeys the hands, mouth, lips and face occupy a disproportionate area. The hands one can easily understand, but it is not obvious why the lips and face should be so prominent. As Adrian[119] said, it is true that monkeys and human babies often examine an object by taking it into their mouth, but this does not explain why the skin of the face particularly that round the nostrils and lips should have such a large representation. He therefore suggested that the explanation might be that we are descended from animals without hands which used the snout and the long whiskers of the face as tactile guides. Adrian continues:

> 'Animals like the cat which hunt their food and use their forelimbs for capturing it have a reasonably large receiving area in the cortex for messages from the forefoot and foreleg. And as the whole body is used for the skilled movements of fighting, a fairly complete sensory map of it is formed in the brain. But many animals have no need to hunt and fight their prey, for their food lies round them. The limbs of a sheep or a horse are mainly employed for supporting the body and for moving it from one pasture to another. A map of the receiving area in the brain of a Shetland pony is shown in [figure 3]. The area is divided into two parts of about equal size. The part in front is solely concerned with sensory messages from the area round the nostrils; the part behind deals with all the rest of the body surface—an area many thousand times as large as that of the nostrils. In the large-scale map of the nostril the messages from different points can be clearly distinguished: in the small-scale map of the limbs there is so much convergence that points several feet apart may use the same afferent fibre to convey their signals.
>
> 'An even more striking illustration is given by the brain of the pig [figure 4]. Here the whole of the tactile receiving area seems to be devoted to the snout, and if messages from the limbs reach the cortex at all it must be in some small area where they have so far escaped recognition. The pig's snout is its chief executive as well as its chief tactile organ, spade as well as hand, whereas the legs are little more than props for the body.'

Adrian[120] found that in addition to the main, contralateral receiving area there is another area lower down, which in some animals receives messages from both sides of the body. As he remarked, the meaning of the dual representation is unclear, but it seems reasonable that each cerebral hemisphere

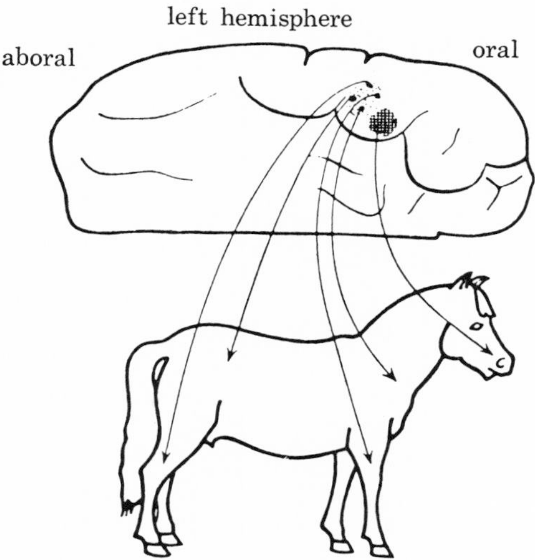


FIGURE 3. Somatic receiving area in the brain of a Shetland pony. The anterior part of the area is concerned entirely with the detailed representation of the nostril. (From Adrian, *Brain*, **69**, 5, 1946.)

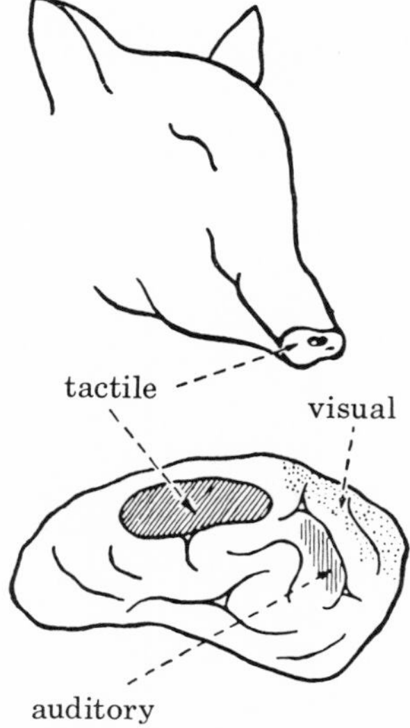


FIGURE 4. Receiving areas in the pig's brain. The tactile area is connected with the opposite half of the snout. (From Adrian, *The Lancet*, 10 July 1943, p. 34.)

should have a smaller map of the whole body besides a larger one of the larger half which it controls.

The work of Adrian and his American friends on the sensory cortex was the forerunner of studies of evoked potentials which can now be exploited with computer-averaging techniques and are of growing clinical importance because they can be recorded through the intact human skull.

### X. Work on nerve gases, 1941

During the early part of the war, Adrian, Feldberg & Kilby[121] carried out experiments on various fluorophosphonate compounds which both Germany and Britain had considered as nerve gases to be used in chemical warfare. Since neither side used these compounds it is unnecessary to make the usual claims that all research work done in one country or the other was wholly defensive in nature, though this may well be true.

Adrian was a member of the Chemical Board and must frequently have been consulted about nerve gases and related matters. The only published work is a short paper with Feldberg & Kilby which appeared in 1947. This showed that the dimethyl and diisopropyl fluorophosphonates have a strong inhibitory effect on cholinesterase, which explains their toxic action and acetylcholine-like effects.

### XI. Final experiments on sense organs, 1937–59

Anyone who tries to give a chronological account of the last 20 years of Adrian's life as an experimental scientist is faced with the difficulty that he was constantly dodging to and fro between subjects as disparate as hearing, the sense of smell, the sensory cortex, the cerebellum and the vestibular apparatus. And as we have seen, the animals used ranged in size and complexity from the water beetle to the Shetland pony or monkey. There is much to be said for such a course of action if you have the knowledge and mental agility to carry it through. When a scientist attempts to follow one paper with another on a closely related subject, there is a distinct possibility that the only new thing to emerge will be minor corrections to the first article. The scientist then has the alternatives of concealing a mistake or writing a dreary paper about some trivial error which will probably turn out to be less serious than he thinks at the time. Tactically it may be better to wait a few years and return to the subject with a fresh mind and improved technique. At all events, Adrian certainly did switch subjects a great many times between 1936 and 1946 although probably not primarily for the tactical reason mentioned above. In reading his papers from this period, one has the feeling that he was desperately anxious to survey the whole of the central nervous system, as well as the principal sense organs, and that he did not know how long he would be able to keep going in the laboratory.

#### (i) *The vestibular receptors*, 1941–43

Adrian's last experiments were on the sense of smell but in order to complete the record we must return to 1936 when one of his post-doctoral visitors,

D. A. Ross,[122] managed to record impulses from single fibres from various parts of the labyrinth in frogs. At about the same time, Sand & Löwenstein[123] made similar records from the dogfish and ray but the technique was not applied to the mammalian vestibular apparatus until Adrian's work in 1942–43.[124] One reason for the delay was the great prominence of cochlear activity in the eighth nerve of mammals; another was the difficulty of reaching the vestibular fibres without interfering with the blood supply to the organ. Adrian overcame these difficulties by using a fine wire electrode thrust into the brain stem in the region of the vestibular nerve, so as to pick up impulses from the entering bundles of vestibular fibres.

The results were beautifully clear and illustrate the principle, first enunciated by Adrian, that for simple sensations the pattern of nerve impulses coincides well with subjective human experience. If we sit in a revolving-chair with the eyes closed, a rapid turn gives a sensation corresponding to the movement, but if the chair is rotated at constant speed we feel rotation at the beginning and then the feeling subsides, to return again in the opposite direction when the chair is brought to rest. Adrian found that the discharge of nerve impulses from the cat's vestibular apparatus followed an exactly similar pattern. A brief turn was reproduced faithfully by the rise and fall in the frequency of nerve impulses, but if the rotation was continued the discharge died away in a few seconds and then reappeared from the opposite canal when the rotation ceased. Some central processing has to go on because the majority of the rotation receptors, though not all, give persistent low-frequency discharges when the head is at rest, and of this we are unaware. This steady discharge is suppressed by acceleration in the non-stimulating sense and by deceleration in the stimulating sense, and it may take 30 s before the resting discharge is fully restored. Hence all that is needed in order to convert the messages in a single fibre into something very like our sensation is to smooth out, or integrate, the intermittent discharge and balance the steady discharge from one side of the head with the corresponding discharge from the other.

In addition to the rotation-sensitive receptors there are also receptors controlled by gravity and by linear acceleration. As would be expected from our own subjective experience these receptors adapt very slowly, or not at all.

### (ii) *The sense of smell*, 1937–59

Adrian worked intermittently on chemoreception during the last 20 years of his life in the laboratory. The first paper, with Ludwig,[125] which dealt with olfaction in fish was published in 1938 and the last note on the olfactory organ of the rabbit appeared in *Journal of Physiology* in 1957.[126]

From 1951 to 1955 Adrian was President of the Royal Society and from 1951 to 1965 he was Master of Trinity College, Cambridge. In addition during this period he was Vice-Chancellor of the University of Cambridge from 1956 to 1958, President of the British Association in 1954, President and later

Chancellor of the University of Leicester from 1955 to 1970, and President of the Royal Society of Medicine in 1960–61; he also held a number of other important and time-consuming posts. It is therefore not surprising that the papers on smell which came out during the last phase of his experimental life are neither as clear nor as incisive as his earlier work. But this is at least partly due to the nature of the subject, rather than to lack of time or increasing age; for there are many reasons why the sense of smell should be particularly difficult to analyse. In man, as Adrian pointed out,[127] there are far more nerve fibres from the nose than from the eye or the ear and we can recognize a great variety of odours. Yet man is not an olfactory animal and smell does not affect thinking in the same way that sound or vision does. The visual or auditory physiologist is guided by a mass of psychophysical information whereas very little that is quantitative can be said about smell. We have a fair idea about the general mechanism of vision and hearing, but know hardly anything about olfaction. The engineer can make instruments such as the television camera and the microphone which will do all that the eye or the ear can do 'but it would take an army of chemists to plan anything like an artificial nose, if it was to signal more than a very limited number of smells'.[128] In his last book[129] Adrian points out that we can distinguish an immense variety of smells and can recognize them again. But 'we cannot analyse the sensation, presumably because for us the visual pattern is so much more worth analysing. A dog can perhaps analyse the pattern of a smell as some of us can analyse the sounds produced by a full orchestra. . . . We are rarely aware of the constituent parts of a smell pattern but probably we recognize different smells by slight differences in the pattern, just as we recognize a familiar face or voice.'[130]

As in much of his earlier work, Adrian made good use of the comparative physiological approach, using animals like hedgehogs and rabbits as well as the all-purpose cat. He was equally catholic in his choice of stimuli, for he plied these animals with odours whose complexity would make a chemist shudder; for example, fresh grass, dried herbs, clove oil, rotten meat and decaying earthworms. The results were much what one might expect. The rabbit's nose reacted well to fruity and aromatic smells like fresh grass or clove oil, but was rather insensitive to foul smells from decaying animal matter. On the other hand, the cat's nose did not react to herbs and flowers but responded strongly to foul smells and animal matter. One rather sensitive preparation gave a strong response 'whenever I came close to it'.

At first Adrian[131] thought that the nose was stimulated by the mechanical effect of air being drawn through it. For he found that a current of air which had no smell that we can appreciate set up electrical activity over two-thirds of the whole surface of the brain of a hedgehog when passed into its nose.[132] Later he found that such activity could be greatly reduced by purifying the air, and the residual effect of a strong air current could probably be explained in terms of the chemicals picked up from the nasal passages. As he says, olfactory stimuli which seem mild to us may have the same kind of effect on a hedgehog's cortex that shining a dazzling light on the cat's eye has on its brain.

One of Adrian's most important contributions on olfaction came from his studies of mitral units each of which receives from some thousand receptors and from which he was able to record unitary action potentials. He found[133] that for each mitral unit isolated there was one odour which would stimulate it at a concentration too low to affect other units in touch with the electrode. The sensitivity was usually greatest for one substance but chemically related compounds might also be effective.

From the outset Adrian had been impressed by the large size of the olfactory area, on which elaborate spatio-temporal patterns of excitation might be formed, as in the eye and the ear. 'It is a striking fact, not always appreciated, that the olfactory organ has a very large sensitive surface, larger than that of the eye in most mammals. . . . There is no reason why a large organ should be more sensitive to smells than a small one, but it will certainly provide a screen on which the pattern of excitation can be mapped in greater detail.'[134] He suspected 'that the great variety of olfactory sensation, and our failure to recognize a few primary smells from which the rest can be compounded, is far more easy to explain on the basis of characteristic patterns of discharge than on the basis of a large number of specific receptors'.[135] And his earlier experiments had seemed to support this hypothesis. The new results on the chemical specificity of mitral units caused him to revise his views. In a final summing-up in 1962 he said: 'We can only distinguish four different tastes, but we can distinguish a vast number of smells: differences in the excitation pattern, if they help at all, would be unlikely to separate more than a few general categories and, although specific receptors could give much more detail, the evidence seems scarcely enough to account for the whole range of olfactory discrimination.' However, 'olfactory recognition, like visual recognition, need not depend on a single method of sensory analysis; it may depend on several methods taken together. If smells can be separated into five categories by the spatial pattern and five more by the temporal and another 50 by the specific receptors, the number of different smells that might be distinguished would be very large. We could pick them out as we pick out a book in a library catalogue by a class mark, a letter and a number'.[136] Adrian had been in the lead in the discovery of all these three factors; and if, in the end, the balance between them eluded even his subtle grasp it is a measure of his greatness that, some quarter of a century after his experimental work ended, the general picture has not finally emerged; but what is emerging is, by and large, Adrian's sketch with the details filled in.

## XII. After the flood: last writings, 1958-77

When Adrian finished his term as President of the Royal Society in 1955 he hoped to spend more time in the laboratory than had been possible during the previous five years. However, Cambridge was having difficulty in finding a suitable Vice-Chancellor and Adrian reluctantly accepted a very pressing offer to serve as Vice-Chancellor for the usual two-year period from 1957.

Nevertheless he managed to keep going with a few experiments on smell and intended to follow this up more vigorously when he retired from the Vice-Chancellorship in 1958. How much he would have done is uncertain. He worked alone and some of his family thought that at the age of 69 he was beginning to dread the strain of a full-scale mammalian experiment. In the event the decision was taken out of his hands because his room in the basement was subjected to a flood of unusual severity, which resulted from a break in a rubber tube connected to a tap in the room above. The tap had been left running at full blast for 12 hours and after it had been turned off next day water continued to fall from the ceiling of Adrian's room for several hours. Adrian was away at the time and his colleagues who tried to salvage records and equipment were forced to use umbrellas as they waded over a floor which had acquired the consistency of a rice paddy from the combination of water and the dust that had accumulated under cupboards for the 40 years that Adrian had occupied the room. The records *were* salvaged but most of the equipment, which was of considerable antiquity, was damaged beyond repair. The damaged apparatus could have been replaced and Adrian who liked new gadgets would formerly have enjoyed using the Tektronix oscilloscopes which were then just coming into general use. But at 69 it was, as he said, too late for him to face rebuilding his equipment and learning to use new instruments and he had not the necessary energy to start work again in earnest.[137]

Adrian remained interested in the nervous system and for the rest of his life was much in demand as a lecturer. He spoke both formally and informally on subjects of general interest such as 'Sleep', 'Dreaming', 'Hysteria', 'Multiple sclerosis' and 'The English Hippocrates'.[138] A few examples mostly taken from a slightly earlier period illustrate the wit and irony which made Adrian's lectures so fascinating to hear or read.

> 'The lower creatures do not meet to discuss the factors which determine their behaviour. "Know thyself" is a precept reserved for *homo sapiens*; indeed the more academic our discussion the better we shall demonstrate our true position in the animal kingdom.'[139]

> 'The earthworm can take to its burrow when it feels the shock of footsteps on the grass, and such an immediate reaction needs only a few hundred nerve cells and fibres; but we can sell out an investment when we hear rumour that the company is unsound, and this reaction needs the ten thousand million cells of the human cerebral cortex.'[140]

On falling asleep:

> 'When we feel sleepy in the train back from London our eyes are more and more difficult to keep open, but we know that we can at least pretend to follow our neighbour's argument. It is their closure and the cutting off of visual stimuli which is the first stage in the catastrophic fall of activity in the brain and the definite loss of consciousness, and it is their opening which makes us fully awake.'[141]

In connection with the principle that the nervous system is organized to extinguish sensory messages and that in man the reaction may involve many generations and centuries of effort:

> 'Thus hunger may lead a cat to its plate and may start the feeding movements which relieve the sensation, but when the human cerebrum is involved hunger may lead to the planting of corn, to tractors and black markets and food conferences.'[142]

Or more pessimistically:

> 'For this reason I think we shall be deluding ourselves if we suppose that what we are going to do in the next hundred years will lead to a permanent increase in the happiness of the human race. I fancy that life will be much the same mixture of happiness and unhappiness that it is now—that our moods must always tend to oscillate about a position of equilibrium which does not greatly depend on external circumstances. . . . What we can be sure of giving is a more vigorous life for mankind and a greater freedom from physical pain; and if we can do more than this, so much the better for everyone.'[143]

## XIII. Adrian's own assessment of his scientific work

At the end of the brief autobiographical notes, which Adrian left in his desk, we find the following sentence 'Looking back on my own scientific work I should say that it shows no great originality but a certain amount of business instinct which leads to the selection of a profitable line'. Adrian certainly was good at picking fruitful lines, but if taken at its face value the statement seems an extreme example of his diffidence about his own abilities, for his papers are full of fascinating, highly original ideas about the way the central nervous system might work. Nor does it say anything about his experimental skill or about his marvellous command of language which makes a book like *The basis of sensation* so elegant and simple to read that it is difficult for a student of today to appreciate the novelty and importance of what is being said. Yet Adrian certainly had some limitation in mind, and one can guess what it was from an earlier discussion of the nature of scientific enquiry.

At the end of his second book *The mechanism of nervous action*, Adrian says:[144]

> 'In all branches of natural science there are two methods of approach, that of the strategist who can devise a series of crucial experiments which will reveal the truth by a sort of Hegelian dialectic, and that of the empiricist who merely looks about to see what he can find. The development of electrical technique has given a new way of looking about, and so much is going on in the nervous system that it is hard to resist the temptation to record anything that turns up. This method has had the merit of showing many unexpected resemblances in the activity of different parts of the nervous apparatus, but it gives us facts rather than theories, and the facts may not always mean very much.'

The first method, that of the strategist or practitioner of Hegelian dialectic, was clearly the one followed by Adrian from 1911 until 1925, leaving out the war years when events beyond his control took charge. It earned him a high reputation, but met with only limited success and by 1925 some of his conclusions were coming unstuck, in spite of the rigorous, self-critical attempts that he and Keith Lucas made to build up a logical structure. Although he never said so, the abandonment of the idea of a continuous decrement in narcotized nerve and of his method of measuring the intensity of the nerve impulse must have come as a bitter blow and might have finished the career of someone less resilient or less curious about nature. Happily, he went ahead with his amplifier and opened up a field which yielded enormous dividends in the next 30 years. During this period his writings are full of original conclusions but the ideas seem to arise naturally from the experiments and are not spun out of nothing by some hypothetical genius sitting in a back room with a blank pad of paper in front of him. This is possibly what Adrian meant when he refers to a sound business instinct for the profitable line but no great originality.

Another interesting point about Adrian's career is to see how the influence of Keith Lucas fades and how his early interest in psychoanalysis, hypnosis and brain–mind problems became of increasing importance in the later part of his life. One might guess that for 10 years after the war he could not bear to think very much about the terrible things that he had seen in the way of brain damage, or the neurasthenia and hysteria resulting from the appalling experiences of those who survived battles like the Somme. But later these experiences reinforced his early interest and the influence of Abrahams and Walshe with the result that the brain and the mind became the dominant interest of his life. Yet it is probably the overlap of the analytical and the descriptive approach which helped to make the years between 1925 and 1930 the high point in Adrian's scientific career.

## XIV. Teaching, administration and public affairs

### (i) *Professor of Physiology*, 1937–51

Adrian succeeded Joseph Barcroft as Professor of Physiology in Cambridge in 1937 and held the chair until 1951 when he became Master of Trinity. This did not cause any obvious reduction in his output of research but it must have made him very busy. He gave all the second year lectures on the central nervous system as well as a set of lectures in the advanced class. A feature of his lectures is that they were often accompanied by ambitious demonstrations: for example, sticking needle electrodes into his arm muscles to record the discharge of motor units, or recording action potentials from single nerve fibres in frogs or decerebrate cats.

In the years before the war, lectures to medical students were noisy affairs, and barracking and practical jokes took the place of student representation, teaching committees and integrated courses. But although lecturing on a difficult subject, Adrian never had any trouble in keeping his large audience quiet. A good example was afforded by a demonstration on the vestibular apparatus. This consisted in Adrian's fishing a duck from a wicker basket, holding it up to the audience and showing that as he rotated the body about its long axis the head remained perfectly still with the beak parallel to the ground. In the ordinary way such a demonstration would have produced stamping and roars of laughter but Adrian always retained complete control.

Adrian did not care much for paper work and as university life grew in complexity the central offices would have preferred typewritten letters to notes dashed off at high speed in his somewhat illegible script. But nothing serious was forgotten and Adrian maintained and strengthened the laboratory's distinguished position in teaching and research. In addition to the group appointed by Barcroft, which included people like Roughton, the Adairs, Rushton, Matthews and Willmer, Adrian found positions for Feldberg, G. W. Harris, A. F. Huxley, D. K. Hill, R. S. Comline and the writer, to name only a few of those who worked in the laboratory during his professorship.

The years of the Second World War cannot have been easy for Adrian. Undergraduates reading medicine had to be put through a quick two-year course by a skeleton staff and there were few demonstrators or research students to help with the experimental classes. Besides his university teaching, which involved lecturing to both first- and second-year classes, Adrian gave elementary courses of lectures on human physiology to students training to be nurses at Addenbrooke's Hospital. He was also involved in experimental work on nerve gases and with meetings of the Chemical Board in London. His wife's accident in 1942 was a source of great distress and although neither he nor Hester complained, the mechanics of everyday life in war-time cannot have been easy for either of them. Adrian took on all the shopping and could often be seen bicycling at high speed or rushing into the laboratory with a rucksack full of provisions on his back.

After the war Adrian obtained a grant from the Rockefeller Foundation which helped to support a group working on the biophysics of nerve and muscle. The original members of the 'unit' were D. K. Hill, A. F. Huxley and myself, but we were soon joined by R. D. Keynes and P. R. Lewis as well as by several distinguished visitors from abroad. Adrian did not interfere with the day-to-day activities of the group but he gave it general encouragement and let its members off with a light teaching load. He himself was much helped in administering the laboratory by H. E. Tunnicliffe and R. S. Comline as well as by the devotion and hard work of his secretary, Miss Sylvia Elton.

### (ii) *Visit to the U.S.S.R. in July* 1945

In July 1945 Sir Robert Robinson represented the Royal Society at the 220th anniversary of the founding of the Academy of Sciences of the U.S.S.R. in Moscow.[145] The Academy also extended an invitation to a number of British scientists of whom Adrian was one. Originally 30 delegates were to have gone but on the night before the group was due to depart the British Government refused to allow nine delegates to leave the country. So the party set out 'shorn of most of our physicists and mathematicians and wondering what we should say about it when we arrived. But our hosts were too polite to question the inscrutable decrees of the Foreign Office and in fact very little was said about it over there'.[146]

As other visitors have discovered, Adrian found it hard to learn all that he would like to know about the organization of scientific research in the U.S.S.R. because his time was crowded with visits to laboratories and physiological talk on the one hand, and excursions and parties on the other. He wrote that science was held in high esteem and was under no necessity to get quick dramatic results. Pavlov was a national hero and physiology was built around the work of classical masters. Superficially there was not a great deal of difference between Russia and war-time Britain. One effect of the war was a renewed pride in the Russia of the past. He saw the famous victory parade at which about 100 000 men headed by Marshal Zhukov on a white horse and Marshal Rokossovsky on a black, filed past Stalin and others on the saluting base. At the theatre, opera and ballet they saw classical performances of Chekov, Tchaikowsky and Glinka. Eisenstein's film, 'Ivan the terrible', had been shown earlier in the year but in July the cinemas in Moscow were in a more light-hearted mood for all seemed to be showing that well-known classic, 'Charley's aunt'. Altogether Adrian found Russia a great deal more invigorating than when he visited it 10 years earlier for the Physiological Congress in 1935.

Today Adrian's account seems somewhat starry-eyed, but one should remember that at that time few of the horrors of Stalin's régime had come to light and in Britain there was universal admiration for Russia's triumph over Germany as well as sympathy for her terrible sufferings. Moreover, if Adrian had any misgivings about the régime he would have been unlikely to voice them in a public lecture.

### (iii) *Foreign Secretary and President of the Royal Society*

Adrian was Foreign Secretary of the Royal Society from 1946 to 1950 and President from 1950 to 1955. His tenure of these offices is particularly remembered for the magnificent speeches that he made at the Society's Anniversary Dinners and on many other public occasions. Like Sir Francis Bacon he was one of the very few people of whom it could be said that when he spoke the only anxiety of the audience was that he would stop.

It is hard to say what made Adrian's speeches so fascinating, but some of the ingredients were a strong sense of history and tradition, great dignity of language and voice, a sharp wit and, above all, the capacity to tune his remarks exactly to the quality of the particular audience he was addressing. Nowadays we regard the ability to make a good speech as at best a minor talent. Indeed it is almost an insult to say 'X is an excellent speaker, but he isn't much good at running things'. This denigration of rhetoric or eloquence is largely a modern fashion. At other times and in other societies, republican Rome for example, rhetoric was valued highly for its own sake; and in our own recent history, the example of Churchill shows that words can be as important as deeds;

indeed military historians[147] have argued strenuously that the war would have gone much better for Britain with fewer of Churchill's deeds.

Adrian's talent was all the more remarkable because he was not naturally a fluent talker. When speaking extempore he had a habit of changing his mind half-way through a sentence and the secretary of the Trinity College Council, who greatly admired Adrian's speeches, used to refer to the Master's 'unfinished symphonies' with some exasperation. The speeches seemed to come out spontaneously but were in fact the product of draft after draft and Adrian went on changing the manuscript right up to the last minute, so that when it was finally delivered his speech had the air of being given off the cuff.

Adrian's name is not associated with any major changes or reforms at the Royal Society of the kind which have become identified with the name of a President like Lord Florey, who once said that he hoped to get something done even if he had to carry the Royal Society kicking and screaming into the twentieth century.[148] Yet the nine years for which Adrian held office, first as Foreign Secretary and then as President, were a time of steady progress and growth, for which Adrian should receive much credit, even though some of the ideas came from scientists like A. V. Hill, who preceded him as Foreign Secretary or Robert Robinson, the previous President. The period between 1945 and 1955 saw a great expansion of international scientific activities, Unesco and W.H.O. were born,[149] the International Council of Scientific Unions increased the scale of its activities by an order of magnitude and great efforts were made to help reconstruct science in Europe, first in the occupied countries[150] and then in Germany itself. The Royal Society played a major part in organizing the Empire Scientific Conference in 1946 which resulted in the setting up of important links within the Commonwealth. What happened formally was that the recommendations of the Royal Society Empire Scientific Conference were endorsed by the British Commonwealth Scientific Conference which succeeded it. The Official Conference set up a Standing Committee to watch and report on the process of implementing the recommendations.[151] Two results which might be mentioned were the setting up of a massive conference on Scientific Information in 1948[152] and perhaps more helpfully the foundation of the Commonwealth Bursaries scheme, a project organized and financed jointly with the Nuffield Foundation.[153] From 1947 to the present day British scientists travelling on scientific business abroad have been greatly helped by the Travelling Expenses Committee which was set up in that year.[154] Another highly beneficial project, the United States Research Fellowship, was started by the National Academy of Sciences of the U.S.A., with the Royal Society cooperating in the selection of candidates. This arrangement which terminated at the end of 1955 enabled up to 25 British post-doctoral fellows to spend two years in the United States.[155] On the side of big science, plans were laid for the International Geophysical Year[156] and discussions started which resulted eventually in the formation of C.E.R.N.[157] (Centre Européen de Recherche Nucléaire) and in the building of optical telescopes first in South Africa[158] and many years later in Australia.

As the cold war slackened and memories of the fate of scientists like N. I. Vavilov[159] faded, relations with the U.S.S.R. were resumed. At the invitation of the Royal Society, the President of the U.S.S.R. Academy of Science and five other Academicians visited Britain for a fortnight in November 1955.[160]

On the administrative side the Royal Society continued to be supported by the voluntary work of a series of devoted officers, as well as by the highly efficient staff built up under the able leadership of the Assistant Secretary, D. C. Martin, who served the Society so well for more than 30 years. David Martin was Robert Robinson's find, but Adrian thoroughly approved of the appointment and was on excellent terms with Martin throughout his period as Foreign Secretary and President.

From all this it is plain that the decade after the war when Adrian was closely associated with the Royal Society was a time of considerable growth and activity. Yet there were those who felt that great opportunities were lost in the post-war years. As Lovell points out in his biography of Blackett,[161] Royal Society policy immediately after the war was (a) that Treasury grants for exceptional and expensive purposes, for example telescopes, nuclear machines and so on, should be made on the advice of the Royal Society, and (b) that the Royal Society's Parliamentary Grant-in-aid should be increased very substantially. This did not satisfy Blackett, an influential member of the Royal Society's Council, who wanted the Society to become the organization primarily responsible for administering the financial support of research on a national basis. Twenty-five years later Blackett changed his mind, or at any rate realized that his earlier views were no longer practicable, but felt that his ambitions for the Royal Society were partly satisfied by the 'gradual growth of a close, even symbiotic relationship between the Society and governmental scientific departments, notably with the Department of Education and Science'.[162] Adrian's views on this debate which was running strongly when he became Foreign Secretary in 1946 are not known. One would guess that he would have argued that independence of Government was more important than financial power in controlling research. But he probably did not say very much as he would have felt that the controversy was essentially one for the physical scientists.

However, there was another major argument, which smoulders on to this day, in which Adrian was to play a decisive if little known part. This was the idea of a Science Centre on the south bank of the Thames which might house all the principal scientific societies, the Royal Society and the Research Councils, and perhaps the Patent Office. The project was originally conceived by Sir Henry Dale[163] during his Presidency and was taken up enthusiastically by his successor, Sir Robert Robinson, P.R.S. As Foreign Secretary and President-elect, Adrian was deeply concerned with this proposal which came to a head in 1950. There were evidently several interrelated questions. Provided Government money to pay rents and rates could be assured in perpetuity it might have been a good thing to have a site for scientific societies on the South Bank. But whether it would have been right for the Research Councils and the Royal Society to be there too is more doubtful. In 1950 the immediate question for

Adrian was not whether the Science Centre should be built on the South Bank, but whether the Royal Society should leave its home at Burlington House and move to the South Bank. Adrian's views are not known with absolute certainty but David Martin told me six or seven years ago that Adrian was dead against the idea. This fits with what happened and with the fact that Adrian's close friend, G. I. Taylor, subsequently wrote a letter to the P.R.S. in which he expressed strong opposition to the plan for the Royal Society to become a part of the Science Centre.[164]

In the autumn of 1950 Adrian was in a position of some difficulty. It would have been alien to his nature to argue against the outgoing President in Council, or to indicate that there was any kind of rift between them. But if he did nothing there was a good chance that during his Presidency the Society would be committed to a course of action of which he deeply disapproved. He dealt with the situation by writing a memorandum which in no way undermined the retiring President's position but which laid down stiff conditions for the Royal Society's participation in the scheme and which made Fellows of the Royal Society realize what they were letting themselves in for. This memorandum which is reproduced below was sent to the Government and later to all Fellows. Meanwhile Sir Robert Robinson in his retiring Presidential address, given on 30 November 1950, stated the case for the Science Centre.[165] Adrian's memorandum[166] was as follows:

> 'It is clearly in the interest of Great Britain and of the Commonwealth that there should be a central Academy of Science, of recognized authority, limited in numbers, electing its members on the grounds of scientific merit and so constituted that election to it is regarded by scientists in every part of the world as a mark of real eminence. The Royal Society occupies this position. Unless its status is greatly changed the letters F.R.S. will remain one of the highest rewards of scientific effort throughout the Commonwealth and its house in London will be recognized as the supreme court in scientific affairs. Its present rooms in Burlington House in the heart of London are not magnificent, but at least they emphasize its independence, one might almost say its aristocratic seclusion. Its position would be lost if it became subject to political interference and identified too closely with Government interests.
>
> 'The Royal Society cannot rely on private endowment and must be free from any dependence on industry. It cannot expect to hold its position without Government support, but under the present arrangement by which it is housed by the State and entrusted with funds for special purposes it has no difficulty in maintaining its prestige as a completely independent body. If the need arose it could dissent strongly from a Government policy based on inadequate scientific knowledge.
>
> 'The proposal to establish a Science Centre where all scientific societies shall be housed, together with some of the Government scientific offices, makes it necessary to consider very carefully what the position of the Royal Society should be in such a centre. It would soon forfeit its

reputation if it lost any of its independence and its aloofness from sectional interests, if it did not occupy a position of dignity in a building worthy of its unique status in the scientific world.

'The ideal solution would be a completely separate building. Failing this the Society's premises must form a complete unit, architecturally marked out in such a way as to express its independence. Its premises should be self-contained: though they might share services like heating with the rest of the buildings they ought not to share corridors, staircases and entrance halls. The Society must have its own meeting rooms, large enough for all ordinary occasions and must not be expected to share its lecture hall with other societies except as a favour. Its Library and its collection of historical documents, pictures, etc., must be properly housed and it must have the entire management of its office and domestic staff.

'The Society has no funds to contribute to the cost of new premises and it could not afford to move to them unless it could be sure that the expenses both of the move itself and of maintaining itself on an increased scale, would be guaranteed by the State.

'These demands are not extravagant. They are justified by the change of emphasis which would follow the establishment of the Science Centre. In Burlington House the Royal Society has no difficulty in maintaining the independence and the almost Olympian dignity and exclusiveness needed for a supreme scientific council. In a Science Centre unless it has a commanding position its prestige is bound to suffer. There is a real danger of its becoming little more than one among many scientific societies and of sinking eventually to the status of a poor relation grudgingly housed by the scientific departments of the Government.

'The Science Centre should be the focus of scientific activity for the whole Commonwealth and the Royal Society must be the principal focus of the Science Centre. It ought not to accept anything less than the best that the site can offer for the whole scheme will suffer if the Royal Society cannot play its part effectively in premises worthy of its pre-eminent role.'

This memorandum was sent to Herbert Morrison, the Lord President of the Council, who referred to it in the following sympathetic if non-committal terms:[167]

'I am thoroughly in sympathy with the statement by Professor Adrian about the status and essential needs of the Royal Society, and would like to confirm that it is the Government's wish that this latest in the list of proposed removals of the Royal Society to new accommodation is designed to help and not in any way to detract from that status, to the preservation of which His Majesty's Government continue to attach the highest importance.'

Adrian's memorandum which did not mention the proposed location of the Science Centre was enclosed with a letter sent to all Fellows of the Royal Society on 18 December 1950[168] and a further letter giving the location and inviting comments was sent to all Fellows on 8 January 1951[169] when permission to divulge the site location had been granted by the Government.

A minute from an officers' meeting dated 24 July 1951[170] indicates the nature of the replies:

'Consideration was given to replies received from Fellows regarding the proposed science centre. 29 replies were carefully considered. 10 replies representing the views of 13 Fellows were not in favour of the proposed move whilst nearly all the other replies referred to other societies which it was proposed should be included in the centre.

'Having noted the replies it was decided to forward to the Ministry of Works the letter approved by Council on 14 July and containing a statement of accommodation requirements. It was, however, decided to defer this until a reply had been received from the Lord President of the Council stating whether the Royal Entomological Society should or should not be included.'

After that the whole scheme gradually petered out without Adrian as President ever having to take any strong public stand. The following extracts from letters and minutes indicate the state of play in 1953.

From a letter of 20 February 1953 from the Royal Society to all members of the Scientific Societies Accommodation Committee:[171]

'Our Architects examined the summary of accommodation requirements which Brunt sent to Burton on 31 July 1951, and the next step would have been a detailed discussion with your people. However, as our Minister explained in the House of Commons on 17 December 1952 in reply to a question by Sir Wavell Wakefield, planning of the Science Centre has had to be deferred in view of the need for economy.'

From Sir Robert Robinson, O.M., F.R.S., to P.R.S., dated 6 March 1953:[172]

'I have received a letter sent to all Members of the Scientific Societies Accommodation Committee explaining the position in regard to the proposed Science Centre. The outcome is very disappointing since it amounts to a complete shelving of the scheme; not even planning is in progress.

'The need for economy is obvious but the application of the principle is arbitrary and relative. Many of us think that the encouragement of science should have a higher priority than is granted.

'The circulation of this letter has had a very bad effect as I had reason to know from attendance at the Chemical Society Council.

'Opponents of the scheme are now able to say "I told you so" and exert an influence altogether disproportionate to their numbers.

'I do hope you can do something to neutralise the depressing activities of the retrogressive element among us.'

By 30 November 1953 the tide was clearly running against building the centre quickly as can be seen from the following minute:[173]

'The Assistant Secretary reported informal discussions he had had with the Secretary to the Lord President of the Council, in which the latter had indicated that because of pressure from the Patent Office to obtain new accommodation there would soon be discussions as to the general layout of the site of the science centre. He had also mentioned that other sites were again being tentatively considered, such as Bloomsbury, South Kensington, the City, and Holland Park, and that the Lord President might discuss the matter informally with the President at the Anniversary Dinner.

'It was agreed that the President should indicate that in the views of the Officers none of those sites, except perhaps the first offered, was particularly attractive and none would provide the same possibilities for architectural development as the site on the South Bank. He would also mention that probably the majority of the Fellows of the Society would prefer to stay at Burlington House, as far as the Royal Society itself is concerned, but that many would be prepared to go from Burlington House because they felt it would be in the general interest of the advancement of science in this country.'

It is not the purpose of this memoir to argue that Adrian was right and Robinson wrong, or vice versa. There clearly was, and is, a good deal to be said on both sides. In any case the words right and wrong have little meaning in history except in terms of some religious or political philosophy, or when applied to actions that either alleviate or increase human suffering and misery.

The writer's own view is that, although much remains to be done, the new arrangements worked out by Lord Florey for the Royal Society at Carlton House Terrace and for the scientific societies housed in its old premises represent a satisfactory compromise between Sir Robert Robinson's grand vision and Lord Adrian's feeling for historical tradition and independence from government.

### (iv) *Membership of the House of Lords*

Adrian, who was one of the last hereditary peers to be created, became Baron Adrian of Cambridge in 1955. He clearly enjoyed this position and attended the House of Lords as regularly as his many academic commitments would allow. He sat on the cross benches and spoke on some ten occasions on the following subjects:

Foot and mouth disease, *Hansard*, **192**, 458–462
Oxford's traffic problems, *Hansard*, **201**, 809–810 (1956–57)
Aircraft industry, *Hansard*, **210**, 1151–1154 (1957–58)
Overseas Information Service, *Hansard*, **210**, 818–821 (1957–58)
Nuclear disarmament, *Hansard*, **214**, 113–117 (1959)
Science in civil life, *Hansard*, **220**, 218–225 (1960)
University and other higher education, *Hansard*, **223**, 691–695 (1960)
Scientific policy, *Hansard*, **226**, 434–439 (1961)
Scientific policy, *Hansard*, **247**, 115–121 (1962)
Chemical and biological warfare, *Hansard*, **299**, 153–157 (1968)

An air of gentle comedy surrounds Adrian's choice of a motto for his coat of arms. Adrian's friend, Andrew Gow, the son of Adrian's headmaster at Westminster, Dr James Gow (see p. 6), first suggested a Greek motto from

Epicharmus: 'μέμνασο ἀπιστεῖν', 'Remember to disbelieve'. As an alternative in Latin, Gow proposed a translation by Quintus Cicero, namely 'Non temere credere', 'Do not believe rashly'—a somewhat weaker sentiment. This was eventually adopted but not without trouble because 'temere' was initially spelt 'timere' thus completely reversing the sense of the original Greek. However, the mistake was found and corrected before it was too late.

There was also much discussion about the crest. Adrian originally intended to use the sign of Aesculapius as the central feature but did not like the result and adopted C. D. Broad's suggestion that he use ☿, the sign for Mercury. The reason according to Broad is that Mercury is *par excellence* the planet which has to do with the mind and the brain. This seems to have been as obscure to Garter Principal King of Arms as it probably is to you or me, but Garter's doubts must have been overcome and ☿ survives.

### (v) *Other activities away from Cambridge*, 1955–70

Adrian became President of the University College of Leicester in 1955 and Chancellor when Leicester became a University in 1957, an office which he held until 1971. He thus helped to promote an expansion from a relatively small institution with a population of 750 students to a fair-sized university teaching 3500 students. During this period there was considerable building activity and his name is commemorated in the fine Adrian building which houses the School of Biological Sciences.

Adrian was President of the British Association in 1954 and of the Royal Society of Medicine in 1960–61; he was a trustee of the Rockefeller University in New York from 1962 to 1965. Another post which he held for many years with much pleasure was that of Governor of Westminster School.

Some of the many honours which Adrian received are listed on pp. 61-63

## XV. Master of Trinity College, Cambridge, 1951–65

When G. M. Trevelyan retired from the Mastership of Trinity in 1951 Adrian was his obvious successor and there was never any question of an alternative candidate. Similarly in 1960, when he reached the initial age of retirement, there was universal agreement that he should be prolonged for the maximum period until 1965. As Master he will probably be best remembered for the splendid speeches that he made each year at the Commemoration Feast, a dinner attended by a large number of fellows and undergraduates and which is regarded by all as a severe test for a speaker. Other notable features of his Mastership were his care for scholars and scholarship and the magnificent way in which he and Hester Adrian entertained both fellows and undergraduates. He also oversaw the initial stages of the great building programme which started during his Mastership and was completed during that of his successor, Lord Butler. From 1957 to 1959 he bore without complaint the office of Vice-Chancellor, which he undertook in an emergency. I asked him once how he was enjoying this and received the characteristic reply, 'Not much, but you learn a great deal about human nature'.

## XVI. Retirement, 1965–77

Adrian retired from the Mastership in 1965 and moved with Hester into a new house beyond the College garden. After leading extremely strenuous and public-spirited lives both looked forward to periods of leisure and holidays together. This was not to be, owing to Hester's unexpected death soon after they had settled in their new home. Those who knew Adrian well felt that Hester's death was a blow from which he never recovered. But he was too stoical to let this show and continued to live a full and active life. He moved back into Trinity where he lived in a beautiful set of rooms in a corner of Nevile's Court. Until failing health intervened, it was his custom to entertain scholars and other undergraduates to lunch or dinner about once a week in term time.

He remained of an adventurous disposition and continued to combine a streak of unorthodoxy with a love of tradition. When he became Chancellor of Cambridge some Trinity rowing men called on Adrian and asked if they might have the honour of rowing him up-river from Trinity to the University Centre. In spite of his 78 years, Adrian accepted and, dressed in formal clothes, he coxed the boat successfully through a succession of up-river bridges.

As Chancellor his principal duty was to preside when Honorary Degrees were given and at other formal occasions. He did this with great dignity and, although it cost him a good deal, continued to produce excellent speeches when required. Adrian was never inclined to interfere in other people's affairs but he knew that running a university can be a lonely as well as a difficult business, and Vice-Chancellors at Cambridge and Leicester have spoken of the help which they received from talking to Adrian, particularly in times of student unrest. He wished to resign the Chancellorship in the summer of 1975 but stayed on till December lest anyone should think he objected to serving with a lady Vice-Chancellor.

Three events gave special satisfaction to Adrian in his last years: the birth of a great-grandson, Robert Keynes; the election of a grandson, Simon Keynes, as a Fellow of Trinity and the election of his son, Richard, to the Fellowship of the Royal Society.

Like many people, Adrian evidently looked forward to old age with some misgiving. In 1948 he wrote:[174]

> 'We must learn to emulate the car manufacturers whose products were constructed to give good service for three years and then to break down so comprehensively that the owners were spared all the anxiety of repairs and had no other course but to order the new model. It is not too much to expect that we shall soon know enough to avoid the particular habits which make us live too long for comfort, which keep our hearts going after our mind has failed.'

During the last two years of his life Adrian suffered from a number of physical and mental infirmities which must have caused him much distress. But it may have been some consolation to him that until a fortnight before his death he continued to live in his beautiful rooms in Nevile's Court in the College which he loved so well.

My thanks are due to Lord Adrian (R. H. A.) for making unpublished material available to me and for much helpful discussion; to Mr Robert Frank for many useful comments and for providing me with an invaluable summary of the Adrian–Forbes correspondence in the Countway Library of Medicine, Boston (of the existence of which I was previously unaware); to Dr P. A. Merton for providing a paragraph summing up Adrian's final views on olfaction; to Professor Zotterman for sending me copies of his letters from Cambridge and to Professor and Mrs. Sandbach of Cambridge for translating these letters; to Sir Bryan Matthews and Lady Rachel Matthews for many helpful comments; to Mrs Alton of the Contemporary Archives Centre, Oxford. I am indebted to the following for permission to reproduce figures: Granada Publishing Ltd London (figure 1), *Brain* (figures 2 and 3), *The Lancet* (figure 4); and unpublished material: The Countway Library and Professor Y. Zotterman; and finally to my secretary, Mrs M. Edwards, for much help in typing the manuscript and searching out references. This memoir, which was written in May–June 1978 and revised in January 1979, was produced independently of the excellent obituary by G. Moruzzi in *Reviews of Physiological and Biochemical Pharmacology*.

The photograph was taken by Lotte Meitner-Graf, London, *ca.* 1953.

HONORARY, FOREIGN, CORRESPONDING OR ASSOCIATE MEMBERSHIPS

1933 Societa Italiana di Biologia Sperimentale
1934 Société de Biologie, Paris
1934 Deutsche Academie der Naturforscher
1935 New York Neurological Society
1935 Academie Royale de Médicine de Belgique
1938 La Société Philomatique de Paris
1938 American Academy of Arts and Sciences
1938 Société Belge de Biologie
1938 Society of British Neurological Surgeons
1940 Academia Nacional de Medicina, Mexico
1940 Academia Nacional de Medicina, Venezuela
1941 National Academy of Science, U.S.A.
1942 Sociedad Argentina de Biología
1943 Academia Nacional de Medicina de Buenos Aires
1944 Royal Society of Medicine
1944 Uppsala Royal Academy of Sciences
1945 Centro Médico Argentino Britannico
1946 Académie de Médicine, Paris
1946 Académie des Sciences
1946 Académie Royal des Sciences d'Amsterdam
1946 Royal Society of Edinburgh
1947 American Neurological Association
1947 Accademia Nazionale dei Lincei
1947 Koninklijhe Vlaamsche Academie Voor Geneeskunde van Belgie (Royal Flemish Academy of Medicine)
1949 Societa Italiana di Fisiologia
1951 Société Française de Psychologie
1951 Sociedad de Neurología y Neurocirugía del Uruguay
1951 Danish Royal Academy of Sciences
1952 Royal Microscopical Society
1952 Deutsche Gesellschaft für Neurologie

1952 Swedish Royal Academy of Science
1954 British Psychological Society
1955 Alpine Club
1955 Royal Institute of Chemistry
1955 The Worshipful Company of Dyers
1956 The Royal Medico Psychological Association
1959 American Physiological Society
1960 Physiological Society
1960 Royal College of Physicians, Edinburgh
1960 Accademia della Scienze dell'Istituto di Bologna
1960 Académie Royal Belgique
1960 Académie Royale des Sciences des Lettres et des Beaux Arts de Belgique
1961 American Philosophical Society
1962 Swedish Medical Society
1962 British Institute of Radiology
1962 Czechoslovak Medical Society
1964 New York Academy of Sciences
1965 Eastern Association of Electroencephalographers

### Honorary degrees

1931 University of Pennsylvania D.Sc.
1934 McGill University LL.D.
1936 Harvard D.Sc.
1936 University of Oxford D.Sc.
1938 University of St Andrews LL.D.
1946 Université de Lyon Hon. Doctorate
1946 University of London D.Sc.
1947 University of Manchester D.Sc.
1949 Catholic University of Louvain M.D.
1949 Université Libre de Bruxelles Hon. Doctorate
1950 Johns Hopkins D.Sc.
1951 University of Glasgow LL.D.
1952 Queen's University Belfast D.Sc.
1953 Université de Montréal M.D.
1955 University of Sheffield D.Sc.
1955 New York University D.Sc.
1957 University of Bologna M.D.
1957 University of Freiburg M.D.
1957 University of Paris Hon. Doctorate
1958 University of Liverpool LL.D.
1958 University of Dalhousie LL.D.
1958 Allahabad D.Sc.
1959 Rockefeller University LL.D.
1961 University of Edinburgh LL.D.
1964 Jagellonian University Cracow M.D.
1965 University of Strathclyde D.Sc.
1965 Royal Veterinary College Stockholm Vet. Med. Doktor
1966 Cambridge Sc.D.
1968 Bucknell University D.Sc.

### Prizes and special lectures

1914 Gedge (Cambridge)
1916 Rolleston (Oxford)
1927 Special Lectures (University of London) (see Adrian 1928a)
1931 Eldridge Reeves Johnson Foundation Lectures for Medical Physics
1931 Croonian Lecture (Royal Society)
1932 Nobel (Stockholm)
1938 Ferrier Lecture (Royal Society)
1946 Waynflete Lecture (Oxford)
1956 Conway Evans Prize (Royal Society and Royal College of Physicians)
1960 Romanes Lecture (Oxford)

### Medals and honours

1912 Walsingham Gold Medal for Physiology (Cambridge)
1929 Baly Medal, Royal College of Physicians
1934 Royal Medal, Royal Society
1942 Order of Merit
1946 Copley Medal, Royal Society
1947 Hughlings Jackson Medal, Royal Society of Medicine
1950 Gold Medal, Royal Society of Medicine
1953 Albert Gold Medal, Royal Society of Arts
1955 Harben Medal
1955 1st Baron Adrian of Cambridge
1956 Chevalier de la Légion d'Honneur
1957 Sherrington Memorial Medal
1958 British Medical Association Medal for Distinguished Merit
1963 Jephcott Medal, Royal Society of Medicine

### Notes and sources

The main sources for this memoir are (1) Adrian's publications listed in the Bibliography, (2) publications by other authors given in the reference list, (3) the Adrian–Forbes correspondence and other Forbes writings in the Francis A. Countway Library of Medicine, Boston Medical Library and Harvard Medical Library, 10 Shattuck Street, Boston, Mass. 02115. Further sources of information are Adrian's autobiographical notes left in his desk for the Royal Society and unpublished lectures and other material in the possession of the Adrian family.

Adrian's collaborators in joint papers are named in the Bibliography but in these notes only Adrian's name is given.

1. Unpublished family history by A. D. Adrian, p. 479.
2. *Dictionary of national biography*, vol. XXV, p. 319.
3. This speculation is based on a comment of Sir Henry Tizard, F.R.S., to R. H. A.
4. Adrian, 1956e.
5. Autobiographical notes.

6, 7 From Cambridge University Natural Science Club (Centenary Record), 1872–1972.

8. Adrian, 1946b.
9. Adrian, 1918a.
10. Trevelyan, 1949; Adrian, 1918a, p. 76.
11. Hardy, 1970.
12. Byron letters, p. 79 of vol. 1, *In my hot youth* (ed. Leslie Marchand). London: John Murray.
13. Adrian, 1934a.
14. Koestler, 1959.
15. Adrian, 1934a.
16. Adrian, 1912a.
17. The quotation is from Lucas's posthumous book (1917) of which the last chapter on central inhibition was written by Adrian.
18. Kato, 1924.
19. Davis, Forbes, Brunswick & Hopkins, 1926.
20. Adrian, 1912b, 1914a.
21. Davis *et al.*, 1926.
22. Adrian, 1913.
23. Adrian, 1914b.
24. Davis *et al.*, 1926.
25. Lucas, 1917.
26. Adrian to Forbes, 16 May, 1914.

27. Adrian, Autobiographical notes. W. S. Farren (1935) mentioned that Keith Lucas was sometimes a guest at 'Chudleigh' and one of these visits may have been the occasion referred to by Adrian (1932a) when he wrote that, a few weeks before his death, Keith Lucas spoke of using thermionic valves in neurophysiology.
28. Adrian. 1916a, 1917a.
29. Lucas, 1907.
30. Lapicque, 1906, 1926.
31. Rushton, 1933.
32. Adrian, 1917b.
33. In the British army deserters were shot until 1916. See *The face of battle*, John Keegan, 1976. London: Jonathan Cape.
34. Adrian, 1943b.
35. Adrian, 1947a.
36. Unpublished MS. The lecture was to the Cambridge University Natural Science Club, see p. 7.
37. Bynum, 1976.
38. Adrian to Forbes, 11 July 1920.
39. The information about Adrian's holidays is based on the Adrian–Forbes correspondence.
40. These letters, which are in Swedish and are in the possession of Professor Y. Zotterman, were translated by Professor F. H. and Mrs Sandbach of Trinity College, Cambridge.
41. Forbes correspondence.
42. Forbes to Adrian, 21 May 1926.
43. Adrian to Forbes, 1 March 1923.
44. Raverat, 1952.
45. Adrian to Forbes, 21 March 1919.
46. Adrian, 1919.
47. Head, Rivers & Sherren, 1905; Rivers & Head, 1908.
48. Adrian, 1920c, 1921a.
49. Adrian to Forbes, 19 October 1919.
50. In winter 13 °C was a common room temperature in the Physiological Laboratory, Cambridge, until about 1952.
51. Lucas, 1912.
52. The machine for moving the photographic plate was also designed and built by Lucas (1909).
53. Adrian to Forbes, 22 May 1922.
54. In March 1922, Adrian and Forbes corresponded about the relative merits of 'all-or-none' or 'all-or-nothing'. Forbes preferred the latter and after 1922 Adrian generally used it too unless writing in a historical context.
55. This information which was kindly provided by Mr R. Frank is based on the Forbes papers. The amplifier had been described by Forbes & Thacher (1920).
56. Forbes's diary indicates that strings were frequently destroyed.
57. E.g. Adrian to Forbes, 30 October 1931; Forbes to Faxon, 21 May 1923.
58. Adrian, 1922b.
59. Adrian, 1954a.
60. Forbes, Campbell & Williams, 1924.
61. Gasser & Erlanger, 1922.
62. Adrian, 1926a.
63. Adrian, 1925b.
64. There is no publication but Zotterman refers to the talk in his letter to Johannson of 28 October 1925.
65. Letters from R. Frank to the writer.
66. Adrian, 1926a, b, d, e.
67. The date is in the Visitors' Book in the Physiological Laboratory, Cambridge.
68. Adrian, 1928a.
69. Professor Y. Zotterman carried out some preliminary experiments with Adrian on the frog's eye in January 1926 (Zotterman 1976).
70. Holmgren, 1880.
71. Fröhlich, 1913.
72. Adrian, 1927a, b; 1928b.
73. Adrian, 1928a.

74. Riccó's (1877) law predicts $IA$ = constant, whereas the Bunsen Roscoe (1862) or Bloch (1885) law predicts $IT$ = constant.
75. Adrian to Forbes, 30 September 1927.
76. Use of loudspeaker: at the suggestion of B. H. C. Matthews, Rachel Matthews and Adrian had previously listened for impulses with telephone earphones.
77. Adrian, 1918b.
78. Adrian, 1928d, e; 1929a. In certain frog muscles and in the intraocular muscles of mammals there are fast and slow muscle fibres supplied respectively by large and small myelinated nerve fibres, so the idea of a separate system for tone does have some validity. But these interesting discoveries do not apply to mammalian skeletal muscle nor do they in any way modify Adrian and Bronk's conclusions.
79. Adrian, 1932a, p. 66.
80. Adrian 1929a.
81. Adrian 1932a, p. 68.
82. Adrian, 1932b.
83. Synchronization might be assisted by the fact that several axons share one Schwann cell to give a Remak bundle.
84. Lucas, 1912.
85. See Rosenberg, 1927.
86. Adrian, 1932a.
87. Adrian, 1931c.
88. Adrian, 1932a, p. 38.
89. Adrian, 1932a, p. 40.
90. No mammalian nerve fibre can carry impulses at a rate higher than about 1000 Hz but a collection of nerve fibres can give rise to a 'composite' electrical effect which follows sound waves of much higher frequency. However, it is doubtful if this has any physiological significance.
91. Adrian, 1938c.
92. Adrian, 1932a, p. 42.
93. Adrian, 1932a, p. 42.
94. Adrian, 1931e.
95. Adrian, 1947a.
96. Adrian is here referring to the experiments of Pfaffmann (1939a, b) who worked with him in the late 1930's.
97. Adrian, 1933a.
98. Adrian, 1932d.
99. Adrian, 1931b.
100. Adrian, 1934b.
101. Adrian, 1934d.
102. Adrian, 1935a.
103. Berger, 1969.
104. Adrian, 1947a. Tönnies (1933) reached this conclusion a little before Adrian & Matthews.
105. Adrian, 1934d.
106. Adrian, 1947a, p. 79.
107. Adrian, 1936b.
108. Adrian, 1939c.
109. Holmes, 1917, 1922.
110. Adrian, 1943e.
111. Moruzzi, 1950.
112. Eccles, Ito & Szentágothai, 1967.
113. Marr, 1969.
114. Adrian, 1947a, p. 31
115. Marshall, Woolsey & Bard, 1937.
116. Adrian, 1941a, b; 1943c; 1946a.
117. Dusser de Barenne, 1916.
118. Marshall *et al.*, 1937; Talbot & Marshall, 1941, and others.
119. Adrian, 1947a, p. 42.
120. Adrian, 1941a.
121. Adrian, 1947d.
122. Ross, 1936.

123. Sand & Löwenstein, 1940.
124. Adrian, 1943a.
125. Adrian, 1938d.
126. Adrian, 1957a.
127. Adrian, 1948a.
128. Adrian, 1948a.
129. Adrian, 1947a, p. 61.
130. Adrian, 1947a, p. 61.
131. Adrian, 1942a.
132. Adrian, 1947a, p. 60.
133. Adrian, 1954b.
134. Adrian, 1951c.
135. Adrian, 1949c.
136. Adrian, 1963e.
137. Autobiographical notes.
138. The first two of these lectures were published (Adrian, 1951b, 1961c); the last three were given to the Eranus Society, a small interdisciplinary group of Cambridge graduates.
139. Adrian, 1936f.
140. Adrian, 1936f.
141. Adrian, 1943b.
142. Adrian, 1947a.
143. Adrian, 1948c.
144. Adrian, 1932a, p. 93.
145. The two hundred and twentieth Anniversary of the Foundation of the Academy of Sciences of the U.S.S.R. *Notes and Records of the Royal Society*, **4**, 65–68.
146. The quotations and other information are from an unpublished lecture given in 1945 to the Society for Cultural Relations with Russia and to Westminster School.
147. Hart, 1970.
148. Quoted in conversation by the late Philip Bowden, F.R.S.
149. Unesco, on 4 November 1946; W.H.O. on 7 April 1948.
150. See Council Report for 1945–46 (*Year Book of the Royal Society*, 1947).
151. See Council Report for 1946–47 (*Year Book of the Royal Society*, 1948).
152. See Council Report for 1947–48 (*Year Book of the Royal Society*, 1949).
153. See Council Report for 1952–53 (*Year Book of the Royal Society*, 1954).
154. See Council Report for 1946–47 (*Year Book of the Royal Society*, 1948).
155. See Council Report for 1951–52 (*Year Book of the Royal Society*, 1953).
156. See Council Report for 1952–53 (*Year Book of the Royal Society*, 1954).
157. See Council Report for 1952–53 (*Year Book of the Royal Society*, 1954).
158. See Council Report for 1954–55 (*Year Book of the Royal Society*, 1956).
159. Medvedev, Z. A. (1969). *The rise and fall of T. D. Lysenko* (translated by I. M. Lerner), p. 74. New York and London: Columbia University Press.
160. Report of Council 1954–55 (*Year Book of the Royal Society*, 1956).
161. Lovell, 1975.
162. Blackett, 1971.
163. Dale, 1944.
164. The letter from G. I. Taylor to Adrian as President of the Royal Society, which is dated 12 December 1950, is in the manuscript collection of G. I. Taylor currently being sorted and catalogued by the Contemporary Archives Society, Oxford, for eventual deposit in the Library of Trinity College, Cambridge. Correspondence in the same collection indicates that G. P. Thomson and others were also strongly opposed to the Science Centre and in July 1951 were planning to support G. I. Taylor in signing a fly-sheet of protest to be submitted to the Council of the Royal Society.
165. Robinson, 1951.
166. Adrian's memorandum was reproduced several times; it appears in typescript first as Royal Society paper A/4(50) dated 18 September 1950.
167. From a letter dated 3 September 1950 from Mr Herbert Morrison to Sir Robert Robinson, P.R.S.
168. Letter to all Fellows of the Royal Society dated 18 December 1950 signed by E. J. Salisbury and D. Brunt (Secretaries).

169. Ditto, dated 8 January 1951.
170. Royal Society paper OM/46(51), Minute 7.
171. From a letter of 20 February 1953 to all members of the Scientific Societies Accommodations Committee.
172. From Sir Robert Robinson, O.M., F.R.S., to P.R.S., 5 February 1953.
173. Officers' meeting 30 November 1953, Minute 3b.
174. Adrian, 1948c.

## References


Bard, P. 1938 *Harvey lectures.* 143 pages. Baltimore: Williams & Wilkins Co.

Berger, Hans 1969 Suppl. 28 to *Electroenceph. clin. Neurophysiol. Ed.* P. Gloor. Elsevier.

Blackett, P. M. S. 1971 *Proc. R. Soc. Lond.* A **321**, 1; *Proc. R. Soc. Lond.* B **177**, 1.

Bloch, A. M. 1885 Expériences sur la vision. Paris: Soc. Biol. Mém. **37**, 493.

Bunsen, R. W. & Roscoe, H. 1862. *Ann. Physik.* **117**, 529.

Bynum, W. F. 1976 *J. Physiol. Lond.* **263**, 23.

Dale, H. H. 1944 *Proc. R. Soc. Lond.* A **182**, 217; *Proc. R. Soc. Lond.* B **132**, 1.

Davis, H., Forbes, A., Brunswick, D. & Hopkins, A. McH. 1926 *Am. J. Physiol.* **76**, 448.

Dusser de Barenne, J. G. 1916 *Q. Jl exp. Physiol.* **9**, 355.

Eccles, J. C., Ito, M. & Szentágothai, J. 1967 *The cerebellum as a neuronal machine.* Berlin, Heidelberg and New York: Springer-Verlag.

Farren, W. S. 1935 Obituary of H. Glauert. *Obit. Not. Fell. R. Soc. Lond.* **1**, 607.

Forbes, A. & Thacher, Catherine 1920 *Am. J. Physiol.* **52**, 409.

Forbes, A., Campbell, C. J. & Williams, H. B. 1924 *Am. J. Physiol.* **69**, 283.

Fröhlich, F. W. 1913 *Z. Sinnesphysiol.* **48**, 28, 354.

Gasser, H. C. & Erlanger, J. 1922 *Am. J. Physiol.* **62**, 496.

Hardy, G. H. 1970 *Bertrand Russell and Trinity.* Cambridge University Press. (1st printed 1942.)

Hart, Liddell 1970 *History of the Second World War.* London: Cassell & Co.

Head, H., Rivers, W. H. R. & Sherren, J. 1905 *Brain* **28**, 99.

Holmes, G. 1917 *Brain* **40**, 461.

Holmes, G. 1922 *Lancet* **202**, 1177–1182, 1231–1237; also **203**, 59–65; 111–115.

Holmgren, F. 1880 *Unters. physiol. Inst., Heidelberg* **3**, 278.

Kato, G. 1924 *The theory of decrementless conduction in narcotised region of nerve.* 166 pages. Tokyo: Nankōdō.

Keegan, J. 1976 *The face of battle.* London: Jonathan Cape.

Koestler, A. 1959 *The sleep walkers. A history of man's changing vision of the universe*, p. 19. London: Hutchinson.

Lapicque, L. & M. 1906 *C.r. Séanc. Soc. Biol., Paris* **58**, 991.

Lapicque, R. & M. 1926 *L'excitabilité en fonction du temps.* Paris: Presses Universitaires de France.

Lovell, A. C. B. 1975 Patrick Maynard Stuart Blackett, Baron Blackett of Chelsea. *Biogr. Mem. Fellows R. Soc. Lond.* **21**, 1.

Lucas, K. 1907 *J. Physiol., Lond.* **35**, 310.

Lucas, K. 1909 *J. Physiol., Lond.* **39**, 208.

Lucas, K. 1912 *J. Physiol., Lond.* **44**, 225.

Lucas, K. 1917 *The conduction of the nervous impulse.* London: Longmans, Green & Co.

Marr, D. 1969 *J. Physiol., Lond.* **202**, 437.

Marshall, W. H., Woolsey, C. N. & Bard, P. 1937 *Science* **85**, 388.

Medvedev, Z. A. 1969 *The rise and fall of T. D. Lysenko*, p. 74. Columbia University Press.

Moruzzi, G. (1950). *Problems in cerebellar physiology.* Thomas: Springfield (Ill.).

Moruzzi, G. (1979). Lord Adrian 1889–1977. *Rev. Physiol. Biochem. Pharmacol.* (In press.)

Pfaffmann, C. 1939a *J. Physiol., Lond.* **97**, 207.

Pfaffmann, C. 1939b *J. Physiol., Lond.* **97**, 220.

Raverat, Gwen 1952 *Period piece.* London: Faber & Faber.

Riccó, A. 1877 *Annali Ottal. Clin. ocul.* **6**, 373.

Rivers, W. H. R. & Head, H. 1908 *Brain* **31**, 323.

Robinson, R. 1951 *Proc. R. Soc. Lond.* A **205**, 1; *Proc. R. Soc. Lond.* B **138**, 1.

Rosenberg, H. 1927 *Pflügers Arch.* **216**, 300.

Ross, D. A. 1936 *J. Physiol., Lond.* **86**, 117.

Rushton, W. A. H. 1933 *J. Physiol., Lond.* **77**, 337.

Sand, A. & Löwenstein, O. 1940 *J. Physiol., Lond.* **99**, 89.

Talbot, S. A. & Marshall, W. H. 1941 *Am. J. Ophthal.* **24**, 1255.
Tönnies, J. F. 1933 *J. f. Psychol u. Neurol.* **45**, 154.
Trevelyan, G. M. 1949 *An autobiography and other essays*. London: Longmans, Green & Co.
Zotterman, Y. 1969, 1971 *Touch, tickle and pain: an autobiography*. Vols 1 and 2. Oxford: Pergamon Press.
Zotterman, Y. 1976 *Sensory function of the skin in primates*. Opening address. Wenner–Gren Center (series). Oxford: Pergamon Press.

## Bibliography

1912a (With Keith Lucas) On the summation of propagated disturbances in nerve and muscle. *J. Physiol., Lond.* **44**, 68–124.
b On the conduction of subnormal disturbances in normal nerve. *J. Physiol., Lond.* **45**, 389–412.
1913 Wedensky inhibition in relation to the 'all-or-none' principle in nerve. *J. Physiol., Lond.* **46**, 384–412.
1914a The all-or-none principle in nerve. *J. Physiol., Lond.* **47**, 460–474.
b The relation between the size of the propagated disturbance and the rate of conduction in nerve. *J. Physiol., Lond.* **48**, 53–72.
c The temperature coefficient of the refractory period in nerve. *J. Physiol., Lond.* **48**, **48**, 453–464.
1916a The electrical reactions of muscles before and after nerve injury. *Brain* **39**, 1–33.
b The recovery of conductivity and of excitability in nerve. *J. Physiol., Lond.* **50**, 345–363.
1917a Physiological basis of electrical tests in peripheral nerve injury. *Archs Radiol. Electrother.* May 1917, pp. 1–14.
b (With L. R. Yealland) The treatment of some common war neuroses. *Lancet* June 1917, pp. 3–24.
1918a *Archibald Don*, ch. 2. A memoir edited by Charles Sayle. London: John Murray.
b Conduction in peripheral nerve and in the central nervous system. *Brain* **41**, 23–47.
1919 The response of human sensory nerves to currents of short duration. *J. Physiol., Lond.* **53**, 70–85.
1920a Muscular tone and the sympathetic system. *Med. Sci. Abstr. Rev.* pp. 454–456.
b A rotating contact breaker designed by Keith Lucas. *J. Physiol., Lond.* **54**, 26*P*.
c The recovery process of excitable tissues. I. *J. Physiol., Lond.* **54**, 1–31.
1921a The recovery process of excitable tissues. II. *J. Physiol. Lond.* **55**, 193–225.
b (With D. R. Owen) The electric response of denervated muscle. *J. Physiol., Lond.* **55**, 326–331.
1922a The relation between the stimulus and the electric response in a single muscle fibre. *Archs néerl. Physiol.* **7**, 330–332.
b (With Alexander Forbes) The all-or-nothing response of sensory nerve fibres. *J. Physiol., Lond.* **56**, 301–330.
c (With J. M. D. Olmsted) The refractory phase in a reflex arc. *J. Physiol., Lond.* **56**, 426–443.
1923a The conception of nervous and mental energy (I). *Br. J. Psychol.* **14**, 121–125.
b Disorders of function in the neurone. *Proc. R. Soc. Med.* **16**, 55–60.
c The time relations of the isometric twitch. *J. Physiol.* **57**, 11–12*P*.
d (With Sybil Cooper) The frequency of discharge from the spinal cord in the frog. *J. Physiol., Lond.* **58**, 209–229.
e (With C. F. Watts) A needle thermo-junction. *J. Physiol., Lond.* **58**, 11*P*.
1924a (With Sybil Cooper) The electric response in reflex contractions of spinal and decerebrate preparations. *Proc. R. Soc. Lond.* B **96**, 243–258.
b A class experiment on the nature of the injury current. *J. Physiol., Lond.* **59**, 1–2*P*.
c (With Sybil Cooper) The maximum frequency of reflex response in the spinal cat. *J. Physiol., Lond.* **59**, 61–81.
d Some recent work on inhibition. *Brain.* **47**, 399–416.
e The chronaxie of frog's ventricular muscle. *J. Physiol., Lond.* **59**, 62–63*P*.
1925a Oliver–Sharpey lectures on the interpretation of the electromyogram. *Lancet* June 1925, pp. 1229–1241, 1282–1293.
b (With Sybil Cooper) Action currents in sensory nerve fibres. *J. Physiol., Lond.* **60**, 42*P*–43*P*.

1925c The spread of activity in the tenuissimus muscle of the cat and in other complex muscles. *J. Physiol., Lond.* **60**, 301–315.

1926a The impulses produced by sensory nerve endings. I. *J. Physiol., Lond.* **61**, 49–72.

b (With Yngve Zotterman) The impulses produced by sensory nerve endings. II. The response of a single end-organ. *J. Physiol., Lond.* **61**, 151–171.

c (With Yngve Zotterman) Impulses from a single sensory end-organ. *J. Physiol., Lond.* **61**, 8*P*.

d (With Yngve Zotterman) The impulses produced by sensory nerve-endings. III. Impulses set up by touch and pressure. *J. Physiol., Lond.* **61**, 465–483.

e The impulses produced by sensory nerve-endings. IV. Impulses from pain receptors. *J. Physiol., Lond.* **62**, 33–51.

f (With Rachel Eckhard) Impulses in the optic nerve. *J. Physiol., Lond.* **62**, 23–24*P*.

1927a (With Rachel Matthews) The action of light on the eye. I. The discharge of impulses in the optic nerve and its relation to the electric changes in the retina. *J. Physiol., Lond.* **63**, 378–414.

b (With Rachel Matthews) The action of light on the eye. II. The processes involved in retinal excitation. *J. Physiol., Lond.* **64**, 279–301.

1928a *The basis of sensation.* London: Christophers.

b (With Rachel Matthews) The action of light on the eye. III. The interaction of retinal neurones. *J. Physiol., Lond.* **65**, 273–298.

c Die Untersuchung der Sinnesorgane mit Hilfe elektrophysiologischer Methoden. *Ergebn. Physiol.* **26**, 501–530.

d (With D. W. Bronk) The discharge of impulses in motor nerve fibres. I. Impulses in single fibres of the phrenic nerve. *J. Physiol., Lond.* **66**, 81–101.

e (With D. W. Bronk) Apparatus for demonstrating nerve and muscle action currents. *J. Physiol., Lond.* **66**, 13*P*.

f Le message sensoriel. *J. Psychol. norm. path.* **25**, 713–720.

1929a (With D. W. Bronk) The discharge of impulses in motor nerve fibres. II. The frequency of discharge in reflex and voluntary contractions. *J. Physiol., Lond.* **67**, 119–151.

b (With Karl Umrath) The impulse discharge from the Pacinian corpuscle. *J. Physiol., Lond.* **68**, 139–154.

1930a The mechanism of the sense organs. *Physiol. Rev.* **10**, 336–347.

b The effects of injury on mammalian nerve fibres. *Proc. R. Soc. Lond.* B **106**, 596–618.

c Impulses in sympathetic fibres and in slow afferent fibres. *J. Physiol., Lond.* **70**, 20–21*P*.

d The activity of the nervous system in the caterpillar. *J. Physiol., Lond.* **70**, 34–35*P*.

1931a The messages in sensory nerve fibres and their interpretation. (Croonian lecture.) *Proc. R. Soc. Lond.* B **109**, 1–18.

b (With F. J. J. Buytendijk) Potential changes in the isolated brain stem of the goldfish. *J. Physiol., Lond.* **71**, 121–135.

c The microphonic action of the cochlea: an interpretation of Wever and Bray's experiments. *J. Physiol., Lond.* **71**, 28–29*P*.

d Potential changes in the isolated nervous system of 'Dytiscus marginalis'. *J. Physiol., Lond.* **72**, 132–151.

e (With McKeen Cattell & H. Hoagland) Sensory discharges in single cutaneous nerve fibres. *J. Physiol., Lond.* **72**, 377–391.

f The microphonic action of the cochlea in relation to theories of hearing. *Report of a discussion on audition at the Physical Society, June 1931*, pp. 5–9.

g (With D. W. Bronk & Gilbert Phillips) The nervous origin of the Wever and Bray effect. *J. Physiol., Lond.* **73**, 2*P*.

1932a *The mechanism of nervous action.* Oxford University Press; Philadelphia: University of Pennsylvania Press.

b (With D. W. Bronk & Gilbert Phillips) Discharges in mammalian sympathetic nerves. *J. Physiol., Lond.* **74**, 115–133.

c Sensory impulses produced by heat and injury. *J. Physiol., Lond.* **74**, 17.

d The activity of the optic ganglion of 'Dytiscus marginalis'. *J. Physiol., Lond.* **75**, 26–27*P*.

e Visceral sense organs. (Horsley lecture, University College London.) *Univ. Coll. Hosp. Mag.*, pp. 1–10.

f The activity of the nerve fibres. (Nobel lecture delivered at Stockholm, 12 December 1932.) *Les prix nobel en 1932.*

1933a (With S. Gelfan) Rhythmic activity in skeletal muscle fibres. *J. Physiol., Lond.* **78,** 271–287.

b Afferent impulses in the vagus and their effect on respiration. *J. Physiol., Lond.* **79,** 332–358.

c The activity of nerve cells. Address to the British Association. *Rep. Br. Ass. Advmt Sci.* pp. 163–170.

d The all-or-nothing reaction. *Ergebn. Physiol.* pp. 744–755.

e (With B. H. C. Matthews) Observations on the electrical activity of the cortex. *J. Physiol., Lond.* **80**, 1–2*P*.

1934a Chapter VII in *Keith Lucas* (ed. W. M. Fisher & Alys Keith-Lucas), p. 87. Cambridge: W. Heffer & Son.

b (With B. H. C. Matthews) The interpretation of potential waves in the cortex. *J. Physiol., Lond.* **8**, 440–471.

c Electrical activity of the nervous system. *Archs. Neurol. Psychiat.*, Chicago, **32**, 1125.

d (With B. H. C. Matthews) The Berger rhythm: potential changes from the occipital lobes in man. *Brain* **57**, 355–385.

e Discharge frequencies in the cerebral and cerebellar cortex. *J. Physiol., Lond.* **83,** 32–33*P*.

1935a (With K. Yamagiwa) The origin of the Berger rhythm. *Brain* **58**, 323–351.

b Recent work on the sensory mechanism of the nervous system. *Adv. mod. biol., Moscow* **4**, 11–15.

c The electric activity of the nervous system. Abstract from *Congr. int. Elettro-radio-Biol.*, pp. 107–110.

1936a L'activité électrique du cerveau humain. *Presse méd.* January, pp. 1–15.

b The electrical activity of the cortex. *Proc. R. Soc. Med.* **29**, 11–14.

c The Berger rhythm in the monkey's brain. *J. Physiol., Lond.* **87**, 83–94*P*.

d The spread of activity in the cerebral cortex. *J. Physiol., Lond.* **88**, 127–161.

e Research on the central nervous system. *Sci. Prog., Lond.* 121, July, 1–13.

f The nervous system. From *Factors determining human behaviour.* Harvard Tercentenary Publications.

g Cortical facilitation with electric stimuli. *J. Physiol., Lond.* **89**, 1*P*.

1937a The frequency range of neurones in the cerebral cortex. From *Volume jubilaire publié en l'honneur du Professeur J. Demoor*, pp. 31–37. Liége: G. Thone.

b The physiology of sleep. (The John Mallet Purser Memorial lecture delivered at the School of Physic, Trinity College, Dublin, 19 May 1937.) *Ir. J. med. Sci.* June, pp. 1–12.

c The psychological interpretation of the electrencephalogram. *XIe int. Congr. Psychol. Paris, July 1937*, pp. 1–8.

d Synchronized reactions in the optic ganglion of Dytiscus. *J. Physiol., Lond.* **91**, 66–89.

e *The brain and the mind*, pp. 1–11. (The Huxley lecture delivered at the Charing Cross Hospital Medical School, 18 November 1937.)

1938a The electro-physiology of the sense organs. *Boll. Soc. ital. Biol. sper.* **13**, 257–262.

b The effect of sound on the ear in reptiles. *J. Physiol., Lond.* **92**, 9*P*.

c (With K. J. W. Craik & R. S. Sturdy) The electrical response of the auditory mechanism in cold-blooded vertebrates. *Proc. R. Soc. Lond.* B **125**, 435–455.

d (With C. Ludwig) Nervous discharges from the olfactory organs of fish. *J. Physiol., Lond.* **94**, 441–460.

1939a The localization of activity in the brain. (Ferrier lecture.) *Proc. R. Soc. Lond.* B **126,** 433–449.

b (With G. Moruzzi) High-frequency discharges from cerebral neurones. *J. Physiol., Lond.* **95**, 27–28*P*.

c (With G. Moruzzi) Impulses in the pyramidal tract. *J. Physiol., Lond.* **97**, 153–199.

d Le développement du sens de l'audition. Lecture printed in *Bull. Soc. philomath. Paris* **122**, 28–42.

e The development of the sense of hearing. (Lecture delivered to the Royal Institution of Great Britain, 10 March 1939.) *Proc. R. Instn Gt Br.* **30**, 1–10.

1940 Double representation of the feet in the sensory cortex of the cat. *J. Physiol., Lond.* **98**, 16–17*P*.

1941a Afferent discharges to the cerebral cortex from peripheral sense organs. *J. Physiol., Lond.* **100**, 159–191.

1941b Visual responses in the cat and monkey. *J. Physiol., Lond.* **100**, 9*P*.
1942a Olfactory reactions in the brain of the hedgehog. *J. Physiol., Lond.* **100**, 459–473.
b The electrical reactions of the cochlea and auditory nerve. Read at the meeting of the Section of Otology, Royal Society of Medicine, 4 December 1942.
1943a Discharges from vestibular receptors in the cat. *J. Physiol., Lond.* **101**, 389–407.
1943b The dominance of vision. (The Doyne memorial lecture delivered at the thirtieth annual meeting of the Oxford Ophthalmological Congress, 8–9 July 1943) *Trans. ophthal. Soc. U.K.* **63**, 194–207.
c Afferent areas on the brain of ungulates. *Brain* **66**, 89–103.
d Sensory areas of the brain. (The Sharpey–Schafer memorial lecture delivered to the Faculty of Medicine, Edinburgh University, 6 May 1943.) *Lancet* July, pp. 33–40.
e Afferent areas in the cerebellum connected with the limbs. *Brain* **66**, 289–315.
1944a Brain rhythms. *Nature, Lond.* **153**, 360–363.
b Localization in the cerebrum and cerebellum. (Bertram Louis Abrahams lecture, delivered to the Royal College of Physicians, 8 June 1944.) *Br. med. J.* **ii**, 137–140.
c Rod and cone responses in the human eye. *Nature, Lond.* **154**, 361–362.
1945 The electric response of the human eye. *J. Physiol., Lond.* **104**, 84–104.
1946a The somatic receiving area in the brain of the Shetland pony. *Brain* **69**, 1–8.
b The mental and the physical origins of behaviour. *Int. J. Psycho-Analysis* **27**, 1–6.
c Rod and cone components in the electric response of the eye. *J. Physiol., Lond.* **105**, 24–37.
1947a *The physical background of perception.* Oxford: Clarendon Press.
b A class demonstration of the alpha rhythm. *J. Physiol., Lond.* **106**, 16*P*.
c General principles of nervous activity. *Brain* **70**, 1–17.
d (With W. Feldberg & B. A. Kilby) The cholinesterase inhibiting action of fluorophosphonates. *Br. J. Pharmacol.* **2**, 56–58.
e Pain and its problems. I. The physiology of pain. *Practitioner* **158**, 76.
f Sir Joseph Barcroft, C.B.E., F.R.S. (Obituary) *Nature, Lond.* **159**, 565.
g Frederick Gowland Hopkins, Kt, O.M., Hon. Sc.D., F.R.C.P. *The Cambridge Review* October 1947, p. 36.
1948a The sense of smell. *Advmt Sci., Lond.* **4**, 287–292.
b The organization of the nervous system. (The Harben lectures, 1947.) *Jl R. Inst. publ. Hlth Hyg.* **11**, 82–110.
c The aims of medicine. *Lancet* **255**, 997–1001.
d El sentido del olfato. *Revta Psicol. gen. apl.* **3**, 615–632.
1949a The development of nerve cell rhythms. *Arch. Psychiat. Z. Neurol.* **183**, 197–205.
b Centenary of Pavlov's birth. *Br. med. J.* **ii**, 553–555.
c *Sensory integration*, pp. 1–20. (The Sherrington lectures.) University Press of Liverpool.
1950a Sensory discrimination: with some recent evidence from the olfactory organ. *Br. med. Bull.* **6**, 330–333.
b The control of nerve-cell activity. *Symp. Soc. exp. Biol.* **4**, 85–91.
c The electrical activity of the mammalian olfactory bulk. *Electroenceph. clin. Neurophysiol.* **2**, 377–388.
d Olfactory adaptation. *J. Physiol., Lond.* **112**, 38*P*.
e Rhythmic discharges from the thalamus. *J. Physiol., Lond.* **113**, 9*P*.
1951a Experiments in the nervous system. (The Stephen Paget memorial lecture delivered at University College London, 22 November 1950.) *Conquest, Res. Def. Soc.* **39**, 2–14.
b Sleep. (The Wilde memorial lecture.) *Mem. Proc. Manchr lit. phil. Soc.* **92**, 10–23.
c Olfactory discrimination. *Année psychol.*, Volume jubilaire **50**, 107–113.
d The role of air movement in olfactory stimulation. *J. Physiol., Lond.* **114**, 4–5*P*.
e High-pass filter for recording axon potentials. *J. Physiol., Lond.* **115**, 41–42*P*.
f Differential sensitivity of olfactory receptors. *J. Physiol., Lond.* **115**, 42*P*.
g The responsibilities of the brain. (Thirty-second Earl Grey memorial lecture delivered at King's College, Newcastle-upon-Tyne, 2 May 1951.)
1952a Address of the President, Professor E. D. Adrian, at the Anniversary Meeting, 30 November 1951. *Proc. R. Soc. Lond.* A **211**, 1–11; *Proc. R. Soc. Lond.* B **139**, 289–299.
b Charles Scott Sherrington, O.M., G.B.E., F.R.S. (Obituary). *J. Physiol., Lond.* **118**, 145–148.

1952c Freedom and responsibility of science. Address delivered at the 89th annual meeting of the National Academy of Sciences, in Washington, D.C., 29 April 1952.

d The discrimination of odours by the nose. *Schweiz. med. Wschr.* **39**, 36–39.

e Sir Charles Sherrington, O.M., G.B.E., F.R.S. (obituary). *Nature, Lond.* **169**, 688–689.

1953a Address of the President, Dr E. D. Adrian, O.M., at the Anniversary Meeting, 1 December 1952. *Proc. R. Soc. Lond.* A **216**, v–xv; *Proc. R. Soc. Lond.* B **140**, 443–453.

b The scientific approach to medical research. *Lect. scient. Basis Med.* **1**, 1–15. University of London, Athlone Press.

c Flavour assessment. Physiological background of flavour assessment. *Chemy Ind.* no. 48, 1274–1276.

d Sensory messages and sensation. Response of the olfactory organ to different smells. *Acta physiol. Scand.* **29**, 5–14.

e The nervous reactions of the retina. (The Trotter–Paterson memorial lecture.) *Trans. illum. Engng Soc., Lond.* **18**, 105–112.

1954a Memorable experiences in research. *Diabetes* **3**, 17–18.

b The basis of sensation. Some recent studies of olfaction. (Banting memorial lecture delivered in Toronto, 16 September 1953.) *Br. med. J.* **i**, 287–290.

c Address of the President, Dr E. D. Adrian, O.M., at the Anniversary Meeting, 30 November 1953. *Proc. R. Soc. Lond.* A **221**, 143–151; *Proc. R. Soc. Lond.* B **142**, 1–9.

d Recent developments in the study of the sense organs. (The Trueman Wood lecture delivered 17 March 1954.) *Jl R. Soc. Arts* **102**, 756–763.

e Science and human nature. Address to the British Association, 1 September 1954.) *Advmt. Sci., Lond.* **11**, 121–128.

f Localisation in the cerebral cortex. (Introduction to the symposium of Section I (Physiology), British Association meeting, Oxford, 1954.) *Advmt Sci., Lond.* **12**, 49–52.

g Synchronised activity in the vomero-nasal nerves with a note on the function of the organ of Jacobson. *Pflügers Arch. ges. Physiol.* **260**, 188–192.

1955a Address of the President, Dr E. D. Adrian, O.M., at the Anniversary Meeting, 30 November 1954. *Proc. R. Soc. Lond.* A **227**, 279–287; *Proc. R. Soc. Lond.* B **143**, 293–301.

b Potential oscillations in the olfactory organ. *J. Physiol., Lond.* **128**, 21P.

c Commemoration Day Address of Imperial College of Science and Technology, delivered in the Royal Albert Hall, 25 October 1955, pp. 1–5

1956a The action of the mammalian olfactory organ. (The Semon lecture, 1955.) *J. Lar. Otol.* **70**, 1–14.

b Transmission of information from the olfactory organ. In *Problems of the modern physiology of the nervous and muscle systems*, pp. 13–19. Academy of Sciences, Georgian S.S.R.

c Address of the President, Lord Adrian, O.M., at the Anniversary Meeting, 30 November 1955. *Proc. R. Soc. Lond.* A **234**, 151–160; *Proc. R. Soc. Lond.* B **144**, 431–440.

d Changing concepts in science. *J. Franklin Inst.* **211**, 33–37.

e Organizers of health. *Br. med. J.* **i**, 1189–1199.

f Academies of science in the modern world. *Proc. Am. phil. Soc.* **100**, 326–330.

g Organizers of health. *Wld ment. Hlth.* **8**, 1.

1957a Electrical oscillations recorded from the olfactory organ. *J. Physiol., Lond.* **136**, 29–30*P*.

b The analysis of the nervous system. (The Sherrington memorial lecture delivered on 27 November 1957.) *Proc. R. Soc. Med.* **50**, 991–998.

c Sir Charles Scott Sherrington, O.M., 1857–1952. *Notes Rec. R. Soc. Lond.* **12**, 211–215.

1958a The control of the nervous system by the sense organs. *Arch. Psychiat. Z. ges. Neurol.* **196**, 482–493.

b Address to the Senate on his retirement as Vice-Chancellor of the University of Cambridge, delivered on 1 October 1958. *Cambridge University Reporter*, October 1958, pp. 231–236.

c Oration on the occasion of the jubilee of the foundation of Queen's College, Belfast, pp. 22–26.

1959a Medical education and its place in the university. (The opening address to the 8th Congress of the Universities of the Commonwealth, 3 September 1958.) Printed in *Eighth Congress of the Universities of the Commonwealth, 1958: Report of Proceedings.* London: Association of Universities of the British Commonwealth.

1959b The place of science in universities past and present. *Nature, Lond.* **183**, 1706–1709.

c Address to the Senate on his retirement as Vice-Chancellor of the University of Cambridge, delivered on 1 October, 1959. *Cambridge University Reporter*, October 1959, pp. 219–225.

d *The risks of progress*, pp. 1–17. (Sixth Fawley Foundation lecture, delivered at the University of Southampton on 17 November 1959.) London and Southampton: Camelot Press.

e Our concern for the mind. *Br. med. J.* **ii**, 78–81.

f Sensory mechanisms—Introduction. In: *Handbook of physiology, neurophysiology I*, Ch. XV, pp. 365–367. Washington, D.C.: Am. Physiol. Soc.

1960 *Factors in mental evolution*, pp. 3–19. (The Romanes lecture delivered in the Sheldonian Theatre, 24 May 1960) Oxford: Clarendon Press.

1961a Francis Bacon: the advocate of science. (Lecture at the Rockefeller Institute on 19 April 1961.) Number 11 of the *Occasional papers of the Rockefeller Institute*, pp. 1–14. New York: Rockefeller Institute Press.

b Instruments in the service of medicine. (Opening address at the annual congress of the British Institute of Radiology on 26 April 1961.) *Br. J. Radiol.* **34**, 404–407.

c Dreaming. *Proc. R. Instn Gt Br.* **38**, 519–525.

1962a *Technology for welfare*, pp. 4–13. (The second annual Lanchester College lecture delivered at the Methodist Central Hall, Coventry, on 23rd October 1962.)

b Creativity in science. (Paper presented at the 3rd World Congress of Psychiatry in Montreal on 7th June 1961.) *Perspect. Biol. Med.* **5**, 269–274.

1963a The reaction of degeneration. (The Samuel Hyde memorial lecture at a meeting of the Section of Physical Medicine on 13 March 1963.) *Proc. R. Soc. Med.* **56**, 439–443.

b Newton's rooms in Trinity. *Notes Rec. R. Soc. Lond.* **18**, 17–24.

c Priorities in medical responsibility. (The Jephcott lecture delivered at a meeting of the Royal Society of Medicine on 8 May 1963.) *Proc. R. Soc. Med.* **56**, 523–528.

d George Macaulay Trevelyan, 1876–1962. *Biogr. Mem. Fellows R. Soc. Lond.* **9**, 315–321.

e Olfaction and taste. Opening address to proceedings of the first Wenner–Gren International Symposium Series. *International Symposium held at the Wenner–Gren Center* (ed. Y. Zotterman), vol. 1, pp. 1–4. Oxford: Pergamon Press.

1968 Address at the memorial service for Lord Florey of Adelaide and Marston, O.M., F.R.S., delivered at Westminster Abbey on 28 March 1968. *Notes Rec. R. Soc. Lond.* **23**, 29–30.

1969 Address at the memorial service for Sir Henry Dale, O.M., G.B.E., F.R.S., at Westminster Abbey on 11 October 1968. *Notes Rec. R. Soc. Lond.* **24**, 145.

1972 Origins of biophysics. From *Three lectures in biophysics*, pp. 5–13. (Lectures delivered on the occasion of the 25th anniversary of the Instituto de Biofisica, Rio de Janeiro, September 1972.) Rio: Universidade federal do Rio de Janeiro Centro de Ciencias Medicas, Instituto de Biofisica.

1976 Detlev Wulf Bronk. *Biogr. Mem. Fellows R. Soc. Lond.* **22**, 1–9.

1977 Fisiologia. Estratto del Volume II della *Enciclopedia del Novicento*, p. 1066. Istituto dell'Enciclopedia Italiana.

W L Bragg.

# WILLIAM LAWRENCE BRAGG

31 March 1890 — 1 July 1971

Elected F.R.S. 1921

By Sir David Phillips, Sec.R.S.

Walking along the Backs in Cambridge one day in the autumn of 1912 William Lawrence Bragg had an idea that led immediately to a dramatic advance in physics and has since transformed chemistry, mineralogy, metallurgy and, most recently, biology. He realized that the observations of X-ray diffraction by a crystal, which had been reported by von Laue and his associates earlier in that year, can be interpreted very simply as arising from reflexion of the X-rays by planes of atoms in the crystal and hence that the X-ray observations provide evidence from which the arrangement of atoms in the crystal may be determined. A few weeks of intensive work on simple inorganic compounds were enough to demonstrate the correctness of these ideas but the development of the method, at first in association with his father and later as the leader or guiding influence of a host of workers, was the labour of a lifetime. When he died on 1 July 1971, X-ray crystallography had revealed the arrangement of atoms in matter of all kinds from the simplest of salts to the macromolecules of the living cell. The story of his life is very largely the story of that achievement and the circumstances that led to his unique part in it.

## Family Background

The Bragg family (*a*)* had its roots in Cumberland where the men farmed or went to sea. In the 1820s one of them, John Bragg, married a Workington girl, Lucy Brown, who had settled near Belfast and they had four children, William, Robert John, James Brown and Mary McCleary. When William the eldest was twelve, in about 1840, his father was lost at sea between Cumberland and Belfast. Some time later the family moved to Birkenhead where William was apprenticed to a chemist, James went into an office and, in 1846, Robert John went to sea as an indentured apprentice in the *Nereides* of Workington, 530 tons. Robert completed his apprenticeship in October 1851 and soon afterwards sailed again for India in the *Nereides*, now as second mate. The outward voyage to Calcutta was uneventful but the return had barely begun, with Robert now chief mate, when the ship was wrecked in the Hoogli River. Only Robert, four crew members and the pilot were saved.

* The labels (*a*) etc. refer to the General References and (*A*) etc. and (1) etc. to the two lists (books and papers respectively) in the Bibliography.

After this disaster he went back to sea again but only until the late 1850s when he bought Stoneraise Place, near Wigton in Cumberland, and settled down to farm there in the parish of Westward within sight of the Solway Firth. In 1861, he married Mary, daughter of the Vicar, the Rev. Robert Wood and his wife Ruth (Hayton). Mary, who was 28, was remembered as a gracious figure with a natural bent for mathematics. On 2 July 1862, when Robert Bragg was returning from a visit to London to see the Great Exhibition of that year, their eldest son, William Henry, was born. Two more sons, John and James, came later.

There are few records of W. H. Bragg's early childhood, but he remembered his mother teaching him to read and then, at the age of five, going to the Westward village school. But in 1869, when he was only seven, his mother died at the early age of 36. It was Uncle William, long accustomed to thinking of himself as head of the family and now established as a chemist in Market Harborough, who came to the rescue. He had just helped to re-establish the old Grammar School in Market Harborough, and the young W. H. Bragg was promptly moved there, to live with his grandmother and uncles (James ran the grocer's shop next door).

Summer holidays were spent in Cumberland and in 1875, at his father's insistence, W. H. Bragg was sent to school at King William's College in the Isle of Man. In 1889 he was awarded an exhibition at Trinity College, Cambridge, but he stayed at school a further year before going up for the long-vacation term in July 1881. At about the same time his father retired to Ramsey, in the Isle of Man, and Market Harborough, not so far from Cambridge and dominated by Uncle William, was clearly the young man's home.

At Cambridge W.H.B.* read mathematics and in 1884 he graduated third in the class with first class honours, Third Wrangler. The following year, encouraged by J. J. Thomson, he applied for the position of Professor of Mathematics and Physics in the University of South Australia. The electors were Horace Lamb (the retiring Professor), J. J. Thomson and the Agent General, Sir Arthur Blyth, but before deciding to send out so young a man they consulted the Government Astronomer of South Australia, Charles Todd, who happened to be in London at the time. He had no objection and the 23-year-old Third Wrangler was appointed to start as soon as possible.

Up to this time W.H.B. had done very little physics, but the electors assumed that he could learn enough as he went along. On the six week voyage to Australia he read *Electricity and magnetism* by Deschanel but on arrival in Adelaide he found that the physics classes were small and elementary and was well able to keep ahead of them. One of the principal difficulties was a shortage of apparatus so he went to work with a firm of instrument makers in the town and helped to equip the laboratories himself. His head mechanic, Rogers, was a key figure who worked with him throughout his period in Australia, initially making apparatus for classes and later the apparatus designed by W.H.B. for his researches.

* From this point it is convenient to distinguish W. H. Bragg from his son, the subject of this memoir, by referring to him as W.H.B.

On the day after his arrival in Adelaide W.H.B. went for supper with the Todd family. Charles Todd, born in England in 1826, and his wife Alice, had been in Australia since 1855 when he was sent out from Greenwich as Government Astronomer with the particular task of installing an electric telegraph system in South Australia. Alice, who came from a Cambridge family named Bell, was 19 and already pregnant when they arrived in Adelaide, a town which had been founded only 19 years earlier by Charles Sturt and William Light and named after the Consort of William IV. By 1872, after years of surveying the bush, the overland telegraph line from Adelaide to Port Darwin in the north was completed and direct communication with Europe by the submarine cable from Darwin was made possible. The final connection was made near an oasis in central Australia, known since as Alice Springs after the Astronomer's wife. Postmaster General and Superintendent of Telegraphs, South Australia, Todd was elected F.R.S. in 1889 and appointed K.C.M.G. in 1893.

The Todds lived at the Observatory in West Terrace, Adelaide, a spacious house surrounded by paddocks and the buildings housing the offices, the transit telescope and other equipment. With six children, Elizabeth, Charles, Headley, Maude, Gwendoline and Lorna, they were at the centre of Adelaide society and they soon made the young professor a regular member of their lively circle. A happy working relationship between the two scientists was quickly established and a closer connection followed. On 1 June 1889, W.H.B. and Gwendoline Todd were married. She was just on 19, lively, sociable, without much formal education but a gifted artist who had been a star pupil at the Design School. They set up house, with a cook and a housemaid not easily managed by the young wife, in Lefevre Terrace, North Adelaide and on 31 March 1890 their elder son, William Lawrence, was born. A second son, Robert Charles, was born a year later and a daughter, Gwendolen Mary, in 1907.

## Adelaide, 1890–1909

W. L. Bragg's earliest memories (*b*) went back to the period following the birth of his brother, Bob, when his mother was convalescing after a difficult delivery. He remembered the pleasures of listening to her stories when she was still in bed but also the indignities of being wheeled out in the pram together with his baby brother and of wearing the blue tunics with red belts and straw hats favoured by his artistic parent. Quite early a nursemaid named Charlotte Schlegel was recruited who stayed with the family for nearly 30 years. She came from the part of Denmark that was lost to Prussia in the war of 1867 which she remembered. Having a fierce and repressive temperament she sternly discouraged any games in which the participants could conceivably get dirty. Writing years after Bragg noted sadly 'I do not think my brother Bob was much affected by her—even as a child he had considerable calm self-confidence—but I was very impressionable and unsure of myself and I am certain that Charlotte was very much the wrong person for me'. Even so there was clearly plenty of fun in the backyards and tree house in Lefevre Street with Eric Gill, later well known as an artist, who lived nearby, the principal playmate.

Even more memorable were the regular Sunday visits to the Observatory, a veritable paradise for small boys with its rambling construction and exciting out-buildings. In the storerooms treasures of all kinds—souvenirs of the Todd's journeys, discarded scientific equipment, old letters and so on—provided the basis for endless play and later for the design and construction of electrical gadgets.

Holidays were spent at the seaside, either on the shore of the Gulf of St Vincent, a horse-tram ride away, or at Port Elliott on the ocean coast. Here the Bragg and Todd families combined to take a large part of a boarding house. Gwendoline Bragg sketched and coached W.H.B. also, so that in time their styles were said to be indistinguishable. W.H.B. also played games of all sorts but Bragg remembered best his happy relationship with his Aunt Lorna, then still in her teens, who 'looked after me, invented games for me, read Grimm's Fairy Tales to me and altogether constituted herself my guardian'.

Bragg started school when he was five, attending a convent school, to which he walked, on the far side of North Adelaide. Then there was a setback. Riding his tricycle one afternoon, he was overturned by his brother and shattered his left elbow. The damage was so serious that the doctor thought nothing could be done but allow the joint to set rigid. But the family intervened. Uncle Charlie (Todd) was himself a doctor and devised an heroic treatment. Every few days Bragg was anaesthetized so that his arm could be flexed to prevent stiffening while a new joint was formed. The treatment worked but he was left with a slightly short and crooked left arm and, 40 years later, in Manchester, had to have an operation to relieve pressure on a nerve that was giving rise to paralysis in his left hand.

This incident involved Bragg in his first encounter with X-rays. While working hard to develop his subjects at the University, W.H.B. took a keen interest in all the latest developments in science as news of them reached him from the other side of the world. In 1895 the greatest excitement was created by Röntgen's discovery of X-rays and W.H.B. eagerly set out to repeat the experiments in Adelaide. The apparatus was ready just in time for examination of Bragg's elbow. The scene was described later by Stanley Addison, W.H.B.'s laboratory assistant (*a*). 'In the area below the laboratory proper the Professor had set up a primitive X-ray apparatus based on the discovery which Dr Röntgen of Würzburg, Germany, had announced to the world a few weeks earlier. Although Professor Bragg's machine [had been] hurriedly brought into being, [it] nevertheless worked, despite its crudity, and was put into motion. Fascinated, the Doctor watched as the big induction coil buzzed loudly, electric sparks crackled and the vacuum tube emitted a weird green glow. Later on there appeared on the screen an X-ray photograph which distinctly showed the extent and location of the injury to the boy's arm. This was the first recorded surgical use of the Röntgen Ray, as it was then called, in Australia'. But W.H.B.'s son remembered (*b*): 'I was scared stiff by the fizzing sparks and smell of ozone and could only be persuaded to submit to the exposure after my much calmer small brother Bob had his radiograph taken to set me an example.'

W. L. Bragg (right) with his mother and brother, *ca.* 1898.

W. L. Bragg photographed *ca.* 1913 by Hills & Saunders, Cambridge.

An account of Röntgen's experiments, with demonstrations, was one of the university extension lectures W.H.B. gave at that time (1896) as he developed his skills and reputation as a popular lecturer. Another of his major interests was the school system in South Australia since he recognized early on that the quality of his students at the university depended in large part on how well they had been taught at school. He gave an address on this subject at the University Commemoration in 1888 and in 1897 the interest led to a momentous decision. He would take a year's leave—it was 12 years after his appointment—and study the educational system in England. But the major inducement, no doubt, was the opportunity this would provide of seeing the uncles again and introducing his family to them.

The family was divided for the journey. W.H.B. and his wife went ahead to make a tour of Egypt and Italy while the two boys followed with Charlotte and Aunt Lizzie, who was now married to a Cambridge solicitor, Charles Squires, and had been visiting her parents. The two parties were reunited at Marseilles and went on together to Market Harborough. Here the boys stayed most of the time while their father visited schools, enquired into the educational system and renewed his acquaintance with leading scientists. But they also visited W.H.B.'s cousins, William Addison and Fanny (now Kemp-Smith) and their families and they stayed in Cambridge near to the Squires family, so that Bragg and his brother Bob got to know their English cousins. And they saw the sights of London. Among many vivid memories Bragg remembered that his father started a series of bed-time stories during these holidays: 'they were always the same—about the properties of atoms'. He also remembered reading a large volume on the voyages of Captain Cook.

On returning to Adelaide the family stayed at first at the Observatory—saddened no doubt by the death of Grandmother Todd during their absence—while a new house was being built for them. It was called Catherwood House, after Uncle William's house in Market Harborough, and looked out across the park lands towards the race-course. It had a large garden in which Bragg had a plot of his own and began his life-long interest in gardening. He also went to a new school, a preparatory school named Queen's on the far side of North Adelaide, which was reached by horse-tram—with a walk at each end of the journey. The headmaster named Hood did not believe in sparing the rod and kept a supply of canes ready to discourage spelling mistakes and other misdemeanours. Looking back, Bragg decided 'I was a misfit at school, being so very immature in some ways and so precocious in others'. He remembered (*b*) being in the same room as a very senior class doing Euclid. 'From what I overheard I realized what it was all about. Somehow Hood must have caught on to what was happening for he pulled me, a very small boy, out of my class and made me explain the theorems to the large boys while he crowed with delight.'

When about 11 years old, he was sent to St Peter's College, the leading Church of England School in South Australia. There were between 300 and 400 day-boys and some 70 boarders under a headmaster named Girdlestone whose main distinction was a passion for good English. Bragg took English language and literature, French, Latin, Greek, scripture, mathematics and chemistry, all to an equal level. The only available subjects that he did not take were German and physics—and he always regretted learning no German. His closest friend was Bob Chapman, son of the Professor of Applied Mathematics at the University, and together they revelled in mathematics, with their fathers' help and encouragement. But again there were difficulties which Bragg attributed later to his being always in a class of older boys and too proud to play with those of his own age and stature. But 'it was a kindly school, because the boys treated me as an amusing freak instead of the teasing and bullying which might so easily have been my lot'. He was in the sixth form at 14 and at 15 his father decided that he should leave and enter the university.

This was in 1905 and the previous year had been a turning point for W.H.B. Throughout his career in Adelaide he had maintained a lively interest in the latest scientific developments and had struggled to repeat the key experiments as they were reported by the leading research workers of the day and to explain them to the interested public. His latest efforts in this direction had been particularly fruitful. In the years following his return from England he had collaborated closely with his father-in-law in emulating Marconi's experiments on wireless telegraphy which had achieved a dramatic success in 1896–97 and must have been much discussed during the visit to Europe. Together they set up a transmitter in the grounds of the Observatory and a receiving station seven miles away at Henley Beach. The successful outcome, described in a popular lecture in 1899, aroused great interest in the isolated community of South Australia and the scientists were local heroes. Bragg remembered this as his first real contact with practical science: 'Bob and I took a great interest in these experiments, especially because it meant a picnic on Sunday afternoons, when my grandfather and father drove to Henley Beach with us in the official Post Office Wagonette to see the signals coming in.' But this was not really original research and W.H.B. had no experience of that until 1904 when he was 41 years old and had been professor for 17 years.

On 7 January 1904 he was to give the Presidential address to the mathematics–physics section of the Australian Association for the Advancement of Science meeting in Dunedin, New Zealand. This was not his first lecture as President of the Section, he had been President at the Hobart meeting in 1892, but now he was to speak on Rutherford's home ground and, stimulated perhaps by the lively interest of his son, he chose to talk on 'Some recent advances in the theory of the ionization of gases'. Reading the published work of Rutherford, Mme Curie and others, he had noticed that the absorption of α- and β-rays had been assumed to be analogous to the exponential decrease in the intensity of a wave traversing an absorbing medium and that this had led to some absurd conclusions. At the same time Mme Curie had described experiments which implied that all of the α- particles emitted by radium travelled about the same distance into the surrounding air. W.H.B. realized that the α-particles must behave 'like bullets fired into a block of wood' and that they must pass through the air atoms that they meet, losing some of their energy with each encounter. He concluded:

'It cannot be correct to say that the amount of the radiation which penetrates a distance $x$ is proportional to the expression $\exp(-ax)$: it must rather be proper to say that (1) the number of $\alpha$-particles penetrating a given distance does not alter much with distance until a certain critical value is passed, when there is a rapid fall; (2) the energy of the $\alpha$-particles penetrating a given distance gradually decreases as the distance is increased and dies out at the same critical value. These statements are the expression of what we should expect if ionization, consuming energy, were alone responsible for absorption of the radiation.'

On his return to Adelaide he obtained some radium, through the generosity of a Mr Barr-Smith, and with the assistance of R. Kleeman set out to test his ideas. They were brilliantly confirmed—$\alpha$-particles of 'four different ranges were shot out from the radium preparation'—and he was able to write to E. Rutherford and J. J. Thomson with the news. Papers describing the results were published in the *Philosophical Magazine* on 8 December 1904. In them he described the absorption of $\beta$-rays with characteristic imagery: 'the general effect will be that of a stream whose borders become ill-defined, which weakens as it goes, and is surrounded by a haze of scattered electrons. At a certain distance from the source all definition is gone and the force of the stream is spent.'

Rutherford replied promptly and generously and thereafter kept closely in touch through the regular exchange of long letters. Proposed by Lamb, with the support of Rutherford and J. J. Thomson, W. H. Bragg was elected F.R.S. on 2 May 1907.

This sudden flowering of his father's research coincided with Bragg's career as an undergraduate at Adelaide University. He read mathematics with subsidiary courses in chemistry and physics, graduating with first class honours in mathematics in 1908 at the age of 18. Most of his tuition was from his father—he even had a desk in his father's office—and from Chapman, the Professor of Applied Mathematics. At his father's suggestion he also took a course in English and was particularly pleased at winning the University prize for the best English essay 'from under the noses of the professionals'. Through it all there were detailed discussions of the latest researches with W.H.B. trying out his ideas and his papers on his son.

The most important of these ideas was broached one day just as they were boarding the horse-tram for the Observatory (*b*). W.H.B. had turned to the consideration of $\gamma$- and X-rays and, building on his earlier studies of the ionizing properties of $\alpha$- and $\beta$-rays, he questioned the commonly held view, proposed by G. G. Stokes, that X-rays are formless pulses of electromagnetic radiation caused by the electrons in the X-ray tube hitting the anticathode. Instead, arguing from the similarities between X- and $\gamma$-rays, he suggested that many of the properties of these rays are easier to explain if the rays are supposed to consist mainly of neutral pairs of material particles (*d*). In a paper 'On the properties and natures of various electric radiations' published in 1907, he compared the known properties of the various rays ($\alpha$-, $\beta$-, X- and $\gamma$-rays and ultraviolet light) and discussed 'the possibility that $\gamma$- and X-rays may be of a material nature'. He noted that earlier corpuscular theories of $\gamma$- and X-rays had been discounted because 'it was always felt that the difficulty of accounting for the great penetration of these radiations was insuperable' and he argued that this difficulty 'was quite exaggerated and even imaginary' since neutral pairs, consisting perhaps of one $\alpha$ or positive particle [the charge of an $\alpha$ particle was not yet known] and one $\beta$ or negative particle' would be expected to have weak ionizing power and hence great penetration. On the other hand, if X-rays were electromagnetic pulses which spread as they travelled why did they not ionize most of the atoms as they passed through a gas, instead of the relatively few actually observed, and how could a spreading pulse concentrate enough energy on an atom to ionize it.

But many physicists at this time believed that X-rays had been shown unequivocally to be electromagnetic pulses by the experiment of C. G. Barkla. These experiments were inspired by J. J. Thomson's theory of X-ray scattering which showed that X-rays, regarded as unpolarized electromagnetic waves, should be scattered through an angle $\theta$ with intensity proportional to $(1+\cos^2\theta)$. In single-scattering and double-scattering experiments Barkla showed that the scattering of relatively soft X-rays is consistent with this formula and that the X-rays can be polarized. Naturally a controversy developed, with Barkla the chief proponent of the ether-pulse theory. It was conducted mainly in *Nature* and the *Philosophical Magazine* and it stimulated both W.H.B. and Barkla to engage in further experiments that were concentrated initially on more detailed studies of the angular distribution of secondary X- and $\gamma$-radiation. W.H.B. emphasized the asymmetric scattering and emission of $\gamma$-rays (with higher intensity at $\theta=0°$ than at 180°) which he claimed was consistent with the neutral pair theory and 'fatal to the ether-pulse theory of the $\gamma$-rays'. Barkla in reply claimed close agreement between his X-ray experiments and the predictions of the electromagnetic pulse theory but had to admit some difficulty with the harder X-rays and $\gamma$-rays: 'My argument has not been concerned with $\gamma$ rays but with the type of radiation with which I am experimentally most familiar—X rays of ordinary penetrating power.'

In retrospect it is easy to see the connection between the properties of X- and $\gamma$-rays that concerned W.H.B. and the quantum properties of light but W.H.B. had not read Einstein's paper on the photoelectric effect and neither he nor Barkla saw the connection. But both made important new discoveries whose true significance was recognized later. Thus Barkla and C. A. Sadler found that secondary X-rays in general consist of two distinct types: (1) the ordinary Thomson-scattered X-rays; and (2) entirely new homogeneous X-rays, the hardness of which is *characteristic* of the emitting element. W.H.B. and J.P.V. Madsen found that $\gamma$-rays excite $\beta$-rays of the same velocity from a number of different scatterers and they proved that the velocity of the $\beta$-rays depends only on the hardness of the primary $\gamma$-rays.

Bragg followed the arguments closely, acting as a sounding board for his father's ideas: he remembered living 'in an inspiring scientific atmosphere'. Then, in 1908 at the height of the debate W.H.B. accepted the Chair of Physics at Leeds University. They left in the *Waratah* in January 1909 and arrived in Plymouth in March. The *Waratah* was lost with all hands on her next voyage.

It was more than 50 years before Bragg saw Australia again but his memory of it remained vivid. He remembered particularly the long summer holidays, in the hills or by the sea to escape the heat in the city; collecting shells on the coastal reefs (including a new *Sepia* that was called in his honour *Sepia Braggi*, Verco); galloping bareback along the sands and into the sea: and learning from his mother, together with the rest of the family, how to draw and paint. England under snow in March 1909 must have seemed very different.

### Cambridge, 1909–14

The family were left in lodgings in Plymouth while W.H.B. and his wife went into Leeds to report for duty and find a house. Initially they rented a furnished house and through the spring and early summer lived rather miserably there, surrounded by the unfamiliar grime of an industrial city. Bragg afterwards regretted not having done something more constructive in this period but eventually, following his father's example, he went up to Trinity College, Cambridge, for the long-vacation term. His brother Bob went to Oundle School, before following him to Trinity in 1912.

Bragg began by reading mathematics at Cambridge. His tutor was the Rev. E. W. Barnes, afterwards well known as a radical Bishop of Birmingham, and he attended lectures by A. N. Whitehead, G. H. Hardy and Professor A. R. Forsyth and was coached by R. A. Herman, all of Trinity. Having been unable to take the Scholarship Examination before going up he sat it in the spring of 1910—while in bed suffering from a serious attack of pneumonia—and was awarded a major scholarship in mathematics, the Master of the College commenting on the brilliant imagination shown in his essays. In the Part I examinations he gained first class honours in mathematics, and then, strongly urged by his father, he transferred to physics for Part II of the degree course. C. T. R. Wilson, who ran the practical class at that time and lectured on optics, made the strongest impression and left him with a love of physical optics which never deserted him. But he also remembered dull lectures from Searle on heat, stimulating fireworks from J. J. Thomson (who staunchly favoured the wave-theory of X-rays) and the excitement of J. H. Jeans's lectures on statistical mechanics and the emerging quantum theory. One of his letters home (*b*) recounts in detail Jeans's discussion of the black-body radiation of a cavity, showing that the observed energy distribution cannot be derived from Maxwell's equations but without mentioning Planck's quantum hypothesis of 1900. He wrote 'I got an awful lot from a Dane who had seen me asking Jeans questions, and after the lecture came up to me and talked over the whole thing. He was awfully sound on it, and most interesting, his name was Böhr or something that sounds like it.' Bohr soon went on to Rutherford in Manchester but he remained one of Bragg's friends for life.

Bragg sat the final examination in Part II Physics in 1911, gaining first class honours, and he spent his third year mainly doing 'a crude research into the velocity of ions in various gases, suggested by J. J. Thomson' (*c*). It was not an encouraging experience since, contrary to popular belief, the facilities for research in the Cavendish at that time were extremely primitive. The large number of research workers attracted there by J. J. Thomson's reputation quite overwhelmed the meagre resources. Bragg remembered for example: 'that there was only one foot bellows between the forty of us for our glass blowing which we had to carry out for ourselves, and it was very hard to get hold of it. I managed to sneak it once from the room of a young lady researcher when she was temporarily absent, and passing her room somewhat later I saw her bowed over her desk in floods of tears. I did not give the foot pump back' (226).

But life in Cambridge, or more particularly in Trinity, had proved to be rewarding and provided compensations. A. L. Goodhart remembered dining regularly in Trinity with Bragg, E. D. Adrian, F. W. Aston and G. P. Thomson, probably during 1913, and listening fascinated to the chaffing of the scientists: Braggs were good at experiments, Thomsons were not!

The beginnings in 1909 were not so happy, perhaps not surprisingly for a young man away from home for the first time, but Bragg's colonial background led to a rewarding activity. On 6 November 1909, following the example of one of his Squires cousins, he enlisted as a Trooper in King Edward's Horse. This Cambridge unit of the Special Reserve had been called originally 'The King's Colonials' and was composed of men who had come from, or had some close connection with, the colonies. They were mounted infantry and trained in the tactics developed during the Boer War, concentrating on marksmanship, riding and the care of horses. Joined by his brother in 1912, Bragg trained during the year and at summer camps for four years until his discharge in November 1913. The company seems to have produced no close friends but it must have helped in the first experience of a new culture to have this link with the old.

It was College life that provided the closest friends. Chief among these was Cecil Hopkinson who came from a family of engineers and was the youngest brother of Bertram Hopkinson the Professor of Engineering in Cambridge at that time. Hopkinson introduced Bragg to skiing, sailing, shooting and climbing and 'dragged him into adventures which he thoroughly enjoyed once he was launched into them'. Sailing remained a particular pleasure, though an early cruise off the south coast of Ireland gave rise to another dangerous bout of pneumonia. The only available hospital was the infirmary of Skibbereen Workhouse, where Bragg was looked after by nuns and spent much time in long conversations with the local schoolmaster, Jeremy O'Regan, who remained a lifelong friend. He went to convalesce with the Townshends at Castle Townshend, a summer resort of hunting people. This and other adventures cemented his friendship with Cecil Hopkinson whom he regarded as a major formative influence.

At Trinity Bragg also became close friends with a group of contemporaries who shared his interest in intellectual exploration. They formed a discussion group, not only sitting up late discussing the world in the universal manner of undergraduates but also reading formal papers to each other on a wide variety of of subjects. H. Townsend was a mathematician, C. S. S. Higham a historian, H. W. St C. Tisdall a classicist and B. S. Gossling a physicist. Bragg remembered giving a joint paper with Townsend on Minkowski's interpretation of relativity and he remembered also a paper by Gossling on the theory of crystal structures with particular emphasis on the latest ideas of Pope and Barlow. This was Bragg's first introduction to crystallography and to the work of W. J. Pope, Professor of Chemistry in the University, 1908–39, which were soon to be of critical importance.

Throughout this undergraduate period, while enjoying new friendships and experiences, Bragg remained closely in touch with his family as they settled down in Leeds. After the initial shock, his mother had come to terms with the industrial north. Securely established in 'Rosehurst', a commodious stone home in Grosvenor Road, and with a cottage near Bolton Abbey in Wharfedale for weekends and holidays, she entered wholeheartedly into the social life of Leeds and its surroundings. According to her son, she was gregarious by nature and clever at making people enjoy themselves and these qualities found full expression in a ceaseless round of visiting, entertaining and welfare work.

For W.H.B. the move to Leeds had been less successful. Reproaching himself for his wife's initial unhappiness and engaged in organizing a large department and giving more formal lectures and courses than those he had given in Adelaide, he found little time or inspiration for new research. The controversy with Barkla was still unresolved, however, and W.H.B. continued to think and to write about the nature of the X- and γ-rays. Early in 1910 he began a correspondence with A. Sommerfeld of Munich (*d*). The occasion was the publication of papers by Sommerfeld and by J. Stark of Aachen in which they advocated rival views of the origin and nature of X-rays. Stark, apparently the first to be stimulated by Einstein, had proposed that X-ray quanta are produced when a beam of electrons collides with electrons in a metal plate and he described the individual collisions on the assumption that momentum is conserved, using the quantum value for that of the X-ray. Sommerfeld, a strong advocate of the view that X-rays are classical electromagnetic radiation, challenged Stark's theory, claiming that the experimental evidence, including the asymmetric emission of the X-rays, could be explained on the pulse theory. W.H.B.s letter to Sommerfeld (7 February 1910) admitted the difficulty he had in accounting for the polarization of X-rays with his neutral-pair theory but emphasized his belief that the difficulties that arise from the spreading of waves are even greater. Sommerfeld's reply conceded the 'weakness of his position regarding the production of the secondary rays' but claimed that 'concerning the emission of the primary rays, we are by contrast on familiar ground'. A year later Sommerfeld sent W.H.B. a reprint of the article in which he showed that if an electron moving at nearly the speed of light is brought to rest in a distance of atomic dimensions nearly all of the resultant radiation (Bremsstrahlung) is emitted into a narrow region between two concentric cones around the direction of motion of the electron. Thus, according to Sommerfeld, the radiation has 'the character of a projectile and in its energy localization is no longer appreciably different from a corpuscular radiation' (*f*). W.H.B. replied immediately (17 May 1911) 'Your hollow cone is most interesting and the ring structure of the γ-ray. But this does not meet the real difficulty to my mind. How do you propose to get the energy back again from this everspreading ring to a single electron ? In other words, how are you going to account for the production of a β-ray by a γ-ray ?' But he went on: 'I am very far from averse to the reconcilement of a corpuscular and a wave theory: I think that some day it must come. But at present it seems to me that it is right to think of the X- or the γ-ray as a self contained quantum which does not alter in form or any other way as it moves along. . . . My chief point is that it does not spread: and it seems that spreading is the inevitable accompaniment of the electromagnetic theory.' Finally he drew attention to C. T. R. Wilson's recently published 'pictures of the fog formed instantly after the passage of ionizing rays through a gas' noting that: 'there is no visible general fog due to the direct action of the X-rays: nor is there any corresponding effect in the γ-ray picture. All that is seen is the track of the [secondary] β-ray like a fine hair right across the chamber.'

Despite these difficulties, Sommerfeld believed at this time that only a demonstration of the diffraction of X-rays was needed to exclude every corpuscular theory of X-rays and early in 1912 he thought he had found such evidence in the diffuse broadening of the image of a wedge-shaped slit illuminated by X-rays. But he had also appointed a young assistant, Walter Friedrich, to investigate whether polarization and directional emission could be found for characteristic radiation. Meanwhile, W.H.B. had been confronted by further evidence that his neutral-pair theory was inadequate to account for all the properties of X-rays: Otto Stuhlmann and R. D. Klee discovered independently that ultraviolet light ejects β-rays asymmetrically from a thin metal plate. Thus a relationship had been established between X-rays and light, an accepted electromagnetic radiation, using the very phenomenon that he had used most often in support of his own theory. Nevertheless, while accepting more and more openly that something new was needed to embrace both the corpuscular and wave concepts, he continued to argue the case for a corpuscular theory, sustained by Whiddington's observations, clearly consistent with such a theory, that X-rays cannot excite the characteristic rays of any substance unless they have themselves been excited by cathode rays of energy exceeding a certain limit. In his book *Studies in radio-activity*' which was published in 1912, he wrote: 'it still seems to me that the neutral pair theory correctly pictures the chief processes of the X-ray, which the old form of the spreading pulse, even the modified Thomson's pulse, are unable to do. But I should now add that we ought to search for a possible scheme of greater comprehensiveness, under which the light wave and the corpuscular X-ray may appear as the extreme presentments of some general effect'.

It was another ten years before A. Compton showed that X-rays are scattered by matter in two ways: for the soft X-rays studied by Barkla, Thomson scattering predominates; for γ-rays and hard X-rays the asymmetric Compton scattering is the more important. And it was longer still before it was accepted that both radiation and matter have particle-like and wave-like properties. Meanwhile, the balance of the argument was pushed dramatically to the side of the wave theory as the result of experiments conducted by W. Friedrich and P. Knipping at the suggestion of Max von Laue in Sommerfeld's Institute for Theoretical Physics in Munich.

These experiments and the ideas underlying them have often been described. (Ewald (*e*), who played a major part in the story, and Forman (*f*) give most detail in somewhat contradictory efforts to recapture the scientific climate of the time.) In brief, Ewald had worked out the theory governing the interaction of electromagnetic radiation with a simple orthorhombic lattice of dipoles and he sought to discuss his results with Laue. Without going deeply into the theory, Laue was struck by the possibility that a crystal irradiated with X-rays might give diffraction effects, if X-rays were indeed electromagnetic radiation. He therefore persuaded Friedrich and Knipping to try an experiment. Friedrich and Knipping first irradiated a copper sulphate crystal and subsequently zinc sulphide (ZnS) and various other crystals of cubic symmetry and observed that the X-rays were scattered by the crystals in discrete directions close to the direction of the incident X-ray beam. The pattern of spots made by the scattered X-rays on a photographic plate depended upon the orientation of the crystal and upon its symmetry so that, for example, cubic crystals irradiated along a four-fold axis gave a characteristic four-fold pattern of spots, though the intensities and absolute positions of the spots varied from substance to substance.

An account of these experiments, with an introduction by Laue on the theory of diffraction by a three-dimensional lattice, was presented at a meeting of the Bavarian Academy on 8 June 1912 followed on 6 July 1912 by Laue's attempt to explain in detail the effects observed with ZnS (*e*).

Unfortunately, after his faultless derivation of the basic conditions for diffraction from a three-dimensional lattice, Laue went wrong in his consideration of the experimental results with ZnS. First, in order to estimate the size of the unit cell of the ZnS crystal structure (which was, of course, unknown at the time and which he needed to derive the wavelengths of the X-rays) Laue assumed that ZnS has a primitive cubic structure with one ZnS molecule per unit cell whereas in fact, as we shall see, the structure is face-centred cubic with four ZnS molecules per cell. Secondly, and more disastrously, he was preoccupied with the idea that the observed effects were associated with characteristic X-rays arising in the crystal. Consequently he sought to explain the results in terms of a limited number of X-ray wavelengths and showed that, *if the conditions for diffraction need be fulfilled only approximately*, the observed spots could be explained in terms of only five different wavelengths. He noticed that some additional spots should be expected to appear, but nevertheless he was strongly persuaded by his success in explaining the observed spots that the phenomenon could be explained by diffraction and hence that it established the wave nature of X-rays.

The papers of Laue and his colleagues appeared in late August 1912 and aroused intense interest, but the conclusions were not immediately accepted, even by convinced advocates of the wave theory. Thus Barkla, writing to Rutherford on 29 October 1912, remarked 'I have had a copy of Laue's paper for some little time and certainly am sceptical of any interference interpretation of the results. A number of features do not point that way . . . this in no way affects my absolute confidence of the truth of the wave theory of X-rays' (*f*). The confusion and the lack of understanding of Laue's theory is well illustrated by the fact that Laue himself, in March 1913 (*e*), was arguing that the effects could not be due to the interaction of a crystal with a continuous range of X-ray wavelengths since this would lead (by analogy with the properties of a simple diffraction grating) to the photographic plate being blackened everywhere. If he had followed up his initial discussion with Ewald, who shortly showed his mastery of the theory, this story would have been different.

Bragg and his father were of course deeply interested in this new evidence on the nature of X-rays and they had the details in time to discuss them during the family holiday, which was spent in 1912 as guests of Leeds friends at Cloughton on the Yorkshire coast. Naturally the first thought was to explain the results in terms of corpuscles and on returning to Leeds Bragg set up an experiment to test whether the spots on the photographs might be due to neutral particles shooting down the avenues between rows of atoms in the crystal structure. The same idea had occurred to Stark (1912) in Aachen and it led to the first mention of Bragg in a published paper. In a letter to *Nature*, written on 18 October 1912, W.H.B. (*g*) noted 'a fact which my son pointed out to me, *viz*. that all the directions of the secondary pencils in this position of the crystal are "avenues" between the crystal atoms'.

Back in Cambridge, Bragg continued to think about Laue's papers and here several bits of knowledge came together to provide the answer. First he remembered that J. J. Thomson had lectured on Stokes's theory of X-rays as very short pulses of electromagnetic radiation, picturing an electron moving with its associated lines of force and X-rays as the whip crack which would run along these lines when the motion of the electron is arrested suddenly at the anticathode of the X-ray tube. Next he recalled C. T. R. Wilson's lectures on the nature of white light which had shown (following Schuster)* that white light could be regarded either as a combination of light of all wavelengths, each wavelength being diffracted at the appropriate angle by a diffraction grating, or as a succession of formless pulses which the lines of the grating converted into a train of waves. Then, drawing on the ideas about crystal lattices that his friend Gossling had described at one of their discussion meetings and remembering that the Laue spots became increasingly elliptical as the photographic plate was moved further from the crystal, he had the idea that the formless X-ray pulses could be regarded as reflected by sheets of atoms in the crystals. The pulses reflected from successive equidistant sheets then would form a wave train, just as in Wilson's treatment of the diffraction grating. Since the path difference between the waves of the reflected train is $2d \sin \theta$, where $\theta$ is the glancing angle at which the radiation falls on the planes and $d$ is their spacing, it followed immediately that the wavelengths ($\lambda$) of the different orders of reflexion

* In the preface to the second edition of his textbook (*h*), Schuster notes 'the treatment of white light and of interference problems has been made more consistent—and I hope clearer—by introducing the theory of impulses at an earlier stage'.

would be given by

$$n\lambda = 2d \sin \theta,$$

where $n$ is an integer.

The critical test was to see whether these ideas explained the observations from ZnS, including the absence of some spots predicted by Laue's analysis. Here Bragg inverted the argument and used the fact that the X-ray pulses can be regarded as equivalent to a 'white-light' spectrum extending over a characteristic range of wavelengths and with maximum energy at a certain wavelength. The intensities of the Laue spots ought, therefore, to fall in a regular series depending upon which part of the spectrum was responsible for each of them. Examination showed that this did not work.

At this juncture Gossling's talk on crystal structures again came to the rescue since his discussion of Pope's ideas (*i*) had embraced not only the simple cubic lattice but also the face-centred lattice. Remembering this Bragg tried to explain the ZnS pattern on the assumption that the structure is face-centred cubic and everything fell into place. Thus he showed that the Laue pictures were made by a continuous range of X-ray wavelengths, a kind of 'white' radiation, and that X-ray diffraction could be used to get information about the crystal structure. This was the start of the X-ray analysis of crystals.

The work was described (1) at a meeting of the Cambridge Philosophical Society on 11 November 1912 and briefly reported in *Nature* of 5 December, though not before W.H.B. (*j*) had remarked in another letter (28 November) 'my son has given a theory which makes it possible to calculate the positions of the spots for all dispositions of crystal and photographic plate'.

The paper, which appeared in January 1913, was called 'The diffraction of short electromagnetic waves by a crystal' because Bragg was still unwilling to relinquish his father's views that the X-rays were particles; he thought they might possibly be particles accompanied by waves. W.H.B., however, did not cling to his ideas but, noting that 'the problem then becomes, it seems to me, not to decide between two theories of X-rays but to find one theory which possesses the capacities of both' (*j*) he went on vigorously to exploit the new possibilities. At this stage they began to lead in two directions, towards the analysis of crystal structures and studies of the nature of X-rays.

Naturally enough, Pope was very pleased at the support for his theories provided by this work on ZnS and he suggested to Bragg that studies of the alkali halides NaCl, KCl, KBr and KI might be even more rewarding, presenting him with suitable crystals. 'The Laue pictures which they gave were simpler than those of zinc blende and led to a complete solution of their structure. These were the first crystals to be analysed by X-rays' (G). But before these results of Bragg's individual work were published (5) there had been other developments.

During the discussion following the presentation of Bragg's epoch-making first paper (1) C. T. R. Wilson suggested to Bragg that crystals with very distinct cleavage planes such as mica might show strong specular reflection of the X-rays. Bragg tried the experiment and well remembered J. J. Thomson's excitement on seeing the still-wet photographic plate with a mirror reflection of X-rays on it (G). This observation was published in *Nature* on 12 December (2) in a letter dated 8 December, the first of Bragg's papers actually to appear in print; and it aroused great interest, not least on the part of W.H.B. who saw at once the possibility of using the effect to study the nature of reflected X-rays by methods with which he was long familiar. On 23 January 1913 (*k*), in a letter dated 17 January, W.H.B. reported in seven lines his success in measuring the ionization produced by X-rays reflected from mica. This urgency illustrates the high excitement of the time and the competitiveness: the following week Moseley and Darwin (*l*), in a letter dated 21 January, published a rather more detailed record of similar experiments in which they acknowledged the stimulus of Bragg's original observation of reflection (2) even though they seem to have had similar ideas independently (*m*).

The apparatus used by W.H.B. in this experiment was rapidly developed in Leeds into the X-ray spectrometer and with this instrument he examined in detail the reflection of X-rays from a number of crystal faces, including those of rock salt. This provided the next great discovery. 'In addition to the "white" X-irradiation of all wavelengths which Bragg had called the X-ray pulses, W.H.B. found that each metal used in the X-ray tube as source of radiation gave a characteristic X-ray spectrum of definite wavelengths, just as elements give spectra in the optical region.' This work was presented at the Royal Society on 7 April 1913 in a joint paper (4). Bragg later (*M*) disclaimed having played more than a general part in the design of the spectrometer or in its use, though his knowledge of the crystals that were studied and which he had been analysing in Cambridge must have been important. Such was the start of X-ray spectroscopy. Moseley and Darwin in similar experiments had missed the characteristic spectra, apparently through the use of too-fine collimating slits, but prompted by details communicated privately by W.H.B. they went on immediately to improve the measurements, discover the fine structure of the spectra and start the classical survey which led Moseley to establish the atomic numbers of the elements.

The development of the X-ray spectrometer by W.H.B. and Jenkinson, his instrument maker in Leeds, highlighted the inadequacies of the Cavendish Laboratory where Bragg had great difficulty in getting on with his experiments. Years later he remembered (*M*) 'When I achieved the first X-ray reflections I worked the Rumkorff coil too hard in my excitement and burnt out the platinum contact. Lincoln, the mechanic, was very annoyed as a contact cost ten shillings [a week's wages at the time], and refused to provide me with another for a month. I could never have exploited my ideas about X-ray diffraction under such conditions'. Furthermore, the X-ray spectrometer promised a far more powerful way of analysing crystal structures than the laborious and indirect method of the Laue photograph. Accordingly it was at this stage, in the early summer of 1913, that Bragg and his father began to work together during the vacations in Leeds. But the Cambridge picture was not entirely black. Pope was always helpful and, although the Professor of Mineralogy had given strict orders that no minerals should ever leave the collections, Bragg got his specimens from Hutchinson, who was then a lecturer and later became Professor (155), and he was able to take them to Leeds with him.

The next papers were published at about the same time in a somewhat strange order. In the first of them W.H.B. (*n*) derived the wavelengths of various radiations and correlated them with Barkla's characterististic radiations, making use of the structure of rock salt which had been worked out by his son, but not yet published. This paper was followed immediately by Bragg's detailed account (5) of NaCl and related structures in a paper described by Ewald (*e*) as 'the great break-through to actual crystal structure determination and to the absolute measurement of X-ray wavelengths'. The analysis depended mainly on Laue photographs taken in Cambridge, supported by some measurements with the spectrometer, and led to a conclusion that was to disturb chemists for many years that 'in sodium chloride the sodium atom has six neighbouring chlorine atoms equally close with which it might pair off to form a molecule of NaCl'.

Finally, in this group of consecutive papers, came a paper jointly by Bragg and his father (7) on the structure of the diamond. Bragg later (234) attributed the credit for this analysis mainly to W.H.B., who succeeded with the spectrometer where he had himself failed with Laue photographs, but as Ewald (*e*) points out, this paper again employed all of the arguments developed in the preceding paper. Ewald goes on to note: 'Diamond was the first example of a structure in which the effective scattering centres did not coincide with the points of a single (Bravais type) lattice. Whereas in the structures of rock salt, zinc blende and fluorite the absence of molecules in the accepted sense created an element of bewilderment, the beautiful confirmation of the tetravalency of carbon on purely optical principles made this structure and the method by which it was obtained immediately acceptable to physicists and chemists alike'.

The summer of 1913 in Leeds was described by Bragg (*G*) in glowing terms. 'The X-ray spectrometer opened up a new world. It proved to be a far more powerful method of analysing crystal structure than the Laue photographs which I had used. One could examine the various faces of a crystal in succession, and by noting the angles at which and the intensity with which they reflected the X-rays, one could deduce the way in which the atoms were arranged in sheets parallel to these faces. The intersections of these sheets pinned down the positions of the atoms in space. . . . It was like discovering an alluvial gold field with nuggets lying around waiting to be picked up. . . . It was a glorious time when we worked far into every night with new worlds unfolding before us in the silent laboratory.'

During this period W.H.B. was more interested in X-rays than he was in crystals and he left the crystal structures to Bragg whose next great paper (10) described a refined analysis of NaCl, using spectrometer measurements of the reflected intensities and went on to describe the structures of zinc blende (ZnS), fluorspar ($CaF_2$), iron pyrites ($FeS_2$) and calcite ($CaCO_3$). This paper represents further remarkable progress, in particular showing how the intensities of the reflexion must be measured and evaluated in a complete structure analysis and in demonstrating the possibility of solving structures in which atomic positions are not fixed by the symmetry but have to be found by a detailed analysis of the X-ray intensities. Iron pyrites and calcite were the first structures involving undefined atomic parameters—one in each structure.

Apart from the structure of copper (11) these were the last to be completed for publication before the outbreak of war in August 1914 brought this period to an end. But even before that happened there were signs of difficulty in the unique working relationship between father and son. As the importance of the work was recognized W.H.B., the established scientist, naturally was consulted or asked to talk about it and, however hard he tried, he did not quite avoid leaving the impression that his was the guiding part: what was no more than fair looked like parental generosity. Thus W.H.B. gave his son credit, though without mentioning him by name, in the earliest *Nature* letters (*g*, *j*) but they were still W.H.B.'s letters and Bragg's first papers came later and were overshadowed by the first joint paper.

Then in 1913 W.H.B. described the work at the annual meeting of the British Association and was invited to the Second Solvay Conference on Physics, 27–31 October 1913. The subject was 'The structure of matter' and Laue, Pope and Barlow were there as well as W.H.B., each of them relying on Bragg's work for major parts of their presentations. They all acknowledged the importance of his contribution and the members of the Conference, including Sommerfeld, Laue, Einstein, Lorentz and Rutherford, sent him a postcard congratulating him on 'advancing the course of natural science'. But there is no doubt that a cloud remained that overshadowed his future relations with W.H.B. and was remembered 60 years later with pain mixed with gratitude for his father's part in making possible the rapid development of the work.

It was in the discussion of the Solvay Conference that Bragg, who was known to family and friends as Willy, was first referred to as W. Lawrence Bragg, to distinguish him more clearly from W.H.B.; and he used this style in his subsequent publications.

Back in Cambridge during 1914 Bragg struggled to extend his methods of analysis to more complex crystals. By this time he had a spectrometer of his father's design but work remained difficult at the Cavendish ('They keep the wretched liquid-air machines going most of the day, which makes the leaf jump all over the shop') and he did not find it easy to get on with writing the book that he and W.H.B. had planned. In a typically undated letter he wrote: 'I find it impossible to do my experiments and write the book at the same time, the book requires one to be absolutely on the spot. I nearly faint when I think of the article for the Jahrbuch. All this kind of thing does make ones brain boil so. Its a curse this continual writing'. But he kept up and extended his contacts with classical crystallographers. Barlow wrote frequently and in March Bragg spent a weekend with W. J. Sollas, the Professor of Mineralogy in Oxford, during which he had a 'great' talk with Barker and visited Moseley who was then near the end of experiments on X-ray spectroscopy that established the idea of atomic number.

In the summer of 1914 Bragg was elected to a lectureship and Fellowship at Trinity College and he occupied a set of rooms there with his close friend Cecil Hopkinson. His brother Bob was also in Trinity, in his second year as an undergraduate, and he had his first research student, E. V. Appleton. At this stage he was working on aragonite, a structure involving several undefined parameters, and writing to his father on 19 July 1914 he said: 'I have been writing up the aragonite but am a bit puzzled about the structure. I would really like to do a little more work on it. I wish I could go over it with you, I don't know quite how infallible I am.' As a postcript he added: 'Could you tell me about our programme in Germany? Where is the meeting and when?' There was no meeting: on 24 August 1914 he was commissioned as a 2nd Lieutenant in the Leicestershire Royal Horse Artillery.

## World War I, 1914–18

On the strength of his service with King Edward's Horse and knowledge of mathematics, Bragg was posted to a Territorial battery of the Leicestershire R.H.A. and spent the first year of the war training at Diss in Norfolk. Describing this experience he wrote (*L*) 'I was very much out of my element as my knowledge of horses was not at all extensive, and my fellow officers and men were Leicestershire hunting enthusiasts'. But he managed and wrote daily letters home describing his new life and yearning to continue his research. Meanwhile, despite the war, recognition of the importance of the new crystallography was growing. In February 1915 'X-rays and crystal structure' (*A*), describing the results obtained so far, was published with a preface in which W.H.B. tried hard to put the record straight: 'I am anxious to make one point clear, viz. that my son is responsible for the "reflection" idea which has made it possible to advance, as well as for much the greater portion of the work of unravelling crystal structure to which the advance has led.' In May the Barnard Medal of Columbia University was awarded to them both jointly. Throughout the early part of 1915 there was much family discussion about W.H.B.'s move to University College London, and all the time there were exchanges about crystal structures.

Then in August 1915 everything changed. The French Army had been experimenting with a method of locating enemy guns from the sound of their firing and the War Office decided that the British Army should follow suit. Bragg was selected to do the work helped by H. Robinson, a member of Rutherford's staff in Manchester, and they left for France at the beginning of September.

Bragg has described the general principle of sound-ranging (*L*) as follows: 'A series of listening posts or microphones are situated in known positions along a base behind the front line. The time differences between the arrival of the report at the posts are measured. Suppose the sound to reach post 1 at time $T_1$, post 2 at time $T_2$ and so forth. Then if one draws a circle on the map around post 2 with radius $V(T_2 - T_1)$, where $V$ is the velocity of sound, and similar circles for the other posts, a great circle which passes through post 1 and touches the other circles represents the form of the report wave, with the gun at its centre.'

The chief requirements for an effective system were to identify the sound due to a particular gun and to record the time intervals precisely. After a study of the French equipment in the front line in the Vosges, Bragg chose the recording equipment developed by Lucien Bull of the Institut Marey in Paris. This was the most elegant and accurate of the recorders but it was complex and required photographic development of a cine film on which the displacements of galvonometer wires were recorded (*L*). The more difficult problem was to find a microphone that distinguished between the report of the gun and the shock wave associated with the shell and this was not solved until late in 1916. Bragg (240) has described how the solution was found. 'We were living in tarred felt huts in bitterly cold weather at the time and we noticed that whereas the shell wave was a deafening crack, the faint gun wave blew jets of very cold air through the readily available holes in the sides of our hut. Now I had in my unit a certain corporal Tucker, who in peace time was a lecturer at Imperial College and who had made experiments on the cooling of heated fine platinum wires by currents of air. The joint brainwave came to us, I think mainly to him, that we could use this effect. We sent to England for a supply of the thin wire. We scrounged some ammunition boxes, bored a hole in each, and stretched the wire across the hole. We incorporated this in one arm of a Wheatstone Bridge, with a sufficient current to heat it to a dull red. . . . The idea was that the high-pitched noises which were so troublesome would have such rapid fluctuations that they would hardly displace the shell of warm air around the wire, whereas the low-pitched gun wave would blow a blast of air through the hole, sweep the warm air away, cool the wire, and so reduce its resistance, upset the bridge, and make the galvanometer record a current.'

The Tucker microphone worked 'like a charm' and this and other developments (*L*), all devised at the Front, made sound ranging a powerful and trusted method.

In the meantime, however, Bragg's personal life was deeply affected during the autumn of 1915 by the death of his brother Bob at Gallipoli, where Moseley was also killed, and by the eventually fatal wounding of his friend Cecil Hopkinson. News of a different kind, the award of the 1915 Nobel Prize for Physics to Bragg and his father, came when he was setting up the first sound-ranging station near the front line south of Ypres. He wrote home on 17 November: 'Just got Dad's letter and yours with the cheery news in it.' The village curé with whom he was billeted produced a bottle of Lachryma Christi.

From the beginning of 1917 to the end of the war Bragg supervised the successful application of sound ranging and a great expansion of the number of units. Many young scientists, including Andrade, were involved. In the process Bragg was awarded the O.B.E. and M.C., was mentioned in dispatches three times, and rose to the rank of Major. This service also brought him new friends. One of them was Harold Hemming, who was in charge of a complementary operation, flash-spotting, and another of lasting importance was R. W. James (232). Bragg and James had been in the same Part II class at Cambridge, where G. R. Crowe, then a precocious lab. boy who had recognized James's more conventional ability, had predicted that: 'Mr. James would get a first and Mr. Bragg might get a first.' James had subsequently had an adventurous time on Shackleton's expedition to the Antarctic and then, returning home, he joined Bragg's unit near Ypres. Later when Bragg moved to G.H.Q., James helped him set up a school for sound rangers where they worked together a great deal and no doubt discussed the future development of crystallography.

As the war drew to an end, their thoughts turned towards jobs and letters home were full of the possibilities. Thus, Bragg wrote to W.H.B. on 21 October 1918: 'I got your letter yesterday about the G.E.C. work. I had never contemplated anything else than a University career . . . training men in the University to take up applied science afterwards.' In December he wrote about James, who was thinking of applying for the Professorship in Cape Town: 'I know that I would feel absolutely happy and confident in taking on any University Chair, such as Leeds even, with a fellow like James to back me up.' But in January 1919, this was followed by 'I am just a bit doubtful of my powers of tackling the Birmingham University job right now as I know so little physics. I've had no experience in lecturing.'

After appropriate celebrations of the end of the war (Major Bragg and Captain G. P. Thomson made their first appearances at the Royal Society Dining Club on 30 November 1918) Bragg returned to Cambridge early in 1919 to take up his duties at Trinity College and demonstrate in G. F. C. Searle's (193) practical class at the Cavendish laboratory. With his brother, Hopkinson and Tisdall all dead it must have been a sad return but he found Cambridge a lively place with the social life dominated by young demobilized officers—Blackett amongst them. He had just enough time to fall in love with Alice Hopkinson, Cecil's first cousin who was then reading History at Newnham College, before accepting the Langworthy Professorship of Physics at Manchester, in succession to Rutherford.

## Manchester, 1919–37

At this time the Vice-Chancellor of Manchester University was Sir Henry Miers, F.R.S., who had previously been Professor of Mineralogy in Oxford (1895–1908). In Manchester the University had created a special Chair of Crystallography for him and he was deeply interested in the development of the subject that had been made possible by Bragg's work. His influence in the appointment is clear. Lecturing on 'the old and the new mineralogy' (*o*) he had said: 'In my opinion, the importance of the study of crystals has now become so great, not only for the identification of substances by crystal measurements but also on account of the new knowledge which modern crystal study is contributing to problems belonging to different sciences, that there is a real need for a department of pure crystallographic research, one in which such studies can be carried out quite independently of elementary teaching or of immediate applications, and without being tied to mineralogy. I venture to hope that it will not be long before some such department is founded either in connection with one of our Universities or elsewhere.' Through Bragg's appointment and the support and encouragement he gave to him Miers was able to realize much of this dream. He also became a firm family friend, godfather to Bragg's younger son David (1926), and his diary records many contacts.

Despite Miers's support, Bragg's early days in Manchester were not easy. Most of the other professors were relatively old—Horace Lamb the Professor of Mathematics had preceded W.H.B. in Adelaide—and they were used to dealing with Rutherford who had made the Physics Department world-famous. Bragg took over at a difficult moment. During the war most of the staff had been away on war work and the teaching had been continued mainly by E. J. Evans and N. Tunstall. When Bragg joined the Department in the autumn of 1919 he brought with him R. W. James and E. C. S. Dickson. H. Robinson (with D. C. H. Florance) had returned a little earlier so that he had at the beginning a nucleus of sound-rangers to support him. He lived with another, a classics lecturer named Drew, in an establishment arranged by his mother with his formidable old nanny, Charlotte, as housekeeper.

The first priority was to organize the teaching and Bragg at the age of 29 was very conscious that he had had essentially no previous experience that was relevant to the elementary teaching—even as an undergraduate. The beginnings were disastrous. Many of the undergraduates were returning ex-servicemen and they had no mercy on the novices. Tunstall remembered that there were 'rowdy, boisterous goings on in the lecture room particularly when medicos were being lectured to. One could hear this not only on the same floor but in the laboratory under the large lecture theatre and there was visible evidence in the fact that panels of the benches were kicked into matchwood during the lecture periods taken by Bragg, James and Dickson'. In one dramatic episode a student set off a firework under the reading desk and Bragg boxed his ears. To make matters worse anonymous letters began to arrive, addressed to the Vice-Chancellor and others, in which Bragg and his young colleagues were accused of incompetence with evidence quoted that was clearly based on a detailed knowledge of events in the department. Bragg was brought close to the edge of breakdown but recovered when the letters began to attack his father and Rutherford and when his research began to flourish again. But he was deeply scarred and it took a year or two for him to gain confident control. Miers gave what support he could and noted laconically in his diary at the end of 1924: 'there was a plague of anonymous letters at the University against certain members of the Professorial staff. But these ceased with the disappearance of one of the Junior staff to another post (with his wife).'

Research had a more promising beginning and in the autumn of 1919 Bragg was writing optimistically, but somewhat guardedly, to his father: 'My own apparatus is nearly set and James and I are eager to get going. I have one or two ideas I am anxious to try right away,' The heart of the apparatus was the X-ray spectrometer made by Jenkinson but it was used initially with a 'very inadequate gas X-ray bulb with a palladium target' (*p*). It wasn't until the following year, when the General Electric Company at Schenectady gave them a Coolidge tube, that rapid progress became possible. In the meantime Bragg returned to the study of zinc oxide that he had begun in 1914 (15) and this work, which included comparisons with related structures, combined with reconsideration of the pre-war analyses in terms of the new ideas about atomic structure and chemical bonding that had emerged during the war led him to the idea that interatomic distances in ionic compounds obey an additive law as if ions had characteristic sizes. He assigned sizes to the common ions and showed that the sums of their radii agreed quite closely with measured interatomic distances (16, 23). This important idea provided the subject for his first Friday Evening Discourse at the Royal Institution, on 28 May 1920, but unfortunately in working it out he had been too ambitious in attempting to embrace the sizes of individual atoms in compound ions (such as $CO_3^{2-}$) and in simple ions (such as $Cl^-$) in the same system. Accordingly, as he was fond of saying later, his scheme was inside out; all the negative ions were too small and the positive ions too large, though the sums of their radii were correct. J. A. Wasastjerna and V. M. Goldschmidt soon corrected Bragg's values (38) and the idea of atomic radii has played an important part in crystal structure analysis ever since.

Established for the first time in his own laboratory Bragg also had to consider the relationship between his own and his father's research programme. W.H.B. was now at University College London with a growing research group and Bragg continued the letter quoted above: 'I have been wondering what you were intending to go on with. I do hope you will never keep from doing any bit of work, Dad, because you think that may be the line I am going on. . . . If we did happen to do the same thing its all to the family credit, isn't it ? and I am sure I would never be the loser if people weren't quite sure which of us did a piece of work.' This philosophy was to prove difficult to live by, and they arrived later at a tacit agreement to work on different aspects of the subject, but at this stage he went on: 'I wish you would go on with some of those experiments on the temperature coefficient of the strength of reflection, you did get such interesting results on the ones you started and I don't think anyone else has done that. I have had one or two brain-waves which I am keen to develop but I want to work at ordinary temperatures and get good numerical results.'

This foreshadowed the research programme in which Bragg, James and Bosanquet (18–20, 24) set themselves the task of making X-ray analysis a quantitative science (240). James (1962) has described how they set themselves to make 'a series of measurements of the absolute intensity of reflexion of X-rays from rocksalt, a crystal whose structure was definitely known, with no uncertain parameters'. The idea was, firstly, to test the applicability of the formulae governing X-ray reflexion which had been derived by C. G. Darwin in 1914. Secondly, they hoped to measure the atomic scattering factors, the ratio of the X-ray amplitude scattered by an atom to that scattered by a simple classical electron under the same conditions, since this would provide evidence of the distribution of electrons in the atoms and fundamental data that would be needed in the analysis of more complex crystal structures. The experimental work was very demanding but they succeeded in showing that the rock-salt crystals reflected X-rays very nearly according to Darwin's formula for an imperfect crystal—a 'mosaic' crystal in Ewald's graphic description—according to which the reflected X-ray intensity is proportional to the square of the structure amplitude (*F*, the effective number of electrons in the unit cell contributing to that reflexion). Furthermore, they were able to derive experimental atomic scattering factors for sodium and chlorine which were 'in fair agreement with what was to be expected from what was known at the time of the electron distribution in those atoms.'

It turned out later that the choice of rock-salt had been fortunate, since the crystals conformed closely to the mosaic model, but the work did much to establish the methods needed for the quantitative analysis of crystal structures. Bragg's unique contribution here was to see the value of making experimental measurements of the absolute intensities of the X-ray reflexions which showed directly the effective number of electrons contributing to each reflexion. The work on rock-salt also stimulated work on the theoretical derivation of the atomic scattering factors that were needed to calculate the intensities of reflexions corresponding to any model structure for comparison with the observed values. In 1925, D. R. Hartree, who was then at Cambridge but soon afterwards became a close colleague as Professor of Applied Mathematics in Manchester, calculated promising atomic scattering factors (*f*-curves) based on the Bohr-orbit model of the atom and, stimulated by the need for better *f*-curves in crystal-structure analysis, he went on to devise the method of the self-consistent field. Recognizing the importance of this work at any early stage, Bragg (33) laid down the criterion that has guided all subsequent structure analysts: 'The structure which leads to the best agreement between observed and calculated values [of the X-ray intensities] is chosen as the closest approximation to the truth.'

The painstaking work of measuring individual X-ray reflexions in detail and studying their dependence upon temperature and crystal perfection was not Bragg's forte. In later years, comparing himself with his father he said that W.H.B. was the better physicist: 'His points always lay on smooth curves; mine didn't,' So from 1922 onwards he left this side of the work to James and concentrated on the analysis of structures.

In the meantime, however, there had been happy domestic changes. Bragg was elected F.R.S. on 12 May 1921 and among the letters of congratulation was one from Alice Hopkinson, then in the final year of the History Tripos, whom he had not seen since leaving Cambridge. They were married in December and moved into a house in Didsbury. Bragg had misgivings about bringing a lively 22-year-old wife to grimy Manchester and introducing her to the sober society of middle-aged professors but she had, after all, been brought up in Manchester, where her father had been a much-loved physician, and she knew the place well and was able to help her rather reserved husband in his developing contacts with the city as well as the university, while he introduced her to the wider scientific world in which he was becoming a leading figure. Earlier in 1921 Bragg (but not W.H.B.) attended the Third Solvay Conference on Physics, the subject was 'Atoms and electrons', and in the autumn of 1922 he had the pleasure of taking his young wife with him to Sweden where he delivered his Nobel lecture

(25) and they established friendly relations with Arrhenius, Westgren and other Swedish scientists. Then, in the summer of 1924 when their first child was a few months old, they made the first of many visits to North America where Bragg lectured at Ann Arbor and they attended the meeting of the British Association in Toronto. In all respects it was an eventful and fruitful marriage which remained a romance to the end. After Stephen Lawrence, born in 1923, there were three other children, David William born in 1926, Margaret Alice in 1931 and Patience Mary in 1935.

Bragg's contacts outside the university had begun early in his career in Manchester. Miers's diary for April 1920 notes that he discussed cotton industry research with the science professors and visited the Tootal Broadhurst Mill. At this time the leading figure in that firm was Kenneth Lee who was a friend of the Hopkinsons and became a close friend of the Braggs and godfather to their daughter Patience. Bragg (243) has described the contact that this friendship gave him with the work of Dr R. S. Willows at the Shirley Institute which certainly coloured his views of scientific research in industry. Important contacts with other firms, especially Metropolitan-Vickers, came later but another Manchester activity must be mentioned here. Bragg's first lecture to the Manchester Literary and Philosophical Society, on 'Sound ranging', was given soon after his arrival in the city (14) and, thereafter, he lectured regularly to the Society. He was President in 1927–28 (49) and Dalton Medallist in 1942.

In 1924 Bragg turned again to the study of aragonite which he had begun in Cambridge just before the war. This analysis required the determination of nine variable parameters and was much the most complex yet attempted (28). The solution depended upon careful absolute measurements of the X-ray intensities made with the spectrometer and Coolidge tube and, for the first time, Bragg discussed the symmetry of the crystals in terms of formal space-group theory.

Miers was deeply interested in this work and his influence, both direct and through his publications, can be discerned in Bragg's next achievement. Having a consuming interest in how best to use physical observations of all kinds to establish the arrangement of atoms in crystals, he turned briefly to the inverse problem of deriving the physical properties of crystals from their atomic structures. He showed that the refractive indices of calcite and aragonite could, with simple assumptions, be calculated essentially from the arrangement of carbonate ions in them (29) and in a second paper (30) he made some progress in generalizing the result and showing how consideration of the refractive indices may help in the analysis of crystal structures. This work aroused considerable attention and Bragg interested Sydney Chapman in it. Chapman had been a contemporary at Cambridge, though not a close friend, and had succeeded Lamb as Professor of Mathematics. In taking a further step they were prompted, perhaps, by a letter from W.H.B. (12 iii 22) discussing the structure of ruby, in which he noted the question 'of why the rhomb takes the particular shape it does', and they showed how the rhombohedral angle of crystals of the calcite type can be predicted quite precisely (31). But Bragg then left this field to

Chapman, who moved away from Manchester shortly afterwards. Although neglected for some time these were important early stages in crystal physics.

The study of aragonite also underlined a problem that struck at the heart of Bragg's quantitative method of structure analysis: the intensities of the reflexions appeared to be more nearly proportional to the structure amplitudes than to their squares (28), as W.H.B. had also observed in his work on diamond and on calcite. This was a consequence of the state of perfection of the crystals, as the theories of Darwin and Ewald had shown, but the mosaic model had worked so well for rock-salt that the theory of 'perfect' crystals was temporarily overlooked. Ewald was aware of the problem, however, and he wrote to W.H.B. about experimental measurements for comparison with his theory. W.H.B.'s response was to send some data but also to write an illuminating letter to Bragg (21 i 25) in which he reported Ewald's suggestion that new measurements on iron pyrites would be useful, and continued: 'I feel this is your province entirely and am thinking of writing to tell him so.' Later in the same letter W.H.B. promised to send an organic paper but in a discussion of mercuric chloride remarks: 'This also is your line rather than mine,' By this time, then, a division of work between W.H.B., who had moved to the Royal Institution in 1923, and Bragg seems to have been understood between them: W.H.B. worked on organic structures (and silica) while Bragg concentrated on inorganic compounds and the physics of crystals and diffraction.

The result of Ewald's interest was a study conference that he organized at Holzhausen in Bavaria in 1925 which was attended by the leading exponents of theory and experiment, including Bragg, James and Darwin. Bragg used to tell how they put forward their champion, Darwin, to present his theories of crystal reflexion only to find that he had forgotten how to derive them. However, the result of the meeting (43) was a much clearer understanding of the role of crystal perfection in determining the intensities of X-ray reflexions and this led, in turn, to increased confidence and success in the quantitative analysis of crystal structures.

From 1925 Bragg concentrated on an intensive programme of research into the structures of silicate minerals. The initial objective was to develop a technique for the analysis of crystals in which the atomic positions were defined by a large number of parameters and the silicates provided excellent material for this purpose owing to their complexity and the ease with which well-formed natural crystals could be obtained (67). The main source of supply was still Hutchinson in Cambridge. The first of these structures to be described were the olivines (40) and this success was soon followed by the analysis of beryl, $Be_3Al_2Si_6O_{18}$ by Bragg in collaboration with J. West (42), who played a large part in the silicate analyses and the training of those who worked on them. This was a remarkable study in a number of ways. The high symmetry of the crystals, which they described by means of the recently published diagrams of Astbury and Yardley, made the analysis very straightforward: Bragg later (59) noted that 'when West and I had determined the space group, I remember well that we found all the atomic positions in about a quarter of an hour, and all subsequent work only altered our first estimates slightly'. This also depended, of course, on their developing knowledge of atomic sizes, which Bragg had discussed again at the Solvay Conference on Chemistry in April 1925 (45), and the expectation that these structures would be defined mainly by the close packing of the oxygen atoms with the other, smaller, atoms tucked in between them (240). Careful measurements were made of absolute intensities and, referring to the earlier difficulties over crystal perfection, they noted that 'accurate allowance for extinction appears to be the key to the analysis of complex structures'. Finally, for the first time in this paper Bragg and West reported their use of a Fourier synthesis of an electron density distribution. Based upon WHB's Bakerian lecture of 1915 and subsequent work by Duane, Compton, Havighurst and others, this synthesis was in only one dimension but it pointed the way ahead and Bragg clearly saw what would follow: 'The Duane method cannot be applied until the signs of the coefficient $F$ (in the Fourier series) are fixed by preliminary analysis, for the observed intensities only give the squares of these quantities. Probably the most convenient procedure will be to combine the trial-and-error method of assuming structures and calculating the spectra to be expected from them, with the Fourier-analysis method, the latter being used to make the final adjustments of atomic position and to indicate the accuracy of the results.'

A discussion of one-dimensional Fourier syntheses as used by various workers, including J. M. Cork in his studies of isomorphous replacement in the alums which were carried out during a visit to Manchester in 1926–27, formed a large part of Bragg's contribution to the 5th Solvay Physics Conference on 'Electrons and photons' in October 1927 (54).

Over the next few years the structures of many silicates were determined by the standard method, of which Bragg and West (55) gave a definitive account in one of his favourite papers, entitled 'A technique for the X-ray examination of crystal structures with many parameters'. Many means 20 or 30. In addition to Bragg himself and West, the workers most involved were W. H. Taylor, a research student who was appointed to a lectureship in 1928, and two of the many visitors from abroad, W. Zachariasen (1927–29) and B. E. Warren (1929).

Bragg introduced Warren to crystal-structure analysis during a visit to M.I.T., where he spent a term lecturing in the spring of 1928. Before leaving Manchester he had begun a study of diopside, $CaMg(SiO_3)_2$, and had encouraged West to make a much more complete set of intensity measurements for this mineral than had been achieved in any previous study. This was made possible by the crystals, provided by Hutchinson (by this time professor in Cambridge), which had been cut perpendicular to the principal axes and permitted the measurement of complete zones of reflexions. Bragg took these data to M.I.T. with him and worked there with Warren on the analysis of the structure which proved to be of key importance (56). Throughout his work on the silicates there was doubt about the extent to which the oxygen atoms were associated more closely with the silicon than with the other atoms, but it was clear in diopside that tetrahedral $SiO_4$ units were joined by their corners to form long chains running through the structure. Systematic analysis of the other structures showed that the essential properties of the various types of silicates were largely determined by the $SiO_4$ tetrahedra which could join together sharing corners or edges, but not faces, to form three-dimensional structures, plates or chains.

The classification of silicate structures on this basis was initiated by Machatschki (236), a visitor in 1928–29, and it was elaborated by Bragg in his review of the whole programme in 1930 (67). Even at this stage, however, Bragg was reluctant to recognize the importance of $SiO_4$ units as complex ions and preferred to consider the individual atoms separately—as had been found appropriate in rocksalt. He was still deeply attached to the views expressed in his Royal Institution Discourse on 20 May 1927 when he had said (48): 'Some of the very earliest structures which were analysed caused us to revise our ideas of what was meant by the "molecule" of the chemist. In sodium chloride there appear to be no molecules of NaCl. The equality in numbers of Na and Cl atoms is arrived at by a chess-board pattern of these atoms; it is a result of geometry and not of a pairing-off of the atoms. This is, of course, not universally true, for this absence of the molecule in solids is in general only found in inorganic compounds. It would appear, however, that the silicates are of this non-molecular type and that in seeking to assign formulae to them, and to the hypothetical acids of silicon on which they are based, it should be borne in mind that they are really extended patterns. The relative numbers of their constituent atoms are characteristic of the extended pattern, and essentially a result of their solid state, so that it is doubtful whether a grouping of the atoms into molecules has in this case a meaning.'*

In contrast with this view, Linus Pauling (*r*), who was a visitor in 1929–30, had proposed a method of describing the structures in terms of $SiO_4$ and other polyhedral units and he went on to propound a set of principles governing the assembly of ionic compounds which depended heavily on the evidence accumulated in Manchester, as Bragg rather sadly remarked (67), and subsumed the less-well-developed rules that had been evolved there (James (*e*)).

Nevertheless, no subsequent analysis can diminish Bragg's achievement in guiding the studies of these complex mineral structures to a fruitful conclusion. His was clearly the guiding hand and his colleagues of those days have written of the excitement of working with him as more and more complex arrangements of atoms yielded to their attack. Silicate chemistry was shown to be inherently a chemistry of the solid state, intelligible only in terms of the three-dimensional structures, and Bragg never tired of using the story of its explanation to illustrate his conviction that the analysis of increasingly complicated structures can lead to the discovery of unimagined new principles.

After 1930 Bragg left further research on mineral structures to others, though he remained closely interested and spent the spring of 1934 at Cornell University

* It was the reporting of this Discourse that provoked H. E. Armstrong's well-known letter to *Nature* (*q*), which included the sentence: 'It were time that chemists took charge of chemistry once more and protected neophytes against the worship of false gods: at least taught them to ask for something more than chess-board evidence.' In his later years, Bragg enjoyed showing a slide of this letter in his lectures—usually a little out of context.

delivering the Baker lectures and writing *The atomic structure of minerals* (E). He was more concerned with crystal physics and the physical methods of structure analysis and he had, by this time, already defined the method that was to dominate crystal-structure determination for the next 20 years. This was another benefit from the work on diopside. Given the complete two-dimensional data that had been measured for the structure analysis he was able to explore the possibility of using Fourier series in two dimensions to calculate the electron density projected on the three faces of the unit cell (60). This was possible because, following the procedure outlined in the paper on beryl (42), the phases (or in this case the signs) of the Fourier coefficients could be calculated from the model of the structure proposed by himself and Warren (56); that is to say, the crystallographic phase problem, which arises because only the structure amplitudes and not their phases are given directly by X-ray observations, was already solved. Unlike most professors, he did not ask someone else to do the calculations for him. Armed only with a slide rule and mathematical tables, he did them himself and so produced the first two-dimensional electron-density projections. The results were very pretty and, although they did not lead to much new structural information since the positioning of the atoms in the original structure analysis had been closely correct, they did show the possibility of identifying atoms (or ions) from their electron counts and they suggested the method of the future. In discussing the results, Bragg posed the question whether the phases could be derived without knowing the complete structure: would partial information do? Investigation showed that the answer could be yes. In the projection on (010), for example, the Ca and Mg atoms overlap giving the equivalent of an atom of atomic number 32. Furthermore, this 'atom' always gives its maximum contribution whereas the other atoms, although they total 74 electrons, tend to cancel out. Consequently only one reflexion differs in phase from that given by the Ca/Mg alone. Bragg was, therefore, able to point the way ahead more precisely than before: 'a preliminary analysis of the crystal which gives approximate positions of the heavy atoms suffixes to fix the signs of the coefficients *F*. The Fourier series may thus be formed and the positions of all the atoms accurately read off on the projections.' In a further paper with West (65) the defects of the image that arise from errors and terminations of the series were defined and possible remedies discussed.

Subsequently, Bragg was sorry not to have published his work on Fourier syntheses jointly with his father, since it derived directly from W.H.B.'s Bakerian lecture and the two of them had discussed it in detail. He did not use the method himself to determine new structures but he encouraged members of his Laboratory to explore it further. In 1929 Zachariasen used two-dimensional projections in his refined determination of the structure of sodium chlorate, in which the oxygen positions were read from the maps; in 1930 West studied potassium dihydrogen phosphate in the same way (incidentally demonstrating the presence of regular $PO_4$ tetrahedra); and in 1932 Parker and Whitehouse re-examined iron pyrites. Characteristically Bragg was content to be thanked for his advice and help at the ends of their papers. He had demonstrated the potential of the method and left it to others to develop in detail: it has been an essential feature of X-ray crystallography ever since.

However, he did not leave it without trying to impress upon others the physical basis of the new method. He began to lecture on X-ray optics (58) and he had the idea of showing directly that the production of an X-ray image was an optical process. Remembering again C. T. R. Wilson's lectures on optics, he knew that a microscope image could be regarded as the superposition of individual waves (or fringes) and that Fourier synthesis was merely a way of adding these waves mathematically instead of experimentally through a lens. He therefore tried to see whether he could produce an image of diopside by superposing fringes on a piece of photographic paper.

Again he carried out the painstaking business himself, with the help of his laboratory superintendent, William Kay. His fringes were the out-of-focus images of a set of parallel rods: each set had to be given the right spacing, orientation, displacement (phase) and exposure to represent the corresponding Fourier coefficient. In spite of the odds against carrying out all these operations without mistakes for about 25 terms, the results were very convincing (61).

Although this analogue method was not taken up generally, and satisfactory numerical methods were devised instead, it is notable as the first of Bragg's instructive developments of optical methods and as a clear illustration of his over-riding interest in the physics of his subject.

At about the same time the possibility of his returning to Cambridge forced Bragg to consider his hopes for the future, and on 3 June 1929 he wrote to Rutherford (*c*) as follows:

> 'I have been thinking very hard about the possible post at Cambridge which you mentioned to me some time ago. . . .
>
> 'To come to Cambridge would in itself be delightful and anything which would bring me there has all the attractions of Cambridge to recommend it. Here on the other hand are a few of the "cons". I have got used to the running of a big physics laboratory, and although I often grumble at the administrative work and would like to be freed from much of it, it is very pleasant to have a constant supply of men eager to do research. I have about twenty or twenty five doing research here and do much of my work through them. Then again I take a great interest in the teaching of physics in general and do not want to drop that. I do not want to label myself a crystallographer as against a physicist and think indeed that though my research is concerned with crystals it is the physical side of it which attracts me. I might at any time wish to switch over into a more purely physical line, and want to feel quite free to do that.
>
> 'Could you tell me what the post at Cambridge might involve ? I realize of course that it is all very much in the air at present. Would it carry with it a laboratory in which I could house a large group of research men ? What funds for research would be available ? What students would come other than men from abroad coming to research under me on crystal problems ? Could I take part in the teaching of physics at the Cavendish ?

'I could perhaps explain my views best by describing what would seem to me a very attractive post. This would be an additional chair of experimental physics with especial charge of the physics of the solid state. You talked to me about the future of the Cavendish, and the possibility that in time to come the work might be divided as the ground to be covered in experimental physics is so great. Is there any possibility of this being done in the next year or two and of your devolving part of the responsibility? If I might put it quite frankly, I feel that such a post would offer unlimited scope for one's energy, whereas the subject of crystallography by itself is very limited. The parts of it which are growing and important are really pure physics, and it would best be developed as part of a big Physics School, not as a subject on its own.'

Nothing came of this negotiation and J. D. Bernal, who had moved from W.H.B.'s group at the Royal Institution to Cambridge in 1927, remained in charge of crystallography there. But it served to focus Bragg's views and may have suggested to him that there would be a danger of losing contact with mainstream physics if he concentrated too much on analysing structures. Disappointment at the outcome may also have contributed to the crisis that overtook him in 1930. In addition to the normal strains of his office, which at this time included the planning of a new building, the introduction of a new series of lectures for industrial physicists and writing a book (*C*), other factors also contributed. There was the excitement but also the tension involved in bringing the silicate work to its climax, especially when understanding the results drew him into the unfamiliar, fast-developing and competitive field of chemical bonding; there was the continuing conflict between his simple enjoyment of family life and his obsessive preoccupation with research at critical moments; there was the distant and guarded relationship with his father,* and the recollection of his lack of rapport with his mother, who had died in 1929 after a long illness; and there was the worsening economic situation which was more evident in Manchester than in many other places.

A real chance to move brought matters to a head. He was offered the Professorship of Physics at Imperial College, London, but, after anxious thought and unhelpful discussion with his father, he refused the appointment, largely through strong feelings of loyalty to the university that had given him so much. His friend G. P. Thomson was appointed instead. It was at this point, fearful that he had lost his last opportunity to move his family to more attractive surroundings, that he broke down.

Bragg's colleagues appear to have been largely unaware of the tensions that produced this crisis and, with the staunch support of his family, Bragg recovered his balance quite quickly. In this he was greatly helped by spending the spring of 1931 on leave in Sommerfeld's laboratory in Munich, where he sought to

* On 17 November 1926, for example, he wrote to W.H.B.: 'I am too lucky in too many ways to have any reason for feeling low at all. I think we ought to talk more about the lines we are doing and I would like to co-operate in the sense that each of us specialized in some particular line which supplemented the work of the other.'

broaden his command of the latest developments in physics, and by the birth in June 1931 of his third child and first daughter, Margaret Alice.

Back in Manchester at Easter, however, he changed his style of working, involving himself less closely in the day-to-day experiments and analysis, and looked for new and more physical lines of research while encouraging the continuation of mineral-structure studies by Taylor and others. With his reputation renewed by the silicate work, he also became somewhat more involved in general scientific affairs which took him outside the university. In 1931 he was awarded the Hughes Medal of the Royal Society and from 1931 to 1933 he served on its Council. He was elected a member of the Dining Club in 1934. During this period, in the summer of 1932, he and his wife made a trip to Russia, together with R. H. Fowler, Dirac, Gurney and the Kapitzas who arranged the trip. This may have made Manchester seem more attractive but, however that may be, everything brightened up in 1933 when he was able to move his family from Didsbury to Alderley Edge, to a house overlooking the Cheshire plain, within sight of the Welsh hills and with a beautiful garden. At the same time research became exciting again and Bragg faced the world with renewed vigour. In 1934 he not only spent a term lecturing at Cornell, he also made his first contribution to broadcasting by giving a course of six lectures on 'Light' and, at the end of the year, delivered the Royal Institution's Christmas lectures to a juvenile auditory on the subject of 'Electricity' (*D*).

Bragg's new research subject was a development of one of his established interests. A short excursion into electron diffraction (76, 79) did not promise much but his attention was attracted by another of Pauling's papers, this time on 'Rotational motions of molecules in crystals', and he made the new idea, that there is a much greater freedom of movement in the solid state than had been suspected, the theme of his lecture at the Centenary Meeting of the British Association in 1931 (77). Although he did not include an account of it in his lecture, this topic was directly related to new work in Manchester that was growing out of the long-standing studies of metals and alloys.

Bragg's first research student in Manchester was A. J. Bradley and, when he had completed his doctorate, Bragg asked him to explore the use of the powder diffraction method, which had been shown by Hull in America and Debye and Scherrer in Switzerland to be valuable in studies of elements and other simple structures. This approach had also been taken up by Westgren in Sweden, whose laboratory had become one of the main centres for the developing study of metals and alloys, so in 1926 Bragg sent Bradley to spend a year with Westgren and Phragmén in Stockholm to learn the trade. This proved extraordinarily successful. Bradley was in his element and was soon solving problems that others had considered impossible. On his return to Manchester he became the leading exponent of powder methods, solving problems of surprising complexity and attaining an accuracy in measurements that has hardly been surpassed in present times (*s*).

Bradley's most outstanding contribution was to determine the structure of $\gamma$-brass, $Cu_5Zn_8$, which has 52 atoms in a cubic unit cell and had defied Westgren and Phragmén whose single crystal Laue and rotation photographs and powder diagrams Bradley used in his analysis. The structure of $\gamma$-brass—an otherwise quite useless alloy—played a considerable part in the development of modern solid-state physics: the $\gamma$-structure was found to exist because its Brillouin zone is more nearly spherical than those of the simpler body-centred and face-centred structures. Bradley was no theoretician, his genius was to provide the evidence, but Bragg saw the importance of his work and discussed it with a succession of lecturers and visitors in the department whose contributions to the development of the theory are universally recognized. They included N. F. Mott (1929–30), W. Hume-Rothery (1932–33), H. A. Bethe (1933–34) and R. E. Peierls (1933–35). The part that Bragg played in this work is not now fully appreciated; he published no original papers on the subject and he would have been the last to claim that he had made any significant contributions. Nevertheless, his role as a catalyst cannot be denied and it is entirely appropriate that the term 'Bragg reflexion' now occurs naturally in solid-state physics and is used by people who have never carried out any X-ray diffraction work themselves.

During the period 1928–32 Bradley was paid by Metropolitan-Vickers, though he continued to work in the university, and it was natural, therefore, for Charles Sykes to consult him when he encountered a problem with iron-aluminium alloys at the Company's Research Laboratories in Trafford Park. Sykes was carrying out an industrial investigation into the properties of these alloys and, during the work, he found that their electrical resistivity varied as a function of aluminium content in what appeared to be a completely haphazard manner. Bragg was immediately drawn into the discussions and suggested, as it turned out correctly, that superlattice formation might be the cause of this behaviour. This started a long and fruitful association with Sykes and it stimulated Bragg's interest in order–disorder phenomena.

Bradley investigated the iron–aluminium system and found that the resistivity effects were due to the difference between an ordered structure of the alloy when cooled slowly and a disordered structure when it was cooled rapidly. The former had the lower resistance. Bradley then gave a colloquium in the department at which he described his results and Bragg put forward some general qualitative ideas about the nature of the order–disorder change. This occasion was attended by E. J. Williams, the Lecturer in Mathematical Physics, who was fascinated and overnight drafted a thermodynamic theory of the phenomena which he showed to Bragg the following day. There is no doubt that the detailed theory which developed from this beginning was very largely due to Williams, as Bragg made clear in his Royal Institution Discourse of 17 March 1933 (81), but Bragg took it up enthusiastically and used it as the basis of his Bakerian lecture in June 1934 which was published, most unusually, in their joint names (83). At this stage they discovered that theoretical treatments on similar lines had been published earlier by other workers and they discussed these, and a new approach to the problem by Bethe (who, together with Peierls, had contributed importantly to the discussions in Manchester), in a second paper (86). Williams rounded off the series of papers with an independent publication in which he acknowledged help from Bragg and from Peierls, who subsequently made further developments to Bethe's approach.

Although the Bragg-Williams contribution was not as original as it first seemed, there is no doubt that it attracted great attention and stimulated much further work all over the world. In Manchester experimental studies were continued in the university in collaboration with Sykes at the research laboratory of Metropolitan-Vickers and they were summarized in joint papers in 1937 (96) and 1940 (111, 113, 114). Meanwhile Bragg encouraged Bradley to devote himself to the study of alloy systems in the hope that X-ray methods, which made possible the unequivocal recognition of individual phases, would clarify the interpretation and use of complex phase diagrams. The work developed naturally into a classification of alloy phases in binary, ternary and even quaternary systems but this did not generally fire Bragg's imagination, though he was excited by the work on magnetic alloys (106), and he left this field in the main for Bradley to develop.

Single-crystal structure analysis continued to be an important part of the work in Manchester during the 1930s but Bragg did not involve himself closely in any particular study after the work on β-alumina which was completed in 1930 (75). But he continued to encourage this branch of research and it is interesting to note that he was present at the Washington meeting of the American Physical Society where Patterson presented his first account of the Fourier syntheses formed with the observables $F^2$ as coefficients which are now known universally as Patterson functions. Patterson, who noted (*e*) that 'Bragg [was] in the audience to ask the right questions', had used West's data on $KH_2PO_4$ in his first tests of the method but Bragg told him about the work by C. A. Beevers and H. Lipson at Liverpool on copper sulphate pentahydrate, which they had had solved by Fourier methods but not yet published, and suggested that he might use their data in more detailed tests. Bragg also described the new numerical methods of Beevers and Lipson for summing Fourier series which Patterson then used, together with the copper sulphate data, to calculate the two-dimensional synthesis that illustrates his classic paper (*t*). First Beevers and then Lipson subsequently moved to Manchester where they continued their development of the famous 'strips' and worked on a number of structures, Lipson for the most part with Bradley. Their work on a method for computing Fourier syntheses of electron density from the structure factors probably stimulated Bragg's invention of a graphical method to solve the inverse problem, the calculation of structure factors from atomic positions (90), which was elaborated in a joint paper with Lipson (91).

By the spring of 1937 there must have been an end-of-term feeling in Bragg's Department in Manchester: W. H. Taylor had left in 1934; West (for a professorship in Rangoon) and Peierls in 1935; Williams in 1936; and James (who now realized his earlier ambition to become professor at Cape Town) in April 1937. In May Bragg was invited to succeed Sir Joseph Petavel as Director of the National Physical Laboratory. He accepted and, arranging for Bradley and Lipson to move with him, took up his new duties on 1 November. He was succeeded at Manchester by Blackett.

In his final departmental report at Manchester, Bragg wrote: 'It is with great regret that I leave a department in which I have spent eighteen happy years. I came to it directly after the war, with no previous teaching experience. Manchester University has taught me all I know about the running of a department, and the fascinating and intricate life of a modern university. I shall always remember with gratitude the kindness of my colleagues and the inspiring atmosphere of this University.' He had certainly served it well, not least by making Manchester the centre of his subject. Visitors came from all over the world and they found him a charming and helpful person, with none of the pomposity they might have expected in so eminent a man. Many have remarked upon the personal kindness of Bragg and his wife and their hospitality at Alderley Edge but Sir Charles Sykes may have provided the most illuminating snapshot: 'when we got down to the serious discussion he would adjourn to the billiard room which contained a full-size billiard table. On all my visits to this room, I never saw any balls on the billiard table; it was covered with reprints of papers and, as the argument developed, Bragg would get up from his chair, wander round the table, pick out the appropriate reprint, and we would then examine it in terms of the ideas we were discussing at the table.'

## The National Physical Laboratory 1937–38

The National Physical Laboratory was at that time administered by the Department of Scientific and Industrial Research whose Secretary, Sir Frank Smith, was much concerned in Bragg's appointment. W.H.B., who was now President of the Royal Society and had strong views on the importance of applied science, very much approved of the move.

But Bragg found the work disappointing. Although some of the research was flourishing, many things were being done that had long ceased to be useful. In taking Bradley (who was then Royal Society Warren Research Fellow) and Lipson with him he hoped to set an example in research. They worked in the Metallurgy Division, whose Superintendent was C. H. Desch, but most of the short time they were there was spent in writing up for publication work done in Manchester. Bragg's only original paper published from the N.P.L. was a short note with Lipson on high-dispersion X-ray photographs of metals (101). One of his few innovations was to attempt the introduction of a series of lectures from prominent scientists: he found that there was no proper lecture room for them; there had been one but it was so little used that it was converted into an extension of the library. But there were plenty of committees and formal occasions, which he did not enjoy.

Rutherford died on 17 October 1947, before Bragg had left Manchester, and there was immediate speculation about who should succeed him as Cavendish Professor of Experimental Physics in the University of Cambridge. Bragg was clearly a possibility but W.H.B., who was himself ill at ease in Cambridge and opposed the move, wrote advising his son's wife not to be disappointed at not being able to go to the Cavendish having just moved to the N.P.L. Sir Frank Smith, who was an elector to the chair, took a different view and with the rest of the Board (The Vice-Chancellor, H. E. Dean; R. H. Fowler; C. G. Darwin; H. Thirkill; W. J. Pope; W. Wilson; O. W. Richardson; and G. I. Taylor) decided to offer Bragg the appointment which was announced in March 1938. Election to a Professorial Fellowship at Trinity College followed shortly afterwards. There was undoubtedly some consternation, especially among nuclear physicists, but Darwin is reported to have remarked that 'nuclear physics is a passing phase' and *Nature* commented: 'The Cavendish laboratory is now so large that no one man can control it all closely and Bragg's tact and gift of leadership form the best possible assurance of the happy cooperation of its many groups of research workers.' The next 15 years showed that this was closer to the mark than most editorial comments.

## Cambridge During World War II, 1938–45

Bragg moved to Cambridge with his wife and four children in October 1938 where, at the age of 48, he succeeded Rutherford in a major appointment for the second time. Again it was not easy since many members of the laboratory had hoped that Rutherford would be succeeded by another nuclear physicist and Bragg not only had different interests, his style of management was quite different also. P. I. Dee and N. Feather were the principal nuclear physicists remaining in Cambridge and the other research interests at the Cavendish were the work of the Mond Low-temperature Laboratory under J. D. Cockcroft, the ionospheric research under E. V. Appleton, and the crystallography, which had been directed hitherto by Bernal. During the previous ten years Bernal had inspired a very lively group which had been particularly successful in starting studies of biologically important molecules and macromolecules, but he had been appointed to succeed Blackett at Birkbeck College in the round of musical chairs that followed Bragg's leaving Manchester. Bragg brought Bradley, with Lipson to assist him, from the N.P.L. to succeed Bernal in charge of the Crystallographic Laboratory and, in the next year, he strengthened metal physics by attracting E. Orowan from Birmingham.

Another change was quickly needed. Appleton, who had been Bragg's first student, resigned the Jacksonian chair in order to succeed Sir Frank Smith as Secretary of the D.S.I.R. and Cockcroft was appointed in his place. In this first year Bragg worked closely with Cockcroft, who had played a large part in designing the new Austin wing of the laboratory and was now supervising its construction—on the understanding that it would be used by the Services in the event of war (138). As war grew increasingly probable, however, ideas for reorganization of the laboratory were set on one side and, by September 1939, most of the basic research work was suspended as the members of staff left for war service or turned their attention to related research.

Nevertheless, Bragg's first year back in Cambridge was scientifically fruitful and, in particular, his first weeks there were marked, most significantly as it turned out, by a dramatic revival of his interest in the analysis of more and more complicated crystal structures. M. F. Perutz, who was the only member of

Bernal's group of biological crystallographers left behind in Cambridge, has described what happened (*u*): 'I waited from day to day, hoping for Bragg to come round the Crystallographic Laboratory to find out what was going on there. After about six weeks of this I plucked up courage and called on him in Rutherford's Victorian office in Free School Lane. When I showed him my X-ray pictures of haemoglobin his face lit up. He realized at once the challenge of extending X-ray analysis to the giant molecules of the living cell. Within less than three months he obtained a grant from the Rockefeller Foundation and appointed me his research assistant. Bragg's action saved my scientific career and enabled me to bring my parents to Britain' (as refugees from Hitler's invasions of Austria and Czechoslovakia).

This meeting with Perutz introduced Bragg to the problem that was to be his main research interest for the rest of his career and his first paper related directly to protein-structure analysis followed almost immediately (107). Here he discussed the problems involved in determining complex structures directly from their Patterson functions and, referring to recently published claims that the Patterson of insulin could be interpreted, he pleaded 'for a due sense of proportion'. This note shows him already thinking about proteins but its main interest now is as an introduction to the two letters that followed immediately afterwards from Bernal and J. M. Robertson. In his letter Bernal paid attention to the then uncertain chemical constitution of proteins, a problem ignored by Bragg, and referred to the difficulty of locating a zinc atom with 28 electrons in a molecule with 20 000 electrons. Robertson, however, while agreeing with Bragg's comments about Patterson diagrams, went on to suggest how the structure of insulin might be determined: 'the molecule does, however, contain a few zinc atoms, and if these could be replaced by mercury, as has been suggested, a very profitable study might ensue'. It was to be a long time before essentially this method was used to solve the structure of a protein crystal and, in the meantime, Bragg played a major part in keeping alive the hope that success would be achieved at last despite the scepticism of most crystallographers—including many of those in his own laboratory.

Meanwhile, in a new burst of creativity, there was time for one more advance before the war intervened to stop most of the research. This was a development of Bragg's earlier attempt to devise an optical method for making Fourier syntheses of electron-density maps (61). Now he had the idea of using Young's fringes instead of the out-of-focus images of a set of rods to represent the Fourier components. Each set of fringes could be produced by a pair of holes with the right orientation and spacing. He suddenly realized that he had rediscovered the reciprocal lattice. The holes had to have areas proportional to the structure amplitudes but there was no easy way of simulating the phases. Nevertheless, the method could be used to synthesize the familar (010) projection of diopside for which all but one of the phase angles were zero. Crowe, the precocious lab. boy of his undergraduate days, built the necessary apparatus—Bragg called it the X-ray microscope—and Chapman, the instrument maker of the crystallography section, drilled the plate simulating the reciprocal lattice. Its diffraction pattern showed clearly the arrangement of atoms in the crystal (108). Bragg was delighted with this result and demonstrated it at a Royal Society Conversazione.

Further developments of these ideas continued intermittently during the war and it is convenient to describe them without interruption here. The first (119) in 1942 was a relatively simple extension of the method just described in which a photographic method was used to produce the reciprocal-lattice plate. This took advantage of a photographic process developed by the British Scientific Instrument Research Association, whose director, A. J. Philpot, was a fellow member of war-time committees, and it made possible the synthesis of a Patterson projection of horse haemoglobin from measurements by Perutz. The possibility of synthesizing centrosymmetrical electron-density projections, for which the phase angles are all 0° or 180°, by using half-wave plates of mica was also described. Having obtained images in this way, Bragg next turned his attention to the opposite problem, how to simulate optically the production of a single crystal X-ray diffraction pattern—in two dimensions. His solution to this problem, first demonstrated at a Royal Institution Discourse in 1942 (128, 136), was to make a set of images of the contents of a unit cell by using a multiple pin-hole camera, in which the holes were arranged on the points of the crystal lattice—the so-called 'fly's eye'. Crowe again carried out the work and it was a success which led to practical results: C. W. Bunn used the device in helping to solve the structure for penicillin.

Finally, Bragg realized that the fly's eye was unnecessary: one image of a unit cell would give rise to a continuous diffraction pattern from which the reciprocal lattice picked out the appropriate intensities. In a joint paper with Lipson, he therefore proposed the use of a simple optical diffractometer and illustrated its value in studies of alloys (123).

These optical devices were taken up and further developed by several people, especially by Lipson and his colleagues. They proved very important educationally in emphasizing the Fourier-transform theory that underlies X-ray diffraction phenomena and they have been used intensively in the analysis of electron micrographs of periodic structures.

But in September 1939 Bragg's main preoccupation was to make what contribution he could to the war effort and he took pains to see that his staff and ex-students were efficiently deployed. His problem then was to carry on the teaching of physics in Cambridge, suitably adapted to meet the demands of the war. Queen Mary College and Bedford College, London, were evacuated to Cambridge and their physics classes and teaching staff were combined with those of the Cavendish. The Queen Mary College professor was an old friend and colleague, H. Robinson, and he stayed with the Braggs. Most remarkably, Searle was brought back from retirement and he took charge of the practical classes until the end of the war (193). Much of the teaching was concentrated on short two-year Honours courses with special classes in electronics for potential radar personnel.

In addition to the X-ray optics already described, Bragg continued the metals research with a good deal of emphasis on practical problems as it had been in

Manchester. Unhappily, however, Bradley was not good at the day-to-day running of a laboratory and he went into a sad decline, finally having to give up charge of the Crystallography Group. Lipson took over responsibility for running the section. Apart from the continued work with Bradley and Sykes on alloys and order–disorder phenomena that has already been mentioned (111, 113, 114) Bragg's most important contribution to metals research in this period was the invention of his remarkably useful bubble model of a metal structure (118). Inspired by his discussions about the strength of metals with Orowan, this simple model illuminated the behaviour of domain boundaries in plastic deformation and, developed further after the war, did much to popularize the theory of dislocations (145, 156). It illustrates very well Bragg's uncanny gift for visualizing atomic arrangements and expressing their essence in simple models, and the fact that Feynman, most unusually, quotes one of Bragg's papers (145) verbatim in his *Lectures on physics* clearly expresses his appreciation of the model and of Bragg's gift for exposition.

Bragg played no part in the war research that was conducted in the Cavendish, by Halban, Kowarski and others, but he did contribute to services research of two main kinds. As early as 1937 he was consulted about the equipment and tactics of the Sound Ranging Section in the Army and he continued throughout the war to advise on its development. The centre of research and teaching was on Salisbury Plain and there he renewed contact with World War I friends, including Hemming who had been in charge of the complementary method of flash spotting. This latter method was no longer useful, since gun flashes had been eliminated, but sound ranging was. Bragg found it in much the state in which he had left it in 1918, without even an effective radio communications system though with some not-very-useful accretions (L). Refined under the pressures of war it again proved valuable and, in addition to being employed in essentially the old way in the main land engagements of the war, the same principles were used in plotting the trajectories of the V2 rockets.

Secondly, Bragg was consulted by the Admiralty on the development of Asdic (sonar). This method of underwater detection by the use of sound waves had been developed to some extent during World War I by a research group led by W. H. Bragg at Parkeston Quay (*a*) but it came into use only in the World War II. Bragg regularly visited the Admiralty Research Station at Fairlie on the Clyde for discussions of the problems encountered in the further development and use of the system. Writing about it later he remarked modestly: 'I find it hard to estimate how much I helped. Only the people on the spot could appreciate the practical difficulties and such help as an outsider could give came from a knowledge of the man to consult about this or that special point. . . Quite apart from direct help, I think the researcher liked talking about their problems to someone who understood and could appreciate their work.' He continued to serve as an advisor on this work for about 15 years.

Bragg also served on committees set up by the Ministry of Supply to keep its scientific activities under review, as Chairman of the General Physics Committee and member of the Metallurgy Committee, and this enabled him to keep the

Ministry closely aware of the work still going on in Cambridge. Other members of these committees included A. V. Hill, Andrade and A. J. Philpot. From the end of 1942 he was also a member of the Advisory Council of the D.S.I.R.

Early in 1941 Appleton asked Bragg to serve a term of six months in Canada as Scientific Liaison Officer between Canada and the U.K., in succession to R. H. Fowler. He sailed to Halifax in March accompanied by C. G. Darwin who was on his way to Washington, D.C., and was attached to the team of scientists working under the leadership of C. J. Mackenzie at the National Research Council Laboratories in Ottawa. Bragg and Mackenzie had met briefly at a sound-ranging course on the Vimy Ridge front in World War I. In Ottawa they collaborated closely and Mackenzie has described Bragg's performance, which was based upon his close relations with the scientific community in Canada and the United States and his standing in the U.K., as that of 'a superb liaison officer for the exchange of secret information and arranging useful and congenial meetings between distinguished allied scientists'. Bragg's report to Appleton on 12 August 1941 advocated the policy of keeping the liaison office small and encouraging experts in each subject to travel backwards and forwards between the two countries that was largely followed. After visits to Vancouver and other centres he flew home in September in a bomber on its way to active service and was succeeded in Ottawa by G. P. Thomson.

A second wartime journey abroad, of a more cultural but possibly equally hazardous nature, took place in 1943 when he visited Sweden at the invitation of the British Council to talk to Anglo-Swedish Societies and re-establish contacts with Swedish scientists. Bragg flew to Stockholm on 16 April and gave some 14 lectures, mainly on his research interests in X-ray optics, proteins, metals and minerals, in six Swedish centres before returning home on 12 May. He met many old friends—Westgren was especially remembered—and his report, which ranged over the availability of scientific journals and the importance of further exchanges, concluded: 'I cannot exaggerate the warmth of my welcome.' With the tide of war changing and thoughts turning more confidently to its end, Bragg clearly made a valuable contribution to Anglo-Swedish relations.

Bragg performed at least one other public function during the war which was of great importance. From October 1939 to September 1943 he served as President of the Institute of Physics and worked hard to maintain the activities of the Institute at as normal a level as possible and to initiate constructive discussions about the likely needs of the postwar world (117). Throughout his time in Manchester he had fostered the activities of the Institute in that area and he had also taken a special interest in the application of X-ray methods to industrial problems (78). At the beginning of his Presidency plans were made to hold a Conference of the Institute on 'X-ray Analysis in Industry' but they were frustrated first by the outbreak of war and then by the events of 1940. It was then decided to publish the papers that had been prepared (116) and a Conference to discuss them was at last held in Cambridge on 10–11 April 1942. The report in *Nature* noted that 'some anxiety was felt by those responsible for the arrangements, lest preoccupation with war work would prevent many from attending, but the decision to proceed was made because the X-ray tool is being widely used for problems directly connected with the war. The large attendance at the Conference (some 280 participated) and the generally expressed appreciation of this opportunity for discussion have shown that this anxiety was unnecessary.' Bragg gave an historical review and mentioned proteins and the 'fine' structure of deformed metal as problems on the threshold of solution.

This meeting was such a success that its members decided to set up an organization under the aegis of the Institute of Physics to arrange similar conferences from time to time. As a result, a discussion meeting on the determination of equilibrium diagrams by X-ray methods was held in September at the Royal Institution, with Bragg in the chair, and a second full conference on X-ray analysis in industry was held in Cambridge on 9–10 April 1943, again with Bragg as chairman. This led to the establishment of the X-ray Analysis Group of the Institute of Physics to arrange meetings and perform other functions connected with X-ray research for a membership drawn from both university departments and industry. The committee of the new group, which met in July 1943, was made up largely of Bragg's associates and he was elected chairman with Lipson as secretary.

The X-ray Analysis Group (XRAG) adopted the pattern of meetings that was set in 1942 and meetings were held regularly in the spring and autumn of each year until the end of the war and, with few exceptions, this has continued to the present time. Bragg remained chairman until April 1947 and was thereafter a vice-chairman until his death.

At the end of the war the XRAG, led by Bragg, played a critical part in the organization of crystallographic research internationally. At the committee meeting held in July 1945, following suggestions by Ewald at the Oxford Meeting a year earlier, there was discussion of the need for a new journal to succeed he then-defunct *Zeitschrift für Kristallographie*. Bragg consulted Wyart, Mauguin, Ewald and others and it was agreed that advantage should be taken of the summer meeting of XRAG in 1946 to hold international discussions of the problem. This XRAG meeting was held with Bragg as chairman on 9–11 July 1946 at the Royal Institution. The subject was 'X-ray analysis during the war years' and it was a memorable occasion which provided the first opportunity after the war for crystallographers of all nationalities to re-establish contacts. In addition to about 250 U.K. participants some 75 visitors from 15 different countries around the world were present, happily including Laue, and many moving accounts were given of research during the hostilities.

On the following two days formal meetings were held at Brown's Hotel of a Provisional International Crystallographic Committee to explore the question of publishing an international journal of crystallography and to consider other questions of crystallographic interest. Bragg opened the meeting which agreed, after much discussion of detail, that a new journal was needed and that it should be called *Structural crystallography*. Bragg then noted that it would be necessary for some organization to assume formal responsibility for the journal and suggested that one possibility would be to form an International Union within the existing framework of Unions, either as a Union of Crystallography or as a Commission of the Union of Physics or of the Union of Chemistry. Unanimous agreement in favour of a separate International Union of Crystallography was quickly reached and Bragg was asked to explore the possibility further.

At this time the General Secretary of the International Council of Scientific Unions was Professor F. J. M. Stratton of Cambridge and Bragg was able quickly to arrange a meeting at which Stratton gave his opinion that a new Union would be acceptable. In this way the International Union of Crystallography was conceived. Bragg was not able to attend its first formal meeting at Cambridge Mass. in 1948 but he was there elected its first President. He also served as a founder member of the Editorial Board of the new journal, which was actually given the fittingly general and international title 'Acta Crystallographica' at the request of the Russians, and he played a large part in raising the money that was needed to launch it.

This account of the International Union has taken the story beyond the end of the war but some brief details of Bragg's personal life in those years remain to be added.

Bragg's knighthood was announced in the New Year Honours list of 1941 and W.H.B. wrote to Lorna Todd in Adelaide on 5 January: 'Isn't that fine ? . . . He will have to be Sir Lawrence: we can't have confusion worse than ever. I am so very glad for his sake. In spite of all care, people mix us up and are apt to give me a first credit on occasions when he should have it: I think he does not worry about that at all now, and will never anyhow have cause to do so now. I think I am more relieved about that than he is' (*a*).

W. H. Bragg died on 12 March 1942, still in his post at the Royal Institution where Bragg had spent part of the day with him. Since 1938, when Bragg was appointed (non-resident) Professor of Natural Philosophy in the Institution in succession to Rutherford, they had met more often and their relationship seems to have grown more easy. Writing about their father 20 years later on the centenary of his birth (223), Bragg and his sister described him in terms which show clearly the qualities that endeared him to so many and reveal to some extent how difficulties arose in family relationships.

From the summer of 1938, Lady Bragg was heavily involved in the work of the Women's Voluntary Service (W.V.S.), initially at the head office in London and subsequently as head of the Service in Cambridge. Bragg took great pride in his wife's work which made her a well-known public figure in Cambridge and led to her election to the Council and, in 1946, to her becoming Mayor. With their four children, the two girls still at school at the end of the war, they had a busy time.

## Cambridge after the war, 1946–53

Bragg's cogitations during the war about the future need for physicists (117) and the organizations that would be needed to provide them (130) prepared him to meet some of the problems that faced him in Cambridge at the end of 1945. He was clear, at least, that the Cavendish Laboratory would no longer be dominated by any single research group under one dominating figure since he believed that 'the ideal research unit is one of six to twelve scientists and a few assistants, together with one or more first-class mechanics and a workshop in which the general run of apparatus can be constructed'. With this model in mind he waited, for the most part, for people to emerge with ideas that engaged his interest.

But the teaching as well as the research had to be reorganized and in both departments he relied heavily on J. A. Ratcliffe who returned early from his war service and became Bragg's most trusted helper, especially in the handling of University Committees at which Bragg did not excel. Ratcliffe's intervention, 'We think, don't we Professor . . .,' seems to have been heard at awkward moments in more than one meeting. To some extent the changes within the laboratory were forced by the veterans returning from the war whose ideas were very different from the old ones: senior members of staff expected an office, a a secretary and a telephone whereas before the war they had none of these. Bragg met these wishes and, as Ratcliffe recalls, 'modernised the very antiquated notepaper, introduced a departmental secretary to help him run the laboratory and opened up the Austin wing. There was a complete transition to a new style laboratory and the place worked in a completely different way from the old one.' A. B. Pippard, one of his successors as Cavendish Professor, wrote long afterwards in 1972: 'Bragg performed a notably excellent job in decentralizing the work of the Cavendish, and thus effectively breaking away from what would have ultimately become the dead hand of the Rutherford tradition. His decision to give each research section as near as possible autonomy, consistent only with very general central principles and of course financial control, has played a significant part in the subsequent developments. Ever since then, the Cavendish has been notable among Cambridge departments for the democratic way in which it conducts its business. There has been no suspicion, I believe, of essential decisions being taken by the head of the department without consultation.'

The development of autonomous sections was made difficult in 1945 by the need to replace staff and fill vacant positions. A. J. Bradley had suffered a serious breakdown and his appointment in charge of the Crystallography Laboratory could not be renewed. To replace him Bragg appointed W. H. Taylor, his most valued and productive associate and successor in the silicate work, who had been Head of the Physics Department at the Manchester College of Science and Technology where Lipson succeeded him. From the end of the war Cockcroft was expected to resign the Jacksonian Chair in order to direct government research in atomic energy but his new appointment was delayed and it was not until 1947 that O. R. Frisch was appointed in his place to take charge of the of the laboratory's continuing effort in nuclear physics. At the same time there were delays in finding a new Plummer Professor of Mathematical Physics before Hartree, another old Manchester colleague, was appointed. However, in November 1946, Bragg was encouraged by the award of a Royal Medal of the Royal Society.

The rapid build up of work after the war and the new range of interests are illustrated broadly by the Departmental reports (printed in the *University Reporter*) and by the public lectures which Bragg gave about the general work of the laboratory (149). In 1948 the major groups were 'nuclear, radio and low-temperature physics, crystallography, metal physics and mathematical physics, with some minor groupings'. Of these Bragg was, of course, most directly interested in the crystallography and metal physics, with the associated electron microscopy under V. E. Cosslett, but his interest had also been engaged in radio physics, which was directed by J. A. Ratcliffe and embraced M. Ryle's developing radio astronomy. Bragg recognized in this latter work a further application of the principles of physical optics to set alongside X-ray crystallography and he supported it vigorously. After he had left Cambridge in 1953 Ryle wrote to him: 'The fact that you were so enthusiastic about our early work on the sun really made me feel that it was worthwhile. The same enthusiasm has made such a tremendous difference ever since—and it has always been a most happy thing to come to you with some new result.'

Nuclear physics, under Frisch and E. S. Shire, remained the largest group in the laboratory but Bragg wrote of it without the same evident enthusiasm. Noting the heavy investment in equipment and the need for technical officers to run it, he must have recalled his thoughts about research institutes (117): 'The strikingly successful places of this kind are those which may be regarded not as a body of men but as a body of equipment. Such a place has a nucleus of permanent staff and accumulates traditions of technique peculiarly its own, but its main service is as a place open to all for short periods of intense work and its main population a changing one'.

Echoing his earlier letter to Rutherford, Bragg described his own central interests as follows (153): 'The department which we call crystallography would perhaps be better described as the department for discovery of the structure of the solid state. . . . Mainly by X-rays we seek to discover the way the atoms are arranged in crystals and in other forms of solids. The scope of the work is very considerable. At one end we are investigating such substances as minerals and alloys in the inorganic field; other researchers are examining complex organic compounds . . .; finally at the other extreme we have a little group which is financed by the Medical Research Council under the direction of Perutz, which is engaged in a gallant attempt to work out the structure of the highly complex molecules which build up living matter, the proteins. . . .

'This section of the laboratory is closely linked to metal physics under Orowan. His students are particularly studying the mechanical properties of metals and relating them to their structure. The effects of cold work on a metal, recrystallisation, the yield point and plastic flow, brittle fracture, distortion under rolling or drawing and so on, are being investigated as physical phenomena. A satisfactory theory of the strength of a metal has yet to be formed.'

Bragg's contributions to research in the early days after the war were concerned mainly with these problems in metal physics, especially through his further development of the bubble-raft model (145, 156) which he discussed now in terms of dislocations. He also promoted the development of X-ray microbeam methods by Taylor's group, with a view to studying directly the variations in grain size in cold-worked metals, and he encouraged J. N. Kellar and P. B. Hirsch to build a big rotating-anode X-ray tube to produce a high-intensity microbeam. With this instrument they produced encouraging pictures of aluminium but work elsewhere then suggested that electron microscopy might provide a better approach. Happily an essential shift in technique in this direction was possible because of Bragg's earlier encouragement of electron microscopy: in 1946 he recruited Cosslett who had proposed a programme of work on electron microscopy. But in 1948 there was an upset. As the new rotating-anode tube came into operation Bragg's interest was becoming more and more focused on proteins and he stunned the metals group by suggesting that it should be diverted to this work. Taylor helped to preserve a balance and, in the end, both lines flourished (*v*).

Perutz had engaged Bragg's interest in proteins in 1938 and this was maintained throughout the war, although Perutz was prevented by internment and subsequent war work from doing much research until he returned to the Cavendish in January 1944. He was joined in January 1946 by J. C. Kendrew. By early 1947 Bragg was seeking some way of ensuring long-term support for the group and on 21 May 1947, with Keilin's encouragement, he wrote a long letter to Sir Edward Mellanby, the Secretary of the Medical Research Council, asking for help. In this letter Bragg gave an outline of the proposed research and its difficulties and described its promise with reference to his earlier experience: 'We thought it a great triumph to analyse quite simple inorganic salts by X-ray methods in the early days, and a complex organic molecule then seemed almost as far beyond our reach as the proteins might seem now. Yet a patient accumulation of clues, and improved techniques, have made it possible to enter the organic field. If the structure of a few molecules of a new type can be analysed, a rich harvest is then reaped, because the structures of many others will then be clear by analogy. I foresee the same happening in the protein field. . . .'

After discussions at the Athenaeum Club, Mellanby agreed that a case could be made to the M.R.C. and, after further talks and correspondence during the summer of 1947, he wrote to Bragg on 20 October: 'Rather to my surprise, your project for the establishment by the M.R.C. of a Research Unit at the Cavendish Laboratory, on molecular structure of biological systems, was adopted by the Council at the meeting on Friday October 17th, although I had put it forward only for a preliminary run.' Such was the birth of the Medical Research Council's most famous Research Unit, now the M.R.C. Laboratory of Molecular Biology. The original application was for a grant of £2550 rising to £2650 per annum to support Perutz, Kendrew and two research assistants for five years.

The work that kept Bragg's enthusiasm for protein research alight was the attempt by Perutz, which had continued on and off through the war years, to derive structural information directly from the diffraction patterns of haemoglobin crystals and, most especially, from a complete three-dimensional Patterson synthesis of horse haemoglobin. On the assumption that the polypeptide chains were arranged in some kind of regular fold (which alone seemed to offer any hope of solution) Perutz devised a model of haemoglobin in which the molecules were shaped like 'pill-boxes' with the chains folded to give prominent repeat distances of about 5 and 10 Å.

At this stage Bragg became deeply interested and, together with Perutz and Kendrew, turned his attention to the possible forms of the folded polypeptide chain. Various models had already been discussed, especially by Astbury, but Bragg was attracted to the idea propounded by Huggins that the most likely structure was a helix because it placed each amino-acid residue in the same kind of position in the chain. There were various observations to take into account, in particular Astbury's studies of α-keratin indicated a repeat distance of 5.1Å, closely similar to one of the distances observed by Perutz whose data also suggested that the number of amino-acid residues in such a repeat was 3.3. Furthermore, it was regarded as very probable that the chain was held in a folded condition by hydrogen bonds between NH and CO and that these bonds were nearly parallel to the axis of the chain.

With these features to guide them Bragg, Kendrew and Perutz (161) tried various forms of helical chain. They allowed free rotation about all the single bonds in the chain and various symmetries in which there were 2, 3 or 4 amino acid residues per turn of helix but they failed to find any structure that was especially convincing. Sadly they concluded: 'In X-ray analysis in general, when a crystal structure has been successfully analysed and a model of it is built, it presents so neat a solution of the requirements of packing and interplay of atomic forces that it carries conviction as to its essential correctness. In the present case the models to which we have been led have no obvious advantages over their alternatives.'

Pauling and Corey showed within a year by their description of the α-helix that Bragg and his colleagues had missed an important feature of protein structure: lacking the necessary chemical insight, they had not realized that the peptide units would be planar—thus reducing the number of possible bends in the chain to one per residue. They had also adhered too firmly to the apparent keratin repeat distances of 5.1Å (which turned out to arise from a higher level of structure) and they had given insufficient consideration to the possibility of non-integral helices.

Otherwise their four-fold helix, which had planar peptide units and the correct hydrogen-bonding pattern, might have been refined to the α-helix with its 3.6 residues per turn and 5.4Å repeat. But the main shortcoming was clearly in the chemistry and Bragg never forgave himself. Years later he wrote (233): 'I have always regarded this paper as the most ill-planned and abortive in which I have ever been involved.' It was especially aggravating to have asked the right question only to have Pauling provide the answer.

Discouraging though this was, the protein work was continued with increasing intensity and Bragg's influence on the next stage can be seen especially in the use of absolute measurements of the X-ray intensities which derived directly from the Manchester methods (55). Following a lead of Crick's, Bragg and

Perutz showed by careful analysis of projection data that the reflexions were too weak to be consistent with a model in which the polypeptide chains were straight and parallel throughout the molecule and this finding raised the possibility that less regular models would have to be considered (171). Analysis of the changes in absolute intensities when a salt solution was substituted for water as the medium permeating a haemoglobin crystal next revealed the approximate outer shape of the molecule (172), a result that was clarified further by examination of different crystal forms (173, 189). Then, in a fourth paper in 1952, Bragg and Perutz (175) at last succeeded in determining the signs (phases) of some protein reflexions. Using the fact that the cell dimensions of haemoglobin crystals change as their liquid content varies, they were able to plot the variation of the molecular transform along the c*-axis of the crystals. Since the projection on the c*-axis had a centre of symmetry the transform was either positive or negative and passed through zero at intervals along the axis. A key question was to decide the minimum wavelength of these variations and Bragg (176) illuminated the problem with a characteristic example, showing that the transform of any random function, such as the times of arrival of the Cambridge trains at Liverpool Street Station on Sundays between 8 a.m. and midnight, contained a set of loops which change sign only at certain minimum intervals. These intervals were determined by the width of the function, $2 \times 16$ hours for the trains (when a centre of symmetry is added) or 38Å for the haemoglobin molecule. Bragg's principle of minimum wavelength was used to determine the signs of the $00l$ reflexions and hence the electron density of the molecule projected on the c*-axis.

This method of plotting the molecular transform was extended by Perutz and it proved especially valuable in providing a check on the working of the much more powerful method that emerged soon afterwards. Bragg's (233) account of its origin illustrates well his enthusiastic involvement in the work: 'I remember going to Perutz in great excitement one day because I had heard from Professor Roughton that an American worker had succeeded in attracting a mercury complex to haemoglobin in stoichiometric proportions, only to have Perutz tell me very coldly that *he* had given this information to Professor Roughton.' The possibilities opened up by this discovery were explored very quickly and Perutz (*u*) remembered that in July 1953 he was able to show Bragg an X-ray photograph from a haemoglobin crystal which had two atoms of mercury attached to each molecule of haemoglobin. At this moment they both realized that the phase problem was solved, at least in principle, and that the way was at last open to unravelling the structure of proteins by X-ray analysis. The signs of the $h0l$ reflexions of haemoglobin were quickly determined by Green, Ingram and Perutz and compared with the other evidence (175, 188): 'Everything checked and double-checked perfectly; it was a thrilling time' (231). This work gave directly an image of the haemoglobin structure projected down the *b*-axis of the crystals (190) and although this told very little about the structure of the protein it paved the way for a detailed investigation in three dimensions. But at this stage Bragg left Cambridge for the Royal Institution and continued his collaboration with Perutz and Kendrew at a distance.

The period 1951–53 during which these critical advances were made in the protein work witnessed also the first great triumph of the M.R.C. Unit. Bragg played no direct part in the study of DNA; indeed at one stage he actively discouraged Crick and Watson from working on it in an attempt to avoid competition with the M.R.C. Unit at King's College, London, but Watson (*w*) has given a colourful and irreverent account of his growing appreciation of its importance, his encouragement at a critical stage and his quick comprehension of the result. Watson also noted Bragg's concern that the chemistry underlying the final model should be checked by A. R. Todd, Pope's successor as Professor of Chemistry and the leading expert on the chemistry of nucleic acids. When Todd approved he was more than willing to promote rapid publication. As Watson saw it: 'The solution to the structure was bringing genuine happiness to Bragg. That the result came out of the Cavendish and not Pasadena was obviously a factor. More important was the unexpectedly marvellous nature of the answer, and the fact that the X-ray method he had developed forty years before was at the heart of a profound insight into the nature of life itself.'

In the report for 1952–3, his final year as Cavendish Professor, Bragg described these dramatic advances in work on 'The molecular structure of biological systems' very briefly together with progress in the other sections of the laboratory. By this time there were seven sections to be listed and their relative sizes were indicated by the distribution of research students between them: nuclear physics 30, radio waves 17; low temperature physics 10; crystallography 16; electron microscopy 4; meteorological physics 4; fluid dynamics 4. In addition there were a number of theoretical physicists housed in the laboratory and working with the various experimental groups. The descriptions of research in progress began with nuclear physics, still the largest group, and recorded the decision to instal a linear accelerator and the work that had been done to implement it. But the longest and most obviously enthusiastic section described the work on radio waves which was divided between the physics of the ionosphere under Ratcliffe and radio astonomy under Ryle. On the last topic the report concluded: 'The new knowledge of the Universe which it is yielding is proving to be of intense interest and, as the Cambridge unit under Mr Ryle has already established a leading position, the opportunity to develop this new science should be exploited vigorously.'

The report on crystallography noted particularly that 'The analysis of crystal structure by X-rays is a typical borderline subject' and went on to record the collaboration with chemistry, metallurgy and mineralogy. Bragg's own papers, which included a description of a simple device for calculating structure factors (174), were included in the list of the M.R.C. Unit and it is remarkable that, although he undoubtedly played a significant part in advising and helping the crystallographers, he scrupulously avoided (as did Taylor) sharing the authorship of papers unless he had made a major contribution to the experiments or theoretical developments recorded in them.

At his Farewell Dinner on 18 December 1953 (*v*) Bragg spoke with pride of the resurgence of the laboratory after the war, attributing the success to advances made by one member of the staff after another. Characteristically he emphasized that the atmosphere of 'affairs of state' was not one that he found easy to breathe and he thanked Ratcliffe particularly for his help with these matters and E. H. K. Dibden, whom he had appointed General Secretary of the laboratory in 1948, for his skilled administration.

From Dibden's point of view Bragg was, in fact, a good administrator because he knew what needed doing and believed in delegation. Ratcliffe has provided a more comprehensive summary which embraces this view: 'A Cavendish Professor plays at least four parts. He must be a scientist, run the laboratory, uphold the interests of the department in the University, and act as an Elder Statesman of Science outside. Bragg was pre-eminently the active scientist, and he ran the laboratory extremely well. I do not think he played the part that some others have done in the University itself, and I am not sure that his part as Elder Statesman was quite as large as theirs would have been. I found him extremely helpful and kindly, and above all things a real gentleman in every way. He was quite open and straight-forward and ready to help anyone who had the good of the laboratory at heart. I think there was an extremely good feeling in the laboratory during his time and all liked him.'

## The Royal Institution, 1953–66

From the time of his appointment to the non-residential Professorship of Natural Philosophy at the Royal Institution in 1938 Bragg had played an increasing part in the affairs of the Royal Institution. At first with his father as Resident Professor and then, after his father's death in March 1942, with Sir Henry Dale (1942–46) and E. K. Rideal (1946–49) as Resident Professors for short periods he lectured regularly in every year except 1941 when he was away in Canada. In this way he remained in touch with the staff after the family connection had been broken and he followed the fortunes of the Institution with close interest as it sought a new role in the difficult post-war period.

When Rideal arrived at the R.I. it was suffering from the inevitable neglect of the wartime period but he established a lively research group, with grants from industry and Government, worked hard at the programme of Friday Evening Discourses and, with his wife's help, struggled to maintain the tradition of weekly dinner parties at a time of shortage and rationing. It seems to have been because of the difficulties associated with this regular entertaining that Rideal suggested unexpectedly in 1949 that E. N. da C. Andrade should take over the Resident Professorship and responsibility for the lectures and entertaining while he remained in charge of the research. When this proved unacceptable to the President, Lord Brabazon, and the Managers, Rideal resigned and Andrade was appointed in his place.

Andrade took up his appointment in January 1950 and began his attempt to refashion the Institution. Unhappily, but perhaps not surprisingly in view of Andrade's temperament and the traditions of the place, this led to trouble. The root of the difficulty was that the Resident Professor, although enjoying the resounding titles of Fullerian Professor of Chemistry, Superintendent of the

House and Director of the Davy–Faraday Research Laboratory, was specifically not the Director of the Royal Institution and much of the responsibility for day-to-day affairs and the staff of the Institution remained with the President, and other honorary officers and the committees of managers and visitors elected by the members. It was widely held at the time that the R.I. had much of the character of a club, though one with scientific objectives, and in Brabazon's opinion the position of Director of a club was unthinkable. Andrade, however, understood that the terms of his appointment gave him powers within the Institution analogous to those of a managing director and this led to friction and discord especially with the honorary secretary, Professor A. O. Rankine. Despite strenuous efforts by many people to find a solution the situation deteriorated rapidly until in March 1952 at a meeting of the members a vote of confidence in Andrade was lost by a substantial majority. Andrade then resigned, though arbitration of his claim for compensation and the litigation that followed were not completed until March 1953.

This unfortunate affair deeply divided the members of the Royal Institution and strong feelings were expressed on both sides. Inevitably Bragg was consulted and, although he tried to stand aside as a servant of the Institution (he was still Professor of Natural Philosophy giving his annual lecture), there was no concealing his concern for the future of the Institution or his disapproval of Andrade's approach. Early in 1950, following the accelerated retirement of W. J. Green who had been the principal lecture assistant in his father's day, he commented in *Nature* 'We shall miss him greatly, for he has come to be a part of the Institution he has served', and later, in a letter to the President, he recalled the difficulties he had encountered when Andrade was in command of one of his Sound-Ranging Sections in France. By mid-1952 he was believed by Sir Henry Dale and other leading figures in the Royal Society to be an advocate, with Brabazon, of a policy to get rid of Andrade and then put the organization of the Institution on a proper basis—a policy that seemed to them grossly unfair and improper on their interpretation of Andrade's letter of appointment. Bragg was faced, therefore, by a difficult and embarrassing decision when the Managers of the Royal Institution in April 1953 offered him the vacant post of Resident Professor. There can be no doubt that he saw it as his duty to revive the fortunes of the Institution but equally he realized that the task was a difficult one and that his motives for intervening at all in the recent troubles would be called into question. Adrian, one of his oldest friends who was now President of the Royal Society and Master of Trinity College, Cambridge, reluctantly acknowledged that he would have to accept the post 'because no-one else would' and he did so, taking up the duties of the Fullerian Professorship immediately and the residential duties on 1 January 1954.

Thus, for the third time Bragg accepted a challenging appointment at a difficult time and against a background of disapproval. But despite the difficulties it was not all gloom. There was a chance to develop a new role for the Institution and, perhaps most important, a chance to continue with the protein research for a few more years just when success seemed imminent and retirement from Cambridge in the normal way, he was already 63, might have deprived him of an active part in it.

From the outset Bragg asserted that his appointment required him to work closely with the Honorary Officers (Brabazon continued as President but the Secretary and Treasurer were new), the Managers, Visitors and members of the Institution and he set out, in the main with their grateful help, to rebuild the reputation of the Institution. His aim above all was to avoid further public discord. Although he knew that the administrative structure would have to be changed he reconciled himself to a patient process of persuasion in order to prepare the ground for his successor and, as it turned out, he was made Director of the R.I. in 1965 when he was about to retire.

In 1953 the immediate problem was financial. The costs of keeping up the premises and running the traditional activities of the R.I. could no longer be covered by the subscriptions of the members and the endowment income and for some years the Institution had been drawing on its reserves. Bragg argued at once that new sources of support would have to be found and that the Institution should seek to provide a public service of some kind, in addition to research, that would justify an appeal for funds. At this time the main activities, apart from research, were the Friday Evening Discourses, occasional Afternoon Lectures on a variety of subjects, and the famous Christmas Lectures adapted to a juvenile auditory. Of these, the Afternoon Lectures no longer attracted large audiences, even though free tickets were issued to undergraduates, and the Discourses were largely reserved for the members and their friends. It was the Christmas Lectures that pointed the way ahead: Bragg offered courses of lectures for London schoolchildren, initially at the sixth form level.

This initiative was based securely on the long experience of the R.I. in presenting science to essentially lay audiences by the lavish use of experimental demonstrations. The idea was to show schoolchildren the experiments they would otherwise only read about, and it received an enthusiastic response from the schools and the Education Authorities. Bragg gave the first course of three lectures on Electricity during the session 1954–55 and it was repeated four times. The lecture theatre holds 500 so that 2000 tickets were issued, but this by no means satisfied demand. Later in the year Bragg gave a further single lecture on 'Famous experimenters in the Royal Institution' for sixth formers that was repeated four times and this eventually set the pattern. The Advisory Committee, which included representative science teachers and members of the Education Authorities, recommended that the demand would best be met by single lectures each repeated four times. They were given usually on the Tuesdays and Wednesdays of consecutive weeks and by 1965 a regular pattern had developed with 20 000 schoolchildren of various ages attending the lectures every year (199, 235).

Armed with this evidence of the Royal Institution's concern for and contribution to the training of future scientists, Bragg turned to Industry and Commerce for support and received a ready response. A new category of Corporate Subscribers was introduced which soon brought in more than the individual members' private subscriptions and allowed the activities both new and old to flourish.

Naturally these activities demanded a great effort from Bragg and the permanent staff of the Institution in developing the contacts with schools and with industry and, especially, in devising and mounting the large number of experimental demonstrations. Here Bragg was supported mainly by Ronald King, who had come to the Institution with Andrade and stayed on as Assistant Director of Research (and later Professor of Metal Physics), Kenneth Vernon the Librarian, and the Lecture Assistant. This important post was held first by Leonard Walden, who left in 1957 to rejoin Andrade, and then by W. A. (Bill) Coates, whom Bragg and King persuaded with some difficulty to leave the research laboratory for this more public role. Together they built up a wide repertoire of demonstrations, exploiting apparatus that had been accumulating in the Institution throughout its existence (208) and drawing on the advice and help of both staff and members. Bragg gave many of the lectures himself and the staff, research workers and office staff alike, would crowd into the gallery to watch him enthral, stimulate and provoke the packed audiences. One week there would be free-hand drawings of highland dances to illustrate the formation of ionic bonds and the next he would be seen lovingly caressing the Paget speech models and beaming with pleasure at every successful 'Ma-Ma'. With a wealth of everyday analogy and a complete avoidance of jargon he inspired a generation of schoolchildren in London and, through the television programmes that followed, the rest of the country.

The public activities of the Institution were also developed in other ways so that throughout his period of office at the R.I. Bragg was engaged continuously with the committees of members and the staff in considering and promoting ideas for new schemes. From 1955 there were 'Research Days' at which teams of workers from various laboratories described their work informally to parties of schoolteachers; television programmes were planned, rehearsed and recorded; films were made; and, towards the end of the period, a new series of lectures to Civil Servants was begun. Bragg's account of this venture (238) brings out well the continuous process of innovation and development in which he was involved with King and others as they sought to create a modern role for the Institution. The general support of industry during this time, the success of a subsequent general appeal, and the continuing vitality of the Institution under his successor are measures of his achievement.

The Friday Evening Discourses were, of course, continued in all their Victorian state accompanied by the traditional entertaining, skilfully managed by Lady Bragg. On each occasion the lecturer was entertained to dinner in the Resident Professor's flat together with a variety of other guests. Bragg attached great importance to this activity and in one of his reports to the Members he wrote: 'The invitations which we send to well known people to meet the lecturer as guests of the Royal Institution have a much greater importance than might perhaps be realized. My wife and I entertain some 120–150 guests in this way during the year. They provide an opportunity to make important people from all walks of life acquainted with the R.I. and its work.' Bragg no doubt enjoyed meeting these people and, for the most part, he also enjoyed listening to the

Discourses which helped him keep abreast of the latest developments in science. He must have listened to some two hundred of these lectures and the experience helped to give final shape to his views on lecturing (239, 250). The lectures were often discussed during the following week in the laboratories and at the daily tea parties for all the staff that helped so much to create a family atmosphere in the Institution. Bragg's favourite criterion for judging the success of a lecture was whether a member of the audience could be expected to remember one idea from it the following morning. More than one failed this test. Bragg also deplored particularly lectures that were read, but he understood too well the difficulties of popularizing science to be over-critical and was always ready to commend a simple explanation or a good experiment.

Two of these Discourses in 1965 gave him particular pleasure. On 7 May, Lady Bragg, who had been a member of the Royal Commission on Marriage and Divorce (1951–55) and was Chairman of the National Marriage Guidance Council, lectured on 'Changing patterns in marriage and divorce'; and on 15 November, Bragg listened with evident pride to the Discourse on 'Oscillations and noise in jet engines' given by his engineer-son Stephen, who was then Chief Scientist at Rolls Royce Ltd and later became Vice-Chancellor of Brunel University.

During this period also Bragg kept up and extended his role as a world figure in science. In 1948 he had been invited to assume the Chairmanship of the Solvay Conferences on Physics and in that year he presided over a discussion of 'Elementary particles'. Conferences followed on 'The solid state' (1951); 'Electrons in metals' (1954); and 'The structure and evolution of the Universe' (1958) until in 1961 he presided over his last conference on the 50th anniversary of the inaugural meeting in 1911. The subject was 'Field theory'—which he confessed to finding 'completely unintelligible'. In 1958 he was the President of the International Science Hall at the Brussels Exhibition (207) and arranged the British contribution to it.

At this time he was also Chairman of the Soirée Committee of the Royal Society. This was one of the few committees that he enjoyed, and he greatly appreciated the contact that it gave him with the growing points of science. In this role he was responsible for organizing the exhibition at the Tercentenary Celebrations of the Society in 1960.

The Davy–Faraday research laboratories are an integral part of the Institution and in Bragg's time they were partly in the basement and partly in the upper floors of the house next door, connected to the main building at the level of the Resident Professor's flat. This intimate arrangement enabled Bragg to visit the laboratories whenever he had a moment to spare or needed relief from the discussion of some tedious difficulty, and he would announce his imminent arrival by a characteristic stamp on the ancient and creaking floor boards.

On his arrival in 1954 there was very little research still in progress. King and a small group were continuing the research in metal physics started with Andrade, and U. W. Arndt was engaged in X-ray studies, partly technical and partly on proteins. Bragg had hoped to persuade Max Perutz or John Kendrew to move with him from Cambridge, but, at this promising moment in their work, they preferred to stay behind. They undertook instead to help Bragg build up protein research at the Royal Institution and they were each given the title of Reader in the Davy–Faraday Research Laboratory. With help and advice from them and from Dorothy Hodgkin and others, a research team was quickly assembled. Helen Scouloudi, who had worked at Birkbeck with Bernal and Carlisle, came first and she was joined in the autumn of 1955 by D. W. Green, who had been a research student with Perutz and had contributed to the critically important development of isomorphous replacement in protein structure analysis, and by A. C. T. North, who had worked on collagen with Randall at King's College. J. D. Dunitz came back from the U.S.A. at the end of the year and D. C. Phillips returned from a post in Canada at the beginning of 1956. This rapid build up was made possible by the support of the Medical Research Council and the Rockefeller Foundation.

Dunitz continued with work on transition-metal compounds until his departure for Zürich in 1957 but the other members of Bragg's research group concentrated on proteins and worked closely for the first few years with their colleagues in Cambridge. Kendrew visited the laboratory nearly every week to keep everyone closely in touch with the rapidly developing work on myoglobin. Bragg was particularly interested in the development of diffractometer methods for measuring the diffraction data needed to produce the first three-dimensional image of a protein molecule (it reminded him of the early days with the X-ray spectrometer) and he sought ways of using such measurements to locate heavy atoms in the isomorphous derivatives that were the key to the analysis. The popular approach was based upon the use of Fourier methods which take into account all of the X-ray reflexions from the native and a derivative crystal at the same time. Bragg realized that determination of the small number of parameters defining a heavy-atom structure is potentially a simple problem, similar to the early analyses of mineral structure (55), and that careful consideration of a few well chosen and carefully measured reflexions might provide the required information. Using data from the studies of myoglobin and oxyhaemoglobin he set to work in characteristic style with pencil and graph paper and devised two new methods which were described in his last research paper (205). Although they have not been generally adopted, computer methods proved too powerful and appealing, they illustrate well Bragg's quick eye for the practical application of basic principles and one of them has proved invaluable in the study of tobacco mosaic virus.

Bragg (233) has given his own account of the period 1956–58 during which Kendrew produced the first image of a protein molecule in three dimensions: 'I remember well the thrill of that time. The collection of the vast body of data needed was shared between the laboratory at Cambridge and the Davy–Faraday Laboratory at the Royal Institution. I made a private test of my own. Kendrew supplied me with sets of data for the *hk*0 and 0*kl* projections, for which general phases had to be determined because they have no symmetry centres. I developed a method for getting the relative positions of the heavy atoms (205) and verified that the phases could be found by drawing vector diagrams, with a very convincing agreement between the results for the different ligands. This investigation played no part in the final analysis. Kendrew fixed the heavy atom positions by a more general and powerful analytical treatment aided by the electronic computer, and the phases for all *hkl* components were systematically determined. My investigation only had a meaning for myself because it showed that the problem had been solved, and that final success was now certain. Kendrew first determined the structure to a resolution of 6 Å. It showed dense rods marking the stretches of α-helix and the flat disc of the haem group. It was a proud day when he brought the model to show it to me.'

In the following two years Phillips, joined by Violet Shore and a team of assistants, continued the collaboration with Kendrew to extend the resolution so that in 1960 a high-resolution image of the myoglobin molecule was obtained in which the detailed atomic arrangement could be seen. During the same period North helped Perutz to produce a low-resolution image of haemoglobin which showed that this large and complex molecule can be regarded roughly as four myoglobin molecules in a tetrahedral arrangement. Bragg was delighted and arranged to take a model of myoglobin with him when, in the autumn of 1960, he went to New Zealand to give the Rutherford Memorial Lecture at the University of Canterbury (219). But his glowing account includes one slightly regretful note: 'The new feature is that the element of guesswork has gone and been replaced by the handling of vast masses of measurements and calculations.'

This engagement in New Zealand gave Bragg a long-looked-for opportunity to take his wife on a visit to Australia where they saw again his favourite Aunt Lorna. It was a great success but there were disappointments: 'I promised my wife I would show her the shells and other fascinating marine life along the shores, where I knew the habitat of all the species, and we arranged to spend a week in a seaside place of my boyhood. Alas, it had all gone except for a few of the hardiest kinds. I suppose the pollution of extending Adelaide must have poisoned the sea for fifty miles along the coast.'

Returning to London, Bragg had the twin pleasures of watching the growing recognition of the Cambridge work and encouraging the development of an independent research programme at the Royal Institution. The most dramatic advances were initiated in 1960 when Roberto Poljak, a visiting research worker, showed that he could prepare promising heavy-atom derivatives of hen egg-white lysozyme. Bragg was immediately interested and encouraged Phillips to join in the work. With the strong support of the Medical Research Council the main resources of the laboratory were put into this study with the result that the the complete structure of this enzyme, the first to be analysed, was ready to be presented to Bragg on his seventy-fifth birthday. He could not have been more delighted and immediately set to work, perched upon a stool in the dusty store room used for model building, making a drawing of the molecular structure for its first publication (*x*). The value of his constant advice, support and encouragement in this work can hardly be overestimated and his evident joy at the result gave the greatest possible pleasure to the people concerned. The work was described at a Royal Society Discussion meeting held at the Royal Institution on 3 February 1966 (245).

There can be little doubt that Bragg's years at the Royal Institution were his happiest despite the shadow of advancing age and illness. Although the Braggs lived most of the time at the Institution they had a family house at Waldringfield in Suffolk where they entertained their growing family—eventually there were ten grandchildren—and enjoyed a country life by the sea with plenty of opportunities for bird watching, gardening, sailing and painting. There too they entertained the members of the laboratory at memorable parties. The Braggs' elder son, Stephen, had married Maureen Roberts in 1951 and had three sons. Their two daughters were married from the Royal Institution, Margaret to Mark Heath a diplomat, and Patience to David Thomson, the son of G.P. and grandson of J.J.: David, their younger son who worked at the Seed Testing Station in Cambridge and was the artist of the family, was married later to Elizabeth Bruno. The Heaths had three children, two boys and a girl, and the Thomsons four, two boys and two girls; and Bragg, who was most at ease with children, spent happy hours entertaining his grandchildren (and any others he encountered) with animal drawings and fairy stories from an apparently inexhaustible store.

At the same time, through his lectures at the Royal Institution and the television series that followed from them, he became a popular lecturer and an admired and recognized public figure. As a University lecturer he had not been a very great success with undergraduates who expected to obtain detailed and complete expositions of important aspects of physics from his lectures whereas he was concerned to identify and explain general principles. In 1927 he had noted 'The air of detachment when one is explaining a general principle and the eager scribbling in notebooks when one comes out with a fact are well known to every lecturer' (49). Throughout his life he sought, in common with his father, to achieve as complete an understanding as possible of every physical phenomenon that he encountered and, although quantum effects presented some difficulty (85), this understanding provided the basis for his popular lectures. What made them unforgettable was his gift of illustration by analogy coupled with an infectious enthusiasm which engaged all but the most sophisticated.

During his time at the Royal Institution also his reputation as a scientist was finally assured. He was certainly aware that the changes he had promoted as Cavendish Professor had attracted criticism from physicists who hardly recognized crystallography, and certainly not molecular biology, as physics. In 1962, when he was critically ill after a serious operation, he heard the news of the Nobel Prizes awarded to Perutz and Kendrew, for their work on proteins, and to Crick, Watson and Wilkins, for their analysis of DNA. This recognition of molecular biology, coupled with exciting developments in the metal physics and radio astronomy which he had promoted, put his standing as Cavendish Professor beyond question.

The 50th anniversary of his Nobel Prize was marked on 15 October 1965 by a splendid party at the Royal Institution, which was attended by the Lord

Chancellor and some twenty British Nobel-Prize winners. Later in the year, with Lady Bragg, he attended the Nobel Prize celebrations in Stockholm and was treated to all the acclaim he had missed 50 years earlier. In his lecture he reviewed his part in the early work, somewhat more bluntly than hitherto, and the subsequent growth of crystal structure analysis (241).

Bragg's retirement from his posts at the Royal Institution was announced in July 1965, to take place on 1 September 1966, but for some time previously he had been concerned to ensure that the members of his research group were found appropriate situations in which to continue their work. In the event, Green moved to Edinburgh where he continued his studies of β-lactoglobulin in the Department of Natural Philosophy, and Phillips, North, Blake, Scouloudi and others who had worked on lysozyme moved to Oxford where they set up a new Laboratory of Molecular Biophysics in the Department of Zoology. With Bragg's strong recommendation, this move to Oxford was supported by the Medical Research Council, but it almost failed at the last stage of the negotiations because of major differences between the salaries which had been paid to senior staff by the M.R.C. and those paid to university lecturers in Oxford. Lecturers in Oxford usually receive additional salaries as Fellows of Colleges but such Fellowships are awarded to meet teaching needs and, at this stage, no College believed that a need had been established for tutorial teaching in molecular biophysics. Nevertheless this suggested a mechanism for saving the situation. Bragg was advised that three Colleges would be prepared to create appropriate Fellowships if a suitable endowment could be found. At this he turned for help to his old friends Sir Kenneth Lee (243) and Harold Hemming and they generously provided the necessary money. In this way Bragg made sure that his last research workers could leave the Royal Institution for attractive new posts when he was succeeded as Resident Professor and Director by Sir George Porter.

In November 1966, when he had at last retired at the age of 76, Bragg was awarded the Copley Medal of the Royal Society. Bernal wrote to him (23 November 1966): 'This is only to congratulate the Society for giving you at last the Copley which you have deserved many times over. It cannot really at this stage mean much to you as you and the whole scientific world know what you have done. Crystal structure may seem now an old story, and it is, but you, its only begetter, are still with us. Three new subjects, mineralogy, metallurgy, and now molecular biology, all first sprang from your head, firmly based on applied optics. You can afford to look back on it all with justified feelings of pride and achievement.' Public recognition of his achievements was confirmed in the New Year Honours list of 1967 when he was made a Companion of Honour.

## Retirement, 1966–71

After his formal retirement, Bragg continued to live in London most of the year and, as Emeritus Professor, he continued to lecture at the Royal Institution. He also lectured elsewhere, wrote a good deal and visited 'his' laboratories, the old one in Cambridge and the new one in Oxford.

During this time he saw his forecast about the study of proteins begin to come true as more and more structures were determined and patterns began to emerge in them. But he also saw and delighted in the application of physical methods and modes of thought to more complex biological problems. Perutz (*y*) has recorded an anecdote that vividly recaptures Bragg's style as a consultant: 'I took him to a young zoologist working on pattern formation in insect cuticles. The zoologist explained how disturbances introduced into these regular patterns pointed to their formation being governed by some kind of gradient. Bragg listened attentively and then exclaimed: "Your disturbed gradient behaves like a stream of sand running downhill and encountering an obstacle." "Good heavens," replied the zoologist, "I had been working on this problem for years before this simple analogy occurred to me and you think of it after twenty minutes." '

This kind of insight into natural phenomena, especially those concerned with optics and three-dimensional relationships, underlay all of Bragg's scientific work and his lecturing and writing about it. Years of discipline had long overcome his early horror of writing and he was able to concentrate immediately on writing anything from a routine circular to a scientific paper. Perutz (*u*) again has described his approach to paper writing: 'He would illustrate his conclusions in a series of neatly drawn sketches, and then write the accompanying paper in a lucid and vivid prose. Some scientists produce such prose as a result of prolonged redrafting and polishing, but Bragg would do it in one evening, all ready to be typed the next day, rather like Mozart writing the overture to "The Marriage of Figaro" in a single night.' Bragg retained this hard-won facility into retirement, and his last book (*M*), which was barely complete when he died, displays all the old vigour and many examples of his ability to summarize a complex problem in a single polished paragraph. Thus, for example, after discussing the wave-particle problem which had so dominated the scientific discussions of his youth, he wrote: 'So the dividing line between the wave or particle nature of matter and radiation is the moment "Now". As this moment steadily advances through time, it coagulates a wavy future into a particle past.'

This book on *The Development of X-ray Analysis* is a history of X-ray crystallography and, since it concentrates particularly on the topics which had interested him most, it is almost Bragg's scientific autobiography. He was writing it in 1970 when crystallographers from all over the world met at the Royal Institution at a meeting to celebrate his eightieth birthday. Organized by W. H. Taylor, this 'Bragg Symposium 1970' was entitled 'X-ray analysis—past, present and future' and it gave many of his old friends and associates a chance to remember old triumphs together and to look to the future. Bragg was himself the liveliest participant. He listened attentively to every session and generally led the discussion—much to everyone's delight.

This Symposium illustrated very well Bragg's essential achievement. The sessions were devoted to most important advances in the forefront of mineralogy, metallurgy, chemistry and molecular biology, subjects which had been revolutionized or in some instances even created by his discoveries. But there were few papers on topics that would be universally recognized as physics by a modern audience of scientists. Centred in physics departments, his achievements had transformed understanding of the natural world and the descriptive sciences in terms of atomic arrangements but his revolution had coincided with others, especially in nuclear and quantum physics, which largely took over physics itself. Bragg remained essentially a classical physicist in the great tradition of those who thought in terms of tangible rather than mathematical models. But he had to struggle to be accepted as a physicist at all and his associates suffered from this, until at last many of them were recognized for their contributions to other fields.

Behind his conventional, even military, appearance as an establishment figure, Bragg had an artistic temperament with strong emotions normally kept in check by stern self-control. He reminded Colin Blake of Elgar, somewhat ironically since Bragg had no appreciation of music at all. But he delighted in painting, a skill he had learned from his mother, and many of his associates treasure examples of his country scenes and portraits. Literature was another of his loves —he instituted special courses in the humanities for physics students in Cambridge—and he delighted in referring to characters in the great novels: the 'philanthropoid' Mrs Norris in Mansfield Park was a great favourite. One of his last broadcasts was a personal choice of verse and prose which he presented 'With great pleasure' on 18 October 1970.

But most of all Bragg was a private family man. The draft autobiography that he was working on at the time of his death abounds with happy memories of family holidays, often sailing on the Broads, and adventures with his adored wife and children. Perutz (*z*) remembered that 'typically one would find him tending his garden, with Lady Bragg, children and grandchildren somewhere in the background, and before getting down to business he would proudly demonstrate his latest roses'. Even there his creativity was for ever bursting out in some new 'venture': only a short time before his death he was enthusiastically promoting a method for supporting tall plants, such as Michaelmas daisies, by letting them grow through sheets of wire netting.

Bragg was certainly one of the great creative scientists yet he often worried about his relative lack of more mundane gifts. Forgetful of names, uneasy on committees, reluctant to face personal problems or angry scenes, he depended a great deal on his wife who sustained him through all the triumphs and difficulties of a long public life. There is no doubt that he found peace at the last and the abiding affection of those that knew him best. He died in hospital near his home at Waldringfield on 1 July 1971.

My first thanks are due to Lady Bragg and to Stephen Bragg for their help in the preparation of this memoir and for their permission to consult and quote from the Bragg Archives at the Royal Institution. The Director of the Institution, Sir George Porter, F.R.S., and the Librarian, Mrs I. M. McCabe, have been most helpful. Mrs A. Caroe, Sir Lawrence Bragg's sister, whose biography of their father has been an invaluable help, has also given aid and counsel without stint and I am deeply indebted to her.

Very many of Bragg's colleagues and students have responded generously to my importunate appeals for help and I am grateful to them for their generous assistance and for allowing me to quote freely from their letters and articles. There are too many to mention all by name but I am particularly indebted to Mr Norman Tunstall for his account of the early days in Manchester, to Mr J. A. Ratcliffe, F.R.S., and to Dr M. F. Perutz, F.R.S. Most especially, however, am I grateful to Professor Henry Lipson, F.R.S. whose prompting, encouragement and help (which included writing his own account of the Manchester, N.P.L. and Cambridge periods) made a vital contribution to the completion of the memoirs.

Finally, I must record my indebtedness to Mrs C. C. F. Blake, whose researches into the details of Bragg's career were invaluable; and to my ex-secretary, Miss Susan Partridge, who made an essential contribution to the literature survey and in many other ways.

The photograph reproduced in the frontispiece was taken by Lotte Meitner-Graf in 1961.

General references

(*a*) Caroe, G. M. 1978 *William Henry Bragg, 1862–1942: Man and Scientist.* Cambridge University Press.

(*b*) Royal Institution archives.

(*c*) Royal Society archives.

(*d*) Stuewer, R. H. 1971 William H. Bragg's corpuscular theory of X-rays and $\gamma$-rays. *Br. J. Hist. Sci.* **5**, 258–281.

(*e*) Ewald, P. P. and numerous crystallographers 1962 *Fifty years of X-ray diffraction.* Published for The International Union of Crystallography by N. V. A. Oosthock's Uitgeversmaatschappij, Utrecht, The Netherlands.

(*f*) Forman, P. 1969 The discovery of the diffraction of X-rays by crystals; a critique of the myths. *Arch. Hist. Exact Sci.* **6,** 38–71.

(*g*) Bragg, W. H. 1912 *Nature, Lond.* **90**, 219.

(*h*) Schuster, A. 1909 *An introduction to the theory of optics* (2nd ed., revised). London: Edward Arnold.

(*i*) Pope, W. J. 1908 *A. Rep. Progr. Chem.* pp. 258–279.

(*j*) Bragg, W. H. 1912 *Nature, Lond.* **90**, 360–361.

(*k*) Bragg, W. H. 1913 *Nature, Lond.* **90**, 372.

(*l*) Moseley, H. & Darwin, C. G. 1913 *Nature, Lond.* **90**, 594.

(*m*) Heilbron, J. L. 1974 *H. J. C. Moseley—the life and letters of an English physicist 1887–1915.* Berkeley, Los Angeles and London: University of California Press.

(*n*) Bragg, W. H. 1913 *Proc. R. Soc. Lond.* A **89**, 246–248.

(*o*) Miers, H. A. 1918 *J. chem. Soc.* **113**, 363–386.

(*p*) James, R. W. 1952 *Trans. R. Soc. S. Afr.* **34**, 1–16.

(*q*) Armstrong, H. E. 1927 *Nature, Lond.* **120**, 478.

(*r*) Pauling, L. 1928 in *Sommerfeld Festschrift.* Leipzig: S. Hirgel.
1929 *J. Am. chem. Soc.* **51**, 1010.

(*s*) Lipson, H. S. 1973 A. J. Bradley (1899–1972). *Biogr. Mem. Fellows R. Soc. Lond.* **19**, 117–128.

(*t*) Patterson, A. L. 1935 *Z.Kristallogr.Kristallgeom.* **90**, 517–542.

(*u*) Perutz, M. F. 1970 *Acta crystallogr.* **A26**, 183–185.

(*v*) Crowther, J. G. 1974 *The Cavendish Laboratory 1874–1974.* London and Basingstoke: Macmillan.

(*w*) Watson, J. D. 1968 *The double helix.* London: Weidenfeld & Nicholson.

(*x*) Blake, C. C. F., Koenig, D. F., Mair, G. A., North, A. C. T., Phillips, D. C. & Sarma, V. R. 1965 *Nature, Lond.* **206**, 757–761.

(*y*) Perutz, M. F. 1971 *New Sci. & Sci. J.* 8 July 1967.

(*z*) Perutz, M. F. 1971 *Nature, Lond.* **233**, 74–76.

## Bibliography


### *Books*

(*A*) 1915 (With W. H. Bragg) *X-rays and crystal structure*. London: G. Bell & Sons Ltd. 2nd ed. 1916, 3rd 1918, 4th (revised) 1924, 5th 1925. Translated into Russian (1916 and 1929) and French (1921).

(*B*) 1930 *The structure of silicates*. 69 pages. Leipzig: Akad. Verlag.

(*C*) 1933 *The crystalline state, a general survey*. London: G. Bell & Sons Ltd. Vol. I of *The crystalline state*, eds, W. H. & W. L. Bragg.

(*D*) 1936 *Electricity*. (The Royal Institution Christmas Lectures, 1934.) London: G. Bell & Sons Ltd. and U.S.A.: Macmillan Company. Translated: Swedish, 1937; Polish, 1939; Czech, 1940; Hungarian, 1948; Finnish, 1950; German, 1951; Japanese, 1951; Italian, 1953.

(*E*) 1937 *Atomic structure of minerals*. Ithaca, N.Y.: Cornell University Press and London: Oxford University Press.

(*F*) 1939 (With A. E. van Arkel, U. R. Evans & N. Parravano) *Chimie Minéral*. Paris: Hermann & Cie.

(*G*) 1943 *History of X-ray analysis*. London: British Council/Longmans. Revised edn 1946; German translation 1947.

(*H*) 1950 (With H. J. Emeleus) *Post-graduate Lectures* (sponsored by the Oil and Colour Chemists Association). Cambridge: W. Heffer & Sons Ltd.

(*I*) 1965 (With G. F. Claringbull) *Crystal structures of minerals*. London: G. Bell & Sons Ltd. Vol. IV of *The crystalline state*, ed. W. L. Bragg.

(*J*) 1967 *The start of X-ray analysis*. London: Longmans/Penguin. (Chemistry Background Books, The Nuffield Foundation.)

(*K*) 1970 *Ideas and discoveries in physics*. London: Longmans. (Longman Physics Topics for 6th form pupils.) Translated: French, 1974; Dutch 1969.

(*L*) 1971 (With A. H. Dawson & H. H. Hemming) *Artillery survey in the First World War*. London: Field Survey Association.

(*M*) 1975 *The Development of X-ray analysis*, (ed. D. C. Phillips & H. Lipson). London: G. Bell & Sons Ltd.

*Editor*

*The crystalline state*. London: G. Bell & Sons Ltd.
Vol. I (1933) (with W. H. Bragg)
Vol. II (1948)
Vol. III (1953)
Vol. IV (1965)

(with G. Porter) *The Royal Institution Library of Science*: *Physical Sciences* (being the Friday Evening Discourses in Physical Sciences held at The Royal Institution, 1851–1939). Amsterdam: Elsevier Publishing Co. (1970). (10 volumes and Index.)

*Consultant Editor*

*Contemporary Physics* (1959–64).

### *Papers*

(1) 1912 The diffraction of short electromagnetic waves by a crystal (lecture 11 November 1912). *Proc. Camb. phil. Soc.* **17**, 43–57. *Nature, Lond.* **90**, 402.

(2) The specular reflection of X-rays. *Nature, Lond.* **90**, 410.

(3) 1913 X-rays and crystals. *Sci. Prog.* **7**, 372–389.

(4) (With W. H. Bragg) The reflection of X-rays by crystals. *Proc. R. Soc. Lond.* A **88**, 428–438.

(5) The structure of some crystals as indicated by their diffraction of X-rays. *Proc. R. Soc. Lond.* A **89**, 248–277.

(6) (With W. H. Bragg) The structure of the diamond. *Nature, Lond.* **91**, 557.

(7) (With W. H. Bragg) The structure of the diamond. *Proc. R. Soc. Lond.* A **89**, 277–291.

(8) 1914 Eine Bemerkung über die Interferenzfiguren hemiedrischer Kristalle. *Phys. Z.* **15**, 77–79.

(9) X-rays and crystals. *J. Röntgen Soc.* **10**, 70–78.

(10) 1914 The analysis of crystals by the X-ray spectrometer. *Proc. R. Soc. Lond.* A **89**, 468–489.

(11) The crystalline structure of copper. *Phil. Mag.* (6) **27**, 355–360.

(12) 1915 (With W. H. Bragg) X-rays and crystal structure. (British Association for the Advancement of Science, Manchester) *Engineering, Lond.* **100**, 305.

(13) (With W. H. Bragg) Die Reflexion von Röntgenstrahlen aus Kristallen (translations of papers in *Proc. Roy. Soc.*, etc., subsequently published by Leopold Voss, 1928). *Z. anorg. Chem.* **90**, 153–296.

(14) 1919 Sound ranging. *Manchester Memoirs* **64**, p. v and *Nature, Lond.* **104**, 187.

(15) 1920 The crystalline structure of zinc oxide. *Phil. Mag.* (6) **39**, 647–651.

(16) The arrangement of atoms in crystals. *Phil. Mag.* (6) **40**, 169–189.

(17) Crystal structure (R. I. Discourse, 28 May 1920). *Proc. R. Instn Gt Br.* **23**, 190–205 and *Nature, Lond.* **105**, 646–648.

(18) 1921 (With R. W. James & C. H. Bosanquet) Über die Streuung der Röntgenstrahlen durch die Atome eines Kristalles. *Z. Phys.* **8**, 77–84.

(19) (With R. W. James & C. H. Bosanquet) The intensity of reflexion of X-rays by rock-salt. *Phil. Mag.* (6) **41**, 309–337.

(20) (With R. W. James & C. H. Bosanquet) The intensity of reflexion of X-rays by rock-salt. II. *Phil. Mag.* (6) **42**, 1–17.

(21) The arrangement of atoms in crystals. *Nature, Lond.* **106**, 725.

(22) (With H. Bell) The dimensions of atoms and molecules. *Nature, Lond.* **107**, 107.

(23) The dimensions of atoms and molecules. *Sci. Prog.* **16**, 45–55.

(24) 1922 (With R. W. James & C. H. Bosanquet) The distribution of electrons around the nucleus in the sodium and chlorine atoms. *Phil. Mag.* (6) **44**, 433–449.

(25) The diffraction of X-rays by crystals. (Nobel Lecture, Stockholm, 6 September 1922.) *Les Prix Nobel en 1921–1922.* (Also published in: *Nobel Lectures, Physics 1901–21.* Amsterdam: Elsevier Publishing Co. (1967), pp. 370–382).

(26) (With R. W. James) The intensity of X-ray reflection. *Nature, Lond.* **110**, 148.

(27) 1923 Sound. *Manchester Memoirs* **67**, p. xii.

(28) 1924 The structure of aragonite. *Proc. R. Soc. Lond.* A **105**, 16–39.

(29) The refractive indices of calcite and aragonite. *Proc. R. Soc. Lond.* A **105**, 370–386.

(30) The influence of atomic arrangement on refractive index. *Proc. R. Soc. Lond.* A **106**, 346–368.

(31) (With S. Chapman) A theoretical calculation of the rhombohedral angle of crystals of the calcite type. *Proc. R. Soc. Lond.* A **106**, 369–377

(32) Crystal structure. *Manchester Memoirs* **68**, pp. xiii-xiv.

(33) 1925 The interpretation of intensity measurements in X-ray analysis of crystal structure. *Phil. Mag.* (6) **50**, 306–310.

(34) Inorganic crystals (address delivered 17 September 1924 on the occasion of the Centenary of The Franklin Institute). *J. Franklin Inst.* **199**, 761–772.

(35) Model gratings to illustrate the diffraction of X-rays by crystals. *Manchester Memoirs* **69**, 35–38.

(36) Model illustrating the formation of crystals. *Manchester Memoirs* **69**, p. xvi.

(37) The sizes of atoms. *Manchester Memoirs* **70**, p. viii.

(38) The crystalline structure of inorganic salts (R.I. Discourse, 1 May 1925). *Proc. R. Instn. Gt. Br.* **24**, 614–620 and *Nature, Lond.* **116**, 249–251.

(39) 1926 (With G. B. Brown) Die Kristallstruktur von Chrysoberyll ($BeAl_2O_4$). *Z. Kristallogr. Kristallgeom.* **63**, 122–143.

(40) (With G. B. Brown) Die Struktur des Olivins. *Z. Kristallogr. Kristallgeom.* **63**, 538–556.

(41) (With G. B. Brown) The crystalline structure of Chrysoberyl. *Proc. R. Soc. Lond.* A **110**, 34–63.

(42) (With J. West) The structure of beryl, $Be_3Al_2Si_6O_{18}$. *Proc. R. Soc. Lond.* A **111**, 691–714.

(43) (With C. G. Darwin & R. W. James) The intensity of reflexion of X-rays by crystals. *Phil. Mag.* (7) **1**, 897–922.

(44) Interatomic distances in crystals. *Phil. Mag.* (7) **2**, 258–266.

(45) X-ray analysis of crystal structures and its relation with chemical constitution. *2ième Cons. Chim. Inst. Intern. Chim. Solvay, 1926*, 44–65.

(46) 1927 The structure of phenacite, $Be_2SiO_4$ *Proc. R. Soc. Lond.* A **113**, 642–657.

(47) 1927 (With J. West) The structure of certain silicates. *Proc. R. Soc. Lond.* A **114**, 450–473.

(48) The structure of silicates (R.I. Discourse, 20 May 1927). *Proc. R. Instn Gt Br.* **25**, 302–310.

(49) Some views on the teaching of science (Presidential Address to the Manchester Library and Philosophical Society, 1927–28 Session). *Manchester Memoirs* **71**, 119–123.

(50) Some recent advances in the physics of the solid state. *Manchester Memoirs* **71**, p. xii.

(51) Crystallography. *Ann. Rep. Prog. Chem.* **22**, 257–279.

(52) (With W. H. Bragg) Stereoscopic photographs of crystal models, to illustrate the results of X-ray crystallography. 2 series (1927, 1930). London: Adam Hilger Ltd.

(53) 1928 The diffraction of short electromagnetic waves by a crystal. *Atti Congr. Internazionale dei Fisici* (Como, September 1927 (V)), 171–180.

(54) L'Intensité de Réflexion des Rayons X. *Inst. Intern. Phys. Solvay. 5ieme Cons. de Physique, 1927*, 1–43.

(55) (With J. West) A technique for the X-ray examination of crystal structures with many parameters. *Z. Kristallogr. Kristallgeom.* **69**, 118–148.

(56) (With B. Warren) The structure of diopside, $CaMg(SiO_3)_2$. *Z. Kristallogr. Kristallgeom.* **69**, 168–193.

(57) 1929 (With R. W. James, J. D. Bernal & A. J. Bradley) Crystallography. *Ann. Rep. Prog. Chem.* **25**, 275–302.

(58) X-ray optics (the 9th Mackenzie Davidson Memorial Lecture). *Br. J. Radiol.* **2**, 65–71.

(59) Atomic arrangement in the silicates. *Trans. Faraday Soc.* **25**, 291–314.

(60) The determination of parameters in crystal structures by means of Fourier series. *Proc. R. Soc. Lond.* A **123**, 537–559.

(61) An optical method of representing the results of X-ray analysis. *Z. Kristallogr. Kristallgeom.* **70**, 475–492.

(62) An optical method of displaying the results of X-ray examination of crystals. *Manchester Memoirs* **72**, pp. xii–xiii.

(63) The diffraction of short electromagnetic waves by a crystal. *Scientia* March 1929, pp. 153–162.

(64) Diffraction of X-rays by two-dimensional crystal lattice. *Nature, Lond.* **124**, 125.

(65) 1930 (With J. West) A note on the representation of crystal structure by Fourier series. *Phil. Mag.* (7) **10**, 823–841.

(66) (With W. H. Zachariasen) The crystalline structure of phenacite, $Be_2SiO_4$ and willemite, $Zn_2SiO_4$. *Z. Kristallogr. Kristallgeom.* **72**, 518–528.

(67) The structure of silicates. *Z. Kristallogr. Kristallgeom.* **74**, 237–305.

(68) (With B. E. Warren) The structure of chrysotile $H_4Mg_3Si_2O_9$. *Z. Kristallogr. Kristallgeom.* **76,** 201–210.

(69) Die Untersuchung der Atomanordnung mittels Röntgenstrahlen. *Metallwirtschaft* **9**, 461–465.

(70) Bau der silikate. *Glastech.* (Frankfurt) **8**, 449–453.

(71) The structure of silicates (lecture to the Mineralogical Society, 18 March 1930). *Nature, Lond.* **125**, 510–511.

(72) Structure of silicates. *J. Soc. Glass Technol.* **14**, 295–305.

(73) X-ray optics. *Photogr. J.* **70**, 179–186.

(74) 1931 The architecture of the solid state (the 22nd Kelvin Lecture, 30 April 1931). *J. Instn elect. Engrs* **69**, 1239–1244 and *Nature, Lond.* **128**, 210–212 and 248–250.

(75) (With C. Gottfried & J. West) The structure of β alumina. *Z. Kristallogr. Kristallgeom.* **77**, 255–274.

(76) (With F. Kirchner) The action of a crystal as a two-dimensional lattice in diffracting electrons. *Nature, Lond.* **127**, 738–739.

(77) 1932 The structure of molecules: the solid state. In: *Chemistry at the Centenary (1931) Meeting of the British Association for the Advancement of Science*, pp. 255–256. Cambridge: W. Heffer & Sons Ltd.

(78) 1932 The application of X-ray methods to industrial problems. (lecture at the University of Manchester, 11 July 1932), pamphlet, 19 pages.

(79) 1932 (With J. A. Darbyshire) The structure of thin films of certain metallic oxides *Trans. Faraday Soc.* **28**, 522–529.

(80) Structure of complex ionic compounds (lecture 20 November 1931). *Trans. Oxf. Univ. jr scient. Club.* Fifth series, no. 5, 151–153.

(81) 1933 The structure of alloys (R.I. Discourse, 17 March 1933). *Proc. R. Instn Gt Br.* **27**, 756–784 and *Nature, Lond.* **131**, 749–753.

(82) Development of Röntgen-ray analysis of crystals (a review). *Usp. fiz. Nauk.* **13**, 195–208.

(83) 1934 (With E. J. Williams) The effect of thermal agitation on atomic arrangements in alloys. *Proc. R. Soc. Lond.* A **145**, 699–730.

(84) The exploration of the mineral world by X-rays. (Evening Discourse to B.A., 10 September 1934.) *Rep. a. Meet Br. Ass. Advmt Sci.* **104**, 437–444 and *Nature, Lond.* **134**, 401–404.

(85) The Physical Sciences (introductory lecture as non-resident Lecturer in Chemistry at Cornell University). *Science, N.Y.* **79**, 237–240.

(86) 1935 (With E. J. Williams) The effect of thermal agitation on atomic arrangement in alloys—II. *Proc. R. Soc. Lond.* A **151**, 540–566.

(87) The new crystallography. *Proc. R. Soc. Edinb.* **55**, 62–71.

(88) Atomic arrangement in metals and alloys (25th May Lecture to the Institute of Metals, 8 May 1935). *J. Inst. Metals* **56**, 275–299.

(89) 1936 L'exploration du monde minéral a l'aide des rayons X. (Conference faite devant la Societé Francaise de Physique, 21 April 1936.) *J. Phys. Radium, Paris* **7**, (série VII) 321–325.

(90) (With H. Lipson) The employment of contoured graphs of structure-factor in crystal analysis. *Z. Kristallogr. Kristallgeom.* **95**, 323–337.

(91) Structure-factor graphs for crystal analysis. *Nature, Lond.* **138**, 362–363.

(92) Anordnung der Atome in den Metallen und Legierungen. *Usp. fiz. Nauk.* **16**, 977–1000.

(93) 1937 Alloys. *Jl R. Soc. Arts* **85**, 431–447.

(94) (With W. H. Bragg) The discovery of X-ray diffraction. *Curr. Sci.* **7** (suppl., special number, 'Laue Diagrams'), 9–13.

(95) Alloys. (Report of lecture to meeting, 2 February 1937.) *Manchester Memoirs* **81**, p. xii.

(96) (With C. Sykes & A. J. Bradley) A study of the order-disorder transformation. *Proc. phys. Soc.* **49**, 96–102 and 108–109.

(97) 1938 The atomic structure of alloys (Watt Anniversary Lecture for 1938). *Pap. Greenock phil. Soc.* 1938.

(98) A discussion on plastic flow in metals (opening address). *Proc. R. Soc. Lond.* A **168**, 302–303.

(99) Forty years of crystal physics. In: *Background to modern science* (eds. W. Pagel & J. Needham), pp. 77–92. Cambridge University Press.

(100) The Physics Department, Manchester University. *J. Univ. Manchester* **1**, 35–41.

(101) (With H. Lipson) Structure of metals. *Nature, Lond.* **141**, 367–368.

(102) General features of atomic structure of silicates: inferences to be drawn from them as to the structure of clay minerals (summary). *Rep. a. Meet. Br. Ass. Advmt Sci.* **108**, 403.

(103) The structure of alloys (being the 39th Robert Boyle Lecture delivered before the Oxford University Junior Scientific Club, 11 June 1937). O.U.P. 1938 (5 pages).

(104) The structure of alloys. *Der Feste Körper* (1938), pp. 24–41. Leipzig: Hirzel.

(105) Röntgenstrahlen in der Industrie. *Indian east. Engr.* **82**, 219.

(106) 1939 Magnets (R.I. Discourse, 5 May 1939). *Proc. R Instn Gt Br.* **30**, 783–787 and *Engineering* **147**, 595–596.

(107) Patterson diagrams in crystal analysis. *Nature, Lond.* **143**, 73–74.

(108) A new type of 'X-ray microscope'. *Nature, Lond.* **143**, 678.

(109) Atomic patterns of metals (Fourth Edward Williams Lecture, Institute of British Foundrymen, 13 June 1939). *Foundry J.* 12–17 *June* 1939, pp. 25–31; *Fndry Trade J.* **60**, 506–508; *Proc. Instn Br. Foundrym.* **32**, 25–31 and *Engineering* **147**, 788.

(110) 1940 The structure of a cold-worked metal. *Proc. phys. Soc.* **52**, 105–109.

(111) 1940 (With A. J. Bradley & C. Sykes) Researches into the structure of alloys. *J. Iron Steel Inst.* **141**, 63P–156P.
(112) The symmetry of patterns (title only) (R.I. Discourse, 3 May 1940). *Proc. R. Instn Gt Br.* **31**, 149.
(113) (With A. J. Bradley & C. Sykes) The structure of alloys: X-ray and thermal analysis. *Iron Steel, Lond.* **13**, (no. 9), 305–307.
(114) (With A. J. Bradley) Part I—Investigation of equilibrium diagrams and theory of order-disorder transformation. *Iron Steel, Lond.* **13**, (no. 9), 308–310.
(115) 1941 Diffraction of monochromatic X-rays by crystals at high temperatures. *Proc. R. Soc. Lond.* A **179**, 61–64.
(116) X-ray analysis in industry. *J. scient. Instrum.* **18**, 69.
(117) 1942 Physicists after the War (Afternoon Lecture at the R.I., 26 March 1942). *Proc. R. Instn Gt Br.* **32**, 253–271 and *Nature, Lond.* **150**, 75–80 and 374.
(118) A model illustrating intercrystalline boundaries and plastic flow in metals. *J. scient. Instrum.* **19,** 148–150.
(119) The X-ray microscope. *Nature, Lond.* **149**, 470–471.
(120) A theory of the strength of metals (R.I. Discourse, 31 March 1942). *Nature, Lond.* **149**, 511–513.
(121) Index of X-ray diffraction data. *Nature, Lond.* **150,** 738.
(122) 1943 Seeing ever-smaller worlds (R.I. Discourse, 12 March 1943). *Proc. R. Instn Gt Br.* **32**, 475–481 and *Nature, Lond.* **151**, 545–547.
(123) (With H. Lipson) A simple method of demonstrating diffraction grating effects. *J. scient. Instrum.* **20,** 110–113.
(124) Tensile strength of metals. *Tek. Tid.* 73, 403–407.
(125) (With R. H. Pickard & A. Findlay) The place of scientists in the community. *Chemy Ind.* **62**, 263.
(126) Metals. *Endeavour* **II**, 43–52; *Trans. Can. Inst. Min. Metall.* **46**, 291–304; and *Can. Mach.* **54**, 95–100.
(127) 1944 The mechanical strength of metals. General discussion on radiological testing. (Introductory Contribution.) *Trans. NE. Cst Instn Engrs Shipbldrs* **60**, 299–306.
(128) Lightning calculations with light (R.I. Discourse, 24 March 1944). *Proc. R. Instn Gt Br.* **33**, 107–113 and *Nature Lond.* **154**, 69–72.
(129) The spirit of science. *The Listener* 10 February 1944, p. 147.
(130) Organization and finance of science in universities. *The Political Quarterly* **15**, 330–341.
(131) Mr. F. Lincoln and the Cavendish Laboratory. *Nature, Lond.* **154**, 643.
(132) Metalle. *Metallurgia Electr.* **8**, 20–26.
(133) 1945 Some problems of the metallic state (14th Andrew Laing Lecture). *Trans. NE. Cst Instn Engrs Shipbldrs* **62**, 25–34 and *Iron Steel, Lond.* **18**, 531–535.
(134) Magnetic materials (Lecture to Measurement Section, 18 May 1945). *J. Instn. elect. Engrs* **92**, (Part I, General), 444–451.
(135) X-ray analysis: past, present and future (R.I. Discourse, 11 May 1945). *Proc. R. Instn Gt Br.* **33**, 393–400.
(136) (With A. R. Stokes) X-ray analysis with the aid of the 'fly's eye'. *Nature, Lond.* **156**, 332–333.
(137) La Cohésion des Métaux *Revue Métall, Paris* **42**, 187–193.
(138) 1946 The Austin Wing of the Cavendish Laboratory. *Nature, Lond.* **158**, 326–327.
(139) (With E. B. Bond) The Rutherford Papers in the Library of the Cavendish Laboratory. *Nature, Lond.* **158**, 714.
(140) X-ray analysis in research and practice today (R.I. Discourse, 24 May 1947). *Proc. R. Instn Gt Br.* **33**, 649–661.
(141) X-rays' part in metallurgical research. In: *Science lifts the veil*, pp. 33–37. London: British Council/Longmans, Green & Co.
(142) 1947 The relationship of the university and the technical college (lecture to the Association of Technical Institutions, 28 February 1947). *Association of Technical Institutions*: miscellaneous pamphlets: London (1947). 6 pages.
(143) The conversion factor for kX units to Ångstrom units. *J. scient. Instrum.* **24**, 27; *Phys. Rev.* **72**, 437; and (with E. A. Wood) *J. Am. chem. Soc.* **69**, 2919.
(144) 1947 Working models of crystals (R.I. Discourse, 9 May 1947). *Proc. R. Instn Gt Br.* **34**, 103–108.

(145) 1947 (With J. F. Nye) A dynamical model of a crystal structure. *Proc. R. Soc. Lond.* A **190**, 474–481 and *Naturwissenschaften* **34**, 328–336.

(146) Effects associated with stresses on a microscopic scale. In: Proceedings of Symposium on Internal Stresses in Metals and Alloys, 15–16 October 1947. *Inst. of Metals Monograph and Report Series No. 5*, 221–226.

(147) Recent advances in X-ray analysis. *Paint Technol.* **12**, 421–425.

(148) 1948 Current researches in the Cavendish Laboratory (lecture to the Manchester Association of Engineers, 9 January 1948). Pamphlet, 10 pages.

(149) Organisation and work of the Cavendish Laboratory (course of 3 lectures given at the R.I., 4, 11, 18 March 1948). *Nature, Lond.* **161,** 627–628.

(150) The standards of advanced studies and research in science and technology. (Address to the 19th Annual Convention of the Yorkshire Council for Further Education, May 1948.) Pamphlet no. 36, 10 pages.

(151) Atomic rearrangement in the metallic state. *Festkr. J. Arvid Hedvall* 1948, 75–81.

(152) Recent advances in the study of the crystalline state. *Science N.Y.* **108**, 455–463 and *Advmt Sci., Lond.* **5**, 165–174.

(153) The Cavendish Laboratory (19th Autumn Lecture, Institute of Metals, 16 September 1948). *J. Inst. Metals* **75**, 107–114.

(154) The yield point of a metal. Rep. Bristol Conf. 'Strength of Solids' (1947). *Phys. Soc. Lond.* (1948) 26–29.

(155) 1949 Acceptance of the Roebling Medal of the Mineralogical Society of America. *Am. Miner.* **34**, 238–241.

(156) (With W. M. Lomer) A dynamical model of a crystal structure. II. *Proc. R. Soc. Lond.* A **196**, 171–181.

(157) Giant molecules (R.I. Discourse, 27 April 1949). *Proc. R. Instn Gt Br.* **34**, 395–405 and *Nature, Lond.* **164**, 7–10.

(158) Slip in metals. *Physica* **15**, 83–91.

(159) The place of technological education in university studies. Conference on the Home Universities (1949). London: Association of Universities of the British Commonwealth, pp. 72–77 (and 24–25, 56–58).

(160) The strength of metals. *Proc. Camb. phil. Soc.* **45**, 125–130.

(161) 1950 (With J. C. Kendrew & M. F. Perutz) Polypeptide chain configurations in crystalline proteins. *Proc. R. Soc. Lond.* A **203**, 321–357.

(162) Famous experiments in the Cavendish Laboratory (R.I. Discourse, 12 May 1950). *Proc. R. Instn Gt Br.* **34**, 626–633 and *Nature, Lond.* **166**, 7–9.

(163) Microscopy by reconstructed wave-fronts. *Nature, Lond.* **166**, 399–400.

(164) Science and the adventure of living (the Radford Mather Lecture, 25 October 1950 at the R.I.). *The British Association of the Advancement of Science* **7**, 279–284. (Also Norwegian translation, 1952.)

(165) Riesenmoleküle. *Usp. fiz. Nauk.* **40**, 108.

(166) Address at Electrical Research Association Annual Lunch, 1950. *E.R.A.*/R720, pamphlet, 18 pages.

(167) 1951 (With G. L. Rogers) Elimination of the unwanted image in diffraction microscopy. *Nature, Lond.* **167**, 190–191.

(168) Crystallographic research in the Cavendish Laboratory (R.I. Discourse, 16 March 1951). *Proc. R. Instn Gt Br.* **35**, 103–113 and *Mitt. naturf. Ges. Bern.* **8**, xi–xiii.

(169) 1952 The atomic patterns of everyday materials (the Keith Lecture, 2 April 1952, Royal Scottish Society of Arts). *Edinb. J. Sci. Technol. photogr. Art*, pp. 47–56.

(170) The Cavendish Laboratory archives (R.I. Discourse, 28 March 1952). *Proc. R. Instn Gt Br.* **35,** 299–304 and *Nature, Lond.* **169**, 684–686.

(171) (With E. R. Howells & M. F. Perutz) Arrangement of polypeptide chains in horse methaemoglobin. *Acta crystallogr.* **5**, 136–141.

(172) (With M. F. Perutz) The external form of the haemoglobin molecule. I. *Acta crystallogr.* **5**, 277–283.

(173) (With M. F. Perutz) The external form of the haemoglobin molecule. II. *Acta crystallogr.* **5**, 323–328.

(174) A device for calculating structure factors. *Acta crystallogr.* **5**, 474–475.

(175) 1952 (With M. F. Perutz) The structure of haemoglobin *Proc. R. Soc. Lond.* A **213**, 425–435.

(176) 1952 X-ray analysis of proteins (36th Guthrie Lecture, 12 March 1952). *Proc. phys. Soc.* **65B**, 833–846.

(177) The Cavendish Laboratories of Cambridge University. *Nucleo* (*Barcelona*) **7**, 447–449.

(178) 1953 The discovery of X-ray diffraction by crystals (R.I. Discourse, 22 May 1953). *Proc. R. Instn Gt Br.* **35**, 552–559.

(179) X-ray analysis of the haemoglobin molecule. (In: A Discussion on the Structure of Proteins.) *Proc. R. Soc. Lond.* B **141**, 67–69.

(180) Budgets of the scientific departments of the University of Cambridge. *Nature, Lond.* **171**, 642–643.

(181) The X-ray analysis of protein molecules (Fison Memorial Lecture, 15 May 1953). *Guy's Hosp. Gaz.* (new ser) **57**, 242–246.

(182) (With A. B. Pippard) The form birefringence of macromolecules. *Acta crystallogr.* **6**, 865–867.

(183) The bubble model of a metal structure (lecture delivered in Johannesburg, 18 July 1952). *A. Proc. ass. tech. Socs S. Afr.* (July 1953), pp. 33–44.

(184) A centre of fundamental research. *Physics to-day* **6**, 18–19.

(185) X-ray analysis of protein structure. *Inst. intern. Chim. Solvay, Conseil. Chim.*, 9th Conseil, Brussels, 1953, pp. 100–109.

(186) 1954 X-ray studies of biological molecules (R.I. Discourse, 29 January 1954). *Proc. R. Instn Gt Br.* **35,** 685–696 and *Nature, Lond.* **174**, 55–59.

(187) Models of metal structure (R.I. Discourse, 19 November 1954). *Proc. R. Instn Gt Br.* **35**, 844–852.

(188) (With E. R. Howells) X-ray diffraction by imidazole methaemoglobin. *Acta crystallogr.* **7**, 409–411.

(189) (With E. R. Howells & M. F. Perutz) The structure of haemoglobin, II. *Proc. R. Soc. Lond.* A **222**, 33–44.

(190) (With M. F. Perutz) The structure of haemoglobin, VI. Fourier projections on the 010 plane. *Proc. R. Soc. Lond.* A **225**, 315–329.

(191) (With M. F. Perutz) I. A Fourier projection of haemoglobin on the 010 plane. II. Sign determination by the isomorphous replacement method (abstracts of the meeting of the International Union of Crystallography, 21–28 July 1954). *Acta crystallogr.* **7**, 653–654.

(192) 1955 X-rays and the molecule (Dunn Memorial Lecture to the Newcastle Section of Soc. of Chemical Industry, 11 May 1955). *Chemy Ind.* 1955, pp. 1164–1169.

(193) Obituary Notice: George Frederick Charles Searle. *Physical Society Year Book*, p. 72.

(194) The Royal Institution—maintaining standards of popular exposition. *The Times Educational Supplement* 3 June 1955, p. 597.

(195) 1966 Masters of modern science, No. V: Michael Faraday—Our greatest experimentalist *The Times Educational Supplement* 9 March 1956, p. 302.

(196) The discovery of useful electricity (R.I. Discourse, 9 December 1955). *Proc. R. Instn Gt Br.* **36**, 278–289.

(197) The diffraction of X-rays (34th Silvanus Thompson Memorial Lecture). *Br. J. Radiol.* **29**, 121–126.

(198) Information centre for science teachers. *The Schoolmaster* 6 July 1956.

(199) 1957 Schools Lectures at The Royal Institution: a new venture. *Discovery* **18**, 66–67 (February 1957).

(200) The interference of waves (Trotter–Patterson Memorial Lecture). *Trans. illum. Engng Soc. Lond.* **22**, 175–181.

(201) Experimental demonstrations (R.I. Discourse, 29 March 1957). *Proc. R. Instn. Gt Br.* **36**, 657–664 and *Nature, Lond.* **179**, 1211–1212.

(202) X-ray analysis. *New Scient.* **3**, 19–21 (21 November 1957).

(203) 1822–1957—135 Years of British Achievement: three great men of physics. *The Sunday Times* 14 July 1957, p. 15.

(204) 1958 Gemstones (R.I. Discourse, 31 January 1958) *Proc. R. Instn Gt Br.* **37**, 1–15.

(205) The determination of the coordinates of heavy atoms in protein crystals. *Acta crystallogr.* **11**, 70–75.

(206) 1958 Interpretation of science to the public. *Nature, Lond.* **181**, 807–808.

(207) 1958 An international survey of recent scientific research. *New Scient.* **3**, 16–17 (27 March 1958).

(208) 1959 Treasures in the collections of apparatus at The Royal Institution (R.I. Discourse, 24 October 1958). *Proc. R. Instn Gt Br.* **37**, 259–275 and *Nature, Lond.* **182**, 1541–1543 (1958).

(209) The diffraction of Röntgen rays by crystals. In: *Beiträge zur Physik und Chemie des 20 Jahrhunderts* (ed. O. R. Frisch, F. A. Paneth, F. Laves & P. Rosbaud), pp. 147–151. Braunschweig: Friedr. Vieweg & Sohn.

(210) The contribution of the Royal Institution to the teaching of science (Presidential Address to the Science Masters' Association, 30 December 1958). *Sch. Sci. Rev.* **40**, (no. 141), 240–245.

(211) Talking and writing about science. (Based on an address given on the occasion of the award of the first Waverley Gold Medal by Butterworths Scientific Publications, 15 October 1956.) *I.R.E. Trans.* **EWS–2**, 69–72.

(212) 1960 Atoms and molecules (R.I. Discourse, 20 November 1959). *Proc. R. Instn Gt Br.* **38**, 87–92 and *Contemp. Phys* **I**, 390–393.

(213) William Henry Bragg. *New Scient.* **7**, 718–720.

(214) British achievements in X-ray crystallography. *Science N.Y.* **131**, 1870–1874.

(215) The Schools Lectures at the Royal Institution. *Public Schools Appointments Bureau*, bulletin no. 89, July 1960, pp. 25–27.

(216) What constitutes life? *The Times* 19 July 1960, p. xiv (special number on The Royal Society Tercentenary).

(217) The nature of light. *Trans. illum. Engng. Soc. Lond.* **25**, 6–10.

(218) Achievements in X-ray crystallography. *Proc. K. ned. Akad. Wet.* B. **63**, 210–220.

(219) 1961 The development of X-ray analysis (Rutherford Memorial Lecture, 1960). *Proc. R. Soc. Lond.* A **262**, 145–158.

(220) The development of X-ray analysis (R.I. Discourse, 3 March 1961). *Proc. R. Instn Gt Br.* **38**, 526–543.

(221) Memoir of Maurice, Duc de Broglie. *Proc. phys. Soc.* **77**, 1232.

(222) Adventures of the mind: what is life made of? *The Saturday Evening Post*, 7 October 1961, Vol. **234** (no. 40), pp. 34–35, 54, 62, 64.

(223) 1962 (With Mrs G. M. Caroe) Sir William Bragg, F.R.S. (1862–1942). *Notes Rec. R. Soc. Lond.* **17**, 169–182.

(224) The analysis of protein molecules by X-rays. (Discourse at the R.I., 26 September 1961, to delegates attending the 9th General Assembly of I.C.S.U.) *ICSU Rev.* **4**, 33–41.

(225) The growing power of X-ray analysis. In: *Fifty years of X-ray diffraction* (ed. P. P. Ewald), pp. 120–135. N. V. A. Oosthoek's Uitgeversmaatschappij, Utrecht.

(226) Personal reminiscences. In *Fifty years of X-ray diffraction*, pp. 531–539.

(227) 1963 X-ray analysis of biological moleculs (Presidential Address to the Madras Symposium, 1963). In: *Aspects of protein structure* (ed. G. N. Ramachandran), pp. 1–9. London: Academic Press.

(228) 1964 The start of X-ray analysis. *Chemistry* **40**, 8–13.

(229) The difference between living and non-living matter (Saha Memorial Lecture). *Sci. Cult.* **30**, 161–167.

(230) Minerals (R.I. Discourse, 28 February 1964). *Proc. R. Instn Gt Br.* **40**, 64–81.

(231) Reginald William James (1891–1964) (Obituary). *Acta crystallogr.* **17**, 1615–1616.

(232) 1965 Reginald William James, 1891–1964. *Biogr. Mem. Fellows R. Soc. Lond.* **11**, 115–125.

(233) First stages in the X-ray analysis of proteins. *Rep. Prog. Phys.* **28**, 1–14.

(234) The history of X-ray analysis. *Contemp. Phys.* **6**, 161–171 and *Phys. Teach.* **3**, 295–300.

(235) The Schools Lectures at The Royal Institution. *Science, N.Y.* **150**, 1420–1423.

(236) Birthday Greeting to F. Machatschki. (Foreword to 70th birthday tribute). *Tschermaks miner. petrogr. Mitt.* **10**, (3rd ser.) p. 3.

(237) The two cultures. *Overseas* vol 50, no. 504, pp. 3, 5, 9. October 1965 (pub. Royal Overseas League).

(238) 1966 The Royal Institution Lectures in Science for Members of the Administrative Class of the Civil Service. *Contemp. Phys.* **7**, 358–361.

(239) 1966 The art of talking about science. *Science, N.Y.* **154**, 1613–1616.

(240) 1966 Reminiscences of fifty years' research (R.I. Discourse, 11 March 1966). *Proc. R. Instn Gt Br.* **41**, 92–100.

(241) Half a century of X-ray analysis. Nobel Guest Lecture, I (read 1 June 1966). *Ark. Fys.* **40**, 585–603 (published in 1974).

(242) 1967 The art of talking about science. *Marine Technol.* **4**, 258–261.

(243) Sir Kenneth Lee. (Obituary.) *Nature, Lond.* **216**, 945.

(244) The spirit of science (James Scott Lecture). *Proc. R. Soc. Edinb.* A **67**, 303–308.

(245) Introduction to 'A Discussion on the Structure and Function of Lysozyme'. *Proc. R. Soc. Lond.* B **167**, 349.

(246) Reminiscences of fifty years of research (Redding Lecture, Annual General Meeting of the Franklin Institute, 18 January 1967). *J. Franklin Inst.* **284**, 211–228.

(247) William Henry Bragg. *The Encyclopaedia Americana.*

(248) 1968 Professor P. P. Ewald (appreciation on 80th birthday). *Acta crystallogr.* A **24**, 4.

(249) X-ray crystallography. *Scient. Am.* **219** (1), 58–70.

(250) More on the art of talking about science (editorial) *Nucl. Appl. Technol.* **4**, (no. 5), 282–283.

(251) Foreword to *The double helix* by J. D. Watson. New York: Atheneum.

(252) How a secret of life was discovered (article about *The double helix*). *The Times* 6 May 1968, p. 13.

(253) The white-coated worker. *Punch* vol. 255 (no. 6679), 11 September 1968, pp. 352–354.

(254) 1969 The early history of intensity measurements. *Acta crystallogr.* A **25**, 1–3.

(255) The history of X-ray analysis. In: *Sources of physics teaching* pt 3, pp. 74–84. London: Taylor & Francis.

(256) What makes a scientist. (Lecture for Civil Servants, 11 December 1968.) *Proc. R. Instn Gt Br.* **42**, 397–410.

(257) 1972 Dame Kathleen Lonsdale. (Obituary.) *Acta crystallogr.* A **28**, 226.

(Some additional articles and reports of lectures are listed in *William Henry Bragg and William Lawrence Bragg: A Bibliography of their Non-Technical Writings* (1978), Office for History of Science and Technology, University of California, Berkeley.)

# JOHN ALFRED VALENTINE BUTLER

14 February 1899 — 16 July 1977

Elected F.R.S. 1956

By W. V. Mayneord, F.R.S.

John Alfred Valentine Butler (always known to his friends and colleagues as J.A.V.) was born on 14 February 1899 at Winchcombe, Gloucestershire. His father Alfred Butler (1860–1930) came from Sedgeberrow near Evesham and was employed by his own father until about 1904. He then set up as a farmer on his own account, first at Postlip near Winchcombe and later at Langley Farm nearer Winchcombe. J.A.V.'s mother (1861–1952), *née* Mary Ann Powell, came from Hartlebury near Kidderminster. She was at one time in the household of the Bishop of Worcester near Hartlebury and later in that of Emma Dent at Sudeley Castle, Winchcombe.

John was the eldest of three children. His sister Frances died in 1914. His younger sister Doris, of whom more later, married W. J. Margrett.

Little is known of the ancestry. J.A.V.'s grandfather (John Butler) was probably born near Berkeley, Gloucestershire, and moved to Evesham and later to Sudeley near Winchcombe, where he farmed Home Farm at Sudeley Castle. J.A.V. was thus of Cotswold farming stock and rightly proud of it.

## School and early education

In his personal memoirs prepared for the Royal Society J.A.V. relates how he 'lived during childhood mainly at Postlip Farm near Winchcombe (1903–1915), a rather remote farm just under the Cotswold escarpment and two and a half miles from the country town of Winchcombe'. He continues, 'I went to [the] local infants and boys school from the age of 5 to 11, when I was successful in obtaining a Chandos Scholarship which paid fees and travelling expenses to Cheltenham Grammar School. This involved cycling three miles to Winchcombe station where a train to Cheltenham was caught soon after 8 a.m. The usual train home left at 5.8 p.m. and I reached home after the three mile cycle ride, mostly uphill, between 6 and 7 p.m. and settled down to do my homework.'

'Nevertheless I did very well in the Oxford Local examination taken in 1915. I believe I was given an excellent basic training in general subjects, maths and in science. At this time the question of going to a university did not arise. It was obvious that I did not want to become a farmer, which my father no doubt would have liked me to do. He had no knowledge of the professions and was not willing to leave me at school after I obtained my School Certificate.' It seemed that John received little encouragement in his quest for higher education. Postlip Farm was remote and isolated and he must have been very largely dependent on his own efforts. His later habit of silent and independent thought with little emergent trivial conversation must have been formed early. The writer of this memoir, brought up in neighbouring Evesham, remembers visiting J.A.V. and his family in a typical Cotswold farm near Winchcombe. The welcome was warm but perhaps taciturn, and interest soon moved to a local potter working in one of the outhouses of the farm. Maybe John's interest throughout life in local crafts and painting stems from these beginnings.

His memoir continues, 'At this time having read books about the achievements of the great engineers, I wanted to be an engineer and having written to a number of firms I was taken on as an apprentice by the British Thomson Houston Co., Rugby. This was not a success. All I remember about it now was that I was put to saw in pieces, with a hack saw, brass rods 2″ [5 cm] in diameter. I suppose I was also acutely homesick as I had never been away from home before; so I exercised the clause in the apprenticeship which enabled me to withdraw after three months'.

A strange beginning indeed for one whose theoretical acuity was to make him a distinguished authority on chemical thermodynamics!

The next venture was, however, rather more successful. The memoir continues, 'I then became apprenticed to A. Lee Hall, Pharmacist, Winchcombe, and spent about 1½ years in his shop, where I quickly learnt how to make up prescriptions and do the hundred and one things required in a small town chemist's shop. Mr Hall, who was also the local banker (Lloyds Bank) and also ran a farm, soon left the chemist's shop pretty well to me'.

## Army experiences

However, world events were to intervene and 'In 1917 I was called to the Forces and not being in a very high medical grade, on account of my knowledge of pharmacy I was put into the R.A.M.C. After training in Blackpool and working in a transit station at Canterbury, I was sent to France in the spring of 1918 and joined a Casualty Clearing Station in [the] neighbourhood of Ypres. Here I was a ward orderly—but did not get any desire to study medicine'.

The story of J.A.V.'s army experience deserves more attention than the few words recorded in his notes and fortunately this is possible as his diary for 1918 was preserved and throws a good deal of light on his character and the origins of his subsequent achievements.

Some of the entries in the diary have a familiar flavour. Pte J. A. Butler 116576 R.A.M.C. records that on 1 January 1918 'Orderly sergeant wished us all a happy New Year on 8.30 parade—he is usually very surly'. But perhaps more worthy of record here (though it may have seemed of less importance at the time!) is the next item, 'Sent 10/6* to H. K. Lewis [booksellers, London] for three months subscription to library'. On 3 January we read, 'Got Bragg's

* 10 shillings and 6 pence. 12 pence = 1 shilling; 20 shillings = £1.

"Radioactivity" (post 5d) from Lewis's. Heard from C.C. (University Correspondence College). Fee for 6 lessons in Calculus £1. 1. 0.' The next day, 'Read all Bragg part on $\alpha$ rays—not so clear as it might be. S.M. gave every man 2 pkts Woodbines'. But the reading was not confined to physics. On 5 January, 'Got Coleridges Lectures on S'peare from Library', and next day 'Read section of Bragg on X-rays. Very interesting and fresh to me'. (It is still 'fresh' to many of us who have spent much of our lives working on X-ray measurement!) On 8 January, 'Sent 16/6 to Lewis's. Also got Lee's "Students History of Shakespeare"—this is rather concise but good', and on 11 January, ' "Borderlands of Science" by A. T. Schofield from Lewis's'. To relieve the intellectual pressure we also note, 'Parcel from home with pork pie, cake and apples'. Surely reasonable recording for a young man of 19!

Intermittently we read of military matters, such as falling in at the double as ward orderlies and comments such as '2 Generals and their staff officers came round. I suppose they decided what is to be done this time'.

In relation to subsequent interests and achievements 16 January must have been a significant day. 'Got Findlay's "Phase Rule and its applications" from Lewis's', while on 21 January we read, 'Findlay's "Phase Rule" difficult reading—wrote to Lewis's about Mellor's "Higher Maths" '. Two days later, 'Getting on with Findlay', and on 25 January, 'Got Mellor's "High Mathematics for students of Physics and Chemistry" from Lewis's. Price 16/6 with pt'. 30 January, 'Got Ramsay's "Gases of the atmosphere" from Lewis's'. The pattern of interest was becoming clear.

J.A.V. went home on leave on 1 February and must somehow have acquired optical equipment, for in the midst of his account of reading matter there suddenly appear references to experimental work. Thus on 6 February, 'Pleased with spectroscope. Staff Garbett and Q.M.S. interested in my spectroscope', and on 8th, 'Made spirit lamp with the help of Staff Garbett. Bandage for wick. Answered fairly well. Got some wick, also $BaCO_3$, $KMnO_4$, $CuSO_4$ down town. $KMnO_4$ gave a fine absorption spectrum when dilute. Gave 4 dark bands in green, increasing in thickness as conc. increased. Staff brought me some S.V.M. and got me a large bottle of conc. HCl'. On 9 February, 'Got "Chemical discovery and Invention"—Sir W. A. Tilden—from Lewis's. A better book than the corresponding Dis. & Inv. of the 20th Century. Though popular, is accurate and contains much new information. Gives references and often quotes from original papers'.

There were other more personal problems! On 16 February, 'Found my belt missing at dinner time. Cant find it anywhere. Must have been taken by someone'. The first appearance of the absent minded professor we later knew so well? The belt never was found!

On 22 February, 'Got Bragg's "X-rays and crystal structure" from Lewis's', a text described five days later as 'most interesting but difficult'. Intermediate reading recorded in the diary includes Moisson's "Electric Furnace", while J.A.V.'s notes on 14 March refer to Einstein and light deflection in a gravitational field and hopes of seeing, during an eclipse, the deflection of stars in its vicinity. On 20 March a significant acquisition was made, Sir J. J. Thomson's 'Positive Rays', again from Lewis's. This book seems to have made a particularly powerful impact since on 27 March, 'Heard from Central Library—on duty at night—wrote essay on Sir J. J. Thomson's positive rays'.

After brief training, largely it seems concerned with gas warfare, on 27 April John embarked for France and naturally the emphasis changes. Much reading is still recorded but now of a more general nature, e.g. Lockhart's 'Scott', 'Bride of Lammermoor', Macaulay, Byron's 'Childe Harold'. Reading Thackeray's 'Book of Snobs' and 'Barry Lyndon' he remarks that, 'The first amusing but true and the latter interesting towards the beginning but B.L. becomes disgusting and cruel after'. Some science intrudes, as, for example, Haldane's 'Air Analysis', 'Most interesting and up to date—getting on well with Maths'.

In view of skill later displayed in so many semi-popular expositions of science, an item for 6 August catches the eye, 'Writing a series of papers as an introduction to science for Doris', his sister, with whom he evidently kept up a close correspondence during the whole of this period. Even at this early stage J.A.V. evidently felt the need to record his own version of the state of knowledge in subjects of interest to him. Students of modern biology should be grateful.

J.A.V. also still continued with some experimental work. 2 August, 'I have started doing some experimental work and made and used volumetric solns. of acid and alkali etc. and spent a good deal of my spare time at this'.

Evidently life was pretty busy at the clearing station near Ypres and there are many notes of small walks and excursions as well as some tragic references to individual 'cases' and events, but we are, naturally, told little of these experiences.

There is then a long gap in the recording but by October hopes were rising of the end of the war. During this period readings of 'Rob Roy' and 'Waverley' are mentioned as well as 'Chemistry of Dyeing' and Jones's 'Examples in Physics'. Also, 'Phill sent me a "Chemist's Pocket Book", very good and meets all my needs'. In October in communication with the 'K.C.C.', 'sent for Self-Ed course in Physics £1. 11. 6. Sent 16/–. Also arranged Preliminary Self-Ed Course in Maths and English for Doris', who is recorded as 'seems anxious to study'. Earlier J.A.V. had received from his mother a letter which he notes as encouraging him to follow his own bent towards chemistry.

### University of Birmingham; early research in physical chemistry

Then came the Armistice and new horizons. The memoir continues, 'I was not demobilised until October 1919 when I applied for and was awarded an ex-service Education Grant which enabled me to go to Birmingham University. I had spent my last year in the R.A.M.C., after the Armistice in 1918, studying science, partly with the help of University Correspondence College, Cambridge, and passed Inter.B.Sc. in June 1919, being granted special leave to return to England for this purpose'.

We should interpolate here that J.A.V. in later years was intensely proud of having 'worn the King's uniform', and made this clear in many conversations. He felt, as was indeed true, that the Army had given him his chance of higher education. Those who knew him well in later years will find it difficult to believe that he was ever the smartest recruit on parade, but clearly by his own tenacity and ability to concentrate on a single objective (a notable characteristic) he had made excellent use of the facilities offered and emerged equipped for a professional career. He continues, 'At Birmingham I was passed B.Sc. with 1st Class Honours in 1921 (1st in the year) but as I had not put in enough residence to qualify for the degree, I had to spend another session which I did doing research with the Lecturer in Physical Chemistry, Dr S. R. Carter'.

Though not mentioned in the diary, while in the R.A.M.C. J.A.V. evidently was in touch with work in a laboratory of the Catholic University of Lille, for we have an appreciative letter from Professor Albert Delerne of 15 November 1919 acknowledging a letter from J.A.V. and telling him how he was now teaching mathematics in l'Ecole des H^tes^ Etudes Industrielles et Commerciales. Delerne asks for English books on mathematics emphasizing their significance to him when a prisoner of war in Germany 'pour occuper leur loisirs pendant les heures parfois si longues de la captivité'. J.A.V. evidently sent him as well a copy of *Nature*, acknowledged on 20 January 1920.

J.A.V.'s outstanding abilities were already becoming very obvious even among students in Birmingham. The writer happened to be in Carter's physical chemistry class at the same time as J.A.V. (though then unacquainted with him personally) and remembers well that J.A.V. was always referred to among us as 'the clever man'.

His first research with Carter was 'An attempt to realise a sulphur electrode' as well as 'work on reduction of $SO_2$' to sulphur by ferrous salts in strongly acid solution'. 'For this', he records, 'I was awarded M.Sc. degree (June 1922).' This work was published jointly with Carter in a paper on the kinetics of the reaction between ferrous phosphate and sulphur dioxide in phosphoric acid solution (1). The forms of the primary and secondary reactions were studied carefully but the resulting differential equations were intractable. It was not found possible to obtain a general solution, 'though a special case' showed 'a very close resemblance'. This paper seems to be J.A.V.'s first published mathematical excursion into reaction kinetics. Further results were promised 'in due course'.

## University College of Swansea

His memoir continues, 'Shortly afterwards I was appointed [October 1922] Assistant Lecturer in the University College of Swansea [then in its second year] by J. E. Coates. Morgan [Professor of Chemistry in Birmingham] advised me to stay in Birmingham—undoubtedly good advice—but I was tired of existence on a pittance and I liked the idea of starting teaching in a new college. From the lectures I gave in Swansea I later constructed two books "The chemical elements and their compounds" (1926) and "Chemical thermodynamics" (1928 and 1932) which went through numerous editions, finally appearing as a paper back in 1965'.

These books, particularly the latter, established J.A.V.'s reputation.

Following his move to Swansea one of his main interests for many years began to be apparent. A paper 'On the seat of the electromotive force in the galvanic cell' (5) attempted a synthesis of the different theories in the long controversy about the seat of that e.m.f. He compares and combines the metal contact p.d. theory and the chemical theory, the Nernst theory and the relation between e.m.f. and total energy change in the Gibbs–Helmholtz equation. He was beginning to handle easily general thermodynamic concepts and associated mathematical techniques. This is shown, for example, in another paper of 1924 on the relation between metal contact potentials and the Peltier effect (4) in which he develops a statistical theory of metal boundary potentials shown to be in accordance with the requirements of the laws of thermodynamics. Other papers of that year (1924–25) show preoccupation with heats of solution, solubility and lattice energy (6) in their most general aspects. Views, then modern, concerning electronic structure in relation to co-valency and the mutual sharing of electrons so as to complete already existent groups, led to the studies of the distinctions between 'co-valency' and 'co-ordination' (7).

J.A.V. was evidently at this time in contact with N. V. Sidgwick who wrote to him in April 1926 from Lincoln College, Oxford, about J.A.V.'s paper in the *Transactions of the Faraday Society* (7) concerning co-valency and shared electrons, asking 'What do you imagine to be the structure of the carbon atom in $CH_4$?' and giving alternative interpretations of 'levels'.

This theory of formation of new groups outside the last group representing the ion are set out in a lecture delivered in November 1925 (7). He also published his first studies in heterogeneous equilibria (2, 3) including papers on the kinetics of solubility of strong electrolytes and a general equation for the solubility of a binary salt.

With Carter and Jones there followed (11) further studies of the mechanism of the oxidizing potential of selenium dioxide–selenium in comparison with sulphur dioxide, as well as studies of solubilities of thallous chloride in salt solutions at various temperatures (9). Also in 1926 we note the first paper to the Royal Society (communicated by F. G. Donnan, F.R.S.) on 'The equilibrium of heterogeneous systems including electrolytes', Part I (12). Part II appeared in 1927 (13).

Part I concerns the fundamental equations and phase rule, Part II the equilibrium at interfaces and the theory of electrocapillarity. One of J.A.V.'s characteristics was 'to study the masters not their pupils', and we often find Willard Gibbs in the first few sentences. J.A.V.'s paper (12) extended the methods employed by Gibbs in his 'Equilibrium of heterogeneous substances' to systems containing electrolytes, by the introduction of another variable, the electrical potential. The general conditions of equilibrium were obtained and a modified form of the phase rule for neutral masses containing electrolytes is given, its applications of equilibrium at interfaces are discussed and analysis made of the changes produced by electrolytic polarization at the interface between mercury and solutions of electrolytes. A theory of electrocapillarity is developed, including a kinetic theory of the adsorption of ions and the effect on the electrocapillary curves. These papers are not only masterly reviews of previous concepts but major extensions of them. In their scope, generality and mathematical skill, they constitute some of his best and most significant work.

Part III of this series on the equilibrium of heterogeneous systems concerning 'The effect of an electric field on the adsorption of organic molecules and the interpretation of electro-capillary curves' was not published until 1929 (17) when it was communicated by Sir James Walker, F.R.S., from the University of Edinburgh. The paper (17) established the form of variation of the amount $\Gamma$ of a substance adsorbed from solution with a given potential difference $V$ at the interface as $\Gamma = \Gamma_0 e^{-aV^2+bV}$, for a series of some hundred compounds including homologous series of alcohols, and series of aldehydes, nitriles, amides and acids.

### University of Edinburgh; contributions to thermodynamics

J.A.V. was now a D.Sc. of the University of Birmingham (1927) and also a Meldola Medallist of the Royal Institute of Chemistry (1929), and had meanwhile (in 1926) been appointed Lecturer in Chemistry in the University of Edinburgh, under Sir James Walker, F.R.S.

A paper in the *Journal of Physical Chemistry* (15) on 'The mutual salting-out of ions' again displays his mathematical skills and ingenuity in devising approximations which are testable.

In reviewing all this work one is left with the impression that J.A.V. was more at home in the theoretical mathematical sphere than in experimental observation. His thermodynamic studies or studies of reaction kinetics are of a very high order. The mathematical treatment is often accompanied by a delightfully clear non-mathematical physical picture of the events, mostly kinetic, supposed to be taking place. This power of non-mathematical description as well as rigorous quantitative treatment is seen again in the many textbooks or review books later published and was doubtless one of the reasons for their success.

In 1929 J.A.V. began the publication in the *Proceedings of the Royal Society* (A) of a series of papers on the behaviour of electrolytes in mixed solvents, work carried out in conjunction with a group of collaborators in the University of Edinburgh, particularly C. M. Robertson, R. Shaw, A. D. Lees, R. T. Hamilton and D. W. Thomson, each of whom joined him in one paper (16, 22, 23, 24, 36). An overall account was given by J.A.V. himself (60) at a meeting of the British Association, when he explained that in a mixed solvent there exist many possibilities of differential interaction between ions and two kinds of solvent molecules. The Royal Society papers emphasize that evidence as to the interaction of ions and molecules may be obtained from the study of such diverse properties as refractivities, vapour pressure, volume changes, free energies and heat effects. It is not sufficient to regard a mixed solvent as a uniform medium, for the electric fields exert differential attraction according to polarizability leading to local changes of ionic density.

In this series of papers more emphasis is laid on experimental results and detail, for example in Part I (16) on the e.m.f. of hydrogen–silver chloride cells at different temperatures in a series of hydrogen chloride in water–alcohol mixtures, in Part II (22) on the effects of lithium chloride in such mixtures; in Part III (23) molecular refractivities and partial molar volumes of lithium chloride, Part IV (24) the partial free energies of zinc chloride, and in Part V (24) on free energy of lithium chloride in water–alcohol mixtures; Part VI (37) was published in 1934.

J.A.V. had a remarkable ability to keep going several major series of papers simultaneously, and in 1932 began a series of three papers to the *Proceedings of the Royal Society* (A) on the kinetics of electrode processes (25, 30, 31), designed 'to elucidate the electromotive behaviour of hydrogen and oxygen at electrodes'. We note the theoretical influence of Gurney and quantum mechanics while the experimental methods included the use of a string electrometer and simple 'valve circuit', or alternatively a Lindemann electrometer to record rapid changes of potential. From much experimental evidence with both platinum and gold electrodes the view emerges that a single layer of adsorbed oxygen atoms is formed at the surface during anodic polarization.

We cannot discuss in detail all the work of this period, but must mention a paper on the thermodynamics of the surfaces of solutions (26) communicated by J. P. Kendall, F.R.S., to the Royal Society in which the basic assumption that there is a single layer of molecules at the interface which differs in their properties from those in the bulk of the solution is developed with great skill and generality based of course on Gibbs's thermodynamics of capillarity. Theoretical results are compared with experimental data concerning, for example, changes of surface tension and concentration. This is surely one of J.A.V.'s outstanding contributions to applied thermodynamics of surfaces.

To retrace our steps a little, studies in electrocapillarity continued in 1930 (in conjunction with Ockrent) (18–21) as well as work on adsorption at the surface of solutions, particularly water–alcohol solutions (27, 28), all much under the influence of his studies of Gibbs.

In 1933 interest ranges from electrostriction produced by salts of lithium, sodium and potassium in aliphatic alcohols, of particular interest perhaps as offering a very direct means of estimating the forces between ions and solvent molecules and possibly distinguishing between electrical and other factors in solvation (33), to free energy of normal aliphatic alcohols in aqueous solution (34).

In 1934 investigations into the factors determining electrolytic dissociation and energies of ionic dissociation of simple salt molecules (38) were published. The theoretical treatment differs from Born and Heisenberg by the introduction of a London resonance term for interacting electronic systems and an exponential form of repulsion similar to that used for crystals. The alkali halides are in agreement with the theory but not halide salts.

Two papers on the solubility of non-electrolytes (43, 44) respectively on the free energy of hydration of some aliphatic alcohols and influence of the polar group on this quantity emphasize again his interest in the nature of the interaction between solutes and water.

He still maintained his interest in hydrogen overvoltage and reversible hydrogen electrodes (32, 47) and anodic polarization as well as the mechanism of electrolytic processes (48–50), and entropy of hydration (52).

The possibilities offered by the properties of deuterium evidently next caught his imagination. A paper by Orr on the exchange of deuterium between deuterium hydroxide and ethyl alcohol was followed by studies of the rate of diffusion of deuterium hydroxide in water (45). Interest again centred on such intermolecular phenomena as electrostriction of water by ions.

With Hornel in 1936 (51) he determined the ratio of hydrolysis of acetal in hydrogen chloride solutions in water and deuterium oxide and showed it was possible to determine the ratio of the dissociation constants of the acid in the two liquids.

In 1937 he published a paper with Orr (whose death he sadly records a few years later (68)) on the 'kinetic and thermodynamic activity of protons and deuterons' in water–deuterium oxide solutions (54). Reaction rates were determined by change of refractive index using a Hilger–Rayleigh interferometer. Possible equilibria were formulated and it was concluded that the rates of hydrolysis of acetal in solutions of hydrogen chloride and deuterium chloride were determined by the 'thermodynamic' proton and deuteron activities of the solution. Later experiments were concerned with the acid hydrolysis of esters and alkaline decomposition of diacetone alcohol (58) and dissociation constants of some nitrophenols in deuterium oxide (61).

The latter publication has a particular interest for us, as the joint author was David Christie Martin, later Executive Secretary of the Royal Society. From 1937 to 1939 Martin worked with J.A.V. in Edinburgh and was awarded a Ph.D. degree in 1939, his thesis being in part concerned with some properties of deuterium compounds. Martin in later years always expressed a very real regard for J.A.V.

It is clear as one reads the papers that J.A.V.'s primary aim throughout was to throw light upon intermolecular forces and the properties of liquids. To this end he was able to bring to bear formidable theoretical powers, whether concerned with thermodynamic or kinetic concepts.

A general review of these subjects by him was included in the *Annual Reports of the Chemical Society* for 1937 (59). There he discusses in detail intermolecular forces and the impact of wave mechanics, equations of state and partition functions of liquids, viscosity, melting, dielectric properties of polar liquids, dispersion of the dielectric constant, hydrogen bonds in associated liquids as well as Raman and infrared spectroscopy. One feels that interest in general thermodynamics is now less prominent and emphasis is moving to more detailed theoretical and experimental attacks on the intermolecular forces in determining the properties of liquids. This feeling is perhaps borne out by the events of the next few years.

But first to sum up. Early in 1924 he had developed kinetic theories of the origin of electrode potentials and these had been substantially confirmed. Up to 1934 his emphasis had been on thermodynamic properties of salts particularly in mixed solvents in order to distinguish effects of solvation. His use of mixed water–alcohol as solvents had indeed been outstanding, as had his studies of the thermodynamics of surfaces of solutions, again of single solute and multi-solute systems and both solution–vapour and solution–mercury interfaces. A general theory of overpotential was developed up to 1939 and he had particularly studied the behaviour of electrolytically formed hydrogen and oxygen films, particularly monomolecular films on metals as well as anodic passivity of gold. Since 1935 he had worked on the free energy and entropy of hydration of organic substances (52) and discovered general relations between heat and entropy of solutions. We have already noted his use of deuterium to study acid and base catalysed reactions.

## Rockefeller Institute for Medical Research; research on physical chemistry of biological materials

A break was imminent as he directed his attention to the molecular kinetics of enzyme action. We enter the period in which he began to turn his physical and chemical techniques and skills to the study of biologically important molecules; to the action of radiomimetic substances, and of ionizing radiations on deoxyribonucleic acid, and finally to the behaviour of isolated nucleoproteins.

His personal memoirs bear out the perhaps almost unconscious urge for change. He records that during the late thirties he became increasingly unhappy at Edinburgh, finding the Chemistry Department 'unstimulating'; 'I was also in difficulty to support my family on my stipend as a University Lecturer, which had increased from £350 in 1926 to £550 per annum in 1939! I applied unsuccessfully for several chairs during this period and by 1939 I felt it was necessary to make a break into a new field. In '39 I was appointed to a Rockefeller Fellowship to work at the Rockefeller Institute for Medical Research, Princeton, in the laboratory of Dr J. H. Northrop. Northrop and his associates in the previous year had isolated and crystallized a number of proteolytic enzymes and their precursors and at his suggestion I studied the homogeneity of these preparations by solubility methods. I also spent some time attempting to prepare crystalline chymotrypsinogen from sheep pancreas, which proved to be difficult owing to large quantities of muco-proteins present. Later I investigated the kinetics of some of these enzyme reactions and showed that their kinetic feature was a low activation energy.'

## War-time activities and return to Edinburgh

'After the outbreak of World War II I offered my services to the British authorities and in 1941 I was appointed Executive Officer at the then newly formed British Scientific Office, of which Sir Charles Darwin was the Director.

'I continued in this capacity until 1944 when Edinburgh University recalled me to take part in teaching there.'

A paper appeared in 1940 on the use of solubility as a criterion of purity of proteins (62) while the results of some of the experiments on the formation of chymotrypsin from chymotrypsinogen were published in 1941 (64). From the study of velocity constants at four temperatures the activation energy was found to be 16 300 calories. 'It seemed probable that the reaction is the opening of peptide bonds in ring structures.'

## Courtauld Research Institute of Biochemistry

However, he did not find conditions in Edinburgh after his return in 1944 'at all congenial'. His memoirs continue, 'At this stage it was my desire to continue to work on the physical chemistry of biological materials, and as there was no encouragement to do this in Edinburgh, in 1946 I obtained an appointment as Courtauld Research Fellow at the Courtauld Institute of Biochemistry, London, Director, Professor (later Sir Charles) Dodds, F.R.S., who wished to study the degradation of various protein hormones with proteolytic enzymes. I began with insulin (with Dr D. M. P. Phillips) to obtain an insight into the methods of separating peptides. We did not know at the time that Dr Sanger's studies of insulin structure were then far advanced. The experience gained was, however, very useful later in the studies of histones at the Chester Beatty Research Institute where later Dr Phillips rejoined my laboratory'.

The only publication during 1946 appears to be an article in *Nature* (67) on life and the second law of thermodynamics. His 'attention was somewhat forcibly drawn to these matters by observing the growth of fungi such as *Penicillium notatum* in flasks', leading to the question, 'What is the free-energy change in the elaboration of a protein?' Calculations were made of configurational entropy per amino acid residue and free-energy change of about 1200 cal per residue. 'If an organism can synthesise peptide bonds, it appears it will have no great difficulty in putting together protein molecules of any degree of complication.' This is an intriguing early application of thermodynamics into his biological studies and his interest in it continued over the years, as shown in conversations with the writer years later when we were both interested in Monod's 'Chance and necessity'.

Before commencing to discuss his Courtauld experience we may recall a note to *Nature* (76) deploring the closing of the Princeton Laboratories of the Rockefeller Institute and transfer to New York. He recalls the fundamental work of Northrop and Stanley and records his own thanks for much kindness and hospitality received in Princeton.

This is perhaps also an appropriate place to note a very interesting lecture by J.A.V. (81) on early scientific links between Scotland and America, in which he ranges widely from Benjamin Franklin to Dr Black but emphasizes 'the great debt of early American science to the Scottish pioneers'.

Apart from a study of a toxic substance from agenized flour (78) his work at the Courtauld Institute seems to have centred on the structure of insulin, but was in the event, as he himself admits, overshadowed by Sanger.

Professor F. Dickens, F.R.S., in notes kindly made for the writer, remarks that possibly Dodds had hopes of breaking down protein hormones with a view to splitting off peptide fractions that would retain the hormone activity of the whole protein molecule. At this period Dodds's success with stilboestrol as an artificial substitute for natural steroidal oestrogens had made him perhaps too optimistic about the possibility of chemically simpler substitutes for the protein hormones also. Earlier with R. H. Noble he had had the same or similar ideas about posterior pituitary extract but the outcome was somewhat disappointing.

As a preliminary, J.A.V. published with Stephen a description (70, 73) of a 'preparative electrophoresis apparatus' which permitted conveniently the complete separation of amino-acids, peptides and proteins when their ionic mobilities differ sufficiently. It consisted of a long tube packed with porous material (asbestos, glass or cotton wool which hindered convection without greatly increasing resistance) with the tube attached to closed silver/silver chloride electrodes so that electroendosmotic flow did not occur. Successful separation of amino-acids and peptide, and proteins was attained in this device, common enough now, but then less well known.

Two papers, respectively on the action of chymotrypsin and trypsin on insulin (74) and the 'action of pepsin on insulin and the plastein question', were published in conjunction with Dodds, Phillips and Stephen in the *Biochemical Journal* (74, 75), but the results were disappointing, as appears from a third communication to the *Biochemical Journal* of 1949 (77).

A paper in *Nature* (72) with Phillips and Stephen on 'The core of the insulin molecule' notes Sanger's advance and his showing that the submolecule of insulin consists of two chains and his ability to identify the amino-acid sequence forming the peptide chains. The review describes electrophoretic experiments on the 'core' of the molecule.

A further paper from the Courtauld was published with Phillips, Stephen and Creeth, again on 'Some properties of the insulin core'(86). Insulin was split by the action of chymotrypsin into a number of peptide fragments of molecular weight about 800 and a large residue (known as 'the core') of molecular mass between 4000 and 5000. This paper describes electrophoretic studies of three or four peptides obtained on oxidation of the core, together with studies of the distribution of cystine and aromatic amino-acids.

While at the Courtauld Institute (September 1947) J.A.V. gave the three Cantor Lectures on 'Enzymes: their isolation, structure, uses, mode of action and place in Nature' (71). It would be difficult to find a clearer, more comprehensive account of this vast subject as it then was. The text might still make admirable preparatory reading for a developing molecular biologist and perhaps illustrates J.A.V.'s habit of writing for his own, as well as anyone else's benefit, a 'state of the subject' review.

## Chester Beatty Research Institute; research on ionizing radiations and histones

The attack with proteolytic enzymes had perhaps been less successful than hoped, and feeling that a change of emphasis and methods was again necessary (to return to J.A.V.'s biographical notes), 'In 1949 I moved to the Chester Beatty [Director, A. Haddow (later Sir Alex)] to establish a Department of Physical Biochemistry. During the next few years all the methods of study of macromolecules (ultracentrifuge, light scattering, viscosity, electrophoresis) were applied to DNA and to nucleoproteins and especially to the products from these of the action of ionizing radiations and of carcinogenic agents such as nitrogen mustards. Later (in the late 1950s) this was extended to an extensive investigation, with Dr A. B. Robins, of the effects of ionizing radiation on enzymes both solid and in solution. In view of the difficulty of interpreting the effects of ionizing radiation on cells, in the 1960s with Dr A. R. Crathorn and Dr T. P. Brent, a system of synchronously dividing Hela cells was established and the effects of irradiation—especially on DNA synthesis in cell division, were investigated'.

'Early in the 1950s I had considerable difficulty in obtaining permission to use radioisotopes in tracer quantities in the Chester Beatty Institute as the Director (Professor Haddow) was afraid that the presence of radioactive materials in the Institute might confuse the experiments on carcinogens being carried out. This difficulty was eventually overcome by building a small radioisotope laboratory (opened in 1957) at the Pollards Wood Research Station, an offshoot of the Chester Beatty. As far as possible work involving isotopes was carried out here, though the prohibition of the use of isotopes in the C.B.R.I. was later relaxed. The investigation of the reaction of mustards with DNA by Dr Brookes, using radioactively marked S-mustard, which led to the demonstration of cross-linking by difunctional mustards was, in part, initiated by me.'

'A long series of studies of histones was begun about 1952, originally with Dr P. F. Davison and later with Dr D. M. P. Phillips and Dr E. W. Johns. (The latter had entered the laboratory from the R.A.F. as a technician, and became B.Sc., Ph.D. and later D.Sc.) Methods of fractionating the histones present were devised—the most valuable of which was undoubtedly the use of alcoholic solutions, which provide separations based on the proportion of hydrophobic amino-acids present which were basically different from those given by chromatography. As a result of this, five main histones, $F_1$, $F_{2a1}$, $F_{2a2}$, $F_{2b}$ and $F_3$ were obtained in a reasonably pure state and fully characterized. It was shown (with L. S. Hnilica) that a number of different tissues (and organisms) had remarkably similar histones, and moreover they differed little in metabolic behaviour (turnover rate). As a result of this work it was suggested that histones functioned in a rather unspecific way.'

Thus ends the memoir deposited with the Royal Society on 12 May 1969, but we must retrace our steps to look in a little more detail at the main outline of progress.

His work at the Chester Beatty Institute soon centred around two main themes. The first was the chemical analogies in the action of ionizing radiations and of radiomimetic chemicals on nucleic acid. The second concerned the proteins associated with DNA in the structure of chromosomes, the histones. The latter was a subject he was to make particularly his own, and probably in the outcome the more significant of the two interests.

In early papers in 1950 attention was concentrated on the analogy between the action of ionizing radiations and radiomimetic chemicals, on thymonucleic acid and later particularly on the nature of changes in viscosity which occur after the irradiation with X-rays has stopped. These changes might be due to short-lived radicals produced and alternative methods of producing these changes were sought. In a paper with Smith (82) it was shown that free radicals produced chemically could cause the dipolymerization of nucleic acid, but a footnote foreshadowed future work with Conway who notes that in solutions carefully freed from oxygen no appreciable change of viscosity occurs after the completion of the X-irradiation. The non-Newtonian viscosity of nucleic acid and its decrease after treatment with mustards was emphasized in a paper to *Nature* with Gilbert and Smith (83). Two groups by reacting at two distinct points, lying either on a single surface or fibre, act as cross-linking agents between nucleo-protein or protein molecules. The theme was developed in a set of four papers on the action of ionizing radiations and of radiomimetic substances on deoxyribonucleic acid; part I (84) on the action of some compounds of the mustard type chiefly concerned with changes of viscosity in irradiated samples, part II (85) with Conway returns to the effects of absence of oxygen and the search for the product of molecular oxygen responsible, $H_2O_2$ being ruled out. Part III (89) on the molecular weight of DNA degraded by X-rays or by treatment with a 'nitrogen mustard', in which molecular masses were determined by sedimentation and diffusion–constant determinations, showed an appreciable lowering in molecular mass but also a considerable degree of polydispersity. The variance clearly increased with X-ray or chemical treatment.

Parts IV (96) and V (97), with Press and Conway respectively, deal with the products of the action of di-(2-chloroethyl) methylamine and experiments on the action of X-rays and free radicals respectively, the latter concerned again with the fact that though hydrogen peroxide might be suspected the initial agent is likely to be the radical $HO_2$. Part VI (99) is again concerned with the action of 'mustards'.

In the same year, in a paper on the gel like behaviour of DNA solutions (91) the usual diffusion pattern, namely that at the boundary moving forward into the solvent, behaved anomalously, the boundary moving into the solvent retaining its sharpness. Schlieren pictures of boundaries revealed some detail of the moving concentration gradients. The phenomena are explained in terms of a gel network, also emphasizing the high structural viscosity of nucleic acid solutions and their streaming birefringence.

A review (92) of the chemical analogies in the action of ionizing radiations and of radiomimetic chemicals on nucleic acid (by J.A.V., Conway, Gilbert and K. A. Smith) appeared in *Acta Un. int. Cancr.* The main interest is perhaps the suggestion of the importance of biradical forms in the connection between carcinogens and nucleotoxic substances.

Work also continued on physical detail of techniques, as for example on the effects of rate of shear on the reduced viscosities of thymus nucleic acid solutions, and on the effects of added salts on viscosity measurements. In *Proceedings of the Royal Society* B (J.A.V. is one of the select band of authors in both A and B!) experiments with Conway are described (104) on the action of radicals generated now by ultraviolet light on deoxyribonucleic acid. It was found that the rate of loss of viscosity of DNA agreed, with certain simple assumptions, 'with that produced by X rays'. The liberation of phosphate from DNA as well as simple nucleotides was studied and the detailed chemical reactions outlined. During the next few years there followed a large number of papers of which we can only select a small number for notice, trying to give a brief outline of the development of ideas and techniques.

In 1952 J.A.V. published in *Endeavour* a review (98) summarizing recent work on the physical chemistry of the type of nucleic acid found in the chromosomes. It represents perhaps one of the last overall accounts before the Crick-Watson hypotheses. J.A.V. remarks 'the function of deoxyribonucleic acid in the chromosome is still obscure. It has often been suggested that it acts as a kind of template in which the highly specific peptide chains from which the proteins are formed are laid down, but it is difficult to see how nucleic acid could be capable of a sufficient number of variations'. He thought that it was 'possible that the nucleic acid may not be the basic self-reproductive system. It may act only as a support for the protein'. J.A.V. notes a number of hypotheses. Again, the detailed physical chemistry seemed destined to be overwhelmed by the new concepts but his conviction as to the importance of the protein, as well as DNA, of the chromosomes leads us directly to the next important phase of his work.

True, studies continued of the effects of salts, X-rays, and ultraviolet light on the reduced specific viscosity of DNA, particularly by, or with, Conway, but increasingly work on the histones of calf thymus deoxyribonucleoprotein predominates (109, 110, 118, 119). Detail must be sought in the original papers.

At first (109) two main components were observed both by electrophoresis and in the ultracentrifuge. It appeared that 'the histone of thymus nucleoprotein is not highly complex', but the idea of a continuous range of physical properties was not supported. Further studies (118) were made by extraction by dilute HCl and $H_2SO_4$. Partial fractionation was observed. The sedimentation diagram revealed an accurate Gaussian normal distribution curve for fraction precipitated by acetone after various times at 60 000 rev/min.

There is, of course, speculation as to the nature of the binding and interaction of protein and DNA.

Interesting light on J.A.V.'s thinking at this period is thrown by two reviews, one published by the Centre National de la Recherche Scientifique (126), where we have 'L'histone elle même est complexe. Nous avons trouvé que l'histone du thymus de bœuf, extrait par $SO_4H_2$, contient au moins deux protéines qu'on peut séparer par une extraction avec les solvents différents. Ces deux protéines ont les compositions très différentes: dans l'une une grande partie de l'arginine est remplacée par de la lysine. L'une contient 4% d'arginine et 33% de lysine; l'autre 16% d'arginine et 9·5% de lysine. Il serait absurde de spéculer sur les fonctions de ces substances. . . .

'Si nous identifions le gène à une particule ou à un groupe de particules d'ADN, il faut qu'elles soint jointes d'une façon ou d'une autre suivant un arrangement linéaire. La chose la plus naturelle à laquelle on puisse penser est qu'elles sont jointes par les ponts d'histone, et si l'on veut spéculer davantage il est permis de suggérer que l'une des histones servirait dans les liaisons linéaires entre les particules d'ADN et l'autre pour les liaisons transversales entre les chaînes multiples.' Subsequent work of course revealed much greater complexity.

He also raised a problem which concerned him for some time. Always somewhat suspicious of the proposed helical structure, he raises in this review the question of sufficient specificity in the possibilities of protein construction and 'Il y a d'autres difficultés, à savoir si l'ADN a une structure spiralée—*in vivo*, comment se fait le déroulement ?' This problem worried him considerably and he attacked it much later (193) in one of his few original detailed 'mechanical' models of synthesis of nucleic acids. There seemed to him (114) there was no good reason that 'these specialized protein materials may not themselves be a necessary part of the gene and contribute to determining the required specificity'.

A second very comprehensive and valuable review (with its 259 references), however, contains and largely accepts Watson and Crick. At about the same time he considers the action of carcinogenic agents and radiations in a paper on some implications of new ideas of the structure of deoxyribonucleic acid (113). The Crick–Watson model may well provide the explanation of the profound biological effects of radiation. J.A.V. always felt that the amount of damage produced by a small quantity of radiation was surprising, 'a very large multiplication factor is required, but it is obvious that the loss of $—NH_2$ at only one point of the nucleotide sequence will interfere with the synthesis of the whole chain and also if a break in the nucleotide chain occurs once it will reappear in all subsequent copies'. The model has, however, he thought only a small degree of specificity and the amount of variation possible is not sufficient to account for the possible variations in a peptide chain. Other objections follow and 'much remains to be done before the molecular basis of genetical phenomena can be explained'.

J.A.V.'s main interest during the years from about 1952 onwards lay in the study of the nature, structure and role of DNA and the basic proteins closely associated with them. Many mysteries remain but he and his colleagues were certainly responsible for much of our present knowledge. It is impossible to follow here in detail those investigations but we may note some of the experimental techniques and overall findings.

True to his usual habits J.A.V. wrote several overall reviews of the situation which severally summarize the concepts in vogue at different times (141, 159, 161, 187, 210, 222).

One of the objects of the research was obviously to throw light on the basic nature of the malignant transformation, though this was seen in the wider context of the significance of the Crick–Watson model in relation to gene control. A useful review of this aspect of the research may be found in a paper on nuclear proteins of normal and cancer cells (198).

At first, progress was slow but as the work proceeded during the early 1960s the methods of purification, separation and analysis became more effective. A short communication (122) on the fractionation of deoxyribonucleoprotein first discussed the ratio of lysine-rich and arginine-rich components of thymus histone, a subject developed with much skill and tenacity later with both normal and malignant tissues. The original fractionation process by column chromatography (168) of whole calf thymus histone gave three fractions, a lysine-rich histone ($F_1$), an arginine-rich histone $F_3$) and an intermediate $F_2$ which later separated into two fractions (182) and finally into three, $F_2a1$, $F_2ab$ and $F_2b$. These five histones remain as 'substantially single components', though many complexities, related for example to minor components, remain.

These studies went hand in hand with work on the effects of ionizing radiation (which J.A.V. always thought surprisingly large) and the 'mustards' (127). It was suggested that anything which breaks the DNA–histone bond will completely upset the mechanism of mitosis and reduplication could not even occur 'if the DNA particle is prevented from being opened up'. The breakage of a comparatively few histone–protein bonds will prevent DNA synthesis. But 'at the moment we are in the position of a man who tries to elucidate the mechanism of a telephone exchange by throwing bricks into it and observing some of the results'.

Much effort was directed by J.A.V. and his team to the study of the heterogeneity of the DNA 'particles' by a wide range of physical techniques. Thus use was made of sedimentation (revealing surprisingly large heterogeneity) (131), light scattering and measurement of viscosity under a range of conditions, as well as chromatographic procedures (155, 156, 161). The results were often discordant and not consistent with 'rigid rod' or 'flexible coil' models, so that there was much speculation as to molecular mass, shape and rigidity.

As the work developed, interest increasingly centred around the histones as part of the mechanism controlling the replication and function of chromosomes, and necessarily with cell differentiation and gene function generally.

Problems of species and tissue specificity of histones were investigated, showing normally surprisingly little, at least within mammalian species.

It was suggested that histones do not distinguish individual genes but classes of genes having different functions, e.g. operator genes or regulator and structural genes. It could well be, it seemed, that histones are involved in a repressor system similar to that postulated by Jacob and Monod for bacteria, but the manner in which particular types of histone could be added or removed from a gene or groups of genes has not become apparent.

Though experimental studies of the interaction of histones and DNA have shown little signs of specificity, the fact that histones decrease the ability of DNA to act as a template for DNA-dependent RNA synthesis *in vitro* is well established. Of course, the composition (amino-acid analysis) for the various fractions has been well determined (222) and the C— and N— terminal groups defined. The difficulty in understanding the nature of the control of the template activity of DNA in differentiated cells by histones lies in lack of knowledge of mechanisms determining the presence or absence of such repressors in genes.

Again the problem of specificity raises its head since the number of types of histone appear quite incapable of coping with the large variety of situations in which particular sets of genes require to be activated. J.A.V. himself suggested (210) that histones occur as unspecific repressors which cover the genes which are to remain inactive throughout the life of the differentiated cell, though, as he recognized, this leaves open the problem of pattern maintenance in successive generations.

It is appropriate to end this account of his research with emphasis on a very fundamental unsolved biological problem. As we shall see, he believed that the main effort in relation to the cancer problem should be directed to basic biological research designed to elucidate the mechanisms of normal cells. Such elucidation could only come by meticulous detailed investigation. He believed that science progresses by what we might call infinitesimal accretion, very rarely by flights of imagination, though clearly both are necessary.

He was always critical and he never claimed to have 'solved' major problems, but it may well be that his work will prove to be of greater significance than at present appears, in relation to cell function, particularly gene control, in both normal and pathological organisms.

Leaving his detailed original research we now turn to another important facet of his activities.

## Published books and general interests

J.A.V. was, as we have seen, one of the most distinguished physical chemists of his day, a man of considerable originality, intellectual power, vast detailed knowledge and tenacity. Living it seemed an inner intellectual life deep within himself, he found it difficult to communicate this activity verbally, yet in the writing of a series of lucid texts, mostly in the form of surveys of existing knowledge, he succeeded admirably in breaking down this real if invisible barrier. He had the power of presenting a simple yet adequate picture of fundamental biological phenomena. 'Students' at all levels of attainment read him with pleasure and are grateful.

Some, indeed, might argue that his greatest influence and significance arose from these books, and though it would be tedious to attempt a detailed review of all of them perhaps some individual comment may be pertinent.

The earliest publications up to about 1950 were of a fairly severe technical character, moderately advanced textbooks, setting out with remarkable clarity and explicitness the foundations, historical, mathematical and experimental of his subject. Later the emphasis changed and though he continued to write some surveys of modern biological science his books reflected wider interests, particularly the social significance of science or such profound questions as the relation between mental phenomena, consciousness and its physical basis.

His first book, *The chemical elements and their compounds*, an introduction to the study of inorganic chemistry from modern standpoints, was based he tells us, on courses of lectures delivered to students working for the B.Sc. degree in the University College of Swansea. The first edition was published in 1927 and the second in 1930 after his move to Edinburgh.

From its nature it naturally contains little that is original except perhaps the order and relative significance in which various facets of the subject are arranged. J.A.V. explains his wish to 'remove the reproach that inorganic chemistry is a great number of uncoordinated facts with no unifying theory'. Very properly, for his audience, the properties of electrolytes are introduced early and immediately followed by an account of an elementary electron theory of valency. These were, of course, the heady days of simple Bohr atoms and their almost architectural electronic shells which provided the unifying principles sought for in inorganic chemistry. The classical Rutherford or Bragg physical contributions to atomic theory were treated extensively later in the book.

The next book, *Chemical thermodynamics*, is probably the most influential he ever wrote, for it became the standard text for students for many years. It was, he explained, the outcome of several years' experience in teaching the subject. Part I, originally published in 1928, contained an account of elementary theory and electrochemistry, and was followed in 1932 by Part II covering more advanced discussion of thermodynamic functions (energy, free energy, entropy and their partial derivatives). The two parts appeared combined in one volume in 1946, were reprinted with corrections in 1949, 1951, 1955 and 1960, with a fifth edition in 1962 and 1965. The introduction explains the two methods of approach to the study of chemical or physical processes, namely the kinetic standpoint or that founded on considerations of energy change. Interestingly, in view of some of his later writing, analogy is drawn with the study of social phenomena, with the behaviour of individuals or of large assemblages. The book kept its place for forty years as an excellent text surveying a very wide field. Part of its success doubtless arises from its limitation of mathematical demonstration to the simplest but still precise form, while at the same time illustrating the theoretical analysis with significant practical examples. As an introduction to more advanced theory, in later editions a chapter was added by W. J. C. Orr of the University of Glasgow on the application of statistical mechanics to the determination of thermodynamic quantities, though some preliminaries of the relationship between entropy and probability had already been given by J.A.V. himself. The book of course reflects the firm grasp of the subject J.A.V. acquired over many years, particularly in his editing of Gibbs's papers.

The next two books may conveniently be linked together. *Electrocapillarity—the chemistry and physics of electrodes and other charged surfaces*, appeared in 1940, but in 1951 J.A.V. combined with several of his friends and colleagues (notably J. M. Creeth, P. A. Charlwood, T. R. Bolum, M. B. M'Ewen, J. O'M. Bockris and W. F. Floyd) to publish *Electrical phenomena at interfaces in chemistry, physics and biology*. This is the first time that 'biology' appears in one of his titles, and J.A.V.'s own development is mirrored here. At first a classical physical chemist, we watch his gradual transfer of interest, via the study of electrical phenomena at surfaces, to the problems of complex biological structures and processes. As he himself expressed it in the preface to *Electrical phenomena at interfaces*, his aim was that 'The biological scientist will, it is hoped, be better able to judge the nature of the physical concepts which enter into their interpretations'. His own contributions to the book are physico-chemical, and concern such subjects as electrical potential differences and their origin, the electrical double layer, electrocapillarity, concentration polarization and the deposition of metals or the behaviour of oxygen and hydrogen at electrodes. Much of the more biological flavour of the volume is due to W. F. Floyd writing on membrane potentials and electrical properties of living cells as well as electrical properties of nerve and muscle.

Henceforth, though some of J.A.V.'s books are still semi-technical guides to the state of biological science, semi-popular descriptions of cellular structures and mechanisms, a new emphasis appears. It now embraces the significance of science, particularly biological science to human society, as well as animadversions on philosophy, art, religion and much else.

*Man is a microcosm* (1950) is described as 'a broad survey and interpretation of present knowledge of the nature and basis of life'. It was to explain 'what science has found out about living things, and also to bring out the repercussions which this knowledge had had on thought of recent times and on the picture which ordinary people have of life and human nature'. The text opens with the question 'What is life?' and, not surprisingly, ends with Newton wondering on the sea shore! Here as elsewhere J.A.V. argues for the significance of man in the Universe. He feels that the demonstration that the Universe can be 'explained' mechanically has depressed man to a 'unit of man-power'. 'Even scientists are referred to today in Government reports, as so much scientific-man-power.' This is a recurrent theme particularly in the earlier books, and doubtless lay at the root of another favourite study of his, namely the nature of consciousness, the structure and mode of working of the human brain. How can consciousness arise and develop in and from a concatenation of atoms and molecules, however complex? How can thought, free will and creative activities arise from such structures? Not surprisingly there are no firm answers but much interesting questioning. It is interesting to re-read the more 'technical' parts of the book and see how, in the nearly thirty years sinces its publication, biological understanding and detailed knowledge of mechanism have moved on. In biology, as yet we had no helix, and little on the structure of proteins or DNA, or the complexity of gene control or the mystery of differentiation. J.A.V.'s books summarize exactly our state of knowledge at a given time and place. They are, as it were, intellectual maps with a notice saying 'You are here', and as such may be valuable historically.

The next of his books, *Science and human life: successes and limitations* (dedicated to his wife Lois and first published in 1957) is, in the present writer's view, perhaps the most interesting of all. It is divided into two parts, 'Science and the individual' and 'Science and human society'.

The approach is almost apolitical and mostly summarizes various viewpoints. One of the most interesting and original chapters is that on 'Imagination in human life'. It emphasizes the importance of imagination in the study of language, in science and the 'creative output of human communities', including such activities as that of the 'story teller' (Homer and Plato).

J.A.V. was an amateur painter of considèrable skill, mostly in a robust imaginative vein. It is therefore interesting to read that he considered 'all primitive art purposeful rather than representational'; it is to create neither accurate representation nor 'beautiful' (but 'significant') objects. In the long tradition of European art 'pictures have hardly ever been merely to convey information but the human meaning of scenes or to induce feelings'.

J.A.V. has much to say of the limitations of 'photography' and liberation of the artist from 'representation'. Is it necessary to have any recognizable features at all, 'any resemblances to the world' ? He roams over a wide field from Braque to Picasso with the latter's symbolic bitter comment on human affairs.

J.A.V.'s own painting was, it would seem to the writer, more influenced by Cézanne or Van Gogh, attempting to stress 'unfamiliar aspects of primal energy'.

His discussion of music as an independent mode of expression of greater abstraction than speech is interesting. He himself had a fine collection of 'discs'. His favourite composers were Schubert and Mahler. I think he would not have claimed to be expert as an instrumental performer on any instrument though the present writer remembers on some few occasions attempting to 'accompany' on the piano J.A.V.'s playing of a recorder! 'Melancholy' is probably the appropriate descriptive adjective!

Returning to the book, a depressing chapter, 'Science and the future of humanity' reminds us of the now even more familiar theme that Science has raised living standards but 'does not seem to produce contentment, or even stability'. Much of the difficulty he thinks lies in communication between individuals. One suspects that J.A.V. felt acutely that the normal method of communicating with others, by means of speech, is a very indirect one. 'You cannot really communicate to another person exactly what you see and still less what you feel about it. You can only communicate in symbols what you hope will call up the response you expect.'

His next book, *Inside the living cell* (1959, 1962), is of a very different character, largely a description of biological research and concepts. It was followed in 1968 by *Gene control in the living cell*, notable for one of the few references he makes to his own work on histones and containing one of his most complete discussions of the cancer problem. The treatment of the subject is wide-ranging and though offering little that is original his account outlines and pulls together admirably the known facts. This text serves as a good introduction to the present scientific position, and includes discussion of methods of treatment of the disease. J.A.V. took little, if any, direct part in clinical day to day treatment of patients, though he expressed the wish to have been able to do more, but maintaining, 'that the best hope for the future will lie in a greater basic knowledge of the functioning of the human body, especially the mechanisms of gene control which will at least lay bare the nature of the disease'. He had great scorn of 'breakthroughs' and solutions 'just around the corner', an attitude which sometimes contrasted sharply with that of his colleagues. Given his character, temperament and abilities, who can doubt that so far as he personally was concerned his judgement was right? In his writings he continually emphasized our ignorance and had little use for the specious certainty of 'the Media' men.

*The life process*, next of his books (1970, 1971), intended for students beginning university studies, lays great stress on the overwhelming evidence that 'the basic mechanisms of life are indeed common to all organisms so that it is now possible to present the life process in a unitary fashion'.

His last book, *Modern biology and its human implications* (1976), reverts to a description of technical advance and chapters on Science and ethics and Science and belief. Again, he discusses the relation of molecules and consciousness. With the decay of traditional beliefs and the great authority which Science has acquired is it possible to establish scientifically a principle of *value* on which conduct can be based? Is the ideal conduct to assist general evolutionary processes, or perhaps improvement of survival of the individual? Science has, he thinks, provided an objective way of studying how societies behave and may be able to assess to some extent the influence of their belief on their way of life.

Brought up, as his diary shows, in the Anglican tradition he emphasizes now the influence of Christianity, interpreting doctrinal elements in Christianity very broadly, and asking that central statements of faith be taken as symbols of profound truth. The Universe is not, he believes, a pointless accident. Is it too much to hope that the Western world can gain unity in a Christianity which does not insist on its supernatural elements?

Looking over the whole extraordinary range of writing one is left with a feeling of an author of great integrity of purpose, of notable originality, able to grasp and convey to others not only the facts, but the fever of intellectual excitement which lies behind the unfolding of the scientific concepts.

## Professional activities

J.A.V. was a Fellow of the Chemical Society and a local representative for the Edinburgh district from 1936–1939. He was also a Fellow of the Royal Institute of Chemistry and of the Biochemical Society. He had particularly close association with the Faraday Society, being a Fellow and on its Council from 1953 to 1960, and a Vice-President from 1957 to 1960. He was Chairman of the Colloid and Biophysics Committee of the Faraday Society from 1957 and Chairman of the Biophysics section of the Society from 1958 to 1959, which resulted in the establishment of the British Biophysical Society. Among his international commitments we note that he was a member of the International Union of Pure and Applied Biophysics from its inception in 1966 and Secretary of the Commission of Molecular Biophysics from 1965 to 1969.

He was elected a Fellow of the Royal Society in 1956.

In view of his many writings it is perhaps not surprising that his skills as an editor were in demand and he edited *Progress in Biophysics and Biophysical Chemistry* (Pergamon) for a number of years with various partners, namely Professor J. T. (now Sir John) Randall, F.R.S. (vols I–V), Professor B. (now Sir Bernard) Katz, F.R.S. (vols. VII–XII), Dr H. E. Huxley, F.R.S. (vols XIII–XVII), and Dr D. Noble (vol. XVIII). Vol. VI he edited alone.

## Family life

In 1929 J.A.V. married Margaret Lois Hope (at Haddington, East Lothian), the daughter of John Deans Hope (1860–1949) Liberal Member of Parliament for West Fife and later for East Lothian, and Elizabeth Holms-Kerr (1872–1954). J.A.V. was fortunate in a gracious and understanding partner, herself a botanist and Cambridge graduate with wide interests. Many of us remember with deep pleasure hospitality received, perhaps sitting in the spacious garden of their home at Nightingale Corner (Rickmansworth).

Their three children have attained success in professions allied to biological and medical science, the eldest son, Gavin, as an adviser on agricultural problems and William as a pathologist interested in cell injury related to carcinogenesis, particularly by aflotoxins. He has supplied illustrations for his father's books. Their daughter Elizabeth Warrington, a D.Sc. of the University of London, is a distinguished neuropathologist with special interest in memory and perceptual disorders in patients with cerebral lesions. There are seven grandchildren.

## Personal characteristics

J.A.V. would certainly be described as a strong personality. Of medium height and sturdy build he gave an impression of physical strength. His fresh complexion, blue eyes, 'outdoor' look and contemplative expression reminded one instantly of his farming origins. His method of walking was characteristic. Slightly bent with shoulders thrust forward, his eyes apparently focused on the ground about a metre ahead (where he was probably contemplating an 'idea' not a physical object) he strode at a brisk pace which it seemed he could maintain indefinitely. He and the writer (during their Birmingham period) went on a walking tour together in Switzerland and Northern Italy and I well remember the physical effort to keep up and the struggle against the ever widening gap as the day went on. Somewhat inhibiting to conversation!

He personally rarely initiated a joke but much appreciated some. If a joke judged worthy of attention was made he would, characteristically, respond with a rather disconcerting grin followed by one or two staccato bursts of hearty and appreciative laughter followed by an equally sudden silence or low chuckle.

He was courteous, thoughtful and friendly. His American friend, Professor Roger M. Herriott of Johns Hopkins, described him as 'a gentleman of the old school', and as having some of the characteristics of an absent minded professor. J.A.V. could be suddenly and surprisingly angry if he thought injustice, for example, was being done.

He evidently preferred to write or paint in front of the drawing room fire in the presence of his family rather than in the study upstairs—a somewhat trying preference for the family!

His absent mindedness was proverbial. Dr Johns, one of his close collaborators, in an obituary notice in *Nature* describes how he had seen him return from an Academic Board meeting with two hats, one on his head and one in his hand, hotly pursued by the rightful owner of the second hat. A few years ago after we had both attended a Royal Society conversazione I had a midnight telephone call from J.A.V. apologizing for having taken my raincoat. In fact, it certainly was not mine—whether the rightful owner was ever identified is unknown. His lack of pens and pencils, the gun-fight he caused in Chicago by losing his briefcase, his complaining about not receiving any change only to find it in his coffee when he stirred it, are local legends. A screech of car brakes in the Fulham Road was often the sign that J.A.V. was crossing the road. While attending an international conference in Moscow, not being readily amenable to restraints, he would recount with feeling his resentment at the large Russian ladies who attempted to pilot him along the correct corridor or through the right door of his hotel, or how the only way to find a seat was to take a sight-seeing bus ride!

In committees he normally said very little and sometimes conveyed by his silence a certain slight contempt for the whole proceedings, doubtless often well justified. Administration, I think, interested him very little.

Modest, but not unaware of some unusual intellectual powers, he must be one of the least 'auto-referring' authors, for he scarcely ever refers in his books to his own contributions.

After his retirement particularly, he was frequently to be seen at the Royal Institution for which he had a special affection, striding up Albemarle Street or in the library which he much appreciated and loved. He might also be seen there with his grandchildren at the Christmas Lectures. He and his wife Lois made a number of tours abroad, particularly to the Mediterranean and the Middle East. These travels evidently pleased him greatly.

A very private man, difficult to know, but one for whom many of us came to have a very real admiration and affection.

The writer wishes to express thanks for information received from Professor Franz Bergel, F.R.S., Professor F. Dickens, F.R.S., and Professor E.

Boyland. Professor Roger M. Herriott kindly commented on J.A.V.'s activities while in the United States.

Dr E. W. Johns kindly read the typescript and made useful comments particularly on the later work on histones.

Mr Dennis Brunning, Librarian of the Institute of Cancer Research, provided a partial bibliography which was of great assistance in the final compilation.

Most valuable of all was the sympathetic help of Mrs Lois Butler who kindly allowed the use of the diary and other personal papers as well as making suggestions as to sources of information and discussing various aspects of the text.

The photograph was taken about 1965 by Mr K. G. Moreman, Head of the Photographic Department of the Institute of Cancer Research.

## Appointments

Oct. 1922–26 Assistant Lecturer in Chemistry, University College of Swansea under Professor J. E. Coates.

1926–39 Lecturer in Chemistry, University of Edinburgh.

1939–41 Rockefeller Fellow at Rockefeller Institute for Medical Research, Princeton, N.J. (In laboratory of Dr J. H. Northrop.)

1941–44 Executive Officer at British Commonwealth Scientific Office, Washington, D.C.

1944–46 Lecturer in Chemistry, University of Edinburgh.

1946–49 Courtauld Research Fellow in Courtauld Institute for Biochemistry, Middlesex Hospital, Medical School, London W1.

1949–52 Physical Chemist at Chester Beatty Research Institute, Royal Cancer Hospital, London.

1952–66 Professor of Physical Chemistry in University of London at Institute of Cancer Research: Royal Cancer Hospital, London. Member of Academic Board and Committee of Management from 1949

## Bibliography

### *Papers*

(1) 1923 (With S. R. Carter) The kinetics of the reaction between ferrous phosphate and sulphur dioxide in phosphoric acid solution. *Trans. chem. Soc.* **123**, 2370.

(2) 1924 Studies in heterogeneous equilibria. I. Conditions at the boundary surface of crystalline solids and liquids. II. The kinetic interpretation of Nernst's theory. III. A kinetic theory of reversible oxidation potentials. *Trans. Faraday Soc.* **19**, 729, 734.

(3) IV. The solubility of strong electrolytes, *J. phys. Chem.* **28**, 438.

(4) On the relation between metal contact potentials and the Peltier effect. *Phil Mag.* **48**, 1924.

(5) On the seat of the electromotive force in the galvanic cell. *Phil. Mag.* **48**, 927.

(6) Löslichkeit, Lösungswärme und Gitterenergie von Salzen. *Z. phys. Chem.* **113**, 279.

(7) 1925 Co-ordination and co-valency. *Trans. Faraday Soc.* **21**, 1.

(8) The relation between the deviations from Raoult's law and the partial heats of solution. *J. Am. chem. Soc.* **47**, 117.

(9) 1926 (With E. S. Hiscocks) The solubilities of thallous chloride in salt solutions at 0°, 25°, and 50°, and its heats of solution. *J. chem. Soc.* p. 2554.

(10) (With W. E. Hugh & D. H. Hey) A note on the effect of the electrode material on oxidation potentials. *Trans. Faraday Soc.* **22**, part 1.

(11) (With S. R. Carter & F. James) The oxidation potential of the system selenium dioxide–selenium. *J. chem. Soc.* p. 930.

(12) The equilibrium of heterogeneous systems including electrolytes. I. Fundamental equations and phase rule. *Proc. R. Soc. Lond.* A **112**, 129.

(13) 1927 The equilibrium of heterogeneous systems including electrolytes. II. Equilibrium at interfaces and the theory of electrocapillarity. *Proc. R. Soc. Lond.* A **113**, 594.

(14) A note on the electric potentials of ions in salt solutions. *Phil. Mag.* **iii**, 213.

(15) 1929 The mutual salting-out of ions. *J. phys. Chem.* **33**, 1015.

(16) (With C. M. Robertson) The behaviour of electrolytes in mixed solvents. I. The free energies and heat contents of hydrogen chloride in water–ethyl alcohol solutions. *Proc. R. Soc. Lond.* A **125**, 694.

(17) The equilibrium of heterogeneous systems including electrolytes. III. The effect of an electric field on the adsorption of organic molecules, and the interpretation of electro-capillary curves. *Proc. R. Soc. Lond.* A **122**, 399.

(18) 1930 (With C. Ockrent) Studies in electrocapillarity. I. The electrocapillarity curves of organic acids and their salts. *J. phys. Chem.* **34**, 2286.

(19) (With C. Ockrent) Studies in electrocapillarity. II. Selective adsorption in solutions containing two active substances. *J. phys. Chem.* **34**, 2297.

(20) (With C. Ockrent) Studies in electrocapillarity. III. The surface tension of solutions containing two surface-active solutes. *J. phys. Chem.* **34**, 2841.

(21) (With C. Ockrent & A. Wightman) Studies in electrocapillarity. IV. The effects of salts on the electrocapillary curves of solutions containing surface active substances. *J. phys. Chem.* **35**, 3296.

(22) (With R. Shaw) The behaviour of electrolytes in mixed solvents. II. The effect of lithium chloride on the activities of water and alcohol in mixed solutions. *Proc. R. Soc. Lond.* A **129**, 519.

(23) (With A. D. Lees) The behaviour of electrolytes in mixed solvents. III. The molecular refractivities and partial molar volumes of lithium chloride in water–ethyl alcohol solutions. *Proc. R. Soc. Lond.* A **131**, 382.

(24) 1932 (With R. T. Hamilton) The behaviour of electrolytes in mixed solvents. IV. The free energy of zinc chloride in water–alcohol solutions. *Proc. R. Soc. Lond.* A **138**, 450.

(25) (With G. Armstrong) The kinetics of electrode processes. Depolarisation effects by hydrogen and oxygen at platinum electrodes. *Proc. R. Soc. Lond.* A **137**, 604.

(26) The thermodynamics of the surfaces of solutions. *Proc. R. Soc. Lond.* A **135**, 348.

(27) (With A. Wightman) Adsorption at the surface of solutions. I. The surface composition of water–alcohol solutions. *J. chem. Soc.* p. 2089.

(28) (With A. D. Lees) Adsorption at the surface of solutions. II. The effect of lithium chloride on the surface of water–alcohol solutions. *J. chem. Soc.* p. 2097.

(29) The mechanism of overvoltage and its relation to the combination of hydrogen atoms at metal electrodes. *Trans. Faraday Soc.* **28**, 379.

(30) 1933 (With G. Armstrong) The kinetics of electrode processes. II. Reversible reduction and oxidation processes. *Proc. R. Soc. Lond.* A **139**, 406.

(31) (With G. Armstrong & F. R. Himsworth) The kinetics of electrode processes. III. The behaviour of platinum and gold electrodes in sulphuric acid and alkaline solutions containing oxygen. *Proc. R. Soc. Lond.* A **143**, 89.

(32) (With G. Armstrong) The rate of decay of hydrogen and oxygen overvoltages. *Trans. Faraday Soc.* **29**, 1261.

(33) (With W. C. Vosburgh & L. C. Connell) The electrostriction produced by salts in some aliphatic alcohols. *J. chem. Soc.* p. 933.

(34) (With D. W. Thomson & W. H. Maclennan) The free energy of the normal aliphatic alcohols in aqueous solution. (I. The partial vapour pressures of aqueous solutions of methyl, n-propyl, and n-butyl alcohols. II. The solubilities of some normal aliphatic alcohols in water. III. The theory of binary solutions, and its application to aqueous–alcoholic solutions.) *J. chem. Soc.* p. 674.

(35) (With G. Armstrong) Electrometric titrations with oxygen electrodes. *Trans. Faraday Soc.* **29**, 862.

(36) (With D. W. Thomson) The behaviour of electrolytes in mixed solvents. V. The free energy of lithium chloride in water–alcohol mixtures and the salting-out of alcohol. *Proc. R. Soc. Lond.* A **141**, 86.

(37) 1934 (With R. T. HAMILTON & L. C. CONNELL) The behaviour of electrolytes in mixed solvents. VI. The electrical conductivities of some salts in water–ethyl alcohol solutions. *Proc. R. Soc. Lond.* A **147**, 418.

(38) (With W. J. ORR) Factors determining electrolytic dissociation and the energy of dissociation of salt molecules. *Phil. Mag.* **18**, 778.

(39) (With G. ARMSTRONG) The anodic passivation of gold in chloride solutions. *Trans. Faraday Soc.* **30**, 1173.

(40) (With A. WIGHTMAN & W. H. MACLENNAN) Adsorption at the surface of solutions. III. The surface structure of solutions of the lower aliphatic alcohols. *J. chem. Soc.* p. 528.

(41) (With F. R. HIMSWORTH) Adsorption at the surface of solutions. IV. Adsorption constants in solutions containing two solutes. *J. chem. Soc.* p. 532.

(42) (With G. ARMSTRONG) The electrolytic properties of hydrogen. (I. Hydrogen as an anodic depolariser. II. Effect of anodic polarisation of the platinum electrodes.) *J. chem. Soc.* p. 743.

(43) 1935 (With C. N. RAMCHANDANI & D. W. THOMSON) The solubility of non-electrolytes. I. The free energy of hydration of some aliphatic alcohols. *J. chem. Soc.* p. 280.

(44) (With C. N. RAMCHANDANI) The solubility of non-electrolytes. II. The influence of the polar group on the free energy of hydration of aliphatic compounds. *J. chem. Soc.* p. 952.

(45) (With W. J. C. ORR) The rate of diffusion of deuterium hydroxide in water. *J. chem. Soc.* p. 1273.

(46) 1936 (With W. S. REID) The solubility of non-electrolytes. III. The entropy of hydration. *J. chem. Soc.* p. 1171.

(47) Hydrogen overvoltage and the reversible hydrogen electrode. *Proc. R. Soc. Lond.* A **157**, 423.

(48) (With G. DREVER) The mechanism of electrolytic processes. I. The anodic oxidation of some metals of the platinum group. *Trans. Faraday Soc.* **32**, 427.

(49) (With W. M. LESLIE) The mechanism of electrolytic processes. II. The electrolytic oxidation of sodium sulphite. *Trans. Faraday Soc.* **32**, 435.

(50) (With W. M. LESLIE) The mechanism of electrolytic processes. III. Irreversible reductions. *Trans. Faraday Soc.* **32**, 989.

(51) (With J. C. HORNEL) The rates of some acid- and base-catalysed reactions and the dissociation constants of weak acids in 'heavy' water. *J. chem. Soc.* p. 1361.

(52) 1937 The energy and entropy of hydration of organic compounds. *Trans. Faraday Soc.* **33**, 229.

(53) (With P. HARROWER) The activities of some aliphatic alcohols and halides in non-polar solvents. *Trans. Faraday Soc.* **33**, 171.

(54) (With W. J. C. ORR) The kinetic and thermodynamic activity of protons and deuterons in water–deuterium oxide solutions. *J. chem. Soc.* p. 330.

(55) 1938 (With J. D. PEARSON) The mechanism of electrolytic processes. IV. A cathode ray oscillographic study of the anodic passivation of gold in chlorine solutions. *Trans. Faraday Soc.* **34**, 806.

(56) (With I. M. BARCLAY) The entropy of solution. *Trans. Faraday Soc.* **34**, 1445.

(57) Die elektrolytische Trennung von Wasserstoff und Deuterium und die katalysierte Austauschreaktion $HD+H_2O = H_2+HDO$. *Z. Elektrochem.* **44**, 55.

(58) (With W. E. NELSON) Experiments with heavy water on the acid hydrolysis of esters and the alkaline decomposition of diacetone alcohol. *J. chem. Soc.* p. 957.

(59) Intermolecular forces and the properties of liquids. *Ann. Rep. Chem. Soc., 1937*, p. 75.

(60) The behaviour of electrolytes in mixed solvents. Meeting of the British Association, p. 65.

(61) 1939 (With D. C. MARTIN) The dissociation constants of some nitrophenols in deuterium oxide. *J. chem. Soc.* p. 1366.

(62) 1940 The use of solubility as a criterion of purity of proteins. (I. Application of the phase rule to the solubility of proteins. II. The solubility curves and purity of chymotrypsinogen.) *J. gen. Physiol.* **24**, 189.

(63) (With I. M. BARCLAY) Some observations on the double layer capacity at mercury electrodes. *Trans. Faraday Soc.* **36**, 128.

(64) 1941 On the formation of chymotrypsin from chymotrypsinogen. *J. Am. chem. Soc.* **63**, 2968.

(65) The theory of the hydrogen overvoltage. *J. chem. Phys.* **9**, 279.

(66) The molecular kinetics of trypsin action. *J. Am. chem. Soc.* **63**, 2971.

(67) 1946 Life and the second law of thermodynamics. *Nature, Lond.* **158**, 153.

(68) William James Coltart Orr 1911–1946 (obituary). *J. chem. Soc.* p. 759.

(69) 1947 (With G. Armstrong) Electrochemical periodicities in the anodic polarisation of platinum electrodes in the presence of hydrogen and their significance. *Discuss. Faraday Soc.* no. 1, p. 122.

(70) (With J. M. L. Stephen) An apparatus for preparative electrophoresis. *Nature, Lond.* **160** 469.

(71) Enzymes: their isolation, structure, uses, mode of action and place in nature. Cantor Lectures. (I. Isolation and nature. II. Their mode of action and structure. III. Their formation and place in nature.) *Jl R. Soc. Arts* **95**, 715.

(72) 1948 (With D. M. P. Phillips & J. M. L. Stephen) The core of the insulin molecule. *Nature, Lond.* **162**, 418.

(73) (With J. M. L. Stephen) A preparative electrophoresis apparatus. *Research* **1**. 525.

(74) (With E. C. Dodds, D. M. P. Phillips & J. M. L. Stephen) The action of chymotrypsin and trypsin on insulin. *Biochem. J.* **42**, 116.

(75) (With E. C. Dodds, D. M. P. Phillips & J. M. L. Stephen) The action of pepsin on insulin and the plastein question. *Biochem. J.* **42**, 122.

(76) Rockefeller Institute for Medical Research, Princeton. *Nature, Lond.* **162**, 479.

(77) 1949 (With E. C. Dodds, D. M. P. Phillips & J. M. L. Stephen) The action of trypsin on insulin. *Biochem. J.* **44**, 224.

(78) (With G. L. Mills) Concentration of the toxic substance from 'agenized' flour. *Nature, Lond.* **163**, 835.

(79) 1950 (With B. E. Conway & K. A. Smith) The degradation of deoxyribonucleic acid (DNA) by chemical agents and by free radicals. *Trans. Faraday Soc.* **46**, 794. (Abstract.)

(80) (With B. E. Conway & L. Gilbert) The molecular weights of degraded deoxyribonucleic acids. *Trans. Faraday Soc.* **46**, 795. (Abstract.)

(81) Early scientific links between Scotland and America. In: *An eighteenth century lectureship in chemistry* (ed. A. Kent), p. 151. Glasgow: Jackson.

(82) (With K. A. Smith) Degradation of deoxyribonucleic acid by free radicals. *Nature, Lond.* **165**, 847.

(83) (With L. A. Gilbert & K. A. Smith) Radiomimetic action of sulphur and nitrogen 'mustards' on deoxyribonucleic acid. *Nature, Lond.* **165**, 714.

(84) (With K. A. Smith) The action of ionizing radiations and of radiomimetic substances on deoxyribonucleic acid. I. The action of some compounds of the 'mustard' type. *J. chem. Soc.* p. 3411.

(85) (With B. E. Conway) The action of ionizing radiations and of radiomimetic substances on deoxyribonucleic acid. II. The effect of oxygen on the degradation of the nucleic acid by X-rays. *J. chem. Soc.* p. 3418.

(86) (With D. M. P. Phillips, J. M. L. Stephen & J. M. Creeth) Some properties of the insulin core. *Biochem. J.* **46**, 74.

(87) Centenary of the second law of thermodynamics. *Nature, Lond.* **165**, 164.

(88) Nature of nucleotoxic substances. *Nature, Lond.* **166**, 18.

(89) (With B. E. Conway & L. Gilbert) The action of ionizing radiations and of radiomimetic substances on deoxyribonucleic acid. III. The molecular weights of deoxyribonucleic acid degraded by X-rays and by treatment with a 'nitrogen mustard'. *J. chem. Soc.* p. 3421.

(90) Commentary: Scientific views of man. *Research* **3**, 485.

(91) 1951 (With D. W. F. James) Gel-like behaviour of deoxyribonucleic acid solutions. *Nature, Lond.* **167**, 844.

(92) (With B. E. Conway, L. Gilbert & K. A. Smith) Chemical analogies in the action of ionizing radiations and of radiomimetic chemicals on nucleic acid. *Acta Un. int. Cancr.* **7**, 443.

(93) (With L. Gilbert, D. W. F. James & W. C. J. Ross) Degradation of deoxyribonucleic acid by a 'nitrogen mustard'. *Nature, Lond.* **168**, 985.

(94) 1951 (With B. E. CONWAY & D. W. F. JAMES) The state of thymonucleic acid solutions and the effect of certain reagents thereon. *J. Chim. phys.* **48**, 609.

(95) 1952 Josiah Willard Gibbs. *Nature, Lond.* **169**, 383.

(96) (With E. M. PRESS) The action of ionizing radiations and of radiomimetic substances on deoxyribonucleic acid. IV. The products of the action of di-(2-chloroethyl)methylamine. *J. chem. Soc.* p. 626.

(97) (With B. E. CONWAY) The action of ionizing radiations and of radiomimetic substances on deoxyribonucleic acid. V. Some experiments on the action of X-rays and free radicals. *J. chem. Soc.* p. 834.

(98) The nucleic acid of the chromosomes. *Endeavour* **11**, 154.

(99) (With L. GILBERT & D. W. F. JAMES) The action of ionizing radiations and of radiomimetic substances on deoxyribonucleic acid. VI: Physicochemical measurements of the action of bischloroethylmethylamine. *J. chem. Soc.* p. 3268.

(100) (With B. E. CONWAY) The action of denaturing agents on deoxyribonucleic acid. *J. chem. Soc.* p. 3075.

(101) 1953 (With B. E. CONWAY) Effects of salts on interactions in polyelectrolyte solutions. *Nature, Lond.* **172**, 153.

(102) (With E. J. AMBROSE) Swelling and orientation phenomena with nucleoprotein films. *Discuss. Faraday Society* no. 13, p. 261.

(103) Biological applications. *Trans. Faraday Soc.* **49**, 575.

(104) (With B. E. CONWAY) The action of photochemically generated radicals from hydrogen peroxide on deoxyribonucleic acid and simple model substances. *Proc. R. Soc. Lond.* B **141**, 562.

(105) (With B. E. CONWAY) Effect of rate of shear on the reduced viscosities of thymus nucleic acid solutions. *J. Polym. Sci.* **11**, 277.

(106) (With B. E. CONWAY) The role of oxygen in the after-effects of X-irradiation on deoxyribonucleic acid. *Trans. Faraday Soc.* **49**, 327.

(107) 1954 Contribution to discussion on the mechanism of the 'after-effect' in the irradiation of aqueous solutions of deoxyribonucleic acid with X rays. *Br. J. Radiol.* **27**, 49.

(108) (With B. E. CONWAY) Effects of salts on the interaction of nucleic acid particles. *J. Polym. Sci.* **12**, 199.

(109) (With P. F. DAVISON, D. W. F. JAMES & K. V. SHOOTER) The histones of calf thymus deoxyribonucleoprotein. I. Preparation and homogeneity. *Biochim. biophys. Acta* **13**, 224.

(110) (With K. V. SHOOTER & P. F. DAVISON) Physical properties of thymus nucleoprotein. *Biochim. biophys. Acta* **13**, 192.

(111) (With P. F. DAVISON & K. V. SHOOTER) The physical state of thymus nucleoprotein. (Abstract.) In: Discussion on structure and properties of nucleic acids and nucleoproteins. *Trans. Faraday Soc.* **50**, 295.

(112) The chemistry of cell reproduction. *Times Sci. Rev.* no. 12, p. 13.

(113) The action of carcinogenic agents and radiations—some implications of new ideas of the structure of deoxyribonucleic acid. *Acta Un. int. Cancr.* **10**, 97.

(114) (With P. F. DAVISON & B. E. CONWAY) The nucleoprotein complex of the cell nucleus and its reactions. *Prog. Biophys. biophys. Chem.* **4**, 148.

(115) (With P. F. DAVISON, D. W. F. JAMES & K. V. SHOOTER) The characteristics of histones from calf thymus nucleoprotein. *Biochem. J.* **57**, 24.

(116) (With B. E. CONWAY & D. W. F. JAMES) The effect of salts on polyelectrolyte interactions, with special reference to deoxyribonucleic acid. *Trans. Faraday Soc.* **50**, 612.

(117) (With J. A. LUCY) Fractionation of deoxyribonucleoprotein by successive extraction with constant salt concentration. *Nature, Lond.* **174**, 32.

(118) (With P. F. DAVISON, D. W. F. JAMES & K. V. SHOOTER) The histones of calf thymus deoxyribonucleoprotein. II. Electrophoretic and sedimentation behaviour and a partial fractionation. *Biochim. biophys. Acta* **15**, 415.

(119) (With P. F. DAVISON) The fractionation and composition of histones from thymus nucleoprotein. *Biochim. biophys. Acta* **15**, 439.

(120) Mind and matter: a monist view. *Science News*, no. 34, p. 95. Harmondsworth.

(121) 1955 (With P. SIMSON) After-effects of irradiation of DNA. In: *Radiobiology Symp., Liège, 1954* (ed. Z. M. Bacq & P. Alexander), p. 46. London: Butterworth.

(122) 1955 (With J. A. LUCY) Fractionation of deoxyribonucleoprotein. *Biochim. biophys. Acta* **16**, 431.

(123) (With K. V. SHOOTER) Apparent heterogeneity of deoxyribonucleic acid: sedimentation experiments at low concentrations. *Nature, Lond.* **175**, 500.

(124) Effects of ultra-violet light on nucleic acid and nucleoproteins and other biological systems. *Experimentia* **11**, 289.

(125) (With B. E. CONWAY) The effect of salts on polyelectrolyte interactions. In: *Int. Symp. macromolec. Chemistry, Milan and Turin, 1954*. Suppl. to *Ricerca scient.* **25**, 920.

(126) L'acide nucléique considéré comme un polyélectrolyte. *Colloques int. Cent. natn Rech. scient.* **57**, 145.

(127) 1956 The action of ionizing radiations on biological materials: facts and theories. *Radiat. Res.* **4**, 20.

(128) (With J. A. LUCY) Fractionation of deoxyribonucleoprotein. *Bull. Soc. chim. Belg.* **65**, 133.

(129) (With K. V. SHOOTER and R. H. PAIN) The sedimentation behaviour of DNA and the effect of heat and X-rays. In: *Int. Congr. Biochem. Brussels, 1955*, p. 139. New York: Academic Press.

(130) (With K. V. SHOOTER) Fractionation of deoxyribonucleic acid by physical procedures. *Nature, Lond.* **177**, 1033.

(131) (With G. D. HUNTER) Stimulation by ribonucleic acid of induced β-galactosidase formation in *Bacillus megaterium*. *Biochim. biophys. Acta* **20**, 405.

(132) Effects of ultra-violet light on nucleic acid and nucleoproteins and other biological systems. In: *Int. Photobiol. Congr. Amsterdam, 1955*, p. 111. Wageningen: Veenman & Zonen.

(133) (With E. W. JOHNS, J. A. LUCY & P. SIMSON) The composition of nucleic acids prepared from rat and mouse tumours. *Br. J. Cancer* **10**, 202.

(134) (With K. V. SHOOTER & R. H. PAIN) The effect of heat and X-rays on deoxyribonucleic acid. *Biochim. biophys. Acta* **20**, 497.

(135) (With K. V. SHOOTER) Sedimentation of deoxyribonucleic acid at low concentrations. *Trans. Faraday Soc.* **52**, 734.

(136) (With P. F. DAVISON) The chemical composition of calf thymus nucleoprotein. *Biochim. biophys. Acta* **21**, 568.

(137) Effects of X-rays and radiomimetic agents on nucleic acids and nucleoproteins. In: *Ciba Fdn symp. on ionizing radiations and cell metabolism* (ed. G. E. W. Wolstenholme & C. M. O'Connor), p. 59. London: Churchill.

(138) 1957 (With K. V. SHOOTER) The physical heterogeneity of DNA. In: *Symp. on the chemical basis of heredity, 1956* (ed. W. D. McElroy & B. Glass), p. 540. Baltimore: Johns Hopkins Press.

(139) (With K. V. SHOOTER) Physical fractionation of DNA by centrifugation and other processes. *J. Polym. Sci.* **23**, 705.

(140) (With R. H. PAIN) The preparation and properties of ribonucleic acids from rat liver. *Biochem. J.* **66**, 299.

(141) (P. D. DAVISON) Deoxyribonucleoprotein, a genetic material. In: *Advances in enzymology and related subjects of biochemistry* (ed. F. F. Nord), vol. 18, p. 161. New York & London: Interscience.

(142) (With P. COHN) Fractionation of microsomal proteins by a non-ionic detergent. *Biochim. biophys. Acta* **25**, 222.

(143) (With G. D. HUNTER & A. R. CRATHORN) Sites of the incorporation of an amino-acid into proteins of *Bacillus megaterium*. *Nature, Lond.* **180**, 383.

(144) (With A. B. ROBINS & K. V. SHOOTER) The viscous behaviour of dilute solutions of a strong polyelectrolyte (polystyrene sulphonate). *Proc. R. Soc. Lond.* A **241**, 299.

(145) The genetical implications of the Watson–Crick model of deoxyribonucleic acid. In: *Congr. int. botanique, Paris, 1954*, sect. 9, p. 21. Paris: Rapports et communications.

(146) (With P. COHN & A. R. CRATHORN) Effects of ionising radiation on the *in vivo* incorporation of amino acids into proteins. In: *Advances in radiobiology* (Int. Congr. Radiol. Biology, Stockholm, 1956) (ed. G. C. de Hevesy, A. G. Forssberg & J. D. Abbatt), p. 33. Edinburgh & London: Oliver & Boyd.

(147) 1957 (With D. M. Phillips & K. V. Shooter) The influence of protein on heterogeneity of DNA. *Archs Biochem. Biophys.* **71**, 423.

(148) (With D. J. R. Laurence, A. B. Robins & K. V. Shooter) Molecular weights and physical properties of deoxyribonucleic acid. *Nature, Lond.* **180**, 1340.

(149) 1958 (With P. Cohn) The study of microsomal protein fractions by means of radioactive amino acids. In: *Radioisotopes in scientific research* (Int. conf. radioisotopes scient. res. (Unesco), Paris, 1957) (ed. R. C. Extermann), **3**, 378. London & New York: Pergamon.

(150) Effects of oxygen on the degradation of DNA by ionizing radiations. In: *Les peroxydes organiques en radiologie* (Colloque sur les peroxydes organiques formés par les radiations et leur rôle en radiobiologie, Institut du Radium, Paris, janvier 1957) (ed. M. Haissinsky), p. 36. Paris: Masson; London: Pergamon.

(151) (With K. V. Shooter) The physical heterogeneity of deoxyribonucleic acid. *Z. phys. Chem.* **15**, 6.

(152) (With R. H. Pain, A. B. Robins and J. Rotblat) The relative effects of direct and indirect actions of ionizing radiations on deoxyribonucleic acid. *Proc. R. Soc. Lond.* B **149**, 12.

(153) (With A. R. Crathorn & G. D. Hunter) The site of protein synthesis in *Bacillus megaterium. Biochem. J.* **69**, 544.

(154) (With P. Cohn) Fractionation of proteins of the microsomes of rat liver by means of a non-ionic detergent. *Biochem. J.* **70**, 254.

(155) 1959 (With D. J. R. Laurence, A. B. Robins & K. V. Shooter) Comparisons of the molecular weights of deoxyribonucleic acids as determined by light scattering and from sedimentation and viscosity. In: Discussion on the structure and physical chemistry of nucleic acids and proteins. *Trans. Faraday Soc.* **55**, 489.

(156) (With D. J. R. Laurence, A. B. Robins & K. V. Shooter) Comparison of the molecular weights of deoxyribonucleic acids as determined from light scattering and from sedimentation and viscosity. *Proc. R. Soc. Lond.* A**250**, 1.

(157) Symposium E: Induced changes in DNA and in chromosome structure. *Radiat. Res.* Suppl. no. 1, p. 403.

(158) Summary of the discussion and some critical remarks. In: Symposium on human DNA with particular reference to DNA of hemopoietic system. Int. Congr. Haemat. Rome, 1958. *Haemat. lat.*, vol. 2, Suppl. no. 2, p. 69. Milan: Istituto per la Diffusione di Opere Scientifiche.

(159) Les histones: leurs structures, variations et rôle dans les organismes animaux. *Exposés à Biochim. méd.* **21**, 41.

(160) (With G. D. Hunter, P. Brookes & A. R. Crathorn) Intermediate reactions in protein synthesis by the isolated cytoplasmic-membrane fraction of *Bacillus megaterium. Biochem. J.* **73**, 369.

(161) Heterogeneity of nucleic acids and effects of chemical and physical agents. *Rapp. Cons. Chim. Solvay*, **11**, 177.

(162) The heterogeneity of nucleic acids. In: *Int. Congr. Biochem. Vienna, 1958*, Symp. 9, p. 77. London: Pergamon.

(163) 1960 (With P. Cohn & P. Simson) The presence of basic proteins in microsomes. *Biochim. biophys. Acta* **38**, 386.

(164) (With A. B. Robins & J. Rotblat) The inactivation of α-chymotrypsin by ionizing radiations. *Proc. R. Soc. Lond.* A **256**, 1.

(165) (With A. B. Robins) Effect of oxygen on the inactivation of trypsin by ionizing radiation. *Nature, Lond.* **186**, 697.

(166) (With F. Sutherland) The incorporation of precursors into the deoxyribonucleic acid of *Bacillus megaterium*. In: *The cell nucleus* (Proc. of an informal meeting held at the Department of Radiotherapeutics, University of Cambridge, 1959, by the Faraday Society), p. 66. London: Butterworth.

(167) (With D. J. R. Laurence) Effect of whole-body radiation *in vivo* on the DNA of rat liver. *Int. J. Radiat. Biol.* **2**, 331.

(168) (With E. W. Johns, D. M. P. Phillips & P. Simson) Improved fractionations of arginine-rich histones from calf thymus. *Biochem. J.* **77**, 631.

(169) 1960 (With A. B. Robins) The flow properties of deoxyribonucleic acid solutions. In: *Flow properties of blood and other biological systems* (ed. A. L. Copley & G. Stainsby), p. 337. London: Pergamon.

(170) Influence of hydrogen-ion and salt concentration on polyelectrolytes. In: *Size and shape changes of contractile polymers: conversion of chemical into mechanical energy* (Proc. of seminars held at University College London) (ed. A. Wassermann), p. 90. London: Pergamon.

(171) (With D. J. R. Laurence) Relative metabolic activities of histones in tumours and liver. *Br. J. Cancer* **14**, 758.

(172) Biochemical actions of ionizing radiations. *Proc. int. Congr. Radiol. Munich, 1959* (ed. B. Rajewsky), p. 1007. Stuttgart: Thieme.

(173) (With P. Bianchi, A. R. Crathorn & K. V. Shooter) Some characteristics of the phosphorylating kinases of neoplastic and normal cells. *Biochem. J.* **77**, 15*P*.

(174) Symposium on human DNA with particular reference to DNA of the hemopoietic system. Introduction. In: *Proc. 7th Int. Congr. Int. Soc. Haematology, Rome, 1958*, **3**, 11. Rome: Il Pensiero Scientifico.

(174a) Summary of the discussions and some critical remarks. In: *Proc. 7th Int. Cong. Int. Soc. Haematology, Rome, 1958*, **3**, 61. Rome: Il Pensiero Scientifico.

(175) 1961 (With P. A. Bianchi, A. R. Crathorn and K. V. Shooter) The thymidine-phosphorylating kinases. *Biochim. biophys. Acta* **48**, 213.

(176) (With A. B. Robins) Effect of pH on the sensitiveness of trypsin to ionizing radiation. *Nature, Lond.* **189**, 852.

(177) (With G. N. Goson & G. D. Hunter) Observations on the site and mechanism of protein biosynthesis in *B. megaterium*. In: *Protein biosynthesis* (Symp. held at Wassenaar, August/September 1960, under the auspices of Unesco and the Council for International Organizations of Medical Sciences) (ed. R. J. C. Harris), p. 349. London: Academic Press.

(178) (With E. W. Johns, D. M. P. Phillips & P. Simson) The electrophoresis of histones and histone fractions on starch gel. *Biochem. J.* **80**, 189.

(179) (With G. N. Godson & G. D. Hunter) Cellular components of *Bacillus megaterium* and their role in protein biosynthesis. *Biochem. J.* **81**, 59.

(180) (With P. A. Bianchi, A. R. Crathorn & K. V. Shooter) The thymidine phosphorylating kinases. *Biochim. biophys. Acta* **53**, 123.

(181) (With P. Bianchi, A. R. Crathorn & K. V. Shooter) The incorporation of thymidine into DNA of various tissues. *J. Chim. phys.* **58**, 972.

(182) 1962 (With E. W. Johns) Further fractionations of histones from calf thymus. *Biochem. J.* **82**, 15.

(183) (With L. Hnilica & E. W. Johns) Observations on the species and tissue specificity of histones. *Biochem. J.* **82**, 123.

(184) (With A. B. Robins) Effects of oxygen on the inactivation of enzymes by ionizing radiations. *Radiat. Res.* **16**, 7.

(185) (With A. B. Robins) Metal ion redox systems as radiation protective agents. *Nature, Lond.* **193**, 673.

(186) (With G. N. Godson) Preparation of a nuclear fraction from *Bacillus megaterium* and its role in biosynthesis of ribonucleic acid. *Nature, Lond.* **193**, 655.

(187) Some researches on histones. *J. gen. Physiol.* **45**, 195.

(188) (With A. B. Robins) Effects of oxygen on the inactivation of enzymes by ionizing radiations. II: Solid trypsin and deoxyribonuclease. *Radiat. Res.* **17**, 63.

(189) (With E. W. Johns) Studies on histones. 4: The histones of wheat germ. *Biochem. J.* **84**, 436.

(190) (With P. Bianchi, A. R. Crathorn & K. V. Shooter) The incorporation of thymidine into DNA of various tissues. In: *Deoxyribonucleic acid, its structure, synthesis and function* (Proc. of 11th annual meeting of the Physical Chemistry Society at Col de Voza, near Chamonix, 1961), p. 96. Oxford: Pergamon.

(191) 1963 (With D. J. R. Laurence & P. Simson) Studies on histones. 5: The histones of the Crocker sarcoma and spontaneous mammary tumours of mice. *Biochem. J.* **87**, 200.

(192) (With P. Cohn) Studies on histones. 6: Observations on the biosynthesis of histones and other proteins in regenerating rat liver. *Biochem. J.* **87**, 330.

(193) 1963 A possible mechanism of synthesis of nucleic acids. *Nature, Lond.* **199**, 68.
(194) (With G. N. Godson) Biosynthesis of nucleic acids in *Bacillus megaterium.* I. The isolation of a nuclear material. *Biochem. J.* **88**, 176.
(195) (With G. C. Barr) Biosynthesis of nucleic acids in *Bacillus megaterium.* 2: The formation of ribonucleic acid by nuclear material *in vitro. Biochem. J.* **88**, 252.
(196) (With G. N. Godson) Biosynthesis of nucleic acids in *Bacillus megaterium.* 3: Biosynthesis of ribonucleic acid *in vivo. Biochem. J.* **88**, 259.
(197) (With G. C. Barr) Ribonucleic acid synthesis in isolated cell fractions of *Bacillus megaterium. Biochem. J.* **87**, 36*P*.
(198) Nuclear proteins of normal and cancer cells. *Expl Cell Res.* suppl. 9, 349.
(199) (With A. B. Robins) Effects of certain metal salts on the inactivation of solid trypsin by ionizing radiation. *Radiat. Res.* **19**, 582.
(200) (With G. C. Barr) Histones and gene function. *Nature, Lond.* **199**, 1170.
(201) 1964 (With G. N. Godson) 'Nuclear' and cytoplasmic ribosomes in *B. megaterium. Nature, Lond.* **201**, 876.
(202) (With E. W. Johns) Interactions between histones and nucleic acids. *Biochem. J.* **91**, 15C.
(203) Fractionation and characteristics of histones. In: *The nucleohistones: proceedings of the first world conference on histone biology and chemistry, Pasadena, 1963* (ed. J. Bonner & P. Ts'o), p. 36. San Francisco: Holden-Day.
(204) (With G. N. Godson) Ribonucleic acid synthesis in *B. megaterium.* In: *Istituto Lombardo Accademia di Scienze e Lettere*, p. 238. (Antonio Baselli conference on nucleic acids and their role in biology). Milan: Istituto Lombardo.
(205) (With G. N. Godson) Biosynthesis of nucleic acids in *Bacillus megaterium.* 4: Roles of the 'nuclear', cytoplasmic and cytoplasmic-membrane components of the cell in the biosynthesis of ribonucleic acid. *Biochem. J.* **93**, 573.
(206) (With E. W. Johns) Specificity of the interactions between histones and deoxyribonucleic acid. *Nature, Lond.* **204**, 853.
(207) 1965 Gene control by histones. *New Scient.* **25**, 712.
(208) (With T. P. Brent & A. R. Crathorn) Variations in phosphokinase activities during the cell cycle in synchronous populations of Hela cells. *Nature, Lond.* **207**, 176.
(209) (With D. J. R. Laurence) Metabolism in malignant tissues and liver of the rat and mouse. *Biochem. J.* **96**, 53.
(210) Role of histones and other proteins in gene control. *Nature, Lond.* **207**, 1041.
(211) (With B. Askonas, F. Jacob, D. C. Phillips, L. Sachs & G. V. Sherbet) Biological systems at the molecular level. *Nature, Lond.* **208**, 1048.
(212) (With G. N. Godson & G. C. Barr) Nuclear synthesis of RNA in *B. megaterium* and the effects of histones on RNA synthesis. In: *Nucleic acids: structure, biosynthesis and function* (Symp. organized by the Regional Research Laboratory, Hyderabad, January 1964), p. 56. New Delhi Council for Industrial Research.
(213) (With J. Palau) The histones of trout liver. *Biochem. J.* **98**, 5P.
(214) (With D. F. Power) Counter-current distribution studies of histones. *Biochem. J.* 97, 32P.
(215) 1966 How genes are controlled. *Sci. J.* **2**, 41.
(216) (With D. J. R. Laurence & D. M. P. Phillips) A comparison of histone fractions from an 'osteogenic' rat tumor and calf thymus. *Archs Biochem. Biophys.* **113**, 338.
(217) (With T. P. Brent & A. R. Crathorn) Effects of irradiation on synthesis of deoxyribonucleic acid and mitosis in synchronous cultures of Hela cells. *Nature, Lond.* **210**, 393.
(218) Complexity and specificity of histones. In: *Ciba Fdn Study Grp no. 24* on *Histones, their role on the transfer of genetic information* (ed. A. V. S. de Reuck & B. Knight), p. 4. London: Churchill.
(219) (With J. Palau) Trout-liver histones. *Biochem. J.* **100**, 779.
(220) 1967 (With D. F. Power & J. Palau) Countercurrent-distribution studies on histones. *Biochem. J.* **102**, 539.
(221) (With A. R. Chipperfield) Inhibition of RNA polymerase by histones. *Nature, Lond.* **215**, 1188.

(222) 1968 (With E. W. Johns & D. M. P. Phillips) Recent investigations on histones and their functions. *Prog. Biophys. Mol. Biol.* **18**, 209.

*Books*

(a) 1927 *The chemical elements and their compounds.* London: Macmillan. (1st ed., 2nd ed. 1930.)

(b) 1928 *Chemical thermodynamics.* London: Macmillan. (1st ed. (two volumes), combined in one volume 1946; reprinted with corrections 1949, 1951, 1955, 1960; 5th ed. 1962, 1965.)

(c) 1940 *Electrocapillarity: the chemistry and physics of electrodes and other charged surfaces.* London: Methuen & Co.

(d) 1951 (Editor) *Electrical phenomena at interfaces in chemistry, physics and biology.* London: Methuen & Co. A revision of (c).

(e) 1950 *Man is a microcosm.* London: Macmillan.

(f) 1951 *Man is a microcosm.* (U.S. edition.) New York: The Macmillan Co. (Swedish translation based on U.S. edition. Stockholm: H. Gibers Förlag.)

(g) 1957 *Science and human life: Successes and limitations.* London: Pergamon Press. New York: Basic Books Inc. (Translated into Japanese and reprinted in 1969.)

(h) 1959 *Inside the living cell.* London: Allen & Unwin. New York: Basic Books Inc. (2nd imp. 1962). (Translated into Mexican, Finnish, Swedish, Italian, Slovene, Dutch, German, Japanese, Polish.)

(i) 1964 *The life of the cell.* London: Allen & Unwin. New York: Basic Books Inc. (Translated into Polish, Spanish, Japanese.)

(j) 1968 *Gene control in the living cell.* London: Allen & Unwin. New York: Basic Books Inc. (Translated into German, Japanese.)

(k) 1970 *The life process.* London: Allen & Unwin. New York: Basic Books Inc. (1971).

(l) 1976 *Modern biology and its human implications.* London: Hodder & Stoughton.

S R Christophers

# SAMUEL RICKARD CHRISTOPHERS

27 November 1873 — 19 February 1978

Elected F.R.S. 1926

By H. E. Shortt, F.R.S., and P. C. C. Garnham, F.R.S.

After a life of great physical and mental activity, Samuel Rickard Christophers died on 19 February 1978, aged 104 years, the greatest age ever reached by a Fellow of the Royal Society. He followed Bacon's 'Regimen of Health—to be free minded and cheerfully disposed at hours of meat and of sleep, and of exercise, is one of the best precepts of long lasting' [i.e. for prolonging life]. He lived through a century of Science in general and medical science in particular including the immense progress in tropical medicine. In the latter field he was one of the great pioneers to rank equally with his famous peers, Sir Patrick Manson, F.R.S., and Sir Ronald Ross, F.R.S.

Christophers was born in Liverpool on 27 November 1873. His father, Samuel Hunt Christophers, was born in Plymouth but the family came from the small village of Maunan in Cornwall and Christophers was vastly proud of the family's Cornish origin. His mother, Mary Selina Rickard, was born at Redruth, Cornwall, and his parents were married at St Michael's-in-the-hamlet near Otterspool on the Mersey. His father came to Liverpool and for many years was head of the Statistical Office of the Mersey Docks and Harbour Board.

Christophers married Elise Emma Sherman, daughter of Fitzroy Sherman, owner of a coffee estate in the Nilgiri Hills in India, and Elise Blacas, daughter of a French admiral. The marriage took place in St Andrew's Church, Westminster, on 27 September 1902. There were two children, a daughter and son. The daughter, Elise Iseult, had considerable talent in mathematics and married a British officer, Captain Cliff Wilson, of the Essex regiment, which he later commanded. They had one son, a naval officer, and one daughter (Mrs Parker) who was a well known ballet dancer.

Christophers' son, Samuel Vagn, married the daughter of the artist, Wix. They had two sons but this marriage was unsuccessful and led to an estrangement between Vagn and his parents. In later life there was, happily, a reconciliation with his parents when Vagn remarried. His second wife was Christian Thompson, a distant relation of J. B. S. Haldane, F.R.S. Vagn had great artistic and scientific potential but as the result of his early domestic trouble he was emotionally insecure and unable to capitalize on his ability. He studied medicine at Cambridge, nearly joined the Indian Police Service but turned instead to art which he studied for seven years, three in Edinburgh and four in London at the Royal College of Art. He showed great promise, especially in sculpture and much of his work was sold, but the outbreak of war in 1914 turned his talents to industrial chemistry and he joined an aircraft firm belonging to his friend, the Duke of Richmond. Here his work on plastics and aerofoils resulted in the incorporation of these products into aircraft propellers which increased the speed of aircraft by 10 miles an hour. Vagn, a man of many talents, was a recognized expert on Chinese porcelain and well known in the world of antiques for the wide range of his knowledge.

## Career

As a boy Christophers was intensely attracted to natural history and from about the age of 14 he became interested in geology when his grandfather gave him access to his collection of minerals and taught him their names. After attending a kindergarten school, he went at the age of 13 to the Liverpool Institute where he did particularly well in mathematics and hydrostatics but subjects such as history, grammar and languages held no appeal, possibly because the subjects were badly taught. To counterbalance this defect he, on his own volition, read widely every form of literature he came across, making the best use of public libraries. As a result he passed the London Matriculation at the age of 16.

He entered University College Liverpool as a medical student in 1889 and qualified M.B. Ch.B. in 1896. Among his professors the one who influenced him most and had a lasting effect on his scientific outlook and work was Sir Charles Sherrington, a debt he often acknowledged.

Christophers's earliest scientific work was on serology and as early as 1898 he studied the effect of normal human serum on *Bacillus coli communis*. This was before his introduction to the tropics as medical officer on a steamer of the Booth Line which was the first ocean steamer to traverse the upper reaches of the Amazon river. The young medical man was fascinated by this experience which undoubtedly influenced him in his decision to adopt a career in the tropics.

An opportunity soon arose; he was appointed a member of the Malaria Commission of the Royal Society and Colonial Office in 1898–1902 and this appointment gave him five years of experience of the tropics in Africa and India with his senior colleague the late Professor J. W. W. Stephens, F.R.S. He was so impressed with the opportunities offered by India for research in tropical problems that on the termination of the Malaria Commission he decided to return to that country and enter the Indian Medical Service by the usual examination. This service offered an almost unlimited scope for work in many scientific disciplines besides medicine and surgery and Christophers's previous experience inevitably marked him out for appointment in the Research Department of the service.

Although the Indian Medical Service was primarily a military service, and junior officers commenced as medical officers in the Indian Army for two years or more before either making a permanent military career or transferring to one of the many other outlets of service available, Christophers's talents were so obvious that this normal procedure was waived. After a short period as medical officer of the 1st Brahmins he was put in charge of anti-malarial operations at Mian Mir, but was soon placed on special duty to investigate the findings of Colonel Donovan in Madras of the newly described cause of kala azar, in patients suffering from the disease.

At this time, 1904, he was appointed to the Directorship of the newly constituted King Institute of Preventive Medicine in Madras, an appointment he held for four years.

In 1908 the occurrence of blackwater fever among planters in the tea gardens of the Duars led to an urgent call for investigation of the causes responsible for this serious condition. To study this Christophers and Dr C. A. Bentley (57) were placed on special duty but in 1909 a more urgent matter led to the recall of Christophers to investigate a serious epidemic of malaria in the Punjab. His appointment to this investigation was to lead to important developments in the organization of malaria research and measures to control the disease in India.

Between 1910 and the outbreak of World War I a great deal of activity took place in the organization of malaria research, including measures to be taken in implementing active anti-malarial measures in the field. Each province now had its own malaria officer with organization and facilities for field work. Under Christophers there was formed a Central Malaria Bureau with a laboratory in the grounds of the Central Research Institute, Kasauli, with provision for workers, literature, collections and other facilities. As officer in charge of the bureau, Christophers was now responsible for all matters relating to malaria in the whole of India and especially for the operation of 'malaria surveys' in order to gain an idea of the distribution and severity of the disease nation wide. In this period Christophers published his standard book on the anopheline mosquitoes of India and in 1915 he was awarded the C.I.E.

After this very brief account of Christophers in his early years in India and before we go on to describe his long and distinguished career in the Indian Medical Service of which he was probably the most outstanding scientist, it seems appropriate to give some account of him as an individual in his relationships to his contemporaries and those with whom he worked and met in everyday contact.

Although, perhaps, rather shy on first acquaintance, his charm captured all of either sex and any age. He could disagree with a friend fundamentally on a particular subject but his dissent would be expressed so understandingly that no one could take offence. In other words while by no means a 'yes' man his 'noes' were expressed so tactfully that no relationship could be strained. One aspect of his personality can never be ignored; in spite of his scientific achievements and the world-wide renown in which he was held, he never lost the modesty which was inborn in his character. To his scientific peers and to humble students alike he was equally approachable and by many of the latter the time and care he took in helping them over their difficulties were always a source of encouragement to them.

The years 1916–18 saw Christophers in an entirely different environment and his adaptation to this was so rapid and so complete that he seemed to assume almost a different personality. The war in Mesopotamia (Iraq) was in progress and, apart from the military operations, many situations arose which posed problems not only for the military personnel but others, affecting their health and welfare directly and indirectly from the close contact between troops and the civil population. It was obvious that some organization capable of dealing with a diversity of problems bearing on the health of the troops had to be provided and to meet this demand a central laboratory was established in Basra under the command of Christophers who was appointed D.A.D.M.S. (San.) to the Mesopotamian Expeditionary Force. This laboratory was accommodated in the Indian naval ship the *Elphinstone* which was moored in the Shatt-el-Arab near the left bank and immediately opposite the city of Basra. The entire ship and its Lascar crew were under the command of the Director of the laboratory and the scientific staff and laboratory personnel all had quarters in the ship. Under Christophers, the senior staff comprised W. D. H. Stephenson, I.M.S. senior bacteriologist, Dr Miskin, a Lebanese bacteriologist trained at the Pasteur Institute, Paris, Dr Bassett, a highly qualified chemist, Dr A. J. Grove, an entomologist, the Reverend Aitken, an amateur entomologist, P. J. Barraud, an entomologist, and H. E. Shortt, I.M.S., a protozoologist and malariologist.

The work of the Central Laboratory was extremely varied; much of it was not strictly medical as many aspects affecting the troops indirectly had to be studied, such as the quality of the rice supplied for the Indian troops and the components in the blankets as regards the amount of 'shoddy' in their composition. Christophers now showed his extraordinary adaptability. As one knew him in India his reaction to any problem was a strictly scientific one. Before forming a conclusion or giving an opinion on any matter he would consider it from every point of view, almost giving an impression of indecisiveness. Now on active service, he became a different person. The scientific side remained, but its expression was completely altered. He quickly realized that the military wanted quick and decisive answers to problems on which to base actions and this became the *modus operandi* with emphasis on practicability.

One of the main operations of the laboratory was to carry out malaria surveys in all areas where troops were operating (101). The area of operations throughout the whole campaign covered a very large area from Basra on the Shatt-el-Arab to Kirkuk in Kurdistan, well beyond Baghdad, and the whole of Persia up to the Caspian Sea. These surveys were chiefly to ascertain the endemicity of malaria by assessing the spleen rates of children, and the results provided information on areas where there was special need for anti-malaria operations.

Another activity, which was of lesser importance in that it did not have a direct impact on military operations, was the study of 'oriental sore' or

'Baghdad boil'. There was a high incidence of this condition, and the phlebotomine flies which were the transmitters rivalled mosquitoes as agents of irritation. In little things as in great Christophers took an equal interest. The wings of these flies were thickly covered with scales which obscured the venation and he evolved a technique for complete elimination of the scales leaving a clear picture of the venation. This was based on a sandfly falling into a drop of soda water which set up an effervescence in the liquid which detached some of the scales. Next day he showed us a specimen with wings completely nude. He had immersed it in acid and then added an alkali which produced a very brisk effervescence which completely detached all the scales!

To most of us in the laboratory the country was completely unknown and ignorance sometimes led to unexpected situations. On one occasion Christophers and one of us (H. E. S.) were swimming in a creek connecting with the main river near Basra when we noticed an increasing number of Arab children collecting on the opposite bank. This became annoying and we shouted across to them in Arabic 'Aesh tusoown hunaker. Imshi' ('What are you doing there? Go away'). They answered back 'Muntazerin le samak al quarsh le yakulakum' ('We are waiting to see the sharks get you!') Although they might be noted for curiosity they were certainly not noted for humour, so we made a quick exit from the water. Our danger was forcibly brought home to us a few days later. H. E. S. developed a slight fever which put him into hospital for a few days, and he found that the soldier in the bed next to his was there on account of severe laceration of one of his legs by a shark. The accident had been sustained close to where we had been swimming. He was saved by his companions by being pulled into a boat.

During the two years Christophers spent as Director of the Central Laboratory it was a pleasure as well as a privilege for all of us to work under his direction and it remains as one of our cherished memories. He was now recalled to India but first went to England on a short period of leave. He then in 1921 returned to India to rejoin his previous post as Assistant Director of the Central Research Institute, Kasauli, until 1925 when, on retirement of the Director, Colonel Harvey, I.M.S., he took over as Director, a post he held until his retirement in 1932. During this period a great deal of important work on malaria was carried out from the Malaria Bureau and was published, such as the volume on Anophelini by Christophers (177), in the Fauna of India series and another by P. J. Barraud in the same series on the Culicidae (volume 5).

Sir Rickard Christophers as he now was (since 1931) found time during this period to pursue many interests outside his strictly service duties and one of these was his interest in geology, pre-history and palaeontology. It was a common sight in Kasauli to see him wandering off down the hillside with his geological hammer, expeditions on which I (H. E. S.) would accompany him. On one occasion, our destination was the fabulously rich fossil beds of the Siwalik hills, a trip which but for a stroke of luck might have had a tragic end. We left Kasauli (6000 ft above sea level) at dawn to motor to Kalka (2000 ft), the railhead for the Simla railway, thence we walked about four miles across an arid plain to the Siwalik Hills, outliers of the Himalayas, and in fact older than the latter. The hills in this area are of low altitude, almost entirely bare of vegetation and dissected by narrow gullies leading from the plain into the hills. At the foot of the hills was a dry river bed which seldom held water. The season was a break in the monsoon, very hot and humid. Having marched the four miles to the hills and done some digging we decided to have a break and eat our lunch of sandwiches, washed down by water from our water bottles. I noticed that Christophers ate hardly anything and threw away many of his sandwiches. After a while we went to explore one of the gullies and started digging where we found signs of fossil materials. It was extremely hot and humid but interest kept us going in the ever present hope of unearthing something of real interest. The work in these narrow gullies, however, was strenuous and we sweated profusely and decided to return to level ground at the mouth of the gully. After some time on the way back Christophers said to me: 'You go ahead, I'll follow soon' and I thought perhaps he had a call of nature but when he did not rejoin me went back to where he had stopped and found him collapsed on the ground. He was a much bigger and heavier man than me; thus it was impossible to carry him, but as he was obviously suffering from heat exhaustion it was essential to get him out of the narrow gully. I succeeded in getting him to his feet and we staggered on with him leaning heavily upon me. After some necessary rests during which one dared not let him get down again we reached the open plain. Here I put him under the only shelter, a small thorn tree giving no real shade and searched for water. We had exhausted our water bottles and I tried to reach water by digging with my hands and geological hammer, both very inadequate tools in the dry river bed but without success. The situation looked dangerous, no water and four miles of hot arid plain to traverse to Kalka with a man who could not even stand, much less walk, when nature intervened. A wind started and a dark heavy cloud appeared in the previously brassy sky; the temperature dropped sharply and rain began to fall. This soon became a torrent and thoroughly soaked us both. Christophers improved enough to sit up but there was still the four miles to Kalka. I saw something moving in the distance which as it came nearer proved to be a string of camels. How could we get him on to a camel and keep him there over the rough going? However, once more we were fortunate, for a line of pack ponies appeared and I immediately commandeered one of these and we managed to hoist a limp Christophers on to it. He was already beginning to improve as the result of the unexpected downpour and after some distance was able to sit up on the pony which accepted him as its pay load. By the time we reached Kalka he was able to walk to the car and we started on our way back to Kasauli. As we reached the conifer line and found the bracing air and the smell of the pines, he became much better and when we arrived at Kasauli he was able to walk home to his house. Christophers's collapse was surprising because he was exceedingly tough. However, he had left home without a meal and had covered the four mile trek over rough ground and the subsequent digging for fossils in the hot and humid atmosphere produced profuse sweating to the point of near dehydration. This was why he ate very little of the sandwiches he had brought and the subsequent further work after lunch in the hot ravine had completed the debilitating dehydration, leading to his collapse. He was so ashamed afterwards of what he considered a personal failure out of character, which it certainly was, that he did not tell Lady Christophers about it! Next day she looked at me rather suspiciously and said: 'Chum [her name for him] seemed rather tired last night after your trip.' I kept my counsel and Christophers never again referred to the incident.

When Christophers finally retired from India he was appointed Professor of Malaria Studies of London University at the London School of Hygiene and Tropical Medicine a post he held between 1932 and 1938. He now showed his versatility in engaging on biochemical studies (see p. 189, 190). It was during this period that Christophers suffered a bad accident in being knocked down by a car on the Kingston by-pass on his return from a geological trip to a gravel pit. He had a multiple fracture of the femur which necessarily immobilized him for a considerable period. The bone did not unite satisfactorily so he was sent to recuperate in a more favourable climate in the Canary Islands, which had the desirable result of leaving him completely mobile without even a limp.

This accident gave rise to a reaction characteristic of Christophers. When taken to hospital and as soon as he was able, he wrote a letter to the person who had run him down apologizing for his carelessness in stepping out on to the road immediately in front of a car and regretting the distress he must have caused the motorist.

Christophers's work in Britain after he had returned from India is related elsewhere in this memoir but the friendship formed by one of us (H. E. S.) over many years of work and close relationships together were continued by occasional meetings after both had retired, especially on each of his birthdays. In his latest years he became very deaf but would not agree to any artificial aid and when his eyesight also became poor it was a double deprivation, but he endured this with the placidity and patience which had been characteristic of him throughout his life. His granddaughter, Mrs P. Parker, found among his papers certain sheets of paper with curious markings which remained a puzzle until it was realized that they indicated the angles at which the sunlight struck upon his desk at different times of the year.

## Scientific contributions

Christophers was distinguished for his work as an entomologist, protozoologist and sanitarian. His immense mastery of histological techniques played a vital part in his researches both on insects and protozoal parasites of man and animals. In all these disciplines he made many discoveries, but probably his greatest originality lay in his synthetic approach to the field of 'malariology'. This word was introduced into medical literature late in the nineteenth century following the visit in October 1899 of Sir Patrick Manson and Dr L. Sambon to the laboratory of Grassi in the University of Rome; the Roman 'malariologists' demonstrated their results on the transmission of human malaria parasites by local anopheline mosquitoes and Manson was greatly impressed by Grassi's beautiful drawings of the anatomy of *Anopheles* and of specific features of the larvae. The word 'malariology', however, did not come into general use until 1915 when the specialist journal *La Malariologia* first appeared in Naples under the editorship of Ernesto Cacace.

Christophers's introduction to malaria began a year before the visit of Manson to Italy. He and J. W. W. Stephens were appointed, in 1898, jointly by the Royal Society and the Colonial Office, as members of a Malaria Commission to study malaria in tropical Africa. They were requested to travel to Italy first in order to learn about the most recent developments in malaria research. At that time, the discoveries of the cycle of the parasite in the mosquito, made by Surgeon-Major R. Ross in India in 1897, had scarcely been recognized; in fact Professor M. Foster, Secretary of the Royal Society, in a letter dated 2 August 1898 to the Colonial Office, stated 'the view that the mosquito is an important agent in propagating the disease has at present advanced very little beyond the stage of hypothesis, and even if proved to be a true view, the important problems to be solved are pathological in nature'.

They spent a month in Italy, first in Pavia to consult Golgi about his recently described periodic cycles in tertian and quartan malaria and secondly in Rome to see the work which Grassi, Bastianelli and Bignami were doing in the San Spirito Hospital on the transmission of human malaria by mosquitoes. Stephens and Christophers left England in December 1898 and eventually arrived at Blantyre on 1 February 1899. They investigated malaria in the surrounding country, then known as British Central Africa, and later successively as Nyasaland and Malawi. After eight months, they decided that conditions for work were unsuitable and they returned to England, with the proposal that they should transfer their operations to West Africa, which they reached in December 1899.

The first report (2) of Stephens and Christophers dealt with the protozoological aspects, their second (3) (and later ones) with the entomological problems, and their fourth, fifth and sixth (4, 5, 6) with sanitation. These two investigators found numerous sporozoites and 'zygotes' in mosquitoes (*Anopheles costalis* = *gambiae*), caught in Sierra Leone; these observations must represent some of the earliest confirmatory evidence of Ross's discovery of the role of the mosquito in the transmission of the human disease in the tropics.

In 1902, Stephens and Christophers moved to Bengal and carried out work on much the same basis as their researches in tropical Africa. But they added a further dimension—the problem of malarial endemiology which was to occupy much of Christophers's time in later years in India. Christophers's interest became extended to other protozoa and he (28) described sporozoan parasites in the salivary glands of *Anopheles rossii* ( = *subpictus*) which he had previously found in *A. costalis* ( = *gambiae*). Half a century later (207) he gave a list of 'parasites in mosquitoes', a subject of increasing importance today in biological control.

Stephens and Christophers embodied the knowledge they had acquired in Africa and India in a little book (39) *The practical study of malaria and other blood parasites* which first appeared in 1903, was translated into French by the Sergent brothers (49) in 1906 and had three editions. A similar, practical work (160) appeared in 1928 with the title of *How to do a malaria survey*, this went through six editions and was under the joint authorship of Christophers and his brother officers in the Indian Medical Service, J. A. Sinton and G. Covell. These books may be out of date today, in view of the development of residual insecticides and the powerful synthetic drugs, but up to the time of World War II they were the constant companions of most malaria workers in the tropics. Their highly scientific approach was responsible for leading many of the latter into the 'research life'.

Christophers's researches are discussed under three headings, malaria, other protozoal diseases and entomology.

### *Malaria*

Stephens and Christophers worked closely together for five years in Africa and India on malaria and this collaboration resulted in major discoveries in all aspects of malariology. Their careful analysis (2, 12, 20, 34, 37) of the possible aetiological factors of blackwater fever in India and Africa demonstrated that three factors are involved: (1) *Plasmodium falciparum* malaria accompanied by very few parasites in the blood, (2) previous attacks of the disease which had been inadequately treated with quinine, and (3) the administration of quinine shortly before the onset of blackwater fever. The exact mechanism of the intravascular haemolysis was not discovered in these researches; it is still not precisely known, though the trigger is now thought to be due to an autoantigen–antibody reaction. As a result of these observations they were able to establish proof of the aetiology of blackwater fever, which previously had been mainly conjecture.

The nature of malaria endemicity in areas of intense transmission of malaria was studied in both continents. They appreciated (8) the different effects, noting that in Africa, once young children had recovered from their first infections, symptoms of the disease disappeared and the population became almost immune; in India, however, the immunity took longer to develop and was less complete. The nature of such immunity resembles the 'salting' of animals with trypanosomiasis and piroplasmosis. As a corollary to these observations, Christophers reported that gametocytes ('crescents') were only to be found in any number in the young children, and recommended (11) that European houses should be sited well away from native villages. Robert Koch, about the same time, and the Dutch workers in the East Indies showed that a similar situation prevailed elsewhere in the tropics, while later in Africa the concept of holoendemicity was developed by Bagster Wilson (1950) as a result of his tutelage at Kasauli in India.

Christophers appreciated the varying degrees of endemicity, and sought to establish statistical standards for its classification. These were based primarily on the incidence of splenomegaly and on parasite rates in the blood in the different populations. His methods (161) for measuring the size of the spleen in relation to the size of the individual (the 'average enlarged spleen') have been widely adopted and add precision to the records. The malaria survey was then completed by investigating the mosquito factor in all its manifold aspects, e.g. species, habits, malaria infection rate and relationship to the various meteorological conditions. The analysis of these data enabled Christophers (67, 180) and others to predict epidemic years. George Macdonald (see Bruce-Chwatt & Glanville 1973) developed these methods with a high degree of sophistication, and made them the basis of modern malaria control and eradication.

As a result of his observations of over 25 years in India, particularly in Mian Mir (35, 42), the Duars (59), throughout the Punjab and into Assam (113), Christophers (1948) came to some surprising conclusions. In regions of hyperendemic malaria, where the population was saturated with the infection, the pathogenicity was low and he (127) considered that malaria was a serious cause of mortality neither in adults nor in children. On the other hand, he (64) found that regional epidemic malaria, as in the Punjab, was accompanied by an enormous degree of morbidity and a very heavy mortality especially in infants and young children. In hyperendemic malaria, infection is nearly 100% throughout the year. In epidemic malaria the initial rate is negligible, but rises to a high level in the course of the epidemic. The explanation of the paradox is to be found in the immune status of the population—almost complete in the hyperendemic region, but practically absent in epidemic conditions.

Early in 1909, mounting records of heavy mortality from the epidemic areas in India began to show the importance and extent of the disease, and when Christophers found that under the official system accurate records of deaths had for many years been kept, he was able to map not only the present epidemic but those that for many years in the past had been occurring at intervals of some six or seven years. He was able from studying these records to confirm that one of the most important causes of heavy mortality from malaria was flooding from the many large rivers crossing the country. The importance of these and other findings led to a meeting under the Viceroy in Simla at which important questions in organization were decided upon. It is difficult to convey any idea of how devastating these epidemics were and how completely they destroyed living conditions in a country of villages dependent on local activities in agricultural pursuits for their very existence.

An eye witness, Captain E. C. Hodgson, I.M.S., described to one of us (H. E. S.) an actual incident. As one approached the distant village a curious low pitched insistent moaning sound could be heard. As one came nearer this was intensified and on arrival turned out to be the constant moaning of the village cows which were neglected and could not be milked as there was no one to milk them. Hardly a soul was moving about; many of the villagers lay on charpoys (native beds) racked with fever, others were lying on the ground incapable of any effort and there were dead bodies lying unburied; community life was completely disrupted; small naked children were neglected and many died; few had the energy to cook and help by neighbour to neighbour was at an end.

Christophers naturally took a great interest in the malaria parasites themselves, and he and Stephens (38) were the first investigators to describe the diagnostic changes which *Plasmodium falciparum* induces in erythrocytes; these changes are usually referred to as 'Maurer's clefts' from the name of the German worker who described them two years later but the term, 'Stephens's and Christophers's clefts', should have precedence.

The correct names of the different species (and genera) of malaria parasites have been debated from the time of their discovery in 1880 by Laveran, and in the course of the succeeding years the situation became increasingly complicated until 1938 when Christophers and Sinton (189) showed conclusively that the name, *Plasmodium falciparum* in common use for the parasite of malignant tertian malaria, was zoologically invalid and that the correct name was *P. malariae* (Marchiafava & Celli 1885). The latter, however, was the name commonly applied to the parasite of quartan malaria and it was abundantly clear that the reversal of these names would cause great confusion in the literature of tropical medicine. Accordingly in 1943 a case was submitted to the International Commission on Zoological Nomenclature, based on the analysis by Christophers and Sinton and supported by malariologists in the U.S.A., for the stabilization of the nomenclature of these important human parasites. A full investigation was then completed by the Secretary of the Commission (Frank Hemmings 1954) in which Christophers played a leading part and in 1954, Opinion 283 was issued which validated the generic and specific names in common use.

Christophers's interest in taxonomy no doubt stemmed from his systematic work in entomology. His old colleague and friend, J. W. W. Stephens, F.R.S., described two other species of human malaria parasites (*Plasmodium ovale* and *P. tenue*), about which there has been much debate. Christophers supported the validity of the former from the start and this is now the general view; he (127) also accepted the existence of *P. tenue* which he had observed himself in the semi-aboriginal races of Central India. (On a visit to Ferryside, Carmarthenshire, in 1945, a year before Professor Stephens's death, the latter reiterated to one of us (P. C. C. G.) his conviction that *P. tenue* was indeed a valid species although the name has still not been generally recognized.)

In Christophers's last years in India, he became familiar with the malaria parasites of Asian monkeys, including *Plasmodium knowlesi*, and on his return to England in 1932 he began a new phase in his career, by studying the biochemical properties of this parasite (184). He had previously ventured into the physical chemistry of acid haemolysis in 1929 (165) with careful electrometric measurements of hydrogen ion uptake, which established the determinant reaction as a rapid equilibrium of acid between the cells and the medium in which they were suspended.

These studies were extended by experiments on the macro- and microelectrophoresis of red cells and their component stroma and haemoglobin

(166); changes in charge on the major constituent, haemoglobin, were concluded to be of primary importance for the acid haemolytic reaction.

In England, a significant later application (1937–40) of this novel electrochemical approach was measurement of the ionization constants of the antimalarial drugs quinine, atebrin and plasmoquine (186, 193). Christophers's early recognition of the importance of drug inonization at blood pH as a factor of fundamental importance in therapeutic activity showed remarkable prescience, and in collaboration with J. D. Fulton during this period, he continued a series of equally innovative studies (187, 188, 191) on the respiratory metabolism of *P. knowlesi* and *Trypanosoma rhodesiense*.

No previous work had ever been done directly on the respiration of malaria parasites, and it was necessary to devise a method of isolating pure schizont-infected red cells from the heavily infected host, *Macaca mulatta*. Defibrination of heart blood, followed by centrifugation, was found to yield an easily separable top layer of infected, pigmented red cells, which could be washed to give a suspension containing over 95% parasitized cells and less than 0·2% white cells. Both this method and a later development, in which saponin haemolysis was used to liberate free parasite material, were used extensively by many workers in the ensuing 30 years as a basis for increasingly detailed studies of plasmodial metabolism.

The pioneer work of Christophers and Fulton, the first in which the Barcroft respirometric technique had been applied to isolated malaria parasites, showed that a very considerable consumption of oxygen occurred in the absence of glucose. In parallel experiments, trypanosomes were also found to be characterized by a high rate of oxygen consumption, dependent in this case on a high glycolysis rate, with large amounts of acid products accumulating. In examining the effect of drugs on this test system, inhibition of oxygen uptake was found to correlate closely with therapeutic effect *in vitro* in the case of trypanosomes; the correlation was marked but less close with anti-malarial drugs, although quinine and atebrin inhibited plasmodial respiration in concentrations (1/50 000–1/500 000) comparable with those associated with therapeutic effect. These sensitive techniques and the results obtained with them represented a great advance in the testing of lethality of drug action *in vitro*.

## *Other protozoal diseases*

### *Leishmaniasis*

In 1904 and 1905, Christophers (41, 43, 45) described a parasite which he had found in patients suffering from splenomegaly in Madras. He was convinced that this was the same organism that Leishman and Donovan had independently found in 1903 in patients ill with 'dam-dam fever' (kala azar or visceral leishmaniasis); later in the same year Ross neatly combined the names of the latter workers in the scientific designation, *Leishmania donovani*.

Rogers in 1904 described the growth of *L. donovani* in culture and Christophers (142) confirmed this and modified the medium.

The classification of *Leishmania* presented difficulties. Christophers at first thought it might be a microsporidian and rejected the interpretation of Laveran and Mesnil who had named it *Piroplasma donovani*. However, when he saw a flagellum growing out of the parasite in culture, he assumed that it must belong to the family of flagellates, and this was soon accepted as the correct solution.

Christophers became greatly interested in the possibility of the transmission of leishmaniasis through the bites of sandflies, and with his fellow workers, Shortt and Barraud (147–150), found that the flagellate stages of *Leishmania* were present in massive numbers in the pharynx and buccal cavity of sandflies. In 1925 Christophers was appointed to the directorship of the Kala-azar Commission of India to investigate the outbreaks of this disease in Assam and Bengal.

In Assam epidemics lasted for almost 10 years and recurred at intervals of almost 20 years, while in the intervening periods the disease smouldered in the areas affected only to break out in a new epidemic and spread eastward. In this way the disease, which had first entered Assam in the Garo Hills from neighbouring Bengal, progressed slowly but inexorably as far as Golaghat and beyond, by the time that the Commission had started work. The area affected was on both banks of the Brahmaputra river and as before had a devastating effect. In the previous epidemic in Nowgong, the impact was so great that about a quarter of the population had perished and one third of the land went out of cultivation. The one additional factor in the 1925 epidemic was that an effective treatment was now available, due to the discovery in Assam of the greater curative effect of pentavalent antimony as compared with the trivalent form of the drug previously in use. The latter was the sodium salt (tartar emetic) but the potassium salt was used as being less toxic. This treatment comprised a long process of intravenous injections lasting usually many weeks and with uncertain results. The pentavalent antimonial, urea stibamine (first produced by a Bengali doctor and his chemists), had been found by one of us (H. E. S.) in Shillong to be extremely effective and, in fact, was a major breakthrough in tropical medicine, which changed a 90% mortality rate in untreated cases to a 90% cure rate. Another advantage was that the treatment required only a small course of injections and was usually completed in about a fortnight or less. Owing to the widespread area of the epidemic and the poor communications it was impossible with the resources available to treat the population of all areas, but the mortality was greatly reduced in all treated areas. It was curious that the epidemic died out in untreated areas at the same time as in those where treatment was available but, of course, with a greatly increased mortality. One infers that owing to the great death rate in epidemic periods most of the cases affected died so that a population without any immunity built up in the periods between epidemics and was ripe for the next epidemic, whatever the trigger mechanism causing it might be.

It was in these conditions that the Commission started work in Assam.

In addition to Christophers as Director, there were Colonel H. E. Shortt, I.M.S., Mr P. J. Barraud, entomologist, Captain A. C. Craighead, I.M.S.,

Mr C. S. Swaminath, entomologist, and Dr Sribas Das, I.M.D., who was enaged in treating cases of kala azar with urea stibamine. An invaluable assistant was Mr James John, of no definite status, but whose unsparing efforts in collecting cases of kala azar by scouring the country on a bicycle meant that there was a continuous supply of fresh cases for all the experimental work.

Christophers now organized the staff in which each had his specific part to play and all the parts were fused in working towards the main object of the Commission which was 'How and by what agent is kala azar transmitted?' Christophers showed his genius in building this machine which worked smoothly without any apparent direction from above and yet his touch was there throughout and unconsciously acknowledged. The atmosphere was one in which there was an interest and a pleasure in working hard inspired by the fact that none worked harder than the Director himself. He took his full share in all the technical work in addition to his duties in administration. Of holidays there were none; the work itself was too interesting with an inspired leader, who commanded the completest loyalty, affection and admiration from every member of his staff. Holidays were impossible because it was essential to maintain a continuous supply of laboratory bred sandflies for the various experiments; each night Barraud and Shortt had to go out to villages to feed the sandflies on kala azar cases found during the day by James John. This involved driving the old Ford car to villages over country without proper roads at night, feeding the flies in unlighted villages and returning to the laboratory with the fed flies. This was done seven days a week and everyone was surprised one day when Christophers said with a rather apologetic smile: 'Oh, well, it's Christmas day—perhaps you could give it a miss tonight!'

Unfortunately for the Commission Christophers was too important a man to be located in the distant province of Assam, as the medical authorities in Simla required his presence where he could immediately be consulted on all matters relating to medical and scientific problems. He was therefore recalled to be Director of the Central Research Institute, Kasauli, and Directorship of the Commission was taken over by Colonel H. E. Shortt.

Although Christophers had no further direct concern with the Commission, he retained his interest so that when another officer visited Assam in a different connection Christophers said to him: 'When you go to Assam tell Shortt that it *must* be the sandfly!' It always seemed a pity in view of his long concern with kala azar from its first discovery that he was not able to remain with the Commission to complete its object in proving that the sandfly was the vector of the infection, but the foundations he had laid materially helped the Commission to achieve the final proof, as was accomplished by Swaminath, Shortt and Anderson in 1941.

## *Piroplasmosis*

The transmission of piroplasms by ticks was discovered by Theobald Smith in 1893, the first time that arthropods had been shown to carry protozoal parasites. Other examples quickly followed, including the incrimination in

1901 by Lounsbury of the tick *Haemaphysalis leachi* as the vector of the common *Babesia canis* of dogs. But unlike the researches on the mosquito transmission of malaria in which the cycle in the insect had been described in great detail, the cycle in the tick remained practically unknown until 1907 when Christophers (54) revealed the stages in *Rhipicephalus sanguineus*. He described the stages in the terminology used in malaria, such as zygotes, sporoblasts and sporozoites, but he was unable, however, at that time to prove that a sexual process was involved and this problem is only now nearing solution with the aid of electron microscopy.

### *Haemogregarines*

These common parasites in the blood of numerous animals quickly attracted Christophers's attention and he studied the transmission of two species in detail. He (1905) first worked (46) with a haemogregarine of the gerbil (*Gerbillus indicus*) which he named *Haemogregarina* ( = *Hepatozoon*) *gerbilli* and described (1906) its life cycle in the louse, *Haematopinus stephensi*, including the formation of large oocysts, filled with sporocysts containing six to eight sporozoites. Later, he expressed a little doubt about the attribution of the structures seen in the body cavity of the louse to the haemogregarines present in the gerbil. This louse was a new species which Christophers and Newstead described and named after their Liverpool colleague J. W. W. Stephens (46). In 1907 Christophers (52, 53) studied the life cycle in the tick (*Rhipicephalus sanguineus*) of *Leucocytozoon* ( = *Hepatozoon*) *canis*, a parasite of the leucocytes of dogs and found a similar cycle to the one in the gerbil parasite. Christophers showed that in the vertebrate host, schizogony took place in the spleen and bone-marrow.

Although many species of haemogregarines have been found in various classes of animals since the early years of the century, the full life cycles have rarely been described. Even the cycle of the well known *Hepatozoon balfouri* of jerboas was not fully described until 1959 by Hoogstraal, working in the department of one of us (P. C. C. G.). He had succeeded in tracing the course of *H. balfouri* through the jerboa and establishing its sporogony in the mite, *Haemolaelaps aegyptius*. Christophers came to the department at this moment, and we took him into Hoogstraal's laboratory, but failed to make introductions; a long conversation ensued in which Hoogstraal, in ignorance of the identity of the visitor, discussed the difficulties he was having in recognizing the different stages of the parasite in sections of the mite, and the failure of the vast majority of the mites to become infected. He deplored the fact that he had had no opportunity of seeking the advice of the man who had originally investigated the problem 50 years earlier. Christophers with typical modesty had not revealed his identity until this point when, of course, the belated introductions were made and the advice given.

### *Entomology*

The above summary of Christophers's scientific work clearly indicates the extreme interest that he had in entomology. From the start Christophers revealed a flair for the study of mosquitoes, sandflies, ticks and other arthropods in all their aspects. His first contributions dating from 1901 were illustrated by meticulous drawings showing histological details of the internal organs and tissues of anopheline and culicine mosquitoes (see figure 1). These drawings were based on the examination of stained sections and of fresh tissues. The excellence of such illustrations were a feature of all his subsequent entomological writings and finally culminated in his masterpiece, *Aedes aegypti*, published in 1960.

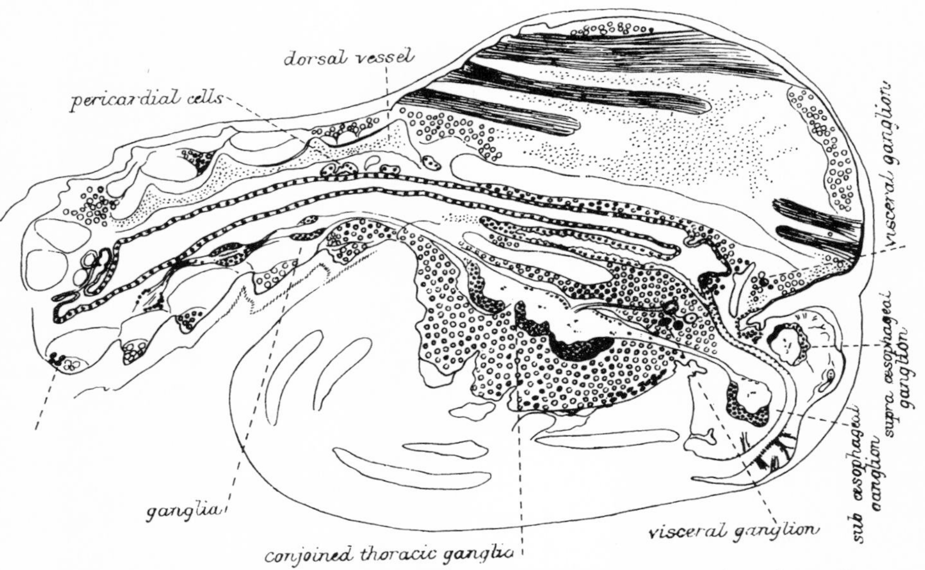


FIGURE 1. Nervous system of female mosquito. Longitudinal section of nymph. (Reproduced from (15).)

Christophers was always aware of the importance of zoology in his work, and in particular of taxonomy, and knew that without correct identification of material he could not hope to achieve a scientific perspective of the problems. When he began his studies on mosquitoes their identification was very largely based on the external characters of the female adult; he soon added the criteria of the larval and, later, of the pupal characters. He also made a point of examining the interior of the insect and studied the various organs with great precision. His work on the structure of the ovary is of prime importance, especially the development of the ovarian follicles and the nurse cells (70); the appearance of the five different stages was found to indicate the age of the mosquito, at least during the first 24 hours after emergence, and also whether it had already oviposited. Christophers placed less importance on the deterioration of the wing fringe as a clue to the age of the insect.

In his early studies on mosquitoes in India with Stephens, Christophers devoted much attention to the species of *Anopheles* and classified them into natural groups, based on the appearance of the adult, larva and egg and their respective habits. At that time (1902) only 16 species had been identified, and no formal subdivisions had been made; by 1933, the number had reached 52 and a classification into two subgenera (*Anopheles* and *Myzomyia*) had become possible. These mosquitoes were described in considerable detail in Christophers's volume (177) on Anophelini in the *Fauna of British India* (1933). Of great importance are his observations on zoogeography and phylogeny which confirmed the grouping of the subgenus, *Myzomyia*, into five (Indian) sections: *Neomyzomyia*, *Myzomyia*, *Paramyzomyia*, *Neocellia* and *Pseudomyzomyia* (133). It is interesting to compare the synonymy of these Indian anophelines in the course of this interval. Christophers (94, 133) himself was responsible for the sinking of many of the well known but incorrect names, though *Anopheles christophersi* ( = *minimus*) and *Anopheles rossi* ( = *subpictus*) were sunk by Edwards. It is unfortunate that the names of these two, most illustrious, malariologists can no longer be attached to anopheline mosquitoes. Christophers carried out original work, either alone or in conjunction with his able assistant P. J. Barraud, on the structure of mosquitoes; e.g. their pilotaxy (92) in systematics; male and female genitalia including the evolution of the terminal abdominal segments and hypopygium (108), and a new terminology for the structures (120); wing venation (124); characteristics of the egg.

Christophers devoted much time to broader studies of mosquitoes and described in detail their bionomics, relations to disease, susceptibility to various parasites and distribution, In this way, he was one of the first entomologists to realize the importance of specific differentiation of the vector in malaria control, i.e. by the introduction of species sanitation, in which the attack is made solely on the known malaria carrier, breeding in what might be a unique situation (e.g. *A. stephensi* in wells), and not on mosquitoes in general.

As early as 1900, Christophers recommended practical measures for control of malaria by reducing the breeding places of *Anopheles* spp. in West Africa, e.g. in Lagos by filling swamps with sand (9), but he was sceptical at that time if any anti-anopheline operations would do much to diminish the prevalence of the disease, and even added that to stamp out malaria from the native population was 'chimerical'. Instead he concentrated on the segregation of Europeans from the illimitable native reservoirs of infection (11). In India, however, he became more optimistic and in conjunction with S. P. James, F.R.S., he reported (40, 58) success in mosquito destruction operations by treatment of the irrigation canals, especially in the notoriously unhealthy conditions of Mian Mir.

In these early years, Christophers stressed the necessity of differentiating prophylaxis of malaria into two groups: (1) as applicable to 'native communities' and (2) as applicable to 'Europeans'. He could not emphasize too strongly the importance of personal precautions, and stated that in over three years of residence in Africa and India, neither he nor J. W. W. Stephens had contracted the disease. He placed the proper use of a mosquito net as 'by far and away the greatest means of individual protection'.

During the Mesopotamian campaigns in World War I, Christophers and Shortt (103) quickly realized the danger that malaria represented and directed their attention to two problems. The first was personal prophylaxis for the troops dispersed in small units, and for this purpose quinine was given daily and mosquito nets were used when practicable. The second problem was to reduce the mosquito population around the Basra base, an area of about 10 square miles. Anopheline breeding places comprised water in excavations and waterlogged ground. Silt was dredged from the river bed and bunds were constructed; the water table sank to 12 ft and mosquito breeding was largely eliminated; the incidence of malaria fell dramatically.

After World War II, Christophers's advice was sought throughout India, particularly in Bombay, Delhi, Assam, and some of his last papers (194, 208) summarized his views on malaria control in India. Naturally, by this time, he emphasized the paramount importance of malaria *in the rural populations* in its different degrees of endemicity, but also he laid great stress on the continuing importance of research; fortunately this aspect is still receiving much attention. He concluded that *organization* is a very essential part of anti-malarial work, and the resurgence of malaria in recent years in the Indian sub-continent illustrates how terrible can be the results of the discontinuation of organized control.

The use of mosquito repellents was investigated by Christophers (197, 200) and he introduced strict methods for the determination of the efficacy of various compounds, and for their proper application. One of the best preparations was devised or modified by him and has the following composition: (DMP cream) dimethyl phthalate 12.5 ml, cera alba (B.P.), 9 g and arachis oil 27.5 ml.

An equally magnificent contribution to the study of mosquitoes was made by Christophers in the last years of his active life, when he produced his monograph on the life history, bionomics and structure of *Aedes aegypti*, 'the yellow fever mosquito'. This work was carried out in the Zoological Laboratories of Cambridge University and was published with addenda in 1960. Although 'yellow fever' figures prominently on the title page, fewer than a dozen pages are devoted to it in the text; nevertheless, it is clear from these pages and other writings (210) that he was intrigued by the complicated life history of the infection in the monkey reservoirs in tropical Africa and America and in a wide variety of curious arboreal mosquitoes (*Aedes aegypti* plays only an accidental role and that outside the forest). Perhaps the most remarkable feature about this book is that it epitomizes the character of Christophers himself; it is thoroughly practical, it is based largely on structure (i.e. the visual aspect of the mosquito) and it contains many original features, including the first ever description of the brain of the mosquito in both larval and imaginal stages. Nearly all the 86 line drawings which accompany the text were made by the author and are of the finest calibre.

Even as late as 1960, Christophers was still fascinated by the *Rules of zoological nomenclature*, and was only too delighted to take up the challenge of

Sir William MacArthur who objected to the use of a diaeresis in the 'generic name Aëdes'; it was typical of him also that at the age of 87 years he (213) was still capable of changing a lifetime's habit and accepting *Aedes* as the correct form (Article 27 of the 1964 *Rules* validates the omission of a diaresis and all diacritical marks). In spite of his advanced age, Christophers was able to include in this monograph, most of the important new developments up to its date of publication, including the mode of action of, and resistance to, insecticides, genetics and chromosome structure, insect hormones and other recently discovered physiological processes.

During the course of Christophers's observations (see p. 193) on haemogregarines in the erythrocytes of dogs in Madras, he noticed that these animals were heavily infested with ticks, in which arthropods he found that the haemogregarine *Leucocytozoon canis* ( = *Hepatozoon canis*) underwent sporogonic development. In order to follow the latter in detail, he had to ascertain the anatomical and histological structure of the internal organs of ticks (50). He took as an example of argasid ticks, the desert-inhabiting *Ornithodorus savignyi*, and of ixodid ticks, *Rhipicephalus annulatus* and *Hyalomma aegyptium*. He found a great similarity in their internal structure, but reported profound differences in their physiological characters. His observations on embryology and the ovum are of much importance in view of the hereditary transmission of parasites in ticks, which process he was one of the first to demonstrate.

Christophers, Shortt and Barraud (153) made a detailed study of the sandfly, *Phlebotomus argentipes*, and especially the mouthparts, while his assistant, Barraud, developed a breeding technique for all stages from oviposition to the emergence of the adult fly. Observations on the detailed histology of specimens enabled these observers to trace the anatomical course of experimental infection from the midgut to the proboscis (see pp. 191 above).

## Honours and prizes

Sir Rickard Christophers received many tributes on the occasion of his centenary in November 1973. The Royal Society of Tropical Medicine and Hygiene (of which he had been President from 1939 to 1943) published in its *Transactions* (**67**, 729–754) messages from 17 of his friends and past colleagues from India, Nigeria, United States, Venezuela, France, Portugal, Italy, Germany and the United Kingdom. The Royal Entomological Society held a special meeting, honouring him as one of the foremost entomologists of the world (1974).

The year before his death, a symposium to commemorate the 'Birth of Medical Entomology' was arranged by Dr Michael Service; its proceedings (published in the *Transactions of the Royal Society of Tropical Medicine and Hygiene* 1968) were dedicated to Christophers who had done so much to nurture the 'Offspring'. In 1979, a 'Christophers Medal' is being endowed by the Royal Society of Tropical Medicine and Hygiene to commemorate his life and achievements.

Before we complete this memoir of a very remarkable man it is of interest to record the observations of his granddaughter, Mrs P. Parker, who knew him in his declining years, looked after him and was greatly attached to him. She writes:

> 'He was by nature very reticent as you know and the characteristic that never changed, even when he was ill, was his gentleness and thoughtfulness for others. At the nursing home not one of the staff had ever had a word of complaint or irritability and he was held in great affection by them all. He was always most anxious that people should not go to any trouble on *his* behalf—yet he never spared himself if he thought he could be of help to others. Examples of his letters show how much time he devoted to requests for help of all kinds and what great pains he took to answer their questions, take up their battles or send donations!
>
> 'He was most determined to look at his advancing age in a scientific manner and it took him a long time to accept a guiding hand across the road, preferring to be entirely independent in his movements.'

Christophers enjoyed a long and happy life with his wife, Lady Christophers, until her death in 1963. She was the ideal foil to the dedicated scientist.

We are grateful to various people for providing personal details and other information; in particular we wish to thank Mrs Patricia Parker, who remained in close contact with her grandfather until the end. We acknowledge also the help of Mr N. H. Robinson, the Librarian of the Royal Society, of Dr M. Service of the Liverpool School of Tropical Medicine, of the late Mr P. G. Shute, O.B.E., who maintained a correspondence with Christophers over a period of 50 years, and of other friends and admirers of the 'verray parfit gentil knight' as Professor Bruce-Chwatt termed him in the centennial publication. We are much indebted to Dr James Williamson of the National Institute of Medical Research, for the summary of Christophers's biochemical investigations (pp. 189, 190). To Mrs Christian Thompson in a personal interview we are indebted for details relating to the career of Christophers's son Vagn.

The photograph of Christophers was taken in 1916 by H. E. Shortt on board the *Elphinstone*, in the former's laboratory, at Basra during the Mesopotamian campaign of World War I.

## Medals and public honours

| | |
|---|---|
| 1892 | Torr Gold Medals for Anatomy and Physiology, University of Liverpool |
| 1898 | Holt Tutorial Scholar in Physiology and Pathology, University of Liverpool |
| 1915 | Commander of the Star of India |
| 1918 | Officer of the British Empire Order (Mil.) |
| 1923 | Barclay Memorial Medal, Royal Asiatic Society |
| 1926 | Fellow of the Royal Society |
| 1928 | Wilhelmina Jubilee Medal (Netherlands-Indies) |
| 1927–30 | Honorary Physician to His Majesty King George V |
| 1931 | Knight Bachelor |
| 1934 | Mary Kingsley Medal, Liverpool School of Tropical Medicine |
| 1944 | Manson Medal, Royal Society of Tropical Medicine and Hygiene |
| 1952 | Buchanan Medal of the Royal Society |
| 1962 | Gaspar Vianna Medal and Decoration, Brazil |

### Honorary appointments and degrees

1908 Corresponding Member, Société de Pathologie Exotique, Paris
1940 Hon. Fellow, National Institute of Sciences of India
1942–45 Member of the Entomological Subcommittee of the Military Personnel Committee of the Medical Research Council
1942 Hon. M.A., Cambridge
1942 Hon. Fellow, Downing College, Cambridge
1943–45 Malaria Committee of the Medical Research Council
1950 Membre d'Honneur, Société de Pathologie Exotique
1951 Hon. Member, American Academy of Tropical Medicine
1953 Hon. Fellow of the National Society of India for Malaria and other Mosquito-borne Diseases

### References

Bacon, F. 1625 *Essays and counsels*. London & Glasgow: Collins (undated).

Bruce-Chwatt, L. J. & Glanville, V. S. 1973 (Editors) *Dynamics of tropical diseases* by the late George Macdonald. London: Oxford University Press.

Foster, M. 1898 Unpublished letter from the Secretary of the Royal Society to the Secretary of State, Colonial Office, London, dated 2 August 1898.

Hemming, F. 1954 *Opinions and declarations rendered by the International Commission of Zoological Nomenclature*, vol. 7. London.

Hoogstraal, H. 1961 The life cycle and incidence of *Hepatozoon balfouri* (Laveran, 1905) in Egyptian jerboas (*Jaculus* spp.) and mites (*Haemolaelaps aegyptius*). *J. Protozool.* **8**, 231–248.

Lounsbury, C. P. 1901 Transmission of malignant jaundice of the dog by a species of tick. *Agric. J. Cape G. H.* **19**, 714–722.

Manson, P. & Sambon, L. 1900 Anonymous editorial on 'A malaria conference in Rome'. *Br. med. J.* 10 February, pp. 323–325.

Rogers, L. 1904 Preliminary note on the development of *Trypanosoma* in cultures of the Cunningham–Leishman–Donovan bodies of cachexial fever and kala-azar. *Lancet* **11**, 215–216.

Smith, T. & Kilborne, F. E. 1893 Investigations into the nature, cause, and prevention of Texas or southern cattle fever. *U.S. Dept. Agric. Bur. Anim. Indust. Bull.* 1.

Swaminath, C. S., Shortt, H. E. & Anderson, L. A. P. 1942 Transmission of Indian kala-azar to man by the bites of *Phlebotomus argentipes*. *Indian J. med. Res.* **30**, 473–477.

Wilson, D. B., Garnham, P. C. C. & Swellengrebel, N. H. 1950 A review of hyperendemic malaria. *Trop. Dis. Bull.* **47**, 677–698.

Symposium to commemorate the 'Birth of Medical Entomology', dedicated to Sir Rickard Christophers on his 100th birthday. 1973. *Trans. R. Soc. trop. Med. Hyg.* **67**, 728–754.

A tribute to Sir Richard Christophers on his 100th birthday. 1974 *Trans. R. ent. Soc. Lond.* **125**, 253–256.

### Bibliography

(1) 1898 Note on the specific action of normal human serum on the *Bacillus coli communis*. *Br. med. J.* **1**, 71–72, 502.

(2) 1900 (With J. W. W. Stephens) The malarial and blackwater fevers of British Central Africa. *Rep. Malar. Comm. R. Soc. Lond.* (1), 12–41.

(3) (With J. W. W. Stephens) Distribution of Anopheles in Sierra Leone. *Rept. Malar. Comm. R. Soc. Lond.* (1), 42–75.

(4) (With J. W. W. Stephens) The native as the prime agent in the malarial infection of Europeans. *Rep. Malar. Comm. R. Soc. Lond.* (2), 3–19.

(5) (With J. W. W. Stephens) Note on certain bodies found in the glands of two species of Culex. *Rep. Malar. Comm. R. Soc. Lond.* (2), 20.

(6) (With J. W. W. Stephens) The malaria of expeditionary forces and the means of its prevention. *Rep. Malar. Comm. R. Soc. Lond.* (2), 20–22.

(7) (With J. W. W. Stephens) The agglutination of sporozoites. *Rep. Malar. Comm. R. Soc. Lond.* (3), 1.

(8) (With J. W. W. Stephens) The malarial infection of native children. *Rep. Malar. Comm. R. Soc. Lond.* (3), 2–13.

(9) 1900 (With J. W. W. Stephens) The destruction of Anopheles in Lagos. *Rep. Malar. Comm. R. Soc. Lond.* (3), 14–19.

(10) (With J. W. W. Stephens) Note on malarial fever on railways under construction. *Rep. Malar. Comm. R. Soc. Lond.* (3), 20.

(11) (With J. W. W. Stephens) The segregation of Europeans. *Rep. Malar. Comm. R. Soc. Lond.* (3), 21–24.

(12) (With J. W. W. Stephens) Blackwater fever and malaria. *Br. med. J.* **2**, 1406–1407.

(13) 1901 The prevention of malaria in tropical Africa. *Thompson Yates Johnston. Lab. Rep.* **3**, part 2, 169–176.

(14) (With J. W. W. Stephens & S. P. James) Note on the occurrence of *Anopheles funestus* and *Anopheles costalis* in India. *Indian med. Gaz.* **36**, 361.

(15) The anatomy and histology of the adult female mosquito. *Rep. Malar. Comm. R. Soc. Lond.* (4), 3–20.

(16) (With J. W. W. W. Stephens) Proposed site for European residents in the Freetown Hills. *Rep. Malar. Comm. R. Soc. Lond.* (5), 1–4.

(17) (With J. W. W. Stephens) Mononuclear leucocytosis diagnostic of malaria. *Rep. Malar. Comm. R. Soc. Lond.* (5), 5–6.

(18) (With J. W. W. Stephens) Malarial fever without parasites. *Rep. Malar. Comm. R. Soc. Lond.* (5), 7–9.

(19) (With J. W. W. Stephens) Tonicity of blood in malaria and blackwater fever. *Rep. Malar. Comm. R. Soc. Lond.* (5), 10–11.

(20) (With J. W. W. Stephens) Blackwater fever: summary and conclusions. *Rep. Malar. Comm. R. Soc. Lond.* (5), 12–27.

(21) 1902 (With J. W. W. Stephens) The relation of malarial endemicity to species of Anopheles. *Rep. Malar. Comm. R. Soc. Lond.* (6), 3–10.

(22) (With J. W. W. Stephens) Some points in the biology of species of Anopheles found in Bengal. *Rep. Malar. Comm. R. Soc. Lond.* (6), 11–19.

(23) (With J. W. W. Stephens) The relation between enlarged spleen and parasite infection. *Rep. Malar. Comm. R. Soc. Lond.* (6), 20–23.

(24) (With J. W. W. Stephens) The classification of Indian Anopheles into natural groups. *Rep. Malar. Comm. R. Soc. Lond.* (7), 3–14.

(25) (With J. W. W. Stephens) The relation of species of Anopheles to malarial endemicity. *Rep. Malar. Comm. R. Soc. Lond.* (7), 15–19.

(26) (With J. W. W. Stephens) The relation of species of Anopheles to malarial endemicity (further report). *Rep. Malar. Comm. R. Soc. Lond.* (7), 20–22.

(27) (With J. W. W. Stephens) An investigation into the factors that determine malarial endemicity. *Rep. Malar. Comm. R. Soc. Lond.* (7), 23–44.

(28) (With J. W. W. Stephens) Note on bodies in the salivary glands of Anopheles. *Rep. Malar. Comm. R. Soc. Lond.* (7), 45–46.

(29) (With J. W. W. Stephens) Malarial fever without parasites in the peripheral blood. *Trans. Malar. Conf. held Nagpur Jan. 1902*, pp. 29–33. Nagpur Jail Press.

(30) (In discussion) The value of the spleen test as an indicator of the prevalence of malaria. *Trans. Malar. Conf. held Nagpur Jan. 1902*, pp. 56–57. Nagpur Jail Press.

(31) (With J. W. W. Stephens) Relation between species of Anopheles and the endemicity of malaria (abstract). *Trans. Malar. Conf. held. Nagpur Jan. 1902*, pp. 85–87. Nagpur Jail Press.

(32) (In discussion) Mosquito eggs and larvae. *Trans. Malar. Conf. held Nagpur Jan. 1902*, p. 99. Nagpur Jail Press.

(33) On the feeding and dissection of mosquitoes. *Trans. Malar. Conf. held Nagpur Jan. 1902*, pp. 101–103. Nagpur Jail Press.

(34) (With J. W. W. Stephens) The occurrence of blackwater fever in India. *Rep. Malar. Comm. R. Soc. Lond.* (8) 1–2.

(35) (With J. W. W. Stephens) Malaria in an Indian cantonment (Mian Mir); an experimental application of antimalarial measures. *Rep. Malar. Comm. R. Soc. Lond.* (8), 3–21.

(36) (With J. W. W. Stephens) Brief summary of conclusions arrived at in previous papers. *Rep. Malar. Comm. R. Soc. Lond.* (8), 22–26.

(37) 1902 (With J. W. W. STEPHENS) Summary of researches on native malaria and malaria prophylaxis; on blackwater fever its nature and prophylaxis. *Thompson Yates Johnston Lab. Rep.* (n.s.) **5**, part 1, 221–233.

(38) (With J. W. W. STEPHENS) Note on the changes in the red cell produced by the malignant tertian parasite. *Br. med. J.* **1**, 730.

(39) (With J. W. W. STEPHENS) *The practical study of malaria and other blood parasites* (1st ed.). London: Longmans Green & Co.

(40) 1904 (With S. P. JAMES) The success of mosquito destructive operations. *Br. med. J.* **2**, 631.

(41) A preliminary report on a parasite found in persons suffering from enlargement of the spleen in India. *Scient. Mem. Offrs med. sanit. Deps India* (n.s.) no. 8.

(42) Second report of the antimalarial operations at Mian Mir, 1901–1903. *Scient. Mem. Offrs med. sanit. Deps India* (n.s.) no. 9.

(43) On a parasite found in persons suffering from enlargement of the spleen in India. (Second rep.) *Scient. Mem. Offrs med. sanit. Deps India* (n.s.) no. **11**.

(44) (With J. W. W. STEPHENS) *The practical study of malaria* (2nd ed.). London: Longmans Green & Co.

(45) 1905 On a parasite found in persons suffering from enlargement of the spleen in India. (Third rep.) *Scient. Mem. Offrs med. sanit. Deps India* (n.s.) no. 15.

(46) *Haemogregarina gerbilli. Scient. Mem. Offrs med. sanit. Deps India* (n.s.) no. 18.

(47) Malaria in the Koraput Hills. *Trans. S. Indian Brch. Brit. med. Ass.* **13**, 5–15.

(48) 1906 (With R. NEWSTEAD) On a new pathogenic louse which acts as the intermediate host of a new haemogregarine in the blood of the Indian field rat (*Gerbillus indica*). *Thompson Yates Johnston Lab. Rep.* (n.s.) **7**, part 1, 3–6.

(49) (With J. W. W. STEPHENS) *Étude pratique du paludisme et des parasites du sang.* (Transl. from the English by Ed. and Et. Sergent.) Paris: Doin.

(50) The anatomy and histology of ticks. *Scient. Mem. Offrs med. sanit. Deps India* (n.s.) no. 23.

(41) On the importance of larval characters in the classification of mosquitoes. *Scient. Mem. Offrs med. sanit. Deps India* (n.s.) no. 25.

(52) *Leucocytozoon canis. Scient. Mem Offrs med. sanit. Deps India* (n.s.) no. 26.

(53) 1907 The sexual cycle of *Leucocytozoon canis* in the tick. *Scient. Mem. Offrs med. sanit. Deps India* (n.s.) no. 28.

(54) *Piroplasma canis* and its life cycle in the tick. *Scient. Mem. Offrs med. sanit. Deps India* (n.s.) no. 29.

(55) 1908 *The practical study of malaria and other blood parasites* (3rd ed.). Liverpool: University Press.

(56) (With C. A. BENTLEY) Note on the phagocytosis of red blood corpuscles in the spleen of a case of blackwater fever. *Indian med. Gaz.* **43**, 81–82.

(57) (With C. A. BENTLEY) Blackwater fever. *Scient. Mem. Offrs med. sanit. Deps India* (n.s.) no. 35.

(58) 1909 (With S. P. JAMES) Malaria in India: what can the state do to prevent it? *Indian med. Gaz.* **44**, 272–274.

(59) (With C. A. BENTLEY) *Malaria in the Duars.* (Second report to the Advisory Committee appointed by the Govt of India to conduct an enquiry regarding blackwater fever and other fevers prevalent in the Duars.) (105 pages.) Simla: Govt Monotype Press.

(60) (With C. A. BENTLEY) The intimate pathology of malaria in relation to blackwater fever. *Trans. Bombay Med. Congr.* pp. 74–76.

(61) (With C. A. BENTLEY) The human factor. An extension of our knowledge regarding the epidemiology of malarial disease. *Trans. Bombay Med. Congr.* pp. 78–83.

(62) (In discussion) Malaria in Mian Mir. *Trans. Bombay Med. Congr.* pp. 90–91.

(63) 1910 A new statistical method of mapping epidemic disease in India with special reference to the mapping of epidemic malaria. *Proc. imp. Malar. Conf. Simla, Oct. 1909*, pp. 16–22. Simla: Govt Central Branch Press.

(64) On malaria in the Punjab. *Proc. imp. Malar. Conf. Simla Oct. 1909*, pp. 29–44. Simla: Govt Central Branch Press.

(65) A short note on syllabus of work done at the malaria class held at Amritsar during the month of April 1910. *Paludism* **1**, 13–15.

(66) 1911 Suggestions on use of available statistics for studying malaria in India. *Paludism* **1**, 16–32.
(67) Epidemic malaria on the Punjab, with notes on a new method of predicting epidemic years. *Paludism* **2**, 17–26.
(68) Notes on mosquitoes; a new anopheline, *Neocellia fowleri* n. sp. *Paludism* **2**, 64–68.
(69) A new culicine, *Leslieomyia taeniorrhynchus* nov. gen. et sp. *Paludism* **2**, 68–72.
(70) Development of the egg follicle in anophelines. *Paludism* **2**, 73–88.
(71) On the selection of unit areas for recording data concerning malaria in India. *Paludism* **3**, 15–23.
(72) Aids to identification of Culicidae other than *Anopheles* with special reference to Indian species. *Paludism* **3**, 40–54.
(73) A system of mounting and preserving mosquitoes. *Paludism* **3**, 57–61.
(74) (With C. A. Gill & H. Acton) *A. turkhudi* at altitude of 6000 feet. *Paludism* **3**, 64.
(75) Revised and new descriptions of Indian *Anopheles*. *Paludism* **3**, 66–67.
(76) Malariometry: observations upon graphs of the spleen rate and average spleen. *Paludism* **3**, 87–102.
(77) The working of the Central Malaria Bureau. *Paludism* **4**, 25–27.
(78) Malaria in the Andamans. *Paludism* **4**, 42–45.
(79) (In discussion) Antimalaria operations in Bombay. *Paludism* **4**, 74–75.
(80) Epidemic malaria in India. *Paludism* **4**, 81–82.
(81) Canals and mosquito breeding. *Paludism* **4**, 97–99.
(82) Prejudices against quinine. *Paludism* **4**, 126–127.
(83) Malaria in the Punjab. *Scient. Mem. Offrs med. sanit. Deps India* (n.s.) no. 46.
(84) 1912 The development of *Leucocytozoon canis* in the tick with a reference to the development of *Piroplasma*. *Parasitology* **5**, 37–48.
(85) Malaria in the Andamans. *Scient. Mem. Offrs med. sanit. Deps India* (n.s.) no. 56.
(86) 1913 Contributions to the study of colour markings and other variable characters of Anophelinae with special reference to the systematic and phylogenetic grouping of species. *Ann. trop. Med. Parasit.* **7**, 45–100.
(87) (With R. Ross & E. L. Perry) The spleen rate in London children. *Indian J. med. Res.* **1**, 385–387.
(88) 1914 (In discussion) Malaria and silting. *Proc. 3rd All India San. Conf. Lucknow, Jan. 1914. Indian J. med. Res., Suppl.* **1**, 44–46.
(89) The spleen rate and other splenic indices: their nature and significance. *Indian J. med. Res.* **2**, 823–866.
(90) (With Khazan Chand) Notes on some anophelines from Arabia and Mesopotamia. *Indian J. med. Res.* **3**, 180–200.
(91) (With K. R. K. Iyengar) The effect of haemolytic drugs, toxins and antisera upon the haemolytic point (so-called isotonic point) and the association between this and haemoglobinuria. *Indian J. med. Res.* **3**, 232–250.
(92) The pilotaxy of *Anopheles*. *Indian J. med. Res.* **3**, 362–370.
(93) The male genitalia of *Anopheles*. *Indian J. med. Res.* **3**, 371–394.
(94) 1916 A revision of the nomenclature of Indian Anophelini. *Indian J. med. Res.* **3**, 454–488.
(95) An Indian tree-hole breeding *Anopheles*. *A. barianensis* James (*A. coelodiazesis plumbeus* Haliday). *Indian J. med. Res.* **3**, 489–496.
(96) (With Khazan Chand) A tree-hole breeding *Anopheles* from Southern India, *A. culiciformis* Cogill. *Indian J. med. Res.* **3**, 638–645.
(97) A new anopheline with unspotted wings from Mesopotamia. *Indian J. med. Res.* **4**, 120–122.
(98) 1917 *Lectures on malaria*. (14 pages.) Simla: Govt Central Press. Reprinted 1924, 1925 as *Hlth Bull.* no. 5.
(99) 1920 A summary of recent observations upon the *Anopheles* of the Middle East. *Indian J. med. Res.* **7**, 710–716.
(100) (With K. R. K. Iyengar & W. F. Harvey) Standardisation of disinfectants with special reference to those used in the chemical sterilisation of water. *Indian J. med. Res.* **7**, 803–809.
(101) 1921 (With H. E. Shortt) Malaria in Mesopotamia. *Indian J. med. Res.* **8**, 508–552.

(102) 1921 (With H. E. Shortt) Incidence of malaria among troops in Mesopotamia, 1916–1919. *Indian J. med. Res.* **8**, 553–570.

(103) (With H. E. Shortt) Antimalarial operations at Busra, 1916–1919. *Indian J. med. Res.* **8**, 571–592.

(104) (With W. F. Harvey & K. R. K. Iyengar) The influence of age and temperature on bacterial vaccines. *Indian J. med. Res.* **8**, 715–730.

(105) The distribution of mosquitoes in relation to the zoogeographical areas of the Indian Empire. *Rep. Proc. 4th Entom. Meeting, Pusa.* Calcutta: Govt Printing Press.

(106) 1922 The geographical distribution of the Anophelini. *Trans. 4th Congr. Far East Ass. Trop. Med.*, pp. 421–430.

(107) (With F. W. Cragg) On the so-called 'penis' of the bed-bug (*Cimex lectularius* L.) and the homologies generally of the male and female genitalia of this insect. *Indian J. med. Res.* **9**, 445–463.

(108) The development and structure of the terminal abdominal segments and hypopygium of the mosquito (with observations on the homologies of the terminal segments of the larva). *Indian J. med. Res.* **10**, 530–572.

(109) (With S. P. James) Malaria: synonyms; definitions; geographical distribution. In: W. Byam and R. G. Archibald, *Practice of medicine in the tropics*, pp. 1500–1507. London: Frowde & Hodder & Stoughton.

(110) (With S. P. James) Malaria: general aetiology. In: W. Byam and R. G. Archibald, *Practice of medicine in the tropics*, pp. 1507–1514.

(111) Malaria: endemic, epidemic and incidental malaria. In W. Byam and R. G. Archibald, *Practice of medicine in the tropics*, pp. 1546–1554.

(112) (With S. P. James) Malaria: serious cases, complications and sequelae. In: W. Byam and R. G. Archibald, *Practice of medicine in the tropics*, pp. 1599–1620.

(113) Report on malaria at Assam sugar estates and factories, Nalbari, Assam, 1921. (20 pages.) Calcutta. Republished with another report in *Indian J. med. Res.* **13**, 363–400, 1925.

(114) 1923 An *Anopheles* of the *Myzorhynchus* group (*Anopheles amazonicus* sp. n.) from South America. *Ann. trop. Med. Parasit.* **17**, 71–75.

(115) Note on outbreaks of malaria on ships leaving Bombay in the autumn of 1922, with some remarks on the new Back Bay Reclamation Scheme and other points connected with malaria in Bombay. (MSS report in Office of Director Publ. Hlth Bombay Presidency, Poona.)

(116) Note on the prevention of the introduction of malaria and of the mosquito nuisance into the New Imperial City of Delhi. (MSS report in Office of Hlth Officer of Delhi Imperial City, Delhi.)

(117) *Enquiry on malaria, blackwater fever and anchylostomiasis in Singhbhum.* Rept no. 1. Preliminary investigation into conditions on the Bengal Iron Company's mines at Manhapur, Jan. 1923. Govt Publ. Behar and Orissa.

(118) The structure and development of the female genital organs and hypopygium of the mosquito. *Indian J. med. Res.* **10**, 698–720.

(119) (With W. F. Harvey) Malaria research and preventive measures against malaria in the F.M.S. and the Dutch East Indies. *Indian J. med. Res.* **10**, 749–771.

(120) (With P. J. Barraud) Descriptive terminology of male genitalia characters. *Indian J. med. Res.* **10**, 827–835.

(121) A new East African anopheline (*A. kingi*) related to *A. natalensis* Hill and Haydon and *A. watsoni* Leicester. *Indian J. med. Res.* **10**, 1008–1019.

(122) 1924 (With Khazan Chand) Measurement in centimetres of the enlarged spleen in children and its correction for size of child by a factor based on an anthropomorphic measurement. *Indian J. med. Res.* **11**, 1065–1080.

(123) The shape and position of the palpable portion of the enlarged spleen in children. *Indian J. med. Res.* **11**, 1081–1102.

(124) (With P. J. Barraud) The tracheation and venation of the wing of the mosquito. *Indian J. med. Res.* **11**, 1103–1118.

(125) The frequency distribution of measurements of the enlarged spleen in a malarious child community. *Indian J. med. Res.* **11**, 1245–1252.

(126) 1924 Some Himalayan and Peninsular varieties of Indian species of *Anopheles. Indian J. med. Res.* **12**, 11–14.

(127) The mechanism of immunity against malaria in communities living under hyper-endemic conditions. *Indian J. med. Res.* **12**, 273–294.

(128) Some further varieties of Indian species of *Anopheles* with notes on the species *A. pallidus* Theobald and *A. philippinensis* Ludlow. *Indian J. med. Res.* **12**, 295–301.

(129) What disease costs India, being a statement of the problem before medical research in India. Presidential Address Med. San. Sect. 5th Indian Sci. Cong., 1924. *Indian med. Gaz.* **59**, 196–200.

(130) Lectures on malaria. *Hlth Bull., Govt of India* no. 5. Simla: Govt Press.

(131) The measurement of the enlarged spleen. *Trans. 5th Congr. Far East Ass. Trop. Med.*, pp. 101–112. London: Bale Sons & Danielsson.

(132) Instructions for collecting and forwarding specimens in connection with the investigation of mosquitoes and malaria. *Hlth Bull., Govt of India* no. 8 (*Malar. Bur. Bull.* no. 1). (3rd ed.)

(133) Provisional list and reference catalogue of the Anophelini. *Indian med. Res. Mem.* no. 3.

(134) 1925 (With H. E. Shortt & P. J. Barraud) The development of the parasite of Indian kala azar in the sandfly *Phlebotomus argentipes* Annandale and Brunetti. *Indian J. med. Res.* **12**, 605–607.

(135) (With E. D. W. Greig) Infection of a monkey (*Macacus rhesus*) with the parasite of Indian kala azar following introduction of infective material into the lumen of the small intestine. *Indian J. med. Res.* **13**, 151–157.

(136) (With H. E. Shortt & P. J. Barraud) Temperature in relation to culture of *Herpetomonas donovani* on NNN medium. *Indian J. med. Res.* **13**, 167–171.

(137) (With H. E. Shortt & P. J. Barraud) The effect of salt solution of different concentrations on the parasite of Indian kala azar. *Indian J. med. Res.* **13**, 177–182.

(138) Two malarial surveys connected with industrial projects in certain very highly malarious localities in India. *Indian J. med. Res.* **13**, 363–406.

(139) Man, Anopheles and the malarial parasite in relation to the faunas. *Indian med. Gaz.* **60**, 279–280.

(140) 1926 Introduction to Report no. 1 (1924–5) of the Kala azar Commission. *Indian med. Res. Mem.* no. 4, 3–18.

(141) (With H. E. Shortt & P. J. Barraud) The morphology and life cycle of the parasite of Indian kala azar in culture. *Indian med. Res. Mem.* no. 4, 19–53.

(142) (With H. E. Shortt & P. J. Barraud) Temperature in relation to culture of *Herpetomonas donovani* on NNN medium. *Indian med. Res. Mem.* no. 4, 55–59.

(143) (With H. E. Shortt & P. J. Barraud) The effect of salt solution of different concentrations on the parasite of Indian kala azar. *Indian med. Res. Mem.* no. 4, 61–66.

(144) (With E. D. W. Greig) Infection of a monkey (*Macacus rhesus*) with the parasite of Indian kala azar following the introduction of infective material into the lumen of the small intestine. *Indian med. Res. Mem.* no. 4, 69–75.

(145) (With H. E. Shortt & P. J. Barraud) The result of intraperitoneal inoculation of mice with cultures of *Leishmania donovani. Indian med. Res. Mem.* no. 4, 77–87.

(146) (With H. E. Shortt & P. J. Barraud) The result of feeding mice with cultures of *Herpetomonas donovani. Indian med. Res. Mem.* no. 4, 89–103.

(147) (With H. E. Shortt & P. J. Barraud) The development of the parasite of Indian kala azar in the sandfly, *Phlebotomus argentipes* Annandale and Brunetti. *Indian med. Res. Mem.* no. 4, 123–125.

(148) (With H. E. Shortt & P. J. Barraud) Further observations on the feeding of sandflies, *Phlebotomus argentipes*, on cases of kala azar. *Indian med. Res. Mem.* no. 4, 127–133.

(149) (With H. E. Shortt & P. J. Barraud) Development of the parasite of Indian kala azar in the sandfly, *Phlebotomus argentipes*: controls. *Indian med. Res. Mem.* no. 4, 135–139.

(150) 1926 (With H. E. Shortt & P. J. Barraud) Development of the parasite of Indian kala azar in the sandfly, *Phlebotomus argentipes*: refed flies and further results in the feeding of sandflies on kala azar cases. *Indian med. Res. Mem.* no. 4, 141–145.

(151) (With H. E. Shortt & P. J. Barraud) The feeding of larvae of *Phlebotomus argentipes* Annandale and Brunetti on cultures of *Leishmania donovani*. *Indian med. Res. Mem.* no. 4, 155–156.

(152) (With H. E. Shortt & P. J. Barraud) Technique employed in breeding *Phlebotomus argentipes* in Assam. *Indian med. Res. Mem.* no. 4, 173–175.

(153) (With H. E. Shortt & P. J. Barraud) The anatomy of the sandfly, *Phlebotomus argentipes*, Ann. and Brun. (Diptera). I. The head and mouthparts. *Indian med. Res. Mem.* no. 4, 177–204.

(154) (*A. Myzomyia*) *pattoni*, a new *Anopheles* from Shan Tung, North China, with notes on some other species of *Anopheles* from the same locality. *Indian J. med. Res.* **13**, 871–876.

(155) (With J. A. Sinton) A malaria map of India. *Indian J. med. Res.* **14**, 173–178.

(156) 1927 (With J. A. Sinton & G. Covell) Synoptic table for identification of the anopheline mosquitoes of India. *Hlth Bull., Govt of India* no. 10 (*Malar. Bur. Bull.* no. 2).

(157) Instructions for collecting and forwarding mosquitoes. *Hlth Bull., Govt of India* no. 13 (*Malar. Bur. Bull.* no. 5).

(158) *Report on malaria in Delhi.* (22 pages.) Govt Publ., Imperial Province of Delhi.

(159) Souvenir: the Indian Empire. A brief description of the chief features of India and its medical and sanitary problems. *7th Congr. Far East. Ass. Trop. Med.* Calcutta: Thacker's Directories.

(160) 1928 (With J. A. Sinton & G. Covell) How to do a malaria survey. *Hlth Bull., Govt of India* no. 14 (*Malar. Bur. Bull.* no. 6).

(161) 1929 A summary of what is known of the significance of the spleen rate and average size of the large spleen in malaria. *Trans. 7th Congr. Far East. Ass. Trop. Med.* **2**, 756–772.

(162) (With I. M. Puri) Why do Anopheles larvae feed at the surface and how? *Trans. 7th Congr. Far East. Ass. Trop. Med.* **3**, 737–738.

(163) Note on a collection of anopheline and culicine mosquitoes from Madeira and the Canary Islands. *Indian J. med. Res.* **17**, 518–530.

(164) The mixture reaction in haemolysis by acids and bases. *Indian J. med. Res.* **17**, 533–543.

(165) Haemolysis by acid and base and by acid and basic salts, including quinine and its salts. *Indian J. med. Res.* **17**, 544–563.

(166) The electric charge of the red blood corpuscle haemoglobin and stroma in relation to haemolysis. *Indian J. med. Res.* **17**, 564–573.

(167) 1931 (With I. M. Puri) Note on some anopheline mosquitoes collected in Sierra Leone including differentiation of *Anopheles d'thali* Patton (Mediterranean) as a distinct species from *A. rhodesiensis* (Ethiopian). *Indian J. med. Res.* **18**, 1133–1166.

(168) (With P. J. Barraud) The eggs of Indian *Anopheles* with descriptions of hitherto undescribed eggs of a number of species. *Rec. Malar. Surv. India* **2**, 161–192.

(169) (With P. J. Barraud) On a collection of anopheline and culicine mosquitoes from Siam. *Rec. Malar. Surv. India* **2**, 269–285.

(170) Studies on the anopheline fauna of India I–IV. *Rec. Malar. Surv. India* **2**, 305–332.

(171) (With I. M. Puri) Species and varieties of the *funestus* series of *Anopheles*. *Rec. Malar. Surv. India* **2**, 481–493.

(172) *The science of disease.* Presidential address 17th Indian Science Congr. held at Allahabad, 1930.

(173) 1932 (With A. C. Craighead) The diffraction (halometric) method of determining the average diameter of red blood corpuscles. *Indian J. med. Res.* **19**, 963–976.

(174) (In discussion) Dr. Giglioli's paper on blackwater fever. *Trans. R. Soc. trop. Med. Hyg.* **26**, 231–232.

(175) 1933 (In discussion) Dr. Kellaway's paper on snake venome. *Trans. R. Soc. trop. Med. Hyg.* **27**, 27–28.

(176) 1933 (With A. Missiroli) Report on housing and malaria; being a summary of what is is known about anophelism in relation to housing and malaria. *Q. Bull. Hlth Org. L. of N.* **2**, 355–482.

(177) Family Culicidae. Tribe Anophelini. *Fauna of British India. Diptera*, vol. 4. London: Taylor & Francis.

(178) 1934 (In discussion) Dr. Hackett's paper on subspecies of *Anopheles maculipennis. Trans. R. Soc. trop. Med. Hyg.* **27**, 132–134.

(178a) Malaria from a zoological point of view. *Proc. R. Soc. Med.* **27**, 991–1000.

(179) 1936 (With J. A. Sinton & G. Covell) How to do a malaria survey (3rd ed.). *Hlth Bull., Govt of India* no. 14 (*Malar. Bur. Bull.* no. 6).

(180) (In discussion) Col. Gill's paper on the malaria epidemic in Ceylon. *Trans. R. Soc. trop. Med. Hyg.* **29**, 466–469.

(181) 1937 (In discussion) Sir R. Archibald's paper on kala azar in the Sudan. *Trans. R. Soc. trop. Med. Hyg.* **30**, 400–401.

(182) (In discussion) Dr Hamilton Fairley and Dr Bromfield's paper on blackwater fever. *Trans. R. Soc. trop. Med. Hyg.* **31**, 171–172.

(183) Dissociation constants and solubilities of bases of antimalarial compounds. I. Quinine. II. Atebrin. *Ann. trop. Med. Parasit.* **31**, 43–69.

(184) Observations on *Plasmodium knowlesi* infection in *Silenus rhesus*, with description of some physico-chemical properties of isolated parasite substance. *Rep. Proc. 2nd Int. Congr. Microbiol., London 1936*, pp. 282–000.

(185) 1938 (With J. A. Sinton) The correct name of the malignant tertian malaria parasite. *Br. med. J.* **2**, 1130–1134.

(186) (With J. D. Fulton) Observations on the respiratory metabolism of malaria parasites and tyrpanosomes. *Ann. trop. Med. Parasit.* **32**, 43–75.

(187) (With J. D. Fulton) Respiratory metabolism of *Trypanosoma rhodesiense* and *Plasmodium knowlesi* with observations on the inhibitory effect of various compounds on $O_2$ uptake by these organisms. *Acta Conventus Tertii de Tropicis atque Malariae Morbis II*, pp. 509–514. Amsterdam: Spin and Zoon.

(188) (With J. D. Fulton) The inhibitive effect of drugs upon oxygen uptake by trypanosomes (*Trypanosoma rhodesiense*) and malaria parasites (*Plasmodium knowlesi*). *Ann. trop. Med. Parasit.* **32**, 77–93.

(189) (With J. D. Fulton) Observations on the course of *Plasmodium knowlesi* infection in monkeys (*Macacus rhesus*), with notes on its treatment by (1) atebrin and (2) 1 : 11 normal undecane diamidine. *Ann. trop. Med. Parasit.* **32**, 257–278.

(190) 1939 (With J. A. Sinton) The correct name of the malignant tertian parasite: correction. *Br. med. J.* **1**, 146.

(191) (With J. D. Fulton) Experiments with isolated malaria parasites (*Plasmodium knowlesi*) free from red cells. *Ann. trop. Med. Parasit.* **33**, 161–168.

(192) Malaria in war. (Presidential address.) *Trans. R. Soc. trop. Med. Hyg.* **33**, 277–292.

(193) 1940 (With J. D. Fulton) The dissociation constants of plasmoquine. *Ann. trop. Med. Parasit.* **34**, 1–11.

(193a) Report on terminology in malaria. *Bull. Hlth Org. L. of N.* **9**, 131–246.

(194) 1942 The treatment of malaria and some points about the drugs in use against this disease. *Trans. R. Soc. trop. Med. Hyg.* **36**, 49–59.

(195) 1943 Measures for the control of malaria in India. *Jl R. Soc. Arts* **91**, 285–295.

(196) The cell metabolism of the malaria parasite in relation to the mode of action of antimalarial drugs. *Trans. Faraday Soc.* **39**, 333–338.

(197) 1945 Structure of the Culex egg-raft in relation to function. (Diptera.) *Trans. R. ent. Soc., Lond.* **95**, 25–34.

(198) Insect repellents. *Br. med. Bull.* **3**, 222–224.

(199) Some remarks on the nomenclature of the malaria parasites of man. *Revta Inst. Salubr. Enferm. trop. Mex.* **6**, 213–227.

(200) 1946 Repelentes de insectos. (Transl. into Spanish of paper in *Br. med. Bull.* 1945.) *Med. Rev. Mexicana* **26**, 318–324.

(201) 1947 Mosquito repellents: being a report of the work of the Mosquito Repellent Enquiry, Cambridge, 1943–5. *J. Hyg.* **45**, 176–231.

(202) Sydney Price James. *Obit. Not. Fell. R. Soc. Lond.* **5**, 507–523.

(203) 1948 John William Watson Stephens. *Obit. Not. Fell. R. Soc. Lond.* **5**, 525–540.
(204) Mr. P. J. Barraud (obit. not.) *Nature, Lond.* **162**, 481.
(205) 1949 Sir Ronald Ross, 1857–1932. *The dictionary of national biography (1931–40)*, pp. 752–754.
(206) Sir David Bruce, 1855–1931. *The dictionary of national biography (1931–40)*, pp. 108–110.
(207) Endemic and epidemic prevalence. Chapter in M. F. Boyd's *Malariology*, vol. 1, pp. 698–721. Philadelphia: Saunders.
(208) Insect vectors. Chapter in M. F. Boyd's *Malariology*, vol. 1, pp. 225–234.
(209) 1951 The *Culex pipiens* complex. *Trans. R. ent. Soc., Lond.* **102**, 231–282.
(210) Yellow fever. *Br. med. J.* **ii**, 833–835.
(211) 1952 The recorded parasites of mosquitoes. *Riv. Parassit.* **13**, 21–28.
(212) 1955 Policy in relation to malaria control. *Indian J. Malar.* **9**, 297–303.
(213) 1960 The generic name Aedes. *Trans. R. Soc. trop. Med. Hyg.* **54**, 407–408.
(214) *Aedes aegypti (L.): the yellow fever mosquito.* Cambridge University Press.
(215) 1967 A note on tropical medicine and protozoology. *Protozoology* **2**, 5–6. (Festschrift for H. E. Shortt.)

James B. Grant

# JAMES BRYANT CONANT

26 March 1893 — 11 February 1978

Elected For.Mem.R.S. 1941

By G. B. Kistiakowsky, For.Mem.R.S., and F. H. Westheimer

## Beginnings

James Bryant Conant was born on 26 March 1893 in the town of Dorchester, Massachusetts; he was the youngest child in the family, having two much older sisters. In 1880, shortly after their marriage, his parents, James Scott Conant and Jennet Bryant Conant, had moved to Dorchester from Joppa Village in the county of Plymouth, a town some 40 miles southeast of Boston, that had been the residence of the Bryant and the Conant families for generations.

Grandfather Bryant was an outspoken Yankee Republican who, to the great distress of his family, became a Democrat in his old age. He owned a prosperous farm, and a shoe factory nearby, in which he manufactured more than 200 000 pairs of shoes for the Union army in the Civil War, proudly stamping his own name on every shoe as a 'warranty of quality'. By contrast, the Conant family was poor, James's grandfather working as a shoe cutter in the Bryant factory. Fortunes changed with the passage of time and the Bryant grandparents spent their old age as guests in the Conants' spacious Dorchester household, where the elder Bryant's Democratic politics conflicted sharply with the Conants' Republican principles.

James's father served in the ranks of the Union Army and Navy in the Civil War, but he saw no action. Afterwards for a time he was a successful developer in Dorchester, which was a low income suburb, where he built utilitarian two- and three-family houses. Later he started a small wood-engraving company, and maintained the profession of engraver thereafter. The invention of the half-tone reproduction process, and its introduction into the printing business, confronted the senior Conant with the need to learn the complicated procedures required for etching copper plates and, although he totally lacked any previous contact with chemistry, he soon added the preparation and developing of wet photographic plates to his chemical techniques. The business prospered, and fortuitously introduced James to chemistry.

James's childhood was spent in Dorchester or at the family's summer cottage in a farming community in southern New Hampshire. He attended kindergarten and a public (that is, tax-supported) primary school in Dorchester, watched over by his mother, by his grandmother Bryant, two sisters and several aunts and female cousins. His earliest contacts with chemistry were the occasional visits to the photoengraving establishment in Boston. His father constructed a small workshop for him in their Dorchester home and, when his son was in his early teens, had gas piped into it. Equipped with a Bunsen burner and a blast lamp worked by foot-bellows, James now ventured into the new world of chemical experiments, acquiring his chemicals in local drugstores.

Observing James's interests in chemistry and electricity, his parents placed him in the Roxbury Latin School for the six years of secondary education. This school, in a suburb next to Dorchester, had the highest reputation in Boston for its college preparatory course, which then emphasized Latin, French, either Greek or German, and extensive preparation in mathematics. Despite its name, Roxbury Latin was also strong in chemistry and physics, maintained laboratories for both subjects, and boasted an outstanding science teacher, Newton Henry Black, who much later taught elementary physics in Harvard College. Black's personal acquaintance with James began with sandwich lunches in the Roxbury school's physics laboratory during James's second year. Learning of the boy's chemical experimentation at home, Black encouraged him to try qualitative analysis, and began to provide him with solutions to analyse. So began what later became an intimate tutorial relationship about which Conant wrote:[1] 'I doubt if any schoolteacher has ever had a greater influence on the intellectual development of a youth than Newton Henry Black had on mine.'

## College

During his last year in school, James Conant had the use of Mr Black's private laboratory and carried out experiments required in Harvard's freshman course in chemistry. Mr Black wrote about Conant to Professor Theodore William Richards, the department chairman; as a consequence of this intervention, the Harvard Chemistry Department voted[2] that 'Conant, considering his extraordinary ability, be allowed to anticipate Chemistry I by taking the final examination in the course next June [1910], and such other tests as the instructor in Chemistry I may deem necessary'. On the assumption that he would get one college credit, Conant, guided by Black, worked out a plan of study which would give him 15 other credits in three years, thus completing Harvard's requirements for the A.B. degree. This plan was strong on science and mathematics but weak in other subjects, in which Conant's scholastic standing at the Roxbury Latin School was by no means distinguished. Not long afterward President Abbott Lawrence Lowell abolished this 'free elective system' which merely required passing grades in any 16 courses.

Sixty years later, commenting on this college education, Conant wrote:[3] 'Regarding as a "case", the admission of J. B. Conant in 1910 to special advanced standing by the department of chemistry at Harvard, largely on the basis of one schoolteacher's judgment, may well be considered a deplorable example of the consequences of the nineteenth-century educational ideas . . .'. Deplorable, perhaps, but it did no harm to J. B. Conant, who found time for a course in philosophy and even 'went out for the *Harvard Crimson*' (the undergraduate daily). This meant being a reporter for the paper for a term, in competition with other candidates for the editorial board. On the second try he succeeded, a most unusual achievement for a science concentrator, since the demands of undergraduate laboratory courses almost precluded extra-curricular activities such as organized athletics and undergraduate publications.

As an editor of *The Harvard Crimson*, he was chosen to join the highly selective undergraduate literary club, the Signet, and there found a sophisticated substitute for the 'distribution' courses of the General Education programme which Harvard, led by Conant, initiated some 30 years later. But his focus on chemistry and on early graduation did preclude a formal education in the humanities. Yet Conant graduated 'with distinction' in three years, and immediately enrolled in the Harvard Graduate School.

He had come to Harvard with the intention, eventually, of doing research with Richards, and of becoming a physical chemist. Richards, at the time was already world famous for his precise determinations of atomic weights and his researches relating to the Third Law of Thermodynamics; soon he became the first American Nobel Laureate in Chemistry. Conant, however, changed his direction on exposure to Professor Elmer Peter Kohler, a great teacher of organic chemistry and a thoughtful investigator. Although Kohler's discoveries were limited, his attitude was vital to the development of organic chemistry in America; he emphasized understanding chemical reactions and was one of the first who was concerned with reaction mechanisms, rather than only with the products of synthesis. Conant quickly adopted this attitude and, while still an undergraduate, began research with Kohler[4] on fundamental cyclopropane chemistry. Later, as he had originally planned, he conducted research on electrochemistry with Richards, and in 1916 received what was in essence a double Ph.D.—in both organic and physical chemistry.

During World War I, he was briefly engaged in an unsuccessful and tragic venture in chemical manufacture, taught organic chemistry briefly in 1916–17 as an Instructor at Harvard, and served in the U.S. Chemical Warfare Service, with a final rank of major. In 1919 he was invited to return to Harvard as an assistant professor, and began his extraordinary career as an independent investigator.

A year after returning to Harvard, Conant proposed to Grace Thayer Richards, Professor Richards's only daughter, whom Conant first met in 1916 while a graduate student working in Richards's laboratory. They were married in the spring of 1921 and spent that summer in England and on the continent of Europe, where Conant made many stimulating visits to the leading organic chemists and chemical laboratories.

## Chemistry

At that time, organic chemistry was totally dominated by European and British scientists: Richard Willstaetter, Leopold Ruzicka, Emil Fischer, Robert Robinson, Arthur Lapworth, Hans Meerwein, Rudolph Criegee, Arthur Stoll and many others. In his autobiography,[5] Conant noted that, 'The first three decades of this century were not a great period in the history of American organic chemistry'. It would be impossible to state the plain facts more gently. The situation soon was otherwise; in the few years, from 1919 when he was appointed Assistant Professor to 1933 when he became President of Harvard, U.S. chemistry pulled itself up by its bootstraps and was on the way to achieving parity with that in Europe.

In particular, Conant achieved an international reputation in both natural products chemistry and in physical-organic chemistry. In his research, he maintained a double-pronged approach that reflected his training with both Kohler and Richards. Although he took greatest pride in the research on natural products, his physical organic chemistry showed the most originality. He spanned the whole spectrum of the field, participating in all the areas of importance and anticipating many discoveries to come. He developed the ideas of superacidity, of measurements of the acid strengths of extremely weak acids, of acid and base catalysis in non-aqueous solvents, and of structure–reactivity series; he contributed to the chemistry of free radicals and steric effects, discovered the effects of pressure on reaction rates, and pioneered in the use of radiocarbon to follow biochemical processes. In his studies on natural products he contributed to the determination of the structure of chlorophyll, to the understanding of the oxidation of haemoglobin to methaemoglobin and to the elucidation of the prosthetic group of haemocyanin.

Perhaps the most striking of his contributions to physical organic chemistry concerned 'superacid' solutions.[6] In 1927, Conant and N. F. Hall carried out an investigation of acids in glacial acetic acid as solvent. They measured electrochemical potentials that corresponded to 'superacid' solutions, that is to say, the potentials corresponded to acidities enormously higher than could be achieved by similar low concentrations of strong acids in water. On the other hand, dilute solutions of sodium acetate in acetic acid gave rise to potentials that suggested that the solutions were in some sense basic.

Conant and his coworkers were able to carry out electrochemical titrations of perchloric acid with sodium acetate in acetic acid as solvent just as one would titrate a strong acid with alkali in water as solvent. Furthermore, Conant and G. M. Bramann demonstrated that the acetylation of β-naphthol by acetic anhydride in acetic acid as solvent was subject to acid catalysis by added perchloric acid (0.2 M acid increased the rate $10^6$-fold) and to basic catalysis by added sodium acetate or pyridine (0.2 M pyridine increased the rate $10^3$-fold). As in the titrations, sodium acetate behaved like a base in acetic acid as solvent. The generalization of acid–base behaviour implied by these experiments is routinely accepted today; the idea was unfamiliar, or even revolutionary, in the 1920s.

In a related series of studies[8] (some of which were completed[9] only after Conant had 'retired' from chemistry to the Presidency of Harvard), Conant investigated extraordinarily weak acids in aprotic solvents. With G. W. Wheland (and later with W. McEwen), he used sodium triphenylmethyl as a strong base in ether solution, and was able to determine the acidities of such weak acids as acetophenone, phenylacetylene, fluorene and diphenylmethane. The work enormously widened the knowledge of weak acids and only recently has it been improved upon. The generalization of the concepts of acids and bases, and in particular an understanding of acids and bases in solvents other than water, owes much to the papers of Conant and his collaborators; their work, along with that of J. N. Bronsted, G. N. Lewis, A. Hantzsch and L. P. Hammett, forms the basis of our modern understanding of acidity.

A recurring theme in Conant's approach to reaction mechanism was the relation between the thermodynamic, or equilibrium, properties of reactions and the corresponding rates. A few investigators had previously explored the reactions of aldehydes and ketones with carbonyl reagents; for example, in 1898, Arthur Lapworth studied the equilibrium constants for cyanohydrin formation. But in an important study, Conant and P. D. Bartlett[10] determined both the rates and equilibria for semicarbazone formation, and sharply distinguished between thermodynamic and kinetic control of chemical reactions. To emphasize the distinction for the preparative chemists of the day, they mixed equal quantities of furfural and cyclohexanone with only one equivalent of semicarbazide in a properly buffered solution, and showed that the first product formed (under kinetic control) was the derivative of cyclohexanone, while the final product (under thermodynamic control) was essentially pure furfural semicarbazone.

Conant's investigations included early studies of the displacement reaction, where he determined the effect of structure on the rate of the displacement of chloride by iodide in a series of alkyl chlorides,[11] and studies (principally with L. F. Fieser)[12] of the effect of structure on the oxidation–reduction potentials of quinones. Conant's investigations of free radical chemistry showed the effect of steric hindrance in the dissociation of highly substituted ethanes; in particular, he and N. H. Bigelow showed that di-t-butyltetraphenylethane dissociates into radicals.[13] In another important area, he collaborated after 1933 with G. B. Kistiakowsky[14] to measure the heats of hydrogenation of unsaturated organic compounds; the work supplied precise thermodynamic data for physical-organic chemistry and led, in the hands of others, to the concept of hyper-conjugation.

An interesting series of investigations concerned the reaction of phosphorus halides, and in particular of $PCl_3$, with carbonyl compounds, and especially with α, β, unsaturated ketones.[15] The products of these investigations were β-halo-phosphonates, and Conant and E. L. Jackson demonstrated and investigated the fragmentation of these compounds in alkaline solution.[16] The reaction was then 'lost' in the literature. Although several papers on the subject had been published in the *Journal of the American Chemical Society*, the chemistry was forgotten until Maynard and Swan,[17] at Monash University in Melbourne, rediscovered it in 1960. The reaction has recently assumed considerable theoretical and practical importance; for example, the Conant–Swan fragmentation of β-chloroethylphosphonate is used today in agriculture as an *in situ* source of ethylene for ripening fruit.[18]

Another highly original and pioneering research project concerned the effects of high pressures on the rates of chemical reactions. In three papers on the subject, initially in collaboration with P. W. Bridgman,[19, 20] Conant showed that the polymerization of isoprene at room temperature is strongly catalysed by traces of peroxides but inhibited by hydroquinone. Nevertheless, even in the presence of hydroquinone, the reaction proceeded, albeit slowly, under pressures of 9000–12 000 atmospheres. Such polymerizations under pressure are today routine industrial procedures.

Conant's interests in structure, reaction mechanisms and electrochemistry, and his feeling for the important problems of biochemistry, all converged upon the respiratory pigments as a major research challenge. His investigations in this area were extraordinarily promising, although the most important project was left incomplete when he assumed the Presidency of Harvard. At that time, he was engaged in an attempt to determine the structure of chlorophyll. He and his coworkers made a number of significant advances in the field; they found the site where phytol is attached[21] to the carbon skeleton of chlorophyll, confirmed that chlorophyll is in a reduced state relative to porphyrins,[22] discovered that the 'phase test' for the pigment involves an oxidative cleavage with alkali,[23] and carried out a number of transformations that were later important in elucidating the structure of the essential pigment of photosynthesis. When he left the field in 1933 he was wrestling with the difficult problem represented by the five-membered ketoester ring of chlorophyll that (together with the reduction of an adjacent pyrrol ring) distinguishes the chlorophyll structure.[24] This structure, in all its details except for the stereochemistry of the reduced ring, was correctly presented by Hans Fischer[25] and his collaborators in Munich in 1940. One can only speculate on what Conant might have contributed to this objective had he remained in chemistry. The problem was a major one, and ripe for solution.

Conant achieved several fine successes in other areas of natural products chemistry. At the time, the oxidation–reduction reactions of haemoglobin were not understood. Methaemoglobin, an oxidation product of haemoglobin, could be reduced to haemoglobin, but could not itself carry oxygen; it was variously thought to be an iron hydroxide or oxide. In a study that combined Conant's interest in biochemistry with his expertise in physical chemistry, Conant and N. D. Scott[26] showed that the oxidation of haemoglobin to methaemoglobin constituted only a one-electron change. Methaemoglobin thus contains ferric iron, whereas oxyhaemoglobin is a complex of oxygen with the ferrous iron of haeme. In a somewhat parallel study, he, D. Dersch and W. E. Mydans investigated haemocyanin, the oxygen-carrying blue blood pigment of crustaceans. They confirmed earlier findings that the compound contained copper and proved that, in sharp contrast to haemoglobin, the prosthetic group contained no porphyrin.[27] The exact structure of this group has still not been elucidated; it remains to be seen whether Conant's findings of sulphur in the pigment will prove a significant clue.

One of the most imaginative of Conant's initiatives came after he assumed the Presidency of Harvard. He stimulated A. B. Hastings, G. B. Kistiakowsky and B. Vennesland[28] to apply $^{11}C$ to a study of the metabolism of lactate in the liver. Since the half-life of $^{11}C$ is only 20 minutes, the information that could be gathered with such an isotope is limited, and the project was not directly fruitful.

But it illustrated Conant's far-reaching and imaginative approach to research, and foreshadowed the immense development of biochemistry that took place when, as an indirect result of the Manhattan Project, $^{14}C$ became available.

No discussion of Conant's chemistry would be complete without mention of the books he published or edited. In 1918, Roger Adams, Conant's Harvard contemporary and then a young member of the faculty of the University of Illinois, suggested that the publication of carefully researched preparative methods would make organic chemicals more readily available to U.S. investigators. The series *Organic Syntheses* evolved from this suggestion, with Conant as one of the original organizers, who served as Editor-in-Chief[29] of volumes II and IX and contributed to others. Among his own books on chemistry was a high-school text he wrote with his respected teacher, N. H. Black.[30] He also wrote a textbook of organic chemistry,[31] and collaborated in later editions with Max Tishler and with Harold Blatt. This book is remarkable in its organization: instead of beginning the study of organic chemistry with hydrocarbons, Conant began with the alcohols. This organization may seem less systematic than that followed by the standard texts; probably, however, it is pedagogically sound as well as imaginative, and, like so many of Conant's innovations, may prove a portent for the future.

Conant was at the height of his productivity as a chemist and a teacher of chemists when the President of Harvard, A. Lawrence Lowell, announced his coming retirement. In the course of the search for his successor, one of the members of the Harvard Corporation (Harvard's governing body) interviewed Conant about the presidential qualifications of one of the candidates. Conant's views on the need and nature of reforms at Harvard so impressed the interviewer that other meetings with the members of the Corporation followed. Out of the almost accidental initial meeting grew the offer to him of the Harvard Presidency, which he accepted with little hesitation.

## The Presidency

The university which Conant took over in the summer of 1933 was quite a different place from the institution he had entered as a college freshman 23 years earlier; in this interval President Lowell had introduced major changes, aimed generally at strengthening the undergraduate college. The degree now firmly required four years of study. The free elective system, which had enabled dedicated athletes and rich undergraduate inhabitants of Harvard's 'Gold Coast' to pass through college with a minimum of mental strain, was abolished. It was replaced by rules of study that combined both concentration and distribution; the new curriculum required undergraduates to combine advanced studies in one of the university departments with less advanced courses well distributed over the wide range of scholarship and arts. The dormitories were greatly expanded, and became undergraduate Houses that provided dining facilities and common rooms for undergraduates as well as living quarters for house masters and some of the tutors. Tutors were brought to Harvard in rather large numbers when Lowell introduced individualized tutorial instruction for undergraduates in the fields of their concentration. In distinction to the tutors in the old English universities, however, most of the Harvard tutors had little allegiance to the Houses in which they tutored, but saw themselves as junior members of the university faculty; they yearned for promotion and the distinction of being responsible for lecture courses.

It was common knowledge in those days that Harvard University lacked a consistent policy of faculty promotion. Some members of the instructional staff remained in the rank of assistant professor into their old age, insecure on term appointments and paid miserably low salaries. Others were promoted into the ranks of tenured faculty on grounds not related to creative scholarship. The whole issue of whom to promote, and when, became acute as the pressure for promotion spread to the tutors in the Harvard Houses, many of whom had been appointed with less regard to their promise of scholarship than to their willingness and ability to engage in tutorial instruction. Had the University acceded to this pressure, it would have risked insolvency, especially since the financial situation was exacerbated by the Great Depression. Moreover, Conant believed that only by filling the senior ranks with eminent and creative scholars could the university hope to become one of the best in the world.

Conant had stressed this point of view to the members of the Harvard Corporation when they had interviewed him for the Presidency, and as the new President he saw the furtherance of faculty quality as his central task. In this endeavour, he received decidedly less than unanimous faculty support, so that the years of his Presidency before World War II were occasionally marked by turbulent faculty meetings. In the matter of promotions Conant was accused of paying no attention to the quality of formal teaching by the faculty, but merely counting their publications. A nation-wide campaign against him, with political overtones, was waged when two tutors in economics, who were active in the teachers' union, were denied promotion into the tenured ranks.

Conant's reforms, which induced such intense and occasionally emotional opposition, involved several procedural changes. One was the 'up or out' rule, which required that no appointee to the teaching staff could be given a term appointment for a total of more than eight years. He or she must either be let go or promoted into a tenured rank (associate or full professor). Conant tried also to couple promotions with systematic increases in the salaries of tenured professors so that the income from the university of all faculty members of the same age group would be approximately the same.

A second element of the reform, which became known as the Graustein scheme, replaced the hitherto common tradition of appointing a successor to a senior faculty member only upon his death or retirement. The authors of the Graustein scheme determined statistically what frequency of new tenure appointments would ensure that, over a long period of time, each university department would remain at the same average size it maintained in the thirties. For example, the Chemistry Department could then add a new tenure member every $4\frac{1}{2}$ years, regardless of the somewhat irregular sequence of future retirements of the active faculty. During Conant's presidency, the Graustein scheme was followed closely, although some departments were deliberately allotted an increase in senior appointments to allow for the long-term trends in student preferences.

The introduction of *ad hoc* committees to approve the qualifications of candidates for tenure appointments was the most crucial of Conant's innovations. It resulted from his observations of British universities during an extended visit to Great Britain before he assumed the office of the President in the spring of 1933. Upon notice from a department of a choice for a tenure appointment, an *ad hoc* committee was constituted by the President; the committee usually included two senior members from related departments of the university plus several distinguished scholars from other institutions in the field of the vacancy. The system, which was introduced in the forties after a delay caused by the war, has functioned successfully ever since. The *ad hoc* proceedings usually lasted most of a day, and had faint overtones of a judicial process: the committee acted as the jury, the chairman of the department that had made the nomination and his witnesses functioned as the defence, the dean of the faculty as the people's attorney and Dr Conant, who attended all such sessions, as the judge. When the committee, after hearing the arguments, began its executive session, Conant without fail asked the same question: Was the departmental nominee among the top scholars, world-wide, in his discipline and age group? In several instances the departmental choice was rejected as inferior to someone else in the field; and the 'someone else' was then brought into the Harvard faculty.

Although Conant was deeply concerned with the quality of the faculty, he also sought to reform the composition of the undergraduate student body. When he came to the Presidency, the students were drawn primarily from among the sons of old graduates, and from families inhabiting the northeast corner of the United States. Many came from private preparatory schools and those select public (i.e. tax-supported) schools in large eastern cities, like Roxbury Latin, that offered exacting college preparatory curricula. To give the Harvard student body a more national character, Conant convinced the Harvard Corporation to create National Scholarships, designed to 'assure that any young man with remarkable talents from any part of the United States may obtain his education at Harvard whether he be rich or penniless'.[32] The stipends, unlike the previous custom of small grants, were made high enough to take care of each student's total expenses insofar as these expenses exceeded family resources. A well designed process for selecting candidates produced a remarkably talented group of Harvard graduates with broad geographic representation who, over the years, have had distinguished careers in scholarly and public domains.

Conant's concern about the composition of the undergraduate student body extended beyond his interest in the select group of National Scholars. The college admissions policy was gradually modified to emphasize the scholastic aptitude of all entering freshmen, to provide more scholarship funds, and to de-emphasize the preferential treatment accorded to sons of Harvard alumni and boys enrolled in select 'preparatory' schools. This trend was naturally not very popular with some Harvard alumni and thus progressed only slowly. It was resumed after the war, resulting gradually in a democratization of the Harvard student body, and in similar trends in most other private colleges in America.

## World War II

Other reforms at Harvard were also interrupted or delayed by the war, when Conant's efforts became centred on national security problems. Lengthy visits to Germany in the twenties and early thirties generated in him an intense distrust and dislike of Hitler and his henchmen, whom he saw as the embodiment of gangster rule on a grand scale, bent on the total suppression of individual freedoms and on ruthless military conquest. When the war broke out in 1939, Conant saw it as the start of a world-wide conflict in which the United States would inevitably become involved and for which it must be prepared.

Throughout the period of the 'phony war' on the western front, in the fall and winter of 1939–40, Conant wrote and spoke publicly about the threat to America from Hitlerism. After the invasion of Norway, he became one of the charter members of the 'Committee to Defend America by Aiding the Allies'. Openly and aggressively an interventionist, he joined the public debate against those who later formed the 'America First Committee'. On specific issues Conant pleaded for changes in the American neutrality act and for the passage of military draft legislation. Much later, in February 1941, he was a key witness before the Senate Committee on Foreign Relations during the consideration of President Roosevelt's Lend–Lease bill.

Soon after the start of Hitler's western offensive in 1940 Conant had occasion to discuss with several individuals, including Vannevar Bush, the President of Carnegie Institution in Washington, the plan of a government-financed organization of American civilian scientists and engineers to pursue the development of new instrumentalities of war. Less than a month later, in mid-June 1940, he was appointed by President Roosevelt as a member of the newly created eight-man National Defense Research Committee (N.D.R.C.).

On Chairman Bush's initiative, the committee decided at its first meeting on a then radical plan to contract for military R. & D. in academic and industrial laboratories where potential leaders—the 'principal investigators' for specific projects—could be identified. This turned out to be a wise decision, in view of the resistance of the Federal bureaucracy to new initiatives while the United States was still formally at peace. The expectation that the United States would soon be involved in war, however, lent urgency to the activity of the N.D.R.C.

For management purposes, the committee created five divisions, each headed by one of its members. Conant headed Division B, which comprised chemical warfare, explosives, certain munitions and a host of chemical matters. The effort began at once to identify urgent problems of military significance through consultations with the military, and simultaneously to recruit leading civilian scientists to work on them. Conant led this organizing drive with great persistence and persuasiveness; his efforts were especially necessary before America entered the war in December 1941, since many members of the scientific community, especially those in interior parts of the United States, harboured isolationist views. Also some military officers believed at that time that civilian scientists should conduct their research under strict military supervision pursuant to 'requirements' defined by military staff work.

Notwithstanding the problems with isolationists and the resistance of conservative military officers, Conant and other members of the N.D.R.C., aided by a small full-time staff, were spectacularly successful in mobilizing a massive American technical effort. The N.D.R.C. preserved its intellectual independence and gave broad authority to private scientists; it even competed aggressively with the military research agencies and, led by Vannevar Bush, appealed directly to high Federal officials, including the President, on disagreements with military officers about what weaponry should be developed, and how.

In early March 1941 Conant travelled to England to establish an N.D.R.C. liaison office in London and so to open channels for systematic exchange of military-technical information. Conant's support for the Lend–Lease bill, which was still being debated in the U.S. Senate, was of course known in England; he was welcomed everywhere he went as friend and messenger of hope. On his arrival, he was met by Brendan Bracken, who conveyed to Conant an invitation to lunch with the Prime Minister. He was graciously received by the King, and met Churchill three times. He also met the key members of Churchill's cabinet, had lengthy discussions with Lord Cherwell, and visited several senior leaders of the British military research establishment, as well as some of his academic friends. His reception augured well for Conant's mission; his visit got the N.D.R.C. office off to an excellent start, led to a rapidly expanding exchange of information, and expedited a stream of American scientists bent on learning from British colleagues something that was not available in Washington: the lessons of war.

## Nuclear Energy

A few months after Conant's return to America he was appointed Chairman of N.D.R.C., which became the larger part of a new Office of Scientific Research and Development (O.S.R.D.) within the Executive Office of the President, and with Bush as director. Conant at that time took over from Bush the task of personally monitoring the work of the N.D.R.C. that was concerned with uranium fission. As optimism about the feasibility of an atom bomb grew, President Roosevelt created a small cabinet-level 'Top Policy Group' which was to supervise this effort, in tight secrecy, with Bush and Conant as its technical members.

One of Conant's main concerns now was that the Nazis would have the atom bomb first. Since none of the methods under development for obtaining weapons-grade fissionable material had either been proved successful or eliminated, Conant recommended in the spring of 1942 that industrial scale plant construction be undertaken simultaneously for four different methods. Within days, Bush had obtained a personal approval to go ahead from President Roosevelt. The work on one method, the centrifugal separation of uranium isotopes, was soon terminated, but the other three projects, the gaseous diffusion and the electromagnetic separation of uranium isotopes, and the plutonium synthesis in nuclear reactors, all proved successful. They all contributed to the making of atom bombs in the spring of 1945, and thus justified the decision to build all these plants without delay.

The industrial phase of the atom bomb project was assigned in 1942 to the Army Corps of Engineers and became known as the Manhattan District, commanded after September 1942 by General L. E. Groves. Policy determination was entrusted to a four-member Military Policy Committee, chaired by Bush with Conant as alternate, to which Groves reported. Of the committee members, it was Conant who maintained personal contacts with the key leaders of this giant undertaking, while critical decisions were generally made jointly by Bush and Conant. This team operated harmoniously throughout the war years and for some time thereafter, Bush concentrating mainly on representing and promoting their undertakings in official Washington, and Conant on managing them along guidelines arrived at by mutual agreement.

In the midst of his involvement with the instrumentalities of war, Conant was drafted by President Roosevelt in the summer of 1942 to serve as a member of a three-man committee chaired by Bernard Baruch to review the synthetic rubber programme, which appeared to be floundering amidst indecisions, competing plans and bickering on the Cabinet level and below. Two months of thorough evaluation led to a report which was accepted by the President, and was the basis of a successful enterprise that later in the war was to produce synthetic rubber at the rate of a million tons a year.

## The Presidency—again

Throughout the war years Conant continued living in Cambridge and between his trips to Washington and elsewhere gave some time and attention to the university; most of the burden of university leadership and administration during the war nevertheless fell to Paul H. Buck, the Provost and Professor of History. While the number of regular Harvard undergraduates soon declined drastically, a dozen or so accelerated military training programmes came into existence, and by the end of the war many thousands of junior army and navy officers had been trained in Cambridge by those faculty members who had not left for wartime assignments. Harvard also administered many military research projects: it was the third largest (behind the Massachusetts and California Institutes of Technology) among N.D.R.C. contractors.

During the seven years of his Presidency after the war, Conant became involved in several major reforms at Harvard. Undergraduate instruction for the women of Radcliffe College, although done by the Harvard faculty, had traditionally required separate classes and hence duplication of lectures. During the war, as a temporary emergency measure, the classes had to be combined; but with the coming of peace, instead of returning to the old custom, the faculty, after some debate, decided to continue many of the coeducational practices. This set in motion a process that has now led to a virtually total integration of Radcliffe and Harvard.

A major new departure in undergraduate teaching was the introduction of the programme for General Education. This programme resulted from a decision by Conant and Buck in 1942 to develop plans for improved undergraduate education in the post-war society. The result was the 1945 'Redbook' report, which recommended setting up a faculty committee on General Education to administer broad interdisciplinary courses in the three domains of human intellectual endeavours—the natural sciences, the social sciences, and the humanities. These courses would be open to undergraduates to meet their distribution requirements.

The Harvard Faculty of Arts and Sciences adopted the plan without substantial change and so began an impressive rejuvenation of elementary college instruction at Harvard. Conant himself developed and taught a General Education course, exploring the nature of intellectual progress, in which he analysed several historically important scientific discoveries, concentrating on those related to chemistry. With some modifications, the concept of General Education has been adopted in the intervening years by many American colleges.

In another development Harvard became almost unique in the United States. Conant ruled that with the coming of peace all 'classified' or secret research at Harvard should cease as soon as practicable. The results of research by Harvard faculty and students were to be freely publishable, regardless of which external agency—governmental or industrial—might finance the project. This rule has remained in force to this day and has spared Harvard many internal conflicts, although costing Harvard some large military funds which went to educational institutions less concerned about the openness of their laboratories.

To strengthen scholarly research at Harvard, Conant proposed the creation of university professorships. These professorships were designed to relieve a few especially productive scholars from the mundane duties that membership in a department at a U.S. university necessarily entails, and thus free them for more productive scholarship.

In most American colleges, intercollegiate sports constitute an important component of college life; their administration is frequently influenced by the alumni associations, which provide athletic scholarships, in effect hire and fire the coaches, apply pressure on the colleges to provide 'soft' curricula for athletes, etc. Being concerned about the impact of this extraneous influence on the student body, Conant placed the administration of all sports in the hands of a faculty committee with the responsibility for the operating budget; athletic scholarships as such were abolished, and athletic coaches could no longer exercise *de facto* control over the admission of promising student athletes. These reforms were initially ridiculed in the national press and may have cost Harvard some victories in intercollegiate competition, but they led to a much healthier involvement in sports by the entire Harvard student body.

In addition to the College, and its associated Graduate School of Arts and Sciences, Harvard comprises several semi-autonomous professional schools, including Architecture, Business Administration, Dentistry, Divinity, Education,

Law, and Medicine. Some of the professional schools at the time suffered from outdated organization and objectives and lack of forceful leadership. Conant dedicated much of his thought and time to the elimination of the worst deficiencies, especially in the Graduate School of Education. This school was supposed to upgrade the scholarship of elementary and secondary school teachers; the teachers, on their part, sought advanced Harvard degrees in large measure to assist in their professional advancement.

Unfortunately, the School of Education was failing in two ways. It set its tuition at a level that was inadequate for self-sustaining operation and it set scholastic standards for acceptable performance considerably lower than those in the Harvard Graduate School of Arts and Sciences. Since the students in the School of Education had to take professional courses given by the faculty of Arts and Sciences, there were continuing conflicts on the issues of double scholastic standards. After the war Conant reoriented the School of Education toward training school administrators rather than school teachers. Led by a young dean, Francis Keppel, the school soon became a nationally recognized success.

## National Affairs

After the war Conant became active in developing the so-called May–Johnson bill to create an American Atomic Energy Commission, and supported this proposal in Congressional hearings. An influential group of scientists who feared that it potentially gave too much authority to the military, strongly opposed the bill and it was defeated. Later the McMahon Act, calling for greater civilian control of atomic energy, was passed by Congress and came into effect by mid-1946. Conant declined Truman's invitation to become the first chairman of the new Atomic Energy Commission (A.E.C.), although he agreed to serve as a member of its part-time General Advisory Committee under the chairmanship of Robert Oppenheimer. For the next six years this committee was highly active and very influential in advising the Commission on a broad range of technical policy matters.

Meanwhile the Cold War came into full force, with the United States suspicious that Stalin planned world-wide aggression; this was reinforced by the hot war in Korea. The A.E.C. was under increasing pressure to undertake a crash development of 'the Super', the hydrogen bomb; its influential advocates included Pentagon civilian officials, some members of Congress, Air Force generals and a number of scientists whose chief spokesman was Edward Teller.

After a thorough discussion led by Oppenheimer, the General Advisory Committee in 1949 unanimously recommended to the A.E.C., on both technical and ethical grounds, against a crash development of the H bomb. But at the end of January 1950, President Truman decided otherwise. These events contributed greatly to Oppenheimer's political downfall. Conant's connection with the A.E.C. ended in 1952; but in 1954, appearing before an A.E.C. security board, he testified unreservedly in Oppenheimer's defence at the secret and highly biased hearings on his loyalty and qualifications to be entrusted with secret materials.

In 1950 Congress passed an act creating the National Science Foundation, with central responsibility to promote American basic scientific research. The President appointed Conant as the chairman of the National Science Board, its policy-making body composed of private citizens. As the chairman, Conant was involved in the appointment of the first Director of the N.S.F., Dr Alan T. Waterman, as well as in guiding the development of the operational policies of the Foundation; these wise policies have undergone only a slow evolution in the intervening decades, although the budget of the Foundation has grown by three orders of magnitude.

## The National Academy

In that same year, Conant suffered from an unpleasant incident that strongly influenced his subsequent choice of career. He agreed to stand for election to the Presidency of the National Academy of Sciences; in accordance with tradition, the nominating committee presented only one candidate to the membership. One of those who urged him to accept the nomination was Detlev W. Bronk, then chairman of the associated National Research Council. The actual election in those days was by vote of those members who attended the annual meeting and was virtually a formality.

Unfortunately for Conant, his forceful leadership of the N.D.R.C. and of the atom bomb project, as well as his defence of the May–Johnson bill in Congress, had antagonized quite a few scientists, some who felt slighted in wartime, others who regarded Conant as high-handed, and still others who mistrusted him as an ally of the military. At any rate, just before the annual meeting, a self-selected group of members of the Academy, resentful of Conant, decided to nominate Detlev Bronk from the floor when the election of the president would be in order. Accounts differ on what took place then but it seems that Bronk, when told of this plan, did not reject it outright. The next day Conant, informed in Cambridge of the situation, withdrew his candidacy and Bronk was duly elected. But the affair angered Conant, as he felt himself unfairly treated and rejected by fellow scientists, and it probably contributed to his withdrawal from all activities involving the American scientific community after his retirement from Harvard in 1953.

Measured chronologically Conant's Harvard Presidency lasted almost 20 years, but five of them were taken up by wartime efforts and during the remainder he gave freely of himself to national affairs. Nonetheless his Presidency constituted an epoch of far reaching changes and reforms at Harvard, resembling in their scope those instituted in late nineteenth century by another chemist-president of Harvard, Charles Elliot. Conant's contributions to many aspects of higher education place him in the very front ranks of modern university administrators.

## Adventure in Diplomacy

In December 1952 Conant was invited by the President-elect, Eisenhower, to become the High Commissioner of the U.S. Zone of Occupation in Germany and later the Ambassador to the Federal Republic of Germany. Conant accepted and arranged for a leave from the Harvard Presidency until the following fall when he would formally retire after 20 years of service. After some delay, caused by a few reactionary senators who objected to his views on public education, Conant was confirmed by the Senate and left for Germany in February 1953. There he oversaw the gradual liquidation of the large staff of the American High Commissioner, later established the Embassy, and made frequent visits to Berlin, largely, it seems, to 'show the flag'. He developed cordial, warm, relations with Chancellor Konrad Adenauer and accompanied him on two visits to the United States.

Conant refreshed his fluency in German, and made many speeches to German audiences. He visited German scientific and educational institutions, became known throughout the Federal Republic as a friendly statesman-chemist who valued German scholarship, and helped in rebuilding German cultural institutions.

Conant had some difficulties with Soviet occupation authorities, largely because of their efforts to seal off East Germany. French fears of a German army led to delays of nearly two years in accepting the emergence of a sovereign Federal Republic. But probably his worst problems had their origin in Washington. While testifying before a Senate committee, he was furiously attacked by the notorious Senator Joseph P. McCarthy, because, according to the Senator, American Information Service libraries in Germany under Conant's jurisdiction contained 30 000 books by communist authors. McCarthy further charged that Conant protected certain of his subordinates who were communists or tinged with communism. In this confrontation Conant received little help or even forewarning from the State Department, which then existed in a state of mortal fear of Joe McCarthy.

Conant had gradually learnt that as an ambassador he had virtually no role in formulation of policy, Secretary of State Dulles issuing a stream of detailed instructions and demanding swift compliance. Somewhat disenchanted therefore with diplomatic life, Conant resigned from the foreign service and returned to the United States in 1957.

## Focus on High Schools

While still in Bonn, Conant decided to become engaged in the problems of American high schools. This was not a sudden interest, as Conant had been active in national educational circles since the thirties. In 1940 he had been elected to the Educational Policies Commission of the National Education Association and even in the war years found time to participate in its activities. In 1948 he published a book *Education in a Divided World* in which he defended the American public high schools, opposed tax support of church-affiliated and other private schools and urged great expansion of community-affiliated two-year junior colleges, to be open to all high school graduates and to serve as the terminal education for the majority. These, of course, have become an important part of the educational edifice in America.

To get the necessary financial support for his post-war project, he enlisted the interest of the Carnegie Foundation in his ideas. After settling in New York, he received a grant which enabled him to engage a competent professional staff of four and in the fall of 1957 to begin extensive travels to visit various kinds of high school. In one year 103 schools in 26 states were visited and assessed in detail, more than half of them by Conant himself.

The timing for this study was ideal. The launching of Sputnik I in the fall of 1957 started a wave of public criticism of the high schools that crested a year later, with school administrators and elected members of school boards full of questions on how to reorganize the schools and what to teach. Conant's book, *The American High School Today*, based on first-hand observations of his team, came out in early 1959. It concluded that some schools were providing satisfactory education, at least to the boys if not the girls, but it also offered specific and sharp recommendations for numerous improvements, especially in teaching foreign language. It also urged consolidation of small schools into comprehensive high schools which could offer broader choice of curricula, including college preparatory courses and various vocational choices.

Conant's findings were called a 'whitewash' by some contemporary critics of American high school education, who were far more harsh, sometimes rejecting the American system altogether and urging European-type schools. On the other hand, the Educational Policies Commission as well as most public school superintendents and principals welcomed the findings. The book was on the American 'best-seller list' for several weeks and gradually brought about extensive school reforms.

Conant's next venture mainly concerned the schools of the 'inner cities', which he scrutinized in visits to Philadelphia, Chicago, Detroit and other cities, as well as to the suburban communities surrounding them. Out of this grew the book *Slums and Suburbs* (1961) in which he warned the American public of the masses of unemployed and out-of-school black youth which he called social dynamite—five years before it triggered the social explosion in American schools.

Conant's proposals for remedies rejected school integration as not practical if it required massive 'bussing' of pupils. He asserted that 'satisfactory education can be provided in all-Negro schools through the expenditure of more money for staff and facilities' and urged the opening of employment opportunities in inner cities for black youth through the use of Federal funds. These ideas seemed close enough to the 'separate but equal' doctrine favoured by outright segregationists to provoke intense anger among black educational leaders, and to make Conant into a *persona non grata* among them and many white liberals.

Conant's attention turned then to a different controversial topic, the training and certification of school teachers; *The Education of American Teachers* followed two years later. The book produced a violent response from professional educational circles and organizations, including some of Conant's old friends in the Educational Policies Commission. Conant had criticized severely both what was being taught by many professors of education and the curricula of teachers' colleges and other schools of education; he aroused greatest indignation by pleading that authority for the certification of teachers should not be given to schools of education, but be retained by independent bodies.

Conant, now a septuagenarian, escaped many antagonistic confrontations with his former colleagues by departing just before the publication date of his latest book for West Berlin on invitation of its mayor, Willi Brandt, who asked Conant's assistance in building an international Pedagogical Centre. While living abroad, Conant's writings on educational matters included a book, *Shaping Educational Policy* (1964), in which he urged greater involvement of state administrations in educational policies and a compact between the states to form an Educational Commission of the States. A few years later this organization came into being and has since played a useful role in shaping consistent educational policies of participating states. After 1965 Conant divided his time between New York in the winters and Hanover, New Hampshire, in the summers. But he continued his writing and publishing for several years.

He became debilitated in the summer of 1977 and died in Hanover on 11 February 1978. He leaves behind his wife and faithful companion in his several lives, Grace Thayer Richards, two sons and five grandchildren.

For all of Conant's prominence, he never showed self-importance, and treated people, young and old, as equals. He judged others as firmly as he judged himself, but on gaining confidence gave them his full loyalty. Straightforward, reserved, yet outspoken and meticulously fair, given to precise rather than brilliant language and writing, he was a true modern descendant of the New England Puritans who held himself as personally accountable as had they. Science, America and particularly Harvard are the beneficiaries of his originality and strength.

The photograph reproduced was taken in 1954 or 1955 by H. Wol, Mehlem, Germany.

## References

1. Conant, J. B. 1970 *My several lives*, p. 15. Harper & Row.
2. *Ibid.*, p. 17.
3. *Ibid.*, p. 19.
4. Kohler, E. P. & Conant, J. B. 1917 *J. Am. chem. Soc.* **34**, 1404, 1699.
5. Reference 1, p. 34.
6. Conant, J. B. & Hall, N. F. 1927 *J. Am. chem. Soc.* **49**, 3047; Conant, J. B. & Werner, T. H. 1930 *J. Am. chem. Soc.* **52**, 4436.
7. Conant, J. B. & Bramann, G. M. 1928 *J. Am. chem. Soc.* **50**, 2305.
8. Conant, J. B. & Wheland, G. W. 1932 *J. Am. chem. Soc.* **54**, 1212.
9. McEwen, W. 1936 *J. Am. chem. Soc.* **58**, 1124.
10. Conant, J. B. & Bartlett, P. D. 1932 *J. Am. chem. Soc.* **54**, 2881.
11. Conant, J. B. & Kirner, W. R. 1924 *J. Am. chem. Soc.* **46**, 232; Conant, J. B. & Hussey, R. E. 1925 *J. Am. chem. Soc.* **47**, 476; Conant, J. B., Kirner, W. R. & Hussey, R. E. 1925 *J. Am. chem. Soc.* **47**, 488.
12. Conant, J. B. & Fieser, L. F. 1923 *J. Am. chem. Soc.* **45**, 2194.
13. Conant, J. B. & Bigelow, N. H. 1928 *J. Am. chem. Soc.* **50**, 2041.
14. Conant, J. B. & Kistiakowsky, G. B. 1937 *Chem. Rev.* **20**, 181.
15. Conant, J. B. & Cook, A. A. 1920 *J. Am. chem. Soc.* **42**, 830; Conant, J. B. & Coyne, B. B. 1922 *J. Am. chem. Soc.* **44**, 2530.
16. Conant, J. B. & Jackson, E. L. 1924 *J. Am. chem. Soc.* **46**, 1033.

17. Maynard, J. A. & Swan, J. M. 1920 *Aust. J. Chem.* **42**, 830.
18. *Chem. & Eng. News* 1978 (9 October) p. 18.
19. Bridgman, P. W. & Conant, J. B. 1929 *Proc. natn Acad Sci. U.S.A.* **15**, 680.
20. Conant, J. B. & Peterson, W. R. 1932 *J. Am. chem. Soc.* **54**, 628.
21. Conant, J. B. & Hyde, J. F. 1929 *J. Am. chem. Soc.* **51**, 3668; Conant, J. B., Dietz, E. M., Bailey, C. F. & Kamerling, S. E. 1931 *J. Am. chem. Soc.* **53**, 2382.
22. Conant, J. B. & Bailey, C. F. 1933 *J. Am. chem. Soc.* **55**, 795.
23. Conant, J. B. & Moyer, W. W. 1930 *J. Am. chem. Soc.* **52**, 3013; Conant, J. B., Kamerling, S. E. & Steele, C. C. 1931 *J. Am. chem. Soc.* **53**, 1615.
24. Conant, J. B. & Dietz, E. M. 1933 *Nature, Lond.* **131**, 131; Conant, J. B., Hyde, J. F., Moyer, W. W. & Dietz, E. M. 1931 *J. Am. chem. Soc.* **53**, 359.
25. Fischer, H. & Wenderoth, H. 1940 *Justus Liebigs Ann. Chem.*, **545**, 140; Fischer, H. & Stern, A. 1940 *Die Chemie des Pyrrols*, vol. II, part 2, pp. 1 ff. Leipzig: Akademische Verlagsgesellschaft.
26. Conant, J. B. & Scott, N. D. 1926 *J. biol. Chem.* **69**, 575.
27. Conant, J. B., Deisch, F. & Mydans, W. E. 1934 *J. biol. Chem.* **107**, 755.
28. Conant, J. B., Cramer, R. D., Hastings, A. B., Klemperer, F. W., Solomon, A. K. & Vennesland, B. 1941 *J. biol. Chem.* **137**, 557.
29. *Organic syntheses*, vols II & IX (ed. J. B. Conant). New York: John Wiley.
30. Black, N. H. & Conant, J. B. 1937 *New practical chemistry*. New York: Macmillan Co.
31. Conant, J. B. 1933 *The chemistry of organic compounds*. New York: Macmillan Co.; 1939 (2nd ed.) Conant, J. B. & Tishler, M.; 1949 (3rd ed.) Conant, J. B. & Blatt, A. H.
32. Conant, J. B. 1934 President's First Annual Report.

## Bibliography

### *Papers*

1916 (With G. L. Kelley) Electrometric titration of vanadium. *J. Am. chem. Soc.* **38**, 341–351.
(With G. L. Kelley) The determination of chromium and vanadium in steel by electrometric titration. *J. ind. Engng Chem.* **8**, 719–723.
(With G. L. Kelley) The use of diphenylglyoxime as an indicator in the volumetric determination of nickel by Frevert's method. *J. ind. Engng Chem.* **8**, 804–807.

1917 (With E. P. Kohler) Cyclopropane series. *J. Am. chem. Soc.* **39**, 1404–1420.
(With E. P. Kohler) Cyclopropane series II. *J. Am. chem. Soc.* **39**, 1699–1715.
Action of phosphorus trichloride on unsaturated ketones. Preliminary paper. *J. Am. chem. Soc.* **39**, 2679.

1919 Preparation of sodium *p*-hydroxyphenylarsonate. *J. Am. chem. Soc.* **41**, 431.

1920 (With E. B. Hartshorn & G. O. Richardson) Mechanism of the reaction between ethylene and sulfur chloride. *J. Am. chem. Soc.* **42**, 585–595.
(With A. A. Cook) A new type of addition reaction. *J. Am. chem. Soc.* **42**, 830–840.
(With A. D. MacDonald) Addition reactions of phosphorus halides. I. Mechanism of the reaction of the trichloride with benzaldehyde. *J. Am. chem. Soc.* **42**, 2337–2348.

1921 (With N. Tuttle) Diacetone alcohol. *Org. Synth.* **I**, 45–47.
(With N. Tuttle) Mesityl oxide. *Org. Synth.* **I**, 53–55.
(With S. M. Pollack) Addition reactions of phosphorus halides. II. The 1,4-addition of phosphenyl chloride. *J. Am. chem. Soc.* **43**, 1665–1669.
(With A. H. Bump & H. S. Holt) Addition reactions of phosphorus halides. III. The reaction with dibenzalacetone and cinnamylidenacetophenone. *J. Am. chem. Soc.* **43**, 1677–1684.
Addition reactions of the carbonyl group involving the increase in valence of a single atom. *J. Am. chem. Soc.* **43**, 1705–1714.
(With A. D. MacDonald & A. McB. Kinney) Addition reactions of phosphorus halides. IV. Action of the trichloride on saturated aldehydes and ketones. *J. Am. chem. Soc.* **43**, 1928–1935.

1922 (With O. R. Quayle) α,γ-Dichloroacetone. *Org. Synth.* **II**, 13–15.
(With O. R. Quayle) Glycerol α,γ-dichlorohydrin. *Org. Synth.* **II**, 29–31.
(With O. R. Quayle) Glycerol α-monochlorohydrin. *Org. Synth.* **II**, 33–35.
(With T. W. Richards) Electrochemical behavior of liquid sodium amalgams. *J. Am. chem. Soc.* **44**, 601–611.
(With H. M. Kahn, L. F. Fieser & S. S. Kurtz, Jr) Electrochemical study of the reversible reduction of organic compounds. *J. Am. chem. Soc.* **44**, 1382–1396.

1922 (With L. F. Fieser) Free and total energy changes in the reduction of quinones. *J. Am. chem. Soc.* **44**, 2480–2493.

(With B. B. Coyne) Addition reactions of the phosphorus halides. V. The formation of an unsaturated phosphonic acid. *J. Am. chem. Soc.* **44**, 2530–2536.

(With H. B. Cutter) Catalytic hydrogenation and the potential of the hydrogen electrode. *J. Am. chem. Soc.* **44**, 2651–2655.

1923 (With R. E. Lutz & B. B. Corson) 1,4-Aminonaphthol hydrochloride. *Org. Synth.* **III**, 7–10.

(With J. B. S. Brauerman & R. E. Hussey) Addition reactions of phosphorus halides. VI. The 1,2- and 1,4-addition of diphenylchlorophosphine. *J. Am. chem. Soc.* **45**, 165–171.

(With V. H. Wallingford & S. S. Gandheker) Addition reactions of the phosphorus halides. VII. Addition of alkoxy- and aroxychlorophosphines to carbonyl compounds. *J. Am. chem. Soc.* **45**, 762–768.

(With R. E. Lutz) An electrochemical method of studying irreversible organic reductions. *J. Am. chem. Soc.* **45**, 1047–1060.

(With R. E. Lutz) A new method of preparing dibenzoylethylene and related compounds. *J. Am. chem. Soc.* **45**, 1303–1307.

(With L. F. Fieser) Reduction potentials of quinones. I. The effect of the solvent on the potential of certain benzoquinones. *J. Am. chem. Soc.* **45**, 2194–2218.

(With A. W. Sloan) Formation of free radicals by reduction with vanadous chloride. *J. Am. chem. Soc.* **45**, 2466–2472.

(With O. R. Quayle) The purity of α,γ-dichlorohydrin prepared by the action of hydrogen chloride on glycerol. *J. Am. chem. Soc.* **45**, 2771–2772.

An electrochemical study of hemoglobin. *J. biol. Chem.* **57**, 401–414.

1924 (With V. H. Wallingford) Addition reactions of the phosphorus halides. VIII. Kinetic evidence in regard to the mechanism of the reaction. *J. Am. chem. Soc.* **46**, 192–202.

(With W. R. Kirner) Relation between the structure of organic halides and the speed of their reaction with inorganic iodides. I. The problem of alternating polarity in chain compounds. *J. Am. chem. Soc.* **46**, 232–252.

(With E. L. Jackson) Mechanisms of the decomposition of β-bromophosphonic acids in alkaline solution. *J. Am. chem. Soc.* **46**, 1003–1018.

(With H. B. Cutter) Irreversible reduction and catalytic hydrogenation. *J. Phys. Chem.* **28**, 1096–1107.

(With R. E. Lutz) Irreversible reduction of organic compounds. I. The relation between apparent reduction potential and hydrogen-ion concentration. *J. Am. chem. Soc.* **46**, 1254–1267.

(With E. L. Jackson) Addition of methyl hypobromite to certain ethylene derivatives. *J. Am. chem. Soc.* **46**, 1727–1730.

(With J. B. Segur & W. R. Kirner) γ-Chloropropyl phenyl ketone. *J. Am. chem. Soc.* **46**, 1882–1885.

(With L. F. Fieser) Reducation potentials of quinones. II. The potentials of certain derivatives of benzoquinone, naphthoquinone and anthraquinone. *J. Am. chem. Soc.* **46**, 1858–1881.

1925 (With S. A. Freeman) 1,4-Naphthoquinone. *Org. Synth.* **V**, 79–82.

(With A. W. Sloan) Dissociation into free radicals of substituted dixanthyls. I. Dibenzyl- and dibutyldixanthyl. *J. Am. chem. Soc.* **47**, 572–580.

(With R. E. Hussey) Relation between the structure of organic halides and the speed of their reaction with inorganic iodides. II. The study of the alkyl chlorides. *J. Am. chem. Soc.* **47**, 476–488.

(With W. R. Kirner & R. E. Hussey) Relation between the structure of organic halides and the speed of their reaction with inorganic iodides. III. The influence of unsaturated groups. *J. Am. chem. Soc.* **47**, 488–501.

(With W. R. Kirner & R. E. Hussey) Problem of alternating polarity in chain compounds. Reply to C. F. van Duin. *J. Am. chem. Soc.* **47**, 587–589.

(With R. E. Lutz) Unsaturated 1,4-diketones. I. Halogen derivatives of dibenzoylethylene and related compounds. *J. Am. chem. Soc.* **47**, 881–892.

(With L. F. Small & B. S. Taylor) Electrochemical relation of free radicals to halochromic salts. *J. Am. chem. Soc.* **47**, 1959–1974.

1925 (With L. F. Small) Dissociation into free radicals of substituted dixanthyls. II. The dissociating influence of the cyclohexyl group. *J. Am. chem. Soc.* **47**, 3068–3077.

(With L. F. Fieser) Methenoglobin. *J. biol. Chem.* **62**, 595–622.

(With L. F. Fieser) A method for determining methemoglobin in the presence of its cleavage products. *J. biol. Chem.* **62**, 623–631.

1926 (With H. B. Cutter) Irreversible reduction of organic compounds. II. The dimolecular reduction of carbony compounds by vanadous and chromous salts. *J. Am. chem. Soc.* **48**, 1016–1030.

(With L. F. Small & A. W. Sloan) Dissociation into free radicals of substituted dixanthyls. III. The effectiveness of secondary alkyl groups in promoting dissociation. *J. Am. chem. Soc.* **48**, 1743–1757.

(With M. F. Pratt) The irreversible reduction of organic compounds. III. The reduction of azo dyes. *J. Am. chem. Soc.* **48**, 2468–2484.

(With M. F. Pratt) Irreversible oxidation of organic compounds. I. The oxidation of aminophenols by reagents of definite potentials. *J. Am. chem. Soc.* **48**, 3178–3192.

(With M. F. Pratt) Irreversible oxidation of organic compounds. II. The apparent oxidation potential of certain phenols and enols. *J. Am. chem. Soc.* **48**, 3220–3232.

(With N. D. Scott) The adsorption of nitrogen by hemoglobin. *J. biol. Chem.* **68**, 107–121.

(With N. D. Scott) The so-called oxygen content of methemoglobin. *J. biol. Chem.* **69**, 575–587.

The electrochemical formulation of the irreversible reduction and oxidation of organic compounds. *Chem. Rev.* **3**, 1–40.

(With E. J. Cohn) Molecular weights of proteins in phenol. *Proc. natn Acad. Sic. U.S.A.* **12**, 433–438.

(With E. J. Cohn) Molecular weight determination of proteins in phenol. *Z. phys. Chem.* **159**, 93–101.

1927 Reduction potentials of quinones. III. The free energy of reduction referred to the gaseous state. *J. Am. chem. Soc.* **49**, 293–297.

(With R. E. Lutz) Irreversible reduction of organic compounds. IV. The apparent reduction potential of unsaturated carbonyl compounds. *J. Am. chem. Soc.* **49**, 1083–1091.

(With B. S. Garvey, Jr) Dissociation into free radicals of substituted dixanthyls. IV. Dixanthyl and dixanthyl-9,9′-dicarboxylic acid. *J. Am. chem. Soc.* **49**, 2080–2088.

(With B. S. Garvey, Jr) Differential cleavage of the carbon to carbon linkage by alkali metals. *J. Am. chem. Soc.* **49**, 2599–2603.

(With N. F. Hall) A study of superacid solutions. I. The use of the chloranil electrode in glacial acetic acid and the strength of certain weak bases. *J. Am. chem. Soc.* **49**, 3047–3061.

1928 (With A. H. Blatt) Action of sodium–potassium alloy on petroleum. *J. Am. chem. Soc.* **50**, 542–550.

(With A. H. Blatt) Action of sodium–potassium alloy on certain hydrocarbons. *J. Am. chem. Soc.* **50**, 551–558.

(With N. M. Bigelow) Di-tert-butyltetraphenylethane. *J. Am. chem. Soc.* **50**, 2051–2059.

(With G. M. Bramann) Acidic and basic catalysis of acetylation reactions. *J. Am. chem. Soc.* **50**, 2305–2311.

(With J. G. Aston) Certain new oxidation reactions of aldehydes. *J. Am. chem. Soc.* **50**, 2783–2798.

(With G. A. Alles & C. D. Tongberg) The electrometric titration of hemin and hematin. *J. biol. Chem.* **79**, 89–93.

(With N. D. Scott) A spectrophotometric study of certain equilibria involving the oxidation of hemoglobin to methemoglobin. *J. biol. Chem.* **76**, 207–222.

(With N. D. Scott & W. F. Douglass) An improved method of determining methemoglobin. *J. biol. Chem.* **76**, 223–227.

Atoms, molecules and ions. *J. chem. Educ.* **5**, 25–35.

1929 (With A. H. Blatt) Action of the Grignard reagent on highly branched carbonyl compounds. *J. Am. chem. Soc.* **51**, 1227–1236.

(With C. N. Webb & W. C. Mendum) Trimethylacetaldehyde and dimethylethylacetaldehyde. *J. Am. chem. Soc.* **51**, 1246–1255.

(With Mildred W. Evans) Dissociation into free radicals of substituted dixanthyls. V. The rate of dissociation. *J. Am. chem. Soc.* **51**, 1925–1935.

1929 (With G. H. CARLSON) Apparent racemization of pinene. *J. Am. chem. Soc.* **51**, 3464–3469.
(With J. F. HYDE) Chlorophyll series. I. Thermal decomposition of the magnesium-free compounds. *J. Am. chem. Soc.* **51**, 3668–3674.
(With J. F. HYDE) Relationship of chlorophyll to the prophyrins. *Science* **70**, 149.
1930 (With J. G. ASTON & C. O. TONGBERG) Irreversible oxidation of organic compounds. *J. Am. chem. Soc.* **52**, 407–419.
(With W. D. PETERSON) Rate of coupling of diazonium salts with phenols in buffer solutions. *J. Am. chem. Soc.* **52**, 1220–1232.
(With F. F. HYDE) Chlorophyll series. II. Reducation and catalytic hydrogenation. *J. Am. chem. Soc.* **52**, 1233–1239.
(With C. O. TONGBERG) Polymerization reactions under high pressure. I. Some experiments with isoprene and butyraldehyde. *J. Am. chem. Soc.* **52**, 1659–1669.
(With W. W. MOYER) Chlorophyll series. III. Products of the phase test. *J. Am. chem. Soc.* **52**, 3013–3023.
(With T. H. WERNER) Superacid solutions. IV. Determination of the strength of weak bases and pseudo bases in glacial acetic acid solution. *J. Am. chem. Soc.* **52**, 4436–4450.
(With R. V. MCGREW) An inquiry into the existence of intermediate compounds in the oxygenation of hemoglobin. *J. biol. Chem.* **85**, 421–434.
(With C. O. TONGBERG) The oxidation–reduction potentials of hemin and related substances. I. The potentials of various hemins and hematins in the absence and presence of pyridine. *J. biol. Chem.* **86**, 733–741.
(With C. O. TONGBERG) The α-oxidation of acetaldehyde and the mechanism of the oxidation of lactic acid. *J. biol. Chem.* **88**, 701–708.
(With W. G. HUMPHREY) Nature of the prosthetic group in *limulus* hemocyanin. *Proc. natn Acad. Sci. U.S.A.* **16**, 543–546.
(With F. H. CRAWFORD) The study of adsorption spectra of organic compounds at liquid-air temperatures. *Proc. natn. Acad. Sci. U.S.A.* **16**, 552–554.
1931 (With B. B. CORSON) 1-Amino-2-nephthol hydrochloride. *Org. Synth.* **XI**, 8–11.
(With J. F. HYDE, W. W. MOYER & E. M. DIETZ) Chlorophyll series. IV. The degradation of chlorophyll and allomerized chlorophyll to simple chlorins. *J. Am. chem. Soc.* **53**, 359–373.
(With N. M. BIGELOW) Reduction of triphenylmethane dyes and related substances with the formation of free radicals. *J. Am. chem. Soc.* **53**, 676–690.
(With S. E. KAMERLING & C. C. STEELE) Allomerization of chlorophyll. *J. Am. chem. Soc.* **53**, 1615–1616.
(With H. W. SCHERP) Addition of free radicals to unsaturated compounds. *J. Am. chem. Soc.* **53**, 1941–1944.
(With EMMA M. DIETZ, C. F. BAILEY & S. E. KAMERLING) Chlorophyll series. V. Structure of chlorophyll a. *J. Am. chem. Soc.* **53**, 2382–2393.
(With S. E. KAMERLING) Chlorophyll series. VII. Evidence as to structure from measurements of absorption spectra. *J. Am. chem. Soc.* **53**, 3522–3529.
(With EMMA M. DIETZ & T. H. WERNER) Chlorophyll series. VIII. Structure of chlorophyll b. *J. Am. chem. Soc.* **53**, 4436–4448.
(With G. PAYLING WRIGHT & S. E. KAMERLING) The catalytic effect of ferricyanide in the oxidation of unsaturated compounds by oxygen. *J. biol. Chem.* **94**, 411–413.
(With E. M. DIETZ & S. E. KAMERLING) The dehydrogenation of chlorophyll and the mechanism of photosynthesis. *Science* **73**, 268.
1932 (With W. R. PETERSON) Polymerization reactions under high pressure. II. Mechanism of the reaction. *J. Am. chem. Soc.* **54**, 629–635.
(With G. W. WHELAND) Study of extremely weak acids. *J. Am. chem. Soc.* **54**, 1212–1221.
(With P. D. BARTLETT) Quantitative study of semicarbazone formation. *J. Am. chem. Soc.* **54**, 2881–2899.
(With A. F. THOMPSON, JR) Free energy of enolization in the gaseous phase of substituted acetoacetic esters. *J. Am. chem. Soc.* **54**, 4039–4047.
(With G. H. CARLSON) Study of the rate of enolization by the polariscopic method. *J. Am. chem. Soc.* **54**, 4048–4059.
(With A. M. PAPPENHEIMER, JR) A redetermination of the oxidation potential of the hemoglobin-methemoglobin system. *J. biol. Chem.* **98**, 57–62.
Equilibria and rates of some organic reactions. *Ind. Engng Chem.* **24**, 466–472.

1933 (With C. F. Bailey) Chlorophyll series. IX. Transformations establishing the nature of the nucleus. *J. Am. chem. Soc.* **55**, 795-800.
(With K. F. Armstrong) Chlorophyll series. X. Esters of chlorin. *J. Am. chem. Soc.* **55**, 829–839.
(With Emma M. Dietz) Chlorophyll series. XI. The position of the methoxyl group. *J. Am. chem. Soc.* **55**, 839–849.
(With R. F. Schultz) Dissociation into free radicals of di-tert-butyltetrakis(phenylphenyl)ethane. *J. Am. chem. Soc.* **55**, 2098–2104.
(With G. W. Wheland) Structure of the acids obtained by the oxidation of triisobutylene. *J. Am. chem. Soc.* **55**, 2499–2504.
(With B. F. Chow) Addition of free radicals to certain dienes, pyrrole and maleic anhydride. *J. Am. chem. Soc.* **55**, 3475–3479.
(With B. F. Chow) Measurement of oxidation–reduction potentials in glacial acetic acid solutions. *J. Am. chem. Soc.* **55**, 3745–3751.
(With B. F. Chow) Potential of free radicals of the triphenylmethyl type in glacial acetic acid solutions. *J. Am. chem. Soc.* **55**, 3752–3758.
(With B. F. Chow & E. B. Schoenbach) The oxidation of hemocyanin. *J. biol. Chem.* **101**, 463–473.
(With Emma M. Dietz) Structural formulas of the chlorophylls. *Nature, Lond.* **131**, 131.
The heat of dissociation of the carbon–carbon linkage. *J. chem. Phys.* **1**, 427–431.

1934 (With B. F. Chow & Emma M. Dietz) Chlorophyll series. XIV. Potentiometric titration in acetic acid solution of the basic groups in chlorophyll derivatives. *J. Am. chem. Soc.* **56**, 2185–2189.
(With F. Dersch & W. E. Mydans) The prosthetic group of *limulus* hemocyanin. *J. biol. Chem.* **107**, 755–766.

1937 (With G. B. Kistiakowsky) Energy changes involved in the addition reactions of unsaturated hydrocarbons. *Chem. Rev.* **20**, 181–194.

1939 Lessons from the past. *Ind. Engng Chem.* **31**, 1215–1217.

1941 (With R. D. Cramer, A. Baird Hastings, F. W. Klemperer, A. K. Solomon & Birgit Vennesland) Metabolism of lactic acid containing radioactive carboxyl carbon. *J. biol. Chem.* **137**, 557–566.
Chemists and the national defense. *Am. chem. Soc. News Edn* **19**, 1237–1238.

1944 Science and the national welfare. *Chem. Engng News* **22**, 1642–1645.

1946 Address on scientific accomplishments of Roger Adams (Richards medalist). *Chem. Engng News* **24**, 1511–1513, 1611.

1948 The role of science in our unique society. *Science* **107**, 77–83.

1951 Scientists, inventors, and executives. *Chem. Engng News* **29**, 2262–2264.
A skeptical chemist looks into the crystal ball. *Chem. Engng News* **29**, 3847–3849.
Chemists and the building of international bridges. *Chem. Engng News* **29**, 4254–4255.

1970 Theodore William Richards and the periodic table. *Science* **168**, 425–428.

*Books*

1920 (With N. H. Black) *Practical chemistry*. (Revised ed. 1929.) New York: Macmillan Co.

1922 (Member, Editorial Board, vols I–XII; Editor-in-chief, vol. II, 1922, and vol. IX, 1929). *Organic syntheses* New York: John Wiley & Sons, Inc.

1928 *Organic chemistry*. New York: Macmillan Co.

1932 *Equilibria and rates of some organic reactions*. Columbia University Press.

1933 *The chemistry of organic compounds*. New York: Macmillan Co.

1936 (Revised with M. Tishler) *Organic chemistry*. New York: Macmillan Co.

1937 (With N. H. Black) *New Practical chemistry*. (Revised ed. 1946.) New York: Macmillan Co.

1939 (Revised with M. Tishler) *The chemistry of organic compounds*. (2nd ed.) New York: Macmillan Co.

1944 *Our fighting faith*. Cambridge: Harvard University Press.

1948 *Education in a divided world*. Cambridge: Harvard University Press; also New York: Greenwood Press.

1947 (With A. H. Blatt) *The chemistry of organic compounds*. (3rd ed.), (4th ed. 1952.) New York: Macmillan Co.

1949 *The growth of experimental sciences, an experiment in general education*. Cambridge: Harvard University Press.

1947 *On understanding science.* New Haven: Yale University Press.
1950 (With A. H. BLATT) *Fundamentals of organic chemistry.* New York: Macmillan Co.
1951 *Science and the common sesnse.* New Haven: Yale University Press.
1953 *Education and liberty.* Cambridge: Harvard University Press.
*Modern science and modern man.* Garden City: Doubleday.
1955 *Gleichheit der Chancen: Erziehung und Gesellschaftsordnung in den Vereinigten Staaten.* Bad Manheim: Christian-Verlag.
1956 *The citadel of learning.* New Haven: Yale University Press.
1957 (With L. K. NASH, Assoc. Ed.) *Case histories in experimental science.* Cambridge: Harvard University Press.
1958 *Deutschland und die Freiheit.* Frankfurt: Ullstein.
1959 *The American high school today.* New York: McGraw-Hill.
*The child, the parent and the state.* Cambridge: Harvard University Press.
1960 *Education in the junior high school years.* New York: McGraw-Hill.
1961 *Slums and suburbs.* New York: McGraw-Hill.
1962 *Thomas Jefferson and the development of American public education.* Berkeley: University of California Press.
1962 *Germany and freedom, a personal appraisal.* New York: Capricorn Books.
1963 *The education of American teachers.* New York: McGraw-Hill.
1964 *Shaping educational policy.* New York: McGraw-Hill.
*Two modes of thought.* New York: Trident Press.
1967 *The comprehensive high school, a second report to interested citizens.* New York: McGraw-Hill.
*Scientific principles and moral conduct.* Cambridge University Press.
1970 *My several lives.* New York: Harper & Row.

*Patents*

(1) J. B. Conant. Benzyl chloride. *U.S. Patent* 1233986, 17 July 1917.
(2) Percy W. Bridgman and J. B. Conant. Polymerizing indene and other unsaturated organic compounds. *U.S. Patent* 1950671, 13 March 1934.

J. Craigie.

# JAMES CRAIGIE

25 June 1899 — 26 August 1978

Elected F.R.S. 1947

By Sir Christopher Andrewes, F.R.S.

James Craigie, who died in Edinburgh on 26 August 1978, was a microbiologist who will be remembered for the part he played in the development of his subject in Canada. It was there that he spent the most active 15 years of his life. When he went there from Scotland in 1931 virology was still in its infancy; he was one of those who helped to raise it to its present position as a discipline in the forefront of biological knowledge.

He was born in Arbroath, Angus, on 25 June 1899, the elder of two brothers. His grandfather, James, was a professional gardener, holding several appointments in large gardens in Scotland. His son, also James, the father of the microbiologist, was a librarian, having experience in several libraries in Scotland and Australia before settling in Perth in 1902 to become librarian to the Sandeman Library there. He was an elder of the church and an active and popular figure in local affairs. His brother, uncle of our Craigie, was Sir William Craigie, an outstanding lexicographer and philologist. He became co-editor of the *Oxford English Dictionary* and also wrote Scottish, American and Icelandic dictionaries. He was familiar, also, with Scandinavian, Anglo-Saxon, Frisian and Gaelic languages and literature.

Craigie's mother, Frances Stewart McHardy, came from a farming family at Inverey, near Braemar, and here he often spent much of his holidays. He early became interested in natural history, first in insects but soon, after being lent a microscope, in pond life. This interest he maintained, reading a paper on Ciliata (1) before the Perthshire Society of Natural Science. He was also interested in music, playing the organ and piano.

On leaving school he went to the University of St Andrew's, intending to take a combined medical/B.Sc. degree. On being called up during World War I, he was promptly sent back to complete his studies for a medical degree.

From University College, Dundee (University of St Andrew's), he qualified M.B., Ch.B. in 1923. Later he took his Ph.D. and D.P.H. His first appointment was as assistant medical officer, Murray Royal, Perth. He was appointed in 1927 assistant in bacteriology under Professor W. J. Tulloch in Dundee. He early showed an interest in bacterial flagella (2, 3) and this led him on to a study of the serological reactions of the flagella of *B. typhosus* (now *Salmonella typhi*) (7). He also worked with Professor Tulloch and W. L. Burgess on a 'variola–vaccinia flocculation test', and with them was concerned in writing two Medical Research Council special monographs on the subject (4, 6).

Before we turn to the scientific side of his work, it will be convenient to sketch his early career, for his studies on vaccinia and typhoid were carried out on both sides of the Atlantic. In 1931 he emigrated to Canada to become a research assistant at the Connaught Laboratories in the University of Toronto. His status was advanced in successive stages; he became lecturer in epidemiology in 1924, associate Professor of Virus Infections in 1940 and, in 1946, Professor of Virus Infections. He remained in Canada for over 15 years, returning to Britain in 1947 to join the staff of the Imperial Cancer Research Fund. Over a period of 10 years (1935–45) he served as Secretary of the School of Hygiene in Toronto.

## Vaccinia and variola

Before the 1930s several workers, particularly M. H. Gordon, had described a 'flocculation reaction', seen when vaccine lymph or small-pox crusts were mixed with appropriate antisera. Such visible reactions with viral materials were unfamiliar and some claimed that they were non-specific, secondary bacterial invaders being concerned. In the first of the two M.R.C. reports with which Craigie was associated (4) evidence was produced that the reaction was specific, varicella crusts being negative. In the second report (6) the reaction was demonstrated with material free from secondary invaders and it was shown to be independent of the organ or species from which the lesions were derived.

Craigie continued his work on vaccinia after he came to Toronto. By that time it was generally recognized that the small particles generally known as elementary bodies were, in fact, infectious viral particles. Craigie added further evidence by means of an improved staining reaction (12) and by showing that purified elementary bodies elicited skin reactions in man similar to those induced by vaccine lymph (10). His main interest was, however, still in viral antigens and antibodies. He showed (8) that the 'flocculation reaction' was really a mixture of agglutination of elementary bodies and precipitation of an antigen which could be separated from the virus particles by filtration. That the same antibody was concerned in both reactions was revealed by absorption tests. These findings were paralleled by others using the complement-fixation test (15). Study of the heat-stability of vaccinia led to the conclusion (13) that the sera under study contained two antibodies directed respectively against a heat-labile (L) and a heat-stable (S) agglutinogen. The L-antigen was also more readily inactivated by some chemicals.

All these studies were finally brought together in three classical papers by Craigie and F. O. Wishart (22, 23, 24). It was shown that soluble precipitable substances, both the L and S antigens, were slowly released *in vitro* from suspensions of washed elementary bodies. Addition of either anti-L or anti-S sera to these suspensions precipitated both antigens and it was therefore concluded that they were components of a complex LS antigen. Both antigens were present also in crude vaccine of dermal origin, whether coming from calf, rabbit or guinea pig. The LS antigen was able to stimulate the production of both L and S antibodies when used to immunize rabbits; the L-antigen, however, had its antigenicity destroyed by heating to 70 °C. A final paper in the field of pox-viruses described how the complement-fixation test using anti-vaccinial serum and variola crusts could be used in diagnosis; the test was eight to ten times more sensitive than the flocculation test and more convenient in practice (25).

## Typhoid

The work that Craigie carried out while in Dundee was put together in a 95-page-long very involved paper (7). As a result of his studies of flagella and antibodies against them, he there put forward cogent criticism of the double receptor hypothesis of Weil and Felix; this had dealt with the relationships and importance of heat-labile and heat-stable antigens of certain enteric bacteria.

By the time he returned to the subject in Canada a few years later, Felix and his co-workers had described another, Vi (virulence), antigen present in freshly isolated typhoid bacilli but lost on sub-cultivation. Strains of the organism either had (V-forms) or had not (W-forms) the Vi-antigen. Craigie and Brandon (21) discovered a bacteriophage active only against V-forms. Such cultures, when treated with the phage, reverted to the W-form. Use of this phage proved of diagnostic value in identifying V-forms of *B. typhosus*; it was quicker in use than the agglutination test, giving positive results in six hours (19).

This work soon led on to what can probably be considered to be Craigie's most important contribution to his subject. It was found that not all Vi-phages were alike. They could, in fact, be grouped into four types, differing in the size of plaques produced, in heat-stability and in the range of typhoid strains they could attack. Three of the strains would lyse any V-form of typhoid. Type 2, however, was different, showing activity only against certain typhoid strains. It proved, however, to be very adaptable; after passage on any strain it acquired the property of lysing that strain in, perhaps, a millionfold higher dilution than was found with a heterologous strain. It became possible on this basis to divide V-form typhoid bacilli into a number of groups according to their susceptibility or otherwise to various adapted strains of type 2 phage. These types proved to be stable. In the first study by Craigie and Yen (28), nearly 99% of strains could be placed in one or other of 6 types, but by 1947 24 types or subtypes had been identified.

The ability to type typhoid strains turned out to have great usefulness epidemiologically, for strains of common origin always belonged to the same type (29). Accordingly, when typhoid cultures were obtained and studied in the laboratory, one could decide which could have had a common origin and which could not. This was particularly useful when it came to blaming a particular typhoid carrier for spreading infection or absolving him.

There came to light some anomalies, necessitating the erection of sub-types; thus things became a little more complicated than in the above simplified account. In 1947 Craigie and Felix made suggestions for standardizing the test and maintaining reference reagents (39). The methods found so useful in typhoid were soon applied to *Salmonella paratyphosus* B and to other salmonellas.

## Other viruses: typhus

During his 15 years in Canada Craigie concerned himself with a number of other viruses, particularly poliomyelitis, on which he wrote three papers (18, 27, 34). He became, in fact, an outstanding leader in the fields of virology and microbiology generally, in Canada. In 1946 he was elected President of the American Society of Bacteriologists and gave a presidential address entitled 'The significance of bacteriophage in bacteriological and virus research' (38). During World War II there were fears that the enemy might introduce rinderpest into America with disastrous results to the cattle industry. Craigie was a member of a joint U.S.–Canadian Commission on the matter (1942–46). Under its aegis a research station was set up on an island in the St Lawrence River, where the infection could be studied under conditions of rigorous isolation.

Another infection of importance in war-time is typhus. Craigie was closely involved in the preparation of vaccines against the disease. He, together with colleagues, wrote five memoranda on this subject for the National Research Council of Canada. His three published papers on typhus concerned an improved staining method for rickettsiae (35), a method of purifying rickettsiae from yolk-sac suspensions at an ether–water interface (36), and the serological relationships of epidemic and murine typhus (37). He described a heat-stable antigen common to both kinds of rickettsiae and a heat-labile specific one; the latter was more important in immunity. For all this work he was awarded a U.S. Typhus Commission medal (1946).

## Cancer

Soon after the end of the war there came a complete change in Craigie's interests. In 1946 W. E. Gye, then Director of the laboratories of the Imperial Cancer Research Fund in London, was touring laboratories in North America to learn of current progress; and Craigie joined him on the tour. Gye was much impressed by his ability and persuaded him to return to Britain to join the staff of the I.C.R.F. with a view to becoming Director in a few years' time. Accordingly, in 1947, Craigie returned to Britain to work in the Fund's laboratories at Mill Hill. These were next door to the National Institute for Medical Research, so that I saw a lot of him during the next few years.

Soon after his return, Craigie collaborated with Gye and others (42) in experiments which showed that tissues of several tumours of mice could survive either freezing or drying. It was felt to be unlikely that intact cells would survive such treatment and that the findings indicated the probability that a virus was present as a continuing cause. It is likely that Craigie himself had reservations about such a conclusion, for in the next few years his work was directed largely to showing that, in fact, tumour cells could survive these treatments.

In the studies on freezing and drying Craigie showed evidence of his love of 'gadgetry'. He designed an improved method for rapid drying of tissues (41). He also described a tissue-mincer which would reduce tumour tissues almost to the state of single cells (40). He had made a 'fail-safe' freezing machine in which tissues were kept frozen in dry ice, but the whole was surrounded by an electric cooling system. There was thus insurance against either breakdown in the electricity supply or failure in supplies of dry ice. Intermittent use of the electrical system also resulted in considerable saving in the consumption of dry ice (48). To all this he brought his close knowledge of the physical principles involved.

There was an important result of this work. It had for many years been necessary for workers in cancer research to propagate transplantable tumours, especially in mice, by means of cell-grafts at fairly frequent intervals. This was expensive in time and labour and, moreover, the tumours could, and often did, change their properties in the course of transplantation. This safe method of preserving tissues *in vitro* over many years overcame these difficulties, and a 'tumour bank' was a consequence. This has proved outstandingly useful.

Two findings were particularly helpful. Many tumours injected intraperitoneally could be induced to grow as 'ascites tumours' with cells multiplying in the exudate they induced. Thus single-cell suspensions of tumour cells became available and quantitative work was correspondingly easier (47). Another finding was that in dextrose, tumour cells would survive particularly well at low temperatures (43), and this had important consequences, for microscopical studies, using phase contrast, showed that nuclei of surviving cells assumed a homogeneous vitreous appearance.

This led to the discovery that in tumour preparations, and especially in those of ascites tumours, survival was due to the presence of greater or smaller numbers of cells in an abnormal 'paramorphic' state (45, 46). These, when seen by phase contrast microscopy, were highly refractile; they were also resistant to hypertonic dextrose, glycerol, freezing and drying. When restored to more 'physiological' conditions they soon returned to normal and could start multiplying. The paramorphic state could not be recognized in fixed and stained preparations.

Craigie's last published work concerned Tyzzer's disease of mice and its causative organism, *Bacillus piliformis*. This has been a cause of outbreaks of disease which have ruined much laboratory work with mice. The organism grows intracellularly and had not been cultivable in bacteriological media. Craigie succeeded in propagating it serially in the yolk-sacs of fertile eggs. The vegetative form of the organism was difficult to preserve until it was found possible to do so by freezing tissue suspensions at $-75$ °C (51). Both the parent strain and a non-sporing variant were pathogenic for mice. Infection was potentiated by cortisone but could be checked with penicillin (52).

## Personality

Craigie was a remarkable man with the originality and curiosity necessary for a good research worker. He was fascinated by gadgetry and techniques; any new piece of apparatus had to be taken to pieces and reassembled so that he thoroughly understood how it worked. He was meticulous in all he did. His best work was done before World War II when he was working by himself or with one technician. At that time he was teaching in the Department of Hygiene, University of Toronto. Dr R. J. Wilson writes that 'he will be remembered by many students . . . as a magnificent teacher'.

It was when he was in charge of a department, first in Canada, later in Mill Hill, that things became more difficult. He was essentially a kindly man and troubles that arose stemmed from a difficulty in communication. In discussing a scientific problem he would start in the middle, assuming that his hearers knew the background and, in particular, his own earlier writings. Junior workers were too shy to admit that this left them all at sea. A number of people have confessed that they were often baffled by a frustrating habit he had; he would start to explain something, break off in the middle of a sentence and look up with a smile, assuming one would know how the exposition would end. As one commonly did not, one was none the wiser. Ensuing difficulties would be overcome only by those with some sense of humour. He was reluctant to delegate and too apt to devote himself to his own research rather than to running the laboratory as a whole. Difficulties had gradually increased from the time he was put in charge of the Mill Hill laboratories in 1949. Accordingly it was suggested to him that he should step down from administrative charge of the laboratories, so that he could concentrate on his own research. This he agreed to do and he was succeeded in 1957 as head of the laboratories by Dr R. J. C. Harris. He was certainly happier and more effective after this had come to pass, and thereafter junior colleagues actually found him more helpful.

Craigie received a number of honours. In 1946 he received the O.B.E. and was elected a Fellow of the Royal Society of Canada. In the following year he was elected F.R.S., London, and was awarded the Medal of Freedom of the U.S.A. He received the Stewart Prize of the British Medical Association in 1950 and the LL.D. of St Andrew's in the same year.

On his return to Britain in 1947 he took a house at Christmas Common in the Chilterns; there were ten acres of grounds. On his retirement in 1964 he found ample occupation in the many problems arising on this estate. He was an enthusiastic gardener, raising many plants from seed and was particularly interested in breeding irises. Another resource derived from his lifelong interest in apparatus, with many items to repair or construct. On his wife's death he moved to Edinburgh, where one of his daughters lived.

I am very grateful for the help I have received from many sources: his two daughters, Mrs Margaret Ridehalgh, herself a microbiologist, and Miss Frances Craigie, Dr E. S. Anderson, Dr K. F. Brandon, Dr R. J. C. Harris, Dr G. Negroni, Dr R. J. Wilson, Professor R. Hare and Mrs J. Orr.

The photograph reproduced was taken by J. Russell & Sons, London, *ca.* 1949–50.

## Bibliography

(1) 1921 The Ciliata. *Trans. Proc. Perthsh. Soc. nat. Sci.* **7**, part 3.

(2) 1928 A method of staining bacterial flagella. *Br. J. exp. Path.* **9**, 55.

(3) 1929 The demonstration of bacterial flagella. *Jl R. microsc. Soc.* **49**, 9.

(4) (With W. L. Burgess & W. J. Tulloch) Diagnostic value of the 'Vaccinia Variola' flocculation test. *Spec. Rep. Ser. med. Res. Coun.* no. 143.

(5) 1931 A method of drying complement from the frozen state. *Br. J. exp. Path.* **12**, 75.

(6) (With W. J. Tulloch) Further investigation on the Variola–Vaccinia flocculation reaction. *Spec. Rep. Ser. med. Res. Coun.* no. 156.

(7) Studies on the serological reactions of the flagella of *B. typhosus. J. Immun.* **25**, 417.

(8) 1932 The nature of the Vaccinia flocculation reaction and observations on the elementary bodies of Vaccinia. *Br. J. exp. Path.* **13**, 259.

(9) Inhibition of the Vaccinia flocculation reaction by fresh rabbit serum. *Trans. R. Soc. Can.* section 5, p. 303.

(10) 1933 (With F. O. Wishart) Skin sensitivity to the elementary bodies of Vaccinia. *Can. publ. Hlth J.* **24**, 72.

(11) Variation in the scarification-intradermal titre ratio of Vaccinia virus. *Trans. R. Soc. Can.* section 5, p. 177.

(12) A method of staining the elementary (Paschen) bodies of Vaccinia. *J. Path. Bact.* **36**, 185.

(13) 1934 (With F. O. Wishart) The agglutinogens of a strain of Vaccinia elementary bodies. *Br. J. exp. Path.* **15**, 390.

(14) Some aspects of virus infection with special reference to virus diseases of childhood. (Second Blackader Lecture.) *Can. med. Ass. J.* **31**, 347.

(15) (With F. O. Wishart) The complement fixation reaction with the elementary bodies of Vaccinia and the specific precipitable substance of Vaccinia. *Trans. R. Soc. Can.* section 5, p. 91.

(16) 1935 (With F. O. Wishart) The titration of the L and S antigens of Vaccinia virus in extracts of the vaccinated skin of the rabbit, calf and guinea pig. *Trans. R. Soc. Can.* section 5, p. 57.

(17) The present status of the antigenic analysis of the elementary bodies of Vaccinia. *J. Iumun.* **29**, 70 (abstract).

(18) 1936 Some problems of poliomyelitis. *Can. publ. Hlth J.* **27**, 6.

(19) (With K. F. Brandon) The laboratory of identification of the V form of *B. typhosus. Can. publ. Hlth J.* **27**, 165.

(20) (With K. F. Brandon) The identification of the V and W forms of *B. typhosus* and the occurrence of the V form in cases of typhoid fever and in carriers. *J. Path. Bact.* **43**, 249

(21) (With K. F. Brandon) Bacteriophage specific for the O-resistant V form of *B. typhosus. J. Path. Bact.* **43**, 233.

(22) (With F. O. Wishart) Studies on the soluble precipitable substances of Vaccinia. I. The dissociation *in vitro* of soluble precipitable substances from elementary bodies of Vaccinia. *J. exp. Med.* **64**, 803.

(23) (With F. O. Wishart) Studies on the soluble precipitable substances of Vaccinia. II. The soluble precipitable substances of dermal vaccine. *J. exp. Med.* **64**, 819.

(24) (With F. O. Wishart) Studies on the soluble precipitable substances of Vaccinia. III. The precipitin responses of rabbits to the LS antigen of Vaccinia. *J. exp. Med.* **64**, 831.

(25) (With F. O. Wishart) The complement fixation reaction in Variola. *Can. publ. Hlth J.* **27**, 371.

(26) 1937 (With C. H. Yen) V bacteriophages for *B. typhosus*. *Trans. R. Soc. Can.* section 5, 79.

(27) Poliomyelitis virus and experimental infection. *Can. publ. Hlth J.* **28**, 1.

(28) 1938 (With C. H. Yen) The demonstration of types of *B. typhosus* by means of preparation of type 2 Vi phage. I. The principles and technique. *Can. publ. Hlth J.* **29**, 448.

(29) (With C. H. Yen) The demonstration of types of *B. typhosus* by means of preparations of type 2 Vi phage. II. The stability and epidemiological significance of V form types of *B. typhosus*. *Can. publ. Hlth J.* **29**, 484.

(30) 1939 Notes on the typing of *B. typhosus*, with special reference to types E2 and F2. *Can. publ. Hlth J.* **30** (abstract).

(31) 1940 Further observations on types of *B. typhosus*. *Can. publ. Hlth J.* **31** (abstract).

(32) 1939 Die Antigenfunktionen und die serologischen Reaktionen der Virusarten *in vitro*. In: *Handbuch der Virusforschung* (ed. R. Doerr & C. Hallauer), vol. 2, pp. 1106–1147. Vienna: Julius Springer.

(33) 1941 Typing of typhoid bacilli with type 2 Vi phage. *Hersol's Cyclopedia of Medicine, Surgery and Specialties*, section of Bacteriology, service volume.

(34) 1943 (With H. A. Howe) The question of spontaneous acquisition of poliomyelitis by rhesus monkeys. *J. Bact.* **45**, 87.

(35) 1944 An alkaline thionin method of staining rickettsiae. *Can. J. Res.* E **22**, 89.

(36) 1945 Application and control of ethyl–ether–water interface effects to the separation of rickettsiae from yolk-sac suspensions. *Can. J. Res.* E **23**, 104.

(37) 1946 (With N. M. Clark, E. Malcomsen & D. W. Watson) The serological relationships of epidemic and murine typhus. *Can. J. Res.* E **24**, 84.

(38) The significance and applications of bacteriophage in bacteriological and virus research. *Bact. Rev.* **10**, 3–4, 73–88. (Presidential Address to Society of American Bacteriologists.)

(39) 1947 (With A. Felix) Typing of typhoid bacilli with Vi bacteriophage. Suggestions for its standardization. *Lancet* **1**, 823.

(40) 1949 A pressure mincer for the preparation of tumour suspensions. *Br. J. Cancer* **3**, 249.

(41) A drying apparatus for the study of tumour transmission. *Br. J. Cancer* **3**, 250.

(42) (With W. E. Gye, A. M. Begg & I. Mann) The survival of activity of mouse sarcoma tissue after freezing and drying. *Br. J. Cancer* **3**, 259.

(43) The preservation of suspensions of tumour cells after freezing and drying. *Br. J. Cancer* **3**, 268.

(44) A quantitative approach to the study of transplantable tumours. *Br. med. J.* **2**, 1485.

(45) 1951 (With P. E. Lind, M. E. Hayward & A. M. Begg) Preliminary observations on a 'dormant' state of sarcoma cells with special reference to resistance to freezing and drying. *J. Path. Bact.* **63**, 177.

(46) 1952 Further observations on tumour cells in the 'paramorphic' or 'dormant' state. *J. Path. Bact.* **64**, 251.

(47) Sarcoma 37 and ascites tumour. *Ann. R. Coll. Surg.* **11**, 287.

(48) 1954 Survival and preservation of tumours in the frozen state. *Adv. Cancer Res.* **2**, 197.

(49) 1955 Some aspects of basic cancer research. *Med. Pract.* **234**, 335.

(50) 1962 *Bacillus piliformis* and Tyzzer's disease of the laboratory mouse. *Proc. 8th Int. Congr. Microbiol.*, abstracts, p. 115.

(51) 1966 '*Bacillus piliformis*' (Tyzzer) and Tyzzer's disease of the laboratory mouse. I. Propagation of the organism in embryonated eggs. *Proc. R. Soc. Lond.* B **165**, 35.

(52) '*Bacillus piliformis*' (Tyzzer) and Tyzzer's disease of the laboratory mouse. II. Mouse pathogenicity of *B. piliformis* grown in embryonated eggs. *Proc. R. Soc. Lond.* B **165**, 61.


The work on cancer is also covered in annual reports of the Imperial Cancer Research Fund. Craigie was responsible for writing those of the years 1949–56.

Pehr Edman

# PEHR VICTOR EDMAN

14 April 1916 — 19 March 1977

Elected F.R.S. 1974,

By S. Miles Partridge, F.R.S., and Birger Blombäck

Pehr Edman died after a short illness at the age of 60 in Munich. His untimely death brought to an end a long and challenging undertaking which although not quite finished to his own satisfaction has brought about a revolution in protein chemistry. Edman's work has provided chemists with a capability undreamt of a generation ago: the power to determine the amino acid sequence of long runs of peptide chain with speed and precision by an automated method. This has put into man's grasp essential information for the study of the genetic replication of enzymes and structural proteins and has completed the graduation of protein chemistry from a branch of colloid science to a fundamental organ of molecular genetics.

It now seems scarcely necessary to say that the sequencing of proteins, combined with X-ray diffraction analysis, provides a powerful tool to aid the determination of their complete spatial configuration including that of the interface with solvent which carries most of the biological activity. Extension of knowledge of protein sequences is essential in the search for evolutionary relationships between different proteins. In addition, studies of numerous heritable diseases are now showing how aberrant enzymes and structural proteins produced by genetic errors affecting the primary sequence may give rise to the malfunctions observed and how this exact knowledge may sometimes be used to alleviate the condition.

Edman set out to solve, in a determined and single-minded way, the problem of rapid and accurate sequencing and has resisted all temptation to deviate from his set course even though this meant leaving to others the rewards of early application to many interesting biological and medical problems. In preparing this memoir the authors have sought some clue to Edman's motivation in providing a highly refined tool for others to use and have found no solution other than his own personal integrity and the satisfaction of a task well done.

## Early life

Pehr Victor Edman was born in Stockholm, Sweden, on 14 April 1916. His father, Victor Edman, was a judge. On the paternal side the male members of the family had for generations served as public officers in state agencies and the armed forces. The father was a serious man and a devoted Christian. The mother, Alba Edman, was of a more joyous nature, lively and neat. As a boy Pehr Edman attended the elementary public school in Stockholm and at the beginning of the thirties started his high school education at the 'Norra Latin-skolan' in Stockholm, which specialized in the humanities. He was very unhappy during his first year at high school. The reason for this appears to have been a sadistic teacher, who made life in school unbearable for the sensitive young boy. He became depressed and confused and put on weight. Finally his father decided to take him out of school. He now started in the 'Norra Real-skolan', where emphasis was put on mathematics and the natural sciences. From now on everything went well in school. He was lucky enough to get a biology teacher, Mr Ringselle, who took good care of him and who was instrumental in awakening his interest in the biological sciences. It was very likely at this time that Pehr Edman finally decided to become a physician, although he had earlier shown an interest in this profession. Important for his development as a scientist were certainly the summers he spent with Mr Ringselle out in the archipelago of Stockholm on an island named Singö, where Mr Ringselle had a house. Under the expert guidance of Mr Ringselle he went out botanizing and bird-watching. His intense interest in nature was certainly formed during these summers. Pehr Edman's brother tells that he sometimes used to join Pehr on excursions in the fields. He recalls how Pehr could sit for hours watching some natural phenomenon—be it live or dead, organic or inorganic. Later on in life the scientist Pehr Edman would sit still for hours, in the same way, at his laboratory bench meticulously watching chemical reactions or physical phenomena. During these summers he developed a keen interest in fishing—mainly for pike and perch. Pehr Edman would often talk with warmth and appreciation about Mr Ringselle and this time of his life. Mr Ringselle, this stout, jovial and warm man, meant in these formative years of Pehr Edman's life a great deal for his eventual development as a scientist. No doubt his natural gift of observing phenomena and making deductive abstractions was sharpened. Already as a boy he gave proof of qualities in his character which later became prominent—i.e. his logical mind and stringency of expression. His brother recalls the burst of laughter Pehr produced when reading an announcement a tenant in their house had put in the elevator: 'Grey gloves found, can be obtained against description.'

In 1935 Pehr Edman passed his matriculation examination with an excellent record. This examination in Sweden is a great step in the career of a young man and on the day of the examination the family and friends usually come to school with flowers and gifts to give to the graduates when they are through. Pehr Edman's family had to wait in vain. He left the school through the back door and went straight home. This episode shows another quality in Pehr Edman's character. He was a shy person and disliked pompous performances especially when he himself was the centre of attention. After the matriculation examination he wanted to study medicine and applied to the Karolinska Institute in

Stockholm, a medical school. He started his medical studies in 1935 and received a bachelor of medicine degree in 1938. He graduated as physician in 1946. During his studies at the Karolinska Institute he joined a Marxist political organization, Clarté. A number of Swedish intellectuals, politicians and artists were members. Among the politicians was Tage Erlander, who later on became prime minister of the Swedish government. Among the artists was a famous poet, Nils Ferlin, whose anarchistic ideas and whims quite often turned the meetings to pandemonium. During his studies Pehr Edman also met his first wife, Barbro Bergström, whom he married in the early forties.

Concurrently with his studies in medicine he started his training in biochemistry with Professor Erik Jorpes. For a short period he also studied with Professor Hugo Theorell. It was in Professor Jorpes's department that he first became interested in protein chemistry. Professor Jorpes's main interest at the time was the biochemistry of mucopolysaccharides, especially heparin. Erik Jorpes had also, with Einar Hammarsten, an interest in secretin. Pehr Edman took some part in the work on secretin together with Professor Gunnar Ågren. However, he soon started on a project of his own, which was the isolation and characterization of angiotensin. As starting material he used bovine blood, obtained in early morning hours from a nearby slaughterhouse. During this work he became acquainted with all of the preparatory and analytical tools used at that time in protein chemistry. One of these tools was column chromatography. Seeing the need for collection of fractions at short regular intervals he invented the first automatic fraction collector. He also developed solvent systems for partition chromatography of amino acids on paper sheets. His work on angiotensin resulted in a preparation which he considered to be chemically pure. He determined the amino acid composition of the compound and other chemical characteristics including molecular mass. This work resulted in a thesis which was presented at the Karolinska Institute in 1946, receiving the highest mark. Pehr Edman's thesis work took place during World War II. For a long period of time he was drafted to serve as a physician in the armed forces. Knowing Pehr Edman's dislike for military establishments, this must have been a rather dull time for him. However, he got some relief by the good fortune of being offered a horse for transportation between the military units. This gave him a good opportunity to practise horse riding which he enjoyed tremendously. After his dissertation, Pehr Edman applied for a 'docentship' (equivalent to lecturer) at the Karolinska Institute and this was granted. He also applied for and received a Rockefeller fellowship at the Rockefeller Institute in Princeton, which resulted in a one year stay with Dr Northrop and Dr Kunitz in their laboratory. Pehr Edman wanted to widen his experience and perspectives in protein chemistry and at that time the laboratory of Northrop and Kunitz was indeed one of the most prestigious places—a laboratory where most of the enzymes known at that time had been prepared and isolated in crystalline form.

## THE ROCKEFELLER INSTITUTE 1946–47

The time spent at the Rockefeller Institute was in a way crucial in Pehr Edman's scientific career since it was here that he made the first attempts towards stepwise degradation of proteins. However, the turning point in his thinking had occurred before that. During his work with angiotensin, it became clear to him that molecular mass and amino acid composition were not parameters that could give information explaining the biological activity of the protein. Obviously this must reside in the amino acid sequence of the protein. That this prediction was correct we can witness today. It is true that for the function of a protein the secondary and tertiary structures are equally as important as the primary structure. However, all evidence is now for the concept that the information necessary to give a protein a particular conformation is inherent in its primary structure. In fact, this latter view was already clearly expressed by Pehr Edman in the early sixties. At the Rockefeller Institute Pehr Edman studied reagents which would allow both carbamylation of the α-amino acid residue in proteins and subsequent rearrangement and release under mild conditions. Abderhalden and Brockmann had previously used phenylisocyanate for carbamylation. On acid hydrolysis the N-terminal amino acid was released as a hydantoin derivative. However, extensive cleavages of other peptide bonds also occurred during the hydrolysis. Edman considered that the use of phenylisothiocyanate would be more advantageous, since hydantoin formation with subsequent release of the N-terminal amino acid could occur under much milder conditions with this reagent. Towards the end of his stay at the Rockefeller Institute he had tried phenylisothiocyanate on model peptides and obtained evidence for the soundness of his idea.

## LUND 1947–57

On his return to Sweden Pehr Edman applied for and was awarded a vacant associate professorship at the University of Lund. In Lund he continued to work on the use of phenylisothiocyanate for sequence analysis. In fact, from there on the problem of sequence analysis was his major scientific interest. He showed that coupling to amino groups of peptides and proteins occurred easily and that the thiocarbamylated N-terminal amino acid was swiftly rearranged and released as thiohydantoin in acid media under conditions when a secondary hydrolysis of peptide bonds did not occur to any appreciable extent. In order to make the method more generally applicable to sequence analysis, Pehr Edman made thorough investigations on the reaction mechanisms involved, as well as procedures for characterization of the thiohydantoins formed during the reaction. It now became evident that the product formed in anhydrous media was not a phenylthiohydantoin derivative but rather the isomeric phenylthiazolinone. This derivative is extremely labile and easily undergoes rearrangement to the corresponding thiohydantoin. The basic experimental work on the phenylisothiocyanate method was done between 1950 and 1956. It was now clear that three discrete reaction steps were involved, i.e. (1) coupling with phenylisothiocyanate, (2) cyclization to phenylthioazolinone under anhydrous conditions and (3) hydrolysis and conversion to phenylthiohydantoins. The following account by his mother reflects the importance Pehr Edman himself put into the discovery of the phenylisothiocyanate reaction: 'One day Pehr came home to me and asked me to sit down with him because he had something interesting to tell me. He then told me that he had discovered a way to analyse proteins which had not been possible before and that this discovery would certainly be of great importance for biochemistry in the future.'*

## Melbourne 1957–72

In 1957 Pehr Edman accepted an offer as Director of Research at St Vincent's School of Medical Research in Melbourne where he remained for 15 years. The reasons for his leaving Sweden were rather complex. Pehr Edman emphasized the circumstance that he did not get enough support in Sweden because of lack of understanding for the work he was engaged in. There were, however, other factors which certainly played an important role in his decision to leave. One of them was the breakdown of his first marriage, ending in separation in 1957 and eventually divorce. Another reason may have been the personal friction in the biochemistry department where Peter Edman worked. As a result of all this Pehr Edman very likely felt himself rather isolated in Lund and there was a lack of scientific stimulation for him at the biochemistry department. The few persons he could enjoy discussing scientific matters with included Arvid Carlsson, professor of pharmacology at the University in Lund, Dr John Sjöquist, his close associate, and Dr Ikuo Yamashina, at the time a visiting scientist from Professor Jorpes's laboratory.

Dr Ikuo Yamashina stayed in Pehr Edman's laboratory at the end of 1956 and the beginning of 1957. He was very likely the first, outside Edman's group in Lund, to learn the phenylisothiocyanate technique. When he returned to Professor Jorpes's laboratory in Stockholm he enthusiastically told about how easily N-terminals in proteins could be determined with this method. At this time Birger and Margareta Blombäck, working in Professor Jorpes's laboratory, had just finished their work on purification of fibrinogen from different species. Stimulated by Dr Yamashina's account they decided to try the method on fibrinogens from different species. This turned out to be worth while since it showed for the first time that the molecule was composed of three pairs of polypeptide chains indicating a dimeric structure of the molecule. Pehr Edman occasionally came to Stockholm to see his mother during this period. During these visits he took time off to come to Professor Jorpes's laboratory. These visits were always welcomed since they gave the young scientists an opportunity to discuss with Pehr Edman the problems which they had had with the method. He gave his advice in a friendly and competent way.

* This quotation is a recollection of a conversation between Birger Blombäck and Pehr Edman's mother during her visit to Australia in the spring of 1962.

Pehr Edman also enjoyed discussing scientific matters with Professor Erik Jorpes, his former teacher. He appreciated Jorpes and his work, which he admired perhaps because it was solid and reliable like his own. This relationship with Erik Jorpes, however, came to an abrupt end in 1963. The background may seem trivial but is worth mentioning since it shows important facets in Pehr Edman's personality—his craving for absolute honesty and his inability to compromise. The background was this: When Professor Jorpes was about to retire in 1963, Pehr Edman and Erik Jorpes had a discussion about the possible candidates to succeed him. A name was mentioned and Pehr Edman was very pleased that Erik Jorpes considered the particular man a strong candidate for the position. However, another candidate eventually got the chair. Later on Pehr Edman happened to read the appraisal on the candidates that Erik Jorpes had delivered to the nomination committee at the Karolinska Institutet. Finding that the candidate he and Erik Jorpes had discussed was not even considered among the first three top names enraged Pehr Edman. For him this was an almost unforgivable deceit. In a letter to Erik Jorpes at Christmas time 1963 he told him this and broke all further communications with him.

During his first years in Australia Pehr Edman did not take much initiative in creating scientific contacts with other laboratories. He may therefore have appeared shy and unsociable to many of his fellow scientists. It is probable that his inclination for withdrawal was a consequence of spells of depression, which he very likely had suffered earlier.

In Australia Pehr Edman finished the work on the manual three-stage degradation technique about 1960. When Birger and Margareta Blombäck came to the laboratory as visiting scientists in 1961 they tried the three-stage technique on human fibrinopeptide A consisting of 16 amino acid residues. Starting with a few micromoles of peptides they were able to make a complete stepwise degradation with excellent yields up to the very last residues. These results impressed Pehr Edman very much. He now became convinced that longer peptides could be degraded in good repetitive yields too. This being the case, the need for automation was evident. Pehr Edman became at this time convinced that automation was absolutely necessary in order to carry out, within a reasonable time, the formidable task which sequence determination of protein molecules required. At the end of 1961 he started to analyse different possibilities to solve the automation problem. The problem was to find a single physical process which could accommodate the various operations in the manual procedure. Guided by his great knowledge, imagination and intuition, he almost at the very start of this endeavour conceived the idea of the spinning cylindrical cup, in which all reaction media were spread out as thin films on the vessel wall. He considered that the rotating film containing the protein would be well suited for extraction with a solvent as this is continuously fed in and glides over the surface of the first film and is subsequently removed in the upper part of the cup. Although the principle for the 'sequenator' was simple and brilliant, a number of technical problems had to be solved before the automation of all 30 individual operations was finally realized. Pehr Edman and his associate Geoffrey Begg started experimental work with rotating glass cups in January 1962. Pehr Edman would sit watching in strobe light the properties of films—monofilms and composite films—formed in the cup under different physical conditions. After finding a cup that was convenient for the purpose they continued step by step to experiment on the remaining operations necessary for automation. In 1964, after two years of hard work he reported, at a meeting of the International Committee on Thrombosis and Haemostasis at Gleneagles in Scotland, that automatic stepwise degradation of proteins could be done. Pehr Edman concluded his presentation with the following: 'Our experience of the performance of this apparatus is as yet limited. However, trial runs have shown that it is capable of an output of at least 15 amino acids in 24 hours. Furthermore, the high repetitive yield of 97% indicates that the determination of extended sequences will be possible. These expectations are supported by the results of sequence determinations on intact proteins currently being made in our laboratory. However, more work is required before a full assessment is possible.' In 1967 the work on the automated sequence analysis was finished and published.

In 1966 Pehr Edman met Agnes Henschen, whom he married in 1968. This encounter changed Pehr Edman's personal life in a more happy direction. He appeared now more relaxed and at peace with himself and the years to follow were certainly among the happiest in his life. In the early seventies Pehr Edman began to contemplate leaving Australia for Europe, where he thought the chances to pursue his scientific work would be better. He accepted an offer to be Director of the Department of Protein Chemistry I of the Max Planck Institut für Biochemie in Munich. He and Agnes Henschen moved there in 1972. During the last years of his life he continued to work on the sequenator with the main objective of improving the yields. He was of the opinion that high repetitive yields are crucial in stepwise sequencing and that all efforts must be directed to this aim. The actual yield of 98% had made possible 60 sequence steps but he believed 99% repetitive yield was possible, which would allow additional sequence steps to be performed.

## Munich 1972–77

After settling down in Munich Pehr Edman and his family visited Sweden every summer where his wife had a summer house in the archipelago of Stockholm. There he had the opportunity to exercise the hobbies of his young days—fishing and bird-watching and to enjoy being close to nature. For the whole of his life nature meant a lot for Pehr Edman. During his years in Australia he took every opportunity to make long excursions to remote places for hiking, fishing and bird-watching. He loved the seashores of Australia and was an eager swimmer and surfer. Bird-watching was no doubt his favourite hobby and he was almost as knowledgeable in ornithology as he was in chemistry.

Pehr Edman was widely read in his profession, and he used to spend much time every day reading scientific journals. He respected and admired thoroughness in scientific work, but, above all, he was sensitive to all sorts of new ideas in science. When he himself had an idea he scrutinized with extreme care the possibilities of proving it in practice. He designed his experiments with the same thoughtfulness. Pehr Edman despised fortuitous experiments for the simple reason that if successful they would be difficult to reproduce. There was a great deal of perseverance and single mindedness in his personality. If he had an idea which he believed must be proved experimentally, there seemed no obstacle that could not be surmounted. This quality of personality was certainly an asset in his scientific work. Though Pehr Edman's most important work was concerned with stepwise degradation of proteins, he worked also in other areas in biochemistry, i.e. on the N–O acyl shift and the cleavage reaction with CNBr. He made at an early stage interesting experiments on coupling of proteins to insoluble matrices. He observed as early as the thirties that some proteins such as fibrinogen had a lower solubility in the cold and consequently could be frozen out of solution.

Pehr Edman preferred to work in a modest setting with only a few people around him. In his group in Lund Dr John Sjöquist worked on a new method for amino acid analysis using their phenylhydantoin derivatives and Dr Lars Josephsson was engaged in studies of the N–O acyl shift. In Melbourne his group consisted also of a small number of people: Dr Frank Morgan and Hugh Nial worked mainly on applications of the phenylisothiocyanate degradation technique. Dr Ilse studied the mechanism of the reaction. His closest associate during his work on the sequenator was Geoffrey Begg, who was of indispensable help in solving the technological problems.

## Awards

In his professional life Pehr Edman was well known throughout the world. He received the following honours for his achievements in science: Britannica Australia Award, the Berzelius Gold Medal, the Gold Medal of the Swedish Academy of Engineering, the Linderström–Lang Medal. Pehr Edman was a Fellow of the Australian Academy of Science, Fellow of the Royal Society of London and a scientific Member of the Max Planck Society.

## Edman as a person

Pehr Edman had broad interests outside science. Of the arts he appreciated music most. He could sit for hours and listen to his favourite records. He enjoyed the company of friends, who mostly were from circles outside the scientific field. Only his friends could fully appreciate the greatness of his genius. They recognized in him a man full of generosity, warmth, humour and sympathy. His thoughts turned not merely to science but to culture, society and politics as well. Pehr Edman had a vast knowledge in many areas. His mind was logical and he was stringent in expression. The integrity on which his opinions were based was admirable and respected and in these opinions he was rock-firm, almost to the extent of stubbornness; but he could change views if well founded reasons were presented. Pehr Edman was not an individual who thoughtlessly followed fashions in scientific or other kinds of thinking for he was too analytical and had too strong a desire to reach for causes on fundamental levels. There was in his personality a certain aloofness, which people who did not know him may mistakenly have taken for snobbishness. His friends enjoyed more than animated discussions with him: an integral part of being together with friends was food; and he was a fine cook. It may have been crispy duck or simply Swedish meatballs. The dishes prepared by Pehr Edman were always cooked in a masterly way—thoughtfully and meticulously.

In trying to describe Pehr Edman's character, words like incorruptible and uncompromising come to mind as do qualities of sincerity and loyalty to his friends. In Pehr Edman's language 'yes' and 'no' stood for fundamentally opposite meanings. He had courage and dared to express, without hesitation and without political or opportunistic consideration, opinions which he felt were morally right. The uncompromising quality of his personality made him distrust politicians with few exceptions. At the core of his personality was a sincere humanism. Therefore he was, on the whole, against violence and oppression and he was a sworn enemy of militarism in the world.

Finally, there was in Pehr Edman's personality an encompassing trait of purism which may be common to many scientists of his calibre—his teacher Erik Jorpes had this quality and J. J. Berzelius, the first professor of chemistry at the Karolinska Institute, had it. This trait may perhaps to some extent be linked with Scandinavian culture since one recognizes it in so many works by Scandinavian novelists, poets and playwrights, e.g. in characters in Ibsen's and Strindberg's plays. Pehr Edman's urge for purity and perfection in life may therefore partly have been a cultural heritage. After all his father was a judge—a profession symbolizing a cornerstone of society. Whatever its origin, indigenous or through influence, this quality was very likely instrumental when he joined the Marxists as a young man in the thirties, when he chose the self-imposed expatriation in the fifties and it was probably a strong driving force in his scientific accomplishments. For a purist nothing except the whole is good enough. He is beset by one idea: to reach perfection and impeccability. We believe that this quality in Pehr Edman's personality was a pre-requisite for his motivation for spending so much time and effort on perfection of the phenylisothiocyanate method.

In February 1977 when leaving a scientific lecture in Munich Pehr Edman suddenly fell down unconscious. After a few weeks of illness he died on 19 March. The disease was caused by a tumour of the brain, which had not given any symptoms before he was struck by unconsciousness.

Pehr Edman leaves his widow, Dr Agnes Henschen, and their children, Karl and Helena. From the first marriage he leaves two children, Martin and Gudrun.

## THE RENAISSANCE OF PROTEIN CHEMISTRY SINCE THE MID-CENTURY; EDMAN'S PAPER ON SEQUENCE DETERMINATION IN 1949

What has been called the modern renaissance of protein chemistry perhaps could be said to have started almost at the turn of the century with Tswett's (1906) demonstration of the chromatographic column (1). However, Tswett's discovery was almost completely neglected and 35 years were to pass before this elegant application of the principle of multi-stage counter-current distribution was to reach recognition as a practical method of solving the complex technical problems of amino acid analysis faced by the protein chemist. What in Tswett's hands was an art was systematized and put on a quantitative basis by Tiselius (2) and by Claesson (3). Early chromatographic separations had made use of molecular adsorbants such as charcoal or alumina which are only marginally useful for separation of mixtures of the 18 or 20 aliphatic amino acids which commonly faced protein chemists and a genuine upsurge in technical capability did not really begin until 1941 when Martin & Synge (4) demonstrated that solutes such as amino acids are distributed selectively between two liquid phases, one of which could be immobilized by mixing it with an absorbent powder such as paper pulp, kieselguhr or silica gel. It was later shown (5) that this 'partition chromatography' could be conducted in a filter paper sheet in a moist chamber by allowing the wick action of the filter paper to propel the solvent phase relative to the stationary water phase held within the fibres. When the technique of paper chromatography was first introduced by Consden *et al.* in 1944 it was regarded by many protein chemists as an amusing toy, but it soon proved to be so rapid and convenient for qualitative identification of mixtures of amino acid that within a few years it was adopted everywhere, and has since had a major influence on the course of protein chemistry.

However, it soon became obvious that the first necessity for the chemical study of proteins is the availability of an accurate and rapid method of amino acid analysis, and for this purpose a number of groups became interested in the use of synthetic ion exchange resins as reversible adsorbents of amino acids. Moore & Stein found that when the sodium form of a strongly acidic cation exchange resin is used and adsorption of an amino acid takes place from a large excess of sodium buffer, the concentration of the adsorbed ion is small compared with the buffer ion concentration and adsorption of the solute is directly proportional to its concentration.

This situation is ideal for quantitative analysis by elution chromatography and Moore & Stein were able to show that symmetrical peaks and high recoveries of amino acids were obtainable by eluting cation exchange columns with buffers or with high concentrations of mineral acids. In their 1951 paper Moore & Stein (6) were able to demonstrate the separation and quantitative determination of the products of acid hydrolysis of about 6 mg of a protein on a 100 cm column for the acidic and neutral amino acids and on a 15 cm column run at 25 °C for the basic amino acids. With synthetic mixtures simulating a protein hydrolysate the estimates from the peak areas were correct to about ±3% and the whole operation could be completed in about two weeks. Today the same information can be obtained in a few hours on a much smaller sample but before the advent of chromatography, the amino acid analysis of a protein was an operation which required at least two years' work by an experienced and skilful chemist.

The availability of accurate amino acid analysis combined with the evidence from the work of Svedberg (7) and Tiselius (8) that purified proteins migrated as single boundaries in a centrifugal or electrical field brought about a changing view about proteins which was eventually accepted by chemists and physicists alike. Traditionally proteins were regarded as biocolloids and few supposed that any protein preparation contained identical molecules; after 1950 the realization dawned that, unlike most carbohydrates, proteins such as haemoglobin contained molecules which were identical replicates, had exact molecular masses and amino acid compositions, and identical packing of the long polypeptide chains. This new view of proteins gained final acceptance when crystalline preparations of various proteins including some enzymes became available and it was found that these crystals gave rise to X-ray diffraction patterns which could be interpreted on the same basis as the crystals of inorganic compounds and organic substances of low molecular weight.

Although the analysis of the amino acid composition of a protein became little more than a matter of routine, the chemistry of the primary structure was still not defined because the sequence of the amino acid in the polypeptide was unknown. Indeed, some chemists, making calculations about the number of possible permutations of sequence in a polypeptide chain some 500 residues long, expressed the view that this was information that would for ever be beyond human reach.

It is not easily possible to be sure if in these early days of the renaissance of protein chemistry Edman had already conceived the ambition to complete the chemistry of peptides by determining amino acid sequences. However, 1948 finds him devising the first of what later became many designs of chromatographic fraction collectors with escapement mechanisms operated by a clock. That of Edman (1948) consisted of a weight-driven circular rack which was prevented from moving by a spiral-cut ratchet engaging a rod. The rod was driven continuously outward by a clock and the ratchet was so designed that equal time intervals elapsed for each notch to be passed.

The first successful attack on the problem of sequence determination in proteins was that mounted by F. Sanger and published during the period 1945–51. As usual with all great scientific enterprises the basic idea was simple. All that is necessary to determine the composition and sequence of a dipeptide is a semiquantitative amino acid analysis and a method of determining which amino acid is N-terminal or which C-terminal. Thus the basic requirement for sequencing is some specific and, hopefully, simple way of recognizing a terminal amino acid.

Sanger was the first to realize that even with a quite complex peptide—say one containing five or six residues—the unique sequence could be established by locating the terminal in the starting molecule and in each of the smaller peptides derived from it by random partial hydrolysis. With this bold concept in mind he devised a method of labelling the N-terminal end of a peptide or polypeptide chain by reacting it with 1 : 2 : 4-fluorodinitrobenzene (FDNB) to form the dinitrophenyl derivative of the N-terminal amino group (9). These dinitrophenyl (DNP) derivatives were substantially stable to acid hydrolysis and their bright yellow colour facilitated qualitative analysis and quantitative colorimetric estimation. Thus, by use of paper chromatography and column chromatography on silica gel both the amino acid composition and the N-terminal amino acid could be recognized with any small peptide and its sequence could be worked out by partial hydrolysis and by fitting the overlapping sequences.

By these simple means Sanger was able to elucidate the order of the amino acid residues in proximity to the free N-terminal amino groups and the lysyl ε-amino group in the A and B chains released from insulin by oxidation with performic acid (10, 11). Two years later these researches resulted in elucidation of the complete sequence of the 30 amino acid residues in the B chain of insulin by Sanger & Tuppy (12, 13). This was indeed a milestone on the road of protein chemistry and was the final convincing evidence required to demonstrate unequivocably a protein carrying a unique primary sequence.

At this point we can return to consider the development of Pehr Edman's researches which were certainly influenced by the frequent publications appearing from Sanger's laboratory. In 1949 Edman's method for the determination of the amino acid sequence in peptides was ready for publication and displayed a concept of sequencing which was basically different from Sanger's, and which, as time was to show, had finally a greater potential for development and for automation.

It is interesting that 10 years before Sanger introduced the FDNB method of end group analysis, Jensen & Evans (14) had been able to isolate the phenylhydantoin of phenylalanine from a hydrolysate of insulin that had been treated with phenylisocyanate, thus demonstrating that some free amino groups of insulin are present on phenylalanine residues.

Edman considered the use of phenylisocyanate for labelling the N-terminal amino acid but soon decided to take advantage of the much greater chemical reactivity of iso*thio*cyanates. What he had in mind was to attempt a stepwise degradation starting from the N-terminal end, with removal and identification of one amino acid at a time. This immediately raised the problem of how to break a terminal peptide bond and leave all the others unaffected. The approach he had in mind was to offer the —CO group of the peptide bond adjacent to the N-terminal a more favourable reaction partner than the $NH_2$— group of the next amino acid in sequence. It was here that the use of phenylisothiocyanate seemed to offer good prospects (figure 1, reaction 2).

This expectation was dramatically fulfilled and the peptide bond was split in a few seconds at room temperature and in an anhydrous acid medium. From the work of Abderhalden & Brockmann (15) on phenylisocyanate, Edman

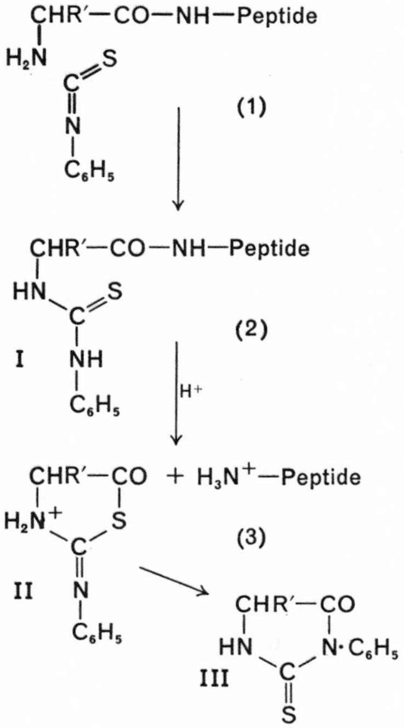

CHR′—CO—NH—Peptide
$H_2N$ S
C
N
$C_6H_5$

↓ (1)

CHR′—CO—NH—Peptide
HN S
C
I NH
$C_6H_5$

↓ $H^+$ (2)

CHR′—CO + $H_3N^+$—Peptide
$H_2N^+$ S
C
II N
$C_6H_5$

(3)

→ CHR′—CO
HN N·$C_6H_5$
III C
S

FIGURE 1

had expected the formation of the phenylthiohydantoin (figure 1, formula III) of the N-terminal amino acid together with the peptide shortened by one residue. He was, therefore, not too surprised when this was what he isolated. It was only some years later that the suspicion arose that this was not the whole story. It was discovered that the first compound to form during the cleavage reaction was not the phenylthiohydantoin but a 2-anilino-5-thiazolinone (figure 1, formula II).

The thiazolinone readily rearranges to the isomeric phenylthiohydantoin (III). This reaction had not previously been described and its extreme facility is explained by the nucleophilic attack of the thioketonic sulphur in reaction (2). Its generality has subsequently been demonstrated in many other stepwise reactions using other reagents but where the key reaction is always the formation of a thiazolinone. The reaction has also proved a general one for peptide bound N-terminal amino acids and is the basis for nearly all the protein sequencing work carried out at the present time.

Unlike the approach adopted by F. Sanger which depended upon the initial cleavage of the protein into rather small peptides, Edman's approach of successively removing and identifying the N-terminal amino acid from a long polypeptide demanded that each step should be as quantitative and as free from side reactions as possible. This stepwise degradation must come to a halt as soon as the product of side reactions reach concentrations comparable with those of the linear degradation.

A very large part of Edman's work since the original description of the method (16) was given in 1950 consisted in identifying and eliminating side reactions. Thus it was discovered that the thiocarbamyl group in reaction (2) easily lost sulphur by oxidation. The resulting carbamyl group was unreactive and the degradation came to an end. This side reaction could be eliminated by performing the reaction in a nitrogen atmosphere. Further, reaction conditions for coupling, cleavage and conversion that were equally suitable for all amino acids had to be found. Thus it appeared that proline was much more slowly released than other amino acids during the cleavage reaction (2) which was normally carried out at 55 °C in heptafluorobutyric acid. Also the position of proline in the sequence was important, since the rate of release of proline could vary considerably depending upon its near neighbours.

## Identification of amino acids and PTH-amino acids

With a few exceptions the chemical stability of PTH-amino acids is excellent, and in general they are easily crystallizable compounds with high melting points. The less stable compounds are those with an —OH or —SH group on the β-carbon of the amino acid chain and these show in varying degrees a tendency for β-elimination. In PTH-cystine and PTH-cysteine the tendency for β-elimination is so strong that the derivatives are not useful for identification purposes. On the other hand, the PTH derivatives of S-alkylated cysteine are more stable as is also PTH-cysteic acid. The tendency for β-elimination becomes important in the identification of the susceptible compounds and it should be borne in mind that β-elimination also occurs in the corresponding thiazolinones.

The PTH-derivatives of asparagine and glutamine are unstable to the extent that the amide group is hydrolysed by acids and alkalis. In sequence determination these PTH-amino acids are found to be contaminated by the corresponding acids. PTH-tryptophan is also susceptible to the action of strong acids, but fortunately the acid conditions of the degradation procedure do not seem to be sufficiently vigorous to affect the tryptophan PTH derivative appreciably. Finally, solutions of PTH-amino acids show a tendency for photodecomposition, which becomes apparent after prolonged exposure to daylight. Solutions must therefore be protected during storage.

All PTH-amino acids show strong absorption in the ultraviolet with a maximum around 268 nm and a minimum around 245 nm. The ratio $A_{245}/A_{269}$ lies around 0.4 and is a useful index in assessing the purity of a PTH-amino acid preparation.

Two different principles have been used in the identification of the amino acid residue removed in a degradation cycle. The *direct* method relies on the positive identification of the residue split off. The *indirect* method depends for the identification on a difference in the peptide before and after a degradation cycle.

The PTH-amino acids tend to be poorly soluble in water and readily soluble in organic solvents and may be separated and identified by chromatography. For this purpose paper chromatography, thin layer chromatography and liquid–liquid and gas–liquid partition chromatography systems have been proposed. Paper and thin layer chromatographic techniques have been most commonly used by Edman and have been worked out in detail. These techniques are not well suited for the identification of some PTH-amino acids with strongly ionized groups in the side chain such as PTH-arginine, PTH-histidine and PTH-cysteic acid but here spot reactions and paper electrophoretic techniques may be used.

The indirect method of identifying the amino acid split off by a difference in analytical composition of the peptide before and after a degradation cycle has been used extensively by Hirs *et al.* (17), in their classical elucidation of the first enzyme structure. It has also been used in a rather different way by Gray & Hartley (18) who determined the new N-terminal amino acid by use of the sensitive dansyl technique after each degradation cycle. This requires complete hydrolysis of a small portion of the peptide after each cycle but the method permits sequence determination on very small amounts of peptide because of the great sensitivity of fluorescence measurements.

Edman clearly favoured the direct identification method for the following reasons:

(1) The chief criticism of the indirect method relates to the fact that it requires complete hydrolysis of the peptide. Therefore the difference in composition before and after hydrolysis relates only to the *hydrolysate* of the peptide. Thus amino acid residues like asparagine, glutamine and tryptophan cannot be identified.

(2) Many proteins contain modified amino acid residues, e.g. by a covalently bound carbohydrate moiety. If these groups are removed by hydrolysis in concentrated acid as they usually are, they cannot be located by the indirect method. They may even escape detection because there is nothing in the method to indicate their presence.

Edman maintained that the weaknesses enumerated above are inherent in the indirect method and cannot be made good by any improvement in technique. He therefore concentrated his effort on improvements in the direct method. Since the value of a sequence technique depends largely on the length of the sequence which may be determined, the important factor is a high repetitive yield, i.e. the yield of amino acid calculated from one degradation cycle to the next. Losses of a small percentage severely limit the practical length of the degradation. This is another reason why it is undesirable to remove samples from the peptide stock for hydrolysis. Perhaps the most telling reason against the use of the indirect method for automation purposes is the length of time required actually to carry out acid hydrolysis. This process is clearly not suitable for rapid automated sequencing techniques and, taking these objections together, Edman decided not to attempt further development of the indirect technique.

The concentration of effort only on the direct technique stimulated improvements in the methods for rapid identification of the PTH-amino acids. This has finally resulted in a whole arsenal of procedures including gas chromatography, mass spectroscopy and recently also high performance liquid chromatography. These methods have been reviewed by Edman & Henschen (1975).

## The protein sequenator

By 1962 the stage was set for automation of the degradation. Standard reaction conditions applicable to all amino acids were already known, and side reactions had largely been eliminated. Thus a high repetitive yield was possible. The importance of the repetitive yield from one degradation cycle to the next was repeatedly emphasized by Edman who illustrated the point with a simple calculation which showed that repetitive yields of 97%, 98% and 99% make possible 30, 60 and 120 degradation cycles, respectively.

It remained to find a suitable technical device in which to perform the reactions of the degradation cycle. Edman and his colleague Begg provided a characteristically ingenious solution to this problem. In order to establish a large surface and the equivalent of rapid stirring they chose to spread out the media in thin films inside a spinning cup (figure 2, Edman & Begg (19)).

The film is very suited for carrying out extractions, dryings and other procedures and the whole degradation cycle may be programmed. The automated instrument was called a sequenator. This instrument allows the degradation of long runs of polypeptide, in favourable cases up to 50 and 60 amino acids. The speed was about 15 amino acids a day in contrast to the one or two amino acids per day possible with the manual technique.

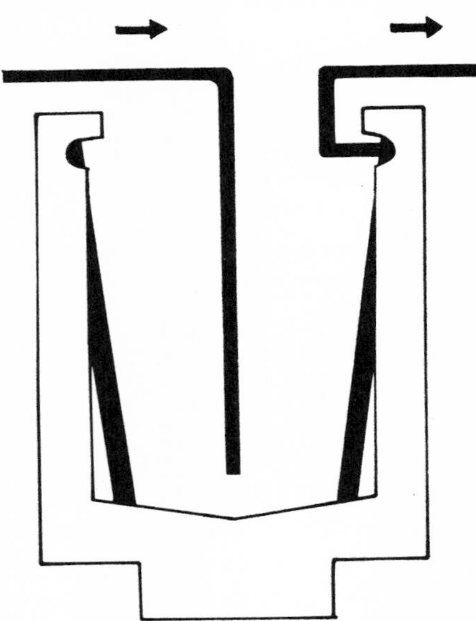

FIGURE 2. Schematic presentation of the operation of the sequenator cup. An aqueous solution (white) is being extracted by an organic solvent (black).

The instrument was designed to contain reservoirs to hold all the reagents required for the reaction cycle together with receivers for effluents and means for controlling reaction temperature. A system of feed tubes and automated valves was provided and programmed to supply the reagents and extraction solvents to the spinning cup in the correct order at preset time intervals. The process embraced the formation of the phenylthiocarbamyl derivation of the protein and splitting off the N-terminal amino acid as thiozolinone. The degradation cycle proceeded at a rate of 15.4 cycles in 24 hours and with a yield in the individual cycle of 98%. The thiazolinones of each N-terminal amino acid were automatically stored in a fraction collector accommodating 50 tubes and they were converted to the corresponding phenylthiohydantoins in a separate operation for later identification by thin layer chromatography.

The process was applied to the whole molecule of apomyoglobin from the humpback whale and it was possible to establish the sequence of the first 60 amino acids from the N-terminal end. About 0.25 μmol of the protein was required for this operation.

Automation has changed the strategy of sequence determination. It is no longer necessary to begin by cleaving the protein backbone into many small peptides since long direct sequences are possible. It is then ideal to work with large and few fragments. At the fragmentation high cleavage yields are of the greatest importance, otherwise the heterogeneity in the cleavage mixture will cause considerable difficulty in the isolation of fragments. As pointed out by Agnes Henschen-Edman (20) it should be taken into account that with incomplete cleavage two cleavage points will give rise to six components, three will give 10, four will give 15 and so forth, thus resulting in increasing difficulty of separating pure cleavage products.

## The strategy and tactics of protein sequence determination as exemplified by work in Edman's laboratory

Since the appearance of Edman's first paper on the isothiocyanate degradation in 1949 and up to the time of his lecture delivered at the Carlsberg Laboratory Centennial in 1976, more than 80 000 amino acids had been put into sequence by various laboratories throughout the world. As Edman commented, 'this figure may seem large but it is dwarfed when compared with the maximum coding capacity in a mammalian genome of 2 billion residues. Most likely only a very small fraction of this capacity is actually used for the coding of protein structures. Even so the number is likely to be large, and this means that the road before us will be long. At present there are several hundred sequencing devices in operation. This will undoubtedly speed up the data accumulation, and it may reasonably be expected that in the next few years the 200 000 mark will be reached.'

Edman's own chief concern up to the time of his death was in the refinement of the methodology and in the necessity for the establishment of adequate arrangements for data storage, data retrieval and data processing. Needless to say, his laboratory in Munich was endowed with a wealth of hard-won experience in sequencing and at the time of his death was engaged in, among other projects, the elucidation of the primary structure of fibrinogen. This work Pehr Edman regarded as exclusively the project of his wife Agnes Henschen-Edman. However, to quote her own words in December 1977, 'It would for certain, not have been possible to proceed with the investigation in such a way without Pehr Edman's insight and his organization of the department. The γ-chain sequence was finished and published half a year ago. The complete β-chain sequence has now appeared in print after just a few months of work. My husband also gave the idea to a workshop on fibrinogen here in Martinsried. It was sad and strange, but perhaps appropriate, that the workshop took place on the day of his death.'

Agnes Henschen-Edman's lecture (20), prepared for the 2nd Solid Phase Symposium, Montpellier, September 1977, gives a very good insight into the strategy and tactics in protein sequence determination current in Pehr Edman's laboratory at Martinsried at the time of his death, and some passages warrant quotation in full.

> 'The first instance when N-terminal analysis might be introduced is already during the isolation of the protein. Once the N-terminal of the chosen protein is known, N-terminal analysis can be a most convenient method for monitoring the progress of purification. It might be much easier to use than, e.g., a biological activity test. It is, of course, very important to use high quality reagents and general caution during the purification procedure, as N-terminals may get blocked and chemical heterogeneity may be introduced already at this stage. Any new heterogeneity in size or charge of the protein molecule or modification of its side chains will substantially increase the difficulties at most subsequent fractionation steps and also at many fragmentation reactions. A few examples may suffice. Blocking of amino groups or loss of amide groups will change the charge and thus change the behaviour in ion-exchange chromatography and electrophoresis. Furthermore, trypsin will not cleave at lysine residues with modified ϵ-amino groups. Cyanogen bromide will not cleave at methionine residues in the sulfoxide form. N-terminal glutamine in the native protein cyclizing to pyroglutamic acid during the purification represents a special, not yet solved problem.
>
> 'As a purity test N-terminal sequence analysis is in many respects superior to physico-chemical analysis, like ultracentrifugation and gel electrophoresis. At the evaluation of sequencing results no assumptions are needed. The result is independent of aggregation or quaternary structure, many foreign substances will not interfere, and, above all, the result is more informative. The probability that a certain sequence will show up by chance is about one in twenty for each step in the sequence. That a contaminating protein by chance will have the same first four amino acid residues as the protein to be purified is then about one in 160 000. This means that even a short sequence will give an excellent characterization of the protein.

'A further application of the N-terminal analysis is for molecular weight determination. The subunit weight is calculated from the quantitative yield of the N-terminal amino acid(s). Again the result is more informative and often complementary to those obtained by physico-chemical measurements. The number of identical or non-identical subunits can be deduced. The N-terminal amino acids in human fibrinogen and fibrin may serve as an example. Fibrinogen contains per molecular weight of 340 000 two moles of alanine and two of tyrosine, fibrin contains four moles of glycine and two of tyrosine (21). The interpretation was that both proteins consist of three pairs of non-identical peptide chains, two of which are cleaved proteolytically at the fibrinogen–fibrin conversion, and that one pair of chains in fibrinogen has a blocked N-terminal.'

Another instance in which N-terminal sequencing was used was for monitoring the isolation of non-identical subunits. The three subunits (Henschen & Edman (22)) of mercaptan-reduced, carboxymethylated fibrin were separated on CM-cellulose, all the chromatographic fractions being identified by their N-terminal yields. For chromatography, buffers containing 8 M urea have to be used and urea is known to form cyanate which blocks amino groups. Earlier, N-terminal yields of only about 20% were obtained after chromatography in such buffers. However, when Tris was introduced as the positive ion of the buffers the yields increased to 90–95%. This is because Tris acts as a scavenger for cyanate and thus protects the protein amino groups. The acetic acid used was free of aldehydes which also could have blocked amino groups.

Agnes Henschen-Edman emphasized the importance of using a highly selective procedure for cleaving the isolated protein subunits into a few fragments of fairly large size. As has already been pointed out, high cleavage yields are of the greatest importance as otherwise the heterogeneity of the cleavage mixture will cause considerable difficulty in isolating the fragments. The selectivity of the cleavage reaction is of equal importance. Many highly specific proteolytic enzymes have been described, but have not found extensive use so far. Two of these, thrombin and plasmin, belong to the blood coagulation system, and a growing group of specific proteolytic enzymes is being isolated from snake venoms. A few selective chemical cleavages have also been described, the most well known being the cyanogen bromide cleavage.

The cleavage reaction may, to great advantage, be studied with N-terminal analysis. A qualitative determination will give information about the number and kind of new N-terminal amino acids or how many different kinds of bonds have been split. A quantitative result can be used for calculating the number of bonds cleaved or the cleavage yield. Furthermore, the time course of the cleavage and the optimal cleavage conditions may conveniently be deduced from these determinations.

To quote again directly from Agnes Henschen-Edman's lecture at Montpellier:

'The fragmentation, isolation of fragments and subsequent sequencing will be illustrated by our own recent work on one of the chains in fibrinogen, the γ-chain. The molecular weight of the chain indicated that it contained about 400 amino acid residues. Thus it was far too large for direct sequencing. The amino acid composition showed that cleaving the chain at methionyl or arginyl bonds should produce a convenient number of fragments having a suitable size. Furthermore, cleavages at these two residues are known to be specific and almost complete.

'First, the γ-chain was split at the eight methionyl bonds (23) with cyanogen bromide [CB↓ in figure 3], and nine fragments were expected to be formed. Six new N-terminals were found in the cleavage mixture. The fragments were then isolated by Sephadex chromatography and CM-cellulose chromatography and characterized by the N-terminal sequence and amino acid composition. The finding that three of the fragments had the same N-terminal amino acid, i.e. lysine, explained why only six new N-terminals were found in the original cleavage mixture.'

It is obvious from this description how all separation procedures were monitored by N-terminal analysis. This was done to reduce the great danger of losing a fragment, which otherwise might easily happen, especially when the fragment is small or is devoid of ultraviolet absorption. With this 'N-terminal book-keeping', all N-terminal amino acids once present in the original cleavage mixture or in a fraction of it have to be accounted for by the N-terminal amino acids of the isolated fragments.

In Edman's laboratory it was found convenient to name the isolated fragments after their N-terminal sequences in one-letter abbreviation (IUPAC–IUB Commission on Biochemical Nomenclature (24)). Such a name gives an almost unambiguous definition of the fraction. The name is easy to remember and independent of how the fragment was isolated.

Out of the nine cyanogen bromide fragments from the γ-chain of fibrinogen one fragment, YVAT-M, can be recognized as the N-terminal by its sequence. Another fragment, KIIP-, is recognized as the C-terminal by the absence of a methionine (represented by a homoserine) residue in the amino acid composition. It now remained to establish the true order of the seven internal fragments. For this purpose eight overlap sequences were needed.

In order to find these overlaps the γ-chain was fragmented in a different way. The 10 arginyl bonds (Henschen & Lottspeich (25)) were selectively cleaved by trypsin after blocking the ε-amino groups of the lysine residues by citraconylation (CT↓ in figure 3). The cleavage should give rise to 11 fragments. Seven new N-terminal amino acids were found in the digest. However, after fractionation on Sephadex and CM-cellulose chromatography the fragments were characterized by N-terminal sequence and amino acid composition and it was obvious that in fact 11 fragments had been formed. Five of these fragments contained all methionine overlaps.

By using this and similar approaches (26) it was possible to place all fragments, obtained by cleaving the γ-chain at the methionyl bonds, in their original order

```
         CT                  CT
1        ↓       10          ↓          20
Y V A T R D N C C I L D E R F G S Y C P T T C G I A D F L S 30

31                40                        50 CHO
T Y Q T K V D K D L Q S L E D I L H Q V E N K T S E V K Q L 60

61                 70                CB     80            CT  CB
                                     ↓                    ↓   ↓90
I K A I Q L T Y N P D E S S K P N M I D A A T L K S R K M L

       CB
91     ↓           100              CT  110
                                    ↓
E E I M K Y E A S I L T H D S S I R Y L Q E I Y N S N N Q K 120

121               130                   140
I V N L K E K V A Q L E A Q C Q E P C K D T V Q I H D I T G 150

151               160                   170
K D C Q D I A N K G A K Q S G L Y F I K P L K A N Q Q F L V 180

                                   CT
181               190              ↓   200
Y C E I D G S G N G W T V F Q K R L D G S V D F K K N W I Q 210

211               220                   230
Y K E G F G H L S P T G T T E F W L G N E K I H L I S T Q S 240

              CT                 CT                 CB
241           ↓  250             ↓     260          ↓
A I P Y A L R V E L E D W N G R T S T A D Y A M F K V G P E 270

          CT
271       ↓       280                   290
A D K Y R L T Y A Y F A G G D A G D A F D G F D F G D D P S 300

                   CB
301               310 ↓                 320
D K F F T S H N G M Q F S T W D N D N D K F E G N C A E Q D 330

            CB
331         ↓      340                  350
G(S)G W(W)M N K C H A G H L N G V Y Y Q G G(T,Y,S)K A S T P 360

                            CT       CB          CB          CT
361               370       ↓        ↓ 380       ↓
N G Y D N G I(I,W,A,T)K T R W Y S M K K T T M K I I P F N R 390↓

391               400                   410
L T I G E G Q Q H H L G G A K Q A G D V
```

FIGURE 3. Amino acid sequence of human fibrin γ-chain. Cyanogen bromide cleavage points are marked by CB↓, trypsin cleavage points after citraconylation by CT↓.

in the chain (figure 3). About 70% of the total γ-chain sequence was obtained by direct sequencing of these fragments. Remaining sections were sequenced after supplementary cleavage by various methods.

The descriptions given by Pehr Edman and Agnes Henschen-Edman and her collaborators in the laboratory at Martinsreid give a good visualization of the remarkable feat required to assign the order of 410 amino acid residues in the γ-chain of fibrinogen as shown in figure 3. But to what biological end does the knowledge of the primary sequences in proteins lead us? From the very first it was clear that the amino acid sequence in a protein does not immediately lead to understanding of its biological function. The active centres of enzymes and the sites of immune affinity on proteins generally concern the three-dimensional description of the molecule as much as the primary sequence; although the tertiary structure is a consequence of the primary structure. One of the most potentially powerful applications of sequence studies lies in the search for evolutionary relationships between different proteins; but this becomes valuable only in proportion to the number of sequences available for comparison. It is to this fact that we can attribute Edman's concern that the opportunity to set up adequate computer storage facilities should not be lost. There are now several hundred automatic sequencing devices in operation and in the next few years we can expect a rapid acceleration in the rate at which sequence data become available for comparison. At present the Atlas of Protein Sequencing provides a facility through its computer service, but this is done on an insecure year to year financial basis and Edman expressed his doubt if this important function is sufficiently safeguarded. In his words 'we may in time expect the unravelling of a new *systema naturalis* among the biomolecules. It would be tragic if this development would be endangered through our own negligence.'

It might be right to conclude with an observation of Pehr Edman's which is perhaps self-revealing. 'People with no experience of structural work sometimes tell me that they believe it is (a) tedious, (b) with automation a routine. This is wide of the mark. It may have been tedious at the time when all sequencing had to be done by hand, but automation has done away with most of that. The belief that the work has become a routine is even more untrue. In fact, the solution of a large structure taxes the investigator's resources of skill and knowledge to the utmost, and luck is not an unessential factor. The comparison to the solution of a super-crossword puzzle is perhaps apt. Anyone, who has experienced the elation in the laboratory when a fragment known to be missing has been found, or a tantalizing inconsistency has been resolved, would know what I mean.'

## References

(1) Tswett, M. 1906 *Ber. dt. bot. Ges.* **24**, 316.
(2) Tiselius, A. 1943 *Ark. Kemi Miner. Geol.* **16A**, no 18.
(3) Claesson, S. 1946 *Ark. Kemi Miner. Geol.* **23A**, no 1.
(4) Martin, A. J. P. & Synge, R. L. M. 1941 *Biochem. J* **35**, 1358.
(5) Consden, R., Gordon, A. H. & Martin, A. J. P 1944 *Biochem. J.* **38**, 224.
(6) Moore, S. & Stein, W. H., 1951 *J. biol. Chem.* **192**, 663.

(7) Svedberg, T., 1926 *Z. phys. Chem.* **121**, 65–77.
(8) Tiselius, A. 1937 *Trans. Faraday Soc.* **33**, 524.
(9) Sanger, F. 1945 *Biochem. J.* **39**, 507.
(10) Sanger, F. 1949 *Biochem. J.* **44**, 126.
(11) Sanger, F. 1949 *Biochem. J.* **45**, 563.
(12) Sanger, F. & Tuppy, H. 1951 *Biochem. J.* **49**, 463.
(13) Sanger, F. & Tuppy, H. 1951 *Biochem. J.* **49**, 481.
(14) Jensen, H. & Evans, F. A. 1935 *J. biol. Chem.* **108**, 1.
(15) Abderhalden, E. & Brockmann, H. 1930 *Biochem. Z.* **225**, 386–408
(16) Edman, P. 1950 *Acta chem. scand.* **4**, 283–293.
(17) Hirs, C. H. W., Moore, S. & Stein, W. H. 1960 *J. biol. Chem.* **235**, 633.
(18) Gray, W. R. & Hartley, B. S. 1963 *Biochem. J.* **89**, 379.
(19) Edman, P. & Begg, G. 1966 *Eur. J. Biochem.* **1**, 180.
(20) Agnes Henschen-Edman 1977 In: *Strategy and tactics in protein sequence determination.* 2nd Solid Phase Symposium, Montpellier.
(21) Blomback, B. & Yamashina, I. 1958 *Ark. Kemi.* **12**, 299–319.
(22) Henschen, A. & Edman, P. 1972 *Biochim. biophys. Acta* **293**, 351.
(23) Henschen, A. & Warbinek, R. 1975 *Hoppe-Seyler's Z. Physiol. Chem.* **356**, 1981–1984.
(24) IUPAC–IUB Commission on Biochemical Nomenclature 1968 *Biochim. biophys. Acta* **168**, 6–10.
(25) Henschen, A. & Lottspeich, F. 1975 *Hoppe-Seyler's Z. Physiol. Chem.* **356**, 1985–1988.
(26) Henschen, A., Lottspeich, F., Sekita, T. & Warbinck, R. 1976 *Hoppe-Seyler's Z. Physiol. Chem.* **357**, 605–608.

## Bibliography

1939 (With E. Jorpes & T. Thaning) Neutralization of action of heparin by protamine. *Lancet* p. 975.

1942 A micromethod for the estimation of cerebrosides in nerve tissue. *J. biol. Chem.* **143**, 219.

(With others) Preparation and some properties of hypertensin (Angiotonin). *J. Physiol.* **101**, 284

1944 On the purification of hypertensin (Angiotonin) *Ark Kemi Miner. Geol.* **18B**, no. 2.

1945 Preliminary report on the purification and the molecular weight of hypertensin. *Nature, Lond.* **155**, 756.

On the purification and chemical composition of hypertensin (Angiotonin). *Ark. Kemi Miner. Geol.* **22A**, no. 3.

(With S. E. G. Ågvist) A micromethod for the estimation of phosphatidyl ethanolamine in nerve tissue. *Acta physiol. scand.* **10**, 144.

1947 (With G. Ågren) The amino acid composition of secretin. *Arch. Biochem.* **13**, 283.

A note on the action of tyrosinase on pepsin, trypsin and chymotrypsin. *J. biol. Chem.* **167**, 301.

The action of tyrosinase on chymotrypsin, trypsin and pepsin. *J. biol. Chem.* **168**, 367.

Note on the cleavage of insulin by chymotrypsin. *Acta chem. Scand.* **1**, 684.

1948 A technique for partition chromatography on starch. *Acta chem. scand.* **2**, 592.

1949 A method for the determination of the amino acid sequences in peptides. *Arch. Biochem.* **22**, 475.

(With others) Partition chromatographic separation of adenine and guanine. *J. biol Chem.* **178**, 395.

(With S. Bergstrom & O. Hall) On the occurrence of isoguanine in pig blood. *Acta chem. scand.* **3**, 1128.

1950 Preparation of phenyl thiohydantoin from some natural amino acids. *Acta chem. scand.* **4**, 277.

Method for determination of the amino acid sequence in peptides. *Acta chem. scand.* **4**, 283.

1952 (With K. Diehl) Reduction of insulin with borohydride. *Trans. 2nd Int. Congr. Biochem.* p. 51.

1953 Note on the stepwise degradation of peptides *via* phenyl thiohydantoin. *Acta chem. scand.* **7**, 700.

Selective cleavage of peptides In: *The chemical structure of proteins* (ed. G. E. W. Wolstenholme, p. 98. London: H. & A. Churchill Ltd.

1955 Den kliniska experimentalforskningens dilemma. *Svenska Läkartidn.* **52**, 97.

1956 (With K. Lauber) Note on the preparation of phenyl thiohydantoins from glutamine, S-carboxymethyl cysteine and cysteic acid. *Acta chem. scand.* **10**, 466.
Mechanism of the phenyl isothiocyanate degradation of peptides. *Nature, Lond.* **177**, 667.
On the mechanism of the phenyl isothiocyanate degradation of peptides. *Acta chem. scand.* **10**, 761.
(With J. Sjöquist) Identification and semiquantitative determination of phenyl thiohydantoins. *Acta chem. scand.* **10**, 1507.

1957 (With K. Heirweg) Purification and N-terminal determination of crystalline pepsin. *Biochim. biophys. Acta* **24**, 219.
Isolation of the red pigment concentrating hormone of the crustacean eyestalk. *Trans. 2nd Int. Symp. Neurosecretion*, p. 119. Berlin: Springer-Verlag.
(With L. Josefsson) Reversible enzyme inactivation due to N,O-peptidyl shift. *Nature, Lond.* **179**, 1189.
Phenylthiohydantoins in protein analysis. *Proc. R. Aust chem. Inst* p. 434.
(With L. Josefsson) Reversible inactivation of lysozyme due to N,O-peptidyl shift. *Biochim. biophys. Acta* **25**, 614.

1958 (With L. Josefsson) Alcoholysis of lysozyme with boron trifluoride. *Ark Kemi* **13**, no. 13.
Reversible enzyme inactivation due to N,O-peptidyl shift. *Trans. 4th Int. Congr. Biochem.* **8**, 42.

1959 Chemistry of amino acids and peptides. *Ann. Rev. Biochem.* **28**, 69.

1960 Phenylthiohydantoins in protein analysis. *Ann. N.Y. Acad. Sci.* **88**, 602.

1962 (With H. Smith & J. A. Owen) N-terminal amino acids of human haptoglobins. *Nature, Lond.* **193**, 286.
(With H. Nial) The N-terminal amino acids of human plasma proteins. *J. gen. Physiol.* **45**, Suppl., 185.
(With B. Blombäck, M. Blombäck & B. Hessel) Amino-acid sequence and the occurrence of phosphorus in human fibrinopeptides. *Nature, Lond.* **193**, 883.

1963 (With D. Ilse) The formation of 3-phenyl-2-thiohydantoins from phenylthiocarbamyl amino acids. *Aust. J. Chem.* **16**, 411.
(With B. Blombäck & M. Blombäck) On the structure of human fibrinopeptides. *Acta chem. scand.* **17**, 1184.
(With B. Blombäck, M. Blombäck, R. F. Doolittle & B. Hessel) Properties of a new human fibrinopeptide. *Biochim. biophys. Acta* **78**, 566.
Determination of amino acid sequences in proteins. *Thromb. Diath. Haemorrh., Suppl.* **13**, 17.

1966 (With B. Blombäck, M. Blombäck & B. Hessel) Human fibrinopeptides; isolation, characterization and structure. *Biochim. biophys. Acta* **115**, 371.

1967 (With G. Begg A protein sequenator. *Eur. J. Biochem.* **1**, 80.
(With H. D. Niall) Two structurally distinct classes of kappa chains in human immunoglobulins. *Nature, Lond.* **216**, 261.

1968 (With A. G. Cooper) Amino acid sequence at the N-terminal end of a cold agglutinin kappa chain. *FEBS Lett.* **2**, 33.

1969 (With K. J. Fraser) On the amino acid sequence of light chains from arsonic antibody. *Proc. Aust. Biochem. Soc.* **2**, 37.
(With G. Mamiya & A. Henschen) Structure of jack bean urease. *Proc. Aust. Biochem. Soc.* **2**, 26.

1970 Sequence determination. In: *Protein sequence determination* (ed. S. B. Needleman), p. 211. Berlin: Springer Verlag.
(With A. Inglis) Mechanism of the cyanogen bromide reaction with methionine in peptides and proteins. I. *Proc. Aust. Biochem. Soc.* **3**, 25.
(With A. Inglis) Mechanism of the cyanogen bromide reaction with methionine in peptides and proteins. II. *Proc. Aust. Biochem. Soc.* **3**, 25.
(With A. Inglis) Mechanism of cyanogen bromide reaction with methionine in peptides and proteins I *Analyt Biochem.* **37**, 73.
(With A. Henschen) Variants in fibrinogen. *Proc. Aust. Biochem. Soc.* **3**, 26.
(With C. Rochat & H. Rochat) Some S-alkyl derivatives of cysteine suitable for sequence determination by the phenylisothiocyanate technique. *Analyt. Biochem.* **37**, 259.
(With H. Rochat, C. Rochat, F. Miranda & S. Lissitzky) The amino acid sequence of neurotoxin I of *Androctonus australis* Hector. *Eur. J. Biochem.* **17**, 262.
Scorpion neurotoxins: a family of homologous proteins. *FEBS Lett.* **10**, 349.

1970 (With K. J. FRASER) The N-terminus of light chains from rabbit arsonic antibody. *FEBS Lett.* **7**, 99.

1972 (With A. HENSCHEN) Large scale preparation of S-carboxymethylated chains of human fibrin and fibrinogen and the occurrence of $\gamma$-chain variants. *Biochim. biophys. Acta* **263**, 351.

1975 (With A. HENSCHEN) In: *Protein sequence determination* (ed. S. B. Needleman) (2nd ed.), p. 232. Berlin: Springer Verlag.

1976 (With W. F. BRANDT, A. HENSCHEN & C. VON HOLT) Abnormal behaviour of proline in the isothiocyanate degradation. *Hoppe-Seyler's Z. Physiol. Chem.* **357**, 1505.

1977 Unwinding the protein. *Carlsberg Res. Comm.* **42**, 1.

A. Erdélyi

# ARTHUR ERDÉLYI

2 October 1908 — 12 December 1977

Elected F.R.S. 1975

By D. S. Jones, F.R.S.

## Life to 1939

Arthur Erdélyi was a gifted expositor and, like prophets, gifted expositors are not welcome in their homeland, particularly when it is controlled by Nazis. So, in 1939, he joined the growing band of refugees from the continent of Europe and arrived in Britain, destined for Edinburgh. At Waverley station, carrying a battered suitcase and very little money, he was met by Barry Spain who had been deputed by Professor E. T. (later Sir Edmund) Whittaker to give him two pounds and fix him up with lodgings. At the same time Walter Ledermann was called in to act as interpreter since Erdélyi spoke practically no English though his German was fluent. From these welcoming signs Arthur realized that he was to be made at home and thus was started an association with Edinburgh which was to flower into a major love of his life, sufficient to bring him back from the U.S.A. many years later at considerable personal sacrifice.

His earlier life had not been without vicissitude. He was born in Budapest on 2 October 1908, the eldest of five children of Ignác József Ármin Diamant and Frieda (*née* Roth) but his name was changed later when he was adopted by his mother's second husband after his father's death. He went to school in Budapest (primary 1914–18, secondary 1918–26) and, while a schoolboy, witnessed the rising of the Communists under Béla Kun. It was during this time that he gained his fluency in German, reading extensively from advanced texts in mathematics.

On completion of the school curriculum he wanted to become a mathematician and was offered a place in Budapest University to study mathematics—no small tribute to his ability in view of the quota on the admission of Jews imposed by the university under the *numerus clausus*. But he was aware that if he accepted the place he would be unable to secure employment in Hungary because no university appointments were allocated to Jews. So he planned to become an engineer and then set up in private practice in Hungary. However, the quota in engineering for Jews in Hungarian universities was zero and consequently, after consulting L. Fejér at Budapest, he decided to go to Brno (then Brünn) in Czechoslovakia to study engineering.

After two years at Brno he passed the first of the state examinations with distinction in 1928 and was awarded both the first and second prize in the mathematics competition. At this stage, he realized that he could obtain employment as a mathematician if he stayed in Czechoslovakia and, with the encouragement of the Professor of Mathematical Analysis, decided to devote himself to mathematics. Thus he never completed his degree at Brno (a not unusual occurrence in Central Europe in those days) but moved into mathematical research and published his first paper in 1934.

No one would have guessed that this was the precursor of a flood but his name was to appear on 40 publications in the next five years. The first few dealt with the oscillations of various mechanical and electrical systems but the remainder were mainly concerned with the confluent hypergeometric function which had been discovered by Whittaker in 1904. By the time he was 30 he had established himself as an international authority on special functions.

In 1938 he submitted a collection of his published papers in lieu of a thesis to the German University of Prague (having matriculated there in 1937 while continuing to live in Brno) for the degree of Dr rer. nat. (Doctor rerum naturalium). His dissertation passed the scrutiny of the principal examiner, Professor Loewner (to whom he was to dedicate a paper (154) nearly 30 years later) without difficulty and he was awarded the degree. He actually graduated at the last *Promotion*, the quaint medieval ceremony at which degrees were handed over, before the university was taken over by the Nazi authorities. Also receiving his doctorate on this occasion was Lipman Bers who was extremely surprised to discover that this well known mathematician was acquiring his first degree!

The occupation of Czechoslovakia by the Nazis meant that Erdélyi's days in that country were numbered. Already in active correspondence with Tricomi because of their related interests in research, he enquired about the possibilities in Italy. Tricomi felt that the surge of anti-Semitism in Italy militated against such a move by Erdélyi and suggested contact with Whittaker in Edinburgh. There followed a desperate and poignant series of letters. Whittaker was willing to help and obtained a grant from the University of Edinburgh but it was insufficient since the British Government refused to issue a visa unless £400 per annum was guaranteed. Whittaker and Professor Brodetsky of Leeds made strenuous efforts and eventually, with the aid of a supplementary grant from the Academic Assistance Council (now the Society for the Protection of Science and Learning Limited), were able to assure Erdélyi at Christmas of 1938 that a visa had been promised. Erdélyi duly appeared in the Mathematical Institute of Edinburgh in February 1939.

There is no doubt that the invitation to Edinburgh saved Erdélyi's life for the whole Jewish community at Brno was wiped out during the war and his two brothers as well as a sister died in a concentration camp. He used to tell, with grim humour, how he had to cross Germany to reach Edinburgh and, being fearful that as a Jew he would have trouble on the journey, approached a German consul to enquire whether this was likely to happen. 'Of course not!' replied the official, 'We are a civilized nation.'

## Edinburgh 1939–49

The refugee was warmly treated by the Mathematical Institute and soon friendships that were to last the rest of his life were forged. Whittaker took to him at once and almost immediately proposed that he undertake the preparation of a new edition of Whittaker and Watson. But, according to Erdélyi, 'We were walking along the street at the time, it was raining and I didn't understand English.' The subject was never mentioned again. It is interesting to speculate how the appearance of *Modern analysis* would have changed under the authorship of Erdélyi. Some clue is offered by *Higher transcendental functions* in which the opening sentence of volume 1 states: 'The work of which this book is the first volume might be described as an up-to-date version of Part II, *The transcendental functions* of Whittaker and Watson's celebrated "Modern Analysis".' The difference in emphasis is dramatic. Whereas the hypergeometric function forms part of *Modern analysis* it becomes in *Higher transcendental functions* the central core about which most of the work is draped.

At about this time Erdélyi met John von Neumann though he was unaware of this until a lengthy interval had elapsed. He had been called to Max Born's room to talk to a visitor who had arrived unexpectedly. No introductions were effected and no names were mentioned so that it was not until some time after the meeting that he was able to identify the rather stout stranger who 'looked like a not very prosperous commercial traveller and spoke German with a Budapest accent.'

Arthur now felt that it was opportune really to get to grips with the English language. He was assisted in this by Nancy Walls (later Mrs W. L. Wilson) who was subsequently appointed Lecturer in the History of Mathematics at Southampton. She directed his reading of the English classics and, under her guidance, he developed a facility and precision in English that he was to retain always. He insisted on good writing from his students; those submitting theses were frequently forced to rewrite them many times over. A counter-example which he sometimes quoted against himself was of a student who 'has learned to write so rapidly that he has published an inordinate amount of material, but he still cannot spell!'

His conversion to English was so wholehearted that, being addressed by Erdös in Hungarian in 1950, he felt obliged to answer in English because his Hungarian was too rusty. However, some 10 years later, he startled Erdös in Haifa by addressing him in Hungarian; the explanation turned out to be that Erdélyi was staying in Israel with relatives who had no other tongue.

During this period his attachment to Edinburgh and its environs grew. As a talented violinist and violist (he also played the piano and recorder) he was an active member of the musical community and he often took part in chamber music recitals. He was a keen walker and spent many happy hours in the Pentland Hills and exploring the Scottish Highlands. His interest was extended to geology on his return to the chair at Edinburgh when he attended extra-mural classes and went on geological excursions, as well as being a member of and constant attender at meetings of the Edinburgh Geological Society. Indeed, he was ever fascinated by the geographical situation of his surroundings so that, when he was at Pasadena, he was frequently to be found hiking in the San Gabriel mountains. Deserts were an abiding attraction. The Mojave and Sonora deserts were thoroughly explored and twice he camped in Death Valley. In Australia he was constantly climbing Mount Wellington and going into the bush, usually taking a camera for he was an avid photographer. His dress was always appropriate—a pair of shorts and sandals—for he said that was the only way to be *ferdinkum* which he explained 'is the Australian slang for real, authentic, pukka, echt'.

Despite his liking for Edinburgh Erdélyi was, in fact, living a hand-to-mouth existence or, as Aitken put it, 'for two or three years, from 1939 on, when he escaped from Hitler's descent on Prague and came to us, he lived like Lazarus on the crumbs from Dives's table while doing all kinds of unobtrusive work in our Department'. In spite of the award of the degree of D.Sc. by the University of Edinburgh in 1940 it was not until 1941 that Whittaker was able to appoint Erdélyi as an assistant lecturer and so dispense with the special grants from the University and the Academic Assistance Council. The event was celebrated by his colleagues at a party graced, wartime austerities and restrictions notwithstanding, by a splendid chocolate cake.

A lectureship followed in 1942. With his future secure he married, on 4 November 1942 in Glasgow, Eva Neuburg, daughter of Frederic Neuburg (of Litoměrice, Czechoslovakia) and Helene (*née* Feitis), second cousin of Max Perutz. The marriage brought him great joy and proved to be a happy and harmonious one.

While participating fully in the teaching duties of his post he was also actively engaged as a scientific consultant to the Admiralty. This entailed frequent visits to London where he met G. E. H. Reuter, D. H. Sadler and J. Todd. One outcome of their discussions was a proposal to form a National Mathematical Laboratory; this eventually materialized as a real entity and became one of the divisions of the National Physical Laboratory.

He also assumed the duties of Editor of the *Proceedings of the Edinburgh Mathematical Society* (of which he had been a member since 1939 and whose meetings he attended faithfully whenever he was in Scotland). Until his departure in 1947 he discharged these duties with customary efficiency and cheerfulness, tempered by an insistence on high quality papers. Once, it is recalled, he was offered a paper as he entered a building and had rejected it by the time he had mounted to the first landing. The Society recognized his service to it by appointing him President in the session 1971–72.

Erdélyi was a magnificent lecturer, with a superb delivery. He polished his lectures until they were complete down to the last iota yet transparently clear and informative. Undergraduates treasured the notes from his courses and regarded him with admiration, if not awe. Graduate students were apt to be swung from previous enthusiasms and to venture into the territory he was charting. Nevertheless, all his students have very warm memories of him. As

J. W. S. Cassels says, 'He was by far the most approachable member of staff at Edinburgh and took a friendly interest in my progress and, indeed, in all the mathematical students.' His postgraduate students found him a constant source of inspiration: he always knew how to improve the exposition and he was fertile with ideas when the students encountered difficulties. When he combined his penetration of thought with his lecturing skill to present a talk at an international colloquium, as he was frequently invited to do, the result was outstanding. Every member of the audience would attest to a better understanding of the subject and the ovation accorded to him was remarkable.

Students' attempts to pronounce Erdélyi's name often caused him to chuckle quietly and once he observed: 'I think I have become a trinity.' But Nancy Walls, his adviser in English, was aghast at some of the pronunciations and tried to circumvent the hurdle by distributing the poem

If once every fortnight a fair day ye
Would take as a clean-and-repair day, ye
Would very soon be
As pleasant to see
As our dear spick-and-span Dr Erdélyi.

Arthur's own prescription was to say that the surname of the Scottish artist Joan Eardley was a good enough approximation to the Hungarian. Apropos of the last line of Nancy Walls's poem, the spotless white shirts, bow tie and dapper dress of Arthur were always being remarked on.

Edinburgh was shortly to lose Erdélyi. In 1946 Harry Bateman, who had emigrated to the California Institute of Technology, died leaving behind a mass of notes which he had intended to edit into a monumental work on special functions. There was dire need for such a work because, notwithstanding the volume of research in the journals, the only available books were Whittaker and Watson's *Modern analysis*, Magnus and Oberhettinger's *Formeln und Sätze für die speziellen Funktionen der mathematischen Physik* and the text *Tables of functions with formulae and curves* by Jahnke and Emde. Whittaker, to whom Bateman had been junior at the same Cambridge college, was the obvious world authority for CalTech to consult. He advised that Erdélyi, who had been elected a Fellow of the Royal Society of Edinburgh in 1945, was unquestionably the most highly qualified expert around. So Erdélyi was granted leave of absence from 1 June 1947 to 30 June 1948 by the University of Edinburgh in order to make a feasibility study while Visiting Professor at CalTech.

On completion of his study he reported that the task of reducing the Bateman manuscripts to order would involve one man for 15 years or four men for 4 years. He then returned to the senior lectureship to which Aitken, who had succeeded Whittaker, had managed to persuade the University of Edinburgh to promote him.

Meanwhile, CalTech had obtained funds from the U.S. Office of Naval Research to support four scholars for 3 years on the 'Bateman Project', the job of sorting the huge box of typescripts that was the legacy of Bateman. Conscious that no one else could command the expertise to take charge of the project, CalTech made an alluring offer to Erdélyi. He could have either a three year contract as Director of the Bateman Project or a permanent appointment as full professor and direct the project as part of his duties. The salary would be double what he was earning at Edinburgh. It was more than Erdélyi could resist and he departed for the professorship in 1949.

## The Bateman Project

He was to remain in the U.S.A. for the next 15 years but the beginning was not auspicious. One of the first things Arthur did was to buy a new Buick. A day or two afterwards, noticing that he was low on fuel, he turned off the road into a service station. Unfamiliar with the characteristics of his powerful new car he went roaring through the service station at 40 miles per hour, demolishing three pumps.

He was also having trouble with his beloved violin. He had particularly requested the shippers to take special care of the valuable instrument, but the sound it produced at Pasadena was excruciating. It transpired that the shippers, to protect the violin from ocean dampness while on board the boat, had varnished it!

Perhaps he regarded these incidents as an augury of events to come; at any rate, during his whole sojourn in the U.S.A. he never gave up the British passport to which he had become entitled by naturalization in 1947.

The British citizenship did not diminish his interest in Jewish affairs. He paid several visits to Israel and spent the session 1956–57 on sabbatical leave as Visiting Professor of Applied Mathematics at the Hebrew University, Jerusalem. He was a member of the Friends of the Hebrew University and, in the U.S.A., served on its Academic Council. For a period he was Vice-President of the Edinburgh section of the British Zionist Association.

In 1949 the collaboration of the team on the Bateman Project started. Erdélyi had successfully induced W. Magnus (of Göttingen), F. Oberhettinger (of Mainz) and F. G. Tricomi (of Turin) to come together for the compilation of the manual on special functions. Tricomi had been granted leave of absence by his ministry but the presence of Oberhettinger necessitated some legerdemain by the U.S. Navy because of government restrictions. To mould the team into a coherent body was not an easy task for Erdélyi. Agreement was essential on the philosophy to be adopted, notation, the space and treatment of various topics, etc. and there were forceful characters among the members. Nevertheless, Erdélyi succeeded in avoiding any unpleasant disagreement by exercising control with tact and courtesy. He displayed, as he was to demonstrate many times in subsequent years, an exceptionally well developed common sense and was absolutely straightforward in his opinions and decisions so that he was soon viewed by the other members of the team as totally reliable both as a person and as a mathematician. By the time the team broke up in 1951 (when Magnus went to a full professorship at New York University) it had produced three volumes of *Higher transcendental functions* and two volumes of *Tables of integral transforms* (following a suggestion of E. R. Love of Melbourne, Arthur often referred to them as 'The TOME', the initials of the four authors in reverse order). Erdélyi, with tenure at CalTech, was left with the gigantic job of seeing the five volumes through the press. It is a remarkable tribute to Arthur that the preparation of the five volumes was accomplished while he was carrying a normal teaching load at CalTech, supervising two research students and looking after his beloved wife Eva who was in a sanatorium for a long time after contracting tuberculosis.

With the labours of Hercules behind him, the next few years were happy ones for Arthur. Attached to one of the great centres of learning of the world, he seized the propitious circumstances to encourage and stimulate the learning of the bright minds around him. He travelled extensively reporting the achievements of himself and his associates. Wherever he was, he took a benign interest in his fellow humans; he conversed happily with all and sundry yet was equally ready to listen and he impressed an unforgettable image on those he met (one postmaster in Stony Brook has a Scottish pound note in his currency collection because Arthur was told of the deficiency and rectified it the next time he was in Scotland). The young were always handled gently, the full power of his intellect never being directed against them, and he was extremely kindly disposed to children. As a result he was much in demand as a baby-sitter, for excursions to the zoo and picnics. Once his benevolence backfired. It was on the occasion of his second visit to Australia in 1970 (his first short trip in 1962 was to lecture at the Summer Research Institute of the Australian Mathematical Society at the instigation of the then President, Sir Thomas Cherry, who shared Arthur's pastime of mountain climbing as well as common mathematical interests). *En route* to Melbourne to help out the University by occupying the Chair of Mathematics for six months on a visiting basis because the University had been unable to find a permanent appointee since the retirement of Sir Thomas Cherry in 1963 he stopped off at Hobart, Tasmania, to participate in another Summer Research Institute. He was one of the three principal speakers, the other two being P. J. Davis (Brown University) and Kurt Mahler (Manchester University and Ohio State). On the day in question a drive was organized and the party included children at Arthur's request. Early on he had pleased everyone by dubbing the Warumbungle mountains of New South Wales as the 'Why Bungle' range and by rejecting a severely pot-holed road on the grounds, not of preserving the car as his colleagues thought, but, as he said with a twinkle, 'of not doing damage to myself'. One of the party (it may have been Mahler) propounded the theorem that all Tasmanian cows point in the same direction. Arthur indicated his disbelief but a quick check of visible fields failed to substantiate his view. Thereafter the fields were carefully scanned but many miles passed before Arthur announced: 'I have a counter-example. Inspection of the group of cows yonder reveals that one is pointing in a different direction'. Almost immediately one of the children shouted: 'But it isn't a cow, it's a horse' and, to Arthur's dismay, so it was.

Erdélyi could easily have stayed in Pasadena for the rest of his life, but the University of Edinburgh decided to create a second Chair of Mathematics in 1963. The post was advertised twice but Erdélyi did not apply. There were numerous good arguments against application. Apart from financial considerations and the low ebb of the Edinburgh department on account of Aitken's ill health, there was the question as to whether his wife's health could stand up to a return to the Edinburgh climate. There would be burdensome administration and secretarial help would be scarce. For Lady Whittaker often said that her husband wrote 3000 letters each year in his own hand and Aitken had, for many years, never used a secretary but dealt with all his correspondence at home. Also many routine matters that ought to have been within the purview of an adequate secretariat were the responsibility of lecturers. Finally, Erdélyi was gravely concerned about his pension because, having cashed in his F.S.S.U. benefits in 1949, he would have to begin superannuation anew.

Fortunately for Edinburgh a catalyst, in the person of I. N. Sneddon of Glasgow, was at hand. While the second advertisement was running Sneddon was visiting CalTech and in conversation one day Arthur remarked that he thought of Edinburgh as his real 'alma mater' because of how well he had been received there as a refugee. He also observed that he missed playing chamber music with his friends. At once Sneddon pressed him to apply but all that Erdélyi would concede was that, if Edinburgh invited him to occupy the chair, he would think about it very seriously. As soon as Sneddon got back to Glasgow three days later he passed on the information by telephone. Shortly thereafter Principal Appleton issued an official invitation. Three months of correspondence ensued but in the end Erdélyi wrote on 1 October 1963, the day before his fifty-fifth birthday, to accept the invitation. It had been a terribly difficult decision but some idea of what swayed him is gathered from the following extract from a reply to a letter of welcome from a former colleague.

> '4th November 1963
>
> I am delighted with your letter: both my wife and I thank you for your good wishes. After we left Scotland in 1949 I felt that you were one of the very few of our friends, if not the only one, who really believed that we should return given the chance—even if this required a considerable sacrifice on our part. As the years passed and no suitable opportunity presented itself I sometimes wondered if you have retained faith in us—indeed I began to wonder if aging as we are we should have the courage to make the move. I am glad to see that my doubts on both counts were unjustified.'

## Return to Edinburgh, 1963–77

There is no doubt that the department at Edinburgh was in bad shape when Erdélyi arrived for his reincarnation. This was primarily due to the poor health of Aitken which prevented him from exerting the proper influence in university committees. Visitors and postgraduate students attracted by Erdélyi's name were at first appalled by the lack of life as compared with the establishments they came from. Arthur set to with a will to put things right. He played his full part in university committees where his interventions were invariably highly pertinent. He was capable of taking a much broader view of things than many and earned the respect of his colleagues on Faculty and Senatus for his considerable intelligence and charm. One reason why his colleagues took to him was that, in spite of his position and distinction, he was astonishingly modest.

Any doubts that the department might have had were soon set at rest. His international standing brought many distinguished visitors to the benefit of all. He took a great deal of interest in the work of everyone and he had the advantage of being extremely widely read. His knowledge of the recent literature in topics which he was not engaged in researching was truly amazing. The postgraduate lectures which he gave on a wide diversity of subjects were another source of life.

To his duties as head of department he brought many attributes. First and foremost he was a perfect gentleman. Everyone, great or small, was accorded full courtesy and faultless manners. He would talk to people on any subject at any level and make them feel completely at ease. Level-headed and tolerant, he was always in command of the situation. Part of his competence stemmed from his ability to recognize the existence of difficulties before they had matured to major magnitude. The authority he wielded was successfully combined with consultation with his staff so that, while they might feel that he had not come to the right conclusion, they could accept his decisions as being informed and reasoned.

One of the first fruits of Erdélyi's endeavours was the move of Professor F. F. Bonsall and his research students to Edinburgh. From that point the department never looked back. Established as a major centre of functional analysis it branched out in other directions and was transformed into a flourishing hive of activity. Undoubtedly Erdélyi, the polymath, was the prime mover in this expansion and any debt which he owed Edinburgh as a refugee had been repaid with interest.

Many honours came Erdélyi's way over the years. Some have already been mentioned. He was elected a Foreign Member of the Academy of Sciences of Torino (Italy) in 1953 and a Fellow of the Royal Society in 1975. In 1977 he had the distinction of being the only mathematician in recent years other than Sir William Hodge to be awarded the Gunning Victoria Jubilee Prize of the Royal Society of Edinburgh. His service to the mathematical community included membership of the Council of the American Mathematical Society as well as several advisory bodies of the National Academy of Sciences. He was involved in an editorial capacity with: *Proceedings of the Edinburgh Mathematical Society*, *Journal of the Indian Mathematical Society*, *Mathematical Tables and Other Aids to Computation*, *Journal of Mathematics and Mechanics*, *Archive for Rational Mechanics and Analysis*, *Society for Industrial and Applied*

*Mathematics*, *Journal of Mathematical Physics*, *Canadian Journal of Mathematics*, *Proceedings of the Royal Society of Edinburgh*, and also found time to contribute innumerable reviews to *Mathematical Reviews*. His seventieth birthday was to have been celebrated by a special issue of *Applicable Analysis* and by the *Proceedings of the 1978 Dundee Conference on Differential Equations*. These will now be dedicated to him as a lasting memorial to his work.

The final years of his life were dogged by bad health and he underwent major surgery in the summer of 1973. Naturally he was given medical leave but at the first postgraduate lecture in October there was Arthur, his rubicund beaming face matching his sunny disposition as ever. On being remonstrated that he was supposed to be convalescing, he gave a typical reply which sums up the spirit of his life: 'My doctor forbade me to teach; he did not forbid me to learn.'

The *joie de vivre* and impish vitality of this gentle cultured scholar continued undimmed until he died suddenly on 12 December 1977 at the age of 69, leaving a widow, Eva, and a stepson, David.

## A MATHEMATICAL ASSESSMENT

The evaluation of the papers of an author as prolific as Erdélyi is likely to be as revealing of the prejudices of the reviewer as the attainments of the reviewed. Today Erdélyi's researches might be roughly classified as applied analysis and as such range from the unfashionable to the chic.

If the first half dozen or so papers, inherited from his apprenticeship as an engineer, are ignored, the publications spanning the years 1930–50 are almost entirely devoted to special functions and the differential equations from which they stem. These investigations, which number nearly 100, are those of a pure mathematician, i.e. the purpose was to unveil the beauty of the underlying pattern without any concern for applications. Particular attention was paid to identities and integral representations as well as expansions in special functions. Some of the results are striking and all the proofs have the fine elegance which was one of Arthur's trademarks. But, by some odd mischance, he did not always discover the most important formulae. For instance, the discoveries of Burchnall (to whose obituary he contributed) and Chaundy about Appell functions are more important than those of Erdélyi. This series of papers may be visualized as giving Erdélyi total mastery of the hypergeometric functions of a single variable. True, there is a group of papers on the hypergeometric function of two variables (62, 88, 90, 92, 94) but their importance is hard to estimate because of the current difficulty in dealing with such functions.

In retrospect, Erdélyi's research on special functions can be viewed as tilling the ground which was to bear the fruit of 'TOME'. Without it he would have had neither the authority nor competence to act as director of the Bateman Project. Both attributes were necessary to weld the team and to correct the numerous analytical errors in the material that had to be coordinated. Making the hypergeometric function the core around which all else revolved created a unity and coherence which otherwise would have been lacking. Erdélyi's intuition and perception on content were extraordinarily sound. He was able to foresee what would be important in the future and ensure its inclusion (e.g. the treatment of orthogonal polynomials and Mellin–Barnes integral representations). As a result, *Higher transcendental functions* was the most comprehensive account of special functions and remains in that position today even after a lapse of 25 years. Its importance to science cannot be overstressed despite Erdélyi's inclination towards the end of his life to play it down in comparison with his subsequent researches. Admittedly, there is a tendency today to decry investigations in special functions because, on the one hand, they are not abstract and, on the other, the digital computer has rendered them superfluous. But real problems must yield concrete answers not abstraction and adequate mathematical preparation is vital to the efficient and economical use of computers; in such preparation the properties and manipulation of special functions are often essential. So the scientific community owes a great debt to Erdélyi for being willing to concentrate his energy in this way; the impact on science of what he accomplished is immeasurable.

The Bateman Project was a watershed in Erdélyi's career. Never again would special functions occupy the centre of his stage; instead he moved his attention to the methods of applied mathematics. There was a brief excursion (103, 108) into diffraction theory but mostly he considered situations in which some singular behaviour arose so that asymptotic analysis or singular integration was involved.

Erdélyi's first essays in asymptotics were concerned with differential equations and integrals containing a large parameter. The problem to be resolved is the finding of suitable approximations to the solution of

$$\mathrm{d}^2y/\mathrm{d}x^2+\{\lambda^2p(x)+q(x,\lambda)\}y = 0,$$

where $\lambda$ is large and $q$ is 'small' compared with $\lambda^2 p$. In addition, $p$ might have a transition point where it had a zero or pole in the region of interest. The W.J.K.B.L. method, developed for half a century, and Langer's provision of formulae which were valid uniformly as $x$ passed through a transition point had already indicated that Poincaré's definition of an asymptotic expansion was insufficient to meet demand and that an adequate error analysis was absent. To this problem Erdélyi brought two ideas. The first (84) was of an expansion based on an asymptotic scale (others, notably Olver, had the same idea simultaneously). In fact, the notion is of some antiquity and can probably be traced back to the last century but its exploitation has awaited the last 25 years. It may be expressed as follows: $\{\phi_n(\lambda)\}$ is an asymptotic scale as $\lambda \to \lambda_0$ (which may be infinite) if $\phi_{n+1} = o(\phi_n)$ and $\sum_{n=0}^{\infty} f_n(\lambda)$ is an asymptotic expansion of $f(\lambda)$ with respect to the scale $\{\phi_n\}$ if for each $N$

$$f-\sum_{n=0}^{N} f_n = o(\phi_N)$$

as $\lambda \to \lambda_0$.

The second idea (128, 152) was a systematic examination of the singular Volterra integral equation so as to demonstrate that a formal expansion was asymptotic. The two ideas provided a basis on which Erdélyi was able to erect a considerable body of general theory. A lucid account is contained in his classic monograph *Asymptotic expansions*. The theory was applied to differential equations (106, 109, 112, 114, 115, 117, 120, 121, 124, 129, 134) to give asymptotic representations of various special functions of practical importance though several of the results were already available as formal expansions. Another area of application was the asymptotic evaluation of integrals and the method of stationary phase (113, 118, 123, 127, 132, 149, 163). These papers are notable not only for a unified treatment of Watson's lemma and Darboux's method but also a general approach to Laplace integrals. The results which he obtained on expansions which are uniformly valid as parameters in the integrand vary are very impressive.

It is perhaps curious that Erdélyi did not apply his theory for differential equations to find error estimates and so missed the theorems of most practical importance in asymptotic analysis. This may have been due to his background which suggested starting from a particular special function and finding its asymptotic expansion whereas the significant step for progress is, as F. W. J. Olver showed, to begin with an asymptotic formula and identify the function which it represents.

Another surprising omission from Erdélyi's investigations of this period is the absence of an integral involving a generalized function, the asymptotic theory of which is both simpler and more general. Erdélyi was thoroughly familiar with generalized functions at the time as can be seen from his marvellously clear description of Mikusiński's work in his book *Generalized functions and operational calculus*. It is possible that the lacuna occurred because Mikusiński's definitions were occupying his mind and they are not a good starting point for the asymptotics of integrals. A decade was to pass before Erdélyi switched to working with spaces of test functions and their duals. Theorems on the fractional integral of generalized functions were evolved immediately (167, 168, 170, 171), employing the fact that the Riemann–Liouville and Weyl operators are adjoints of one another so that the construction of test functions on which one is continuous leads to a class of generalized functions on which the other can operate. A similar concept in respect of the Stieltjes transform (176) was being actively pursued at the time of his death.

Asymptotics appeared in another guise in a further series of researches. These were stimulated by studies of the nonlinear equations of fluid mechanics which were being carried out at CalTech in the 1950s. It had been found by Kaplun and Lagerstrom that when a certain parameter $\varepsilon$ was small different expansions in $\varepsilon$ were necessary in different regions but that the expansions could be linked if a recipe for matching them was followed. The technique is now known as the method of matched asymptotic expansions for singular perturbation problems.

Kaplun and Lagerstrom proposed that the two expansions (called inner and outer respectively) should be combined into a single composite expansion which would then hold uniformly in space. After simplifying the mathematics (130), Erdélyi took a typical problem, namely

$$\varepsilon y'' + F(t, y, y', \varepsilon) = 0$$

subject to $y(0) = \alpha(\varepsilon)$, $y(1) = \beta(\varepsilon)$, and showed rigorously that the solution possessed a composite expansion of the type desired. His conditions were less restrictive than previous writers and, moreover, he proved that the error bound held uniformly. This and papers on related topics (135, 137, 138, 140, 141, 144, 160) set the scene for subsequent authors. The rigorous theory of the two-variable expansions in which the composite expansion is constructed directly without the intervening matching of inner and outer expansions was also initiated by Erdélyi (158, 159) and was made possible by his theory of asymptotic scales. Research in the subject exploded afterwards but Erdélyi kept in touch as is evidenced by his surveys (144, 172, 175) which have been invaluable in clarifying issues and pointing out future directions to travel.

With any active research worker a tool which has been forged in one area often turns out to be an effective weapon elsewhere and fractional integration was one such for Erdélyi. Its use in connection with generalized functions has already been alluded to but for conventional functions he had employed it much earlier (50, 57, 58). A short while after he, in conjunction with H. Kober, was responsible for a major advance by introducing what are now termed the Erdélyi–Kober operators. These operators are defined by

$$I_{\eta,\alpha} f(x) = \frac{x^{-\eta-\alpha}}{(\alpha-1)!} \int_0^x (x-y)^{\alpha-1} y^{\eta} f(y)\, dy,$$

$$K_{\eta,\alpha} f(x) = \frac{x^{\eta}}{(\alpha-1)!} \int_x^{\infty} (y-x)^{\alpha-1} y^{-\eta-\alpha} f(y)\, dy.$$

In two papers (59, 60) the properties of these operators were laid out and their relation to the Hankel transform was elucidated via the operator

$$S_{\eta,\alpha} f(x) = x^{-\frac{1}{2}\alpha} \int_0^x y^{-\frac{1}{2}\alpha} J_{2\eta+\alpha}(2\sqrt{(xy)})\, f(y)\, dy.$$

The three operators are intimately connected as a glance at the identities, successfully obtained in the papers referred to,

$$\begin{aligned} I_{\eta+\alpha,\beta} S_{\eta,\alpha} &= S_{\eta,\alpha+\beta}, \\ K_{\eta,\alpha} S_{\eta+\alpha,\beta} &= S_{\eta,\alpha+\beta}, \\ S_{\eta+\alpha,\beta} S_{\eta,\alpha} &= I_{\eta,\alpha+\beta}, \\ S_{\eta,\alpha} S_{\eta+\alpha,\beta} &= K_{\eta,\alpha+\beta} \end{aligned}$$

will confirm. Surprisingly, these operators are relevant to dual integral equations though it took a chance remark by I. N. Sneddon, lecturing on the topic at a

Summer School in Montreal during 1961, to provoke the necessary research. The consequence was a joint paper (139) in which a general class of dual integral equations (which appear in a number of branches of mathematical physics) was solved in a systematic and unified way, thereby displacing the *ad hoc* methods which had been prevalent until then.

Another place where Erdélyi deployed fractional integration was in singular partial differential equations in a paper (119) published in 1956. He was not a newcomer to the subject because he had earlier shown (90, 98) how to derive a fundamental system of solutions in a neighbourhood of singular points where three singular curves intersect for the resolution of a problem in Appell series. In (119) he considered the generalized axially symmetric potential equation which has a regular singular line. By adding an imaginary part to a real independent variable Erdélyi discovered a correlation between the singularities of regular solutions of the partial differential equation and singularities in the complex plane. Many authors were to build on this and, in many ways, the paper can be thought of as initiating the extensive developments which have occurred subsequently in the analytical theory of partial differential equations and ill-posed problems. Erdélyi himself continued to apply fractional integral operators to singular partial differential equations in a number of contexts (122, 154, 155, 164).

The breadth of Erdélyi's interests, the brilliance of his exposition and his uncanny ability to forecast profitable lines made him not only an innovator but also an instigator of an abundance of research. The many who have followed where his footsteps led have reason to be glad that he painted such magnificent signposts and exhorted them to tread the path. They and the scientific community are the losers by his death.

What is written above is based on information derived from many sources but the responsibility for what is actually set down is mine. I wish to express my sincere thanks to all those, too numerous to mention by name, who have contributed to my knowledge of Arthur Erdélyi.

The photograph reproduced was taken in 1973 by Professor I. N. Sneddon with technical assistance by Audio-Visual Services, New Haven University.

## Bibliography

(1) 1934 Ueber die freien Schwingungen in Kondensatorkreisen mit periodisch veränderlicher Kapazität. *Annln Phys.* (5) **19**, 585–622.

(2) Ueber die kleinen Schwingungen eines Pendels mit oszillierendem Aufhängepunkt. *Z. angew. Math. Mech.* **14**, 235–247.

(3) 1935 Ueber Schwingungskreise mit langsam pulsierender Dämpfung (zur Theorie des Pendelrückkopplungsempfängers). *Annln Phys.* (5) **23**, 21–43.

(4) Ueber die rechnerische Ermittlung der Schwingungsvorgänge in Kreisen mit periodisch schwankenden Parametern. *Arch. Elektrotech.* **29**, 475–489. Cf. also *Elektrotech. Z.* **56**, 1128.

(5) Ueber die freien Schwingungen in Schwingungskreisen mit periodisch veränderlicher Selbstinduktivität. *HochfreqTech. Elektroakust.* **46**, 73–77.

(6) Schwingungskreise mit veränderlichen Parametern. Bemerkungen zu einer Arbeit von C. L. Kober. *HochfreqTech. Elektroakust.* **46**, 178.

(7) 1935 Bemerkungen zur Ableitung des Snelliusschen Brechungsgesetzes. *Z. Phys.* **95**, 115–132.

(8) 1936 Ueber einige bestimmte Integrale in denen die Whittakerschen $M_{k,m}$ Funktionen auftreten. *Math. Z.* **40**, 693–702.

(9) Ueber die kleinen Schwingungen eines Pendels mit oszillierendem Aufhängepunkt. Zweite Mitteilung. *Z. angew. Math. Mech.* **16**, 171–182.

(10) Sulla generalizzazione di una formula di Tricomi. *Atti Accad. naz. Lincei Rc.* **24**, 347–350.

(11) Ueber die Integration der Mathieuschen Differentialgleichung durch Laplacesche Integrale. *Math. Z.* **41**, 653–664.

(12) Ueber eine Methode zur Gewinnung von Funktionalbeziehungen zwischen konfluenten hypergeometrischen Funktionen. *Mh. Math. Phys.* **45**, 31–57.

(13) Funktionalrelationen mit konfluenten hypergeometrischen Funktionene. Erste Mitteilung. Additions und Multiplikationstheoreme. *Math. Z.* **42**, 125–143.

(14) Entwicklung einer analytischen Funktion nach Whittakerschen Funktionen. *Proc. Sect. Sci. K. ned. Akad. Wet.* **39**, 1092–1098.

(15) Ueber eine Integraldarstellung der $W_{k,m}$ Funktionen und ihre Darstellung durch die Funktionen des parabolischen Zylinders. *Math. Annln* **113**, 347–356.

(16) Ueber eine Integraldarstellung der $M_{k,m}$ Funktionen und ihre asymptotische Darstellung für grosse Werte von $R(k)$. *Math. Annln* **113**, 357–362.

(17) 1936–37 Sulla transformazione di Hankel pluridimensionale. *Atti Accad. Sci., Torino* **72**, 96–108.

(18) 1937 Funktionalrelationen mit konfluenten hypergeometrischen Funktionen. Zweite Mitteilung. Reihenenwicklungen. *Math. Z.* **42**, 641–670.

(19) Ueber gewisse Funktionalbeziehungen. *Mh. Math. Phys.* **45**, 251–279.

(20) Ueber die Integration der Whittakerschen Differentialgleichung in geschlossener Form. *Mh. Math. Phys.* **46**, 1–9.

(21) Gewisse Reihentransformationen die mit der linearen Transformationsformel der Thetafunktion zusammenhänge. *Compositio math.* **4**, 406–423.

(22) Untersuchungen über Produkte von Whittakerschen Funktionen. *Mh. Math. Phys.* **46**, 132–156.

(23) Der Zusammenhang zwischen verschiedenen Integraldarstellungen hypergeometrischer Funktionen. *Q. Jl Math.* **8**, 200–213.

(24) Integraldarstellungen hypergeometrischer Funktionen. *Q. Jl Math.* **8**, 267–277.

(25) Beitrag zur Theorie der konfluenten hypergeometrischen Funktionen von mehreren Veränderlichen. *Sber. Akad. Wiss. Wien* **146**, 431–467.

(26) Zur Theorie der Kugelwellen. *Physica, 's Grav.* **4**, 107–120.

(27) Ueber die erzeugende Funktion der Jacobischen Polynome. *J. Lond. math. Soc.* **12**, 56–57.

(28) Inhomogene Saiten mit parabolischer Dichteverteilung. *Sber. Akad. Wiss. Wien* **146**, 589–604.

(29) Sulla connessione fra due problemi di calcolo delle probabilità. *G. Ist. ital. Attuari* **8**, 328–337.

(30) 1938 Eigenfrequenzen inhomogener Saiten. *Z. angew. Math. Mech.* **18**, 177–185.

(31) A Sturm–Liouville féle határértékfeladat sajátértékeiröl. *Magy. tudom Akad. mat. Természettud. Ért.* **57**, 1–6.

(32) Bemerkungen zur Integration der Mathieuschen Differentialgleichung durch Laplacesche Integrale. *Compositio math.* **5**, 435–441.

(33) Eine Verallgemeinerung der Neumannschen Polynome. *Mh. Math. Phys.* **47**, 87–103.

(34) Asymptotische Darstellung der Whittakerschen Funktionen für grosse reele Werte des Argumentes und der Parameter. *Čas. Pěst. Mat. Fys.* **67**, 240–248.

(35) Bilineare Reihen der verallgemeinerten Laguerreschen Polynome. *Sber. Akad. Wiss. Wien* **147**, 513–520.

(36) Ueber eine erzeugende Funktion von Produkten Hermitescher Polynome. *Math. Z.* **44**, 201–211.

(37) Die Funksche Integralgleichung der Kugelflächenfunktionen und ihre Uebertragung auf die Ueberkugel. *Math. Annln* **115**, 456–465.

(38) The Hankel transform of a product of Whittaker functions. *J. Lond. math. Soc.* **13**, 146–154.

(39) 1938 On some expansion in Laguerre polynomials. *J. Lond. math. Soc.* **13**, 154–156.
(40) Einige Integralformeln für Whittakersche Funktionen. *Proc. K. ned. Akad. Wet.* **41**, 481–486.
(41) On certain Hankel transforms. *Q. Jl Math.* **9**, 196–198.
(42) The Hankel transform of Whittaker's function $W_{k,m}(z)$. *Proc. Camb. phil. Soc.* **34**, 28–29.
(43) Integral representations for products of Whittaker functions. *Phil. Mag.* (7) **26** 871–877.
(44) 1939 Einige nach Produkten von Laguerreschen Polynomen fortschreitende Reihen. *Sber. Akad. Wiss. Wien* **148**, 33–39.
(45) An integral representation for a product of two Whittaker functions. *J. Lond. math. Soc.* **14**, 23–30.
(46) Infinite integrals involving Whittaker functions. *J. Indian math. Soc.* new series, 3, 169–181.
(47) Integraldarstellungen für Produkte Whittakerscher Funktionen. *Nieuw Archf Wisk.* **20**, 1–34.
(48) Integral representations for Whittaker functions. *Proc. Benares math. Soc.* new series, 1, 39–53.
(49) Note on the transformation of Eulerian hypergeometric integrals. *Q. Jl Math* **10**, 129–134.
(50) Transformation of hypergeometric integrals by means of fractional integration by parts. *Q. Jl Math.* **10**, 176–189.
(51) Transformation einer gewissen nach Produkten konfluenter hypergeometrischer Funktionen fortschreitenden Reihe. *Compositio math.* **6**, 336–347.
(52) Transformation of a certain series of products of confluent hypergeometric functions Applications to Laguerre and Charlier polynomials. *Compositio math.* **7**, 340–352.
(53) On a paper of Copson and Ferrar. *Proc. Edinb. math Soc.* (2), **6**, 11.
(54) Two infinite integrals. *Proc. Edinb. math. Soc.* (2), **6**, 94–104.
(55) Integration of a certain system of linear partial differential equations of the hypergeometric type. *Proc. R. Soc. Edinb.* **59**, 224–241.
(56) 1940 On Lambe's infinite integral formula. *Proc. Edinb. math. Soc.* (2) **6**, 147–148.
(57) On some biorthogonal sets of functions. *Q. Jl Math.* **11**, 111–123.
(58) Some integral representations of the associated Legendre functions. *Phil. Mag.* (7) **30**, 168–171.
(59) (With H. Kober) Some remarks on Hankel transforms. *Q. Jl Math.* **11**, 212–221.
(60) On fractional integration and its application to the theory of Hankel transforms. *Q. Jl Math.* **11**, 293–303.
(61) A class of hypergeometric transforms. *J. Lond. math. Soc.* **15**, 209–212.
(62) Some confluent hypergeometric functions of two variables. *Proc. R. Soc. Edinb.* **60**, 344–361.
(63) 1941 On some generalisations of Laguerre polynomials *Proc. Edinb. math. Soc.* (2) **6**, 193–221.
(64) On Lamé functions. *Phil. Mag.* (7) **31**, 123–130.
(65) On the connection between Hankel transforms of different order. *J. Lond. math. Soc.* **16**, 113–117.
(66) Generating functions of certain continuous orthogonal systems. *Proc. R. Soc. Edinb.* A **61**, 61–70.
(67) Integration of the differential equation of Appell's function $F_4$. *Q. Jl Math.* **12**, 68–77.
(68) (With I. M. H. Etherington) Some problems of non-associative combinations II. *Edinb. math. Notes* no. 32, 7–12.
(69) Note on Heine's integral representation of associated Legendre functions. *Phil. Mag.* (7) **32**, 351–352.
(70) On algebraic Lamé functions *Phil. Mag.* (7) **32**, 348–350.
(71) Tullio Levi-Civita. Obituary notice. *Yb. R. Soc. Edinb.* pp. 1941–1942.
(72) 1942 On certain expansions of the solutions of Mathieu's differential equation. *Proc. Camb. phil. Soc.* **38**, 28–33.
(73) The Fuchsian equation of second order with four singularities. *Duke math. J.* **9**, 48–58.

(74) 1942 Integral equations for Lamé functions. *Proc. Edinb. math. Soc.* (2) **7**, 3–15.

(75) On certain expansions of the solutions of the general Lamé equation. *Proc. Camb. phil. Soc.* **38**, 364–367.

(76) Integral equations for Heun functions. *Q. Jl Math.* **13**, 107–112.

(77) 1943 Inversion formulae for the Laplace transformation. *Phil. Mag.* (7) **34**, 533–537.

(78) Note on an inversion formula for the Laplace transformation. *J. Lond. math. Soc.* **18**, 72–77.

(79) 1944 Certain expansions of the solutions of the Heun equation. *Q. Jl Math.* **15**, 62–69.

(80) 1945 (With W. O. Kermack) Note on the equation $f(x)\,K_n'(z)-g(z)\,K_n(z) = 0$. *Proc. Camb. phil Soc.* **41**, 74–75.

(81) 1944–46 (With J. Cossar) *Dictionary of Laplace transforms.* Admiralty Computing Service.

(82) 1946 (With J. Todd) Advanced instruction in practical mathematics. *Nature, Lond.* **158**, 690.

(83) Harry Bateman. Obituary notice. *J. Lond. math. Soc.* **21**, 300–310.

(84) 1947 Asymptotic representation of Laplace transforms with an application to inverse factorial series. *Proc. Edinb. math. Soc.* (2) **8**, 20–24.

(85) On certain discontinuous wave functions. *Proc. Edinb. math. Soc.* (2) **7**, 39–42.

(86) Harry Bateman. *Obit. Not. Fell. R. Soc. Lond.* **5**, 591–618.

(87) 1948 Expansions of Lamé functions into series of Legendre functions. *Proc. R. Soc. Edinb.* A **62**, 247–267.

(88) Transformations of hypergeometric functions of two variables. *Proc. R. Soc. Edinb.* A **62**, 378–385.

(89) Lamé–Wangerin functions. *J. Lond. math. Soc.* **23**, 64–69.

(90) 1950 Hypergeometric functions of two variables. *Acta Math.* **83**, 131–164.

(91) The inversion of the Laplace transformation. *Math. Mag.* **24**, 1–6.

(92) The general form of hypergeometric series of two variables. *Proc. Int. Congr. Math.* **1**, 413–414.

(93) 1950–51 On some functional transformations. *Rc. Semin. mat. Univ. Torino* **10**, 217–234.

(94) 1951 The general form of hypergeometric series of two variables. *Proc. Am. math. Soc.* **2**, 374–379.

(95) 'Operational calculus' by B. van der Pol & H. Bremmer (book review). *Bull. Am. math. Soc.* **57**, 319–323.

(96) (With F. G. Tricomi) The asymptotic expansion of a ratio of gamma functions. *Pacif. J. Math.* **1**, 133–142.

(97) Parametric equations and proper interpretation of mathematical symbols. *Am. math. Mon.* **58**, 629–630.

(98) The analytic theory of systems of partial differential equations. *Bull. Am. math. Soc.* **57**, 339–353.

(99) Nota ad una lavoro di L. Toscano. *Atti Accad. naz. Lincei Rc.* (8) **11**, 44–45.

(100) 1952 'Die zweidimensionale Laplace-Transformation' by D. Voelker & G. Doetsch (book review). *Bull. Am. math. Soc.* **58**, 88–94.

(101) (With Maria Weber) On the finite difference analogue of Rodrigues' formula. *Am. math. Mon.* **59**, 163–186.

(102) 'Randwertprobleme und andere Anwandungsgebiete der hoeheren Analysis fuer Physiker, Mathematiker und Ingenieure' by F. Schwark (book review). *Bull. Am. math. Soc.* **58**, 274–276.

(103) 1952–53 Variational principles in the mathematical theory of diffraction. *Atti Accad. Sci., Torino,* **87**, 1–13.

(104) 1953 'Bessel functions. II. Functions of positive integer order' by W. G. Bickley *et al.* (book review). *Bull. Am. math. Soc.* **59**, 189–191.

(105) Funzioni epicicliodali. *Atti Accad. naz. Lincei Rc.* (8) **14**, 393–394.

(106) (With H. F. Bohnenblust *et al.*) Asymptotic solutions of differential equations with turning points. Review of the literature. *Technical Report* 1, ref. no. NR 043–121. Pasadena: Cal. Inst. Tech.

(107) 1954 'Lezioni sulle funzioni ipergeometriche confluenti' by F. G. Tricomi. 'Die konfluente hypergeometrische Funktion mit besonderer Berucksichtigung ihrer Anwendendungen' by Herbert Buchholz (book review). *Bull. Am. math. Soc.* **60**, 185–189.

(108) (With C. H. Papas) On diffraction by a strip. *Proc. natn Acad. Sci. U.S.A.* **40**, 128–132.

(109) 1954 (With M. Kennedy & J. L. McGregor) Parabolic cylinder functions of large order. *J. ration. Mech. Anal.* **3**, 459–485.

(110) 'Hypergeometric and Legendre functions with application to integral equations of potential theory' by Chester Snow (book review). *Bull. Am. math. Soc.* **60**, 580–582.

(111) On a generalization of the Laplace transformation. *Proc. Edinb. math. Soc.* (2) **10**, 53–55.

(112) 1955 (With M. Kennedy, J. L. McGregor & C. A. Swanson) Asymptotic forms of Coulomb wave functions, I. *Technical Report* 4, ref. no. NR 043–121. Pasadena (29 pages.)

(113) Asymptotic representations of Fourier integrals and the method of stationary phase. *J. Soc. ind. appl. Math.* **3**, 17–27.

(114) (With C. A. Swanson) Asymptotic forms of Coulomb wave functions, II. *Technical Report* 5, ref. no. NR 043–121. Pasadena (24 pages.)

(115) Differential equations with transition points. I. The first approximation. *Technical Report* 6, ref. no. NR 043–121. Pasadena (22 pages.)

(116) Review of F. G. Tricomi's book 'Funzioni ipergeometriche confluenti'. *Bull. Am. math. Soc.* **61**, 456–460.

(117) 1956 Asymptotic factorization of ordinary linear differential operators containing a large parameter. *Technical Report* 8. Pasadena (25 pages.)

(118) Asymptotic expansions of Fourier integrals involving logarithmic singularities. *J. Soc. ind. appl. Math.* **4**, 38–47.

(119) Singularities of generalized axially symmetric potentials. *Communs Pure appl. Math.* IX, 403–414.

(120) Asymptotic solutions of differential equations with transition points. *Proc. Int. Congr. Math.* **3**, 92–101.

(121) 1957 (With C. A. Swanson) Asymptotic forms of Whittaker's confluent hypergeometric functions. *Memoirs, Amer. Math. Soc.* no. 25, 1–49.

(122) 1958 (With E. T. Copson) On a partial differential equation with two singular lines. *Archs Ration. Mech. Analysis* **2**, 76–86.

(123) 1959 On the principle of stationary phase. *Proc. Fourth Can. Math. Congr. Toronto*, pp. 137–146.

(124) 1960 Asymptotic solutions of differential equations with transition points or singularities. *J. math. Phys.* **1**, 16–26.

(125) Elliptic function and integral. *McGraw-Hill encyclopedia of science and technology* pp. 561–563.

(126) Spherical harmonics. *McGraw-Hill encyclopedia of science and technology* pp. 609–611.

(127) General asymptotic expansions of Laplace integrals. *MRC tech. Summ. Rep.* no. 188. Mathematics Research Centre, U.S. Army, University of Wisconsin, Madison (38 pages).

(128) Singular Volterra integral equations and their use in asymptotic expansions. *MRC tech. Summ. Rep.* no. 194. Mathematics Research Centre, U.S. Army, University of Wisconsin, Madison, Wisconsin (87 pages).

(129) Asymptotic forms for Laguerre polynomials. *J. Indian math. Soc.* **24**, 235–250.

(130) 1960–61 An expansion procedure for singular perturbations. *Atti Accad. Sci., Torino* **95**, 651–672.

(131) 1961 From delta functions to distributions. In *Modern mathematics for the engineer*, second series (ed. E. F. Beckenbach), pp. 5–50. McGraw-Hill.

(132) General asymptotic expansions of Laplace integrals. *Archs ration. Mech. Anal.* **7**, 1–20.

(133) Review of F. G. Tricomi's book 'Vorlesungen ueber Orthogonalreihen'. *Bull. Am. math. Soc.* **67**, 447–449.

(134) Asymptotic solutions of ordinary differential equations. (Mimeographed.) California Institute of Technology. (75 pages).

(135) 1962 An example in singular perturbations. *Mh. Math.* **66**, 123–128.

(136) Review of 'Transzendente Funktionen' by A. Kratzer & W. Franz. *Bull. Am. math. Soc.* **68**, 51–55.

(137) Singular perturbations. *Bull. Am. Math. Soc.* **68**, 420–424.

(138) 1962 On a problem in singular perturbations. *Report on the 2nd Summer Research Institute of the Australian Mathematical Society*, pp. 11–21.

(139) (With I. N. Sneddon) Fractional integration and dual integral equations. *Can. J. Math.* **14**, 685–693.

(140) A result on non-linear Volterra integral equations. In *Studies in mathematical analysis and related topics* (*essays in honour of George Polya*), pp. 104–109. Stanford University Press.

(141) On a nonlinear boundary value problem involving a small parameter. *J. Aust. math. Soc.* **2**, 425–439.

(142) 1963 Review of 'Polynomials orthogonal on a circle and interval' by Ya. L. Geronimus. *Scr. Math.* **26**, 264–265.

(143) Note on a paper by Titchmarsh. *Q. Jl Math.* (2) **14**, 147–152.

(144) Singular perturbations of boundary value problems involving ordinary differential equations. *J. Soc. ind. appl. Math.* **11**, 105–116.

(145) An integral equation involving Legendre's polynomial. *Am. math. Mon.* **70**, 651–652.

(146) Some applications of fractional integration. *Mathematical Note, Boeing Scientific Research Laboratories*, no. 316. (23 pages.)

(147) An extension of the concept of real number. *Proc. Fifth Can. math. Congr.* pp. 173–183.

(148) Remarks at a Research Policy seminar. *Proc. Fifth Can. math. Congr.* pp. 82–86.

(149) (With M. Wyman) The asymptotic evaluation of certain integrals. *Archs ration. mech. Anal.* **14**, 217–260.

(150) (With R. P. Gillespie) Thomas Murray MacRobert (obituary notice). *Proc. Glasg. math. Ass.* **6**, 57–64.

(151) 1964 An integral equation involving Legendre functions. *J. Soc. ind. appl. Math.* **12**, 15–30.

(152) The integral equations of asymptotic theory. In *Asymptotic solutions of differential equations and their applications* (ed. Calvin H. Wilcox), pp. 211–229.

(153) Review of 'Les transformations intégrales à plusieurs variables et leurs applications' by Mlle Huguette Delavault. *Scr. Math.* **27**, 173.

(154) 1965 An application of fractional integrals. *J. Analyse math.* **14**, 113–126.

(155) Axially symmetric potentials and fractional integration. *J. Soc. ind. appl. Maths.* **13**, 216–229.

(156) 1967 Some integral equations involving finite parts of divergent integrals. *Glasg. math. J.* **8**, part 1, 50–54.

(157) Review of 'Partial differential equations of parabolic type' by Avner Friedman 1964 (Prentice-Hall). *Mathl Gaz.*

(158) Two-variable expansions for singular perturbations. *Report, College of Engineering, State University of New York at Stony Brook*, no. 86.

(159) 1968 Two-variable expansions for singular perturbations. *J. Inst. Maths. Applics.* **4**, 113–119.

(160) Approximate solutions of a nonlinear boundary value problem. *Archs ration. Mech. Anal.* **29**, 1–17.

(161) Some dual integral equations. *SIAM J. Appl. Math.* **16**, 1338–1340.

(162) 1969 Review of 'Formulaire pour le calcul opérationnel' by V. A. Ditkin & A. P. Prudnikov, 1967 (Masson & Cie, Paris). *Mathl Gaz.* **53**, 110–111.

(163) 1970 Uniform asymptotic expansion of integrals. In *Analytic methods in mathematical physics* (eds R. P. Gilbert & R. G. Newton), pp. 149–168. Gordon & Breach.

(164) On the Euler–Poisson–Darboux equation. *J. Analyse Math.* **23**, 89–102.

(165) Reviews of 'Special functions for scientists and engineers' by W. W. Bell and 'Basic equations and special functions of mathematical physics' by V. Ya. Arsenin, translated from the Russian by S. Chomet. *Mathl Gaz.* **54**, 97–98.

(166) Lectures on Generalized functions and integral transformations. In *Report on the 10th Summer Research Institute of the Australian Mathematical Society*, pp. 20–44.

(167) (With A. C. McBride) Fractional integrals of distribution. *SIAM J. Math. Anal.* **1**, 547–557.

(168) 1972 Reviews: 'The functions of mathematical physics' by Harry Hochstadt and 'Solved problems in analysis' by O. J. Farrell & Bertram Ross. *Mathl Gaz.* **56**, 354–355.

(169) 1972 Fractional integrals of generalised functions. *J. Aust. math. Soc.* **14**, 30–37.
(170) 1974 Asymptotic evaluation of integrals involving a fractional derivative. *SIAM J. Math. Anal.* **5**, 159–171.
(171) 1975 Fractional integrals of generalised functions. In *Fractional calculus and its applications* (ed. B. Ross), Springer Verlag Lecture Notes in Mathematics, no. 457, 151–170.
(172) A case history in singular perturbations. In *International conference on differention equations* (ed. H. A. Antosiewicz), pp. 266–286. New York: Academic Press.
(173) Fourier transforms of integrable generalized functions. *Philips Res. Rep.* **30**, 23–30.
(174) 1976 Review of 'Constructive methods for elliptic equations' by R. P. Gilbert. *Bull. Am. math. Soc.* **81**, 1036–1037.
(175) Singular perturbations. In *Trends in applications of pure mathematics to mechanics* (ed. G. Fichera), pp. 53–62. London: Pitman Publishing.
(176) 1977 Stieltjes transforms of generalized function. *Proc. R. Soc. Edinb.* **76A**, 221–249.
(177) 1978 An extension of a Hardy–Littlewood–Polya inequality. *Proc. Edinb. math. Soc.* **21**, 11–15.
(178) The Stieljes transformation on weighted $L_p$ spaces. *App. Anal.* **7**, 213–219.

BOOKS

(179) 1953–55 (With W. MAGNUS, F. OBERHETTINGER & F. G. TRICOMI) *Higher transcendental functions*, 3 volumes. New York: McGraw-Hill.
1965–66 Russian translation.
(180) 1954 (With W. MAGNUS, F. OBERHETTINGER & F. G. TRICOMI) *Tables of integral transforms*, 2 volumes. New York: McGraw-Hill.
(181) 1955 *Asymptotic expansions*. Pasadena: Cal. Inst. Tech.
1956 Dover.
1962 Russian translation.
1967 Polish translation.
(182) 1962 *Operational calculus and generalized functions*. New York: Holt, Rinehart and Winston.
1971 French translation.

Francis C. Fraser

# FRANCIS CHARLES FRASER

16 June 1903 — 21 October 1978

Elected F.R.S. 1966

By N. B. Marshall, F.R.S.

Francis Charles Fraser, internationally respected as a leading authority on whales, dolphins and porpoises, spent most of his career (1933–69) in the British Museum (Natural History). His introduction to cetology could not have been better. From 1925 to 1933 he was a zoologist on '*Discovery* Investigations', charged with the main task of studying the life and death of whales in relation to their physical and biological surroundings in the Southern Ocean. Fraser's *Discovery* research, as will be seen, was considerably more than that represented in his definitive study on the development of krill (*Euphausia superba*), the food of the large baleen whales. His publications from the Museum were almost entirely concerned with cetaceans. That he was able to pursue this research, despite the heavy and increasing demands of museum and other duties, was due to his adroitness as an organizer and the disciplined way he divided his time. There was also his determination, which matched his sturdy figure. His personal qualities will emerge as this memoir proceeds. But it is right now to say that many remember him with affection and miss the warmth of his company.

## Early days

Francis Charles Fraser, born 16 June 1903, was the youngest son of James and Barbara Anne Fraser. There were six boys and four girls in the family. His father was a master-saddler with a business (founded 1817) in Dingwall, Ross and Cromarty, Scotland. Like his brothers and sisters, Francis went to school from infants to Higher Leaving Certificate grades at Dingwall Academy, where, writes his brother Robert ('Roy') Fraser: 'Homework was plentiful and in his family it was seen to that it was done. One might have an hour or so free before tea (5.0 p.m.) and then homework was the rule and I can't remember that there was any expressed objection to that.'

Francis was seven when his father died. The management of the business then passed to the second son (Louie), who was barely out of his apprenticeship. The oldest son, James, had already gone to university. Like his two brothers just older than himself, Francis had to do his stint in the saddling and harness workshop, where hands were most busy just before harvest time. Here beside learning the skills of 'Fraser the Saddler', he learnt something else. The men in the saddler's shop used to tease him by saying that Francis was a 'lassie's name' (there was a girl, Frances, daughter of the next door shop owner). And, as his brother Robert writes: 'Francis stoutly renounced her appellation, saying, "My name's Peter." And that stuck. To me and most members of the family he was Peter. At university he was Peter, sometimes Francis Peter by those who thought that really was his name.'

Robert also recalls: 'As a child he heard someone say that he had a face like an angel. So he dubbed himself Francis Charles Gabriel Fraser. That did not stick. He wasn't quite an angel.'

## University days

In 1921, Francis Fraser went straight from school to Glasgow University, where he attended classes in various departments including botany (Professor F. O. Bower), zoology (Professor J. Graham Kerr), geology (Professor J. W. Gregory) and natural philosophy (Professor Andrew Young). He admired Professor Bower's approach to plants through functional morphology and certainly obtained a good grounding in zoology (though he once said that Graham Kerr placed too much emphasis on lung fishes). While at university he was a member of the Shinty Club and frequently played in the first twelve. Despite injuries, he much enjoyed this boisterous Highland kind of hockey.

At Glasgow University he was joined by his brother Robert, who had served in the army for two years. Robert writes that they '. . . went through university together and enjoyed graduating on the same day—he as B.Sc. "Pure Science" and his brother as B.Sc. "Engineering" (not so pure!). It amused them too that Francis graduated a few minutes before his older brother' (in 1924).

## *Discovery* days

After a year as Demonstrator in the Department of Geology, Glasgow University, Francis Fraser was appointed zoologist to '*Discovery* Investigations'. This research organization arose from the recommendations of an interdepartmental committee set up in 1917 by the Secretary of State for the Colonies to advise him on research and development in the Dependencies of the Falkland Islands. During World War I the number of licences granted by the Dependencies to whaling companies had been relaxed, for whale oil was used to provide glycerine for munitions. Whale stocks in the Dependencies might well be endangered at the end of the war. Thus, the terms of reference of the committee were: 'To consider what can now be done to facilitate prompt action at the conclusion of the war in regard to the preservation of the whaling industry and to the development of other industries in the Dependencies of the Falkland Islands; and to consider not only the economic questions above referred to, and to scheme for the employment of a research vessel, but also what purely scientific investigations are most required in connection with these regions and whether any preliminary inquiries by experts in this country should be instituted.'

As Fraser (1964) wrote: 'Within this precise official statement lies the germ of a new phase of Antarctic discovery, lacking the glamour and public appeal that goes hand in hand with geographical exploration but in natural sequence to it, and from the point of view of the advancement of knowledge, of equal rank. For the first time in the history of the Antarctic, investigations were to be made into its biology as a main objective and not as a subsidiary to some other principal activity.'

The germ took form in 1923 with the purchase from the Hudson Bay Company of the *Discovery*, the ship originally built for the National Antarctic Expedition (1901–3) of which Captain (then Lieutenant) R. F. Scott was leader. The *Discovery* was extensively refitted for her new work.

Dr Stanley Kemp was appointed Leader of the Expedition and Director of Research. Fraser was appointed as zoologist in 1925. When he told Kemp that his first name was Francis, he was told: 'We've got one of those already; you'll be Jimmie.' Later, this was more elegantly changed to 'James' by Anne, his wife. They were married in 1938.

The Royal Research Ship *Discovery* eventually sailed for the south on 5 October 1925. Before she sailed, an advance party consisting of N. A. Mackintosh (in charge), L. H. Matthews, J. F. G. Wheeler and A. J. Clowes had left for South Georgia the previous autumn. After establishing themselves in the newly built Marine Station at Grytviken, South Georgia, their task was to make a start on whale research during the coming season.

'Jimmie' Fraser did not sail with the *Discovery*. He and another recently appointed zoologist, David Dilwyn John, awaited the maiden voyage of R.S.S. *William Scoresby*, a full powered steamship of whale-catcher type specially built for *Discovery* Investigations.

The *Scoresby*, as Sir Alister Hardy (1967) wrote, was built '. . . to satisfy three distinct purposes: whale-hunter, trawler and research ship. She has the whaler's look-out barrel at the mast-head, her built-up bow (for firing marking darts instead of harpoons) and a good turn of speed (12 knots). On her port side she is a trawler with the typical steel gallows fore and aft for handling the otter boards of a full-sized commercial trawl; and she is equipped, of course, with the necessary powerful winch. On her starboard side she is the research ship with the small winches and davits similar to those on the *Discovery* for operating water sampling bottles and plankton nets, but without the outboard platforms which are not necessary.'

To devise suitable means for whale marking, the *Discovery* Committee had the valuable help and advice of the distinguished Norwegian oceanographer and biologist, Johan Hjort. Their first trials were with a cross-bow. Fraser (1964) was charmed to recall: 'One has the mental picture of three men in the garden of a London square, behind the Natural History Museum, practising with a cross-bow and firing arrows into a piece of whale blubber. Here was the other end of the link between Aristotle's dolphin tail nicking and the twentieth century. The three men were J. T. Hjort, Sir Sidney Harmer and the senior scientist of *Discovery* Investigations, now Sir Alister Hardy. They carried out many experiments to find the most satisfactory method of marking whales and finally decided on a shoulder harpoon gun which fired a shafted, enlarged drawing-pin-like mark into the blubber of the whale. This, however, was later replaced by an improved form of stout pencil shape, which continues to be used. Old harpoons of unfamiliar design recovered from whales killed in the Arctic contributed to the idea of marking whales and, of course, the tagging of fish had been practised for many years before whale marking was considered. The positions of firing and recovery of these markes give the most precise evidence of the movements of whales in the ocean; the data they furnish give information of a kind not available at present by any other method.'

Before Fraser and John sailed in the *William Scoresby* they were busy assembling and checking the scientific equipment. On 1 August 1926 they arrived at Simonstown, South Africa, and later were no doubt happy to meet their colleagues on *Discovery* at Cape Town (the *Discovery* had reached South Georgia on 20 January 1926, and after a stay and investigations round the island, sailed northwards towards South Africa to work more biological and hydrographical stations). At Cape Town John transferred to *Discovery*, while Fraser continued southward on the *William Scoresby*. Later, in South Georgia he joined the *Discovery*, where he stayed until the end of her first commission.

During Fraser's time on *Discovery* much of his work aboard was to assist in the setting, shooting and hauling of the plankton nets and then to fix and preserve the catches. There is an enchanting photograph* facing p. 304 of Sir Alister Hardy's 1967 book *Great waters* with this caption: 'Working a vertical net on the *Discovery*. F. C. Fraser is on the outboard platform adjusting the net before it goes down and the author is at the winch ready to let it out and to control its speed of hauling with stop watch and depth recording wheel.' One sees the upright Sherlock Holmesian figure of Alister Hardy (with deer-stalker ? hat), and above the rail the head and shoulders of the intent Jimmie Fraser, topped by a trilby hat. When writing of the plankton stations, Sir Alister acknowledges the magnificent work of his fellow zoologists Rolfe Gunther and Jimmie Fraser.

After a period at home, Fraser returned south late in 1927 to take charge of the Marine Biological Station at Grytviken, South Georgia, where '. . . for a period of years a succession of biologists kept pace in the observations on whales with the catch coming into the whaling station. Thousands of whales, blue, fin, sei, humpback and sperm, were measured, sexed and examined externally and internally. Observations were made on colour, baleen plates, ventral grooves, stomach contents, internal and external parasites, reproductive condition, chronological incidence of the catch and relative abundance of the species represented. Samples of testes were sectioned for histological examination and corpora lutea in ovaries counted. Foetuses were measured and the date of their finding noted. As with the results obtained by the pre-Linnean anatomists, much of what was established by these biologists has come to be acceptable matter of fact by those who followed, and used as the basis for further investigation and for development of new lines of research' (Fraser 1964).

At Grytriken he was soon joined by his fellow zoologist, D. Dilwyn John, who writes: 'Fraser was from the beginning my particular friend and confidant. . . . I enjoyed the qualities you will know of: his humour, his friendliness, his

* The photograph originally appeared as Plate XI, Fig. 1 in Kemp, Hardy & Mackintosh (1929).

full and "giving" membership of a small community, his delight in seeing animals new to him and in learning about them. I respected his capacity for hard and, on the flensing platform, unpleasant work, and admired his tact in managing those working under his charge.'

He returned home in April 1929 with D. Dilwyn John and G. E. R. Deacon on the Norwegian transport ship *Peder Bogen*. After his return it was not long (December 1929) before he went south again, this time on a fine new research vessel, the R.R.S. *Discovery II*, on her first commission. Stanley Kemp (1932) wrote: 'Our new ship, the R.R.S. *Discovery II*, built in 1929, was specially designed for the Committee's work and has proved an unqualified success. Her comparatively high speed and very large bunker capacity have allowed us to use our time to better advantage, and we have been able to put through scientific programmes far more expeditiously than before.' During her first commission from 1929 to 1931 these programmes were centred in the Atlantic sector of the Southern Ocean.

The work of '*Discovery* Investigations', guided by Dr Stanley Kemp, attained a high standard. The cruises had to be carefully and fully planned (in the light of past findings) so as to increase and improve the vertical and horizontal coverage of the oceanic region to be investigated, both hydrographically and biologically. In the vertical plane an invaluable feature of the biological investigations was the frequent use of closing devices on the nets. Indeed, the smaller nets (mouth diameter of 70 or 100 cm) were, with few exceptions, closed (by a messenger activating the closing mechanism) before they were hauled. The biologists were concerned particularly to catch young and adult krill, and they found that oblique or horizontal tows generally yielded better catches than those made vertically. At a given station a series of hauls at or between different depth levels, guided by length of wire and depth gauge, enabled the biologists, after quantitative analysis of the samples, to plot the distribution in depth of a particular organism.

Many of the catches contained the young stages of krill (*Euphausia superba*), the shrimp-like organisms well known to whaling men as prime whale food. Moreover, the early work of L. H. Matthews, N. A. Mackintosh and J. F. G. Wheeler at the Marine Station on South Georgia showed clearly that krill is almost exclusively the food of blue, fin and humpback whales in southern waters. But little was then known of the life history of krill, the investigation of which was entrusted to Fraser.

## The life of krill

Fraser's (1936) *Discovery Report* on his research, entitled 'On the development and distribution of the young stages of krill (*Euphausia superba*)', was completed after his appointment (in 1933) to the scientific staff of the British Museum (Natural History). The material at his disposal was taken between 1927 and 1931 and came largely from the Atlantic sector of the Southern Ocean. In all there were enough samples to trace the development of krill during the first 15 months of its growth.

The opening main section of this definitive report is given to careful description, fine illustration and critical analysis of the various young stages of krill: eggs, first nauplius, second nauplius, metanauplius, first calyptopis, second calyptopis, third calyptopis and furcilia. Most of these stages were clearly recognizable but there were two outstanding problems concerning the furcilia. Fraser's observations, like those of Macdonald (1927) on a northern euphausiid, *Meganyctiphanes norvegica*, showed clearly that '. . . distinctive stages nearly always seem to occur as though certain stages are dominant' (in numbers of individuals). In both species there were two dominant furcilia phases and the earlier could be related to the later through changes in the complement and structure of the swimming legs (pleopods) on the abdomen. 'The less advanced dominant phase becomes in each species the more advanced by the provision of setae on the non-setose pleopods present in the earlier stage and the addition of one or more pairs of non-setose pleopods.' Indeed, '. . . in the light of the data supplied by the present material and the interpretation of known larval histories the actual number of stages in early furcilia development is much smaller than previously acknowledged'.

The other outstanding problem concerned the end of the furcilia phase. The stages just before the change to the adolescent phase had been given the name cyrtopia by certain earlier investigators. In their scheme the last furcilia were distinguished from the cyrtopia stages by the setting and structure of the antennae. In the former the antennae had an unjointed flagellum and their lateral direction was correlated with their use as swimming legs; in the latter stages these appendages were directed forward and bore a jointed flagellum. But Fraser's analysis led him to abandon the term cyrtopia. 'Considering the indefinite nature of later euphausian development, which has already been demonstrated . . . it seems that the recognition of the cyrtopia places too much stress on the alteration of form and function of one particular appendage. The larvae designated Cyrtopia are not recognizable from Furcilia by any sudden increase as they change from the old to the altered form. The change in the antenna does not necessarily coincide with equally significant changes in the form of other appendages . . . .'

Fraser concluded by distinguishing six furcilia stages: the first with non-setose pleopods; the second with setose pleopods (up to five pairs); the third with all the pleopods setose and a seven-spined telson; the fourth, fifth and sixth with respectively five, three and one terminal spines on the telson. Dilwyn John, who had also joined the scientific staff of the B.M.(N.H.) and whose fine *Discovery Report* on 'The Southern species of the genus *Euphausia*' follows immediately after Fraser's, found good reason to support his colleague's conclusions on the life history stages of euphausiids.

During his analysis of young krill, Fraser found that some of the larvae in their second season were considerably larger than the majority. Dilwyn John's suggestion was that the larger larvae might have fed on the rich diatom flora for longer periods than had the smaller. When Fraser plotted the average length of adolescent krill against the abundance of a dominant diatom,

*Thalassiosira antarctica* at a number of stations, it certainly looked as though growth was greatest where the populations of this diatom were most dense. The overall growth curve indicated that young krill reach a length of 10 mm by the end of their first summer season. At the end of the first year or 14 months they grew to over 24 mm in length. But the growth rate was not regular, being retarded during the winter months.

Study of the distribution in time of larval and adolescent krill led him to an important conclusion. The eggs were taken over a period of 4½ months, mostly during the earlier part of the summer; the calyptopis and early furcilia stages were predominant from January onwards, but were not found at the beginning of the next summer season; the later furcilia were prominent in the second half of the summer and a few were taken after the winter. The adolescents were recorded over a still greater period of time. Thus, '. . . the wide range of time in which the older forms are found is important ecologically as it ensures a constant supply of food for the whalebone whales of the South'.

Lastly, his analysis of the vertical distribution and migrations of the young stages seemed to have implications concerning the distribution and maintenance of krill stocks. After considering the distribution of eggs, nauplii and metanauplii at depth below the surface waters, the diurnal vertical migrations of calyptopis and earlier furcilia stages in the warm deep water and Antarctic surface waters, and the persistent presence of adolescents at the surface, he postulated '. . . that the continued abundance of *E. superba* in Antarctic waters and the replenishment of the stock of adolescents at the ice-edge is brought about by the rotary movement resulting from the assemblage of the earlier development stages chiefly in the southward flowing warm deep water and that of the later stages in the northward flowing Antarctic surface water. This movement is suggested as an alternative to the hypothesis which involves the return of adults to ice-edge by rotary movements in the surface water alone.'

While forming his hypothesis, Fraser consulted his colleague, Mr G. E. R. Deacon, whose '. . . valuable help where hydrographical problems are concerned . . .' is acknowledged. There were also acknowledgements to Dr S. W. Kemp, F.R.S., for much helpful criticism and advice. The assistance of Dr W. T. Calman, F.R.S. (then Keeper of Zoology at the Natural History Museum and whose knowledge of the Crustacea was unrivalled), and that of his former *Discovery* colleagues, Dr N. A. Mackintosh and Dr Helene Bargmann, is also acknowledged.

When presenting his understanding of euphausiid life histories in a paper read to the Linnean Society, Fraser (1937) returned especially to his conception of evolutionary trends in modes of development. In Crustacea generally, Gurney (1924) had contrasted a primitive, continuous mode of larval development with the marked metamorphosis of more advanced forms. Fraser regarded the euphausiids as falling somewhere between the two extremes. They are arthropods in which 'continuous' development (with numerous moults and slight change at each one) is giving way to metamorphosis (with a reduced number of moults, each marked by considerable change). Such metamorphosis is well marked in the nauplius, metanauplius and calyptopis stages, but is less well defined in the early furcilia (owing to the presence of dominant forms), and becomes still less discernible in the later stages of development.

He continued: 'There is a further consideration to which attention may be drawn. In the more specialized forms with fewer ecdyses the position of each moult on the scale of development, and therefore the changes occurring at each, becomes as it were standardized. In the more primitive cases with so-called "continuous" development the position of the moult may vary and the changes at each one are not always identical. The series of moults may, in fact, be regarded as a kind of "grid" superposed on the course of actually continuous development. In the more primitive cases this grid may still shift slightly backwards and forwards; in the more specialized cases the "grid" has become fixed and all individuals show the same changes at each moult.'

Robert Gurney (1942), whose knowledge of crustacean development was unmatched, became intrigued by Fraser's concept of a 'grid'. But his review of euphausiids led him to conclude that inconstancy in development or shifting of the grid is found only in certain species that cannot be judged more primitive than others in which such variability is absent. Indeed, variability is exceptional and as a specific character is inexplicable. He wrote:

> 'As I understand it, a shifting grid implies a series of fixed compartments, through which portions of a continuous background can be seen, and these compartments must be fixed in area and represent fixed units of development. A shifting of such a grid would only cause different parts of the background to be picked out in each compartment, and could not effect any rearrangement of the sequence of the elements of the background.'
>
> 'The development of *Euphausia superba* seems to fulfil the postulated conditions. Without the remarkably thorough study of a large material which Fraser has made it would have been difficult to delimit certain stages, since, as his figures show, every possible gradation in development of the appendages can be found, and it is only by giving weight to certain points, such as the number of spines on the telson and number of setose pleopods, and establishing the frequency of combinations of certain characters, that a grouping can be made. All the appendages of head, thorax and abdomen, "keep step" in development and it could be said with reason that the conception of a grid with six compartments shifting slightly to and fro across a continuous background would agree with the facts.'

After acknowledging that Fraser's work on *Euphausia superba* is the most complete study of development in a euphausiid that we have, Gurney considered it to be '. . . an exceptional species, partly by reason of the great individual variability, and partly from the very early development of the thoracic appendages'. Moreover, after comparing the development of euphausiids and decapod crustaceans, he thought it right to retain the earlier distinction of a cyrtopia stage as the first of the post-larval series of changes towards the adult form.

But later comparison of development in *E. superba* with that of other euphausiids, particularly with species of the same genus, led Mauchline and

Fisher (1969) to conclude that there are few variant forms in this species. And, like other modern students of the euphausiids, they do not distinguish a cyrtopia stage. Such larvae are included with phase 4 larvae as furcilia. Indeed, Mauchline's (1959) designation of four phases in the series of furcilia stages is essentially similar to that proposed by Fraser (if one groups his stages 4, 5 and 6 in Mauchline's phase 4).

To conclude Fraser's major contribution to euphausiid biology, how far has his rotary hypothesis concerning the distribution of krill populations been supported? For much of the macroplankton a northerly drift in the surface waters followed, after descending migrations, by a southerly return in warm deep water is seen now as an underlying means of containing and maintaining distributions (Mackintosh 1937, Foxton 1964). But for *Euphausia superba* there is still much uncertainty, even in the relatively well sampled Atlantic sector. Changes in the vertical distribution of krill, whether seasonal or developmental, have yet to be properly traced. In his monumental *Discovery Report* on krill, Marr (1964) concluded: 'On the Atlantic or Weddell side of Antarctica the only mechanism we can see clearly working to maintain the krill population within its normal geographic limits is the eastward and southward dispersal of the very early larvae as they rise towards the surface through the warm deep layer.' Recently, with this problem in mind, Deacon (1976) remarked that it will not be solved until we know more about the surface currents and the rates of transport in the deeper layer of the Weddell Sea.

For his part in the exploration of Antarctica, Fraser was awarded the Polar Medal in 1942. There was also his personal contribution. Dilwyn John writes: 'I think—I have told Anne this—that he was the most well-liked of all the *Discovery* scientists. This was reflected in the fact (I believe it to be so) that in after years none of them visited the Museum without going to his room—and that welcoming smile met them.'

## Museum career

Francis Fraser joined the staff of the British Museum (Natural History) in 1933 as an Assistant Keeper in the Department of Zoology. He was assigned to the Osteological Room, which houses the skeletons of Mammalia. Here, as will be seen, he was confronted by a daunting disarray. Perhaps he entertained nostalgic memories of *Discovery* days; he was a good sailor and much at home in a ship. But sea-going soon came his way once more, as told by Sir Frederick Russell:

> 'In January 1933 Col. E. T. Peel (later Sir Edward), of the cotton firm in Alexandria, Egypt, invited W. P. Pyecraft of the British Museum (Nat. Hist.) to take part in a cruise to the Faroe Isles "for the purpose of investigating the movements of the tunny". Pyecraft declined and wrote to E. J. Allen, Director of the Plymouth laboratory, suggesting that he might like to go. Allen kindly gave me the chance instead. Very soon after I heard from F. C. Fraser that he was applying for leave of absence to the Trustees so that he might accompany the cruise to get dolphins for the Museum.

'We joined the 350 ton M.Y. *St. George* at Southampton on July 3rd. Although luxurious in our eyes she proved extremely seaworthy, being designed on the lines of a trawler with a high foc'sle deck. I had not met Fraser before but I at once realised that I was to have a delightful and good humoured companion. We were to pick Col. Peel up at Scarborough on July 5th and his friend Col. Stapleton Cotton a couple of days later at Peterhead. While we were at Peterhead I remember Francis Fraser visiting an old whaling captain with whom he enjoyed a talk about the early days of whaling.

'We then set course for the Faroes. The venture proved a useful scientific cruise. We took water samples, collected plankton and released drift bottles en route. We arrived at Thorshaven on July 10 where Francis talked with fishermen about whaling, and then visited the whaling station and factory at Lopri. On the islands we collected birds and snails for the Museum. We sighted a school of pilot whales. We returned from the Faroes to the Shetland Isles where a lesser rorqual was seen. We visited Loch Eriboll and arrived back at Peterhead on July 16 for a week of dolphin hunting. The yacht would cruise slowly ahead with shoals of dolphins in and around the bow wave. Col. Cotton, with a small harpoon gun, sitting in the bows of a dinghy with outboard motor gave chase. After many attempts two dolphins were secured—a white nosed dolphin 7 ft 6 in [2.3 m] long and a common dolphin of 6 ft 10 in [2.1 m].

'By now the tunny were being reported as numerous in the North Sea and we went south to North Berwick where I have vivid memories of seeing the two dolphins wrapped in sacking taken away in a lorry for rail transport to London. After this Francis and I climbed Berwick Law and he left for home on July 28th. I returned to *St. George* for Scarborough, where the real work on tunny was to begin, after an enjoyable time with a kind and friendly cetacean expert who introduced me to a number of whales and dolphins I had never seen before.'

Fraser returned to the Osteological Room, where he studied and laboured until World War II, when he was seconded for service in the Admiralty.

When he returned to his duties in the Museum, there was soon to be another chance of sea-going, which came from the University of Copenhagen. As Professor R. Spärck (1950) recalled, a few days (in 1945) after the University had received the offer (from Mr Viggo Jarl) of his yacht *Atlantide* for a marine expedition (to West African waters), Professor A. V. Hill, then Foreign Secretary of the Royal Society, was visiting Copenhagen. Spärck approached A. V. to propose possible collaboration in the projected expedition between marine zoologists of Denmark and the British Museum (Natural History). The collaboration was to be in the form of Dr F. C. Fraser, who became a member of the Danish *Atlantide* Expedition to West Africa (during late 1945 and the first half of 1946). Though the expedition obtained but one dolphin (Fraser 1950), he became interested, as will be seen, in the sounds made by dolphins. His Danish zoologist colleagues much enjoyed his company, and he theirs.

And there were times when his good nature and sound advice were appreciated.

Fraser became Deputy Keeper of the Department of Zoology in 1948 and so did his friend and colleague, Dr D. Dilwyn John. In 1957 he was appointed Keeper of Zoology in succession to Dr H. W. Parker. He relinquished the keepership in 1964 in order to devote more time to his research. After his retirement in 1969 he regularly visited the Museum to continue his studies. He much appreciated the room that was allotted to him. It was near his beloved Whale Hall.

## The Whale Hall

When Fraser joined the Museum, there was a new whale hall, which had been completed in 1931. The first exhibit was of the skeleton of an 82 ft [25 m] blue whale. The skeleton came from an animal stranded in 1891 and as Fraser (1934) wrote, it had remained in the Osteological Room for 42 years for lack of space in which to exhibit it. Later he was concerned dimensionally and logistically with the magnificent cast of a 91 ft [28 m] blue whale, prepared by Mr P. Stammwitz and his son Stuart. They also prepared casts from dolphins stranded on British shores, which are mentioned elsewhere, as are certain of the fine exhibits prepared by P. E. Purves.

Under Fraser's guidance and administration the Whale Hall attained its present-day excellence. The blue whale cast is now suspended below the original exhibit and the skeletons of other whales. Around the hall and in part of the upper gallery are the casts of dolphins and porpoises. The upper gallery also houses exhibits on skeletal modifications in marine mammals, on cetacean anatomy, including some of the superb dissections by R. H. Burne (see Fraser 1952), locomotion, hearing organs, development and the oceanography of whale feeding grounds.

Today and every day, the Whale Hall attracts many visitors. Here is enchantment and education for children, diversion, at the very least, for their parents, and much for all manner of students, from young naturalists to serious cetologists.

## The Osteological Room

When Fraser began his duties in the Osteological Room in 1933, the state of the collection was not ship-shape and *Discovery* fashion. A. J. E. Cave, now Emeritus Professor of Anatomy, University of London, who worked in the Osteological Room during Fraser's period of curatorship and who became his friend, remembers vividly the early days.

Fraser had '. . . inherited a deplorable "dump" of extensive mammalian osteological material, inadequately housed (hence difficult of access) in ill lit, unkempt and somewhat depressing basement premises and long overdue for reorganization in keeping with modern practice'. Fraser was '. . . confronted therefore with an Augean task' which evoked his '. . . latent talent for order and organization. He initiated and sustained for years a well planned and vigorous programme of reorganization, which embraced: improved lighting and equipment of premises; improved maceration and labelling methods; installation of modern storage cabinets (and better conservation of specimens); a new, more informative and more convenient system of cataloguing; the multiplication of research facilities; the instructive supervision and encouragement of junior (professional and technical staff), and the adequate provision for future accessions.'

This programme transformed the Osteological Room '. . . into an active, efficient and reorganized centre of research, the Mecca of comparative and human anatomists, cetologists and others, from home and overseas. The prestige of the B.M.(N.H.) was enhanced in consequence.' Moreover, visitors to the Osteological Room were given '. . . a cordial welcome and indefatigable assistance in their enquiries, an important factor in the maximization of the Section's scientific potential'.

Fraser had two first class members on his staff, Miss Judith E. King (now Mrs Basil Marlow) and P. E. Purves, who later obtained his doctorate from Reading University. Beside their official duties, Fraser encouraged them to pursue their own lines of research, which included the study of soft anatomy. Mrs Marlow is now a world authority on seals and Dr Purves an outstanding student of the functional anatomy and hydrodynamics of cetaceans.

There was also his own research. His reorganization of the cetacean material enabled him to make special anatomical and morphometric studies, thus as Professor Cave writes, '. . . laying the foundation of his expertise in cetology and ultimate international reputation as arbiter of cetacean taxonomy'.

Cave concludes: 'In brief, by his curatorial supervision, infective enthusiasm for research and generous encouragement of colleagues, he transformed a depressing ossuary into an active and productive research centre for mammalian morphology and taxonomy.'

## The systematics of Cetacea

During and after his museum career nearly all of Fraser's publications were concerned with cetaceans. Indeed, five were published before the appearance of his *Discovery Report* on krill. The first is on Cetacea stranded on British coasts from 1927 to 1932. This and other such reports will be considered before his papers on individual species. In his last paper (1977) Fraser wrote:

> 'In Britain there is a long tradition of interest in cetology: John Ray . . . (1625–1705), Edward Tyson (1651–1708), John Hunter (1728–1793), Sir Richard Owen (1804–1892), Sir William Flower (1831–1899), Sir William Turner (1832–1916), to mention a few of the most accomplished.
>
> 'It may have been with this tradition in mind that Sir Sidney Harmer (1862–1950) coming to the British Museum (Natural History) in 1909 as Keeper of Zoology, resuscitated a personal interest in cetology that had been dormant from 1893 when, along with T. Southwell, he produced a paper 'Notes on a specimen of Sowerby's Whale (*Mesoplodon bidens*) stranded on the Norfolk coast'. Harmer was clearly aware of the potentially

rich source of information and material that stranded cetaceans could provide and through the Museum's Trustees negotiated an arrangement with the Board of Trade, the outcome of which was that in 1914 the first 'Report on the Cetacea stranded on the British coasts during 1913' was published. The Receivers of Wreck had been instructed by the Board of Trade at the request of the Trustees of the British Museum to send telegraphic reports of the stranding of specimens of whales to the Museum. They were provided by the Museum with a description sheet to help towards a provisional identification of animals stranded, together with a key for their specific determination. They were asked by the Museum to fill in a form partly descriptive, partly of measurements of the animal, but it was normally on the information received in the initial telegram from the reporting officer that the Museum decided its requirements in the way of a report, and the whole or some part of the animal—head, lower jaw, flipper, baleen—that could be of diagnostic use for specific determination or for anatomical purposes. The Museum was to pay the cost of securing, packing and forwarding the specimens and was permitted to pay a small honorarium to the officer actually involved in dealing with the stranding. Rail transport charges were under the salt-fish rate—an economically useful concession, even if anachronistic in relation to Linnean classification.

'Harmer continued to produce annual reports of strandings up to 1918, followed by biennial reports covering the next six years to 1924. In 1927 he produced his final report in which he covered the two years up to the end of 1926 and summarized the results of the period 1913–26. Subsequent to Harmer's retirement four reports were published covering the period 1927 to 1966 (Fraser 1934, 1946, 1953, 1974.)'

As Fraser continued: 'Advancement of cetological knowledge has been retarded over the years because of the inaccessibility of the animals themselves unless they are economically important'. Apart from the odd harpooned or netted individual, smaller cetaceans must be studied largely from stranded animals. There were also the studies of a few species in dolphinaria, where: 'The bottle-nosed dolphin has become the prima donna of the cetacean fraternity' (Hm!).

The records of stranding between 1913 and 1966 ranged in frequency from the common porpoise (*Phocoena phocoena*) (631 records) to the pygmy sperm whale (*Kogia breviceps*) and white whale (*Delphinapterus leucas*) (one record each). In his reports that covered in all the stranding of 22 species, Fraser was concerned not only with features of taxonomic interest (especially colour pattern, morphometric features, dentition and sexual features) but also with their derivation. He concluded '. . . that the British cetacean fauna is derived from populations that are partly world-wide in their distribution, partly more local and partly resident—the Common Porpoise. The North Atlantic provides the source of several species—Bottle-nosed Dolphin, Pilot Whale, Bottle-nosed Whale, Risso's Dolphin, Pygmy Sperm Whale and the implication of the North Atlantic Current and its branches is evident. The incidence of the

White-beaked and White-sided Dolphin and of the Narwhal, White Whale and Killer Whale is regarded as a manifestation of the peripheral role of British waters in a series of concentrations of population north of the British Isles. . . . All in all the "stranded whales" arrangement has led to a better conception of the composition and distribution of the British cetacean fauna and to the appreciation that about a quarter of all the known species of cetaceans throughout the world are to be found in British waters' (Fraser 1977). To help in the recognition and reporting of these species he prepared successive editions entitled, *Guide for the identification and reporting of stranded whales, dolphins and porpoises on the British coasts* (see Fraser and Parker,* 1949, 1953, Fraser 1969, 1976). There is also his book with his colleague J. R. Norman on *Giant fishes, whales and dolphins*', first published in 1937. They wrote the book mainly for travellers, seafaring men and sportsmen. There are many fine illustrations in colour and line by Lt-Col. W. P. C. Tenison and keys for the identification of the species concerned. Fraser's section on whales and dolphins is not only given to careful description of colour patterns and form but contains much on other aspects of their natural history. The book was, and still is, a valuable guide for marine observers.

There were further bounties from British beaches. All the 'British Dolphins' are exhibited in the Whale Hall of the Natural History Museum and they were cast from stranded animals. Stranded animals were also the source of the excellent exhibits of cetacean anatomy in the Whale Hall. In particular, there are preparations by Dr P. E. Purves of the middle ear air-sac system in various cetaceans by means of plastic injection. 'The preparation of the sacs in the Common Porpoise, Pilot Whale, White beaked Dolphin, Risso's Dolphin, Bottle-nosed Dolphin and Common Dolphin were all made possible by the availability of stranded whales material. Together with the other dissections associated with them they provide a unique morphological series relating to the way by which cetaceans hear' (Fraser 1977). Furthermore, such preparations and others were the basis of the outstanding work of Fraser and Purves on hearing in cetaceans.

There are some 60 species of cetaceans. This seems an easy assignment, but a cetologist needs more than one lifetime to make a proper systematic study of the Order. Much of the research on the larger kinds must fall to biologists concerned with whaling; the smaller forms tantalize the cetologist. Indeed, if to tantalize is to tease by keeping something desirable in view but out of reach, dolphins and porpoises seem to be arch tantalizers. As Fraser (1977) wrote: 'It is difficult to obtain a precise indication of the pigmentation patterns of living cetaceans in the sea. So little of the body is normally exposed above the surface of the water and then usually only momentarily that the impression is a fleeting one. Even when the cetaceans are dead and cast up on the beach, rapid decomposition and desiccation of the skin blur the finer details of pigmentation.' Even so, by one means or another, Fraser was able to make taxonomic studies on about half the known species of smaller cetaceans.

* The jointly authored guides contain a section on turtles by Dr H. W. Parker.

More often than not he had to be content with a skull. For instance, his 1950 paper on Hector's beaked whale, *Mesoplodon hectori* (Gray), was based on a skull collected on a Falkland Island beach by his old *Discovery* colleague Dr J. E. Hamilton, Government Naturalist to the Falkland Islands. After study of various morphometric features and the dentition, aided by radiographs, he found the skull compared well with the type specimen skull in the Museum collections. When he wrote, the species was known only from the above two specimens and one in the United States National Museum, of which there was no published description.

Even if no material was available, much might be learnt from photographs and sightings of easily recognizable species. Thus, early in 1952 three southern right whale dolphins (*Lissodelphis peroni* (Lacépède)) became stranded on the beach at Onekaka, Golden Bay, South Island, New Zealand. After they were filmed in colour, 'They were eventually returned to the sea and swam away, apparently none the worse for their temporary sojourn on dry land' (Fraser 1955). Study of these photographs and published records showed that *Lissodelphis peroni* was clearly distinguishable from its northern congener, *L. borealis*. Moreover, the charting of all records and sightings at sea indicated that the southern right whale dolphin '. . . probably ranges round the world in the southern hemisphere. Although it is not entirely restricted to the West Wind Drift, it appears to have some predilection for it, because . . . those records to the north of the Sub-tropical Convergence are for the most part close to that boundary, and except for one sight record, there is no evidence that it penetrates into the Antarctic Ocean' (Fraser 1955).

But one might find there was material enough for tangible and substantial study. Thus, the mass stranding of electra dolphins (*Peponocephala electra*) at Crowdy Heads, about 200 miles [320 km] north of Sydney, Australia, in August 1958 prompted the paper by Dawbin, Noble & Fraser (1970). There were between 150 and 250 animals in the school and evidently all came ashore. Good photographs were taken but as usual the carcases were soon removed. Fortunately one had fallen off a truck. The skull was removed by a local resident who generously gave it to Dawbin (in 1962). Dawbin also obtained a half skull from one animal stranded in the Port Macquarie area in January 1962. It had been used as bait in a fish trap. These two specimens, together with 10 others (5 from the B.M.(N.H.)), formed the basis of the joint paper. There was not only material enough to prepare a much needed and thorough redescription of the electra dolphin, but also to make a quantitative assessment of skull features. Topographical survey of four skulls of increasing age enabled them to trace the changes in skull form from birth to physical maturity and they also provided comparative notes on certain alternations in the axial skeleton with age. Their measurements of the skull indicated, *inter alia*, that brain growth is largely achieved in youth.

There was also a treasure in store, which came to Fraser's attention during a reorganization of the Museum's cetacean collection. It was a dolphin skeleton (registered number 1895.5.9) labelled 'White Porpoise ? *Lagenorhynchus* sp.

purchased from Dr. C. Hose, Lutong River, Baram, Borneo'. Like his predecessor, Sir Sidney Harmer, who had provisionally labelled the skeleton *Lagenorhynchus* sp., Fraser realized that the name *Sotalia borneensis* (the 'white dolphin' of Bornean waters) could not be applied to the skeleton from Sarawak. Indeed, the two forms were not even generically related. Close examination and description of this skeleton, followed by comparison with skeletons of *Lagenorhynchus*, *Delphinus* and *Lissodelphis* species, convinced Fraser that he was dealing with a new genus and species of dolphin. He named it *Lagenodelphis hosei*, Hose's Sarawak dolphin (Fraser 1956).

Dolphins display their colour patterns to each other rather than to man. Those of the genus *Stenella* are handsome animals with attractive markings that seem to be unique to each species. But, there may be specific variations in pigmentation pattern, as in Meyen's dolphin, *Stenella coeruleoalba*, the subject of a fine paper by Fraser & Noble (1972). In all they examined photographs and drawings of 24 individuals which came from the Western Mediterranean, the North Atlantic, the North Pacific and the western Indian Ocean. They concluded:

> 'Certain dolphins of the genus *Stenella* can be distinguished from the rest by the presence of a band of pigmentation, the main plimsoll line, running from the eye along the flank to the anal region. They can also be distinguished, in addition, by a promontory extending from the dorsal pigmentation antero-ventrally. There are subsidiary features which, in association with the main ones, provide a framework for the identification and classification of the animals concerned. Within this framework subtle differences of pattern occur, such as intensity of shading, definition, extent and orientation.
>
> 'No association of the variations recognized and described can be made with geographical distribution, sex or body length (age).
>
> 'The indications gained from examination of the pigmentation pattern are that the animals described can be included in one species for which the name of *Stenella coeruleoalba*, having priority, is available. The final distinction between *S. coeruleoalba* and other species of *Stenella* must be the result of the combined examination of external and osteological morphology.'

The caveat in the two last paragraphs is a reminder that systematic cetologists, more than most other systematists, have to live with uncertainty. Students of dolphins and porpoises may even have to be long suffering Micawbers. Fraser looked forward to revising the genus *Stenella*, which was 'in him' but was not to be. The selection of just four of his papers is to show the range of approach he needed to study the smaller cetaceans. As stated already, his papers cover about half of these forms. There was also his wide experience and inner fund of knowledge. His opinions were sought and freely given to cetologists all over the world. But he was well aware of the extent of ignorance concerning the smaller cetaceans. In his paper to the First Conference on Cetology held at Washington in 1964 he was concerned to stress (Fraser 1966):

'As compared with the commercially exploited baleen whales, the sperm whale or even the few commercially important delphinoids, the information available about the rest of the delphinoids is deplorably scanty. Although the overall number of species of living delphinoids is not very large, their identity in many instances has not been finally established, and their affinities with one another are still vague and uncertain. This state of affairs is owing in part to their perfect adaptation to the aquatic habitat, resulting in an extent of convergence which obscures indications of phylogenetic affinity, but it has come about because there has been no concentrated effort to obtain representative series of the animals (except as a by-product of commercial exploitation) to which modern taxonomic methods could be applied.'

## Hearing in cetaceans

During the voyage of the Danish *Atlantide* Expedition to West Africa, 1945–46, the sounds of dolphins were heard on several occasions. Fraser could not hear them, but they were described to him by Dr A. F. Bruun as high-pitched whistles. Moreover, dolphins were evidently sensitive to high-pitched notes, which was supported by an observation he did make on the *Atlantide*. 'On December 30th 1945, a school of about a hundred *Delphinus delphis* was near the ship in calm waters, splashing, diving and leaping vertically out of the water. The dolphins suddenly dashed away at great speed and their disappearance coincided with the switching on of the ship's supersonic echo-sounding machine. This sensitiveness to supersonic emissions was confirmed on a later occasion' (Fraser 1947).

By the time that Fraser and Purves (1954) presented their preliminary paper on hearing in cetaceans, there was considerable evidence that bottle-nosed dolphins both emitted trains of high frequency sound (creaking or clicking sound trains) and used them in echolocation. When their main paper appeared (Fraser & Purves 1960) there was still more evidence. But how do cetaceans hear ? Through close anatomical and experimental study of cetacean ears, which are connected to a system of air sinuses, Fraser and Purves strove to elucidate the evolutionary and functional aspects of cetacean hearing. In anticipation of this paper, Fraser presented their anatomical and functional considerations in a paper read at a meeting of the Royal Society (Fraser & Purves 1960).

The main paper opens with an admirable review of earlier anatomical work on the cetacean ear. This review showed them the way ahead and how much needed to be done in a general study of hearing in cetaceans. The base of the skull, where the air sacs are housed, had to be investigated first. After a topographical study of the pterygoid and nasopharyngeal muscles of the common dolphin (*Delphinus delphis*), which they compared with those of other toothed cetaceans and the baleen whales, their anatomical studies led them deeper to the vascular system associated with the air sacs. This system was splendidly revealed by coloured plastic, which Purves injected through the common carotid artery and jugular vein of stranded specimens representing five species: the common porpoise (*Phocaena phocoena*), Risso's dolphin (*Grampus griseus*), the bottle-nosed dolphin (*Tursiops truncatus*), the pilot whale (*Globicephala melaena*) and the white-beaked dolphin (*Lagenorhynchus albirostris*). They wrote: 'The general impression of the vascular system in the region of the base of the skull is of an elaborate plexus of vessels investing the whole of the air sac system, and apparently subservient to the proper functioning of the latter.' The air sacs are filled with foam and lined, as they found, by a mucous membrane overlying two layers of fibrous tissue separated by an open plexus of arteries and veins.

There was need also for study of basal aspects of the skull. Here they assumed that '. . . the form of the various bones and the distribution of the smoothed areas was associated with the state of development of the air sinuses connected with the tympanic cavity, and that these sinuses occupied the space between mesial and lateral laminae of bones such as the pterygoid, alisphenoid and palatine'. Their survey covered the baleen whales and a wide range of toothed forms (5 species of ziphioids, the pygmy sperm whale, 3 river dolphins, the narwhal, 2 porpoises and 17 delphinids). In most of these species the greater part of the lateral and superior laminae of the pterygoid, alisphenoid and palatine bones was absent, but they assumed that at some stage in the evolution of the air sinuses the entire parts of all four laminae (lateral, mesial, superior and inferior) were present. This hypothesis led them to examine the distribution of the air sinuses in detail, which in most instances was through the injection of a polyester resin and the entire dissolution of the soft parts by bacterial maceration. By such means a three-dimensional cast of the entire system of air spaces was obtained. Purves made preparations of the air sacs of two river dolphins, Risso's dolphin, the white-beaked dolphin, the pilot whale, the bottle-nosed dolphin, the common dolphin and the common porpoise.

After describing the extent of the air sinuses in these species, which were compared with published accounts of those in a beaked whale and the lesser rorqual, Fraser and Purves considered the evolution of the air sacs. But first they had '. . . to consider the possible mode of evolution of the sinuses from the typical mammalian middle ear. The periotic portion of the tympano-periotic bones of terrestrial mammals forms a part of the cranial wall and is closely contiguous with adjacent cranial bones. Further, the tympanic cavity is simple and circumscribed and communicates directly with the narial cavity through the Eustachian tube. '. . . In the Cetacea the tympano-periotic bones are excluded and more or less distant from the cranial wall, and the tympanic cavity is extended into an elaborate system of sinuses.' Indeed, as they show and figure so well, starting with a terrestrial mammal and passing through the following series of cetaceans; *Caperea* (the pygmy right whale), *Balaena* (right whales), *Balaenoptera* (rorquals), *Kogia* (pygmy sperm whale), *Physeter* (sperm whale), Ziphioidea (beaked whales), Platanistoidea (river dolphins) and delphinoids, there is a progressive dissociation of the tympano-periotic bones from adjacent bones of the skull. In the same series there is also a progressive invasion of the pterygoid plate by the pterygoid air sinus. Moreover, there is also progressive expansion in the horizontal plane of the air sac system. There is a comparable expansion in the delphinoids in a series extending from the river dolphins to the pelagic dolphins and within the dolphin genus *Lagenorhynchus*.

For the most part, they concluded that the ventral aspect of the cetacean skull with its associated system of air spaces provided a fairly reliable guide to the systematics of the order Cetacea. Considering these parts of their anatomy, the baleen whales (Mysticeti) are more primitive than the toothed whales (Odontoceti). In the more advanced odontocetes '. . . there is a gradation of development and specialization of the sinus system within the sub-order as a whole, from the relatively primitive River Dolphins through the estuarine forms to those which are pelagic'.

Fraser and Purves began their section on functional aspects thus:

> 'The mode of hearing of whales has for long been a subject for controversy among cetologists. Apart from those who maintained that cetaceans are unable to hear water-borne sounds, the most generally accepted hypothesis has been that these animals hear by bone conduction, that is by the perception of vibrations through the skull directly to the cochlea. It is proposed to show that this method of hearing is not only undesirable but also that it is impossible in normal circumstances in the cetaceans.'

The anatomy of the external ear canal is first considered, and they note that the external opening is less than 1 mm in diameter in the smaller toothed cetaceans; in the larger baleen whales this opening is lenticular in shape and measures about 1 cm along its major axis. Their dissections of the ear canal in the pilot whale, the lesser rorqual and the fin whale were compared with published accounts of this structure in other species. In the rorquals and humpback whale the meatus is closed along part of its length by a wax plug which caps the 'glove-finger' extension of the tympanic cavity; in the delphinids and the Greenland right whale the meatus is open throughout its length. Moreover, as in the rorquals and the humpback whale, the auditory meatus of other cetaceans connects with the open end of a glove-finger-like extension of the tympanic cavity, the apex of which is attached to the malleus, the outermost ear ossicle. After comparing their findings with those of others, they regarded the tympanic membrane as composed of two distinct parts, a fibrous portion with an external cavity and a non-fibrous portion which projects into the external ear canal.

Like other mammals, cetaceans have three ear ossicles, which are described in numerous publications. Thus, Fraser and Purves concentrated mainly on structural features that had not been previously emphasized. The processus gracilis of the malleus '. . . is closely associated with the sigmoid process of the tympanic bulla which forms a buttress attached to about four fifths of its lateral border. The mesial border of the process is free from any attachment throughout its length.' The manubrium of the malleus, 'Unlike the typical, handle-shaped structure of most mammals, is short, stout and roughly conical in the baleen whales or globular in form in the toothed cetaceans.' . . . 'The massive head of the malleus is deeply marked by two large facets making a re-entrant angle on its posterior aspect. Both these facets have smoothly convex surfaces covered with articular cartilage, which, with corresponding facets on the incus, form part of a synovial joint.' The incus looks something rather like a wide-based cone, the base forming the larger of two facets articulating with the malleus. The apex curves inwards to end in a facet forming a joint with a corresponding facet of the stapes. The stapes is not so obviously stirrup-shaped as in most other mammals. Above all, Fraser and Purves wished to present the ossicles of cetaceans as forming a fully functional system. Their observations did not cover the inner ear, but drawing on previous investigations they felt that the cetacean cochlea is fully comparable with that of terrestrial mammals.

The hydrodynamic function of the air sacs was next considered. The mobile chain of ossicles, the moveability of the stapes in the oval window and the functional fenestra rotunda seemed to imply that the cochlear fluids are moved by molar rather than molecular disturbances. In turn this pointed to the maintenance of an air space in the middle ear. If so, how is this maintained against changes of hydrostatic pressure during changes of depth? In land mammals pressure in the middle ear is adjusted through the Eustachian tube, but in cetaceans the only chance of making such adjustment is when the animal surfaces for breath. 'It seems likely that the pterygoid air sinuses form a reservoir for this process of pressure regulation, and that the maximum depth to which an animal can dive is in relation to the ultimate compressibility of the air sacs and the size of the tympanic cavity.'

Since the sinuses and tympanic cavity are filled with foamed, oil–mucus secretions, the compressibility of the air sacs must depend ultimately on that of the foam and the rigidity of the surrounding tissues. After tests on the effects of varying pressures on gelatinous, albuminous and detergent foams, they concluded that if '. . . the naturally-occurring foam behaves in a similar manner to that of gelatinous and albuminous foams, it may be deduced that, even at the greatest depth to which cetaceans normally dive, air bubbles would persist and there would be a sound reflecting system surrounding the essential organ of hearing'. But if an air space is maintained in the middle ear cavity, the greatest safe depth of a dive is presumably above the level where fracture of the tympanic bulla would occur. Their examination of bullae showed that fracture was infrequent. Moreover, they suggested that an obviating device is provided by erectile tissue in the corpus cavernosum tympanicum, which could occupy the tympanic cavity sufficiently to prevent fracture.

In cetaceans, as they had shown so well, the periotic bone is separated from the adjacent bones of the skull and is surrounded by the air sinus system. What then, is the most effective sound path to the cochlea? To answer this question they had to consider the likely acoustic function of the air sacs. Since an air space virtually surrounds the periotic bone, and since the transmission or reflexion of sound energy between two media depends on the ratio of their acoustic resistances, and to some degree on frequency, the periotic interface could be regarded as infinite in area as compared to the wavelength. Thus, the normal conditions of sound reflexion should apply. Their study of published work on the reflexion of sound from air–water mixtures led them to state: 'Since all sounds travelling in the direction of the cochlea by way of the bones of the skull and the soft tissues, with the exception of the meatus, must encounter the foam filled spaces, it is reasonable to assume that they must be almost completely reflected or absorbed.' The essential organs of hearing thus being acoustically isolated, they proceeded to examine the external auditory meatus as a possible conduit of vibrations.

They used a deep frozen part of the squamo-mastoid region of a fin whale, which, when thawed, was dissected to expose the middle ear, the wax plug and meatus as far laterally as the blind portion. The latter was dissected to expose the cord between the inner part of the meatus and its external aperture. To find the attenuation of sound down the meatus they used a transducer in the form of a barium titanate probe, which was connected to the output of a variable frequency oscillator. A similar probe was attached to an amplifier and a cathode ray oscilloscope, the output of which was monitored by a rectifying voltmeter. For a reference level they obtained a calibrated deflexion on the time base of the oscilloscope equivalent to a 2 cm distance between the two probes. The second of these was then moved along the blind part of the meatus and readings taken at 2 cm intervals. (To obtain each reading, the volume control of the oscillator was increased until the deflexion on the oscilloscope reached the reference level.) Similar readings were taken for the inner part of the meatus, the wax plug, the tympanic ligament, the wax plug to ligament and fibrous tissue parallel with the meatus. They then graphed the attenuation in decibels along these tissues for frequencies of 100 kHz, 50 kHz and 10 kHz. The curves obtained for the highest frequency, as might be expected, showed the greatest attenuation, but that in the fibrous tissue surrounding the meatus was considerably higher than that measured along the lumen of the meatus, between the wax plug and the tympanic ligament and along the blind section of the meatus. The attenuation down the last section was appreciably the lowest at 100 kHz and 50 kHz. They concluded: 'From these qualitative results it would appear that any vibrations transmitted by the meatus, blind section, lumen or wax plug would be received at the malleolar end of the ligament at an intensity greater than that of vibrations from the same source transmitted simultaneously by the surrounding fibrous tissue. Underlying bone transmissions, conveyed through tissues further away from the meatus, would suffer reflexion at the bulla–tympanic cavity interface. Since the sound transmitted by the meatal path would be dominant at any level of intensity, the animal must be subject to an intensity and/or phase difference at the two cochleae, due to the screening effect of the head and distance apart of the two meatal openings.' Their conclusions from similar sonic tests along the external end of the meatus of a sperm whale were much the same.

To complete this section of their research, there was need to remember that the tympanic bulla is closely encased in a fibro-elastic tissue some 10 cm thick in a large whale. Tests of the sound conductivity of 10 cm of this tissue at

100 kHz showed that the attenuation was about 8 dB above the reference level, which was some 5 dB below that for 10 cm of the blind meatal section and about half that for 10 cm of the meatal lumen. Evidently, the acoustic impedance of the encasing tissue is high relative to that of the meatal tissue, and should thus have a marked damping effect on molar vibrations of the tympanic bulla. They submitted 'that one of the effects of the great weight and density of the tympano-periotic bones is the avoidance of forced oscillations of the bones within the frequency band of the animal's normal auditory range'. Moreover, their tests showed that the malleus exhibits torsional vibrations independently of the bulla.

But how is sound pressure amplitude maintained and displacement amplitude increased by the ear ossicles ? To test such acoustic matching they used a barium titanate probe to the end of which was soldered a thin steel wire. The end of the wire was attached to the tip of the manubrium of the malleus, at the point where the tympanic ligament is normally attached. The wire simulated the ligament in length and position. The angle of attachment of the wire was altered by raising or lowering the transducer, relative to the position of the manubrium, over a friction-free pulley, the tension being kept constant by a small weight attached to the cable connecting oscillator and transducer. The incus, kept in its natural disposition with respect to the malleus, was separated from the latter by a thin film of petroleum jelly. The stylus of a micro-groove, crystal pick-up, which simulated the stapes, was connected to an amplifier and an oscilloscope. The entire equipment demonstrated changes in the amplitude of torsional oscillations of the malleus (in its bullary setting) when actuated by a simulated tympanic ligament vibrating longitudinally at various frequencies (10–100 kHz) and angles of traction.

They recorded considerable differences in the height of deflexion of the time base on the oscilloscope in relation to the angle the steel wire made with the long axis of the manubrium mallei. When the wire was pulling at a sharp angle (*ca.* 5°) the deflexion was about ten times the height attained when the pull was at right angles to the manubial axis. Evidently the malleus was being thrown into torsional vibrations and the manubrium was acting like a crank, actuated by the piston-like movements of the crystal face. When the wire, simulating the tympanic ligament, was pulling at right angles to the manubrium, the relationship between the pressure displacement amplitudes of the crystal face and the manubrium would be about unity: when the pull was at a sharp angle to the manubrium, the displacement ratio would be increased. 'Thus in the middle ear of the cetacean there exists a mechanism for the increase of displacement amplitude of water-borne sounds. It might be pointed out that this method of amplification is self-compensating, since the smaller the displacement amplitude of the sound wave the greater the relative amplification.'

Fraser and Purves ended this section by comparing and contrasting the ossicular mechanisms of cetaceans and terrestrial mammals. After considering differences in the amplification factors of their ossicles and the much greater pressure amplitude of water-borne sounds as compared to that of similar sounds in air, they concluded that the pressure amplitude of sounds finally reaching the inner ears is likely to be much the same in mammals of both media.

Their final section is on theories of cetacean hearing. In it they were at pains to show that Yamada's (1953) contentions that the external auditory meatus of cetaceans is vestigial (based on the assumption that it is unable to transmit sound vibrations), that the auditory bones are not acoustically isolated, and that the tympano-periotic bone is 'a dynamic unit of seismographic principle', are in no way supported by their investigations. Their main concern was with Reysenbach de Haan's (1957) very comprehensive work on cetacean hearing, which they did not receive until their work was nearly completed. While he had shown '. . . by experimental and quantitative treatment of the anatomical data that the conclusions reached by the writers (Fraser & Purves 1954) are in almost every respect in agreement with his own', he did not accept the possibility that the external auditory meatus transmits sounds to the middle ear. Consideration of this disagreement led them to supplement their findings by a further dissection of the auditory system of a fin whale (60 ft in length). The dissection reinforced their interpretations.

This outstanding and absorbing contribution to hearing in cetaceans, founded on careful and far-ranging anatomical work that led Fraser and Purves not only to new insights into the classification and evolution of the Cetacea, but also to undertake bold experimental studies of their auditory mechanisms, closed thus: 'The qualities of hearing referred to have been achieved by modification of typically mammalian auditory structures; so far from being non-functional, the meatus, the tympanic membrane, the auditory ossicles, tympanic bulla, the cochlea, the tympanic cavity and sinus system are all perfectly adapted for underwater hearing.'

Since the publication of this monograph, experimental evidence continues to show that the auditory capacities of the smaller toothed cetaceans, at least, are as sensitive as those found in land mammals. But electrophysiological recordings from the posterior colliculus and lower auditory centres of the brain in three genera of dolphins (*Steno*, *Stenella* and *Tursiops*), which were subjected to a range of ultrasonic frequencies, show that when the overall acoustic sensitivity of the head is mapped, the most sensitive area is that over the posterior mandible, where the outer bone is very thin. Here, Norris (1969) suggests, the impinging sound enters the mandibular channel and is guided by a fat body (with an acoustic impedance much like that of water) towards the ear. Sounds presumably enter the middle ear via the tympanic bulla and are then transmitted through the processus gracilis of the malleus to the ossicular chain and thence to the cochlea.

It would thus seem that the lower jaw is an important channel for ultrasound detection in dolphins. For instance, at 95 kHz the response in this region may be about six times that obtained over the external auditory meatus. But at lower frequencies ($<20$ kHz) recent tests of sound localization by the bottle-nosed dolphin indicate, after consideration of binaural factors, that the animal may have been using the region around each auditory meatus as a detector (Renaud

& Popper 1975). These authors conclude that their data '. . . most closely fit an hypothesis involving the external ear canals in low frequency sound detection or at least in localization'. One wonders if the auditory capacities of the large baleen whales, the subject of combined anatomical and experimental studies by Fraser and Purves, are like those of dolphins. The experimental prospect, if one is thinking of a live animal, is daunting.

## Historical aspects of cetology

As perusal of *Giant fishes, whales and dolphins* (Norman & Fraser, 1937) soon shows, Fraser was attracted to the historical side of his subject. He wrote short papers on early Japanese whaling (1937) and on some letters of William Scoresby Junior (1949). But little else appeared until he had retired, when, urged by Professor R. J. Harrison, he produced 'Royal fishes: the importance of the dolphin' in 1977. After the introduction there are sections on Fishes Royal, the Dolphin in Heraldry, De Praerogativa Regis—the Royal Prerogative, the Thames (or Commonwealth) Whale 1658, recent legislation and some results obtained from the availability of stranded cetaceans. The last section is considered elsewhere (pp. 298-300).

The purpose of his compilation, as he explained in the introduction, had two main purposes 'the one an attempt to convey the extent of human interest in cetaceans and particularly in the dolphin from very early time up to the present'. The other was '. . . to convey the benefit to cetologists of the exercise of the royal prerogative where whales and dolphins are concerned. Concerning Fishes Royal, he reminds us that in pre-Linnaean times the classification of animals depended not on their structure but on their surroundings. Thus, there were jellyfish, starfish, "shell fish" and fishes (aquatic vertebrates). In 1693 John Ray recognised the true nature of cetaceans but to Linnaeus they were still fishes in the 1735 edition of his Systema Naturae; proper recognition had to await the tenth edition (1758).

'The situation therefore is that with reference to the cetaceans, a great proportion of the available information relates to them as fish. And indeed, as recently as 1971, the Lord Chancellor indicated that whales, porpoises and dolphins (and the sturgeon), so far as the law is concerned are *fish* "whatever the scientists may say" (Hansard 1971, vol. 314, no. 46, col. 714).'

The charming sections on Fishes Royal, the Dolphin in Heraldry and the early history of the Royal Prerogative may be left to the interested reader. Whales and sturgeon are Royal Fish and belong to the Sovereign. But along certain stretches of coastline, the right to Fishes Royal has passed from the Crown to landowner, corporation or holder of Crown appointment. One such stretch, from the Naze, Essex, to a point near Newhaven comes under the Lord Warden of the Cinque Ports. Here Fraser recalled: 'When Sir Winston Churchill was Lord Warden his attention was drawn by the Director, British Museum (Natural History) to the right to Fishes Royal that he enjoyed by reason of that office. In his reply Sir Winston expressed interest in his claim to stranded cetaceans in the Cinque Port area and generously prayed the Museum to do whatever it wished in regard to such material. His successor Sir Robert Menzies was equally generous.'

The operation of the prerogative so far as it involves the Museum is quoted elsewhere (pp. 298–99). Turning to recent legislation, Fraser became concerned. In 1970 a Bill was presented to the House of Lords for the abolition of the Crown's ancient prerogative to wild creatures (but without affecting the Queen's right to swans).

> 'At the second reading of the Bill on 25 January 1971 attention was drawn to the Museum's interest in royal fish from the point of view of the advancement of knowledge of cetaceans and the improvement of the national collections of these animals'.
>
> 'At the Committee stage 4 February 1971, an amendment was moved (by the Earl of Cranbrook, then a Trustee of the British Museum (Natural History)) to leave out "royal fish" and also to insert "sturgeons", in the Bill for the abolition of Crown prerogative as to wild creatures, and franchises derived therefrom. The debate was interesting and informative and in the division the amendment was carried. So whales, porpoises and dolphins continue to be accepted, not as belonging to the Phylum Mammalia, but inclusively with the sturgeon, as royal fish . . . .'

Fraser completed the last sentence by quoting once more the Lord Chancellor's disregard of scientific pronouncement. Perhaps there had been a crossing of swords.

## THE MAN, THE MUSEUM AND OTHER CONCERNS

Fraser grew attached to the Museum. Like his garden, the 'Museum', pronounced with full relish of each vowel, became part of him. Both flourished under his curatorship.

Sir Terence Morrison-Scott, for reasons that appear in his letter, was uniquely placed to appreciate Fraser's outstanding qualities.

> 'I joined the Museum three years after him and from the beginning we worked closely together: there was that curious division of the mammals—the Mammal Room with skins and skulls (save pinnipedes, Cetacea and Proboscidea) and the Osteological Room (mammalian only!) with the rest of the skeletons. I was assigned to the Mammal Room but we didn't pay any attention to demarcation lines and had the mutual freedom of our rooms. In fact I early developed an interest in elephant dentition so spent a good deal of time in the Osteological Room (I don't think I had any elephant skins with which to reciprocate).
>
> 'By the time I went off to the Science Museum (1956) he was Deputy Keeper and I came under him. He was a most kind and tolerant master; patient, helpful and wise and I could not have asked for anyone better to report to and consult.
>
> 'Later on, when I became Director he was already Keeper and our friendship was further cemented by having to cope for several years with a very troublesome personnel problem.

'At no time during our joint career do I remember either of us giving the other an instruction of any sort: our mutual understanding of the right approach to science and administration was so close that the necessity never arose. We may, of course, have been wrong—but what a perfect relationship it was'

Dr Gordon Sheals, the present Keeper of Zoology at the Museum, recalls:

'It is probably fair to say that Dr Fraser had no great love for administrative chores. Nevertheless, having accepted the responsibilities of Keeper, he managed a large department most efficiently and guided it through a difficult period. He was always concerned for the welfare of his staff. Those who served with him during this period remember him as a kindly man with a keen sense of humour and a great respect for scholarship.'

In 1962, two years before his retirement as Keeper, he was created C.B.E.

There were many duties outside the Museum. Throughout his career he was active in the affairs of the Zoological Society of London, serving several terms on Council, on several of its committees and as Vice President 1965–67. After his election to the fellowship of the Royal Society in 1966 (particularly in recognition of his work on the functional anatomy and evolutionary biology of cetaceans) he served on Sectional Committee 7, the Aldabra Research Committee, the Coelacanth Research Committee, the Southern Zone Research Committee, the Leverhulme Studentships Committee and the British National Committee on Antarctic Research. David Griffin recalls:

'He was a member of the Aldabra Research Committee from its establishment by the Council of the Royal Society on 14 December 1967 until 31 December 1973. He was a member of the Research Committee's Projects Subcommittee throughout its existence from its formation on 31 October 1968 to its last meeting on 18 December 1973, and on several occasions took the chair; the subcommittee was set up to consider applications for projects on Aldabra and assign priorities to them, and also to stimulate interest in the relevant areas of research. On this last aspect Fraser did much to promote the study of the Aldabra giant tortoises and turtles. In 1968 he gathered information from the B.M.(N.H.) and the Zoological Society of London on possible methods of marking the tortoises. His contacts with the B.M.(N.H.) staff, Professor L. D. Brongersma of the Rijks museum in the Netherlands, and others were invaluable in establishing and promoting the tortoise and turtle research, and other aspects of the Aldabra programme, such as data recording, received the benefit of his wide experience and wise counsel.

'I now turn to Fraser's involvement with the coelacanth project. Following approaches by the U.S. National Academy of Sciences, the Council of the Royal Society established the Coelacanth Research Committee in July 1967 to further the study of *Latimeria*. Fraser was asked to be chairman. He asked the Biological Secretary (Sir Ashley Miles) why he had been so invited, since he was neither an ichthyologist nor a molecular biologist (both of these fields being well represented on the new committee) and Sir

Ashley replied "That is exactly why we wish you to be chairman". [Fraser told this story many times in my presence!] Under Fraser's energetic guidance, the Committee mounted two international expeditions to the Indian Ocean in search of live coelacanths. The second, in 1972, was fortunate enough to obtain two specimens (both at the Comoro Islands), one of which was filmed while still alive—the first time ever this had been done. Fraser's committee had prepared a plan for the distribution of fresh tissues to a world-wide list of research workers, and this was put into effect. The operation would have had little chance of success without the coopera-tion of the French authorities, and this Fraser had secured through the good offices of the principal French research worker in the field, Professor Jean Anthony of the Paris Natural History Museum, who later wrote about the approach made to him by Fraser (*Opération Coelacanthe*, by Jean Anthony; Paris: Librairie Arthaud, 1976):

> "Fraser est un ami de longue date. . . C'est un solide Ecossais. Un organisateur excellent et de naturel optimiste; il a monté l'admirable salle des Cétacés au British Museum. Il a navigué sur toutes les mers. Ses publications font autorité. S'il mêle d'une expédition aux Comores, l'affaire est sérieuse. . . J'accepte. J'écris le jour même à Londres et donne accord de principe."
>
> ("Fraser was a friend of long standing. . . A staunch Scotsman. An excellent organiser and optimistic by nature; he had established the admirable cetacean room at the British Museum. He had sailed the seven seas. His publications were a recognized authority. If he was involved in an expedition to the Comores, it was a responsible enterprise . . . I accepted. I wrote to London the same day and gave my agreement in principle.")

'The extensive advances in knowledge about *Latimeria* resulting from the expedition have been recently described by N. A. Locket in a Royal Society review lecture (*Proc. R. Soc. Lond.* B, in the press).'

He was a member also of the Expeditions Committee of the Royal Geographical Society, London, and the Advisory Committee of the British Antarctic Survey. Again he could draw on wide experience and his services were much appreciated.

Fraser had a well balanced pride in his forebears and country; he was not a drum-banging Scot. In a letter to his brother Robert, written from Takaradi on 20 January 1946 during his absence on the Danish *Atlantide* Expedition to West Africa, he wrote of all the Scots he had met ashore and concluded: 'I know now where Scots go when they leave their country; my experience indicates that they far exceed in number the rest of the European populations in these places. . . . I have *not* however exploited my nationality and try to be the cosmopolite.'

During his early years in the Museum and at Christmas time, his colleague C. C. A. Munro wished him a 'Happy Knoxmas'. This was in jest: Fraser had a keen sense of duty but he was not a puritan. He did not even like a traditional

Scottish means of plain living. When William Schevill, the distinguished American cetologist, was staying with the Frasers (their welcome to all visitors was warm and generous), he asked why there was no porridge for breakfast. 'I've been liberated' was the reply. Whisky, especially a malted kind, was better appreciated.

Indeed, Fraser was closer to classical Greece than Calvinism. He enjoyed a symposium; a drinking together—whether after a banquet or at a bar. At such a latter occasion, probably after a meeting of the Challenger Society, Professor D'Arcy Thompson (later Sir D'Arcy), an authority on the classical symposium, was one of the company. During the evening Fraser upset a pint of beer, some of which ran into a capacious pocket of the great man's jacket. His profuse apology was brushed aside with 'Think nothing of it, brother'.

Fraser liked to recall such events, including some that went against him. He also had a fund of 'stories' ranging from liberated drawing-room to middling bawdy. He liked stories involving a play on words. There was also a certain pawkiness (in the mischievous rather than the sly sense). He could, in seeming solemnity, say the most serious things. Before his broad smile and laugh appeared one's credulity might be showing. His brother Robert recalls one such 'seriousness' less than a week before he died.

A fine tribute to the man and his work appears in Volume III of *Investigations on Cetacea*, published in Berne (Switzerland), 1971. Dr G. Pilleri, the editor, dedicated this volume to Fraser thus:

> 'As I finish this third volume, my thoughts turn to the quiet peaceful atmosphere in the rooms of a well-known institute where investigations on Cetaceans have reached a level rarely attained. This haven of research is the section concerned with cetology in the Department of Zoology, British Museum (Natural History), the image of which is inextricably linked with the man who, until recently, was in charge and who has guided its steps for many years with his far-reaching knowledge and unparalleled experience:
>
> FRANCIS CHARLES FRASER
> C.B.E., D.Sc., F.R.S.
>
> 'Dear Doctor Fraser,
>
> Your unique knowledge of our field of research and your vast experience as a biologist have been a source of continuous enrichment for us. Each time we meet, and each time we are drawn together in a discussion on your life's work, I am deeply stirred by your essential human personality and boundless knowledge. Today I should like to offer you an outward token of my gratitude by dedicating this book to you with my sincerest wish that you may continue the studies you so deeply cherish in peace and happiness for many years to come.'

Those well aware of the man and his work are sad that there were not 'many years to come'.

In writing this memoir I have been much helped by Mrs Anne Fraser and Mr R. W. Fraser. The written appreciations from Professor A. J. E. Cave, Mr D. J. H. Griffin, Dr D. Dilwyn John, Sir Terence Morrison-Scott, Sir Frederick Russell and Dr J. G. Sheals are gratefully acknowledged, as are conversations with Sir Alister Hardy, Dr L. H. Matthews and Mr W. E. Schevill.

## References

(1) Deacon, G. E. R. 1976 The cyclonic circulation in the Weddell Sea. *Deep Sea Res.* **23**, 125–126.

(2) Foxton, P. 1964 Seasonal variations in the plankton of Antarctic waters. *Biologie antarctique, Premier (SCAR) symposium* (ed. R. Garrick, M. Holdgate & J. Prevost), Paris: Hermann 651 pp.

(3) Gurney, R. 1924 Crustacea—Part IX Decapod larvae. *Br. Antarct. Terra Nova Exped.* 1910 *Zool.* **8**, 37–202.

(4) Gurney, R. 1942 Larvae of decapod Crustacea. *Ray Soc. Publs*, p. 306.

(5) Hardy, A. C. 1967 *Great waters.* London: Collins. 542 pages.

(6) Kemp, S. 1932 The voyage of the R.R.S. *Discovery II*: Surveys and soundings. *Geogrl J.* **79** (3), 168–185.

(7) Kemp, S., Hardy, A. C. & Mackintosh, N. A. 1929 Objects, equipment and methods. *'Discovery' Rep.* **1**, 143–232.

(8) Macdonald, R. 1927 Irregular development in the larval history of *Meganyctiphanes norvegica. J. mar. biol. Ass. U.K.* **14**, 785–794.

(9) Mackintosh, N. A. 1937 The seasonal circulation of the Antarctic macroplankton. *'Discovery' Rep.* **16**, 365–412.

(10) Marr, J. W. S. 1964 The natural history and geography of the Antarctic krill (*Euphausia superba* Dana). *'Discovery' Rep.* **32**, 33–464.

(11) Mauchline, J. 1959 The development of the Euphausiacea, especially that of *Meganctiphanes norvegica* (M. Sars). *Proc. zool. Soc. Lond.* **132**, 627–639.

(12) Mauchline, J. & Fisher, L. R. 1969 The biology of euphausiids. *Adv. mar. Biol.* **7**, 1–454.

(13) Norris, K. S. 1969 The echolocation of marine mammals. pp. 391–423. In: *The biology of marine mammals* (ed. H. T. Andersen), p. 511. Academic Press: New York & London.

(14) Renaud, Donna L. & Popper, A. N. 1975 Sound localization by the bottlenose porpoise *Tursiops truncatus. J. exp. Biol.* **63**, 569–585.

(15) Reysenbach de Haan, F. W. 1957 Hearing in whales. *Acta oto-lar.* Supplementum **134**, 1–114.

(16) Spärck, R. 1950 Foreword to Atlantide Rep. no. 1.

(17) Yamada, M. 1953 Contribution to the anatomy of the organ of hearing of whales. *Sci. Rep. Whales Res. Unit (Japan)* no. 8, pp. 1–79.

## Bibliography

1934 *Report on Cetacea stranded on the British coasts from 1927 to 1932*, pp. 1–41. London: Trustees British Museum.

Biological observations made during a cruise to the Faröe Islands and off the coast of Scotland in July 1933. *Proc. Linn. Soc. Lond.* **146**, 38.

(With G. F. H. Smith) The Blue Whale skeleton in the Whale Hall. *Nat. Hist. Mag.* **4**, 228–232.

1935 The Finless Black Porpoise (*Neomeris phocaenoides*). *Nat. Hist. Mag.* **5**, 90–92.

Zoological notes from the voyage of Peter Munday 1644–56. (b) Sea-elephant at St Helena; whale at Greenwich. *Proc. Linn. Soc. Lond.* **147**, 33–37.

1936 Recent strandings of the False Killer Whale, *Pseudorca crassidens* with special reference to those found at Donna Nook, Lincolnshire. *Scott. Nat.* pp. 105–114.

On the development and distribution of the young stages of krill (*Euphausia superba*). *'Discovery' Rep.* **14**, 1–192.

Vestigial teeth in specimens of Cuvier's Whale (*Ziphius cavirostris*) stranded on the Scottish coast. *Scott. Nat.* pp. 153–157.

1937 Early Japanese whaling. *Proc. Linn. Soc. Lond.* **150**, 19–20.
Early larval development of the Euphausiacea. *Proc. Linn. Soc. Lond.* **149**, 89–94.
Common Dolphins in the North Sea. *Scott. Nat.* pp. 103–105.
(With J. R. NORMAN) *Giant fishes, whales and dolphins.* xxvii + 361 (Cetacea, pp. 203–349). London: Putnam.

1938 The effect of control measures on sealing. *Anim. Yb.* **5**, 40–50.
Vestigial teeth in the Narwhal. *Proc. Linn. Soc. Lond.* **150**, 155–162.

1940 Three anomalous dolphins from Blacksod Bay, Ireland. *Proc. R. Ir. Acad.* **45B**, 413–455.

1942 The mesorostral ossification of *Ziphius cavirostris*. *Proc. zool. Soc. Lond.* **112A**, 21–30.

1943 (With W. L. SCLATER) *Zoological Record.* Pt 18: *Mammalia.*

1945 On a specimen of the Southern Bottle-nosed whale, *Hyperoodon planifrons*. *'Discovery' Rep.* **23**, 19–36.
Cetacea stranded on the British coast during 1944. *Ann. Mag. nat. Hist.* (11) **12**, 347–350.

1946 *No. 12 Report on cetacea stranded on the British coasts from 1933 to 1934*, pp. 1–56. London: British Museum (Nat. Hist.).

1947 Fish or flesh? *Ill. Lond. News* **210**, 121.
Porpoises and dolphins. *Ill. Lond. News* **211**, 668.
Curiosities of the seashore—4. Ambergris. *Ill. Lond. News* **211**, 160.
Stranded grampuses. *Country Life Lond.* **101**, 719.
Sound emitted by dolphins. *Nature, Lond.* **160**, 759.

1949 A Narwhal in the Thames estuary. *Nature, Lond.* **163**, 575.
A specimen of *Sotalia tëuszii* Kukenthal from the coast of Senegal. *J. Mammal.* **30**, 274–276.
Some letters of William Scoresby Junior. *Polar Rec.* **5**, 306–308.
(With J. E. KING) The bone remains from Star Carr, Seamer (Yorkshire). *Proc. prehist.* **6**, 67–69.
(With H. W. PARKER) *Guide for the identification and reporting of stranded whales, dolphins, porpoises and turtles on the British coasts.* (viii + 42.) London: British Museum (Nat. Hist.).

1950 Two skulls of *Globicephala macrorhyncha* (Gray) from Dakar. *Atlantide Rep.* **1**, 49–60.
Description of a dolphin *Stenella frontalis* (Cuvier) from the coast of French Equatorial Africa. *Atlantide Rep.* **1**, 61–83.
Note on a skull of Hector's Beaked whale, *Mesoplodon hectori* (Gray) from the Falkland Islands. *Proc. Linn. Soc. Lond.* **162**, 50–52.
The world of the whale. *Leader Magazine*, 28 January.

1951 Vestigial metapodials in the Okapi and Giraffe. *Proc. zool. Soc. Lond.* **121**, 315–317.
Skull of the foetal Narwhal. *Nature, Lond.* **167**, 765.
The specific name of the Northern Pilot whale or Blackfish. *Ann. Mag. nat. Hist.* (12) **4**, 942–944.
On the 'thorn' or 'claw' in panthers' tails. *J. Bombay nat. Hist. Soc.* **49**, 777–779.
(With J. E. KING) Second interim report on the animal remains from Star Carr, Seamer. *Proc. prehist. Soc.* (1950) no. 9, 124–129.

1952 *Handbook of R. H. Burne's Cetacean dissections.* pp. 1–70. London: British Museum (Nat. Hist.).

1953 *Report on Cetacea stranded on the British coasts from 1938 to 1947*, pp. 1–48. London: British Museum (Nat. Hist.).
(With H. W. PARKER) *Guide for the identification and reporting of stranded whales, dolphins, porpoises and turtles of the British coasts* (2nd edn), pp. 1–42. London: British Museum (Nat. Hist.).

1954 Notes on the exhibition of two specimens of *Sotalia lentiginosa*. *Agenda Abstr. scient. Mtgs zool. Soc. Lond.* no. 4, 2.

1954 Faunal remains. In: *Excavations at Star Carr, an early mesolithic site at Seamer near Scarborough, Yorkshire* (ed. J. G. D. Clark), pp. 70–89. Cambridge University Press.
(With P. E. PURVES) Fractured earbones of Blue whales. *Scott. Nat.* **65**, 154–156.
(With P. E. PURVES) Hearing in Cetaceans. *Bull. Br. Mus. nat. Hist. Zool.* **2**, 101–114.

1955 The southern Right whale dolphin, *Lissodelphis peroni* (Lacepède). External characters and distribution. *Bull. Br. Mus. nat. Hist. Zool.* **2**, 339–346.
A skull of *Mesoplodon gervaisi* (Deslongchamps) from Trinidad, West Indies. *Ann. Mag. nat. Hist.* (12) **8**, 624–630.
The dolphin family. *Zoo Life* **10**, 74–78.
(With P. E. PURVES) The 'blow' of whales. *Nature, Lond.* **176**, 1221–1222.

1956 A new Sarawak dolphin. *Sarawak Mus. J.* **7**, 478–503.

1957 Cetaceans stranded on the British coasts during 1956. *Bull. Mammal Soc. Br. Isl.* no. 7, 21–22.

Opononi Jack, the friendly dolphin. *Zoo Life* no. 1, **12**, 14–15.

1958 Common or Harbour porpoises from French West Africa. *Bull. Inst. fr. Arf. noire* **20A**, 276–285.

1959 Some aquatic adaptions of whales and dolphins. *Proc. R. Instn. Gt Br.* **37**, 319–333.

Whales and porpoises. *Zoo Mag.* no. 3, 12–14.

(With P. E. Purves) Hearing in whales. *Endeavour* **18**, 93–98.

1960 A specimen of the genus *Feresa* from Senegal. *Bull. Inst. fr. Afr. noire* **22A**, 669–707.

(With P. E. Purves) Anatomy and function of the Cetacean ear. *Proc. R. Soc. Lond.* B **192**, 62–77.

(With P. E. Purves) Hearing in Cetaceans. Evolution of the accessory air sacs and the structure and function of the outer and middle ear in recent Cetaceans. *Bull. Br. Mus. nat. Hist.* **7**, 1–140.

1963 (With P. E. Purves) Hearing in Cetacea. A reply to Dudok van Heel's publication on 'Sound and Cetacea'. *Neth. J. Sea Res.* **2**, 95–101.

1964 Whales and whaling. In: *Antarctic research. A review of British scientific achievment in Antarctica* (eds R. Priestley *et al.*), pp. 191–206. London: Butterworths.

1965 Sea cows off Sierra Leone. *Mar. Obsr* **35**, no. 208, p. 63.

1966 *Guide for the identification and reporting of stranded whales, dolphins, porpoises on the British coasts* (3rd edn), pp. 1–34. London: British Museum (Nat. Hist.).

Whales and porpoises. *Zool. Soc. Lond. Leaflet.*

Comments on the Delphinoidea. In: *Whales, dolphins and porpoises* (ed. K. S. Norris), pp. 7–31. University of California Press, 1966.

1968 Notes on a specimen of *Phocoena dioptrica* from South Georgia. *Bull. Br. Antarct. Surv.* no. 16, 51–56.

(With B. A. Noble) Skull of *Lagenorhynchus cruciger* from Livingstone Island, South Shetland Islands. *Bull. Br. Antarct. Surv.* no. 15, 29–38.

(With R. G. Busnel & G. Pilleri) Notes concernant le dauphin *Stenella styx* Gray 1846. *Mammalia* **32**, 192–203.

1969 *Guide for the identification and reporting of stranded whales, dolphins, and porpoises on the British coasts* (4th edn), pp. 1–34. London: British Museum (Nat. Hist.).

Review of 'The Whale' (ed. L. H. Matthews), *Advmt Sci., Lond.* **25**, no. 126, June, p. 400.

Whales of Liberia. *Mar. Obsr* **39**, no. 225, July, p. 113.

(With A. J. E. Cave) Congenital jugal bipartism in mysticetes. *J. Zool., Lond.* **157**, 383–390.

1971 Scientific value of the 'Fishes Royale'. *The Times*, 23 January.

(With B. A. Noble) Description of a skeleton and supplementary notes on the skull of a rare porpoise *Phocoena sinus* Norris & McFarland 1958. *J. nat. Hist.* **5**, 447–464.

(With B. A. Noble) Rare porpoise from the Gulf of California. *Nature, Lond.* **323**, 90.

(With W. H. Dawbin & B. A. Noble) Observations on the electra dolphin, *Peponocephala electra. Bull. Br. Mus. nat. Hist. Zool.* **20**, 173–201.

1972 An early 17th century record of the California grey whale in Icelandic waters. In: *Investigations of Cetacea* (ed. G. Pilleri), vol. 2, pp. 13–20. University of Berne.

(With B. A. Noble) Variation of pigmentation pattern in Meyen's dolphin, *Stenella coeruleoalba* (Meyen). In: *Investigations on Cetecea* (ed. G. Pilleri), vol. 2, pp. 147–163. University of Berne.

1973 Record of a dolphin (*Sousa teuszii*) from the coast of Mauritania. *Trans. N.Y. Acad. Sci.* (2), **352**, 132–135.

1974 *Report on Cetacea stranded on the British coasts from 1948–1966*, pp. 1–65. London: Trustees British Museum.

1976 *Guide for the identification and reporting of stranded whales, dolphins and porpoises on the British coasts* (5th edn), pp. 1–34. London: British Museum (Nat. Hist.).

1977 Royal fishes: the importance of the dolphin. In: *Functional anatomy of marine mammals* (ed. R. J. Harrison), vol. 3, pp. 1–44. London, New York, San Francisco.

W. Hudson

# WILLIAM HUDSON

27 April 1896 — 12 September 1978

Elected F.R.S. 1964

By Sir Angus Paton, F.R.S.

'His works constitute his biography.' Thus wrote Samuel Smiles concluding his life of John Rennie. Rarely is one man's name permanently associated with a single great engineering feat. But this was most certainly the case with Sir William Hudson and the Snowy Mountains Scheme in Australia. For 18 years from its inception in August 1949 he was the heart, soul and inspiration of the works, driving himself and the scheme along and expecting, perhaps demanding, that everyone else associated with it did likewise.

## Early career

William (Bill) Hudson, the son of a doctor, was born in 1896 at Nelson in the South Island of New Zealand and was educated at Nelson College where he excelled in rugby, cricket, swimming and gymnastics. He was the youngest of seven sons of a doctor who expected all his sons to read medicine but Bill had set his heart on being a civil engineer. According to his own account, when he summoned up courage in his matriculation year to tell his father of this decision, his father went purple in the face, jumped up from his chair, walked round the study about three times, looked Bill straight in the eye and said: 'Bill, that is about all you are bloody well good for.'

He left New Zealand in July 1914 and read engineering at University College London where he completed the first two years of a course before enlisting in the 4th Yorkshire Regiment. He was wounded in the right thigh at Bullecourt after two and a half months. When he was considered fit again he was trained for service in the tanks in the London Regiment. By that time however the war was over. He returned to university and graduated with first class honours in 1920.

He then took a post-graduate course at Grenoble in hydro-electric engineering, the field he had chosen for his life's work, and despite difficulty in unscrambling his notes in the French language he successfully completed the course.

After a period of service with Sir W. G. Armstrong Whitworth & Co. Ltd, in England, he returned to New Zealand in 1922 and joined the Public Works Department. He was employed first on railway construction and later as assistant engineer in the Mangahao hydro-electric scheme, 113 km north of

Wellington. From 1924 to 1927 he rejoined Armstrong Whitworth on the construction of the Arapuni Dam.

While there he met and married Annie Eileen Trotter, daughter of a South Canterbury farmer. Their first daughter Margaret was born at Arapuni.

Hudson left New Zealand in 1927 to work for the Public Works Department of New South Wales and a year later transferred to the Metropolitan Water Sewerage and Drainage Board as supervising engineer of the construction of Nepean Dam, some 64 km south of Sydney. However, like many other large projects the depression caught up with it and the job was closed down with dramatic suddenness.

## Galloway Hydro-electric Scheme

In 1931 he decided to try his luck in London, called on Sir Alexander Gibb & Partners and was immediately offered a job in Scotland as engineer-in-charge of the supervision of construction of the Galloway power scheme. Gibb had been previously advising Armstrong Whitworth on certain aspects of the Arapuni Dam and one of their partners, John Ferguson, had been particularly impressed during a visit with the competence of Hudson on his section of the scheme. So it was fortunate for Gibb and Hudson that their paths crossed again, particularly as the Scottish scheme was immensely challenging. Although on a much smaller scale, it was very similar to the vast scheme which climaxed Hudson's career.

The Galloway hydro-electric project was in a remote and beautiful area in the southwest corner of Scotland. The waters to be harnessed were mainly those of the Dee and Ken in Kirkcudbright and of the Doon in Ayrshire. The complete installation was then the largest of its kind in Great Britain, far outstripping its forerunners of Rannoch, Tummel and Lochaber. Seven dams were built and the water was brought by tunnels and aqueducts to five power stations at Kendoon, Carsfad, Earlstoun, Glenlee and Tongland. Except for Glenlee which was served by a separate reservoir at Clatteringshaws, the other four power stations were in series (see plate 1). The total installed capacity was 103 250 kW, the output in a normal year being 182 million kWh and the cost of the scheme, completed in 1936, about £3 million.

The impression Hudson made in his five years on the Galloway scheme is well expressed in the following extract from a note of one of his resident engineers:

> 'My memories of Bill Hudson go back to a pouring wet day at Glenlochar Bridge in Galloway in 1931. I, a young engineer of 22, was engaged with a chainman or two in the damp and unpleasant task of river gauging in the boiling flood waters. I looked up and there was our Chief Engineer, James Williamson, a white-haired Scot whose word was law, not warm and snug in Westminster as I had supposed, and beside him an odd figure, a thin face peering out from under a wide brimmed stetson and huddled in a huge waterproof. When it spoke it had a dry Antipodean accent. This was Bill Hudson, who was to be my boss for the next five years.

'He absorbed facts and figures like blotting paper. He was not an easy person to get on with, monosyllabic, almost taciturn, tho' a wintry smile would break through from time to time at some of my more outrageous sallies. But it did not take long for his fame and his influence to percolate and to spread. He was one of the most efficient and dedicated engineers under whom I have worked. His industry was fantastic and he expected the same from us, and got it. He was a magnificent teacher and leader and when things did go wrong, and inevitably they must on construction schemes, there were no recriminations; just a wry smile and hopes for no repeats. He dealt with contractors firmly and fairly, and like us they too learnt a lot from him.'

The many facets of the Galloway scheme proved to be valuable experience not only for Hudson later on Snowy, but also for the Gibb team in developing the hydro-electric resources of Scotland after World War II and subsequently on schemes in various parts of the world. In addition to normal engineering, Hudson, as the firm's representative, was involved in a fascinating range of other problems. The acquisition of land, negotiation for way-leaves and like matters, with most of the landowners bitterly opposed to the scheme, called for tact and infinite patience. Then there were fishery problems, as both the Ken and the Dee were valuable salmon rivers. In conjunction with the authorities and with the advice of the company's fishery expert, salmon ladders or passes were designed and constructed to allow the fish to ascend or descend the various dams and barrages. Of the whole capital cost nearly a quarter went to safeguard the rights and privileges of persons interested in the land and water, persons of course including the fish. Hudson paid great attention to these matters, as well as to the importance of keeping the staff and labour happy with football and boxing matches and other activities.

In the 44 years since its completion the Galloway scheme has been operated with the minimum of major maintenance on the works. The output has been 20% higher than estimated, averaging 220 million kWh per annum. Hudson could not resist, when he very occasionally came over to Great Britain during the Snowy period, visiting the scheme on two occasions.

### Metropolitan Water Sewerage and Drainage Board of Sydney

Following the completion of the Galloway scheme, Hudson rejoined the Metropolitan Water Sewerage and Drainage Board of Sydney in 1937 as Resident Engineer in charge of construction of Woronora Dam. He had been at Woronora less than a year when the then Chief Engineer (Mr S. T. Farnsworth) noted that the 'overall efficiency has vastly increased and there now exists a genuine *esprit-de-corps* among the whole staff and the employees . . . to my mind it has simply been a question of the men as a whole recognizing that the man in charge knew his job'.

In December 1937 Hudson was appointed Inspecting Engineer working from head office. His field of activity covered the major works in construction and in this position he continued his practice of very long working hours—a 'work-aholic' as one of his staff recalls. 'Deep down he had a great sense of loyalty and gratitude for anyone who worked for him. He had no time for "yes-men". He was considered ambitious and utterly ruthless and it was thought that he mischievously enjoyed the ruthless reputation.'

Hudson tried very hard to enlist in the Services in World War II. However, he was not accepted and found himself taking charge in mid-1943 as Chief Construction Engineer for the Board of the concrete work of the Captain Cook graving dock, the largest in the southern hemisphere, and desperately needed for the maintenance of capital ships.

Hudson completed the construction work with his usual drive and efficiency in 1945. This was much to the relief of Gibb who were responsible for the design in England in close liaison with the Admiralty. They had initially been somewhat concerned with the hesitant start of the work at the Garden Island site in Sydney harbour. As an indication of the close liaison on the work, one of Gibb's supervising engineers recalled that 'he used to hand out drawings through the back window of the office to Bill Hudson to get on with construction and then hand another issue to the Department of Works whereafter it would take some time to reach the Water Board's construction force.'

Now comes the most important period in Hudson's career when 15 months after succeeding Mr S. T. Farnsworth as Engineer-in-chief of the Sydney Water Board he was put in charge of the Snowy Mountains Hydro-electric Scheme in July 1949.

## The Snowy Mountains Hydro-electric Scheme

This scheme is located in the southeast corner of Australia midway between Sydney and Melbourne and close to the capital of the Commonwealth at Canberra. It embraced an area of over 5200 km$^2$ of mountainous country containing the most reliable source of water for the driest continent in the world with an annual rainfall except on the coastal belt of 254 mm or less. Snow covered the mountains for five to six months of each year. The mountains were the source of three great rivers, the Murray and Murrumbidgee flowing westward and the Snowy River flowing generally southward across high rainfall coastal land to waste itself in the Tasman Sea.

Various proposals had been advanced in the last hundred years for the inland diversion of the Snowy River, schemes being put forward in the 1920s and 1930s but it was not until 1944 that the first dual-purpose scheme for both power and irrigation was submitted to the New South Wales Government. In 1946 the Commonwealth Government and the Governments of New South Wales and Victoria appointed a committee who reported first in November 1948. This report pointed out that not only could the total flow of the Snowy and the Eucumbene be made available for irrigation in the Murray and Murrumbidgee valleys, but the fall of nearly 914 m of diverted waters as they travelled inland through tunnels and shafts could provide a power capacity ten times as large as that of any scheme previously contemplated.

THE GALLOWAY HYDRO-ELECTRIC SCHEME. A PICTORIAL REPRESENTATION

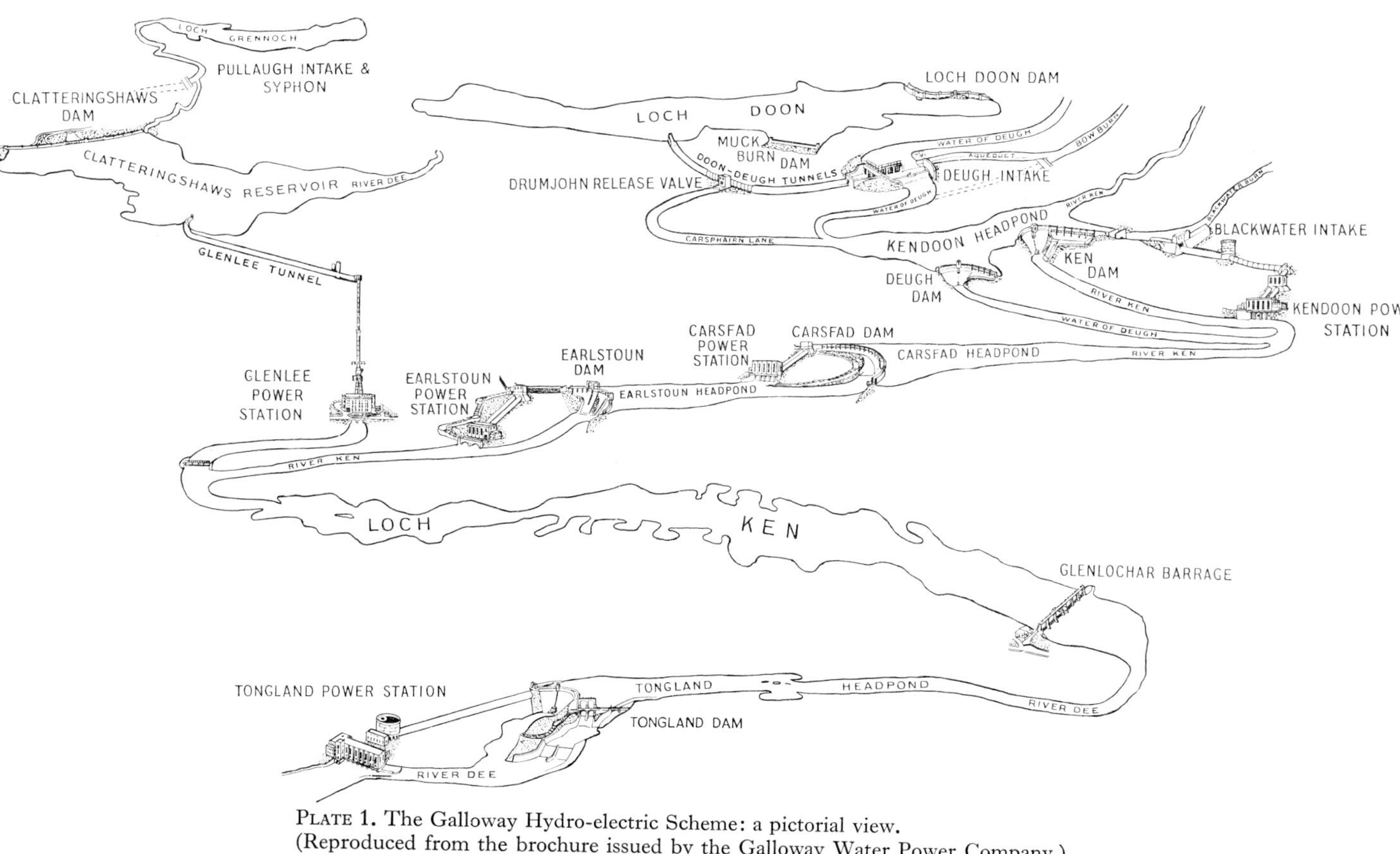


Plate 1. The Galloway Hydro-electric Scheme: a pictorial view.
(Reproduced from the brochure issued by the Galloway Water Power Company.)

PLATE 2. The Snowy Mountains Scheme: a pictorial view.

Action was taken to implement the committee's recommendations. The 'Scheme' would convert the Snowy Mountains into a huge power-house for two States and ultimately supply water equivalent to that required for over 400 000 hectares of new agricultural lands.

The Snowy Mountains Hydro-electric Power Act was passed by the Commonwealth Government in July 1949. The Snowy Mountains Authority, a statutory body constituted under the Act, came into being on 1 August 1949. Planning, detailed investigations, design and preliminary construction operations started immediately.

The Act provided that there should be only one Commissioner; that the role of two Associate Commissioners would be to advise and assist him; and that he would embody and exercise the very extensive powers given to the Authority.

The Act was later supported by a comprehensive agreement between the Commonwealth, New South Wales and Victoria, covering the construction and operation of the Scheme, the distribution of power and water and other relevant matters.

The Snowy Scheme is not only the biggest electric power generation and water conservation project ever attempted in Australia, but also one of the largest engineering achievements of the world. Contained within a radius of 64 km is a complex of 16 large dams and many smaller ones, nearly 161 km of tunnels, seven power stations, over 129 km of high mountain aqueducts to catch the mountain streams which would otherwise miss reservoirs and tunnels, hundreds of kilometres of power transmission lines, a network of roads and several new townships (see plate 2).

The Scheme has an installed capacity of 3 740 000 kW with an annual output of 5000 million kWh. It will also provide some 2.5 km$^3$ of diverted and regulated water each year for irrigation.

### Hudson's appointment as Commissioner

Hudson was not the first name on the short list for the position of Commissioner of the Authority. In fact, he was seventh. The first gave the then responsible Minister (Nelson Lemmon, Minister for Works and Housing) the impression that he would 'concern himself with the Snowy Scheme largely by means of monthly board meetings rather than giving it his whole attention'. The qualifications of five other possibilities were studied and soon afterwards the Chairman of the Commonwealth Public Service Board handed the Minister an envelope which had been given to him at a cricket match by an acquaintance. It contained a note suggesting that the man for the job was Bill Hudson.

The note was from a senior member of the staff of the Metropolitan Water Sewerage and Drainage Board, Sydney. He had told Hudson that he had an appointment to see the Chairman and mentioned incidentally that the Commonwealth was 'looking for a man to run the Snowy Scheme'. Hudson responded at the time, more for something to say than because of any serious intent, 'Well, tell him I'm interested'. From this came the job to which Hudson was to devote himself.

The Minister has described a subsequent interview:

> 'When Hudson walked into my office he was bent on one side and wore a rather crumpled coat. I couldn't measure him up at first sight, but we got talking. I said: "I don't think you look strong enough for the job." He said: "I have a sleeping appendicitis." I said: "You won't start the Snowy job until you get it out."
>
> 'The more I talked with him the more impressed I became. I took him to "Chif" (Hon. J. B. Chifley, the then Prime Minister). Ben sat back sucking his pipe and said: "Well, Mr Hudson, tell me about yourself." Hudson looked embarrassed and said: "I don't like talking about myself." Ben said: "That's a pretty fair sort of answer." I told Hudson afterwards that the Prime Minister would back him in Cabinet. Hudson got his appendix out two days later.'

Hudson, when asked by the Minister about starting salary (he was receiving £2475 p.a. from the Board), said he would like to start on £3000. The Minister said: 'We will give you £5000.' This made Hudson one of the highest paid government employees in Australia.

When Hudson took up his appointment in August 1949 at the age of 53, he accepted immense responsibilities. He shouldered the responsibility of constructing one of the largest hydro-electric and irrigation developments in the world. In fact, it was frequently referred to as the 'Eighth Wonder of the World'. Hudson approached it with the single-mindedness and tremendous capacity for work that characterized the whole of his engineering career. He dedicated himself to the Snowy Scheme. The general success of the Scheme is due in large measure to his untiring efforts.

## Organization and recruitment

The setting up of such a large organization in such a short time was a masterpiece of administration. There were few people in Australia with experience in the type of works involved.

Hudson gathered, indeed attracted, a team of associates, engineers, all manner of other technical experts, and administrators, of many nationalities, which had little parallel elsewhere. He insisted on loyalty to the Scheme. He saw the need for the establishment of the strongest possible team spirit and went out of his way to meet regularly with workers at all levels, to listen to and where possible solve their problems and never to be backward in giving full recognition for achievement. Many of his staff were towering personalities themselves, but it was the team and its great spirit which, under his leadership, caused the Snowy Mountains Scheme to unfold. It was this teamwork which motivated the Commonwealth Government, after his retirement and the completion of the Scheme, to set up the Snowy Mountains Engineering Corporation to carry on other great engineering works.

One of Hudson's achievements was to weld the New Australians into the Australian scene. He did this by ensuring that they were treated as equals with their Australian counterparts and by personal efforts with specific ethnic groups.

As a result New Australians—many of whom were recruited to work on the Scheme in their native country (eventually from 29 nations)—were accepted as individuals, with never a thought as to their actual nationality.

Apart from recruitment of staff with specialized experience from overseas and the use of consultants, the Authority embarked on a training programme with the United States Bureau of Reclamation, which led to over 100 of the Authority's junior engineers receiving training with the Bureau for periods up to one year. In the later years of the Scheme, the Authority was able to play a similar role in training Army engineers, both from Britain and Australia.

Perhaps Hudson often gave the impression of being single-minded to the point of being fanatical about the Snowy Scheme. He developed a concept he called 'Usefulness to the Scheme' to serve as a general criterion for judging policy and management issues. Employees who had demonstrated special usefulness to the Scheme would be rewarded at the Annual Staff Review at Christmas by being granted multiple annual increments in salary, or even promotion to a higher classification. Conversely, the unsatisfactory performers would lose an increment or two, or be advised to look for another position. His 'Usefulness to the Scheme' criterion survived the occasional exceptions and became generally accepted by employees and others as a rule which, while appearing strict at times, was scrupulously fair and just.

## Initial stages

Hudson saw the need for the quickest possible action in getting this Scheme firmly committed before any reservations could arise on the political scene. These, in fact, had already been illustrated by the refusal of the then Opposition to participate in the Scheme's inauguration ceremony. An election shortly thereafter, in fact, meant that the Opposition which had publicly shown such reservations became the Government which was to see the Scheme through virtually to completion.

Having regard to these factors and to the critical shortage of electricity at that time, particularly in N.S.W., early emphasis was given to construction of the first project. The Guthega project was selected as the one section which could stand by itself and then fit into the ultimate development. This 60 000 kW development came into service by April 1955, i.e. less than six years after the establishment of the Authority. This demonstration of Hudson's ability, drive and enthusiasm for the Scheme was justly recognized by his being created a Knight Commander of the Order of the British Empire in The Queen's Birthday Honours in the same year.

Apart from the works directly comprising this first project (a concrete gravity dam 33.5 m high, a tunnel almost 4.8 km long, steel penstocks 975 m in length, together with the surface power station), achievement of this early generating capacity (using turbo-generators bought 'off the shelf' with conditions adapted to their particular characteristics) had necessitated significant progress being made with the construction of the headquarters at Cooma and works townships at Jindabyne and Island Bend, and the commencement of construction of a major mountain road system to give access to the previously inaccessible sites, provision of initial accommodation and construction power supplies.

Construction of these large ancillary facilities had depended to a large extent on the establishment of a substantial direct labour work force which became a continuing feature of the Scheme and allowed contractors to commence real construction very quickly on the major works.

Despite this emphasis on the earliest possible visible evidence of construction activity, Hudson also recognized the need for the soundest possible basic investigation and research facilities if the Scheme was to be developed in the most economical manner to fit in with the States' thermal generating systems. One of the earliest actions was the establishment of engineering laboratories (known as Scientific Services) providing basic advice on hydraulic problems (including where necessary model studies), physical sciences (matters such as photo-elasticity, ultrasonic testing and chemical analyses), geology and soil conservation and investigation of materials required in the construction of the various works. These laboratories assisted greatly in ensuring that the Authority not only kept up to date with world-wide practice, but was also prepared to adapt and innovate as required.

As more information became available from the field and following intensive office investigations the original proposals were modified. Whereas the original proposals envisaged two virtually separate developments with a total installed capacity of 2 820 000 kW in 16 power stations, the Scheme, as finally constructed, became one fully integrated development with a total installed capacity of 3 740 000 kW in seven power stations. This major change was able to be achieved with very little reduction in energy output. In addition to the seven power stations, one pumping station was included and one of the power stations provided also for pumped storage capacity (1 500 000 kW generating capacity, 750 000 kW pumping capacity).

The various interests of the Governments concerned and the rapidly increasing population as a result of post-war immigration (and hence the rapidly developing industrial requirements for energy and other resources) emphasized the need for the closest possible liaison in deciding the ultimate development to be adopted. Despite this critical need, it was not until January 1959 that the States passed the necessary underpinning legislation which gave the Authority complete certainty as to its legality.

## Public relations

Public relations was an aspect of the Scheme in which Hudson gave a tremendous lead to many other bodies concerned with spending public monies.

The Scheme came under political attack during its early years and the Authority also received some bad press publicity for alleged waste and ineptitude. Hudson met these criticisms in his typical forthright fashion by encouraging and assisting the people of Australia to see the Snowy Scheme for themselves and learn the truth. From modest beginnings, public relations became a highly organized and successful feature of Hudson's administration.

The public relations aspects of the Scheme, including literature, tours and accommodation for viewing, were without doubt more far-reaching than any similar scheme in Australia. Hudson also paid particular attention to discussion of the Scheme in Parliament and other forums and moved immediately to correct any interpretations or impressions which he felt were contrary to the facts or were damaging to the general concept. This particularly related to monitoring events in the Commonwealth Parliament and maintaining close relationships with the Ministers and Treasury officials most concerned with the Scheme. On one occasion during which record progress had been made in a financial year on many of the Scheme's contracts, it was necessary to seek additional funds or slow the contractors down. Accordingly, Hudson set off for Canberra to seek to persuade the Government of the day to meet the extra payments to the contractors. He returned from Canberra and said to a colleague: 'There you are, we secured this afternoon an additional £4½ million against an original budget allocation of £24 million—our public relations program has paid for itself in a single afternoon.'

The decision to encourage the average citizen to visit the Scheme and make his own judgement started in the early days when the Guthega project was the main activity to be seen. Many became enthusiastic advocates and helped turn the tide of public opinion solidly behind the Authority. Frequent news releases to press and radio ensured that interest was maintained. It became accepted practice for any distinguished persons visiting Canberra to have included in the itinerary for that visit a few days inspecting the Snowy Scheme. Sir William Spooner, when Minister for the Scheme, used to refer to it as 'the brightest star in my crown'.

It is estimated that, with organized bus tours, car convoys and casual visitors, at the peak of the Authority's activity some 60 000 people were visiting the works each year.

## Contract system

Before World War II most engineering construction in Australia was carried out by direct labour using the State Department's own labour forces. The major works on the Snowy Scheme were among the first in Australia to be carried out by contract, as Hudson realized from his previous experience in private practice that this was the most efficient way to achieve his targets in time and cost.

He was instrumental in introducing and building the confidence of the authorities in the contracting method of construction and arranged that the dams and tunnels should be built by contractors with good experience in these fields.

Hudson believed that contractors would tender keener prices if contingencies could be reduced to an absolute minimum; if they could be assured of continuing payments if progress went ahead of target and if they could see some reward for speeding up the works by a bonus system for earlier completion. Accordingly, he ensured that contracts were written whereby the

Authority was a very active party to the contract, and problems as they arose were handled promptly.

### Industrial relations

Under Hudson's leadership the Snowy Scheme had an enviable industrial record; in fact, there were no major strikes during his commissionership. He always took the view that management had to be, in his own words, 'lily white'. He was a firm believer in the Australian worker, if treated properly. Invariably when a union problem was brought to his notice his starting point would be —there could be substance in the union's claim—and he sought and took advice from level-headed union leaders.

He instigated and made sure that his senior staff followed strict procedures with the trade union movement. This included regular monthly conferences with union representatives.

In addition, for the early years, formal industrial proceedings concerning contractors on the Scheme were conducted by the President of the N.S.W. Industrial Commission, Mr Justice Taylor. On the retirement from the Bench of Judge Taylor, Hudson saw the advantage, in the interests of continuing industrial harmony, in appointing Taylor as Independent Arbitrator on the Scheme, to whom all industrial disputes would be referred and whose judgement thereon would be observed. This required agreement of all contractors on the Scheme and all unions representative of the workforce and, in particular, their agreement to abide by the judgements, which of course did not carry the force of law. It was a triumph particularly for Hudson and a tribute to the respect in which he was held by both unions and contractors that, not without considerable misgivings, they entered upon the scheme and supported it, even when decisions were unfavourable to them.

### Safety

Hudson was determined to make working conditions on the Snowy Scheme amongst the safest in the world. His conviction was that this could only be achieved if safety was given attention by the project managers for the contractors, i.e. safety started at the top. He established a Joint Safety Council with monthly meetings of which he was chairman and required the contractors' project managers to sit on the council with him. Under Hudson's guidance the council achieved a remarkable record. The men became safety conscious, and the Scheme's excellent safety record made it possible for contractors to secure lower insurance premiums.

The Joint Safety Council primarily at Hudson's instigation also operated a rehabilitation centre to expedite the recovery and return to work of injured employees. This centre established such a name in this field that it also came to be used by persons who had suffered injuries elsewhere.

Apart from subsidizing safety bonus schemes operated by its contractors, the Authority also introduced programmes for its own workers to encourage safety to the maximum possible extent. For instance, a safety award lottery was held quarterly with cash prizes being provided to wages personnel and their supervisors who had accident-free records.

Another major innovation by Hudson was the requirement that all the Authority's vehicles be fitted with seat belts and that wearing of these belts was compulsory for all employees. Despite an annual distance travel by the Authority's vehicles of the order of 9.65 Gm, no fatality was recorded as a result of a road accident for a number of years following the introduction of seat belts. The adoption of the compulsory wearing of seat belts in road vehicles has since been followed in a number of Australian States.

### Soil conservation

The Scheme had laid a heavy hand on the wilderness areas of the Snowy Mountains and none deplored this more than Hudson. He hated the despoilation that construction caused, and the fact that it could silt the reservoirs and damage the earthworks. So, while the words 'environment' and 'ecology' tend to be regarded as of somewhat recent development, in the early 1950s Hudson's innovative interest in such matters was reflected in pioneering work being carried out on such diverse items as eels, trout, phasmatids (stick insects), cloud seeding and catchment management.

In these specialized fields the Authority ensured that close liaison was maintained with other interested bodies. On the soil conservation side, regular meetings were held with the State organization responsible for such work. To deal with the effect of the Scheme on the sport fishing potential of the area, a committee was established representing two States, the Commonwealth Scientific and Industrial Research Organization and local fishing interests.

### Communications

Hudson had an acute sense of the need for proper and adequate communications. The inadequate telephone facilities was a continuing source of frustration to him in the earlier days of the Scheme. Accordingly, he arranged to provide the Scheme with its own system and he won permission to interconnect this to the national network. The Snowy radio communications system was highly efficient and operated effectively over the mountains and through all weather conditions.

In addition, Hudson had several airstrips constructed and acquired and made great use of a number of light aircraft in order to ensure there was rapid communication on a face-to-face basis between those in the field and senior people at head office. His attitude was 'Let's jump in a plane and go and settle the problem on the spot'. This had a tremendous morale effect on those working in isolated areas. To connect Cooma to the civil airline system, he was the driving force behind construction of an airport for the town.

### Construction techniques

In the previous sections of this memoir the emphasis has been largely on organization and management. In the technical field many new innovations and construction techniques, particularly in underground construction, were introduced by the Authority for the first time. Hudson had a high regard for American know-how. He also had a particular interest in pressure grouting and rock bolting, the latter being developed by the Authority to such a stage that by 1954 its use in underground power station works involved roof spans of nearly 23 m. The research work on rock bolting was eagerly sought overseas.

A special feature of the construction was the high speed driving of tunnels through hard rock which represented a large proportion of the work on the Scheme. World records for speed of advance were broken time and time again.

Research work on steel and associated welding, primarily for pipe lines, was in addition given particular attention in the Snowy laboratories. Hudson also realized that wider resources were necessary and became a great advocate of the Australian Welding Research Association of which he was the first Chairman in 1965.

## Snowy period conclusions

It was typical that, for a man of such natural reserve, Hudson disciplined himself to become an accomplished public speaker on the technical, economic and social benefits of the Snowy Mountains Scheme. It was a subject close to his heart. He spent many hours giving speeches to groups about the Snowy Scheme, its effects and potential effects on Australia and the South East Asian region. One of his favourite expressions was that 'the Scheme was like a factory which made motor cars cheaper than anybody else' (here he was referring to the peak load electricity which it generated) and 'it gave away trucks free'. The latter reference was to the water being sent westward to irrigate additional areas in the Murray and Murrumbidgee valleys—the water was a complete bonus. Hudson saw this as probably the greater of the two benefits which the Scheme would have in the long term. He was firmly of the view that Australia could produce foodstuffs for the rapidly increasing populations in the South East Asian region generally. He saw, in fact, Australia being a food bowl for this area and saw the Scheme's contribution through its irrigation water as being highly significant in this respect. None of the many important personages, who visited the Scheme and experienced one of Hudson's public relations talks on the Scheme before they set out on tours of inspection, could have failed to have been captivated by his eloquence and enthusiasm for the project.

The following extract illustrates his interest in his employees: in the introduction to the *S.M.A. Magazine* in December 1951 he wrote:

> 'I have always maintained that notwithstanding anything that may be said by those who barrack for us or by those who damn us, we shall ultimately be judged on *one thing and one thing only*, namely on our achievement. We may talk of our plans, of what we shall do this year—or next year—or in the next ten years. Australians are so used to hearing of plans and programmes for great developments like ours that they are liable

to be sceptical. As a race they are hard-headed with a practical outlook. What they look for—in fact what they have a right to demand—are "results".

'On reaching the close of 1951, let us take stock. What have we achieved during the past twelve months? Some things have gone wrong, we have made some mistakes, but by and large I am indeed proud of what the staff and men of S.M.A. have to show. For instance, twelve months ago the Guthega project was no more than a few lines on a drawing. Today men from the other side of the world are at work with their machines blasting the granite to make way for structures which will force the falling waters of the hitherto untamed Upper Snowy to give up their power for the use of mankind. This stage was reached only by hard work in the office and in the field—by S.M.A. men with slide rules and log tables, by geologists and surveyors, by diamond drillers, and by tradesmen and all other grades of workers, not forgetting the bulldozer drivers and other road builders working in the rain and snow on the steep mountainsides —thrusting aside trees and rock to give access to the Munyang and the Guthega and so pave the way for the tunnellers and dam builders to commence their jobs.

'What has been done on the Upper Snowy is now under way on the approaches to the precipitous gorges of the Upper Tumut. Here the Authority's men are up against an even tougher proposition—one which calls for determination and guts. . . .'

The economic soundness of the Scheme as finally decided was amply justified by the approval of the International Bank for Reconstruction and Development (World Bank) to grant a loan of £100M Aust. to the Commonwealth of Australia for financing the Murray Project of the Scheme. A comprehensive examination of the feasibility and economics of the Scheme which preceded the loan covered both the ability of the project to pay for itself as well as its part in assisting the overall development of the country.

With the installed capacity in the power stations of 3 740 000 kW the average annual output of electricity is now 5200 million kWh. The supply of water for irrigation has been increased by 80%, the Snowy Scheme diverting an annual average of 1130 million $m^3$ which with the associated storages at the outlets of the scheme provides additional regulation to give a total of 2.5 $km^3$ annually.

In a way, one might look on the Snowy as the coming of age of engineering in Australia. It was a scheme which captured the imagination of all Australians—in a sense it was the point of national maturity. The Scheme showed that under good leadership Australians could, themselves, tackle the most major projects. Many things had been done before but none as big, none with all the post-war problems of resources of both men and materials, and certainly none within the pre-estimated cost and time. Hudson was the man who made all these things happen. In addition, he laid the basis for an international engineering consultancy group that has prospered, but probably even more, provided training, experience and confidence to many hundreds of his employees to Australia's benefit.

### Retirement

The usual retiring age for senior men of Hudson's standing in the Australian Government's employment is 65. It was a tribute to his high standing in Government and the Opposition circles that the Commonwealth Parliament, on two separate occasions, passed legislation extending his term in office by a total of six years. He retired in 1967 at the age of 71 years, to live in Canberra.

Retirement from the Scheme opened up other avenues of endeavour. He was elected to the board of a large organization making and distributing an internationally known brand of earth-moving and mechanical equipment. He continued his association with the Australian Welding Research Association and took up active association and chairmanship of the Road Safety Council of N.S.W. and presidency of the National Safety Council of Australia. Both these followed his original activity in installing seat belts in all Authority vehicles in the 1950s. Hudson also entered the arbitration field and arbitrated on several important engineering-oriented contract disputes in his retirement, as well as acting as a consultant in many fields.

### Recreations

Hudson's main recreation was bushwalking, which became his greatest interest outside work when he moved to Cooma. In New Zealand and later in Sydney, when he lived near the harbour, he was extremely interested in yachting. In Sydney he owned a 24 foot yacht *Roxane*. He also was keen on astronomy and pursued this hobby whilst working on the Nepean Dam. Sir William had a particular interest in the Geehi Club, a group of bushwalking enthusiasts made up primarily of Snowy people. Many still treasure the memory of the 'Chief', complete with leggings and walking stick, marching down Hannels Spur from Mt Kosciusko to Geehi, with scores of others trying to keep pace with him on that 1830 m descent. Hudson had looked forward to pursuing his astronomy interests in his retirement, but failing eyesight precluded this.

### Character

For all the acclaim and honours he received Hudson, a great engineer and conservationist, outstanding administrator, a man of great strength of character and tremendous vision, remained a man of modesty and simplicity. He was surprisingly quiet, shy and reserved, tough, not particularly tolerant and with a quick temper, but an honest and fair person and justly proud of himself and his achievements.

He did, however, have a great deal of reserve, particularly when in the presence of politicians. It almost seemed he would travel to Canberra only when commanded by the Minister in charge of the Scheme or the Prime

Minister. It is said that he was once described as the Lion of Cooma and the Lamb of Canberra. Hudson also believed in going full bore, to use his own phrase, for what he wanted. Colleagues would often say to him: 'Don't use up all your points on the first round, save some for the next round.' Hudson's view, however, was to put all the cards on the table and go to it, if that is what you want. Usually he was successful. A senior colleague once said of him that his tactic was to plough his lonely straight furrow while others politicked about in zigzag courses, often to find that Hudson had achieved his objective while they were still negotiating in fancy manoeuvres.

A simple true story epitomizes how Snowy people felt about Sir William Hudson. One day a small boy, the son of a Snowy engineer, was walking to school. Sir William, passing in his car, offered him a lift. The boy, now an engineer himself, employed by the Snowy Mountains Engineering Corporation, and with his own family, gazed at the great man in awe and wonder. When he got home he told his mother of the experience and concluded—'Sir William Hudson, he's next to God, isn't he?'

A story told about him concerned a conference about mid-Sunday afternoon at which it was finally decided what tactics would be employed on a certain major problem. One of those present asked Hudson if he wanted to finish the operation that afternoon. Hudson replied: 'No, let's not spoil the whole weekend, leave it until Monday.'

As another example of his interest in the 'hard core' of his employees, Hudson instituted an 'Old Hands' gathering. These were for people who joined the Scheme in the first 12 months, and the gatherings were held in various parts of the Scheme. Hudson always attended and joined in the associated revelries, at one of which he was invested aborigine style with a gorget and given the name of King Billy. Although less formally given, but nevertheless with the same feeling, Hudson became known as Snowy Bill, the Old Man or just Bill.

Like all who would manage a large project efficiently, Hudson appeared to become isolated, remote and lonely. His whole life and all his time were devoted to the Scheme. He was fond of two quotations. The one—

The man who once so wisely said
'Be sure you're right, then go ahead'
Might well have added this to wit—
'Be sure you're wrong before you quit'

he had in his home, at the Water Board and also in his Snowy office.

His other was—

'Rules should be one's servant,
Not one's master.'

It is significant that he wished to be buried at Cooma near the Scheme he made come true. Many hundreds attended the simple service; it was a day when the town of Cooma came to a halt to honour a great man; when memories were relived by people who came from near and far and talked with other friends long after the actual event. It was mentioned many times: 'It was just as the Old Man would have wanted it—he couldn't have organized it better himself.'

A home for aged persons will be built in Cooma and named the 'Sir William Hudson Memorial Home' as a tangible community form of remembrance to a man who did so much for Australia and the Cooma district in particular.

'Si monumentum quaeris, circumspice.'

No account of Sir William would be complete without mention of his wife Eileen (Trotter) whom he married in 1926. Eileen is a remarkable and talented person and the years have shown how she complemented her husband's talents and working pattern. This was demonstrated in 1959 when, in her own right, she was made an Officer of the Order of the British Empire in recognition of her unremitting labours to foster an understanding of the Snowy Mountains enterprise among the many Australian and overseas visitors. Two daughters, Margaret (Mrs Unger) of Wahroonga and Anne (Mrs Taylor) of Mimmitabel, made up the family as well as six grandchildren.

Sir William left no written biographical material. I have been greatly helped in preparing this memoir by Lady Hudson and her daughter Margaret, who from time to time was able to persuade her father, despite his reticence, to talk about his early life and career and kept a record. For the Galloway and Captain Cook Graving Dock periods I was able to cover these from personal knowledge with the help of Charles Marshall and Stuart Harrison.

But this biography would have been sadly deficient without the very comprehensive notes compiled by Ross McIntyre as a result of discussions he had with many colleagues and friends who worked closely with Bill on the Snowy and previous schemes, in particular Eric Warrell, Doug Price, Peter Collins and Tim Besley. Others who have also been of great help are Sir Mark Oliphant, F.R.S., Sir John Holland and Peter Reeves. I am also indebted to Lionel Wigmore for extracts from his book *Struggle for the Snowy*.

### Honours and distinctions

Knight Commander of the Order of the British Empire, 1955
Australian Engineering Award, 1957
Kernot Memorial Medal for distinguished engineering achievements in Australia, 1959
Fellow of University College London, 1961
Hon. Member Australian Institution of Mining and Metallurgy, 1961
Hon. Member Institution of Engineers, Australia, 1962
Hon. Doctor of Laws, Australian National University, 1962
Fellow of the Royal Society, 1964
James Cook Medal of the Royal Society of New South Wales, 1966
Hon. Doctor of Engineering, Monash University, Melbourne, 1968
Hon. Fellow of the Royal Australian Institute of Architects, 1968
Hon. Member of the Institution of Royal Engineers, 1968
Australian Welding Institute Annual Award, 1975
Order of the White Cross Annual Award for services to Australia, 1975
Foundation Fellow of the Australian Academy of Technological Sciences, 1975
Life Governor, Braille Library of Victoria, 1976
Life Member of the Returned Services League of Australia

BIBLIOGRAPHY

(Summary of more important papers and articles)

1938 (With J. K. HUNTER) The Galloway hydro-electric development. *Proc. J. Instn civ. Engrs* **8**, 323, no. 5164.

1954 The contribution of hydro-electric power to Australian power resources. Australian Institution of Political Science.

1956 The Snowy Mountains Scheme. *Yb. Commonw. Australia.*

1959 The Snowy Mountains Scheme. *Financial Times* (London).

1960 A key to Australia's future. *The Young Scientist.*

The contribution of hydro-electric power to Australian power resources. *Snowy Mountains Authority.*

1961 Australian Snowy Scheme. *Geogrl Mag. Lond.* July.

The Snowy Murray development of the Snowy Mountains Scheme. *Victorian Resour. J.* February.

1962 Snowy Mountains Scheme. *Proc. Instn civ. Engrs.*

Snowy Mountains Scheme. *British Electric Power Convention, London.*

Snowy Mountain Scheme. *Nature, Lond.* 7 July.

Snowy Mountains Scheme. *Pacific Neighbours*, vol. 17, no. 1.

Management on the Snowy Mountains Scheme. *Australian Institute of Management.*

The Snowy Mountains hydro-electric project. *Proc. Instn Engineers, Australia.*

Electric supply in Australia with special reference to the Snowy Mountains Scheme. *Financial Times* (London), 7 May.

The Snowy Scheme. *Life, USA*, February.

1963 Multi-purpose water HUD conservation development projects in USA, USSR and Australia with special reference to the Snowy Mountains Scheme. *Instn Production Engineers.*

Snowy Mountains Scheme, Cooma, NSW. *Snowy Mountains Hydro-electric Authority.*

The Snowy Mountains Scheme. *Encyclopaedia Britannica.*

1964 The development of Australia's water resources with particular reference to irrigation. *CEPO Instn civ. Engrs* no. 95.

The role of water resources in the development of Northern Australia. *Living Earth*, vol. 9, December; and *Union Recorder, Sydney*, vol. 44, 15 October.

1965 Snowy Power Scheme. *Manufacturers Monthly, Sydney*, vol. 4, January.

1967 Snowy Scheme. *The Age*, 6 May.

The 25 year plan stays on schedule. *The Age*, 8 May.

1970 The development of Australia's water resources—the need for research. *Proc. Instn Engineers, Australia*, vol. 42, January/February.

Benefits for commerce and industry from road accident prevention. *South Aust. Road Transport J.* vol. 21, April; and *J. Ind.* vol. 38, April.

1971 The structure and work of the Australian Welding Research Association. *Aust. Weld. J.* vol. 15, November/December.

The Snowy Mountains hydroelectric and irrigation scheme (Australia). *Proc. R. Soc. Lond.* A **326**, 23–37.

W. O. James

# WILLIAM OWEN JAMES

1900 — 1978

Elected F.R.S. 1952

By A. R. Clapham, F.R.S., and J. L. Harley, F.R.S.

William Owen James was born on 21 May 1900 at 'Ravenscroft', Mount Pleasant Road, Tottenham, London N.17, the elder of the two sons of William Benjamin James and his wife Agnes Ursula, *née* Collins; there were no daughters. The father, born in 1866, was for 32 years a successful primary school headmaster under the Tottenham Education Committee; he was especially interested in art teaching and had a reputation for training headmasters for other primary schools in the Committee's area. He was a keen amateur botanist and, while working for his external B.Sc. of London University, had attended early classes in zoology run by H. G. Wells. His father's enthusiasms for biology and art were recognized by James as important factors directing his own early interests. James's mother was born in 1869 and the marriage, extending from 1894 until she died early in 1931, was described by James as 'conspicuously happy'. After her death James's father lived with his son in Islip, near Oxford, until he died in 1939.

James was not aware of ancestors with scientific achievements or interests. There was a distant relationship, on the mother's side, with Horatio Nelson, a connection admitted with reluctance by grandmother Ann Ursula Collins because of 'the sort of man he was'.

## Early years

James went to Tottenham Grammar School from 1910 until 1916. His younger brother, Dr A. L. James, who was for a time at Tottenham Grammar School with him, remembers him as a rather quiet boy, regarded from an early age as of delicate health but, nevertheless, always maintaining a high standard in his classwork. The brother had an accident during this period and on the advice of a doctor transferred to a school in Southend-on-Sea, where the two spent their weekends together. James's chief interest at the time was photography, and his brother relates that he constructed 'an apparatus with which he could take telephoto pictures of ships in the River. He was fond of sailing model yachts, of which he had a few, including one quite good boat. He also constructed a fleet of small model warships, and we spent a lot of time fishing'.

Physics and chemistry were the only scientific subjects taught at Tottenham Grammar School, but the teacher in chemistry discovered in James some aptitude for experimentation and did what he could to encourage it. In due course he was awarded a Middlesex County Junior Scholarship and in 1916 took the London Higher School Certificate and Matriculation Examination. During his later years at school he developed a special interest in English and a desire to write, but at school-leaving age he did not feel strong enough to face 'the initial starvation incidental to whole-time authorship' and therefore accepted an invitation from his paternal uncle, Charles James, to enter the flourishing family firm of chartered accountants in Birmingham. There he painfully acquired a fair degree of proficiency in the basic skills of accountancy which proved very useful in later life. But he did not enjoy the work, and a breakdown in health, caused by the first of a series of tubercular outbreaks, compelled him to leave the firm in 1918, when his state of health also brought about his rejection for national service. His two year experience of the business world induced in him a deep and lasting appreciation of the privileges of the academic life.

On recovering from his illness, and while awaiting the start of the university year, James taught for a single term at St John's School, Southend-on-Sea, a private preparatory school where his teaching subjects were English and geography, no science being taught. He found that he did not care for school teaching and he had already been accepted for admission to University College, Reading (now Reading University), so he proceeded there in the autumn of 1919. He set out to read agriculture but during his first year he changed to botany, in which the principal teachers were Theodora Prankerd, who much impressed him by her enthusiastic sincerity, and Professor Walter Stiles, who first interested him in plant physiology. His subsidiary subjects were chemistry and geology, and the quality of the teaching of palaeontology by Professor H. L. Watkins almost induced a further change of primary subject. But he much enjoyed the classes in botany, including the botanical excursions organized by the department. He became secretary of 'Kosmos', the student scientific society, and impressed his fellow students with his organizing capacity. His recreation was chiefly on the river, but he also sang tenor in one of the College choirs, acted in plays produced by the Dramatic Society, went to dances in College and in Hall and played a little tennis.

## Research at Cambridge and at Rothamsted

His period as an undergraduate at Reading was extended by a year through a recurrence of his ill-health, and it was not until 1923 that he took his London External B.Sc. degree with first class honours in botany. He was then awarded a training grant from the Department of Scientific and Industrial Research to work under Dr F. F. Blackman, F.R.S., at the Botany School, Cambridge, for the two years from September 1924 to the summer of 1926. He was admitted as a postgraduate student of St John's College, of which Dr Blackman was a Fellow and Dr Udney Yule, a distinguished statistician, Director of Natural Sciences.

F. F. Blackman, then the leading British investigator in the field of plant physiology, agreed to supervise a project suggested to James by Professor

Walter Stiles, a study of the effects of variations in the supply of carbon dioxide on the rate of photosynthesis of submerged water plants. James threw himself wholeheartedly into his research, sometimes staying up throughout the night to complete long-running experiments. Gladys James remembers him as often saying that the part of the work that he enjoyed most was bench work in the laboratory. He designed and built his own apparatus for measuring rates of photosynthesis in the aquatic moss *Fontinalis antipyretica*. The size and imposing appearance of this apparatus led to its designation by his fellow research students as 'the cathedral'. He was always neat and capable with his hands, ingenious in devising apparatus and meticulous in all his experimental work. Gladys James states that his main pleasure apart from his research was in punting on the Cam, and the use for his research of the submerged moss *Fontinalis* gave him frequent excuses for short collecting trips on the river, often accompanied by a fellow research student appreciative of a pleasant afternoon break. He took a great interest in architectural features of the Cambridge colleges and churches and much enjoyed the numerous opportunities for hearing concerts of classical music. Other evenings were spent in playing bridge with a small circle of friends among graduate research workers in the Botany School or attached to St John's. There seems no doubt that this was a happy episode in James's life.

He finished his investigation in the summer of 1926 and then left Cambridge to join the team under Professor V. H. Blackman (brother of F. F. Blackman) at the Research Institute for Plant Physiology at the Imperial College of Science. Meanwhile, he completed and submitted his thesis and was duly awarded his Ph.D. degree in 1927, an account of his findings appearing in the *Proceedings of the Royal Society* in the following year.

Professor Blackman's team had an experimental garden and a small field laboratory at the Rothamsted Experimental Station in Harpenden, and James now spent much of his time working there. His problem was to study the potassium nutrition of potatoes grown in the plots of a field experiment laid out in accordance with the new statistical concepts being developed by Dr R. A. Fisher, Head of the Statistical Department at Rothamsted. James adopted Fisher's statistical procedures but by the end of his second season of work he became convinced that his physiological findings could have been obtained more easily through controlled experiments in the laboratory. During his time at Rothamsted he enjoyed a close association not only with R. A. Fisher but also with the plant physiologist F. G. Gregory, then a member of Professor Blackman's team spending each summer at Rothamsted. James much admired Gregory's scientific work and relished his effervescent enthusiasms, and the two often sat up till the small hours listening to records of classical music in James's flat in Harpenden.

## Oxford, 1927–59

Early in 1927, A. G. Tansley (later Sir Arthur Tansley and first Chairman of the Nature Conservancy), who had just been appointed to the Sherardian

Chair of Botany at Oxford, invited James to join his small staff, then consisting only of the distinguished morphologist Dr A. H. Church and the mycologist Mr (later Dr) W. H. Wilkins. Tansley recognized the need for a specialist teacher in plant physiology, since he was not himself qualified to undertake the task that had been assumed by his two immediate predecessors in the Sherardian Chair, Professors Sidney Vines and Sir Frederick Keeble: Vines, indeed, had been mainly responsible for introducing the teaching of plant physiology into courses of botany in British universities. James was initially offered the modest and temporary post of Departmental Demonstrator in Botany, which he was nevertheless delighted to accept. He was made University Demonstrator in the following year and remained in Oxford for the 32 years until his election to a Chair of Botany in the Imperial College of Science in 1959. He was awarded the title of Reader in Botany at Oxford in 1947.

In 1927 the Oxford Department of Botany occupied the two ranges of buildings standing between the old Botanic Garden and the High Street, opposite Magdalen College. The range nearer the River Cherwell housed the Library and Herbarium, while the teaching accommodation and the private rooms of members of the departmental staff were mostly in the range to the west of the entrance to the Garden through the Danby Gate of 1632. Both ranges had been built during the tenure of the Sherardian Chair by Charles G. B. Daubeny (1834–67). He had been given permission to reside at the Garden and in 1835, soon after his accession to office, he erected for himself a new dwelling house at the back of and over the Library and including space for the Herbarium and a lecture room as well as his private apartments. In 1847 Magdalen College permitted him to erect a building on the other (western) side of the Danby Gate and thenceforward he delivered his lectures there. It was in this 80 year old building, with the sole additions of a classroom and laboratory extending the original block towards the Danby Gate in 1876, that Professor Tansley and his staff had to make provision for teaching and research in modern experimental botany. University funds for improvements to accommodation were scanty, and it was clear that the utmost economy must be observed. The Library and Herbarium were adequately, if somewhat modestly, housed in the eastern block, but there were certainly no more than minimal facilities for experimental classwork in the old Daubeny teaching block, even with the additions of 1876, and there was no provision for modern research in plant physiology. This presented James with a serious challenge, but he faced it with characteristic determination and resourcefulness. He first created a teaching laboratory for plant physiology from a first floor room at an awkwardly lower level than the adjoining corridors and smaller rooms. Then, during the early 1930s, he, his technician and some research students converted with their own hands the old Daubeny lecture room, long notable for the all-pervading smell of damp and decay for which Daubeny's ghost was held responsible, into a reasonably spacious and well equipped research laboratory for plant physiology. A smaller room, adjacent to James's private room, served as additional research space.

At the time of James's arrival in Oxford there was a preliminary course in botany, primarily for medical students who had still to qualify in the basic sciences before embarking on their preclinical courses. It was attended also by first-year undergraduates who proposed to read a biological subject but had neither passed nor gained exemption from the First Public Examination in Natural Sciences before reaching the university. There was, in addition, a course in botany for first-year foresters, a sizeable group in those days. Tansley initially gave the lectures for both courses, basing them on his well known book *Elements of plant biology*, written while he was on the staff of the Cambridge Botany School and responsible for teaching the 1st M.B. course in plant biology. The course and book were both notable for their pioneering and successful attempt to introduce fundamental biological concepts into the elementary teaching of botany. James took over the lectures for the 'Prelim.' course for some time during the 1930s, and he assisted substantially with successive revisions of *Elements of plant biology*, his name being added to Tansley's in the 1935 edition and replacing it completely after the revision of 1949. His own elementary textbook, *An introduction to plant physiology*, which sought 'to give a balanced account of the more elementary aspects of plant physiology' for 'readers of senior school or junior university status', was first published in 1931 and has continued in demand up to the present decade, a seventh edition appearing in 1973.

Those first-year Oxford undergraduates who had already passed or gained exemption from the First Public Examination, and had been admitted to read botany in the Final Honours School of Natural Sciences, were required to attend lectures and practical classes in no subject other than botany for the whole of their three years or more before graduation, though they might be recommended to go to certain classes offered by other departments. This meant that very few opted to read botany unless they had a genuine interest in the subject and ensured a generally high level of competence as well as of interest. A complete three-year course was designed for them, a day and a half in each week being reserved exclusively for plant physiology, the detailed planning of which was left entirely to James. He found from the start that he was attracting a steady stream of able undergraduates to a special interest in his branch of the subject, leading several of them to seek to work for a research degree under his supervision, provided that they obtained sufficiently good degrees. Among these were Rhodes Scholars from Commonwealth countries and from the U.S.A., and there were, in addition, those with first degrees from other universities, including some graduate Rhodes Scholars, who asked to do research under his direction. James was soon the centre of a small but very active research school and his reputation both as teacher and research worker grew steadily. The early problems of inadequate accommodation had been overcome and the national standing of the still quite small department had risen markedly.

It was important to Tansley that James should as soon as possible become an M.A. and therefore a full member of the University, since he would otherwise be unable to assume certain important functions or to sit on boards and committees where his presence would be valuable for the department. Had he held the corresponding degree either of Cambridge University or of Trinity College, Dublin, he could have incorporated as an M.A., but, in the event, he was obliged to accept a D.Phil. on the basis of his Cambridge doctorate. It was only some years later that he was given the degree of M.A. by decree.

On 7 April 1928, at Chapel Allerton, Leeds, James married his fellow student of botany at Reading, Gladys Macphail Redfern, daughter of Ernest William Redfern and his wife Charlotte Elizabeth, *née* Lowe. They had remained in very close touch throughout his three years in Cambridge and at Rothamsted, while she was doing research in plant physiology under Professor Stiles, and they took early advantage of such security of outlook as was afforded by the junior post in Tansley's department. They found a comfortable house in Islip, about five miles north of Oxford, and they continued to live there, maintaining a very attractive garden and entertaining their friends, until they left for London in 1959. Their elder daughter, Daphne, was born in 1930 and the younger, Agnes Anne, in 1932. Both went to the Oxford High School and both spent the war years from 1940 to 1945 in the United States, as did many other children of Oxford academics during that anxious period.

From his marriage onwards, the house and garden in Islip became the centre for James's deep family devotion and provided his main outlet for relaxation, though his concern for his undergraduate and graduate students and his absorption in his teaching and research remained undiminished. Gladys records that he was never completely happy when unable to be at work and that this caused him great distress during periods of illness. But although he was of frail physique and was compelled to be very careful about his health, it would be misleading to imply that he was in constant or even very frequent ill-health. He spent a good deal of time in tending the garden at Islip, avoiding only the really heavy work, and for long periods was free even from common colds. He did, however, have a further serious tubercular outbreak in the late 1930s and was unable to work for about 18 months, part of that time being spent in a sanatorium at Mundesley on the Norfolk coast. After his recovery he resumed a quite active life, first in Oxford and later in London, until another bout of poor health led him to retire, a year early, from the headship of the Botany Department at Imperial College.

After his mother died in 1931 James's father spent a good deal of time at Islip, and his younger brother 'John' (A. L. James) was frequently there during his years at Oxford first as an undergraduate and then as one of James's research students. James took an active part in the village life of Islip and greatly enjoyed the companionship of numerous friends from many different walks of life. In Oxford, too, he steadily acquired a circle of friends and acquaintances in other departments of the University and also in Oriel College, to which he was admitted as a member of Senior Common Room soon after his arrival in Oxford. He dined there fairly regularly but was never deeply involved in college affairs.

During these early years in Oxford, James found plenty of opportunity for indulging his pleasure in writing by the production of a continuous stream of research papers and review articles as well as his *Introduction to plant physiology* and a succession of contributions on plant physiological topics to the *School Science Review*. His deep interest in draughtsmanship was less readily satisfied, but he provided many of the illustrations for his *Introduction* and also, out of sheer delight in the task, all the original drawings for *The biology of flowers*, for which the text was written by his colleague A. R. Clapham.

In 1931 Tansley invited James to join with H. Godwin and A. R. Clapham in taking over the ownership and editorship of the *New Phytologist*, the general botanical journal which he had founded in 1901. All three consented and continued as editors for a further 30 years before they, in their turn, handed over to others in 1961.

Tansley retired from the Sherardian Chair in 1937. He had held a great respect for James, whom he regarded as showing notable distinction both of mind and manner and whose pungency of expression, whether in writing or in speech, he much appreciated. He had always been happy to give James a free hand in organizing the teaching of plant physiology and gave him his unstinting support.

Tansley's successor was T. G. B. Osborn, who had left Manchester in 1912 to become Professor of Botany first in Adelaide until 1927 and then in Sydney until his move to Oxford. Osborn's specialist interests as a botanist were, like Tansley's, primarily in ecology but also in the morphology and life history of certain groups of plants, notably the gymnosperms. James's relations with the new departmental head were as smooth as with Tansley. By now the department had grown appreciably in size of staff and in numbers of students, and Osborn soon embarked on the lengthy task of securing better accommodation for botany on a site less distant from the other science departments of the University. But the difficult period of World War II was not far ahead, with its extensive changes in the length and content of courses and the early direction of students into the armed forces or other forms of national service. James saw a way in which he might be of some real help to the country in this time of emergency. The outcome was the Oxford Medicinal Plants Scheme (O.M.P.S.), which began with attempts to grow medicinal plants, more especially deadly nightshade (belladonna), the source of the important alkaloid atropine, in the garden at Islip, as a basis for exploring the feasibility of the home production of such plants. This led to laboratory investigation of the mode and place of synthesis of atropine within the plant, later extended to a wide range of alkaloid-producing species and to a general study of alkaloid formation in plants. James also explored the organization of the collection of wild medicinal plants, such as foxglove, by interested members of the general public. In all this laborious activity he was greatly assisted by his wife and by numbers of undergraduates and research students who gave many hours of their time on summer evenings and during weekends. The study of alkaloids also became an important part of the research in plant physiology in Oxford both during the war and for some years afterwards. The idea of the Medicinal Plants Scheme, and its pursuit to the point at which it received national recognition and contributed modestly to the war effort, showed very clearly both James's creative imagination and also his considerable capacity for organization.

## Post-war Oxford

The work of the Oxford Medicinal Plants Scheme brought James into close contact with a wider group of scientists in Oxford than before. The isolated position of the Department of Botany in the Botanical Gardens had always been a factor separating the botanists from the other biological and the physical scientists, but now his cooperation with physiologists, biochemists and pharmacologists broadened his outlook and his interests, for, up to this, his deepest interests had been in the catabolic rather than the synthetic aspects of intermediary biochemistry. As he became better known to a wider acquaintance of scientists, his scientific perception and experimental skill were more admired and appreciated. At this time too, the end of the war saw the return of members of the teaching staff and students of the Botany Department, all of whom owed much to him and held him in high regard.

This was a period of expansion and soon J. L. Harley, E. F. Warburg, J. H. Burnett, F. A. L. Clowes and J. F. Hope-Simpson were appointed as University Demonstrators, although A. R. Clapham and N. V. Polunin had left to take chairs elsewhere. The undergraduate classes were remarkable for their liveliness and enthusiasm as well as for their numbers. The botanical laboratories were full to overflowing, and lectures had to be given in the Examinations Schools as well as in the departmental lecture rooms. All these factors combined to make the immediate post-war years a happy and scientifically productive period for James. It is true that he was at times extremely irritated by the crowded conditions in the Department and indeed he had some sharp disagreements with Osborn and with his other colleagues. His researches, however, prospered and he returned to the study of terminal oxidases and developed an interest in plant mitochondria, the study of which was fast expanding. In 1952 his election to a Fellowship of the Royal Society gave great pleasure to his many friends and colleagues and it seemed then that he finally realized how high he stood in their esteem.

It was during this time that he once again began to entertain his colleagues and their families at Islip. In winter his study could be converted into a complicated permanent way on which model trains of many kinds could be run on elaborate timetables designed in collaboration with his colleagues' children. In summer the garden was a great attraction and indeed on several occasions was the scene of an 'After Schools' evening party.

In these post-war years, thanks to the untiring efforts of T. G. B. Osborn, who relinquished scientific research for the purpose, the new Botany Department was planned, financed and built on the edge of the University Parks in the Science area. The move to it took place in 1951. The new laboratories were well designed and convenient, and the move so well planned that work was soon resumed without much confusion. However, following the retirement of T. G. B. Osborn from the Sherardian Chair in 1953, major changes occurred in the Department of Botany at Oxford, including the resignation of two of James's closest friends and colleagues. He therefore decided in 1958 to accept an invitation to the Chair of Botany at Imperial College, London, taking with him F. H. Whitehead who became his Reader in Taxonomic Botany.

## Imperial College, 1959–70

James had acted as Head of Department for a year in Oxford during the absence of Osborn on sabbatical leave and he so disliked the experience that he had said he would not wish to be head of a department again. In the event, however, the move to Imperial College seems to have suited him well. He and Gladys found a very convenient house in Roehampton, with a pleasant garden running down to the edge of the park, and from there he was able to travel by car daily to Prince Consort Road without difficulty. In the Department he at once brought about changes: one of his colleagues remarked that 'the glass-fronted cases filled with jars of plant specimens were removed from the corridors and there was an air of changes afoot'. At first, rather than carefully feeling his way, James brought about changes in a somewhat autocratic manner, but, as he learnt to know his colleagues better, he consulted them more fully and often took their advice. It was a period of expansion in the College and he was able to promote new lines of study by making appointments in Plant Taxonomy, Plant Genetics, Palaeobotany and Nitrogen Fixation. In particular he established a research group in Analytical Cytology, with Dr Denis Greenwood to further the electron microscopy and structural studies, and his pupil Dr (now Professor) Rachel Leech to pursue the biochemical and metabolic problems.

In all sorts of ways the Department became a more closely knit and friendly community under James. He fostered closer relations between staff and students, especially by introducing a tutorial system. He himself made every effort to acquaint himself with the personal interests of his students and their aspirations. Tea in the afternoon became a daily social meeting of all members of the Department who got to know each other as never before. Gladys and Will James became acquainted with the staff of the Botany Department and their families, for they were regular and well organized in entertaining as long as their health was good. In Roehampton as in Oxford, Will's model railway was a delight to the children of his colleagues, who were bidden to lunch and to spend the afternoon running trains on the permanent way in the loft.

James's hobby of gardening continued throughout his life, both at Islip and at Roehampton. Much of his spare time was spent, in fine weather, in the garden. In 1957 he had written a gardening book, *The background to gardening*, in which much of the valuable advice is given in the form of sayings of Giles, whose behaviour, language and character are based upon the James's gardener at Islip. This book became very much a best-seller because of its wit and humour as well as of its sound advice. During the years at Imperial College James took a great interest in the Chelsea Physic Garden for he was the representative of the Royal Society on its board of management. On this board he was a prime mover in the improvement and reconstruction of the laboratories of the Garden, as well as interesting himself in the more horticultural aspects of its activities.

## Retirement, 1970–78

James retired from the headship of the Department of Botany at Imperial College in 1967, but was appointed Emeritus Professor and Senior Research Fellow, and in 1969 Honorary Fellow of Imperial College. During his tenure of the Research Fellowship, which he relinquished in 1970, he spent his time in writing. He published *Cell respiration*, a detailed consideration of respiration of a whole range of living cells and its control, in 1971. In 1973 the final seventh edition of his *Introduction to plant physiology* appeared.

Towards the end of 1977 Will and Gladys decided, owing to ill-health, to emigrate to New Zealand to join their two daughters who, with their families, had lived there for many years. They had only once before seen their grandchildren when, a few years previously, James had been persuaded to lecture in Singapore and Hong Kong, and, having got so far, was more easily persuaded to go to New Zealand. Now they set up house in Wellington, quite near their elder daughter. In April they celebrated their golden wedding anniversary, and Will wrote that 'Anne brought her family down from Hamilton and a number of friends from our visit four years ago also joined in. We had a very enjoyable time'. Only five months later, on 15 September 1978, Will James died very suddenly, but peacefully, in his sleep after a stroke. He was 78. His last months had been very happy. He loved the company of his daughters, son-in-law and grandchildren, and they were very fond of him. Gladys James has written: 'It was characteristic that at the age of 77, when he felt that his life's main work was finished, he could make up his mind to uproot himself, travel to the other end of the world, and settle comfortably and happily in a completely new environment. Only someone who remained young in spirit could have done that.'

## Lecturing and teaching

James's love of words and the exact expression of ideas showed itself in his writings, as in chapter I of his book *Plant respiration*, but it was more clearly manifest in his lectures. He took the greatest pains over the preparation of these, whether they were to be given to a learned audience or to undergraduates. Each was so carefully planned and so clearly and logically spoken that the audience was almost effortlessly led through intricate and difficult subjects. He used experimental examples, illustrated by wall diagrams of graphs and tables of figures to arrive at his generalizations. He emphasized, in each example, difficulties of experimental procedure and chemical analysis and derived estimates of its limits of reliability. In this way he conveyed to undergraduate audiences the difficulties of achieving reliable information, the need for self-criticism and the joys of success in experimental work. Often he was also witty and amusing, as those who heard his inaugural lecture, *Botany here and now*, at Imperial College will remember.

His laboratory classes were also carefully prepared. Although some of the experiments seemed at first to be extremely simple, others required intricate manipulation and careful attention to detail. Those undergraduates who 'cut' his laboratory classes, even for the afternoon, earned his wrath and acid comments. Although it was customary in pre-war years for undergraduates to attend the laboratory conscientiously in the morning and to return in the evening after spending the afternoon on the river or the playing field, that would not do for James. He demanded attendance morning, afternoon and after tea, whether the experimental work was worthwhile or uninteresting, and, indeed, in a sense he was right. For he had taken pains to provide and prepare suitable living material and it was a rudeness, at the very least, not to use it properly.

As a tutor, James was less successful than as a lecturer. His old pupils seem to agree that he did not easily enter into general discussion after considering the subject that had been set. Questioning pupils were most often referred to a source book or research paper after a very short explanation; rarely did a lively discussion develop. On the other hand, with his graduate students discussion did develop and experiments were designed and conclusions reached in unison. However, James seemed to view himself always as the dominant partner, as of course he usually was, but it was for this reason that few of those he supervised, especially among the men, became his very close friends in spite of all they were aware they owed to him.

It would be wrong if this account of his career as a teacher leads to the view that he was austere or difficult. Of course there were times when the strain of ill-health made him irritable and acid in his comments, but at other times he was friendly, approachable and helpful in every way to students and colleagues alike.

## Administration

During Tansley's tenure of the Sherardian Chair James had no opportunities for acquiring experience in administration beyond that required for the efficient organization of departmental teaching and research in plant physiology. During World War II, however, he demonstrated real administrative capacity in his successful establishment and running of the Oxford Medicinal Plants Scheme. In this he was helped a very great deal by Gladys James, who organized the collection of drug-yielding plants by local people and assisted in many other ways. In 1952 James was Acting Head of the Department of Botany during Professor Osborn's absence in Australia, and performed the duties very competently though with no great enjoyment. It was therefore a matter of considerable interest to his friends to see how he would fare as Head of the much larger Botany Department at the Imperial College, the post to which he was appointed in 1959. Some reference has been made to the speed with which he made his presence felt and to the very positive and independent way in which he began to run the Department, giving rise to a feeling among his colleagues that there should have been more discussion with them before decisions were taken. Later he became more communicative and more flexible, though without relinquishing his ultimate complete control, and was increasingly appreciated as a forward-looking and decisive Head and a good leader.

James went to Imperial College at a time of university expansion and soon set about enlarging the staff of the Botany Department by adding members who could lead teaching and research in important fields so far not represented. In particular he aimed to develop 'analytical cytology', the study of the role of the fine structure of cells in controlling their activity and therefore that of the whole organism. To strengthen this new group he purchased an electron microscope and invited Dr Denis Greenwood from Leeds to take charge of it. Electron microscopy has gone from strength to strength in the Department, which now houses a unit also serving Zoology and Biochemistry, a tribute to James's early recognition of its importance.

There can be no doubt that James displayed considerable administrative competence in this final phase of his academic career. It had its roots in his clear-headedness and practical common sense and owed much also to his ready perception of likely and desirable directions of advance in plant biology and to a notable capacity for taking and implementing appropriate decisions. His constant concern for the best interests of the Department gained him, from the start, a general respect tinged with some awe, but those who knew him best developed a considerable affection for him.

## Scientific work

### *Photosynthesis*

James's scientific work passed through a number of phases during which he contributed to different aspects of his subject. After taking his first degree from Reading in 1923 he went to Cambridge to work with F. F. Blackman. Some years earlier Blackman & A. M. Smith (1911), using multicellular water plants in slowly flowing solutions of carbon dioxide and studying the relation between carbon dioxide concentration and rate of photosynthesis at a range of light intensities but at constant and fairly high temperatures, had obtained curves approximating to two straight lines. The photosynthetic rate first rose linearly with increasing concentration but then, after an abrupt change of direction, remained constant although the carbon dioxide concentration continued to rise. This became familiar as the 'limiting factor' form of relationship, interpreted as implying that after a phase of proportionality of rate with concentration, some other factor, such as light intensity, imposed a restriction on any further rise with increasing concentration. Later, however, O. Warburg (1919, 1920) and R. Harder (1921), both using the unicellular alga *Chlorella* in still solutions of sodium bicarbonate, found rate–concentration curves resembling rectangular hyperbolae. Some explanation of such discrepancies had been proposed by E. J. Maskell when a research student working in Cambridge with G. E. Briggs. In his Ph.D. thesis, Maskell evolved a theoretical scheme for land plants which required that variations in the diffusion resistances to the passage of carbon dioxide to the chloroplast surface must affect the form of the curve relating external concentration of carbon dioxide to rate of photosynthesis. The smaller the total diffusion resistance the more nearly the curve should resemble a rectangular hyperbola and the more it should depart from two straight lines.

James set himself the task of exploring more closely the control of photosynthetic rate in submerged aquatic plants and decided to use the moss *Fontinalis*, selected because it was multicellular but structurally simple and devoid of stomata, and to compare rates of photosynthesis in varying concentrations of carbon dioxide and of sodium bicarbonate and with varying rates of flow. He was able to show that uptake from bicarbonate solutions was in accordance with the prevalent view that the plant did not take up the bicarbonate ion in photosynthesis but only carbon dioxide in solution or carbonic acid, $H_2CO_3$. The rates of dissociation of sodium bicarbonate and of reduction of bicarbonate ion to carbonic acid being rapid compared with photosynthesis, any uptake in photosynthesis is immediately made good by further dissociation and reduction. The effect is equivalent to a considerable shortening of the diffusion path of carbon dioxide in solution and makes possible the prolonged maintenance of the initial rate of photosynthesis in still or slowly moving solutions. He showed also that rates of photosynthesis increased with increasing rates of flow of carbon dioxide solutions but were independent of the rate of flow of bicarbonate solutions. He demonstrated that, at constant light intensity, rates of photosynthesis in still or slowly flowing solutions, adjusted to give equivalent concentrations of carbon dioxide or carbonic acid, were always higher in bicarbonate solutions than in solutions of carbon dioxide. He showed further that curves relating rates of photosynthesis to concentrations of carbon dioxide or carbonic acid varied in form with inferred variations in diffusion resistance as predicted by Maskell and others. He thus reconciled the findings of Blackman & Smith with those of Warburg and Harder and made a valuable contribution towards resolving what had become a controversial matter. The paper describing his investigations, which appeared in 1928, revealed the care and thought that characterized his experimentation throughout his life. This experimental work carried out in Cambridge was followed by a theoretical discussion of the dynamics of photosynthesis first given as lectures to his undergraduate classes in Oxford, where he had been invited by Tansley in 1927, and later published in *The New Phytologist* in 1934. In this he considered photosynthesis as a sequence of reactions, diffusion-dependent, light-dependent and light-independent, and demonstrated that the form of the quantitative relationships between external factors and the rate could be readily explained and predicted.

### *The function of mineral elements*

As a member of V. H. Blackman's research group at Rothamsted, James investigated in particular the function of potassium in the green plant and he published in 1930 the first of a series of papers under the title *Studies in the physiological importance of mineral elements in plants*. In that paper he set out to explain the conclusions of E. J. Maskell (1927) that the application of potassium sulphate to potatoes results in a rise in starch formation in the leaves and an increase of translocation of carbohydrate to the tubers. James collected data from pot and field experiments on the number, weight, area and senescence of leaves; he also estimated rate of starch formation and translocation. He showed that potassium supply might reduce the number and area of leaves while leaving their dry weight unaffected. Senescence of leaves was delayed by potassium, and starch formation per unit area was increased, as was translocation of carbohydrate to the tubers. A further important conclusion was that potassium increased catalytic activity, leading to a greater efficiency of starch formation.

Later, at Oxford, in cooperation with his first research students, Nora Penston and Margaret Cattle, he followed up these conclusions, using improved analytical methods for potassium and chloride perfected by these workers. Potassium was found to be especially high in concentration in growing apices, in reproductive bodies and in the sieve tubes. It had a close relationship in distribution with protein concentration, enzyme activity and active growth. During the life of the plant, potassium was found to move from ageing leaves into the younger developing ones and to circulate through the plant in the phloem. Potassium and chloride were found to affect the action of the enzymes diastase, invertase and catalase in broad bean.

James himself examined the effects of nutrient deficiency on the respiration of detached leaves kept in dark chambers on the lines of work done with cherry laurel leaves by F. F. Blackman in Cambridge. This subject was taken up by a research pupil, E. W. Yemm (later Professor and Head of the Botany Department in Bristol), using broad beans and barley grown in water and sand culture. It soon, however, became clear that the interpretation of the complex sequence of respiratory drift was likely to be very difficult to achieve until much more was known of the respiratory behaviour and mechanism of normal leaves. James's interest in the respiration of plants, their organs and their cells seems to have originated at this time and it was to remain his central research interest throughout his life, as described later.

### *Transpiration and root pressure*

Among the research activities of his early years in Oxford, James cooperated with H. Baker, then a departmental demonstrator in Botany, to study transpiration and water movement. The two papers that they wrote were the outcome of the mating of Baker's skill with scalpel and razor with James's aptitude for physiological experiment. They approached these muddled physiological problems by asking the question whether the fluid in the xylem of a transpiring plant is under tension. They showed, using *Acer pseudoplatanus* (the sycamore), that if the wall of a xylem vessel was perforated under dye, the colour moves both upwards and downwards. It may later move tangentially and radially in the vessels only, not in the bark or pith, but it may move from the xylem of one annual ring to another through pits in adjacent walls of vessels. The initial rate of upward movement of dye was greater than the downward movement if transpiration was active, but the movements in the two directions were equal if transpiration was slow. During transpiration the water columns in the vessels were clearly under tension and the movement in a normal plant was in an upward direction through the lumina of the vessels, and laterally from vessel to vessel by pits according to the difference in tension of the neighbouring vessels. It was clearly impossible that a downward movement of carbohydrate could occur in the vessels of a transpiring plant against the mass flow upward. In a subsequent paper, James and Baker examined the exudation of fluid from the cut ends of segments of roots of sycamore (which like other maples is active in exudation). In early spring exudation occurred only from the morphologically upper end of a detached segment, while water might enter through the lower end. Clearly this gave rise to grave doubts of the usual dogma that exudation took place from the xylem vessels and they showed that in their material it did not. By the examination of previous writings they showed that the usual assumption that root exudation takes place from xylem vessels was not founded then upon much observation and was not a credible generalization. Of course this work is now much dated but at the time it was a small but significant contribution to a difficult subject.

### *Alkaloids in plants*

During World War II James was one of the prime movers in the Oxford Medicinal Plants Scheme (O.M.P.S.), aimed at organizing the supply, within the country, from both wild plants and those that could readily be grown in gardens, of such medicinal drugs, especially alkaloids, as could be satisfactorily and economically extracted. This led to laboratory studies of the chemical techniques available for identifying and estimating alkaloids and of their distribution within the plant at different stages of growth, and developed into investigations of the place and mode of alkaloid synthesis in a number of plant species. An active group of plant physiologists and biochemists, many of whom have since gained world-wide reputations, were associated with James in this 'applied' work, and they made very significant contributions not only to the maintenance of the country's medical services during the war but also, in researches continued well into the 1950s, to the scientific understanding of alkaloid structure, synthesis and transport within the plant.

The Belgian botanist Errera and his co-workers showed during the period 1886–1906 that alkaloids tend to accumulate in very active plant tissues and in particular in the growing apices of roots and stems. Others showed later that the cells of root and stem meristems normally contain no detectable amounts of alkaloids until the onset of vacuolation, and that they are then present in the vacuoles as water-soluble salts. James made confirmatory observations on germinating seeds of *Atropa belladonna* and *Datura stramonium*. He reported in 1946 that the small amount of alkaloid in the resting seed soon disappears and that the first appearance in the embryo is in the radicle and at a very early stage of growth: in *Datura* when the radicles are only 2 mm long, though never any earlier. Appearance in the young radicle seemed, nevertheless, to be *de novo* and not as a result of transport from elsewhere, James being able to detect it even when all alkaloid-containing peripheral tissues had been removed from the seed well in advance. Chaze had reported in 1932 that in radicles of *Nicotiana tabacum* aleurone grains of storage protein in the meristematic cells break down and are replaced by fluid droplets which give positive alkaloid reactions and later coalesce to form the vacuoles.

It had been known for some time that leaf primordia are, like radicles, devoid of alkaloids in their very early stages but accumulate them during vacuolation. Amounts rise rapidly but may subsequently fall again. James's group showed by macroscopic analysis a similar rise to a maximum in the basal leaves of *Atropa*, with a decline setting in at a fairly early stage of leaf development. Here, then, were several problems to be solved, including the initial source of the alkaloid in leaf primordia and the reasons for the decline from a maximum amount, whether because of transport out of the leaf or through decomposition *in situ*.

There was already a good deal of evidence for the view that the initial synthesis of alkaloids takes place in the roots and that for the most part what appears in the leaves is derived from the roots, upward transport being in the transpiration stream. This was the simplest interpretation of the well established facts that *Atropa* and related members of the Solanaceae, if bud-grafted on tomato stocks, develop in their leaves no more than traces of their usual alkaloids; and, conversely, that tomato scions grafted on stocks of other alkaloid-forming plants acquire the alkaloids characteristic of the stocks. Gladys James & B. H. Thewlis published in 1952 the results of reciprocal grafts between *Atropa* and *Datura* showing that the scion always contains the alkaloids hyoscine and hyoscyamine in the proportions characteristic of the plant used as stock, these being very different in the two species. This provided further impressive support for regarding the root as the source of alkaloids which later appear in the shoots.

In 1944 James reported the outcome of an experiment in which he approach-grafted *Atropa* and tomato plants, afterwards removing the *Atropa* roots and the tomato shoots. Analysis subsequently revealed very small amounts of alkaloids in both tomato stock and *Atropa* scion. Pamela Wilson (P. M. Warren Wilson 1952), working with James, sought to clarify these unexpected findings in a series of further grafting experiments. She first showed that the leaves of *Atropa* scions side-grafted on tomato stocks remained completely free of 'solanaceous alkaloids', that is, of the atropine, hyoscine and hyoscyamine characteristic of self-rooted *Atropa*. The oldest leaves of side-grafts on *Physalis alkekengi* contained a trace of these alkaloids, but younger leaves were quite devoid of them, as were both the tomato and *Physalis* stocks. Differences from James's own findings seemed likely to be due to his use of approach-grafting and the consequent lapse of some days before the *Atropa* roots could be removed. The next step was to detach alkaloid-free *Atropa* leaves from grafts on tomato stocks and to stand them in moist sand when, in due course, roots grew from the callused cut ends of their petioles. Analysis showed that alkaloids soon appeared in these roots in amounts typical of normal *Atropa* root systems and could be found also in the leaves. In more elaborate experiments Pamela Wilson induced roots to grow from the lower part of alkaloid-free *Atropa* scions while still attached to rooted *Physalis* stocks. After 2–3 months the *Atropa* roots were found to contain 'solanaceous alkaloids' which were also present in *Atropa* stems and leaves above the scion-roots and, interestingly, in the *Physalis* stem below the graft union and in the *Physalis* roots. These results show that organic connection with *Physalis* roots does not impair the capacity of *Atropa* roots to produce alkaloids, and that these alkaloids can pass not only upwards into the stems and leaves of *Atropa* but also downwards into the *Physalis* stock.

This demonstration of downward movement of alkaloids was confirmed in further highly ingenious grafting experiments which made it very difficult to avoid the conclusion that transport must be in the phloem. Direct analytical evidence for this, by separating phloem from xylem before analysis, is made very difficult because of the presence of internal phloem in members of the Solanaceae, nor is histochemical examination for alkaloids conclusive owing to the small size and dense contents of the sieve tubes. It is, nevertheless, the most reasonable inference, from the many instances of the appearance of alkaloids at points below their presumed source, that they are moving unchanged chemically and via the phloem. This seems the most likely explanation, too, of the decline in amounts of alkaloid in basal leaves of *Atropa* (p. 353), though there is here a possibility of some breakdown in the leaf. That both synthesis and breakdown of alkaloids can in some circumstances take place in the leaf was demonstrated later by James (p. 354 below).

## *Alkaloid synthesis*

The results of experiments on *Atropa* and *Datura* already described point to the conclusion that the final steps of alkaloid synthesis under natural conditions take place predominantly in meristematic cells of the root, initially in the seedling radicle, and this is confirmed by numerous observations on other solanaceous plants and a number of non-solanaceous plants including opium poppy, cinchona and barley. When James began his investigations of alkaloid synthesis it was supposed to depend on the initial presence of an appropriate amino acid such as ornithine for the 'solanaceous alkaloids', proline for the nicotine series and tyrosine for the hordenine of barley. He concluded that the first step towards elucidating the stages of biosynthesis of alkaloids in *Atropa* must be to identify the one or more amino acids functioning in this way and, early in the war, he initiated a series of 'feeding experiments'. Leaves were detached from cultivated plants of the same age and as far as possible from corresponding nodes. Their petioles were trimmed with a sharp razor and the cut bases stood in beakers containing the feeding solutions, these being renewed after 1–2 days. Leaves in distilled water or sucrose solutions were found to remain healthy and did not change appreciably in alkaloid content during 3 days at 25 °C. The alkaloid content was determined by well tested methods, in later experiments that of Roberts & James (1947), and expressed as grams of (−)-hyoscyamine per 100 g dry mass. Establishment of the occurrence of synthesis depended on showing an increase in amount of alkaloid in the leaf, and this necessitated a careful sampling procedure in which the samples compared were equal both in numbers of leaves and in initial fresh weights. In his final report on these experiments (*New Phytol.* **48**, 1949), James was able to claim a number of advances in knowledge of the behaviour of alkaloids in *Atropa*. It was shown at an early stage of the work that when leaves were picked while still in rapid expansion and kept at 25 °C in the dark, there was no measurable change in alkaloid content until, after the third day, they began to turn yellow. The accompanying breakdown of protein led to an increase in soluble nitrogen and a small but significant increase in alkaloid. This showed that alkaloids can indeed be synthesized in *Atropa* leaves as well as in the young roots, and strongly suggests an origin from products of protein breakdown. At a more advanced stage of yellowing there was a loss of alkaloid, presumably through decomposition *in situ*.

Further exploration was by feeding experiments using possible starting points for alkaloid synthesis, M/100 L-arginine in 1–2% sucrose being tested first. Small but statistically significant increases in alkaloid were found within 3 days and similar results were obtained with L-ornithine, but neither L-proline nor ammonium sulphate was effective. It was therefore concluded that 'L-arginine and L-ornithine can act as precursors of the tropane alkaloids formed in young belladonna leaves'. There were thus solid grounds for presuming that 'the nitrogen of the tropane alkaloids is derived from the δ-amino group provided by the arginine–ornithine group of amino acids, and that the α-amino nitrogen of the other acids and the ring nitrogen of proline are not utilizable in the synthesis' (James, *Nature* **158**, 1946), an important clarification of the position.

The other alkaloid whose path of biosynthesis was investigated by James and his co-workers was the hordenine of barley. A possible mechanism by two successive methylations of tyrosine had been suggested by Raoul in 1937, and the products of methylation, first tyramine and then *N*-methyltyramine, were later identified by Mrs S. V. Barber, working with James, by paper chromatography. V. S. Butt, also working in Oxford, isolated *N*-methyltyramine in much larger quantities by the use of a cellulose column. Feeding experiments, comparable with those undertaken successfully with *Atropa*, were made more difficult with barley because hordenine is formed only in the seedling stage and also because microorganisms on the surface of the seedlings may affect external solutions. Mrs Barber overcame these problems by using excised barley embryos, deprived of their endosperm, in sterile culture. She found that in these circumstances no hordenine was formed but that it appeared when an endosperm extract was added to the external medium. Addition of tyramine or *N*-methyltyramine in place of endosperm extract was ineffective, perhaps because there was no suitable methyl donor. When methionine, known as a methyl donor in plant tissues, was added with tyramine or with *N*-methyltyramine, some hordenine was duly formed, but no evidence could be obtained in support of the view that the tyramine in the plant derived from tyrosine. No tyrosine decarboxylase could be detected, but a glutamic decarboxylase was shown to be present and hordenine might therefore originate from glutamic acid rather than tyrosine, though the origin of the phenol would then be uncertain. Here again James's research group in Oxford contributed substantially to the solution of a biosynthetic problem, and again by using essentially plant physiological as well as biochemical concepts and methods.

### *Respiration of plants*

Early in his time at Oxford James began work on plant respiration by observing the gas exchange of detached leaves kept in the dark in a current of carbon dioxide-free air at constant temperature. The changes in rate of carbon dioxide emission were correlated with results of detailed analyses of internal concentrations of carbohydrates, amino acids and other carbon compounds, by James's pupil, E. W. Yemm. It soon became apparent that only the initial phase of carbon dioxide emission could be accounted for by carbohydrate breakdown. When the carbohydrate reserves became exhausted, the rate of emission fell at first but later rose again to a high level which was associated with protein and amino acid breakdown, which eventually led to ammonium production, death and saprophytic colonization. The careful analytical methods of Yemm, coupled with the flair that both he and James had for the design of experimental apparatus, set the scene for much of the research during the 1930s. An account of some of the more elaborate pieces of apparatus that they invented in collaboration with F. B. Hora, S. E. Arney and A. L. ('John') James is given in a paper published by the James brothers in 1940. This includes a description of the automatic system of sampling gases for RQ estimation which was an improved and complex version of a simple system used by Yemm in 1932. It employed large quantities of mercury and was named by Bayard Hora 'H. G. Wells'.

The artificiality of the starving detached leaves and the complexity of their problems led James to use other types of plant material, such as germinating grains, young seedlings and excised barley embryos. All these could, if desired, be supplied with substrates, inhibitors or other substances in the solution or the gas phase. In addition he and his associates used tissue extracts, breis and separated, partially purified enzymes. It must be remembered that comparative biochemistry was not in those days accepted as reputable although the realization of the similarity of biochemical reactions in the cells of all organisms was on the way. However, James began to test how far the ideas concerning the process of respiration in animal cells and yeast might apply to those of the green plant, using all these kinds of plant material.

Between 1933 and 1936, with I. P. Norval, James examined the decomposition of pyruvic acid by crushed acetone-treated barley tissue ('barley zymin') and germinating seedlings. 'On account of the analogy with yeast, and currently accepted theories of fermentation', it could be assumed that pyruvic acid might well be the precursor of acetaldehyde already identified in plants. Their tissue preparations broke down pyruvic acid to produce acetaldehyde and carbon dioxide by means of a heat-labile carboxylase system, and embryos treated with pyruvic acid had an increased carbon dioxide production with a rise of RQ. They concluded that pyruvic acid was a normal intermediate in aerobic respiration of barley.

Gladys and Will James later showed that pyruvic acid accumulated in barley tissues poisoned with aromatic sulphonic acids or excess acetaldehyde. The further demonstration by James and Arney that phosphate supply was important to respiration of barley embryos and that phosphate esters were involved in the process of carbohydrate breakdown enabled James to suggest a possible scheme for glycolysis which was described in a letter to *Nature* in 1938. His ideas were amplified by further work summarized in a paper written with his pupil, A. H. Bunting (later Professor Bunting of Reading University). In this they expressed the view that glycolysis involved phosphorylation of glucose and fructose and that a phosphate cycle, in which adenylic acid acted as a phosphate carrier, took place:

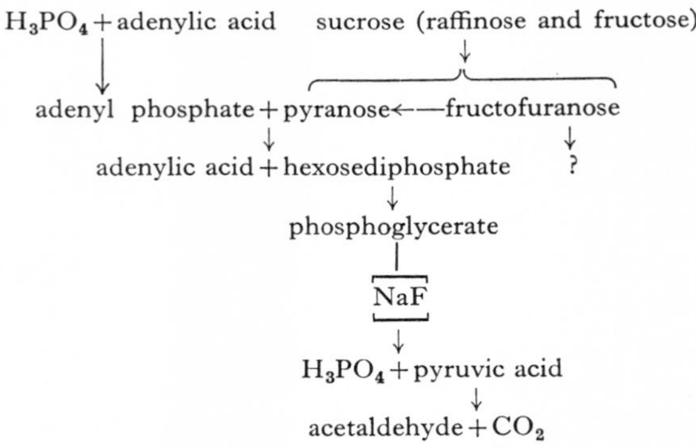


This scheme was believed to be valid both in the presence and absence of oxygen, but they stated that their work did not amount to a demonstration of a 'mechanism of respiration' but the reactions were 'a possible, even a probable means by which the plant may utilize its sugars'.

Although it was known that the cytochromes were intracellular respiratory catalysts common in animals, bacteria, yeast and higher plants and that they were inhibited by dilute cyanide, at any rate from the time of Keilin's work in 1925, there was little interest in the terminal oxidase of higher plants. Until the late 1930s James's research group had used respiratory poisons such as cyanide for specific experimental purposes, but there was little in their writings to indicate an interest in the point of entry of oxygen into the respiratory sequence. James & Hora in 1940 showed that respiration of intact barley tissues was highly sensitive to cyanide, and in 1943 James & Cragg suggested that it was 'therefore likely that heavy metal systems such as polyphenol, cytochrome or ascorbic acid oxidase should play an important part in the respiration' of barley. From that time James became interested in the terminal oxidases, always keeping it in mind that the actual oxidase system might vary from species to species and from one phase of development or from one organ to another. With Joan Cragg (Dr Joan Webb), C. R. C. Heard and Natalie Garton, he examined the possible intervention of ascorbic acid oxidase in barley respiration. It was shown that diethyldithiocarbonate, if suitably applied, inhibited extracted ascorbic acid oxidase and polyphenolase at a concentration of M/5000 but left cytochrome oxidase unaffected. This reagent was shown to inhibit the oxygen uptake of barley root tips very strongly (*ca* 60%) and that was taken as evidence that ascorbic acid oxidase was likely to be responsible for the greater part of the respiratory oxygen uptake by them. James reverted to this problem of the terminal oxidase of growing roots several times in the ensuing years. In the meantime Dr Harry Beevers, one of the research men of the Medicinal Drugs Scheme, had been studying the respiration of *Arum* spadices because of the report of Van Herk & Badenhuizen many years before that *Sauromatum* spadix was 'feebly inhibited' by cyanide (50% by M/1000). In a paper with James, they concluded, as a result of detailed study of the effect of many factors on spadix respiration, that the abnormally high rate of oxygen uptake is a process in which metalloenzymes play no part but which might be dependent on a flavoprotein enzyme. James wrote two further papers on *Arum* respiration with Dr Daphne Elliott which showed that mitochondria capable of oxidizing TCA cycle intermediates could be extracted for *Arum* spadix and that their oxygen uptake was largely cyanide-insensitive. Again, they extracted a flavoprotein from these mitochondria which had an FAD prosthetic group: it behaved as an autoxidizable cytochrome *c* reductase with a high specificity for NAD.

The work on the terminal oxidases of barley roots continued, in cooperation with successive research students, till 1958, when James spent some months working in Sweden with H. Lundegårdh, with whom he had had some correspondence and difference of opinion. The visit came about because James travelled to Russia during a year-long sabbatical leave and took the opportunity not only to visit the Biological Station at Naples, but also to work with Professor Lundegårdh. James and his colleagues, using selective inhibitors, had sought to determine what terminal oxidase was functioning in barley roots at successive stages of development. James, in 1953, showed that the oxygen uptake of barley embryos was sensitive to cyanide, azide and carbon monoxide, so that it was concluded that cytochrome oxidase, the presence of which was verified spectroscopically, was responsible for at least 80% of the uptake. The small inhibiting effect of dieca (diethyldithiocarbonate) was held to indicate the absence of copper-containing enzymes such as ascorbic acid oxidase or polyphenol oxidase. By contrast, young roots 10 days old were apparently deficient in the cytochrome system, uninhibited by carbon monoxide, yet extremely dieca-sensitive. This was taken to imply that electron transfer to oxygen was by way of the ascorbic oxidase. This apparent change of terminal oxidase was studied with D. Boulter (later Professor Boulter of Durham University) over the first seven days of root growth, and similar conclusions were reached. Professor Lundegårdh's work with wheat roots, published in 1951 and 1952, had not shown in them any such change in terminal oxidase during development, so James, with Marigold Ward, made comparisons of wheat and barley. They confirmed the difference that whereas the terminal oxidase of wheat remained cytochrome oxidase, that of barley changed to an oxidase sensitive to dieca but not to carbon monoxide in the dark. When James met Lundegårdh at Penningby they examined the cytochrome spectrum of barley and wheat. They concluded that the spectra were similar but that there was 'a marked sluggishness of reduction and oxidation' in barley which came almost to a standstill after 7 days' growth of the roots, at which time they were much less sensitive to carbon monoxide in the dark.

Although much of James's research on respiration during the 1950s concentrated on the oxidase systems involved, he still enquired into carbon pathways. Two aspects deserve comment here, both of which concern the anaerobic respiration of plants when they are kept in oxygen-deficient surroundings. It was a general observation from the time of F. F. Blackman's researches on apples that the amount of carbon dioxide eliminated during anaerobiosis might exceed, or at any rate nearly equal, that eliminated in an equal time in air. Since at the same time alcohol or acetaldehyde was observed or believed to accumulate in the tissue, it followed either that there was an increased rate of glycolysis under anaerobiosis, or that it was constant in rate, but that in the presence of oxygen some of the products were built back to carbohydrate ('oxidative anabolism'). James was in some doubt that alcohol often accumulated in anaerobic conditions and indeed he gave a very amusing lecture to Bios, the senior biological scientific society at Oxford, on the validity of the various claims that alcohol was produced and the difficulties of its accurate estimation. Later, with Ann Ritchie (Mrs J. K. Brierley), he showed that in carrot 97% of the carbohydrate anaerobically consumed was recoverable as ethanol and carbon dioxide in proportions according to the accepted equation. They concluded that it was at present unknown whether this uncomplicated behaviour was typical of plant tissues. One cannot but believe that it was a surprise for James to meet uncomplicated behaviour at that period of his researches! A further paper with W. O. Slater attempted to determine the possibility that oxidative anabolism occurred in apple tissue (apples were used by F. F. Blackman) and barley. They fed $^{14}C$-labelled pyruvate under aerobic conditions but failed in any case to find radioactive carbon in any carbohydrate, although it entered the TCA cycle and amino acids and their derivatives. They concluded that the results 'do not, of course, preclude the possibility of a back-synthesis from an energy-richer precursor such as phosphoenolpyruvate'. Such a sequence of reactions has been observed in germinating castor bean seeds by Professor H. Beevers as a special reaction sequence of fatty seeds, but it does not seem to be active in adult plants or starchy seeds.

In 1953 James's book *Plant respiration* was published and may be said to have concluded and summarized an epoch in the study of plant respiration which ended about 1950. After that, not only did the new tools such as chromatography, isotopic labelling and electron microscopy become readily avilable, but also the respiratory functions of subcellular organelles, which were being extracted with increased efficiency, were recognized. It is significant in this regard that there is no mention in the index of *Plant respiration* of 'mitochondrion', 'subcellular particle' or 'organelle', nor is the localization of respiratory reactions within the plant cell given more than trifling mention. Nor again is it really accepted that the cytochrome oxidase system is a universal feature of respiration in plants. The absence of discussion of localization of respiratory reactions underlines more than anything else that an epoch had ended, for James, ever since 1930, had considered and discussed in detail problems of the localization of enzymic reactions. In his lectures to undergraduates he had emphasized the difficulties and importance of gaining knowledge of the subject, even to the point of giving much time (excessive time, some thought) to the physical state of protoplasm and the physical chemistry of colloids. It is not surprising, therefore, that with new methods available James and his colleagues in Oxford and at Imperial College put a good deal of their research effort into the study of subcellular particles from the middle 1950s onwards. It is significant that almost as soon as the ink was dry on *Plant respiration* James was writing an article 'Plant mitochondria and respiration' for *New Biology*, which he concluded with the words 'it may well turn out that the successful isolation and manipulation of mitochondrial particles will come to be looked upon as one of the historical landmarks in the study of plant respiration'.

In the laboratory, the new methods of organelle preparation were examined and tested, and it was concluded that the enzymes of glycolysis occur in the 'soluble cytoplasm' outside the mitochondrion, but the first published paper was with V. S. R. Das (now Professor and Head of Department at Tiraputi), entitled 'The organization of respiration in chlorophyllous cells', which was illustrated with electron micrographs of extracted particles. In this they showed that their chloroplast preparations were active in the Hill reaction but did not consume oxygen nor could they oxidize Krebs's cycle acids or cytochrome *c*. By contrast, their mitochondrial preparations from the same tissue had no Hill reaction but carried out both the oxidations with oxygen uptake.

From 1958 when he moved to Imperial College, James did less work with his own hands but he supervised and actively encouraged the work of his analytical cytology group in the study of both structure and function. Subcellular particles were isolated, purified and analysed and their integrity monitored. James published little in his own name except for reviews, but one particularly interesting paper is that written with Anne Richens on energy transport from mitochondria to nuclei. In this they showed that isolated nuclei could synthesize complex nitrogen compounds if presented with amino acids and ATP. The ATP supply might be substituted by active mitochondria supplied with substrate, cofactors, inorganic phosphate and ADP.

His last research paper, with Rachel Leech, concerned the cytochromes of the chloroplasts of *Vicia*. The organelles were purified by a method similar to that used previously with V. S. R. Das to separate chloroplasts and mitochondria. After confirming by electron microscopy that the chloroplasts were free from other cell material, their cytochromes were examined and found to be cytochrome *f* and cytochrome $b_6$, with no trace of cytochromes *a* or *c*. In the chloroplasts the cytochromes were positioned in the grana near to the chlorophylls. The relative proportions of chlorophyll *a*, chlorophyll *b*, cytochrome *f* and cytochrome $b_6$ were estimated and it was calculated on the assumption that each photosynthetic unit ('quantosome') contained one cytochrome molecule, that it also contained between 165 and 379 chlorophyll molecules, a figure that confirmed some previous estimates by others.

It is remarkable that, having contributed so much to research on plant respiration in the earlier epoch, James quite late in his scientific career could master a range of new techniques and remain near the forefront of research.

## Membership of scientific bodies and public service

James took little pleasure in attending meetings even when they concerned his major scientific interests, and the only scientific societies of which he became a member were the Biochemical Society and the Society for Experimental Biology, serving for a time on the Council of the latter. Apart from his 30 years as an editor of *The New Phytologist*, he served for various periods on the editorial panels of the *Journal of Experimental Botany*, the *School Science Review* and *Endeavour*, contributing to the two last a number of articles of general botanical or biological interest as well as reviews, written for non-specialists, of progress in his own fields of research.

He was a member of the Governing Bodies of the Chelsea Physic Garden, East Malling Research Station and the John Innes Horticultural Institution. He took a special interest in the Chelsea Physic Garden and was largely instrumental in securing the reconstruction of the lecture room, laboratories and greenhouses there. When he retired he made the Garden a generous gift of 191 books from his personal library and these now form the basis of the Garden's modern library.

As a result of his involvement in the Oxford Medicinal Plants Scheme he was invited to join both the Vegetable Drugs Committee of the Ministry of

Health (later of the Ministry of Supply) and the County Garden Produce Central Committee of the Ministry of Agriculture, serving for a time as chairman of the local committees in Oxfordshire and the West Midlands. Later he was appointed to the Biology Subcommittee of the D.S.I.R. and became Botanical Adviser to the Commonwealth Scholarships Scheme.

He served on the Council of the Royal Society for the two years 1944–46 and on various of its committees, including the Botany Sectional Committee (Chairman 1956–57), Government Grant Board F and the Library Committee.

## Honours and distinctions

James was given the title of Reader in Botany at Oxford in 1947 and in the following year was granted the definitive appointment to a University Readership, holding this rank until he left Oxford to become Professor and Head of the Botany Department at the Imperial College in 1959. During the absence of Professor T. G. B. Osborn in Australia in 1952 he was made Deputy Sherardian Professor and Acting Head of the Department.

He was elected to the Fellowship of the Royal Society in 1952.

In 1965, just before he relinquished his Chair of Botany, he was elected an Honorary A.R.C.S., and on his retirement in 1967 was made Emeritus Professor of the Imperial College and Senior Research Fellow in the Botany Department. In 1969 he was elected an Honorary Fellow of the College.

James's high international standing was shown by his Corresponding Membership of the American Society of Plant Physiologists and his election as Foreign Member of the Deutsche Akademie der Naturforscher, of the Swedish Royal Academy of Science and of the Leopoldina.

## Concluding remarks

James will long be remembered as a man of great distinction, both as a person and as a scientist, and as one who in spite of an enforced continual concern for his health led a surprisingly full and active life. His appearance was made striking by his being at the same time thin and frail-looking and yet carrying himself with an almost military erectness. His voice, too, was rather thin and high-pitched but his utterance was nevertheless brisk and precise. His keen blue eyes and sharp features framed by spreading brown hair warned that he was not one to be trifled with, and his whole aspect suggested a real and even somewhat formidable personality. During the last decade or so of his life a crown of white hair brought about a change which in no way lessened the impressiveness of his appearance.

That there was something of the formidable in James's personality cannot be denied, but there was certainly another side of which his colleagues and students have always been well aware. Professor Rachel Leech relates, for example, how his former students at Imperial College speak with affection of his personal interest in their progress and careers. He was, moreover, a gracious host and his wit and humour could be very entertaining even though he tended to retain some of his habitual reserve. With his close friends he opened up more completely and revealed the extent of his basic warmth and kindliness.

These concluding remarks would be incomplete without an emphatic reference to James's capacity for clear and simple yet elegant writing. The great success of his texts for schools and universities and of his semi-popular articles and books stemmed largely from this outstanding gift for exposition, though a further contributing factor was the high standard of the illustrations in all his publications, many of which were drawn by himself and others especially by Mrs E. W. Yemm (Marie Solari) and Dr Pamela Warren Wilson.

Finally, tribute must certainly be paid to the magnificent way in which his wife Gladys supported Will at all times and in all his activities. She assisted him in his teaching and research and watched over his health, and her warm and outgoing personality complemented his more reserved nature in their relations with other people.

For their indispensable assistance in the preparation of this Memoir, we wish to thank Gladys James, Dr A. L. James (Will's younger brother), Professor Harry Beevers, Professor Rachel Leech, Professor A. L. Rutter, Professor R. K. S. Wood, Dr Vernon Butt, Dr F. A. L. Clowes, Mrs J. L. Harley, Dr C. C. McCready, Mr E. F. Hemmings, Mrs Hilda Pengelly and Mr W. G. MacKenzie, formerly Curator of the Chelsea Physic Garden.

The photograph was taken by Walter Stoneman in 1952.

## Bibliography

1928 Experimental researches on vegetable assimilation and respiration. XIX. The effect of variations of carbon dioxide supply upon the rate of assimilation of submerged water plants. *Proc. R. Soc. Lond.* B **103**, 1–42.

1930 Studies of the physiological importance of the mineral elements in plants. I. The relation of potassium to the properties and functions of the leaf. *Ann. Bot.* **44**, 173–198.

Some important aspects of plant physiology. *Sch. Sci. Rev.* **11**, 113, 259, 351.

1931 *Introduction to plant physiology*. 259 pages. (7th ed. 1973.) Oxford: Clarendon Press.

Potassium: its distribution, movement and relation to growth in the potato. *Ann. Bot.* **45**, 425–442.

1932 The physical state of protoplasm. *Sch. Sci. Rev.* **52**, 348–356.

1933 (With N. L. Penston) Studies of the physiological importance of the mineral elements in plants. IV. The quantitative distribution of potassium in the potato plant. *Ann. Bot.* **47**, 279–292.

(With M. Cattle) Studies of the physiological importance of the mineral elements in plants. VI. The influence of potassium chloride on rate of diastatic hydrolysis of starch. *Biochem. J.* **27**, 1805–1809.

(With H. Baker) The behaviour of dyes in the transpiration stream of sycamore. *New Phytol.* **32**, 245–260.

(With H. Baker) Sap pressure and the movement of sap. *New Phytol.* **32**, 317–343.

The energetics of plant protoplasm. *Sch. Sci. Rev.* **14**, 18–26.

1934 The dynamics of photosynthesis. *New Phytol.* **33**, 8–40.

1935 (With M. Cattle) Studies of the physiological importance of the mineral elements in plants. VII. The effects of potassium and chloride ions on the diastase of broad beans. *New Phytol.* **34**, 283–295.

(With A. R. Clapham) *The biology of flowers*. 115 pages. Oxford: Clarendon Press.

(With A. C. Tansley) *Elements of plant biology*. (Revised ed.) London: George Allen & Unwin.

1936 (With A. L. James) The estimation of small quantities of fermentable sugars by carbon dioxide production. *New Phytol.* **35**, 1–10.

The chemistry of plant respiration. *Sch. Sci. Rev.* **17**, 265–281.

1938 (With I. P. NORVAL) The respiratory decomposition of pyruvic acid by barley. *New Phytol.* **37**, 455–473.
Glycolysis in barley. *Nature, Lond.* **142**, 1119–1120.
1939 (With S. E. ARNEY) Phosphorylation and respiration in barley. *New Phytol.* **38**, 340–363.
(With G. M. JAMES & A. H. BUNTING) On the method of formation of pyruvic acid by barley. *Biochem. J.* **35**, 588–594.
1940 (With G. M. JAMES) The formation of pyruvic acid in barley respiration. *New Phytol.* **39**, 266–270.
(With F. B. HORA) The effect of cyanide on the respiration of barley. *Ann. Bot.* (n.s.) **4**, 107–118.
(With A. L. JAMES) The respiration of barley germinating in the dark. *New Phytol.* **39**, 145–177.
1941 British drug plants. *Biology* **7**, 1–6.
The cultivation of drug plants. *Sch. Sci. Rev.* **23**, 76–87.
Drug plants native to Britain. *Nature, Lond.* **148**, 217.
(With G. M. WATSON) Variations in samples of *Digitalis* leaves from British sources. *Q. Jl Pharm. Pharmac.* **14**, 214–216.
(With G. M. WATSON & C. R. C. HEARD) A comparison of the biological and chemical assays of *Belladonna* and *Stramonium*. *Q. Jl Pharm. Pharmac.* **14**, 253–258.
(With A. H. BUNTING) On the mechanism of glycolysis in barley. *New Phytol.* **40** 268–275.
(With G. M. JAMES & A. H. BUNTING) On the method of formation of pyruvic acid by barley. *Biochem. J.* **35**, 588–594.
(With A. H. BUNTING) Carboxylase and co-carboxylase in barley. *New Phytol.* **40**, 262–267.
(With J. M. CRAGG) Ascorbic acid system in barley. *Nature, Lond.* **148**, 726–727.
1942 (With K. WOHL) The energy changes associated with plant respiration. *New Phytol.* **41**, 230–255.
1943 (With J. M. CRAGG) The ascorbic acid system as an agent in barley respiration. *New Phytol.* **42**, 28–44.
Phosphorylation, especially in plants. *Sch. Sci. Rev.* **24**, 310–319.
1944 (With C. R. C. HEARD & G. M. JAMES) On the oxidative decomposition of hexosediphosphate by barley. The role of ascorbic acid. *New Phytol.* **43**, 62–74.
1945 (With M. ROBERTS) The nature and specificity of the Vitali–Morin reaction for solanaceous alkaloids. *Q. Jl Pharm. Pharmac.* **18**, 29–35.
1946 The respiration of plants. *Annu. Rev. Biochem.* **15**, 417–434.
Demonstration of alkaloids in solanaceous meristems. *Nature, Lond.* **158**, 377–378.
Biosynthesis of the *Belladonna* alkaloids. *Nature, Lond.* **158**, 654–656.
1947 (With M. ROBERTS) A method for the estimation of total alkaloids in *Belladonna* and *Stramonium*. *Q. Jl Pharm. Pharmac.* **20**, 1–16.
1948 Demonstration and separation of noradrenaline, adrenaline and methyladrenaline. *Nature, Lond.* **161**, 851–852.
(With H. BEEVERS) The behaviour of secondary and tertiary amines in the presence of catechol and *Belladonna* catechol oxidase. *Biochem. J.* **43**, 636–639.
The oxidation of L-ornithine in the presence of *Belladonna* polyphenolase. *Biochem. J.* **43**, xi.
(With E. A. H. ROBERTS, H. BEEVERS & P. C. DE KOCK) The secondary oxidation of amino acids by the catechol oxidase of *Belladonna*. *Biochem. J.* **43**, 626–636.
1949 The amino acid precursors of the *Belladonna* alkaloide. *New Phytol.* **48**, 172–185.
*Elements of plant biology*. London: George Allen & Unwin.
Teleology and the experimental biologist. *Sch. Sci. Rev.* **31**, 92–95.
1950 (With H. BEEVERS) The respiration of *Arum* spadix. A rapid respiration, resistant to cyanide. *New Phytol.* **49**, 353–374.
Alkaloids in the plant. In: *The alkaloids* (ed. R. H. F. Manske & H. L. Holmes). New York: Academic Press.
(With N. KILBEY) The separation of noradrenaline and adrenaline. *Nature, Lond.* **166**, 67–68.
Plant respiration. Article in the new *Chambers Encyclopedia*.
(With G. M. JAMES) The use of solanaceous grafts in the study of alkaloid formation. *Proc. 7th Int. bot. Congr., Sweden*, pp. 774–775.

1951 (With N. Kilbey) A method for the estimation of adrenaline and noradrenaline in mixtures. *J. Pharm. Pharmac.* **3**, 22–26.
1952 (With N. Garton) The use of sodium diethyldithiocarbamate as a respiratory inhibitor. *J. exp. Bot.* **3**, 310–318.
1953 Alkaloids in plants. *Endeavour* **12**, 46.
The use of respiratory inhibitors. *A. Rev. Pl. Physiol.* **4**, 59–90.
Alkaloid formation in plants. *J. Pharm. Pharmac.* **5**, 809–822.
The terminal oxidases of plant respiration. *Biol. Rev.* **28**, 245–260.
The terminal oxidases in the respiration of the embryos and young roots of barley. *Proc. R. Soc. Lond.* B **141**, 289–299.
*Plant respiration.* 382 pages. Oxford: Clarendon Press.
1954 Reaction paths in plant respiration. *Endeavour* **13**, 155–162.
Terminal oxidases of cereal seedlings. *Advmt Sci., Lond.* **11**, 273–276.
1955 (With D. C. Elliott) Cyanide-resistant mitochondria from the spadix of an *Arum*. *Nature, Lond.* **175**, 89.
(With A. F. Ritchie) The anaerobic respiration of carrot tissue. *Proc. R. Soc. Lond.* B **143**, 302–310.
(With D. Boulter) Further studies of the terminal oxidases in the embryos and young roots of barley. *New Phytol.* **54**, 1–12.
Plant mitochondria and respiration. *New Biol.* **19**, 90–102.
1956 Sir Arthur Tansley, 1891–1955. *New Phytol.* **55**, 145–146.
(With V. S. Butt) Die Biogenese von Hordenin in Gerstenkeimlingen. *Abh. dt. Akad. Wiss. Berl.* **7**, 182–187.
The effect of 2,2′-dipyridyl on plant respiration. *New Phytol.* **55**, 269–279.
*Dachanye rasteni.* (Russian translation by A. A. Nitchiporovitch, Moscow, 1956, of *Plant respiration.* Oxford: Claredon Press, 1953.)
1957 Linnaeus (1707–1778). *Endeavour* **16**, 107–112.
(With V. S. R. Das) The organization of respiration in chlorophyllous cells. *New Phytol.* **56**, 325–343.
1957 (With M. M. Ward) The dieca effect in the respiration of barley. *Proc. R. Soc. Lond.* B **147**, 309–315.
Reaction paths in the respiration of the higher plants. *Adv. Enzymol.* **18**, 281–318.
*Background to gardening.* 224 pages. London: Allen & Unwin.
1958 (With D. C. Elliott) A flavoprotein from *Arum* spadix. *New Phytol.* **57**, 230–234.
Succulent plants. *Endeavour* **17**, 90–95.
Cytochromes in chloroplasts. *Nature, Lond.* **182**, 1684–1685.
1959 (With H. Lundegårdh) The cytochrome system of young barley roots. *Proc. R. Soc. Lond.* B **150**, 7–12.
(With R. M. Leech) Some observations on the cytochromes of isolated chloroplasts. *Pubbl. Staz. zool. Napoli* **XXI**/1, 36–42.
*Botany—here and now.* Inaugural lecture, Imperial College of Science and Technology, University of London, May 1959.
(With W. G. Slater) The aerobic utilization of pyruvate in plant tissues. *Proc. R. Soc. Lond.* B **150**, 192–199.
1960 (With R. M. Leech) The plant cytochromes. *Endeavour* **19**, 108–114.
The Chelsea Physic Garden. *Endeavour* **19**, 179–180.
(With A. M. Richens) The occurrence and distribution of cytochrome a and $a_3$ in plant cells. *Nature, Lond.* **188**, 423–424.
(With A. M. Richards) Carboxylase in carrots and potatoes. *New Phytol.* **59**, 292–297.
(With C. Lowe) Carrot tissue and ethanol. *New Phytol.* **59**, 288–291.
1962 Plant respiration and the microstructure of plant cells. Presidential address, Manchester meeting of British Association. *Advmt Sci., Lond.* **19**, 1–7.
(With A. M. Richens) Energy transport from mitochondria to nuclei. *Proc. R. Soc. Lond.* B **157**, 149–159.
1964 (With R. M. Leech) The cytochromes of isolated chloroplasts. *Proc. R. Soc. Lond.* B **160**, 13–24.
1967 Walter Stiles. *Biogr. Mem. Fellows R. Soc. Lond.* **13**, 343–357.
1971 *Cell respiration.* 138 pages. London: English Universities Press.

J. Kenyon N. Jones

# JOHN KENYON NETHERTON JONES

28 January 1912—13 April 1977

Elected F.R.S. 1957

By M. Stacey, F.R.S.

J. K. N. Jones was born in Birmingham, England, on 28 January 1912 and died in Kingston, Ontario, Canada on 13 April 1977. He was the eldest son of George Edward Netherton Jones and Florence Jones (*née* Goodchild). His family had long been established in the Midlands, his paternal grandfather James Jones, being a well known ironmaster in Walsall, a town which prospered during the Industrial Revolution. His maternal grandparents (the Goodchilds) lived in Swansea, Wales, and his mother was the eldest of their seven children. His father, who also was one of seven children, was for most of his career a shipping agent for the Elder Dempster line. Unhappily he was badly gassed in the World War I; this left him in poor health and he died in the early 1920s from tuberculosis. During the next few years Jones's mother (who was well known as an athlete) was left to struggle on and she had to fight bitterly to secure a pension for herself and her seven children. Life was very hard for the family for the pension was not granted until 1926 and shortly afterwards his mother died from blood poisoning. The family was now separated, the six eldest children were made Wards of the Ministry of Pensions and were split up among five families. The youngest, who was born after the war ended in 1918, was not supported by the Ministry of Pensions and was sent to an orphanage. Jones had a particular affection for this brother, Geoffrey David, and suffered great grief when the boy who was a bomber pilot in World War II, was shot down with his crew in June 1944 and was killed. Jones lived with several aunts and uncles in Birmingham during his school days and was very well looked after. He recalled happy summer days when he was able to cycle out to the home of a paternal uncle, Jack Jones, who, with his wife Lucy, lived in the country near Ross-on-Wye, Herefordshire. He spent his holidays with them and these visits sparked off his great love of plants and flowers and lifelong interest in gardening.

He attended the local Bordesley Green Council School between 1917 and 1923 and received much encouragement from the headmistress, Miss Boddy. He gained a scholarship to the Waverley Grammar School, a school noted for producing good science and engineering students especially for Birmingham University.

He often said that he read widely and studied hard at both schools in order to forget the harsh times and the separation from his brothers and sisters, for he rarely saw them at this time. Later both reading and studying became a habit and then a pleasure for him. He always paid tribute to the headmaster of Waverley Grammar School, Mr F. P. Whitely, to the chemistry master, Mr S. Owen, and to a Miss Lucy Barrows, J.P., all of whom gave him great encouragement. He developed into a fine physical specimen, eventually over 6 ft 2 in. (1.88 m) tall and he inherited his mother's athletic talents. He was captain of the school's association football team in 1929 and also athletics champion in that year. From the grammar school he won a polytechnic bursary and a Kitchener scholarship to Birmingham University which he entered in 1930. Following a cycling trip to France and Germany to improve his languages, he began his studies with great enthusiasm, particularly in the laboratories. He related that he had been given a chemistry set when he was 12 years old and frequently experimented with the growing of crystals. He fitted up an outhouse as a laboratory and earned money for his test tubes and chemicals by working as a bread round delivery boy. A near disaster of an experiment with ammonium chloride and sodium nitrate impressed him with the need to be cautious! He had been advised by his headmaster to take a degree in metallurgy and he studied this subject in his first year along with chemistry and physics. He found physical chemistry difficult and his whole interest turned to organic chemistry, inspired no doubt by experience during the vacations when he assisted Dr W. J. Hickinbottom with his researches on *n*-butylaniline. He graduated B.Sc. with first class honours in 1933, winning the coveted Frankland Medal as top man of the year. He tried to secure financial assistance in order to work on platinum compounds with Dr William Wardlaw but was unsuccessful. He was happy to accept a research scholarship to read for his Ph.D. under Professor Haworth and Dr Hirst. The writer, then a Research Fellow, had got to know him well through a mutual interest in athletics, for Jones had become a powerful member of the university cross-country team. He was allocated to the writer for day to day supervision. The chemistry department at that time was aglow with excitement because the structure and synthesis of ascorbic acid had just been achieved. He was assigned the topic of repeating, on a large scale, the synthesis of ascorbic acid and of working out the structure of some of the intermediates. When the writer departed for London, late in 1933, Jones joined forces with the late Fred Smith, both working long hours in the laboratory under Edmund Hirst's general direction. Progress was rapid, particularly with an early attempt to produce ascorbic acid on a commercial scale. For his work he was given, in 1936, a special award of £100 and this enabled him to marry, in June 1937, Marjorie Ingles Noon (with Fred Smith as best man).

The couple first met as teenagers in family circles, for Jones's uncle, Tom, with whom he lived for a time, had married Marjorie's aunt, Elsie, and later they met at school dances and enjoyed happy walks and tandem cycling together. Marjorie quickly appreciated his passion for laboratory work and spent long evenings, Sundays and holidays with him in the laboratory—eventually learning enough chemical language to check his proofs! She was the only child of T. Noon and Mabel Noon of Birmingham where they still reside. Marjorie's father was for many years a maintenance and electrical engineer at the offices of the *Birmingham Post and Mail*, Birmingham's leading newspaper. Her maternal grandfather was a top hatted, frock coated stationmaster at Bromsgrove, a small town near Birmingham.

When Edmund Hirst accepted a Chair at Bristol University in 1936 he invited Jones (now Dr Jones) to go with him as an assistant lecturer. Thus began a partnership as close and productive as the famous Haworth/Hirst partnership and it lasted until Hirst moved to Edinburgh in 1948. Jones always acknowledged that it was Hirst who inspired him to work so hard and, regarding him essentially in the role of a father, tried to emulate him in every way. Hirst in his turn owed much to his devotion for all their publications were shared.

The writer had provided Hirst with several pounds of damson gum gathered in Shropshire and Jones's first topic of research in Bristol was the unravelling of the structure of this complex material—a truly formidable task. Undaunted, he went ahead, rapidly establishing himself as a team leader building up, with colleagues such as G. T. Young, a powerful carbohydrate research team and extending their interests into other plant gums, alginates and unusual starches. However, major researches on carbohydrates were suspended in 1940 for the Bristol University Chemistry Department, under the headship of Professor W. E. Garner, was asked to house Professor Bennett of King's College, London, and his Chemistry Department and also to find accommodation for sections of Woolwich Arsenal staff. The organic chemists accepted an invitation to do 'war-work' with Professors Garner and Cecil Bawn on problems concerning explosives, such as the use of low grade toluene to make TNT, to assist with work on RDX and on plastic explosives.

Jones supervised the laboratory work, enabling Hirst to travel extensively[1] in order to attend government committee meetings and to visit ordnance factories, etc. The team, over a period of six years, made a very significant contribution to the war effort, but because of the nature of the work received very little publicity. Jones kept rigidly to the terms of the Official Secrets Act.

In 1945 Hirst moved to Manchester University and he invited Jones to go with him as Senior Lecturer in Organic Chemistry. Here again it was necessary for Hirst to spend much of his time on university administration work and government committees and so Jones took charge of the carbohydrate research group and supervised the completion of the explosives work. He was fortunate in having a brilliant assistant in the person of Dr T. G. Halsall. The stay at Manchester was short, for Hirst moved on to Edinburgh University in 1948 and Jones returned to Bristol University as Reader in Organic Chemistry. Their close association resulted in some 50 joint publications on carbohydrates.

The arrival of their children had relieved Marjorie of the need to spend long hours at her husband's side in the laboratory at Bristol and Manchester and, whenever possible, they sought recreation with the Hirsts and the Gordon Coxes by walking, climbing and rock climbing in the not too distant mountains of Snowdonia in Wales.

In Bristol, Jones rapidly built up a carbohydrate research group and impressed his colleagues with the need to develop biochemistry and the chemistry of natural products. He had the able assistance of Leslie Hough.

In 1951 he was invited to spend six months at the Institute of Paper Chemistry, in Appleton, Wisconsin, and, to quote his own words written in his Royal Society Record, 'I stayed there from April to September. The people were very kind and helpful and the weather was hot and sunny. The scenery was good and I liked the large open areas. When I saw the advert. for the Chown Research Chair in 1953 I put in for it. I have never regretted moving here. Facilities at first were poor but J. A. McRae, Dean Ettinger and the National Research Council gave me funds to buy apparatus and with the assistance of devoted graduate students we have never looked back.'

He moved to the Chown Research Chair of Chemistry at Queen's University, Kingston, Ontario, in 1953 and despite early difficulties it was an ideal Chair for him. It gave him the minimum time for administration and teaching and the maximum time for research. At Bristol and Manchester he had always played his full part as a university lecturer and had had a wide experience of lecturing and laboratory organization and teaching of a variety of classes but research was always his absorbing passion.

One early disappointment in Canada was the lack of Canadian graduates available for research but this was soon overcome by his ability to attract research students and postdoctoral researchers from overseas, particularly from Bristol. It was some time before he could understand the insatiable demands of North American industry for chemistry graduates. In course of time, however, he did succeed in attracting Canadian graduates into his research group and had great help from men such as Walter Szarek. His research group steadily grew. In 1957 there were twelve members, while in October of the following year the *Kingston Whig Standard* described briefly 'the researches of Professor J. K. N. Jones and his eighteen graduate students!'

In 1961 the following poem signed by fourteen students appeared at a presentation in the department and was much appreciated. He was always kind

There's a certain chap in Kingston,
And research he's fated to do;
'E came to Canada from England,
And brought 'alf Bristol 'ere too.

They gave 'im some labs and classes,
And a Chown Professor's chair,
And some gums and sticky messes
To see 'ow 'e would fare.

Now at sugars 'e was quite a master,
And out the results would fall;
The papers came faster and faster,
'Fact nothin' could stop 'im at all.

'Is gumption could scarce be denied,
And such was the world acclaim,
That at last they 'ad to decide
To add F.R.S. to 'is name.

Now I said research was 'is mission,
Which is really not quite true,
'Cause 'e's quite a dab 'and at fishin',
And pullin' out big ones, too.

So to mark this great occasion,
Some present we wanted to find,
And after some confusion,
A fishin' rod came to mind.

To please him we think it oughta;
To use it he should not shirk,
And spend all 'is time by t'water,
Instead of makin' us work.

to his students and was much inspired and beloved by them. He continued to work steadily, expanding his interests continually as will be described under his research activities. He found excellent senior collaborators in Kingston in the persons of M. B. Perry until 1962 and then Dr (later Professor) W. A. Szarek from 1967 to 1977.

One of the sensible advantages to the holder of the Chown Chair was the possession of a generous travel allowance and Jones took advantage of this, for he loved to travel.

He revisited the United Kingdom many times, taking the opportunity to attend national and international chemical congresses and to spend a few days at various centres of carbohydrate research. He lectured in a number of European cities. He spent a month in Russia in 1967. In 1969 he gave the first plenary lecture to the fifth Caribbean Chemical Congress in Barbados. Previously he spent a sabbatical leave from September 1967 to March 1968 in Curitiba, Brazil, and from March 1968 to June 1968 in South Africa. During that time he also lectured in Uganda, Kenya, Zambia and Malawi. He again spent the first six months of 1976 in Curitiba. He invariably gave a public report on his travels on his return to Kingston.

## Family life

None of Jones's brothers and sisters went to university, though one sister, Marjorie, married a physicist and another, Kathleen, an engineer. He took great pleasure in keeping in touch with them all. He undoubtedly found an ideal partner in his wife Marjorie. She had great sympathy in his early struggles and fully understood his passion for research, his need to spend such long hours in the laboratory and to do so much 'chemistry homework', especially on his publications. She gave him three fine children, Stephanie Netherton, Stephen

Howard and Jonathan Ingles Netherton, who from 1953 onwards rapidly became 'real' Canadians, enjoying life to the full.

At first he was worried and impatient with the Canadian schools system, contrasting it with the rigid discipline and hard work of his own school days. However, he eventually accepted the more leisurely approach and the wider curriculum. School concerts gave both him and Marjorie particular pleasure. He was delighted when both boys graduated, Stephen in engineering from Queen's and Jonathan in biology from Brock University. Stephanie, a graduate nurse, had married S. N. Buckeridge, an officer in the Canadian Navy, and they greatly pleased her parents when they moved, with their two children, back to the Kingston area from the West Coast.

The first family home was in Kingston itself and some time later they found what became their beautiful and indeed romantic home on Treasure Island, on the riverside, a short distance outside the city. Here, from their back garden jetty, they could, with the children, swim, boat, fish and enjoy one of the world's most beautiful views over the St Lawrence river. Here they were able to create from a small rocky area a lovely and interesting garden, bringing plants and soil samples from their trips into the Canadian bush.

There was a time when I approached Jones in regard to the possibility of returning to a Chair in Britain but he felt that he could never deprive Marjorie and their children of their love of the open air life of Canada. His hobbies, which he could share with the family, were simple—music, photography, foreign stamps, chess and the collecting of plants. He took a general interest in military affairs for he was quite proud of the active role he played in Bristol where, between 1939 and 1949, he was a part time officer in the Royal Corps of Signals attached to the University Training Corps.

One recalls an occasion when he visited Birmingham, resplendent in his captain's uniform, causing Sir Norman Haworth to remark: 'By Jove, Jones looks so smart and handsome that they surely must make him into a general and send him to fight.' In Kingston he occasionally gave a series of lectures on carbohydrates to students at the neighbouring Royal Military College, where he maintained close contact with the science departments.

## Academic Interests in Canada

### *Teaching*

In addition to the supervision of the research of a large number of graduate students, postdoctoral fellows and fourth year undergraduates, he taught courses in natural products chemistry and carbohydrate chemistry; these were graduate level courses, but were open also to fourth year undergraduates.

### *Committee and administrative responsibilities at Queen's University*

Department of Chemistry Graduate Committee; served one term as Chairman of Division IV of the School of Graduate Studies and Research (this division encompasses the physical sciences; the chairmen of the various divisions are members of the Council of the School of Graduate Studies); served as Secretary of the Committee on Scientific Research (this committee considered applications from faculty members for financial support of research); designer of some of the laboratory renovations (completed in 1964) in Gordon Hall of the Department of Chemistry.

*Participation in professional societies and affairs outside the university*

Served as Rapporteur for the Royal Society of Canada (Chemical Section) in 1971 and as Convener in 1972; served on the Advisory Committee to the Atlantic Regional Laboratories of the National Research Council in Halifax, Nova Scotia; was a member of the Board of Governors of the Ontario Research Foundation; was a member of the Board of Advisers for the British Commonwealth for *Advances in Carbohydrate Chemistry and Biochemistry*; was a member of the Editorial Advisory Board of *Carbohydrate Research*; was chairman and chief organizer of the fourth International Conference on Carbohydrate Chemistry which was held in Kingston in 1967; was a Corresponding Member of the Nomenclature Committee of the American Chemical Society Division of Carbohydrate Chemistry; served as External Examiner of graduate theses for Brazilian and Indian universities.

*Membership in professional societies*

The Chemical Society; the Biochemical Society; the Royal Institute of Chemistry (Associate); the Chemical Institute of Canada; the American Chemical Society; the New York Academy of Sciences.

*Honours and recognitions*

Elected Fellow of the Royal Society of London (1957); elected Fellow of the Royal Society of Canada (1959); elected Fellow of the Chemical Institute of Canada (1959); received the Claude S. Hudson Award from the Division of Carbohydrate Chemistry of the American Chemical Society (1969); received the Anselme Payen Award from the Cellulose, Paper and Textile Division (1975); received in 1975 the third Sir Norman Haworth Memorial Medal of the Chemical Society (London).

## TRIBUTES FROM HIS COLLEAGUES AND STUDENTS

One of the happiest days in the Jones family life was on the occasion of the award to him of the Hudson Medal in New York in 1969. His former colleagues, including particularly Professor Leslie Hough, collected world wide tributes from friends and students and these were transmitted on tape and read out at the dinner. They all showed the great respect and affection felt for him; two special tributes will convey, perhaps, a better picture of him than I have given. From Professor Leslie Hough of Queen Elizabeth College, London, comes:

'Upon graduation at Manchester in 1945, I joined the formidable carbohydrate research group of E. L. Hirst and J. K. N. Jones, in the main because I was so impressed by J. K.'s personal qualities and his enthusiastic approach to research. They had revived their pre-war Bristol studies on the starches, gums and mucilages, a difficult and challenging area of natural polymer chemistry of major importance and of relevance to the food, textile, paper and related industries. It was perhaps ironic that the first major advance came from the extremely effective separation of complex mixtures of sugars and their derivatives on cellulose, i.e. by paper chromatography. Armed with this facile technique, J. K. was in his element; the full flow of his ideas could now be quickly evaluated; horrendous analyses became child's play, and the research flowed at great pace. With the departure of Edmund Hirst for Edinburgh in 1948, J. K. accepted a readership in Professor Wilson Baker's department at Bristol, and by joining him I achieved one of my ambitions to move south.

'Initially we set up the paper chromatography equipment by persuading the neighbouring museum to give us glass display domes, which we promptly inverted and covered with a glass plate lid. It was not long before he convinced Freddie Pollard to apply the technique to inorganic analyses, with far-reaching success. One of our first objectives was to scale up the paper chromatogram to a column and, after trying sawdust as a packing, we finally settled on a cellulose powder from "ashless filter tablets". Then Hugh Wadman, a chemistry graduate with a good knowledge of electronics, designed and built an automatic fraction collector from ex-War Department equipment; this was probably the first collector of its kind. J. K. used to delight in pointing out a push button labelled "bombs gone" on the control device. Involvement in a new interdisciplinary degree course in biological chemistry stimulated J. K. to initiate a new and important area of research on the biosynthesis of carbohydrates. At this stage requests for reprints of his publications on techniques poured in by their hundreds, greatly adding to J. K.'s collection of foreign stamps. One of my most vivid recollections of J. K. was his daily ritual of inserting his paper chromatograms into their tanks before he departed in the evening and the enthusiastic rush on the following morning to remove, dry, spray and heat the chromatograms, usually with the aid of an electric fire. Occasionally, in his eagerness, the paper would inflame as it came dangerously close to the bars of the fire or it would char due to overheating, with a mild curse from J. K. at the temporary loss of a valuable diagnosis.

'At his Victorian home opposite Redland Green he tended his garden with loving care, taking particular pride in the yucca in the front and the peach tree in the back. He loved the countryside and among his other talents he could find the rare wild orchids. There are many pleasant memories of expeditions with him in the beautiful country around Bristol, fishing at Abbots pool for frog and toad spawn, harvesting seaweed on the beach at Clevedon and collecting fruit gum at Long Ashton.

'J. K. was at his best in the laboratory and never happier than when at the bench, except possibly when in his garden, encouraging his research students and enriching his conversation with stories of past experiences at Birmingham, Manchester and Bristol. He had the ability to create a stimulating and happy relationship with his colleagues, a flair for opening new and important problems by doing a halfpennyworth of research a day, and an ingenious knack of making one feel that his ideas were perhaps one's own. When the mood took him he would scratch away at the many syrups (collected over the years and stored in large desiccators in his room) that stubbornly refused to crystallize, and had an unusual habit of tasting many of his sugary products. It was difficult not to be impressed by J. K.'s infectious enthusiasm which coupled with his sincerity, modesty and quiet sense of humour made him the best and most respected of one's friends and colleagues.

'In 1953 he departed for Canada to take up the Chown Research Professorship at Queen's University, the ideal post since research came naturally to him whereas the administrative side was not quite so attractive. It was most appropriate that he and Marjorie should settle in such a delightful setting as Treasure Island. Not surprisingly there was a steady flow of graduates from Bristol to Queen's, thereby establishing a strong bond of friendship and collaboration between our research groups. His friends, many of them his former students, recall with considerable pleasure the warmth of their welcome to the home of Ken and Marjorie on Treasure Island, the glorious view over the lake, the many interesting books lining the shelves of the timbered walls, the grand piano, the hunting horn, the cacti (some grown by J. K. from a packet of Woolworth's seed), the fishing jetty and the causeway back to civilization and Queen's where he had created a carbohydrate research group of such great distinction.'

and from Professor Walter A. Szarek of Queen's University, Kingston, Ontario:

'My association with Professor Jones began in 1962 when I came to Queen's University to complete my graduate studies under his supervision. Following the completion of my graduate work, and after a period of three years in the United States, I was fortunate to be able to return to Queen's in 1967 as a member of the faculty of the Department of Chemistry. It was in that year that J. K. was chairman and chief organizer of the 4th International Conference on Carbohydrate Chemistry which was held in Kingston. I will always remember 1967 as a milestone in my own career, since it marked the beginning of my very close association and collaboration with J. K. In the fall of 1967 he went away on sabbatical leave and I was asked to assume the responsibility of supervising his entire research group; we continued our association for the remainder of his time at Queen's. Those were indeed happy years! Not only was he a most genuine and valued friend, but also a constant source of inspiration and wisdom.

'He greatly enjoyed discussions of carbohydrate chemistry, and during these discussions he frequently delighted in reminiscing about famous chemists. He thus imbued our entire research group with a feeling of continuity with the past and a spirit of belonging to the world's carbohydrate community. We were always impressed with the universality of his interests and the great depth of his chemical insight.

'Professor Jones was at all times an educator of the highest rank, and from his graduate students he evoked tremendous respect and affection as a result of his enthusiasm, sincerity, and gentle character. In all the years that I knew J. K., I never heard anyone speak ill of him, and similarly I had only seen him to be kind and generous in his opinions of others.

'Although he derived great pleasure from his work, he did have a number of other interests. Together with his wife Marjorie, he had an active interest in the cultural affairs of Kingston such as the promotion of live theatre and the symphony orchestra. He was an experienced and extremely eager traveller. He had a great love of the outdoors and took much pride and joy in cultivating and displaying his flowers and garden at his beautiful home on Treasure Island on the St Lawrence River. In fact, his office at the University sometimes looked like a florist's shop.

'I owe this truly fine and outstanding gentleman a great debt for the effect he has had on my own life.'

The following tribute was read in the Senate of the Queen's University on 28 April 1977 by Mr Heyding:

'John Kenyon Netherton Jones, a native of Birmingham, was appointed Chown Research Professor in Chemistry in 1953. In his 24 years at Queen's he developed a school of carbohydrate chemistry which gained an international reputation of the highest order. He supervised over one hundred and twenty M.Sc. and Ph.D. theses, published well over three hundred research papers and contributed nine chapters to books on his discipline. His laboratory attracted postdoctoral fellows and research associates to Queen's from all over the world.

'Dr Jones was a Fellow of the Royal Society of Canada and of the Royal Society. He was in great demand as a lecturer, and in recent years established a strong bond with the Universidade Federal do Parana in Brazil. Recent honors include the Anselme Payen Award by the Cellulose Division of the American Chemical Society, and the Haworth Memorial Medal by the Chemical Society (London).

'Professor Jones was, above all, a brilliant academic and an inspiration to his colleagues and his students. His enthusiasm, modesty and gentle character evoked tremendous respect and affection from all who knew him. With his passing the University has lost a great man who brought much credit to us all.'

The Senate wished to have this tribute recorded in its Minutes.

An International Meeting on 'Perspectives in Carbohydrate Chemistry' was arranged in Kingston to honour Jones on his sixty-fifth birthday and his retirement. Alas, a few weeks previously, he did not survive a second major operation and this event was held as a Memorial Meeting for him.

It was attended by over one hundred and fifty of his friends and former students and the meeting was organized to serve as a thanksgiving for the life and work of a fine scientist and true gentleman.

I, personally, have lost a great friend for we had many common interests apart from carbohydrates and gardening. In early days we shared a close interest in the books of Francis Brett Young who wrote so brilliantly about the Midland places and characters we knew so well. He tended to equate his mother's hard struggles with those of Jenny Hadley the heroine of *Far forest*, though I was usually able to 'talk him out' of the bitterness he often felt about his early days. We had a close interest in the progress of chemistry in Curitiba where he had been surprised and pleased to see my photograph adorning the wall of the director's office. Once he drove over 500 miles to divert me on an American tour so that he could show me his department and Treasure Island and later he and Marjorie often provided excellent hospitality for members of my family and former students. At the time of his death he had completed arrangements to spend, with Marjorie, the early months of 1978 at Shivagi University in India and together they had made many plans for retirement activities.

Sadly this was not to be and we record our deep sympathy to Marjorie and all the family.

## Researches

Jones joined the Birmingham carbohydrate research school after graduation in the summer of 1933 when the excitement of the ascorbic acid work was still present and he was assigned by Haworth to Edmund Hirst and the writer for supervision. He began work on the intermediates in the syntheses of analogues of ascorbic acid.

When the writer left for London later in that year he worked closely with the late Fred Smith who had been requested by Haworth to repeat the whole of the ascorbic acid work on a large scale. This was an intense and very interesting period for Jones, a happy outcome for him being the rapid success of the work and the modest financial grant from a patent which, as he often put it, 'enabled him to marry Marjorie and live happily ever after'. Four papers and the patent came from the ascorbic acid work.

His enthusiasm and skill impressed Edmund Hirst who, on moving to Bristol in 1936, invited him to a post on his staff. Having gained his Ph.D. Jones was happy to accept.

Fred Smith's work was now mainly concerned with the structures of gum arabic and gum tragacanth, topics suggested by Hirst, and they agreed to maintain a general collaboration in order to avoid overlap. The early Bristol work indeed owed much to the generous provision by Fred Smith of reference samples of partially methylated sugars. Jones undertook the major task of working out the structures of damson gum and various pectic substances.

The next four years was a period of tremendous activity for him, necessitating spending even longer hours than previously in the laboratory, since few research students were available. The techniques used for structural determination of the highly complex acidic carbohydrate polymers were initially those developed by the Birmingham school for determination of polysaccharide structures, namely exhaustive methylation of the gum, or its acid-degraded derivative, followed by partial and complete hydrolysis and then quantitative separation and identfiication of the constituent methylated mono-, di- and oligo-saccharides. He realized that new techniques were urgently needed to cut down the enormous labour needed for these investigations. He began to study new methods of methylation using thallium compounds and methyl iodide, to apply various chromatography techniques for separation of simple saccharides and their methyl ethers and to develop oxidative methods for determination of end groups in saccharide chains. In the four intensive years a succession of papers was published on parts of the structures of damson gum, peanut araban, pectic acids, cherry gum, slippery elm mucilage, citrus araban, etc.

The researches had to close down in 1940 for the whole of the team was transferred to work on explosives, as mentioned earlier. Jones never discussed his work on explosives, which in total represented a major contribution to the war effort, his responsibility being the direction of the experimental work involved. It was possible for him to get some relaxation during his duties with the Officer Training Corps and by 'pottering in the lab during late evenings and weekends on his gum work'.

The move to Manchester in 1945 made a welcome change though he had to build up a new research team. He was greatly helped by T. G. Halsall who proved to be a brilliant, hard working colleague. He was able to round off the work on explosives and to continue more leisurely with carbohydrate studies. The considerable achievements of the Hirst/Jones carbohydrate school is shown by the fact that more than seventy publications came from a partnership which lasted more than twenty years. Outstanding was the assignment of structures to the major parts of the complex macromolecules of damson gum, cherry gum and peach gum. Damson gum is an exudate gathered in the form of resin-like nodules from the bark of the tree *Prunus insitia* and it was isolated in the form of an ash free, water soluble, acidic white powder. On hydrolysis with mineral acid, D-xylose, L-arabinose, D-galactose, D-mannose and D-glucuronic acid were liberated and identified. It differed from gum arabic by its content of D-mannose and D-xylose and its lack of an L-rhamnose constituent. As with gum arabic, the L-arabinose was liberated by autolysis and was present in the furanose form. No less than eighteen methylated saccharide derivatives were isolated from the hydrolysed, methylated gum and the methylated, degraded gum. From the quantitative separation of these constituents and from the examination of their mode of union it was possible to assign a structure to a large part of the highly branched molecule.

Similar studies were made on cherry gum, where periodic oxidation techniques were successfully applied. In the many gum exudates and mucilages studied, striking similarities and yet often wide differences in saccharide constituents and their mode of linkage were disclosed. The work was speeded up by Jones's remarkable development of automated fraction separation devices ('fraction cutters') which were rapidly taken up by instrument manufacturers during the second Bristol period. The work up to 1969[2] was summarized by F. Smith and R. Montgomery in their book *Chemistry of plant gums and mucilages*. Paper and partition chromatography became a fine art at Bristol owing to Jones's skill and that of his students such as A. E. Flood, F. Brown, W. H. Wadman, and L. Hough. Collaboration in a small way was maintained with the writer in some studies on hexuronic acids and derivatives of arabinose.

## Research at Kingston

Once settled at Kingston, Jones's mind was seething with ideas for following new lines of research.

He had made a resolution to work mainly in areas which would be of direct interest and possible value to his new country. It meant slowing down his work on gums and devoting more time to forest products, particularly celluloses and hemicelluloses. During his last year at Bristol he had become more biochemically oriented and had read a great deal on the chemistry of microorganisms and on components of antibiotics. He realized that he would need to carry out a good deal more organic syntheses in order to identify and provide novel mono- and disaccharide derivatives of widely differing structures.

It is of interest to note his annual output of papers from Queen's University. Of necessity the output between 1953 and 1956 was low, consisting mainly of papers describing completion of work begun at Bristol. Then we begin to see his change of direction in 1957–58 with papers on 'The hemicelluloses present in aspen wood', 'The hemicellulose of loblolly pine', 'The action of alkali containing metaborates on wood cellulose', etc. and on synthesis: 'The preparation of L-sorbose from 5-keto-D-gluconic acid', 'A synthesis of 3-*O*-β-D-galactopyranosyl-D-galactose', 'A synthesis of D-tagatose', etc. His aspirations to work on the polysaccharides of microorganisms were fulfilled by collaboration with Michael Heidelberger enabling him to publish with M. B. Perry 'The structure of the type VIII *Pneumococcus* polysaccharide', where they showed the presence of a linear chain of a repeating unit, -*O*-β-D-glucopyranosyluronic acid-(1–4)-*O*-β-D-glucopyranosyl(1–4)-*O*-α-D-glucopyranosyl-(1–4)-*O*-D-galactopyranosyl-(1–4)- . . . -. Further work on other pneumococcal polysaccharides was carried out later.

From 1959 onwards output began to boom with papers on a wide variety of topics in the carbohydrate field, rarely fewer than fifteen per annum. The nature of these will be seen from a study of the Bibliography. It is impossible to describe all his work even in brief detail and the writer proposes to outline only a few of his more interesting papers. One of these was the discovery (with J. C. Turner) of a sugar derivative with nitrogen as the heteroatom in the ring. 5-Acetamido-5-deoxy-L-arabinose was synthesized and found to exist in two forms which differ in the position of ring closure of the terminal aldehyde group. One form has a normal five membered furanose ring and the other a six membered ring in which the heteroatom is nitrogen instead of oxygen. Further papers, e.g. on a D-xylose derivative, were published with W. A. Szarek. A great deal of attention was paid to the reaction of sulphuryl chloride with reducing sugars, the products being fully substituted compounds containing both chlorosulphate and chlorodeoxy groups. A series of papers was published on this topic. Several papers were published on the synthesis of aminodeoxy sugars. Thus (with D. T. Williams) a new synthesis of 3-acetamido-3-deoxy-D-glucose (kanosamine) was achieved; this involved the replacement by azide ion, with inversion, of the sulphonate group in 1,2:5,6-di-*O*-isopropylidene-3-*O*-p-tolylsulphonyl-D-allofuranose. 4-Acetamido-4-deoxy-D- and L-arabinoses were also synthesized. Publication from 1968 onwards carry the name of W. A. Szarek whose presence as lieutenant greatly eased Jones's burdens and stimulated the researches, especially on branched chain sugars and components of antibiotics. A typical example is the paper on lincomycin which is an important antibiotic produced by *Streptomyces lincolnensis* and active against Gram-positive microorganisms. With G. B. Howarth, 6-acetamido-6,8-dideoxy-D-*erythro*-D-galactoctose (*N*-acetyl-lincosamine), the *N*-acetyl derivative of the free carbohydrate moiety in lincomycin, was synthesized from 1,2:3,4-di-*O*-isopropylidene-α-D-galactohexodialdo-1,5-pyranose by two routes. A great triumph was the working out, by patient experiment over a number of years and using all the techniques developed for gum chemistry, of the structure of cholla gum. This acidic polysaccharide is exuded by the white cactus *Opuntia fulgida* native to the United States southern states and Mexico, and its formation, usually in old plants, follows long hot dry spells. Its constituent sugars are D-galactopyranose, L-rhamnopyranose, D-xylopyranose, L-arabofuranose and D-glucuronic acid. The suggested structure for the degraded gum (xylose and arabinose free) was a repeating unit of thirty six sugar residues with a backbone of 1–6 linked galactose units. For the cholla gum itself, the structure shown in figure 1 was devised. Had this plant product been an antibiotic or a hormone what publicity it would have received!

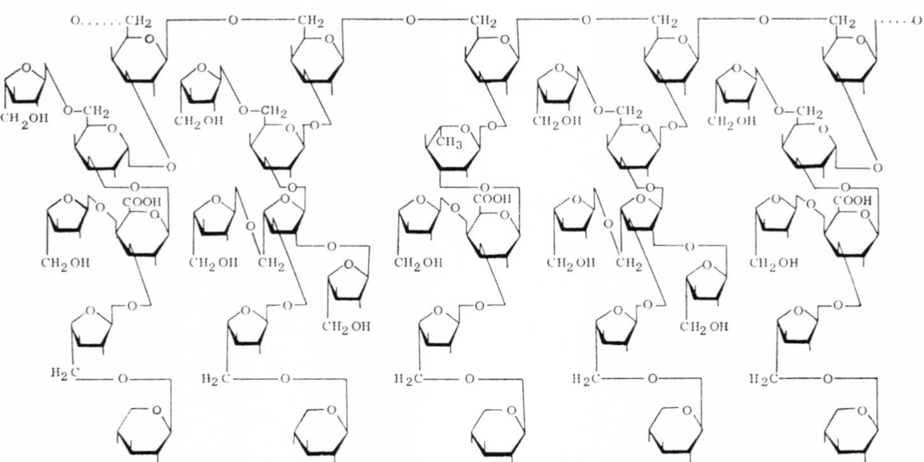

FIGURE 1. Proposed structure of cholla gum.

The high quality of the Queen's University carbohydrate chemistry school has been recognized by the creation, on the suggestion of Professor Walter Szarek, of a Carbohydrate Research Institute at Queen's University within the

Chemistry Department. J. K. N. Jones will be honoured there by the foundation of a research fellowship in his name.

The Institute, the idea of which Jones strongly supported, will undoubtedly be of great value to Canadian industry and Government.

The writer is grateful to many friends and pupils of Professor Jones and thanks in particular Mrs Marjorie Jones, Professor Walter Szarek and Professor Leslie Hough for help in preparing this memoir.

The photograph is by courtesy of Professor Szarek; it was taken in New York in 1959.

References

1. Hirst, E. L. 1976 *Biogr. Mem. Fellows R. Soc. Lond.* **137**, 22.
2. Smith, F. & Montgomery, R. 1959 *Chemistry of plant gums and mucilages.* ACS Monographs. New York.

Bibliography

1934 (With W. N. Haworth, E. L. Hirst & F. Smith) Synthesis of ascorbic acid and its analogues: the addition of hydrogen cyanide to osone. *J. chem. Soc.* p. 1192.

1936 (With W. N. Haworth & E. L. Hirst) Manufacture of vitamin C. *Brit. Pat.* 443901.

1937 (With W. N. Haworth & E. L. Hirst) D-Glucoascorbic acid. *J. chem. Soc.* p. 549.

1938 (With E. L. Hirst) Pectic substances. I. The araban and pectic acid of the peanut. *J. chem. Soc.* p. 496.

(With W. N. Haworth & E. L. Hirst) Analogues of ascorbic acid containing six-membered rings. *J. chem. Soc.* p. 710.

(With E. L. Hirst) The constitution of damson gum. 1. Composition of damson gum and the structure of an aldobiouronic acid (glucuronosido-2-mannose) derived from it. *J. chem. Soc.* p. 1174.

(With C. C. Barker & E. L. Hirst) The methylation of α-methylglucoside by thallous hydroxide and methyl iodide. *J. chem. Soc.* p. 1695.

1939 (With E. G. E. Hawkins & E. L. Hirst) Methyl ethers of D-araboascorbic acid and their isomerism. *J. chem. Soc.* p. 146.

(With E. L. Hirst) Pectic substances. II. Isolation of an araban from the carbohydrate constituents of the peanut. *J. chem. Soc.* p. 452.

(With E. L. Hirst) Pectic substances. III. Composition of apple pectin and the molecular structure of the araban component of the apple pectin. *J. chem. Soc.* p. 454.

The constitution of cherry gum. I. Composition. *J. chem. Soc.* p. 558.

(With R. E. Gill & E. L. Hirst) The constitution of the bark from *Ulmus fulva* (slippery elm mucilage). I. The aldobiouronic acid obtained by hydrolysis of the mucilage. *J. chem. Soc.* p. 1469.

(With E. L. Hirst) The constitution of damson gum. II. Hydrolysis products from methylated degraded (arabinose-free) damson gum. *J. chem. Soc.* p. 1469.

(With G. H. Beaven & E. L. Hirst) Pectic substances. IV. Citrus araban. *J. chem. Soc.* p. 1865.

(With F. A. Isherwood, W. N. Haworth & E. L. Hirst) 2,3,4-trimethyl-D-mannose. *J. chem. Soc.* p. 1878.

(With E. L. Hirst & Winifred O. Jones) The structure of alginic acid. I. *J. Chem. Soc.* p. 1880.

(With E. L. Hirst & Winifred O. Jones) The structure of alginic acid. *Nature, Lond.* **143**, 857.

(With G. H. Beaven) The molecular structure of pectic acid. *Chemy Ind.* p. 363.

1940 (With E. C. E. Hawkins & G. T. Young) The constitution of banana starch. *J. chem. Soc.* p. 390.

1941 (With E. L. Hirst & W. G. Campbell) ε-Galactan of larch wood. *Nature, Lond.* **147**, 25.

1944 The separation of methylated methylglycosides by adsorption on alumina. *J. chem. Soc.* p. 333.

1945 The condensation of glucose and β-diketones. *J. chem. Soc.* p. 116.
(With L. J. Breddy) The quantitative estimation of xylose. *J. chem. Soc.* p. 738.
(With A. H. Campbell, M. E. Foss & E. L. Hirst) Nitrogenous substances synthesized by moulds. *Nature, Lond.* **155**, 141.
(With F. Brown, Sonia Dunstan, T. G. Halsall & E. L. Hirst) Application of new methods of end groups determination to structural problems in the polysaccharides. *Nature, Lond.* **156**, 785.

1946 (With E. L. Hirst) The constitution of damson gum. III. Hydrolysis products from methylated damson gum. *J. chem. Soc.* p. 506.
(With C. C. Barker & E. L. Hirst) The methylation of α-methylglucopyranoside and α-methylxylopyranosides by thallous hydroxide and methyl iodide. *J. chem. Soc.* p. 783.
(With R. E. Gill & E. L. Hirst) The constitution of the mucilage from the bark of *Ulmus fulva* (slippery elm mucilage). II. The sugars formed in the hydrolysis of the methylated mucilage. *J. chem. Soc.* p. 1025.
(With E. L. Hirst) The chemistry of the pectic materials. *Adv. Carbohyd. Chem.* **2**, 235.

1947 (With T. G. Halsall & E. L. Hirst) The structure of starch and cellulose. *Nature, Lond.* **160**, 899.
(With E. L. Hirst) The chemistry of some plant gums and mucilages. *J. Soc. Dyers Colour.* **63**, 249.
The constitution of cherry gum. II. The products of hydrolysis of methylated cherry gum. *J. chem. Soc.* p. 1655.
(With E. L. Hirst & E. A. Woods) The quantitative determination of galactose, mannose, arabinose and rhamnose. *J. chem. Soc.* p. 1048.
(With E. L. Hirst & (Miss) E. Williams) The synthesis of 3-methyl- and 3,5-dimethyl-L-arabinose. *J. chem. Soc.* p. 1062.
(With E. L. Hirst) The constitution of egg-plum gum. I. *J. chem. Soc.* p. 1064.
(With G. H. Beaven) Pectic substances. V. The molecular structure of strawberry and apple pectic acids. *J. chem. Soc.* p. 1218.
(With E. L. Hirst) Pectic substances. VI. The structure of the araban from *Arachis hypogea*. *J. chem. Soc.* p. 1221.
(With E. L. Hirst & (Mrs) W. O. Walder) Pectic substances. VII. The constitution of the galactan from *Lupinus albus*. *J. chem. Soc.* p. 1225.
(With M. Stacey) Some derivatives of D-galacturonic acid. *J. chem. Soc.* p. 1340.
(With P. W. Kent & M. Stacey) Synthesis of some derivatives of D- and L-arabinose. *J. chem. Soc.* p. 1341.
(With T. G. Halsall & E. L. Hirst) The structure of glycogen. Ratio of non-terminal to terminal glucose residues. *J. chem. Soc.* p. 1399.
(With F. Brown) The quantitative separation of methylated sugars. *J. chem. Soc.* p. 1344.
(With T. G. Halsall & E. L. Hirst) Oxidation of carbohydrates by the periodate ion. *J. chem. Soc.* p. 1427.
(With E. L. Hirst & Winifred O. Walder) The galactomannan of the lucerne seed. *J. chem. Soc.* p. 1443.
(With A. E. Flood & E. L. Hirst) Quantitative estimation of mixtures of sugars by the paper chromatogram method. *Nature, Lond.* **160**, 86.

1948 (With F. Brown, T. G. Halsall & E. L. Hirst) The structure of starch. The ratio of non-terminal to terminal groups. *J. chem. Soc.* p. 27.
(With E. L. Hirst) The structure of egg-plum gum. II. The hydrolysis products obtained from the methylated degraded gums. *J. chem. Soc.* p. 120.
(With W. G. Campbell & E. L. Hirst) The ε-galactan of larch wood (*Larix decidua*). *J. chem. Soc.* p. 774.
(With E. L. Hirst) The galacto mannan of carob-seed gum (gum gatto). *J. chem. Soc.* p. 1677.
(With F. Brown & E. L. Hirst) The structure of almond tree gum. I. The constitution of the aldobiouronic acid derived from the gum. *J. chem. Soc.* p. 1677.
(With A. E. Flood & E. L. Hirst) Quantitative analysis of mixtures of sugars by the method of partition chromatography. I. Standardization of the procedure. *J. chem. Soc.* p. 1679.
(With E. L. Hirst & A. J. Roudier) Structure of acorn starch. *J. chem. Soc.* p. 1779.
(With E. L. Hirst) Pectic substances. VIII. The araban component of sugar beet pectin. *J. chem. Soc.* p. 2311.

1948 (With F. BROWN, E. L. HIRST, L. HOUGH & H. WADMAN) Separation of methylated sugars on the paper chromatogram. *Nature, Lond.* **161**, 720.

(With L. HOUGH & H. WADMAN) The application of partition chromatography to the separation of sugars and their methylated derivatives on a column of powdered cellulose. *Nature, Lond.* **162**, 448.

(With T. G. HALSALL, E. L. HIRST & E. W. SANSOME) The amylose content of the starch present in the growing potato tuber. *Biochem. J.* **43**, 70.

Cherry gum. III. An examination of the products of hydrolysis of methylated degraded cherry gum, using the method of paper partition chromatography. *J. chem. Soc.* p. 3141.

1949 (With E. L. HIRST & L. HOUGH) Composition of the gum of *Sterculia setigera*: occurrence of D-tagatose in nature. *Nature, Lond.* **163**, 177.

(With E. L. HIRST & L. HOUGH) Quantitative analysis of mixtures of sugars by the method of partition chromatography. II. The separation and determination of methylated aldoses. *J. chem. Soc.* p. 928.

(With V. C. BARRY, T. C. HALSALL & E. L. HIRST) The polysaccharides of the *Florideas.* Floridean starch. *J. chem. Soc.* p. 1468.

(With F. BROWN & E. L. HIRST) The constitution of egg plum gum. III. The hydrolysis products obtained from the methylated gum. *J. chem. Soc.* p. 1757.

(With F. BROWN & E. L. HIRST) Cholla gum. *J. chem. Soc.* p. 1761.

(With T. URBANSKI) Reactions of nitroparaffins. II. The reaction of 2-nitropropane with formaldehyde and ammonia. *J. chem. Soc.* p. 1766.

(With E. L. HIRST, F. A. ISHERWOOD & M. A. JERMYN) Pear cell wall cellulose. *J. chem. Soc.* p. 182.

(With E. L. HIRST) Quantitative analysis of mixtures of sugars by the method of parition chromatography. III. Determination of the sugars by periodate oxidation. *J. chem. Soc.* p. 1659.

(With L. HOUGH & W. H. WADMAN) Quantitative analysis of mixtures of sugars by the method of partition chromatography. IV. The separation of the sugars and their methylated derivatives on columns of cellulose. *J. chem. Soc.* p. 2511.

(With T. G. HALSALL, E. L. HIRST & L. HOUGH) The action of β-amylase on amylopectin and glycogen. *J. chem. Soc.* p. 3200.

(With E. L. HIRST) The application of partition chromatography to the separation of the sugars and their derivatives. *Discuss. Faraday Society* no. 7, p. 268.

(With F. SMITH) Plant gums and mucilages. *Adv. Carbohyd. Chem.* vol. 4.

1950 (With F. BROWN & L. HOUGH) Synthesis of 2,3-dimethyl-L-rhamnose. The action of sodium metaperiodate on 2,3- and 3,4-dimethyl-D-rhamnose. *J. chem. Soc.* p. 1125.

(With L. HOUGH & W. H. WADMAN) Quantitative analysis of mixtures of sugars by the method of partition chromatography. V. Improved methods for the separation and detection of the sugars and their methylated derivatives on the paper chromatogram. *J. chem. Soc.* p. 1702.

(With J. J. CONNELL, (Miss) R. M. HAINSWORTH & E. L. HIRST) Grapefruit and lemon gums. I. *J. chem. Soc.* p. 1696.

(With B. F. FOLKES & A. A. GRANT) Frog spawn mucin. *J. chem. Soc.* p. 2136.

(With M. E. FOSS, E. L. HIRST, A. T. THOMAS, T. URBANSKY & H. D. SPRINGALL) On the structure of Knudsen's base and related compounds. *J. chem. Soc.* p. 624.

(With M. E. FOSS, E. L. HIRST, H. D. SPRINGALL, A. T. THOMAS & T. URBANSKI) On the structure of Knudsen's base and related compounds. II. *J. chem. Soc.* p. 1691.

(With E. L. HIRST & L. HOUGH) Chemical constitution of slippery elm mucilage; isolation of 3-methyl-D-galactose from the hydrolysis products. *Nature, Lond.* **165**, 34; *J. chem. Soc.* p. 323.

(With D. G. EASTERBY) Composition of linseed mucilage. *Nature, Lond.* **165**, 614.

(With S. K. CHANDA, E. L. HIRST & E. G. V. PERCIVAL) The constitution of xylan from esparto grass (*Stipa tenacissima* L.). *J. chem. Soc.* p. 1289.

The structure of peach gum. I. The sugars produced on hydrolysis of the gum. *J. chem. Soc.* p. 534.

The mannan present in *Porphyra umbilicalis*. *J. chem. Soc.* p. 3292.

1951 (With L. HOUGH) The synthesis of sugars from simpler substances. I. *J. chem. Soc.* p. 1122.

1951 (With L. Hough) The synthesis of sugars from simpler substances. II. *J. chem. Soc.* p. 3191.

The chemical composition and properties of pectins. *Chemy Ind.* p. 430.

(With J. K. Bartlett & L. Hough) The colorimetric determination of methylated sugars. An improved micromethod of end group assay. *Chemy Ind.* p. 76.

(With L. Hough) The origin of the sugars. *Nature, Lond.* **167**, 180.

(With E. L. Hirst & L. Hough) Constitution of the mucilage from the bark of *Ulmus fulva*. III. *J. chem. Soc.* p. 323.

(With D. G. Wasterby & L. Hough) Toluene-*p*-sulphonylhydrazine derivatives of the pentose sugars. *J. chem. Soc.* p. 3416.

1952 (With L. Hough & W. H. Wadman) Some observations on the constitution of gum myrrh. *J. chem. Soc.* p. 796.

(With L. Hough & M. S. Mayson) Methylene derivatives of D-galactose and of D-glucose. *J. chem. Soc.* p. 1525.

(With Louis E. Wise) The hemicelluloses present in aspen wood. I. *J. Chem. Soc.* p. 2750.

(With L. Hough & W. H. Wadman) An investigation of the polysaccharide components of certain fresh-water algae. *J. chem. Soc.* p. 3393.

(With P. Andrews & L. Hough) Mannose-containing polysaccharides. I. *J. Am. chem. Soc.* **74**, 4029.

(With P. Andrews & L. Hough) Mannose-containing polysaccharides. II. *J. chem. Soc.* p. 2744.

(With L. Hough) Methylation of carbohydrates using diazomethane. *Chemy Ind.* p. 380.

(With Louis E. Wise) The hemicelluloses present in aspen wood. II. *J. chem. Soc.* p. 3389.

(With L. Hough) A synthesis of 3,4-dimethyl-D-xylose. *J. chem. Soc.* p. 4349.

(With L. Hough) The synthesis of sugars from simpler substances. III. The enzymatic synthesis of D-xylulose. *J. chem. Soc.* p. 4047.

(With L. Hough) The synthesis of sugars from simpler substances. IV. The enzymatic synthesis of 6-deoxy-D-fructose and 6-deoxy-L-sorbose. *J. chem. Soc.* p. 4052.

(With L. Hough & E. L. Richards) The action of ammonia on sugars. *J. chem. Soc.* p. 3854.

(With L. Hough) The synthesis of sugars from simpler substances. The enzymic synthesis of sedoheptulose. *Chemy Ind.* p. 181.

The occurrence of L-arabopyranose residues in ε-galactan. *Chemy Ind.* p. 183.

1953 Larch ε-galactan. II. The isolation of 3-*O*-β-L-Arabopyranosyl-L-arabinose. *J. chem. Soc.* p. 1672.

(With P. Andrews & L. Hough) Mannose-containing polysaccharides. II. The polysaccharides in the seeds of *Iris ochroleuca* and *I. sibirica*. *J. chem. Soc.* p. 1186.

(With P. Andrews & D. H. Ball) The isolation of oligosaccharides from gums and mucilages. I. *J. chem. Soc.* p. 4090.

(With L. Hough) The synthesis of sugars from simpler substances. V. Enzymic synthesis of sedoheptulose. *J. chem. Soc.* p. 342.

(With P. A. J. Gorin) The synthesis of sugars from simpler substances. VI. Enzymic synthesis of D-idoheptulose. *J. chem. Soc.* p. 2140.

(With P. A. J. Gorin & L. Hough) The synthesis of sugars from simpler substances. VII. Enzymic synthesis of 5-deoxy-D-xylulose. *J. chem. Soc.* p. 2140.

(With L. Hough & E. L. Richards) The reaction of amino-compounds with sugars. II. The action of ammonia on glucose, maltose and lactose. *J. chem. Soc.* p. 2005.

Structure of the 'triuronide' from pectic acid. *Chemy Ind.* p. 303.

1954 (With L. Hough & E. L. Richards) Some observations on the browning reaction between glucose and ammonia. *Chemy Ind.* p. 545.

(With P. Andrews & L. Hough) Methylene derivatives of L-rhamnose. *J. Am. chem. Soc.* **77**, 125.

(With P. Andrews) The isolation of oligosaccharides from gums and mucilages. II. *J. chem. Soc.* p. 1724.

(With P. Andrews) The isolation of oligosaccharides from gums and mucilages. III. Golden apple gum. *J. chem. Soc.* p. 4134.

(With P. Andrews) Isolation of oligosaccharides from gums and mucilages. IV. Isolation of 3-*O*-β-L-arabopyranosyl-L-arabinose from lemon gum. *J. chem. Soc.* p. 583.

1954 (With P. A. J. Gorin & L. Hough) A synthesis of 4-deoxy-D-*erythro*-hexulose. *J. chem. Soc.* p. 4700.

(With J. B. Pridham) A colorimetric estimation of sugars using benzidine. *Biochem. J.* **58**, 288.

The synthesis of sugars from smaller fragments. VIII. The synthesis of D-idoheptulosan from D-xylose. *J. chem. Soc.* p. 3643.

The structure of the oligosaccharides produced by the enzymatic breakdown of pectic acid. I. *J. chem. Soc.* p. 1361.

(With A. R. N. Gorrod) The hemicelluloses of Scots pine (*Pinus sylvestris*) and black spruce (*Picea nigra*) woods. *J. chem. Soc.* p. 2522.

(With G. Guzman) Las hemicelulosas del esparto (*Stipa tenacissima*). *An. R. Soc. esp. Fís. Quim.* Serie B—Quimica, col. L(B), no. 5, p. 565.

1955 (With P. A. J. Gorin & L. Hough) An improved synthesis of D-xylose-5-(barium phosphate). *J. chem. Soc.* p. 582.

(With E. L. Hirst) The analysis of plant gums and mucilages. *Modern Methods of Plant Analysis* (ed. H. Peach & M. V. Tracey), vol. II, chapter II, p. 275. Berlin.

Chemistry of the carbohydrates. *A. Rev. Biochem.* **24**, 113.

(With P. A. J. Gorin & L. Hough) The synthesis of L-glycerotetrulose and related compounds. *J. chem. Soc.* p. 2699.

(With J. R. Nunn) The constitution of gum myrrh. II. *J. chem. Soc.* p. 3001.

(With W. W. Reid) The preparation of L-sorbose from 5-keto-D-gluconic acid (L-sorburonic acid). *J. chem. Soc.* p. 1682.

(With P. A. J. Gorin & L. Hough) The synthesis of sugars from simpler substances. IX. The enzymic synthesis 5,6-dideoxy-D-*threo*-hexulose. *J. chem. Soc.* p. 3843.

(With W. H. Nicholson) The epimerisation of sugars. *J. chem. Soc.* p. 3050.

(With J. R. Nunn) The structure of frankincense gum. *J. Am. chem. Soc.* **77**, 5745.

(With R. B. Kelly) The synthesis of sugars from simpler fragments. X. Synthesis of L-glucoheptulose. *Can. J. Chem.* **34**, 95.

(With W. W. Reid) The structure of the oligosaccharides produced by the enzymic breakdown of pectic acid. II. *J. chem. Soc.* p. 1890.

(With P. A. J. Gorin & W. W. Reid) A synthesis of D-tagatose from D-galacturonic acid. *Can. J. Chem.* **33**, 1116.

(With D. H. Ball, R. H. Butler & W. H. Cook) The separation of an essential oil and of methylated sugars by thermal diffusion. *Chemy Ind.* p. 1740.

1956 (With P. Andrews & L. Hough) Mannose-containing polysaccharides. IV. The glucomannans of lily bulbs. *J. chem. Soc.* p. 181.

A synthesis of 5-*O*-methyl-D-glucose and of 2-*O*-methyl-D-glyceronamide. *Can. J. Chem.* **34**, 310.

The hemicelluloses of the fossilized wood of *Cedrus penhallowii*. *Can. J. Chem.* **34**, 840.

4,6-*O*-isopropylidenemethyl-α-D-glucoside. *Can. J. Chem.* **34**, 840.

(With A. J. Erskine) Fractionation of polysaccharides. *Can. J. Chem.* **34**, 821.

(With W. H. Nicholson, T. J. Painter & D. H. Ball) The structure of the hemicelluloses of loblolly pine. *TAPPI* p. 438.

The synthesis of 3-hexuloses. I. 2-*O*-methyl-L-xylo-3-hexulose. *J. Am. chem. Soc.* **78**, 2855.

(With L. E. Wise & Josephine P. Joppe) The action of alkali containing metaborates on wood cellulose. *TAPPI* p. 139.

1957 (With M. B. Perry) The structure of type VIII *Pneumocuccus* polysaccharide. *J. Am. chem. Soc.* **79**, 2787.

(With T. J. Painter) The hemicelluloses of loblolly pine (*Pinus taeda*) wood. I. The isolation of five oligosaccharide fragments. *J. chem. Soc.* p. 669.

(With D. H. Ball) The synthesis of disaccharides. *J. chem. Soc.* p. 4871.

(With A. J. Erskine) The structure of linseed mucilage. I. *Can. J. Chem.* **35**, 1174.

(With L. Hirst) Carbohydrate biogenesis. *J. scient. ind. Res.* **10A**, p. 271.

(With R. Kolinski, H. Piotrowska & T. Urbanski) On the formation of derivatives of 1,5-diazabicyclo-(3,3,3)-undekane from 1-nitropropane, formaldehyde and ammonia. *Bull. Acad. pol. Sci.* **8**, 521.

(With D. L. Mitchell) The synthesis of 1-deoxy-1-*S*-ethylpolyols. *Can. J. Chem.* **36**, 206.

1957 (With E. MERLER & L. E. WISE) The hemicelluloses present in aspen wood. *Can. J. Chem.* **35**, 634.

(With J. L. THOMPSON) A synthesis of 5,6-dideoxy-D-xylohexose (5-deoxy-5-*C*-methyl-D-xylose). *Can. J. Chem.* **35**, 955.

(With B. O. LINDGREN) Isolation of disaccharides from golden apple gum. *Acta chem. scand.* **11**, 1365.

1958 (With D. H. BALL) A synthesis of 3-*O*-β-D-galactopyranosyl-D-galactose. *J. chem. Soc.* p. 905.

(With D. H. BALL) The acid catalysed reversion of D-xylose. *J. chem. Soc.* p. 33.

(With W. H. NICHOLSON) The acid catalysed reversion of D-arabinose and D-mannose. *J. chem. Soc.* p. 27.

Carbohydrate chemistry at Queen's University. *Pulp Pap. Can. Tech. Sect.* p. 145.

(With L. HOUGH & D. L. MITCHELL) The preparation of some derivatives of D-ribo-(1–4)lactone and D-ribitol. *Can. J. Chem.* **36**, 1720.

1959 (With K. C. B. WILKIE) Structural studies on clinical dextrans. I. Methylation and periodate oxidation studies. *Can. J. Biochem. Phys.* **37**, 377.

(With P. D. BRAGG) The characterization of tri-*O*-tosylsucrose. *Can. J. Chem.* **37**, 575.

(With E. J. C. CURTIS) The synthesis of 4-*O*-β-D-galactosyl-D-glucose(lactose) *Can. J. Chem.* **37**, 358.

(With T. J. PAINTER) The hemicelluloses of loblolly pine (*Pinus taeda*) wood. II. The constitution of hexosan and pentosan components. *J. chem. Soc.* p. 573.

(With D. E. MITCHELL) The oxidation of some terminal substituted polyhydric alcohols by *Acetobacter suboxydans*. *Can. J. Chem.* **37**, 725.

(With D. J. BRASCH, T. J. PAINTER & P. E. REID) Structure of some water-soluble polysaccharides from wood. *Pulp Pap. Can. Tech. Sect.* p. 342.

(With M. J. ABERCROMBIE) The reaction of sodium metaperiodate with some nitrogen derivatives of carbohydrates. *Can. J. Chem.* **38**, 308.

(With D. J. BRASCH) Investigations of some ancient woods. *TAPPI* **42**, 913.

(With D. H. BALL & A. O. PITTET) Separation of sugars on ion-exchange resins. *Chemy Ind.* p. 1196.

(With D. D. MITCHELL) The synthesis of 5-deoxy-5-*S*-ethyl-D-threopentulose. *Can. J. Chem.* **37**, 1561.

(With N. K. MATHESON) Synthesis of sugars from smaller fragments. XI. Synthesis of L-galactoheptulose. *Can. J. Chem.* **37**, 1754.

(With D. J. BRASCH) The structure of an arabogalactan from Monterey pine (*Pinus radiata*). *Can. J. Chem.* **37**, 1538.

(With D. H. BALL & A. E. FLOOD) 5,6-dideoxy-L-arabinohexose (5-deoxy-5-*C*-methyl-L-arabinose). *Can. J. Chem.* **37**, 1018.

1960 (With H. H. SEPHTON) Synthesis of sugars from smaller fragments. XII. Synthesis of D-glycero-L-altro-, L-galacto-D-glycero-L-gluco-, and D-glycero-L-octulose. *Can. J. Chem.* **38**, 753.

(With E. J. C. CURTIS) Some open-chain derivatives of glucose and mannose. *Can. J. Chem.* **38**, 890.

(With P. E. REID) The synthesis of 2-*O*-β-D-glucopyranosyl-D-xylose. *Can. J. Chem.* **38**, 944.

(With P. D. BRAGG & J. C. TURNER) The reaction of sulphuryl chloride with glycosides and sugar alcohols. I. *Can. J. Chem.* **37**, 1412.

(With M. B. PERRY & E. J. C. CURTIS) The reaction of sulphuryl chloride with glycosides and sugar alcohols. II. *Can. J. Chem.* **38**, 1122.

(With E. J. C. CURTIS) The synthesis of 3-*O*-β-D-xylopyranosyl-D-xylose and the re-characterization of some benzylidene derivatives. D-xylose. *Can. J. Chem.* **38**, 1305.

(With M. J. ABERCROMBIE, M. V. LOCK, M. B. PERRY & R. J. STOODLEY) The polysaccharides of *Cryptococcus laurentii* (MRLY-1401). I. *Can. J. Chem.* **38**, 1617.

1961 (With C. B. PURVES & T. E. TIMELL) Constitution of a 4-*O*-methylglucuronoxylan from the wood of trembling aspen (*Populus tremuloides*). *Can. J. Chem.* **39**, 1059.

(With B. GRASER-REID & M. B. PERRY) The demethylation of sugars with hydrogen peroxide. *Can. J. Chem.* **39**, 555.

(With G. H. S. THOMAS) The structure of the gum asafoetida polysaccharide. *Can. J. Chem.* **39**, 192.

1961 (R. A. WALL and in part A. O. PITTET) The separations of sugars on ion-exchange resins. I. *Can. J. Chem.* **38**, 2285.

(With R. A. WALL) The separations of sugars on ion-exchange resins. II. *Can. J. Chem.* **38**, 2290.

(With M. J. ABERCROMBIE & M. B. PERRY) The polysaccharides of *Cryptococcus laurentii* (Y1401). II. Biosynthesis of the carbohydrates found in the acidic polysaccharide. *Can. J. Chem.* **38**, 2007.

(With B. SHELTON, D. J. WALTON & M. B. PERRY) The carbohydrate protein linkage in glycoproteins. I. The syntheses of some model substituted amides and an L-seryl-D-glucosaminide. *Can. J. Chem.* **39**, 1005.

(With M. B. PERRY) The synthesis of acetamidodeoxyketoses by *Acetobacter suboxydans*. Part I. *Can. J. Chem.* **39**, 965.

(With M. B. PERRY) The synthesis of acetamidodeoxyketoses by *Acetobacter suboxydans*. Part II. *Can. J. Chem.* **39**, 2400.

(With S. W. GUNNER & M. B. PERRY) Analysis of sugar mixtures by gas–liquid partition chromatography. *Chemy Ind.* p. 255.

*Biochemie des glucides*, vol. VII, p. 187. Paris: Edition du Centre National de la Recherche Scientifique.

(With S. W. GUNNER & M. B. PERRY) The gas–liquid partition chromatography of carbohydrate derivatives. I. *Can. J. Chem.* **39**, 1892.

1962 (With M. B. PERRY & J. C. TURNER) The synthesis of acetamidodeoxyketoses by *Acetobacter suboxydans. Can. J. Chem.* **40**, 502.

(With M. B. PERRY & R. J. STOODLEY) Biosynthesis of sugars found in bacterial polysaccharides. *Can. J. Chem.* **40**, 856.

(With J. P. MILLINGTON & M. B. PERRY) The carbohydrate protein linkage in glycoproteins II. *Can. J. Chem.* **40**, 2229.

(With W. A. SZAREK) Synthesis of a sugar derivative with nitrogen in the ring. *Can. J. Chem.* **40**, 636.

(With J. C. TURNER) 5-Acetamido-5-deoxy-L-arabinose. *J. chem. Soc.* p. 4699.

(With R. J. STOODLEY) Determination of isotopic carbon distribution in aldoses. *Meth. Carbohyd. Chem.* **2**, 489.

The biological and chemical synthesis of polysaccharides. *J. Pure appl. Chem.* **4**, 468.

Biogenesis of carbohydrate in wood. *J. Pure appl. Chem.* **5**, 21.

(With K. HUNT) The structure of linseed mucilage. II. *Can. J. Chem.* **40**, 1266.

(With R. J. JENNINGS) The reaction of sulphuryl chloride with reducing sugars. *Can. J. Chem.* **40**, 1408.

(With H. G. JONES & M. B. PERRY) The gas–liquid partition chromatography of carbohydrate derivatives. III. *Can. J. Chem.* **40**, 1559.

(With M. B. PERRY & R. J. STOODLEY) Biosynthesis of sugars found in bacterial polysaccharides. II. D-glycero-D-mannoheptose. *Can. J. Chem.* **40**, 1798.

(With L. HOUGH) Chromatography on paper. *Meth. Carbohyd. Chem.* **1**, 21.

(With L. HOUGH) Enzyme methods for the determination of D-glucose. *Meth. Carbohyd. Chem.* **1**, 400.

1963 (With H. J. JENNINGS) The reaction of chlorosulphate esters of sugars with pyridine. *Can. J. Chem.* **41**, 1151.

(With P. E. REID) Structural studies on the water-soluble arabinogalactans of mountain and European larch. *J. Polym. Sci. C.* no. 2, p. 63.

(With R. K. HULYALKAR & M. B. PERRY) The synthesis of D-glycero-D-mannoheptose. *Can. J. Chem.* **41**, 1490.

(With J. W. BIRD) The synthesis of 3-hexuloses. II. Derivatives of 1-deoxy-L-arabo-3-hexulose (syn. 6-deoxy-L-lyxo-4-hexulose). *Can. J. Chem.* **41**, 1877.

(With R. K. HULYALKAR) Synthesis of L-arabinose-5-$C^{14}$. *Can. J. Chem.* **41**, 1898.

(With P. B. REID) The synthesis of 5-*O*-β-glucopyranosyl-D-xylose and 3,5-di-*O*-β-D-glucopyranosyl-D-xylose. *Can. J. Chem.* **41**, 2382.

(With M. B. PERRY & W. SOWA) The occurrence of D-glycero-D-mannoheptose in the extracellular polysaccharide produced by *Azobacter indicum. Can. J. Chem.* **41**, 2712.

(With V. M. PARIKH) The structure of the extracellular polysaccharide of *Azobacter indicum. Can. J. Chem.* **41**, 2826.

(With M. B. PERRY) Elucidation of structures by physical and chemical methods: II. Carbon–oxygen fission: degradation of polysaccharides. *Technique of Organic Chemistry KI.*

1964 (With W. Z. Szarek) Synthesis of methyl-4-acetamido-4-deoxy-L-*erythro*furanoside: a sugar with nitrogen in a five-membered ring. *Can. J. Chem.* **42**, 20.

(With D. T. Williams) The chemistry of apiose. I. *Can. J. Chem.* **42**, 69.

(With W. A. Szarek & Saul Wolfe) Hindered internal rotation in carbohydrates containing nitrogen in the ring. *Tetrahedron Lett.* no. 38, p. 2743.

(With W. Sowa) Polysaccharides from the seeds of the huacra pona palm (*Iriartea ventricosa*). *Can. J. Chem.* **42**, 1751.

(With J. L. Thompson) The glucomannan of bluebell seed (*Scylla monscripta* L.). *Can. J. Chem.* **42**, 1688.

1965 (With K. G. A. Jackson) The *C*- and *O*-benzylation of L-ascorbic acid. *Can. J. Chem.* **43**, 450.

(With L. Buncel & K. G. A. Jackson) The L-ascorbate ion as an ambient nucleophile. *Chemy Ind.* **9**, 89.

(With D. T. Williams) The oxidation of sugar acetals and thioacetals by *Acetobacter suboxydans*. *Can. J. Chem.* **43**, 955.

(With A. J. Dick) Synthesis of 4-acetamido-4-deoxysugars. *Can. J. Chem.* **43**, 977.

(With P. Reid & J. R. Turvey) The reaction of galactose with hydrazine at elevated temperature. *Can. J. Chem.* **43**, 983.

(With R. K. Hulgalkar & M. B. Perry) The chemistry of D-apiose. II. The configuration of D-apiin. *Can. J. Chem.* **43**, 2085.

(With W. A. Szarek) Carbohydrates containing nitrogen in a five-membered ring and an attempted synthesis of a carbohydrate with nitrogen in a seven-membered ring. *Can. J. Chem.* **43**, 2345.

(With H. J. Jennings) Reactions of sugar chlorosulfates. V. The synthesis of chlorodeoxy sugars. *Can. J. Chem.* **43**, 2372.

(With E. J. C. Curtis) Synthesis of 4-*O*-β-galactopyranosyl-D-galactose. *Can. J. Chem.* **43**, 2508.

Some aspects of carbohydrate biosynthesis in plants. *Chimie et biochemie de la lignine, de la cellulose et des hemicelluloses. Actes du symposium International de Grenoble*, July.

(With H. J. Jennings) Reactions of sugar chlorosulfates. VI. The structure of unsaturated chlorodeoxy sugars. *Can. J. Chem.* **43**, 3018.

(With M. S. Patel) Synthesis of 5-benzamido-5-deoxy-D-xylopyranose. *Can. J. Chem.* **43**, 3105.

(With S. C. Williams) Direct displacement of a primary tolyl-*p*-sulfonyloxy group by the methoxide ion: a more direct route to 5-*O*-methyl-L-arabinose and 3,5-di-*O*-methyl-L-arabinose. *Can. J. Chem.* **43**, 3440.

(With V. M. Parikh) Oxidation of sugars with Ruthenium dioxide–sodium periodate: a simple method for the preparation of substituted keto sugars. *Can. J. Chem.* **43**, 3452.

(With V. M. Parikh) Structure of cholla gum (*Opuntia fulgida*). *J. Polym. Sci.* Part C, no. 11, p. 139.

1966 (With R. J. Dick) Selective nucleophilic substitution and preferential epoxide formation. *Can. J. Chem.* **44**, 79.

(With V. M. Parikh) Cholla gum. I. Structure of the degraded cholla gum. *Can. J. Chem.* **44**, 327.

(With D. T. Williams) The separation of aldopentose and aldohexose diethyl dithioacetal derivatives by gas–liquid partition chromatography. *Can. J. Chem.* **44**, 412.

(With A. G. Cottrell & E. Buncel) Chlorosulphate as a leaving group: the synthesis of a methyltetrachlorotetradeoxyhexoside. *Chemy Ind.* p. 552.

(With A. G. Cottrell & E. Buncel) Reactions of sugar chlorosulfates. VII. Some conformational aspects. *Can. J. Chem.* **44**, 1483.

(With V. M. Parikh) Cholla gum. II. Structure of the undegraded cholla gum. *Can. J. Chem.* **44**, 1531.

(With J. R. Campbell & S. Wolfe) A one step conversion of cyclohexene oxide into *cis*-1,2-dichlorocyclohexane. *Can. J. Chem.* **44**, 2339.

(With J. A. Cifonelli, P. Rebers & M. B. Perry) The capsular polysaccharide of *Pneumococcus* type XII, SXII. *Biochemistry* **5**, 3066.

1967 (With D. T. Williams) A new synthesis of 3-acetamido-3-deoxy-D-glucose. *Can. J. Chem.* **45**, 7.

(With S. C. Williams) The synthesis, separation, and identification of the methyl ethers of arabinose and their derivatives. *Can. J. Chem.* **45**, 275.

1967 (With D. T. Williams) Further experiments on the oxidation of sugar acetals and thioacetals by *Acetobacter suboxydans*. *Can. J. Chem.* **45**, 741.

(With D. G. Lance) Acetonation of D-xylosediethyldithioacetal. *Can. J. Chem.* **45**, 1533.

(With R. L. Colbran, N. K. Matheson & Irene Rosema) A synthesis of dihydroxyacetone phosphate from dihydroxyacetone. *Carbohyd. Res.* **4**, 355.

(With D. G. Lance) Gas chromatography of derivatives of the methyl ethers of D-xylose. *Can. J. Chem.* **45**, 1995.

(With G. B. Howarth) The synthesis of L-mycarose and L-cladinose. *Can. J. Chem.* **45**, 2253.

(With T. Sivakumaran) Selective benzoylation of benzyl-β-L-arabinopyranoside and benzyl-α-D-xylopyranoside. *Can. J. Chem.* **45**, 2493.

(With S. S. Ali, T. J. Mepham, I. M. E. Thiel & E. Buncel) Reactions of sugar chlorosulfates. VIII. D-Ribose and its derivatives. *Carbohyd. Res.* **5**, 118.

(With A. J. Dick) Epoxide ring opening of methyl-2,3-anhydro-4-azido-4-deoxypentopyranosides. *Can. J. Chem.* **45**, 2879.

1968 (With A. J. Dick) Synthesis of derivatives of 4-acetamido-4-deoxy-D- and L-arabinose. *Can. J. Chem.* **46**, 425.

(With G. B. Howarth & W. A. Szarek) The synthesis of D-arcanose. *Chem. Commun.* p. 62.

(With R. C. Chalk, J. F. Stoddart & W. A. Szarek) Isolation of two arabinobioses from *Acacia nilotica* gum. *Can. J. Chem.* **46**, 2311.

(With G. B. Howarth & W. A. Szarek) The synthesis of D-arcanose. *Carbohyd. Res.* **7**, 284.

(With J. F. Stoddart) Some structural features of *Citrus liminia* gum (lemon gum). *Carbohyd. Res.* **8**, 29.

(With G. B. Howarth & W. A. Szarek) Synthesis of 6-deoxy-3-*C*-methyl-2-*O*-methyl-*D*-allose. *Can. J. Chem.* **46**, 3375.

(With G. B. Howarth & W. A. Szarek) Synthesis of 6-chloro-9-(6′-deoxy,3′-*C*-methyl-2′,3′,4′-tri-*O*-methyl-β-D-allopyranosylpurine: a branched-chain nucleoside. *Can. J. Chem.* **46**, 3691.

(With G. B. Howarth, D. G. Lance & W. A. Szarek) Photolysis of carbohydrate nitro olefins. *Chem. Commun.* p. 1349.

1969 (With G. B. Howarth, D. G. Lance & W. A. Szarek) Photolysis of a carbohydrate nitroolefin. *Can. J. Chem.* **47**, 81.

(With G. B. Howarth, D. G. Lance & W. A. Szarek) Syntheses related to the carbohydrate moiety in lincomycin. *Can. J. Chem.* **47**, 75.

(With R. J. Beveridge, J. F. Stoddart & W. A. Szarek) Some structural features of the mucilage from the bark of *Ulmus fulva* (slippery elm mucilage). *Carbohyd. Res.* **9**, 429.

(With G. B. Howarth & W. A. Szarek) Branched-chain sugar nucleosides. Synthesis of a purine nucleoside of 4-*O*-acetyl-L-arcanose. *J. org. Chem.* **34**, 476.

(With K. G. A. Jackson) Synthesis of 3-hexuloses. *Can. J. Chem.* **47**, 2498.

(With D. G. Lance, W. A. Szarek & G. B. Howarth) Synthesis of 8-deoxy-D-*erythro*-D-galactooctose. Determination of the configuration of two octenoses. *Can. J. Chem.* **47**, 2871.

(With D. G. Lance & W. A. Szarek) Some *O*-isopropylidene derivatives of *D*-ribosediethyldithioacetal. *Can. J. Chem.* **47**, 2889.

(With B. T. Lawton, D. J. Ward & W. A. Szarek) Synthesis of D-chalcose. *Can. J. Chem.* **47**, 2899.

(With E. Buncel, H. J. Jennings & I. M. E. Thiel) Carbohydrate fluorosulfates. *Carbohyd. Res.* **10**, 331.

(With B. T. Lawton & W. A. Szarek) An improved procedure for oxidation of carbohydrate derivatives with ruthenium tetraoxide. *Carbohyd. Res.* **10**, 456.

(With J. F. Stoddard & W. A. Szarek) Large heterocyclic rings from carbohydrate precursors. *Can. J. Chem.* **47**, 3213.

(With H. G. Jones) Separation and identification of methyl ethers of D-glucose and D-glucitol by gas–liquid chromatography. *Can. J. Chem.* **47**, 3269.

(With Toshio Miyazaki) Structure feature of *Pneumocuccus* type XIX specific polysaccharide. *Chem. pharm. Bull., Tokyo* **17**, 1531.

(With B. T. Lawton & W. A. Szarek) A simple synthesis of azidodeoxy sugars via chlorodeoxy sugars. *Chem. Commun.* p. 787.

1969 (With G. B. Howarth & W. A. Szarek) Reaction of methyl 4,6-*O*-benzylidene-3-*C*-methyl-2-*O*-*p*-tolylsulfonyl-D-allopyranoside with sodium methoxide in methyl sulfoxide: synthesis of 6-deoxy-3-*C*-methyl-3-*O*-methyl-D-allose (2-hydroxy-D-caldinose). *Carbohyd Res.* **11**, 257.

(With W. H. Newsome, F. E. French & A. S. West) The isolation and properties of the skin-reactive substance in *Aedes aegypti* oral secretion. *Can. J. Biochem.* **47**, 1129.

(With E. H. Williams & W. A. Szarek) Synthesis of olivomycose (2,6-dideoxy-3-*C*-methyl-L-arabino-hexose). *Can. J. Chem.* **47**, 4467.

(With G. B. Howarth & W. A. Szarek) The synthesis of *N*-acetyl lincosamine (6-acetamido-6,8-dideoxy-D-*erythro*-D-galactooctose), a derivative of the free carbohydrate moiety in lincomycin. *Chem. Commun.* p. 1339.

(With W. A. Szarek & B. T. Lawton) (*N*-(4,6-*O*-benzylidene-1-*O*-methyl-3-oximino-D-ribohexopyranos-2-yl)-pyridinium-*p*-toluenesulfonate, a novel versatile carbohydrate substrate. *Tetrahedron Lett.* no. 55, p. 4867.

1970 (With B. T. Lawton & W. A. Szarek) A facile synthesis of 4,6-dideoxy-D-xylohexose. *Carbohydrate Res.* **14**, 255.

(With G. B. Howarth & W. A. Szarek) The synthesis of lincomycin. *J. chem. Soc.* (C) p. 2218.

(With Toshio Miyazaki & Toshiro Yadomae) Polysaccharides of type XIX *Pneumococcus*. I. Isolation of type XIX specific polysaccharide. *J. Biochem., Tokyo* **68**, 755.

(With B. T. Lawton & W. A. Szarek) Synthesis of deoxy and aminodeoxy sugars by way of chlorodeoxy sugars. *Carbohyd Res.* **15**, 397.

1971 (With J. H. Duarte) Some structural studies on the galactan from the albumen glands of the snail, *Strophocheilus oblongus*. *Carbohyd. Res.* **16**, 327.

(With E. H. Williams & W. A. Szarek) Synthesis of paratose (3,6-dideoxy-D-ribo hexose) and tyvelose (3,6-dideoxy-D-arabino hexose). *Can. J. Chem.* **49**, 796.

(With R. J. Beveridge & W. A. Szarek) Isolation of three oligosaccharides from the mucilage from the bark of *Ulmus fulva* (slippery-elm mucilage). Synthesis of *O*-(3-*O*-methyl-β-D-galactopyranosyl)-(1–4)-L-rhamnose. *Carbohyd. Res.* **19**, 107.

(With H. Parolis & W. A. Szarek) Reaction of methyl-4,6-dichloro-4,6-dideoxy-D-galactopyranoside-2,3-di-*O*-(chlorosulfate) with sodium azide, and with sodium bromide in *N*,*N*-dimethylformamide. *Carbohyd. Res.* **19**, 97.

(With B. A. Dmitriev, N. A. Hinton & R. W. Lowe) Studies on lipopolysaccharides of *Proteus*. *Can. J. Microbiol.* **17**, 1385.

(With E. H. Williams & W. A. Szarek) Preparation of unsaturated carbohydrates from methyl-4,6-*O*-benzylidene-3-chloro-3-deoxy-β-D-allopyranoside, and their utility in the synthesis of sugars of biological importance. *Carbohyd. Res.* **20**, 49.

(With A. Dmytraczenko & W. A. Szarek) Reactions of carbohydrate α-keto-toluene-*p*-sulphonates. Reaction of methyl-4,6-*O*-benzylidene-2-*O*-toluene-*p*-sulphonyl-α-D-ribohexopyranosid-3-ulose with triethylamine-methanol. *Chem. Commun.* p. 1220.

1972 (With D. J. Ward & W. A. Szarek) An evaluation of methods for the preparation of 1,2:3,4-di-*O*-isopropylidene-α-D-galactohexodialdo-1,2-pyranose. Oxidation of 1,2:3,4-di-*O*-isopropylidene-α-D-galactopyranose with lead tetraacetate-pyridine. *Carbohyd. Res.* **21**, 305.

(With R. J. Beveridge, R. W. Lowe & W. A. Szarek) Structure of slippery elm mucilage (*Ulmus fulva*). *J. Polym. Sci.* Part C, no. 36, p. 461.

(With I. Szczerek, J. S. Jewell, R. G. S. Ritchie & W. A. Szarek) Some reactions of unsaturated carbohydrates in the presence of iodine. *Carbohyd. Res.* **22**, 163.

(With G. W. Hay) Ethers of sugars. *The carbohydrates* (ed. W. Pigman & D. Horton), vol. 1A, pp. 403–422. New York: Academic Press.

(With A. Zamojski & W. A. Szarek) Amination of sugar derivatives with a mixture of phthalimide, triphenylphosphine, and diethylazodicarboxylate. *Carbohyd. Res.* **23**, 460.

(With T. B. Grindley, J. W. Bird & W. A. Szarek) Selective oxidation of a diol with methyl sulfoxide–acetic anhydride. *Carbohyd. Res.* **24**, 212.

(With C. S. Wu & W. A. Szarek) Synthesis of carbohydrate furoxan derivatives. *Chem. Commun.* p. 1117.

1973 (With W. A. Szarek) The total synthesis of carbohydrates. In: *The total synthesis of natural products*, vol. III, pp. 1–80. Chichester: John Wiley & Sons Ltd.

1973 (With A. Dmytraczenko & W. A. Szarek) Reaction of methyl-2,3-*O*-isopropylidene-6-*O*-*p*-tolylsulfonyl-α-D-lyxohexofuranosid-5-ulose with triethylamine-methanol. *Carbohyd. Res.* **26**, 297.

(With A. Zamojski & W. A. Szarek) Reaction of some di-*O*-isopropylidene-hexoses with cyanuric chloride. *Carbohyd. Res.* **26**, 208.

(With R. W. Lowe & W. A. Szarek) Conversion of 2-hexuloses into 3-heptuloses: synthesis of D-manno-3-heptulose. *Carbohyd. Res.* **28**, 281.

(With H. C. Jarrell, R. G. S. Ritchie & W. A. Szarek) Reductive cleavage of carbohydrate *p*-toluenesulfonates with sodium naphthalene. *Can. J. Chem.* **51**, 1767.

Lipopolysaccharides of *Proteus*. *Colloques Internationaux du Centre National de la Recherche Scientifique* no. 221 (Villenauve d'Ascq, 20–27 June 1973)

1974 (With Daphne M. Dean & W. A. Szarek) A reinvestigation of the reaction of methyl-β-D-glucopyranoside with sulfuryl chloride. *Carbohyd. Res.* **33**, 383.

(With W. A. Szarek & A. Dmytraczenko) Reaction of hexopyranoside-α-keto-toluene-*p*-sulfonates with triethylamine-methanol. *Carbohyd. Res.* **35**, 203.

(With Barbara Achmatowicz, W. A. Szarek & E. H. Williams) Reaction of methyl-pentofuranosides with sulfuryl chloride. *Carbohyd. Res.* **36**, C14.

1975 (With W. A. Szarek, Catherine Depew & H. C. Jarrell) Synthesis of nucleosides by direct replacement of the anomeric hydroxy group. *Chem. Commun.* p. 648.

(With H. C. Jarrell, W. A. Szarek, A. Dmytraczenko & E. B. Rathbone) Syntheses related to dendroketose. *Carbohyd. Res.* **45**, 151.

1976 (With D. J. Ward & W. A. Szarek) Decarbonylation of aldehydo sugar derivatives with chlorotris-(methyldiphenylphosphine)rhodium(I). *Chemy Ind.* 21 February, p. 162.

(With G. R. Woolard, E. Rathbone & W. A. Szarek) Syntheses towards the carbohydrate moiety of lincomycin. *J. chem. Soc. Perkin Trans.* I, p. 950.

(With W. A. Szarek & C. Depew) Synthesis of carbohydrate-saccharin conjugates. *Heterocyclic Chem.* **13**, 1131.

(With W. A. Szarek, A. Zamojski, A. R. Gibson & D. M. Vyas) Selective, reductive dechlorination of chlorodeoxy sugars, structural determination of chlorodeoxy and deoxy sugars by $^{13}$C nuclear magnetic resonance spectroscopy. *Can. J. Chem.* **54**, 3783.

1977 (With W. A. Szarek, G. Wayne Schnarr & H. C. Jarrell) Oxidation of a branched-chain alditol by *Acetobacter suboxydans*: a stereospecific synthesis of L-dendroketose. *Carbohyd. Res.* **53**, 101.

(With G. W. Schnarr & W. A. Szarek) Preparation and activity of immobilized *Acetobacter suboxydans* cells. *Appl. Envir. Microbiol.* **33**, 732.

(With W. A. Szarek & H. C. Jarrell) Synthesis of glycosides: reactions of the anomeric hydroxyl group with nitrogen–phosphorus betaines. *Carbohyd. Res.* **57**, 13.

## Patents

1917 Benzyl chloride. *U.S. Patent* 1233986.

1934 (With P. W. Bridgman) Polymerizing indene and other unsaturated organic compounds. *U.S. Patent* 1950671.

G. W. Kenner.

# GEORGE WALLACE KENNER

16 November 1922 — 26 June 1978

Elected F.R.S. 1964

By Lord Todd, O.M., P.R.S.

George Wallace Kenner was born on 16 November 1922 at Sheffield, the younger son of a well known organic chemist James Kenner (1885–1974) who was at that time a lecturer in chemistry at the University of Sheffield. Details of the Kenner family's origins are to be found in the biographical memoir of James Kenner (*Biographical Memoirs of Fellows of the Royal Society*, 1975, **21**, 389) and need not be repeated here. His mother, herself a chemist, I can recall only as a rather ebullient, talkative woman devoted to her two sons, Donald and George, in a family dominated by an aggressive father and kept very much to itself as a result. Before George was two years old the family left England for Australia where in late 1924 his father became Professor of Organic Chemistry (Pure and Applied) in the University of Sydney. Not surprisingly, we know little of George's time there since the family returned to England in January 1928 when James Kenner was appointed Professor of Technological Chemistry at the Manchester College of Technology. The Kenners took up residence in the Manchester suburb of Withington where the family home remained (nominally at least) until James Kenner's death in 1974.

George Kenner had his first encounter with formal education at Didsbury Preparatory School where he enrolled in 1928 and where he remained until he moved on in 1934 to Manchester Grammar School. No science was taught at his small preparatory school, the emphasis being on classics and mathematics; not unnaturally therefore young George went on the classical side at Manchester Grammar School and only moved to science after matriculation. The course of his education was almost certainly determined by his father; a domineering man now embittered by his experience in the College of Technology, he held strong views on the education of his younger son who he was determined should be a great scientist and upon whom he constantly impressed that anything short of excellence should be regarded as equivalent to failure. This constant parental pressure could not have been helpful to the young George and may well have contributed to his later health problems. In his preparatory school days he suffered from a bad stammer and although he largely conquered it later in his university days and became an excellent lecturer the impediment could even then recur in moments of stress. He had an outstanding record at Manchester Grammar School and was recognized from his earliest days there as quite unusually gifted intellectually. His contemporaries recall him as a quiet, rather slight boy who had a friendly disposition and could be a voluble talker on almost any subject when coaxed out of his shell. Not given to sport, he found an outlet for his energy and satisfaction of his social instincts in scouting. Dr William Brockbank, school medical officer at the time and leader of the scout troop, still speaks with enthusiasm of Kenner's membership. It was while a member of the troop that his interest in hill walking and climbing developed, aided no doubt by the Kenner family excursions which were its chief relaxation, at weekends near Manchester and, on holidays, in North Wales or South-west England either walking or cycling.

I first met George Kenner in the autumn of 1939 when, shortly before his seventeenth birthday, he entered the Honours School of Chemistry in the University of Manchester where I had, just one year earlier, become Professor of Chemistry and Director of the Chemical Laboratories. At the time I awaited his arrival with some trepidation for the following reason. At the time of my appointment as a very young and inexperienced academic to the Manchester Chair in 1938 there were many who thought—and indeed warned me—that I could expect to be roughly handled by James Kenner, a notoriously quarrelsome and much older man who would be my opposite number in the College of Technology. In this they were wrong for James Kenner proved both friendly and helpful to me in my new surroundings and I saw him almost daily at lunch in the University Staff Club. As a result of these lunchtime meetings I quickly became aware of the intense pride he had in the ability of his son George and his determination that he should have the best available training in chemistry. When, early in 1939, he told me that George would come to me I was understandably alarmed, for woe betide me if I failed to measure up to his exacting standards. But I need not have worried; George Kenner was both outstandingly able and unusually precocious. He had a brilliant career as an undergraduate and I really believe that the result would have been the same whatever the quality of the teaching. During his undergraduate career, which culminated predictably in the degree of B.Sc. with first class honours in 1942, I had only rather casual contact with him but thereafter when he took up research under my supervision first for the M.Sc. degree (standard Manchester practice in those days) and then in Manchester and Cambridge for his Ph.D., I saw him daily (and was indeed to do so for some 15 years) and came to know him well—and in certain respects perhaps even better than his contemporaries did. Wartime conditions made life hard for all of us but there is no doubt that the common involvement of staff and students in fire-watching and civil defence brought us all much more together than we would otherwise have been. Certainly it forged a lasting bond between those of us who shared life in the Manchester chemical school at that time.

In those days George Kenner was a quiet, rather reserved young man, deeply interested in chemistry, who seemed to get rather easily depressed when, as is common in research, all was not going according to plan. Slight of build, he took no part in organized sport but threw himself with vigour and at times, it seemed, with almost excessive enthusiasm into all departmental activities. To some extent I regarded this latter trait as being, at least in part, a reaction to what was clearly a rather difficult home life in a family where a domineering father was continually exhorting and urging him on in his studies. But it certainly helped to forge the close and lasting friendships which he developed with his fellow research students and with A. R. Gilson, my young and outstandingly able laboratory superintendent, from whom Kenner derived much of his unusual knowledge and skill in scientific instrumentation and laboratory arts. When Kenner graduated in 1942 I was in the early stages of a large series of investigations on nucleotides and nucleotide coenzymes which I had planned when I went to Manchester and which was getting under way as far as the exigencies of wartime allowed. He elected to join me in this endeavour and threw himself into it with enthusiasm; indeed he continued in it as one of my most valued colleagues for 15 years. During that time he made outstanding contributions to our knowledge of phosphorylation and organic phosphate chemistry and jointly we completed syntheses of flavin-adenine dinucleotide (26), codehydrogenase I (nicotinamide-adenine dinucleotide) (52), uridine diphosphate glucose (33) and various other biologically important polyphosphate esters. His interests were not, however, confined to natural product chemistry, although that was and remained his main field; he had remarkable theoretical insight and constantly brought it to bear on all his experimental studies. Some idea of his originality of mind and of his precocity can be gathered from his presentation to me during his first year as a research student of a wholly original and significant theoretical paper on the structure and reactivity of halogenobenzenes. This paper was accepted by the Royal Society and published in its *Proceedings* (5); there must be few young chemists who have matched that achievement.

Tragedy, however, struck the Kenner family in September 1943, towards the end of George's first year as a research student. In those war years the Kenners usually sought relaxation and recreation in family cycling expeditions into the surrounding countryside at weekends and on holiday further afield. On one of these latter George had the appalling experience of seeing his mother, to whom he was deeply attached, killed in a road accident in Devon. A further blow came within weeks when news came that his brother, Donald, with whom again he had close bonds, had been killed in action in Italy. These losses were felt very deeply by him—so much was clear to his intimates in the laboratory but George himself never talked about or even mentioned them. Nor did he reveal that very shortly thereafter two male cousins were also killed in action, leaving him the sole male Kenner of his generation. The shock of these happenings also had a profound effect on his father who took every opportunity to impress on George that the family's scientific future rested entirely upon him. The impact of the tragedy on James Kenner had a strange effect on his behaviour towards his son; not only did he now constantly goad George to greater and greater effort but at the same time criticized and denigrated his achievements, presumably in the hope of spurring him further. This, needless to say, led to a worsening of relations between them and to an intensification of George's moods of depression. The human mind is complex and its workings little understood but it has always seemed to me that it was the devastating experience of the young Kenner at this time and his attempt to shut it out completely from his consciousness that initiated or brought into active existence the illness which was eventually to destroy him.

In these circumstances it was fortunate that in 1944 I was appointed to the Chair of Organic Chemistry at Cambridge and George (together with a large group of his friends and contemporaries) elected to move to Cambridge to build up a new centre of chemistry there. This broke the intimate and enforced contact with his father and gave him the chance to live and work normally without constant interference. He took full advantage of this chance and the next 13 years in Cambridge were not only productive but, perhaps, also the happiest of his life. In the absence of continual parental oversight he blossomed both socially and scientifically. True the alternating moods of elation and gloom which I had noticed in the latter part of his Manchester days were still there, but they gradually diminished in frequency and intensity and probably passed unnoticed by most people within a year or two of the move. As a University Lecturer and Fellow of Trinity Hall he took a full part in the life of the University. In the University Chemical Laboratory he quickly acquired a reputation not only as a good teacher and organizer of seminars and discussions but as one who was always ready to discuss other people's problems both sympathetically and seriously and accordingly give real help and guidance to others not always as able as himself. He had a hand in all departmental activities except cricket, which game he claimed required a far better coordination of eye and hand than he possessed. That claim many of his friends would dispute for he displayed such a capacity to absorb and to put into operation new and demanding laboratory techniques that he would have made a first-class craftsman. This capacity in practical matters showed itself in his passionate and lifelong devotion to sailing and to motor cars; of both he had an encyclopaedic knowledge and he sought perfection in them as he did in his scientific work. In his early days in Cambridge he was a great enthusiast for the Morgan three-wheeler and it was interesting to watch his progression through various makes of sports car. Not only did he give technical advice to all his fellow-workers in the laboratory but he seemed to have a touch of missionary zeal to judge by the way they seemed to change cars at George's whim. This continued for many years long after the members of that group of my early camp followers in Cambridge (now known as the Toddlers Club) dispersed to academic and industrial positions elsewhere. Indeed I know of four or five Alfa Romeo cars, owned by members of that group in recent years, which were bought as a direct result of George's recommendation.

In 1948–49 Kenner spent a sabbatical year in Zürich in the laboratory of Professor V. Prelog. In collaboration with him he published a couple of papers on *Erythrina* alkaloids (14, 17) but, perhaps more important for his career, he seems there to have had his interest aroused in peptide chemistry. In Zürich, too, he formed a lasting friendship with H. G. Khorana who later joined us in Cambridge and with whom he subsequently published two papers on peptide synthesis (22, 27). On his return to Cambridge Kenner continued his work in the nucleotide coenzyme field but also began to develop an independent attack on the chemistry of peptides and polypeptides. This was very much in line with the factors that had taken me into the nucleotide field ten years earlier and which had clearly attracted him then. Here again was a group of compounds of obvious and ever-growing biological interest which offered an alluring prospect to anyone who was prepared to devise new methods of approach to synthesis and bring to bear on the subject the rigorous discipline of organic chemistry with its insistence on the purity and individuality of all synthetic intermediate and final products. Moreover, the problems faced and surmounted in phosphorylation were in essence not dissimilar from those likely to be encountered in aminoacylation. His first paper on peptide chemistry appeared in 1951 (18) and this topic, together with his work on the pyrrole pigments (again a relatively ill-explored field of great biological interest) which he commenced about 1955, were to occupy the whole of his subsequent career in research.

On the personal side, the most important event in Kenner's Cambridge period was his marriage in 1951 to Jillian Bird. The daughter of Angus Bird, a Cambridge businessman, she was for a time on the secretarial staff of the Chemical Laboratory following completion of her degree course at Reading University. The marriage was not only a happy one but was also a highly significant factor in Kenner's career. A charming and lively young lady, Jill gave Kenner the affection and stability he sorely needed and provided him with a home life such as he had probably never before known. Their two daughters, who brought him great joy, were both born in Cambridge before, in 1957, George was invited to take the Heath Harrison Chair of Organic Chemistry in the University of Liverpool in succession to Professor Alexander Robertson. By this time George had become stable and confident to a degree I had not known before and he was able to seize this opportunity to widen his scope and really open up his chosen field of research. It seemed at last that earlier troubles were over and he set about his new tasks with vigour and enthusiasm. Both qualities were required in Liverpool at that time for the laboratories were somewhat antiquated and very ill equipped for modern chemistry. Kenner was accordingly plunged at once into planning, building and equipping a new department to the highest modern standards. Before taking up the Liverpool chair he had been a participant in the building of the new University Chemical Laboratory in Lensfield Road, Cambridge, which was the latest in this country and incorporated many novel features in design. It is said that Kenner on being faced with a similar task in Liverpool said that he intended to make a laboratory "like Lensfield but better". Whether he was entirely successful in that may be a matter for partisan debate, but certain it is that the Robert Robinson Laboratories in Liverpool, completed in 1961, stand today virtually unmodified as a lasting tribute to Kenner's enthusiasm, drive, and his mastery of the details of modern laboratory construction. The effort involved in the building programme was not allowed to interfere with the building up of the Liverpool department as a centre of modernized teaching and research which, with the cooperation of staff and an increasing flow of research students from home and abroad, went on apace in the peptide and porphyrin fields. Members of the Liverpool staff and senior research workers uniformly praise his selfless work for the school together with his friendliness, his informality and his readiness at all times to advise and to help individuals. George Kenner was well aware of the need to have continuity of leadership in a scientific department and the consequent necessity of ensuring that it is not allowed to become a 'one man band'. So it was that in 1962 he persuaded the University of Liverpool to take the radical step of creating a second chair of organic chemistry to which A. R. Battersby was appointed. The combination so formed of two independent research groups working none the less in harmony was a great success and contributed in no small measure to Liverpool becoming in a few years one of the leading organic chemical schools in Britain.

On top of all he did for his department and in the promotion of research, Kenner was also active in the service of the University and served on a variety of its boards and committees. Outside the University he held office in the Chemical Society and, following his election to the Fellowship in 1964, he served on various Royal Society committees. Throughout his career he maintained close and friendly contacts with the chemical and scientific instrument industries where his advice was frequently sought and greatly valued.

In all that he did Kenner was a perfectionist—nothing but the best was good enough whether in administration, teaching or research and he expected all associated with him to adopt the same standards even though they were at times almost impossible of achievement. Research to him had to be on the frontiers of science and he despised the trivial. In research he would never tolerate shoddy work and woe betide any charlatan who came his way. These characteristics are, indeed, evident both in his choice of topics and in the operation of his researches. He had a passionate belief in the need to apply the full rigour of organic chemistry to complex fields such as protein and porphyrin chemistry. To him all intermediates in synthesis must be prepared and characterized unambiguously and he would not relax his standards. I think it is fair to say that by his work he confounded the belief of many that this could not be done and thereby performed a major service to the study of polypeptides and proteins.

In his passion for accuracy and his scorn of the second rate, one could see in George Kenner something of his father, James, who was also a chemical perfectionist with unbounded faith in the power of organic chemistry. Like his father, too, George could display a mulish and even, at times, an aggressive obstinacy. But in him, unlike his father, these qualities were tempered by compassion; it was perhaps this quality that so endeared him to all who knew him. It may be that he drove himself too hard in Liverpool and that the stress of all his activities proved his undoing. That we shall never know, but certainly the moods of elation and enthusiasm interspersed with bouts of depression, which had first evidenced themselves to me following the tragic events of 1943 but which seemed to have subsided during the Cambridge days, began to reassert themselves progressively. Those deepening moods of depression he concealed from his colleagues as, aided by his wife Jill, he battled manfully to resist and overcome them. Both he and all his friends hoped that his election in 1976 to a Royal Society Research Professorship which allowed him to shed all his administrative burdens might relieve the stress under which he had laboured and enable him to conquer the illness which had dogged him for so long. But—alas!—it was not to be; attacks persisted and became more severe and in the summer of 1978, in a remote corner of the Welsh hills he loved so well, George Kenner ended a life which he believed had become an intolerable burden for himself and for his family.

In 1977 George Kenner wrote an obituary of the great Swiss chemist, Leopold Ruzicka (199) of whom he said 'his work exemplifies that combination of severely disciplined empiricism with intellectual fantasy and imagination which is the hallmark of first-class organic chemistry'. That statement could be applied equally to his own work. The pity is that Kenner did not live to see the seal set on his efforts by the completion of his carefully planned synthesis of a lysozyme analogue, of proven purity, containing 129 amino acid residues joined in a rigorously defined order, although he reached the final stage. Indeed, a lesser man might well have claimed completion on the basis of preliminary experiments on the final condensation step which were carried out shortly before his death. Others will in due course realize his dream of making a wholly synthetic enzyme but the value of Kenner's contributions to the methodology of peptide and porphyrin chemistry will be increasingly recognized and will profoundly influence future developments in these fields. Ill-health may have denied him the final triumph but it cannot deny him a permanent place in the history of organic chemical synthesis. And to those who were privileged to know him he has left a memory which will shine 'as the stars for ever and ever'.

## *Scientific work*

Although throughout his career Kenner retained an interest in theoretical organic chemistry and indeed published occasional papers on theoretical topics (e.g. 5, 74, 88, 89, 127) his main researches fall neatly into three sections—nucleotide, peptide and porphyrin chemistry. Of these one could regard nucleotide chemistry as his apprenticeship since it was there that he began his career, first as research student and, later, as a senior worker in the large group developing this field under my guidance in Manchester and Cambridge. There is no doubt that this early work profoundly influenced both Kenner's choice of topics for independent development and the general type of approach to be followed in exploiting them. At the same time it is likely that he elected to enter upon nucleotide research rather than some other line when he graduated, because the philosophy behind it happened to fit with his own ideas on research in general; for he was at once very gifted intellectually, very independently minded and unusually precocious as a student.

Kenner's gifts as an organic chemist and in research leadership come out clearly in his Liverpool work on peptides and porphyrins. In dealing with his prodigious output of research I have consulted, and am most grateful to, a number of his former students and associates. In particular Dr R. C. Sheppard and Professor A. H. Jackson took great pains to provide me with detailed reviews of the peptide and porphyrin work with which they had been closely associated. So excellent were they that in the accounts of Kenner's contributions which follow I have essentially reproduced them subject to abbreviation and editorial modification; to both these former students I am extremely indebted.

George Kenner died just as his research career was approaching its peak, but already its brilliance had brought him recognition from his peers and his wisdom and capacity to lead were recognized in scientific circles. He was awarded the Meldola Medal (1951) and the Corday–Morgan Medal (1957) and was in succession Tilden (1955), Simonsen (1972) and Pedler (1976) Lecturer of the Chemical Society of whose Perkin Division he was President from 1974 to 1976. He was also President of Section B of the British Association for the Advancement of Science in 1974. Elected into the Fellowship of the Royal Society in 1964 he was the Society's Bakerian Lecturer for 1976 and was elected to a Royal Society Research Professorship in 1976. George's passionate interest in science and in the promotion of scientific research was underlined not long before his death by his generous setting up of a fund to be known as the Binmore–Kenner Fund based on his father's estate. This fund is now administered by the Royal Society and used to provide additional support for the work of the Society's research appointees.

### *Nucleotides and nucleotide coenzymes*

Kenner entered this field as a research student reading for the Ph.D. degree in Manchester and Cambridge and continued as postdoctoral worker and later as staff colleague to play a vitally important role in its development by a large group operating under my direction until he left Cambridge for Liverpool. He played a major role in the development of a general and unambiguous synthetic route to purine nucleosides (3, 4, 6–12) including adenosine (11) and over a long period in the researches on pyrophosphate esters and methods for their synthesis (20, 40, 42, 43, 56, 57) although the true significance of work published in papers bearing his name as co-author can only be fully understood when taken in conjunction with all the other numerous publications of the Todd group in this field. Among nucleotide coenzymes Kenner was joint author of syntheses of flavin-adenine dinucleotide (26, 31), uridine (32) and adenosine (43) triphosphates, uridine diphosphate glucose (33), cytidine diphosphate (57) and several $P^1P^2$-dinucleoside pyrophosphates (28, 57), as well as cozymase (now usually described as nicotinamide-adenine dinucleotide or NAD) (52).

### *Peptides and proteins*

From the outset Kenner saw the desirability of using free amino acids and peptides as amino components in polypeptide synthesis and the need for water-soluble acylating species. This was evident in his first papers (18, 21) where he introduced the sulphur trioxide–dimethylformamide complex for the formation of mixed anhydrides with sulphuric acid. Evaluation of his new reagent included a careful racemization study (46) for which he devised one of the first sensitive racemization tests involving separation of diastereoisomers by the then novel technique of countercurrent distribution. The sulphuric anhydride method never achieved wide popularity because of the difficulties in preparing and handling the sulphur trioxide reagent, but his colleagues who used it regularly in Cambridge vouched for its efficiency and cleanliness. Kenner remained true to it to the end (e.g. 199) and it is still one of the very few techniques which, when used in anydrous media, have never been shown to cause racemization.

Kenner had met H. Gobind Khorana in 1948 at Prelog's laboratory in Zürich where they worked together on the structures of *Erythrina* alkaloids. Their collaboration was continued in Cambridge and produced several new methods for peptide degradation. Their use of dialkylxanthates with elimination of amino-terminal residues as thiazolidiones (22) was conceptually similar to Edman's procedure. Reaction of peptide acids with diphenylphosphoroisothiocyanatidate was shown to lead to acylthiohydantoins, from which the original carboxy-terminal residue could be cleaved as a thiohydantoin by the action of alkali (27). Methods for selective cleavage at internal amino-acid residues were also investigated, and two papers describe cyclization reactions of glutamic acid sidechains in this connection (29, 41). Kenner's main interest was always chemical synthesis, and his research returned to this theme with studies of activated ester derivatives (37, 47). *p*-Nitrothiophenyl esters were preferred because of their favourable reactivity ratio towards amines and water, and Kenner devised a new preparative procedure from carboxylic acids and tri-*p*-nitrophenyl phosphorotrithioite (37). These esters were used in the synthesis of *cyclo*-(glycyl-L-leucyl-glycyl-L-leucylglycine) (38), probably the first synthetic cyclic peptide, and subsequently for a range of other cyclic peptides (59, 80). The relation between ease of cyclization and stereochemistry within the peptide chain was investigated, beginning a long interest in the conformations of linear and cyclic peptides (80, 100, 135). Peptide phenylesters which proved too stable to function as acylating agents were considered as potential carboxy protecting groups (61), a possibility brought to an important practical realization many years later with the recognition of peroxide anion catalysts of phenyl ester hydrolysis (158, 166).

From 1957 in Liverpool, synthesis continued to be his main theme in peptide research with increasing attention being devoted to natural products. Already, in Cambridge, studies had begun on a peptide antibiotic which had yielded a series of unusual amino acids on hydrolysis. The identification of *threo*-β-hydroxyleucine and *cis*-γ-methylproline (55) initiated a series of synthetic and stereochemical studies on these and related amino acids from various sources (66, 70, 75, 76, 83, 95), Characteristically, the presence of α-methylalanine in the same antibiotic prompted Kenner to tackle the difficult problem of synthesis of peptides from massively hindered, geminally substituted amino acids with complete success (69, 103, 104, 105).

Another antibiotic under investigation at this time furnished a series of thiazole derivatives, identified as condensation products of cysteine and an adjacent amino acid residue. A series of these novel derivatives was synthesized (63, 80) and their formation by dehydrogenation of intermediate thiazolines investigated (113).

Early in the 1960s, Kenner and his colleagues began a series of investigations which together were to constitute perhaps the most important completed contribution of the Liverpool group to peptide (and medical) research. The antral hormone gastrin had been sought intermittently since 1905 when its existence was first mooted. When successful isolation was finally achieved by Gregory and Tracy working in the Physiological Laboratory at Liverpool (*Gut*, 1964, **5**, 103) the peptide chemists were on hand and eager to tackle the structural and synthetic problems. Despite some surprises, elucidation of the 17-residue sequence of the porcine hormone was soon complete (91), and synthesis followed a year later (92, 101, 114, 118). Intermediate fragments were tested for biological activity producing the quite unexpected result that only the terminal tetrapeptideamide sequence was essential for full gastrin-like action (Tracy & Evans, *Nature, Lond.* 1964, **204**, 935). This observation permitted very extensive structure–function studies within the pharmaceutical industry (Morley, *Proc. R. Soc. Lond.* B 1968, **170**, 97) resulting in the marketing of a pentapeptide derivative (pentagastrin) as a diagnostic stimulant of gastric secretion. In Liverpool, chemical studies continued with the structural elucidation of human gastrin (160), its synthesis (107, 122) and that of several analogues (130, 131). Gastrins from ovine (134, 139), bovine (134, 139), canine (138, 140) and feline (142) species were identified and in most cases synthesized. In the last of these, mass spectrometry of methylated derivatives (133) was used exclusively for structure determination (142). An immunological differentiation of gastrin from related peptides was also devised (150).

Glu-Gly-Pro-Trp-Leu-(Glu)$_5$-Ala-Tyr-Gly-Trp-Met-Asp-Phe-$NH_2$
*Human Gastrin I*

(*Gastrin II* = tyrosine sulphated form of *Gastrin I*)

In 1976 (198), the gastrin story was taken a stage further with the synthesis of the sequence assigned to 'big gastrin', the presumed prohormone. This work is worthy of special mention because it provides a complete vindication of one of Kenner's strongly held views, namely that unambiguous synthesis, besides providing pure material for biological and other studies, should also perform the role traditional for less complex molecules, that of final arbiter of correctness of structure. Others have argued that it is difficult or impossible to compare natural and synthetic macromolecules with the precision required to establish identity and that accordingly the labour involved in total synthesis cannot be justified on these grounds. In the case of big gastrin, radioimmunoassay was able to detect small differences between the natural and synthetic 34-residue peptides (205). Further synthesis and the availability of specific site directed antibodies have enabled the sequence error to be located in the region comprising residues 5–12, and new degradative data now suggest a simple sequence inversion (Dockray, Contribution to Symposium on Gastrin and the Vagus, Aarhus, August 1978). Combination of synthesis and immunological techniques may be expected to play an increasing role in structure determination of large peptides following this pioneering example.

Even while the early gastrin work was in progress, Kenner was considering more ambitious targets. The ultimate goal of rational protein synthesis had long been in his mind, and in 1969 he determined to tackle the synthesis of an enzyme. Experience elsewhere in attempts to assemble defined polypeptide chains of more than 100 residues in length was not encouraging. Kenner recognized the limitations of the classical synthetic approach applied to complex macromolecules, but saw even more clearly the absolute necessity for strict analytical control and rigorous purification of intermediates. These last criteria could not be met by contemporary solid phase procedures. His solution to this dilemma was to tailor the synthetic target so as to reduce the overall problem to manageable proportions while still producing a molecule with the desired physico-chemical and biological properties.

The target chosen by him was a 129-residue analogue of lysozyme containing 28 changes from the hen egg white sequence. In devising this revised sequence the overall aim was to reduce the difficulties of the synthesis to manageable proportions while still producing a molecule with essentially the same compact folded structure as the natural enzyme. It was appreciated that, while it was possible to satisfy the space filling requirements of a globular structure in a modified sequence, lack of information about protein folding mechanisms made such an endeavour highly speculative, but all possible precautions were taken to minimize the risk of producing a non-viable molecule. It was incidentally hoped that a study of this and other similarly conceived enzyme analogues might shed light on the protein folding process. His selection of lysozyme as the basic enzyme structure was strongly influenced by the assured collaboration of the crystallographer D. C. Phillips in predicting the effects of sequence changes on structure. A full molecular model of the enzyme was assembled in Liverpool from Phillips's X-ray data and simplifying changes in the natural sequence were made on the basis of consideration of this model, of natural sequence variants and of factors known to influence the stability of protein secondary structures. In this way, changes made in one part of the sequence were sterically compensated by changes elsewhere, but no modification was permitted of residues thought to be involved in the enzymic process.

```
                 Arg                              Met      Arg-His          Asp-Asn
Lys-Val-Phe-Gly-Orn-Cys-Glu-Leu-Ala-Ala-Ala-Nle-Lys-Ala-Leu-Gly-Leu-Ala-Gly-
1                5                    10                    15

   Arg                              Val                                 Asn
Tyr-Orn-Gly-Tyr-Ser-Leu-Gly-Asn-Trp-Nva-Cys-Ala-Ala-Lys-Phe-Glu-Ser-Gly-Phe-
20                 25                    30                   35

                     Arg        Asp                                 Ile
Asn-Thr-Gln-Ala-Thr-Asn-Orn-Asn-Thr-Glu-Gly-Ser-Thr-Asp-Tyr-Gly-Leu-Leu-Gln-
    40                 45                    50                          55

       Arg              Asn         Arg                    Arg    Leu
Ile-Asn-Ser-Orn-Trp-Trp-Cys-Ala-Asp-Gly-Orn-Thr-Pro-Gly-Ser-Ala-Asn-Gly-Cys-
        60                 65                    70                    75

              Ser         Leu     Ser                           Asn
Asn-Ile-Pro-Cys-Ala-Ala-Leu-Nva-Ser-Gly-Asp-Ile-Thr-Ala-Ser-Val-Gly-Cys-Ala-
            80                    85                   90                    95

                                  Met                              Arg
Lys-Lys-Ile-Val-Ser-Asp-Gly-Asn-Gly-Nle-Asn-Ala-Trp-Val-Ala-Trp-Orn-Asn-Arg-
                 100                   105                 110

            Thr          Gln         Ile-Arg          Arg
Cys-Lys-Gly-Ser-Asp-Val-Ser-Ala-Trp-Val-Orn-Gly-Cys-Gly-Leu
115                 120                  125              129
```

FIGURE. 1. Sequence of lysozyme analogue being synthesized in Liverpool. Superimposed residues at positions 5, 12, 14, 15, 18, 19, 21, 29, 37, 45, 48, 55, 61, 65, 68, 73, 75, 82, 84, 86, 93, 105, 112, 118, 121, 124, 125 and 128 show sequence of hen's egg lysozyme. (Reproduced from 198.)

This, then, was the formidable target which Kenner set himself and his many willing colleagues in Liverpool. The strategy of essentially complete sidechain protection was adopted for synthesis—probably a wise move in view of the interference by free carboxyl groups in minimal protection strategies. The solubility problems expected as a result of this decision, although severe, were not overwhelming, special devices such as chromatography on polyacrylmorpholide in N-methylpyrrolidone being used in difficult cases; several publications issued during the course of the synthesis deal with improved chromatographic techniques for handling large sparingly soluble peptide derivatives (183, 189, 203, 204). Particular care was taken in the selection of permanent sidechain protecting groups so as to confer adequate protection and complete stability throughout the very many synthetic operations involved. Thus sidechain *t*-butoxycarbonyl protection of lysine and ornithine was discarded in favour of the more stable adamantyloxycarbonyl group. On the other hand, temporary protecting groups for terminal amino- and carboxy-functions were chosen, with equal care, to be removable under the mildest possible conditions. Benzyloxycarbonyl and biphenylisopropoxycarbonyl were used for α-amino groups and notably the labile phenyl esters for α-carboxy groups. Development of new synthetic methods (184, 191) and protecting groups (190) based on phosphorus compounds continued alongside the assembly of the lysozyme analogue sequence.

The 129-residue sequence was divided into 12 sections each having glycine at its carboxy terminus. In his brilliant Bakerian Lecture (198) Kenner not only summarized the problems to be faced in protein synthesis but reported the synthesis of the two protected fragments containing residues 1–75 and 76–129 respectively. Dicyclohexylcarbodiimide in combination with hydroxy-succinimide was used as the principal condensing agent but other reagents were mentioned including the dimethylformamide–sulphur trioxide complex introduced in Kenner's first foray into the field of peptide synthesis (18). Which particular method will prove most suitable for effecting the final linkage remains to be seen but preliminary experiments have shown promise. Although Kenner is no longer with us the work will no doubt continue in the hands of his former colleagues in Liverpool. Final success in preparing an enzymically active molecule will be the most fitting tribute to George Kenner's courage, innovative ability, foresight and judgement.

### *Porphyrins and related compounds*

When George Kenner began his work on the porphyrin group in the mid-1950s it was a relatively unfashionable field for chemists, notwithstanding the central role of porphyrin derivatives in living organisms. After the massive researches of Hans Fischer and his school between the wars, activity had

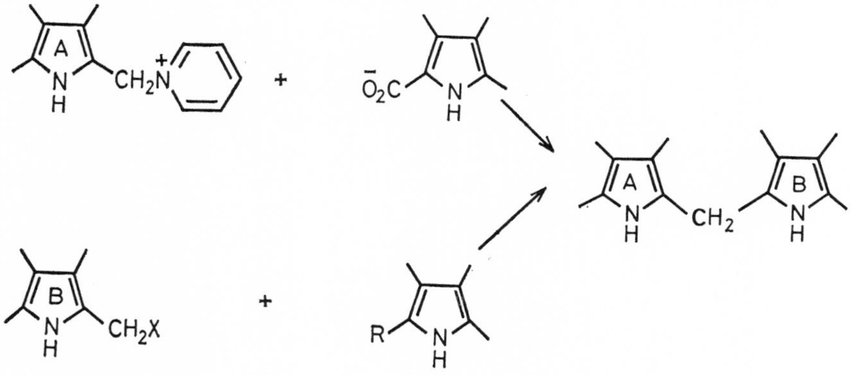

Scheme 1. X = Halogen or OAc; R = H or $CO_2H$.

lessened and there was only a handful of small pockets of research left, led by Plieninger, Strell and Treibs in Germany, by S. F. MacDonald in Canada and by Corwin in the United States of America; of these leaders the first four were all former associates of Fischer. On the biosynthetic front, however, considerable progress was being made following the advent of radiotracer and stable isotope techniques and Shemin and Neuberger's groups had established the broad outline of porphyrin biosynthesis from aliphatic precursors *via* the monopyrrolic porphobilinogen. The structural and biogenetic relationship of the chlorophylls and vitamin $B_{12}$ to the porphyrins had also been established. What caused Kenner to enter the field, we do not know, but it is likely that it attracted him because of the coenzyme function of many porphyrin derivatives and he may well have been influenced too by S. F. MacDonald who worked in the Cambridge laboratory from 1949–1951 and by the structural work on vitamin $B_{12}$ which was going on there during the early fifties. At any rate, he clearly recognized it as a somewhat neglected field, the further development of which would require a new chemical approach.

Kenner's first two papers on porphyrins (58, 60), summarizing the work carried out in Cambridge between 1955 and 1957, clearly set the stage for nearly all his work during the next 20 years. It was clear to him that his first major task was the development of new mild methods for porphyrin synthesis which could be utilized in structural and biosynthetic studies of haem and chlorophyll and related compounds. When he started, the Fischer synthesis (involving the acid-catalysed fusion of two pyrromethanes at temperatures up to 200 °C) was virtually the only effective method of synthesizing porphyrins with an unsymmetrical arrangement of peripheral substituents, such as is found in naturally occurring porphyrins; the yields by the Fischer procedure were, however, generally rather low (except in the preparation of centrosymmetric porphyrins); mixtures of products were sometimes obtained, and the method could not readily be applied to porphyrins with labile sidechains, owing to the vigorous conditions employed. His first paper (58) described two new methods for coupling monopyrrolic units to form pyrromethanes (scheme 1), and foreshadowed the subsequent development of mild stepwise methods for constructing open chain tetrapyrrolic intermediates which could then be cyclized to porphyrins. Further improvements involved the use of more polar solvents (94) (e.g. formamide), and later of toluene-*p*-sulphonic acid in methanol, to facilitate the coupling reaction (155, 168); the limitations of these reactions were also investigated in relation to the pattern of substitution in the pyrromethanes employed.

The second paper (6) was concerned with experiments relating to a possible model for the genesis of the 'isocyclic' ring of chlorophyll, involving intramolecular cyclization of a β-ketoester sidechain, and in this work Kenner showed that pyrromethenes would undergo a Michael-type nucleophilic addition reaction at the central methine carbon atom. In the event other, closer models (137, 157, 176) of the biosynthetic process were subsequently discovered, and much of Kenner's later work in this area revolved around aspects of the chemistry and biosynthesis of the *Chlorobium* chlorophylls (187).

At Liverpool Kenner's initial objective was to extend the new pyrromethane synthesis to tri- and eventually to tetrapyrranes (bilanes), in a manner somewhat analogous to the natural biosynthetic route. However, the limitations of this approach soon became apparent (86, 94), especially because of the relative instability of the tripyrranes and bilanes towards aerial oxidation, and their acid-catalysed rearrangements leading to 'scrambling' of the rings. This approach was, therefore, abandoned in favour of the preparation of more stable tetrapyrrolic intermediates containing carbonyl groups, or unsaturated linkages, between the pyrrole rings. In this manner, four new porphyrin syntheses were developed (123, 188), namely the *a*-oxobilane, *b*-oxobilane, the *b*-bilene and the tripyrrene (123, 188) *ac*-biladiene routes. Each of these involved the construction by rational methods of an open-chain tetrapyrrole which could then be cyclized to an unsymmetrical porphyrin. It should be noted that the original Fischer synthesis (from dipyrromethenes) and the later MacDonald synthesis (from $\alpha\alpha'$-diformylpyrromethanes and $\alpha\alpha'$-disubstituted pyrromethanes) both suffer from the disadvantage that one of the dipyrrolic intermediates must of necessity be symmetrical, or mixtures of products will be obtained.

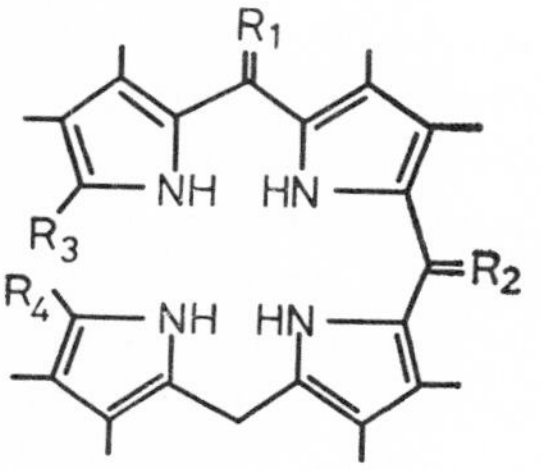

R1 NH HN R3 R2 R4 NH HN

**1**

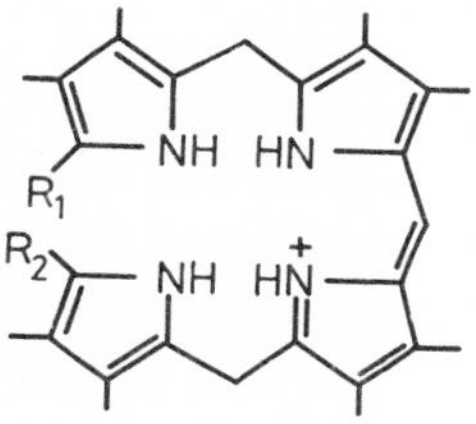

NH HN R1 R2 NH HN +

**2**

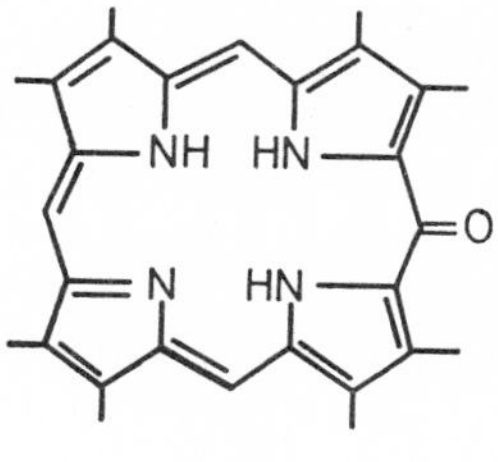

NH HN O N HN

**3**

The *a*-oxobilane route (93, 121) depended for its success upon the initial development of a new synthesis of di- and tripyrroketones (109), utilizing a variant of the Vilsmeier–Haack formylation reaction (109). The $\alpha'$-benzyloxy-carbonyl-$\alpha$-methylpyrroketones readily undergo chlorination of the $\alpha$-methyl group, and the products can be coupled with the alkali metal salts of $\alpha'$-benzyl-oxycarbonylpyrromethane-$\alpha$-carboxylic acids to give stable crystalline *a*-oxo-bilanes bearing benzyloxycarbonyl groups at the $\alpha$-positions of both terminal rings (**1**; $R_1 = O$; $R_2 = H_2$; $R_3 = R_4 = PhCH_2OCO$). The corresponding dicarboxylic acids (obtained by catalytic hydrogenolysis of the benzyl groups) could not, however, be cyclized to porphyrin derivatives for the oxo group not only provided a strong stabilizing influence on the tetrapyrrole, but at the same time inhibited electrophilic attack on the α-position of the A ring of the oxobilane. The *a*-oxobilanes were, however, readily reduced by diborane to the corresponding bilanes, but the latter gave mixtures of porphyrins after removal of benzyl groups and cyclization with one-carbon electrophiles. In consequence the bilanedicarboxylic acids were oxidized to *b*-bilenes (**2**; $R_1 = R_2 =$ COOH) and the latter cyclized to porphyrins under mildly acidic conditions with triethylorthoformate. The overall yields of porphyrin from *a*-oxobilane diester were generally in the 20–30% range even though five stages were involved (hydrogenolysis, oxidation to bilene, decarboxylation, cyclization and dehydrogenation).

In the *b*-oxobilane route (93, 123, 128) a pyrromethane amide activated by phosphorylchloride was coupled with an α-free pyrromethane, and the intermediate imine salt hydrolysed under mildly basic conditions. The resulting *b*-oxobilane-dibenzylester (**1**; $R_1 = H_2$; $R_2 = O$; $R_3 = R_4 = PhCH_2OCO$) was then hydrogenolyzed and cyclized with triethylorthoformate under similar conditions to those used in the final step of the *a*-oxobilane method. The products were the deep blue *oxophlorins* (**3**) (tautomeric forms of the corresponding *meso*-hydroxyporphyrins) whose structures were clearly demonstrated by their visible and i.r. absorption spectra. These oxophlorins were transformed into the corresponding *meso*-unsubstituted porphyrins by conversion to *meso*-acetoxyporphyrins followed by hydrogenolysis and re-oxidation. The overall yields of porphyrins obtained from the *b*-oxobilane-diesters were again of the order of 25%.

Both the *a*- and the *b*-oxobilane routes depended in part for their success upon the use of protecting groups such as benzyl and *t*-butyl, and studies of other ester protecting groups were also initiated (145), reflecting a cross fertilization of ideas from Kenner's other main interests in the peptide and nucleotide fields. Among the 20 or so porphyrins synthesized in Liverpool at the time and demonstrating the versatility of these two methods were mesoporphyrin IX (121), protoporphyrin IX (124, 146), coproporphyrin III (171) and IV (128, 171), rhodoporphyrin XV (173), pempto- and *iso*pemptoporphyrins (125, 171), hardero- and *iso*harderoporphyrins (144, 193) and chlorocruoroporphyrin (171) (scheme 2). This work was also instrumental in establishing the structures of pempto- and harderoporphyrins and in confirming Fischer's original assignment of structure to chlorocruoroporphyrin (from the oxygen carrying pigment of *Spirographis spallanzanii*).

The third and fourth porphyrin syntheses developed in Liverpool also relied heavily upon the use of ester protecting groups. Thus a pyrromethane α′-*t*-butoxycarbonyl-α-carboxylic acid was prepared from the corresponding α-benzylester by hydrogenolysis and coupled under acidic conditions with an α-formyl-α′-*t*-butoxycarbonylpyrromethane to give a *b*-bilene di-*t*-butylester (**2**; $R_1 = R_2 =$ *t*-BuOCO). Removal of the terminal ester groups by brief treatment with cold trifluoroacetic acid, followed by cyclization with triethylorthoformate under mild acid conditions and aerial oxidation, then afforded the desired porphyrins in good overall yield (126). These included mesoporphyrins VI and X and two *meso*-alkylporphyrins structurally related to the *Chlorobium* chlorophylls (153). Attempts to extend the method to the synthesis of porphyrins with nuclear carboxyl groups led to lower yields and production of mixtures (126).

The most recently developed synthesis was a logical extension of this *b*-bilene route involving (a) coupling of an $\alpha'$-*t*-butoxycarbonylpyrromethane-$\alpha$-carboxylic acid with a formyl pyrrole to form a crystalline tripyrrene, (b) deprotection of the latter by treatment with cold trifluoracetic acid, (c) coupling of the tripyrrene with a second, but different, formylpyrrole and (d) cyclization of the resulting *ac*-biladiene (**4**) in presence of copper salts (186, 188). This method gave excellent yields of porphyrins and it was used to effect the first

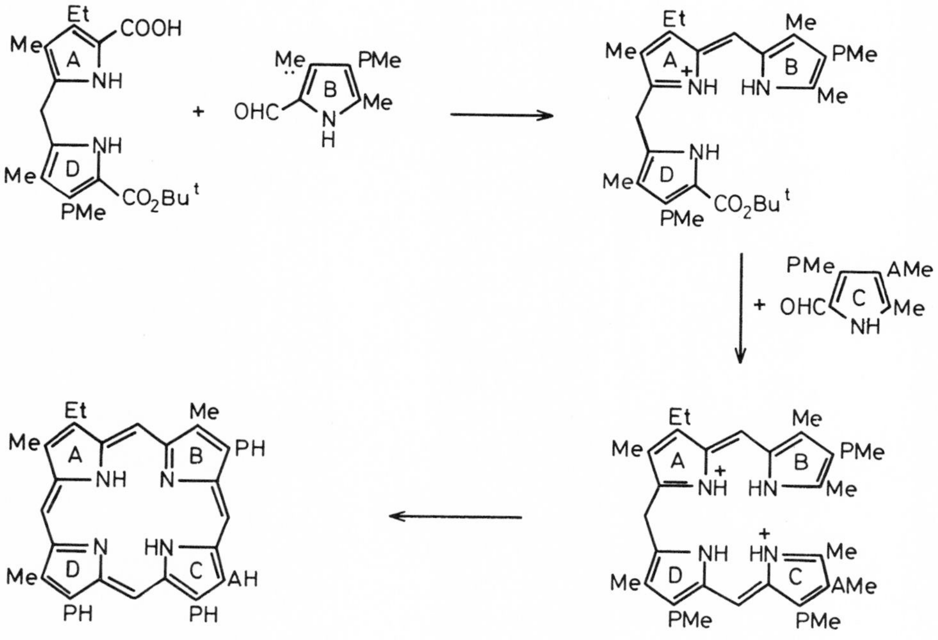

**5** **4**

Scheme 2. A = $CH_2COO$–; P = $CH_2CH_2COO$–.

synthesis of isocoproporphyrin (**5**) (illustrated in scheme 2), a faecal metabolite excreted by rats poisoned with hexachlorobenzene and by patients suffering from symptomatic cutaneous porphyria. This *ac*-biladiene synthesis (186, 188) represents the first truly stepwise synthesis of unsymmetrical porphyrins *via* di-, tri- and tetrapyrrolic intermediates, in contrast to previously known routes all of which involve the coupling of two dipyrrolic units.

The development of these four new syntheses of unsymmetrical porphyrins must rank as a major achievement and extensive use of them has since been made by other workers. In most cases the products are isomerically pure porphyrins formed in reasonable yields, under mildly acidic conditions and at room temperature. Kenner, however, did not eschew other methods of porphyrin synthesis when these were more efficient e.g. the MacDonald method in which $\alpha\alpha'$-unsubstituted pyrromethanes are brought into reaction with $\alpha\alpha'$-diformylpyrromethanes. Alternative cyclization techniques were also developed, e.g. the use of toluene-*p*-sulphonic acid in methanol (rather than hydrogen iodide in acetic acid) and of zinc salts to facilitate the cyclization step.

The syntheses of hardero- and isoharderoporphyrins led to biosynthetic studies in which it was shown that harderoporphyrinogen was much more efficiently converted into protoporphyrin IX by *Euglena gracilis* than its isomer (178), thus providing support for earlier suggestions (144) concerning the specificity of the natural pathway between coproporphyrinogen III and protoporphyrin IX.

A very notable offshoot of the *b*-oxobilane route to porphyrins was the confirmation of the importance of the iron complexes of oxophlorins (oxyporphyrins) (**3**) in the metabolism of haem to bile pigments. Oxyporphyrins and their metal complexes had previously been prepared by direct oxidation of metalloporphyrins by Lemberg and by Fischer, but unsymmetrical porphyrins gave mixtures of products. $\alpha$-Hydroxymesoporphyrin IX and the $\beta$-hydroxy isomer were readily synthesized by the *b*-oxobilane route (112, 128, 152) and the *meso*-tritiated iron complexes were injected into rats with biliary fistulae; isolation of the bilirubin fraction from the bile showed that only the $\alpha$-isomer was converted into mesobilirubin (151) (the diethyl analogue of bilirubin). This provided circumstantial evidence for the intermediacy of $\alpha$-hydroxyhaem in the metabolism of haem. Attempts to prepare $\alpha$-hydroxyhaem itself were unfortunately frustrated by cyclization involving an incipient vinyl group and the *meso*-hydroxyl (146). A number of interesting facets of oxophlorin chemistry, however, were also studied (129) including spectroscopic aspects, their behaviour in acid, deuteriation at the *meso* position opposite to the oxygen function and acylation and alkylation on oxygen. Subsequently other aspects of the *meso* reactivity of porphyrins were also studied including *meso*-deuteration and -tritiation (155, 163, 169) and this together with an interest in the role of cation radical intermediates in the chemistry and biology of porphyrins led to syntheses of *meso*-methylated porphyrins (200).

Kenner was very interested in the structures and properties of the biologically important haemoproteins. Thus his earlier syntheses of porphyrins bearing formyl and vinyl groups were followed by preliminary studies of methods for introducing long alkyl sidechains into porphyrins such as are needed for porphyrin *a* synthesis (148, 176). At about the same time, work on the synthesis of porphyrins bridged with a peptide chain containing imidazole residues was also initiated (C. J. Suckling, Ph.D. Thesis, Liverpool, 1970); in this way it was hoped that models for the oxygen carrying pigments haemoglobin and myoglobin might be developed and their properties studied. It is of considerable interest to note that this work was started in 1967, long before the vogue for synthesising model porphyrins with 'picket fences', 'bridges', 'straps', or 'caps' etc. had even begun, and it is a great pity that these early studies were not followed up.

A more successful project was the synthesis of protoporphyrins specifically deuterated in the methyl groups and *meso* positions using suitably deuterated pyrrolic intermediates in the MacDonald and *b*-oxobilane procedures (179, 180). The specifically labelled compounds were utilized in a joint study (182), with Schulman and his colleagues at the Bell Telephone laboratories, of the assignment of the methyl resonances in n.m.r. spectra of myoglobin, their variation with temperature, and the development of accurate quantum mechanical models to explain the results.

In the course of the synthetic work on porphyrins a number of other significant results were obtained. For example, a new pyrrole synthesis was developed (77, 97) from *N*-tosylglycine esters and αβ-unsaturated carbonyl compounds, which is useful for the preparation of α-free α′-pyrrolecarboxylic esters. Additionally a new synthesis of porphobilinogen (the monopyrrolic precursor of all naturally occurring porphyrins and bile pigments) was devised (162, 195); a key step in this synthesis was the thallium III oxidative rearrangement of a β-acetylpyrrole to a pyrrole bearing a β-aceticester sidechain. It was used for the preparation of labelled porphobilinogen required for biosynthetic studies of *Chlorobium* chlorophylls, (187) and provided a new route to a key intermediate in porphyrin synthesis (168).

Various transformations of the vinyl groups of protoporphyrin IX were also studied (161, 165, 193). These involved the thallium III oxidation of the vinyl groups to acetals (2,2-dimethoxyethylporphyrin derivatives) which in a further series of reactions enabled pempto- and harderoporphyrin and their isomers (193) as well as coproporphyrin III to be prepared directly from protoporphyrin IX (readily available by demetallation of haem). These compounds are much more readily prepared in this manner than by ring synthesis, and the methods used are also capable of adaptation to the preparation of specially labelled compounds for biosynthetic studies.

Kenner's first major incursion into the chlorophyll field, following his original model experiments with pyrromethenes, had to wait until his new porphyrin syntheses had been developed. These allowed the rational development of new routes to porphyrins with nuclear ester groups, especially in the rhodoporphyrin series (173, 174, 175). Rhodoporphyrindimethylester and mono- and divinyl analogues were synthesized and, following the success of model experiments with pyrrole esters, were converted into porphyrin-β-keto-esters (174, 175); these did not undergo base-catalysed nucleophilic substitution into the neighbouring *meso* position, as originally expected, but could be cyclized oxidatively to the corresponding phaeoporphyrin derivatives (137, 157). Initially the magnesium complexes were oxidized with iodine (following Mauzerell's demonstration of the formation of a cation radical in similar oxidations of magnesium octaethylporphyrin). The yields were low and the primary product underwent a further oxidation to give a methoxy derivative

(137) (the methoxyl group being derived from the solvent methanol); however, in spite of the low yields this reaction may be regarded as a very good model for the mode of formation of the isocyclic ring in the chlorophylls. Subsequently much higher yields of the phaeoporphyrin derivatives (157, 176) were obtained by oxidation with thallium III trifluoracetate (175, 176).

Preliminary biosynthetic studies using an isolated chloroplast system confirmed (137) that protoporphyrin IX is a biosynthetic precursor of the plant chlorophylls, although the conclusive demonstration of the (presumed) role of the β-keto esters has not yet been achieved, owing to the ready loss of tritium labels from the *meso* positions (185). In the course of this work a new method for the large scale separation of derivatives of chlorophylls *a* and *b* using Girard reagents was worked out (170) and some oxidation reactions leading to purpurins were also studied.

During the course of his work on the synthesis of porphyrin-β-ketoesters the structure of chlorophyll *c* was published, and this led Kenner to devise new routes for the preparation of porphyrins with acrylic sidechains (185). Work on the total synthesis of both chlorophylls *a* and *c* was actively in progress at the time of Kenner's death. Improved methods for the introduction of magnesium into the porphyrin ring were also developed involving magnesium viologen or magnesium pyridyls; an offshoot of this work was the finding that the magnesium complexes undergo extremely facile hydrogen exchange at the *meso* positions, and this observation led to a useful new way of introducing deuterium or tritium labels into the porphyrin nucleus.

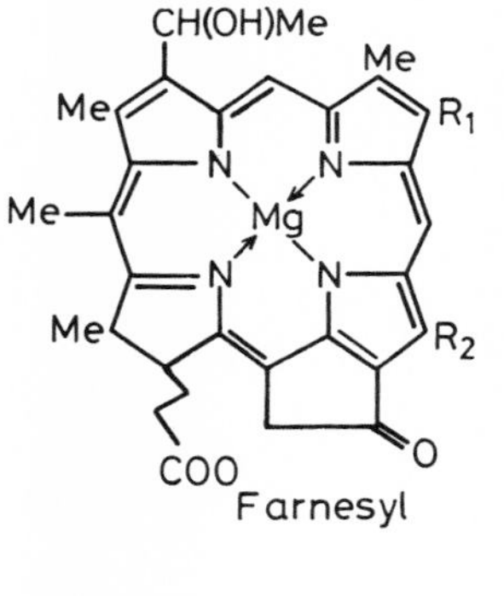

**6** $R_1$ = Et, n–Pr, i – Bu; $R_2$=Me, Et.

A growing interest towards the end of Kenner's life was the biosynthetic origin of the additional methyl groups in the *meso* position and the sidechains of the B and C rings of the *Chlorobium* chlorophylls. His initial interest in these marine pigments had arisen as a result of conflicting structural assignments in the literature in the mid-1960s; some of the discrepancies were resolved by mass spectrometry and the use of the *b*-bilene synthesis to synthesize two phylloporphyrins (146) (*meso*-substituted porphyrins) obtained by Holt and MacDonald in Canada as degradation products of the *Chlorobium* chlorophylls 660 (**6**). Later, [$^{13}$C]n.m.r. studies confirmed that the *meso*-methyl group was in the δ-position in these substances (not α- as had been suggested at one point by Rapoport). It was also shown that this methyl group and the additional carbon atoms in the B and C ring sidechains are all derived from methionine, by biosynthetic experiments feeding [$^{14}$C] and [$^{13}$C]methionine to cultures of *Chloropseudomonas ethylicum* (187). Low, but probably significant, incorporations of porphobilinogen (58%), uroporphyrinogen III ($>2\%$), coproporphyrinogen III (0·4%) and protoporphyrin and protoporphyrinogen IX (0·3%) (all labelled with $^{14}$C at $C_6$) into the *Chlorobium* chlorophylls were also obtained in other experiments with suspensions of *C. ethylicum*. In the important paper outlining this work (187) detailed hypotheses on the sequence of methylation steps were advanced and work on these and related topics was actively in progress at the time of Kenner's untimely death. An interesting by-product of this work was the discovery of an acetylbilatriene in the culture medium (187); this was thought to arise from oxidative ring opening of the *Chlorobium* chlorophylls at the β-*meso* position (which bears the *meso*-methyl group) and may well be of considerable significance in relation to the mode of degradation of chlorophylls in senescent leaves.

In preparing this memoir the author has had invaluable help from a large number of George Kenner's friends and contemporaries from his Manchester and Cambridge days, and from students and colleagues in Liverpool. To all of them and perhaps especially to Professor C. W. Rees, F.R.S., Professor A. R. Battersby, F.R.S., Dr R. C. Sheppard and Professor A. H. Jackson, he wishes to express his sincere thanks.

The photograph reproduced was taken by G. Argent in 1976.

## Bibliography

(1) 1943 (With B. Lythgoe, A. R. Todd & A. Topham) Some reactions of amidines with derivatives of malonic acid. *J. chem. Soc.* p. 388.

(2) (With B. Lythgoe, A. R. Todd & A. Topham) Experiments on the synthesis of purine nucleosides. IV. 4:6 Diaminopyrimidine. A new synthesis of pyrimidine derivatives. *J. chem. Soc.* p. 574.

(3) 1944 (With B. Lythgoe & A. R. Todd) Experiments on the synthesis of purine nucleosides. IX. A synthesis of D-xylopyranosidoadenine. *J. chem. Soc.* p. 652.

(4) (With J. Baddiley, B. Lythgoe & A. R. Todd) Experiments on the synthesis of purine nucleosides. X. A synthesis of D-ribopyranosidoadenine. *J. chem. Soc.* p. 657.

(5) 1945 The structure and reactivity of the halogenobenzenes. *Proc. R. Soc. Lond.* A **185**, 119.

(6) 1946 (With A. R. Todd) Experiments on the synthesis of purine nucleosides. XIII. An improved method for the cyclisation of 4-glycosidamino-5-thioformamidopyrimidines. *J. chem. Soc.* p. 852.

(7) (With G. A. Howard, B. Lythgoe & A. R. Todd) Experiments on the synthesis of purine nucleosides. XIV. An interpretation of some interconversion reactions of N-glycosides. *J. chem. Soc.* p. 855.

(8) (With G. A. Howard, B. Lythgoe & A. R. Todd) Experiments on the synthesis of purine nucleosides. XV. The configuration of some synthetic purine and pyrimidine glycosides. *J. chem. Soc.* p. 861.

(9) 1948 (With B. Lythgoe & A. R. Todd) Experiments on the synthesis of purine nucleosides. XVII. The preparation of 4-glycofuranosidaminopyrimidines and a synthesis of 9-L-arabofuranosido-2-methylthioadenine. *J. chem. Soc.* p. 957.

(10) 1949 (With H. J. Rodda & A. R. Todd) Experiments on the synthesis of purine nucleosides. XXII. The synthesis of the α- and β-forms of 9-triacetyl-D-ribopyranosido-2-methylthioadenine and further studies on the synthesis of 9-glycofuranosido purines. *J. chem. Soc.* p. 1613.

(11) (With C. W. Taylor & A. R. Todd) Experiments on the synthesis of purine nucleosides. XXIII. A new synthesis of adenosine. *J. chem. Soc.* p. 1620.

(12) (With K. J. M. Andrews & A. R. Todd) Experiments on the synthesis of purine nucleosides. XXIV. 9-D-galactosido-2-methylthioadenines. *J. chem. Soc.* p. 2302.

(13) (With M. A. Murray) The cleavage of sulphonic esters with Raney nickel catalysts. *J. chem. Soc.* p. 5178.

(14) (With V. Prelog, K. Wiesner & H. G. Khorana) *Erythrina*-Alkaloide I. Über Erythralin und Erysodin, die Hauptalkaloide der *Erythrina abyssinica* Lam. *Helv. chim. Acta* **32**, 453.

(15) 1950 (With M. A. Murray) The reduction of toluene-*p*-sulphonic esters. *J. chem. Soc.* p. 406.

(16) Pyrimidines. In *Thorpe's dictionary of applied chemistry* (4th ed.) (ed. M. A. Whiteley), vol. 10, p. 317. London: Longmans, Green and Co.

(17) 1951 (With H. G. Khorana & V. Prelog) *Erythrina*-Alkaloide 3. Über der Hofmann'schen Abbau des Tetrahydroerysotrins und des Tetrahydro-erythralins. *Helv. chim. Acta* **34**, 1969.

(18) A new synthesis of peptides. *Chemy Ind.* p. 15.

(19) The chemistry of nucleotides. *Fortschr. Chem. org. NatStoffe* **8**, 96.

(20) 1952 (With N. S. Corby & A. R. Todd) Studies on phosphorylation. X. The preparation of tetra-esters of pyrophosphoric acid from diesters of phosphoric acid by means of exchange reactions. *J. chem. Soc.* p. 1234.

(21) (With R. J. Stedman) Peptides. I. The synthesis of peptides through anhydrides of sulphuric acid. *J. chem. Soc.* p. 2069.

(22) (With H.G. H. G. Khorana) Peptides. II. Selective degradation by removal of the terminal amino acid bearing a free amino group. The use of alkyl alkoxydithioformates (dialkyl xanthates). *J. chem. Soc.* p. 2076.

(23) (With R. J. Stedman) The compounds of alkylamines with esters of azodicarboxylic acid. *J. chem. Soc.* p. 2089.

(24) (With N. S. Corby & A. R. Todd) Nucleotides. XVI. Ribonucleoside-5′ phosphites. A new method for the preparation of mixed secondary phosphites. *J. chem. Soc.* p. 3669.

(25) (With A. R. Todd & F. J. Weymouth) Nucleotides. XVII. N-chloroamides as reagents for the chlorination of diesters of phosphorous acid. A new synthesis of uridine-5′ pyrophosphate. *J. chem. Soc.* p. 3675.

(26) (With S. M. H. Christie & A. R. Todd) Total synthesis of flavine-adenine-dinucleotide. *Nature, Lond.* **170** 924.

(27) 1953 (With H. G. Khorana & R. J. Stedman) Peptides. IV. Selective removal of the C-terminal residue as a thiohydantoin. The use of diphenyl phosphor*iso*thiocyanatidate. *J. chem. Soc.* p. 673.

(28) (With S. M. H. Christie, D. T. Elmore, A. R. Todd & F. J. Weymouth) Nucleotides. XXII. Synthesis of $P^1P^2$-diadenosine-5′ and $P^1P^2$-diuridine-5′ pyrophosphates. *J. chem. Soc.* p. 2947.

(29) (With D. W. Clayton) Conversion of an α-glutamyl peptide derivative into the γ-isomer. *Chemy Ind.* p. 1205.

(30) The synthesis of pyrophosphate coenzymes. *Rec. chem. Prog.* **14**, 131.

(31) 1954 (With S. M. H. Christie & A. R. Todd) Nucleotides. XXV. A synthesis of flavin-adenine dinucleotide. *J. chem. Soc.* p. 46.

(32) (With A. R. Todd, R. F. Webb & F. J. Weymouth) Nucleotides. XXVIII. A synthesis of uridine-5′ triphosphate (UTP). *J. chem. Soc.* p. 2288.

(33) (With A. R. Todd & R. F. Webb) Nucleotides. XXIX. Synthetic uridine-diphosphate-glucose (UDPG). *J. chem. Soc.* p. 2843.

(34) General methods. *Ann. Rep. Prog. Chem.* **51**, 174.

(35) 1955 (With N. R. Williams) A method of reducing phenols to aromatic hydrocarbons. *J. chem. Soc.* p. 522.

(36) 1955 (With C. B. Reese & Sir Alexander Todd) The acylation of 3-methylcytosine. *J. chem. Soc.* p. 855.

(37) (With J. A. Farrington & J. M. Turner) The preparation of *p*-nitrophenyl thiolesters and their application to peptide synthesis. *Chemy Ind.* p. 601.

(38) (With J. M. Turner) Cycloglycyl-L-leucylglycyl-L-leucylglycyl, a synthetic cyclic peptide. *Chemy Ind.* p. 602.

(39) The use of mixed anhydrides in peptide synthesis. *Spec. Publs chem. Soc.* no. 2, p. 103.

(40) (With F. R. Atherton, A. L. Morrison, R. J. W. Cremlyn, Sir Alexander Todd & R. F. Webb) The use of imidoyl phosphates as intermediates in the synthesis of pyrophosphates. *Chemy Ind.* p. 1183.

(41) 1956 (With D. W. Clayton & R. C. Sheppard) Peptides. V. Condensation of the γ-carboxyl group of α-glutamyl peptides with the peptide chain. *J. chem. Soc.* p. 371.

(42) (With Sir Alexander Todd & R. F. Webb) Studies on phosphorylation. XIII. Ketoxime sulphonates as intermediates in pyrophosphate formation. *J. chem. Soc.* p. 1231.

(43) (With B. H. Chase, Sir Alexander Todd & R. F. Webb) Nucleotides XXXV. *cyclo*-Pentanone oxime *p*-nitrobenzenesulphonate as an intermediate in the synthesis of nucleotide derivatives; an alternative synthesis of adenosine-5′ triphosphate. *J. chem. Soc.* p. 1371.

(44) (With J. Mather) Studies on phosphorylation. XIV. The solvolysis by phenols of benzyl phosphates. *J. chem. Soc.* p. 3523.

(45) Recent progress in the chemistry of peptides. *J. chem. Soc.* p. 3689.

(46) 1957 (With D. W. Clayton, J. A. Farrington & J. M. Turner) Peptides. VI. Further studies of the synthesis of peptides through anhydrides of sulphuric acid. *J. chem. Soc.* p. 1398.

(47) (With J. A. Farrington, P. J. Hextall & J. M. Turner) Peptides. VII. The preparation and use of *p*-nitrophenyl thiolesters. *J. chem. Soc.* p. 1407.

(48) The present and future scope of peptide synthesis. *J. Soc. Leath. Trades Chem.* **41**, 75.

(49) (With Sir Alexander Todd) Pyrimidine and its derivatives. Ch. 7, p. 234 in vol. 6 of *Heterocyclic compounds* (ed. R. C. Elderfield). New York: J. Wiley and Sons.

(50) (With F. Cramer, N. A. Hughes & Sir Alexander Todd) Nucleotides. XLII. The preparation of the 2′:5′- and 3′:5′-diphosphates of adenosine. *J. chem. Soc.* p. 3297.

(51) (With L. J. Haynes, N. A. Hughes & Sir Alexander Todd) Codehydrogenases. II. A synthesis of nicotinamide nucleotide. *J. chem. Soc.* p. 3727.

(52) (With N. A. Hughes & Sir Alexander Todd) Codehydrogenases. III. A synthesis of diphosphopyridine nucleotide (cozymase), and some observations on the synthesis of triphosphopyridine nucleotide. *J. chem. Soc.* p. 3733.

(53) (With M. A. Murray & C. M. B. Taylor) Oxidative cyclisation of diphenyl-2-carboxylic acid. *Tetrahedron* **1**, 259.

(54) (With M. Goodman) The synthesis of peptides. *Adv. Protein Chem.* vol. XII, p. 465.

(55) 1958 (With R. C. Sheppard) α-Aminoisobutyric acid, β-hydroxyleucine and γ-methylproline from the hydrolysis of a natural product. *Nature, Lond.* **181**, 48.

(56) (With R. J. W. Cremlyn, J. Mather & Sir Alexander Todd) Studies on phosphorylation. XVI. Iodides as debenzylating and dealkylating agents. *J. chem. Soc.* p. 528.

(57) (With C. B. Reese & Sir Alexander Todd) Nucleotides. XLIII. The use of cyanamide derivatives in pyrophosphate synthesis. Syntheses of P¹-adenosine-5′, P²-uridine-5′-pyrophosphate and of Cytidine-5′-pyrophosphate.

(58) (With A. Hayes & N. R. Williams) Pyrroles and related compounds. 1. Syntheses of some unsymmetrical pyrrolylmethylpyrroles (pyrromethanes) *J. chem. Soc.* p. 3779.

(59) (With P. J. Thompson & J. M. Turner) Peptides. VIII. Cyclic peptides derived from leucine and glycine. *J. chem. Soc.* p. 4148.

(60) 1959 (With A. C. Jain) Pyrroles and related compounds. II. Michael addition to pyrromethanes. *J. chem. Soc.* p. 185.

(61) Phenyl-Ester als Carboxyl-Schutzgruppen. *Angew. Chem.* **71**, 741.

(62) (With R. S. Coffey & M. Green) Peptides. IX. Preparation of L-phenylalanine from L- tyrosine. *J. chem. Soc.* p. 4100.

(63) 1960 (With R. C. Sheppard and C. E. Stehr) Synthesis of thiazole amino-acids derived from natural peptides. *Tetrahedron Lett.* no. 1, 23.

(64) (With J. Ellis, A. H. Jackson & J. Lee) Porphyrin nuclear magnetic resonance spectra. *Tetrahedron Lett.* no. 2, p. 23.

(65) (With K. Chambers, M. J. Robinson & B. R. Webster) The biosynthesis of certain coumarins, particularly of novobiocin. *Proc. chem. Soc.* p. 291.

(66) (With Shirley Dalby & R. C. Sheppard) Peptides. X. β-Hydroxyleucine. *J. chem. Soc.* p. 968.

(67) (With R. J. Cremlyn & Sir Alexander Todd) Studies on phosphorylation. XXI. Keten imides as reagents in pyrophosphate synthesis. *J. chem. Soc.* p. 4511.

(68) With G. Baluja, B.H. Chase & Sir Alexander Todd) Nucleotides. XLV. Derivatives of β-2-amino-2-deoxy-D-glucose (β-D-glucosamine) 1-phosphate. *J. chem. Soc.* p. 4678.

(69) (With M. T. Leplawy, D. S. Jones & R. C. Sheppard) Peptides. XI. Synthesis of peptides derived from α-methylalanine. *Tetrahedron* **11**, 39.

(70) 1961 (With L. F. Burrough, S. Dalby & R. C. Sheppard) Absolute configuration of 4-Methylproline from Perry. *Nature, Lond.* **189**, 394.

(71) (With R. J. Abraham & A. H. Jackson) The proton magnetic resonance spectra of porphyrins. 1. The effect of β-substitution on the proton chemical shifts of porphyrins. *J. chem. Soc.* p. 3468.

(72) (With C. N. C. Drey, H. D. Law, R. C. Sheppard, M. Bodanszky, J. Fried, N. J. Williams & J. T. Sheehan) Degradation of thiostrepton. Derivatives of 8-hydroxyquinoline. *J. Am. chem. Soc.* **83**, 3906.

(73) (With R. J. Abraham, K. A. McLaughlin, Shirley Dalby, R. C. Sheppard & L. F. Burroughs) Structures and conformations of some naturally occurring derivatives of proline. *Nature, Lond.* **192**, 1150.

(74) 1962 (With M. J. T. Robinson, C. M. B. Tylor & B. R. Webster) Reactions between strongly basic nucleophiles and fluorenones. *J. chem. Soc.* p. 1756.

(75) (With Marion Bethell & R. C. Sheppard) 4-Methyleneproline: synthetic studies. *Nature, Lond.* **194**, 864.

(76) (With J. Shirley Dalby & R. C. Sheppard) Peptides. XII. The stereoisomers of 4-methylproline. *J. chem. Soc.* p. 4387.

(77) (With A. H. Jackson & W. G. Terry) A new synthesis of pyrroles. *Tetrahedron Lett.* no. 20, p. 921.

(78) 1963 (With A. H. Jackson) Porphyrins—key molecules of life. *Discovery, Lond.* vol. XXIV, p. 24.

(79) (With D. S. Jones & R. C. Sheppard) A synthetic cyclol tripeptide. *Experientia* **19**, 126.

(80) (With P. M. Hardy & R. C. Sheppard) Peptides. XIII. Effects of configuration on dielectric increments and cyclization of some simple peptides. *Tetrahedron* **19**, 95.

(81) (With R. J. Abraham, A. H. Jackson & D. Warburton) The proton magnetic resonance spectra of porphyrins. III. *meso*-Substituted porphyrins. *J. chem. Soc.* p. 853.

(82) (With D. F. W. Cross, R. C. Sheppard & C. E. Stehr) Peptides. XIV. Thiazol-amino-acids. degradation products of thiostrepton. *J. chem. Soc.* p. 2143.

(83) (With M. Bethell & D. B. Bigley) Stereoselective synthesis of 4-hydroxymethyl-L-proline. *Chemy Ind.* p. 653.

(84) (With R. J. Abraham, P. A. Burbridge & A. H. Jackson) Concentration effects in proton magnetic resonance spectra of porphyrins. *Proc. chem. Soc.* p. 134.

(85) (With C. A. Bunton, M. J. Robinson & B. R. Webster) Experiments related to the biosynthesis of novobiocin and other coumarins. *Tetrahedron* **19**, 1001.

(86) 1964 (With J. Ellis, A. H. Jackson & A. C. Jain) Pyrroles and related compounds. III. Syntheses of porphyrins from pyrromethanes and pyrromethenes. *J. chem. Soc.* p. 1935.

(87) 1964 (With H. BUDZIKIEWICS, C. DJERASSI, A. H. JACKSON, D. J. NEWMAN & J. M. WILSON) Pyrroles and related compounds. IV. Mass spectrometry in structural and stereochemical problems—XX. Mass spectra of monocyclic derivatives of pyrrole. *J. chem. Soc.* p. 1949.

(88) (With B. J. ARMITAGE & M. J. T. ROBINSON) Conformational effects in compounds with six-membered rings. 1. Synthesis of the stereoisomers of 5-alkylcyclohexane-1,3-dicarboxylic acids. *Tetrahedron* **20**, 723.

(89) (With B. J. ARMITAGE & M. J. T. ROBINSON) Conformational effects in compounds with six-membered rings. II. Conformational equilibria in monosubstituted and *cis*-1,3-disubstituted cyclohexanes. *Tetrahedron* **20**, 747.

(90) (With E. STENHAGEN) Location of double bonds by mass spectrometry. *Acta chem. Scand.* **18**, 1551.

(91) (With H. GREGORY, P. M. HARDY, D. S. JONES & R. C. SHEPPARD) Structure of gastrin. *Nature, Lond.* **204**, 931.

(92) (With J. C. ANDERSON, MOIRA A. BARTON, R. A. GREGORY, P. M. HARDY, J. K. MACLEOD, J. PRESTON, R. C. SHEPPARD and J. S. MORLEY) Synthesis of gastrin. *Nature, Lond.* **204**, 933.

(93) 1965 (With A. H. JACKSON, G. MCGILLIVRAY & G. S. SACH) Two new porphyrin syntheses. *J. Am. chem. Soc.* **87**, 676.

(94) (With A. H. JACKSON & D. WARBURTON) Pyrroles and related compounds. V. Syntheses of some pyrromethanes, tripyrranes, and porphyrins. *J. chem Soc.* p. 1328.

(95) (With MARION BETHELL) Peptides. XV. 4-Methyleneproline and 4-hydroxymethylproline. *J. chem. Soc.* p. 3850.

(96) (With A. HAYES, A. H. JACKSON & J. M. JUDGE) Pyrroles and related compounds. VI. Pyrrolylethylenes. *J. chem. Soc.* p. 4385.

(97) (With W. G. TERRY, A. H. JACKSON & G. KORNIS) Pyrroles and related compounds. VII. A synthesis of pyrroles from esters of toluene-*p*-sulphonylglycine. *J. chem. Soc.* p. 4389.

(98) (With D. S. JONES & R. C. SHEPPARD) Peptides. XVI. Experiments related to acyl cyanides. *J. chem. Soc.* p. 4393.

(99) (With A. H. LAIRD) Resistance of a cyclic peptide to enzymic attack. *J. chem. Soc., Chem. Commun.* p. 305.

(100) (With J. BEACHAM, V. T. IVANOV & R. C. SHEPPARD) Dielectric effects and conformations of small peptides in aqueous solution. *J. chem. Soc., Chem. Commun.* p. 386.

(101) (With J. C. ANDERSON, MOIRA A. BARTON, P. M. HARDY, J. K. MACLEOD, J. PRESTON, R. C. SHEPPARD & J. S. MORLEY) Synthesis of peptides related to gastrin. *Acta chim. Hung.* **44**, 187.

(102) (With A. H. JACKSON, K. M. SMITH, R. T. APLIN, H. BUDZIKIEWICZ & C. DJERASSI) Pyrroles and related compounds. VIII. Mass spectrometry in structural and stereochemical problems—LXXVI. The mass spectra of porphyrins. *Tetrahedron* **21**, 2913.

(103) (With D. S. JONES, J. PRESTON & R. C. SHEPPARD) Peptides. XVII. Synthesis of peptides and polymers of some sterically hindered amino-acids via oxazolone intermediates. *J. chem. Soc.* p. 6227.

(104) (With J. PRESTON & R. C. SHEPPARD) Peptides. XVIII. Derivatives of 1-aminocyclohexanecarboxylic acid. *J. chem. Soc.* p. 6239.

(105) (With D. S. JONES, J. PRESTON & R. C. SHEPPARD) Peptides. XIX. The isomerization of some oxazolones derived from tripeptides. *Tetrahedron* **21**, 3209.

(106) 1966 (With P. H. BENTLEY & R. C. SHEPPARD) Structures of human gastrins I and II. *Nature, Lond.* **209**, 583

(107) (With J. BEACHAM, P. H. BENTLEY, R. A. GREGORY, J. K. MACLEOD & R. C. SHEPPARD). Synthesis of human gastrin I. *Nature, Lond.* **209**, 585.

(108) (With G. L. COLLIER & A. H. JACKSON) A novel conversion of porphyrins into chlorins. *J. chem. Soc., Chem. Commun.* p. 299.

(109) (With J. A. BALLANTINE, A. H. JACKSON & G. MCGILLIVRAY) Pyrroles and related compounds. IX. Syntheses and properties of certain pyrroketones. *Tetrahedron* Suppl. **7**, 241.

(110) 1966 (With D. S. Jones, J. Preston & R. C. Sheppard) *Proc. Sixth European Peptide Symp., Athens, 1963,* p. 313. Oxford: Pergamon Press.

(111) (With J. Beacham, P. H. Bentley, R. A. Gregory, J. K. MacLeod & R. C. Sheppard) Recent developments in the chemistry of gastrin. *Proc. Int. Symp. Hypotensive Peptides, Florence, 1963,* p. 34. Berlin: Springer-Verlag.

(112) (With A. H. Jackson & K. M. Smith). Oxyporphyrins. *J. Am. chem. Soc.* **88**. 4539.

(113) (With Moira A. Barton & R. C. Sheppard) Peptides. XXI. Dehydrogenation of some thiazolines derived from cysteine. *J. chem. Soc.* C, p. 1061.

(114) (With J. C. Anderson, J. K. MacLeod & R. C. Sheppard) Peptides. XXII. Syntheses of porcine gastrin I. *Tetrahedron,* Suppl. **8**, 39.

(115) (With Moira A. Barton & R. C. Sheppard) Peptides. XXIII. Experiments on the oxidation of thiostrepton. *J. chem. Soc.* C, p. 2115.

(116) 1967 (With A. H. Jackson, H. Budzikiewicz, C. Djerassi & J. M. Wilson) Pyrroles and related compounds—X[1]. Mass spectrometry in structural and stereochemical problems—X[2]. Mass spectra of linear di-, tri- and tetrapyrrolic compounds. *Tetrahedron* **23**, 603.

(117) (With G. L. Collier & A. H. Jackson). Pyrroles and related compounds. XI. Synthesis of two acetamidoethyl porphyrins and their conversion into vinyl porphyrins and chlorins. *J. chem. Soc.* C, p. 66.

(118) (With J. C. Anderson, M. A. Barton, P. M. Hardy, J. Preston & R. C. Sheppard) Peptides. XXIV. Syntheses of the N-terminal pentapeptide and C-terminal tetrapeptide sequences of porcine gastrin. *J. chem. Soc.* C, p. 108.

(119) (With P. A. Burbidge, G. L. Collier & A. H. Jackson) The proton magnetic resonance spectra of porphyrins. V. Syntheses and spectra of some *meso*-methylated prophyrins. *J. chem. Soc.* B, p. 930.

(120) (With J. Beacham, P. H. Bentley, J. J. Mendive & R. C. Sheppard) Gastrins of some mammalian species. *Proc. Eighth European Peptide Symp., Noordwijk, 1966,* p. 235. Amsterdam: North Holland Publishing Co.

(121) (With A. H. Jackson &. G. S. Sach) Pyrroles and related compounds. XII. Stepwise synthesis of porphyrins through *a*-oxo-bilanes. *J. chem. Soc.* p. 2045.

(122) (With J. Beacham, P. H. Bentley, J. K. MacLeod, J. J. Mendive & R. C. Sheppard) Peptides. XXV. The structure and synthesis of human gastrin. *J. chem. Soc.* C, p. 2520.

(123) (With A. H. Jackson) New syntheses of porphyrins and related tetrapyrroles. *Nature, Lond.* **215**, 1126.

(124) (With R. P. Carr, P. J. Crook & A. H. Jackson). New syntheses of protoporphyrin-IX. *J. chem. Soc., Chem. Commun.* p. 1025.

(125) (With A. H. Jackson & J. Wass) Rational syntheses of chlorocruoroporphyrin (*Spirographis* porphyrin) and pemptoporphyrin. *J. chem. Soc., Chem. Commun.* p. 1027.

(126) (With M. T. Cox, R. Fletcher, A. H. Jackson & K. M. Smith) Syntheses of porphyrins through *b*-bilenes. *J. chem. Soc., Chem. Commun.* p. 1141.

(127) 1968 (With D. Bethell & P. J. Powers) Isomerisation of epoxides to carbonyl compounds induced by iodides in dimethyl sulphoxide. *J. chem. Soc., Chem. Commun.* p. 227.

(128) (With A. H. Jackson, G. McGillivray & K. M. Smith) Pyrroles and related compounds. XIII. Porphyrin synthesis through *b*-oxobilanes and oxophlorins (oxyporphyrins). *J. chem. Soc.* p. 294.

(129) (With A. H. Jackson & K. M. Smith) Pyrroles and related compounds. XIV. The structure and transformations of oxophlorins (oxyporphyrins). *J. chem. Soc.* p. 302.

(130) (With J. J. Mendive & R. C. Sheppard) Peptides. XXVI. Analogues of gastrin containing leucine in place of methionine. *J. chem. Soc.* C, p. 761.

(131) (With K. L. Agarwal & R. C. Sheppard) Peptides. XVII. Synthesis of five heptadecapeptides related to human gastrin. *J. chem. Soc.* C, p. 1384.

(132) (With R. C. Sheppard) Chemical studies of some mammalian gastrins. *Proc. R. Soc. Lond.* B **170**, 89.

(133) (With K. L. Agarwal, R. A. W. Johnstone, D. S. Millington & R. C. Mass spectrometry of N-methylated peptide derivatives. *Nature, Lond.* **219**, Sheppard) 498.

(134) 1968 (With K. L. Agarwal, J. Beacham, P. H. Bentley, R. A. Gregory, R. C. Sheppard & Hilda J. Tracy) Isolation, structure and synthesis of ovine and bovine gastrins. *Nature, Lond.* **219**, 614.

(135) (With G. Gawne, N. H. Rogers, R. C. Sheppard & Kirsten Titlestad) Diamagnetic shielding effects and the conformations of small peptides. *Proc. Ninth European Peptide Symp., Orsay, 1968*, p. 28. Amsterdam: North Holland Publishing Co.

(136) (With A. H. Jackson) Recent developments in porphyrin chemistry. *Biochem. Soc. Symp.* no. 28. Porphyrins and related compounds (ed. T. W. Goodwin), p. 3. New York: Academic Press.

(137) 1969 (With M. T. Cox, T. T. Howarth & A. H. Jackson) Formation of the isocyclic ring in chlorophyll. *J. Am. chem. Soc.* **91**, 1232.

(138) (With K. L. Agarwal & R. C. Sheppard) Structure and synthesis of canine gastrin. *Experientia* **25**, 346.

(139) (With K. L. Agarwal & R. C. Sheppard) Peptides. XXVIII. Synthesis of ovine-bovine astrin I. *J. chem. Soc.* C, p. 954.

(140) (With K. L. Agarwal & R. C. Sheppard) Peptides. XXIX. Synthesis of canine gastrin and a new synthesis of human gastrin. *J. chem. Soc.* C, p. 2213.

(141) (With K. L. Agarwal & R. C. Sheppard) Peptides. XXX. Synthesis of the decapeptide Leu-Ala-Ala-Gly-Lys-Val-Glu-Asp-Ser-Asp. *J. chem. Soc.* C, p. 2218.

(142) (With K. L. Agarwal & R. C. Sheppard) Feline gastrin. An example of peptide sequence analysis by mass spectrometry. *J. Am. chem. Soc.* **91**, 3036.

(143) (With G. Gawne & R. C. Sheppard) Acyloxyphosphonium salts as acylating agents. A new synthesis of peptides. *J. Am. chem. Soc.* **91**, 5669.

(144) 1970 (With G. Y. Kennedy, A. H. Jackson & C. J. Suckling) Isolation, structure and synthesis of a tricarboxylic porphyrin from the Harderian glands of the rat. *FEBS Lett.* **6**, 9.

(145) 1971 (With P. J. Crook & A. H. Jackson) Pyrroles and related compounds. XV. Differential protection of pyrrole rings during porphyrin synthesis. Syntheses of mesoporphyrin-XI. *J. chem. Soc.* C, p. 474.

(146) (With R. P. Carr, A. H. Jackson & G. S. Sach) Pyrroles and related compounds. XVI. Synthesis of protoporphyrin-IX by the *a*- and *b*-oxobilane routes. *J. chem. Soc.*, p. 487.

(147) (With A. H. Jackson & K. M. Smith) Pyrroles and related compounds. XVII. Porphyrin synthesis through *b*-bilenes. *J. chem. Soc.* C, p. 502.

(148) (With R. V. H. Jones, T. Lewis & K. M. Smith) Porphyrin ketones. *Chemy Ind.* p. 129.

(149) (With G. Gawne & R. C. Sheppard) The synthesis of peptides through activated derivatives of hexamethylphosphoramide. *Proc. Tenth European Peptide Symp., Abano Terme, Italy, 1969*, p. 23. Amsterdam: North Holland Publishing Co.

(150) (With K. L. Agarwal, S. Grudzinski, N. H. Rogers, R. C. Sheppard & J. E. McGuigan) Immunochemical differentiation between gastrin and related peptide hormones through a novel conjugation of peptides to proteins. *Experientia* **27**, 514.

(151) (With T. Kondo, D. C. Nicholson & A. H. Jackson) Isotopic studies of the conversion of oxophlorins and their ferrihaems into bile pigments in the rat. *Biochem. J.* **121**, 601.

(152) (With P. J. Crook & A. H. Jackson) Pyrroles and related compounds. XVIII. Synthese von-α-oxy-mesoporphyrin-IX. *Liebigs Ann. Chem.* **748**, 26.

(153) (With M. T. Cox & A. H. Jackson) Pyrroles and related compounds. XIX. Synthesis of phylloporphyrins related to *Chlorobium* chlorophyll (660). *J. chem. Soc.* C, p. 1974.

(154) (With J. R. McDermott & R. C. Sheppard) The safety catch principle in solid phase peptide synthesis. *J. chem. Soc., Chem. Commun.* p. 636.

(155) (With A. M. d'A. R. Gonsalves & K. M. Smith) Novel synthesis of deuteriated derivatives of protoporphyrin-IX. *J. chem. Soc., Chem. Commun.* p. 1304.

(156) 1972 (With A. H. Jackson & J. Wass) Pyrroles and related compounds. XX. Syntheses of coproporphyrins. *J. chem. Soc., Perkin Trans. 1*, p. 1475.

(157) 1972 (With S. W. McCombie & K. M. Smith) Porphyrin β-keto-esters and their cyclisation to phaeoporphyrin. *J. chem. Soc., Chem. Commun.* p. 844.

(158) (With J. SEELY) Phenyl esters for C-terminal protection in peptide synthesis. *J. Am. chem. Soc.* **94**, 3259.

(159) (With A. M. D'A. R. GONSALVES & K. M. SMITH) Pyrromethane (dipyrrylmethane) and tripyrrane synthesis. *Tetrahedron Lett.* p. 2203.

(160) The chemistry of gastrin, a peptide hormone. *Chemy Ind.* p. 791.

(161) (With S. W. McCOMBIE &. K. M. SMITH) Coproporphyrin-III from protoporphyrin—IX. *J. chem. Soc., Chem. Commun.* p. 1347.

(162) 1973 (With K. M. SMITH & J. F. UNSWORTH) Porphobilinogen synthesis. *J. chem. Soc., Chem. Commun.* p. 43.

(163) (With K. M. SMITH & M. J. SUTTON) *meso*-Deuteriation of magnesium porphyrins. *Tetrahedron Lett.* p. 1303.

(164) (With J. A. S. CAVALEIRO &. K. M. SMITH) Biosynthetic intermediates between coproporphyrinogen-III and protoporphyrin-IX. *J. chem. Soc., Chem. Commun.* p. 183.

(165) (With S. W. McCOMBIE & K. M. SMITH) Pyrrole und verwandte Verbindungen XXI[1]. Schutz der Porphyrinvinylgruppen. Eine Synthese von Korpoporphyrin-III aus Protoporphyrin-IX[2]. *Liebigs Ann. Chem.* p. 1329.

(166) (With D. HUDSON, B. MASON, B. MORGAN, R. RAMAGE, B. SINGH & R. TYSON) Phenyl esters for C-terminal protection. *Proc. Twelfth European Peptide Symp., Reinhardsbrunn, D.D.R.*, **1972**, p. 70. Amsterdam: North Holland Publishing Co.

(167) (With A. J. BATES, R. RAMAGE & R. C. SHEPPARD) Activation of hexamethylphosphoramide in peptide synthesis: a reinvestigation. *Proc. Twelfth European Peptide Symp., Reinhardsbrunn, D.D.R., 1972*, p. 124. Amsterdam: North Holland Publishing Co.

(168) (With J. A. S. CAVALEIRO, A. R. GONSALVES & K. M. SMITH) Pyrroles and related compounds. XXII. Syntheses of pyrromethanes and a tripyrrane. *J. chem. Soc., Perkin Trans. 1*, p. 2471.

(168a) (With K. M. SMITH) Synthetic studies on porphyrin systems. *Ann. N.Y. Acad. Sci.* **206**, 138.

(169) (With J. A. S. CAVALEIRO & K. M. SMITH) Pyrroles and related compounds. XXIII. Protoporphyrin-I. *J. chem. Soc., Perkin Trans. 1*, p. 2478.

(170) (With S. W. McCOMBIE & K. M. SMITH) Pyrroles and related compounds. XXIV. Separation and oxidative degradation of chlorophyll derivatives. *J. chem. Soc., Perkin Trans. 1*, p. 2517.

(171) 1974 (With A. H. JACKSON & J. WASS) Pyrroles and related compounds. XXV. Pemptoporphyrin, isopemptoporphyrin and chlorocruoroporphyrin (*Spirographis* porphyrin) *J. chem. Soc., Perkin Trans. 1*, p. 480.

(172) (With T. T. HOWARTH, A. H. JACKSON & J. JUDGE) Pyrroles and related compounds. XXVI. Pyrrole β-keto-esters. *J. chem. Soc., Perkin Trans. 1*, p. 490.

(173) (With T. T. HOWARTH & A. H. JACKSON) Pyrroles and related compounds. XXVII. Syntheses of porphyrins with a nuclear carboxy-group. *J. chem. Soc., Perkin Trans. 1*, p. 502.

(174) (With M. T. COX, T. T. HOWARTH & A. H. JACKSON) Pyrroles and related compounds. XXVIII. β-Keto-esters in the porphyrin series. *J. chem. Soc., Perkin Trans. 1*, p. 512.

(175) (With M. T. COX, A. H. JACKSON & S. W. McCOMBIE) Pyrroles and related compounds. XXIX. Vinylporphyrin β-keto-esters. *J. chem. Soc., Perkin Trans. 1*, p. 516.

(176) (With S. W. McCOMBIE & K. M. SMITH) Pyrroles and related compounds. XXX. Cyclisation of porphyrin β-keto-esters to phaeoporphyrins. *J. chem. Soc., Perkin Trans. 1*, p. 527.

(177) (With R. V. H. JONES & K. M. SMITH) Pyrroles and related compounds. XXXI. Porphyrin ketones. *J. chem. Soc., Perkin Trans. 1*, p. 531.

(178) (With J. A. S. CAVALEIRO & K. M. SMITH) Pyrroles and related compounds. XXXII. Biosynthesis of protoporphyrin-IX from coproporphyrinogen-III. *J. chem. Soc., Perkin Trans. 1*, p. 1188.

(179) (With J. A. S. CAVALEIRO, A. R. GONSALVES & K. M. SMITH) Pyrroles and related compounds. XXXIII. Total synthesis of deuteriated derivatives of protoporphyrin-IX for NMR studies of haemoproteins. *J. chem. Soc., Perkin Trans. 1*, p. 1777.

(180) (With J. A. S. Cavaleiro, A. R. Gonsalves & K. M. Smith) Assignments of the paramagnetically shifted methyl resonances in the nuclear magnetic resonance spectrum of iron (III). Protoporphyrin-IX cyanide by selective deuteriation. *J. chem. Soc., Chem. Commun.* p. 392.

(181) (With R. Arshady & A. Ledwith) Phenolic resins for solid-phase peptide synthesis; copolymerization of styrene and *p*-acetoxystyrene. *J. Polym. Sci.* **12**, 2017.

(182) (With A. Mayer, S. Ogawa, R. G. Shulman, T. Yamane, J. A. S. Cavaleiro, A. R. Gonsalves & K. M. Smith) Assignments of the paramagnetically shifted heme methyl nuclear magnetic resonance peaks of cyanomeimyoglobin by selective deuteration. *J. molec. Biol.* **86**, 749.

(183) 1975 (With I. J. Galpin, S. R. Ohlsen & R. Ramage) Gel filtration of protected peptides on Sephadex G-50 in hexamethylphosphoramide containing 5% water. *J. Chromatogr.* **106**, 125.

(184) (With A. J. Bates, I. J. Galpin, A. Hallett, D. Hudson & R. Ramage) A new reagent for polypeptide synthesis; µ-oxo-bis-tris-(dimethylamino)-phosphonium-bis-tetrafluoroborate. *Helv. Chim. Acta* **58**, 688.

(185) (With G. F. Griffiths, S. W. McCombie, K. M. Smith & M. J. Sutton) Pyrroles and related compounds. XXXIV. Acrylic esters in the porphyrin series. *Tetrahedron* **32**, 275.

(186) (With J. A. P. Baptista de Almeida, K. M. Smith & M. J. Sutton) Stepwise synthesis of unsymmetrically substituted porphyrins: isocoproporphyrin. *J. chem. Soc., Chem. Commun.* p. 111.

(187) 1976 (With J. Rimmer, K. M. Smith & J. F. Unsworth) Studies on the biosynthesis of the *Chlorobium* chlorophylls. *Phil. Trans. R. Soc. Lond.* B **273**, 255.

(188) (With J. A. P. Baptista de Almeida, J. Rimmer & K. M. Smith) Pyrroles and related compounds. XXXV. A stepwise general synthesis of unsymmetrically substituted porphyrins. *Tetrahedron* **32**, 1793.

(189) (With I. J. Galpin, B. K. Handa, S. Moore & R. Ramage) Gel filtration of protected peptides on enzacryl K2 in dimethylformamide and N-methyl-2-pyrrolidone. *J. Chromatogr.* **123**, 237.

(190) (With G. A Moore & R. Ramage) Phosphinamides—A new class of amino protecting groups in peptide chemistry. *Tetrahedron Lett.* p. 3623.

(191) (With A. G. Jackson, G. A. Moore, R. Ramage & W. D. Thorpe) Activation of carboxylic acids as diphenylphosphinic mixed anhydrides: application to peptide chemistry. *Tetrahedron Lett.* p. 3627.

(192) (With R. Arshady & A. Ledwith) The introduction of chloromethyl groups into styrene-based polymer, 1. Synthesis of 4-chloromethylstyrene and 4-methoxymethylstyrene and their copolymerisations with styrene. *Makromolek. Chem.* **177**, 2911.

(193) (With J. M. E. Quirke & K. M. Smith) Pyrroles and related compounds. XXXVI, Transformations of protoporphyrin-X into harderoporphyrin, pemptoporphyrin. chlorocruoroporphyrin and their isomers. *Tetrahedron* **32**, 273.

(194) (With A. H. Jackson, K. M. Smith & C. J. Suckling) Pyrroles and related compounds. XXXVII. Harderoporphyrin. *Tetrahedron* **32**, 2757.

(195) 1977 (With J. Rimmer, K. M. Smith & J. F. Unsworth) Pyrroles and related compounds. XXXVIII. Porphobilinogen synthesis. *J. chem. Soc., Perkin Trans. 1*, p. 332.

(196) (With I. J. Galpin, B. K. Handa, D. Hudson, A. G. Jackson, S. R. Omse, R. Ramage, B. Singh & R. G. Tyson) Studies on the synthesis of 1–75 fragment of a lysozyme analogue. *Proc. Fourteenth European Peptide Symp., Wepion, Belgium*, **1976**, p. 247. Brussels: Editions de l'Université de Bruxelles.

(197) (With A. M. Choudhury, S. Moore, R. Ramage, P. M. Richards, W. D. L. Moroder, G. Wendlberger & E. Wünsch) Synthesis of human big gastrin-I. *Proc. Fourteenth European Peptide Symp., Wepion, Belgium, 1976*, p. 257. Brussels: Editions de l'Université de Bruxelles.

(198) 1977 Towardsthe synthesis of proteins (Bakerian Lecture). *Proc. R. Soc. Lond.* A **353**, 441.

(199) 'Leopold Ruzicka'. *Nature, Lond.* **266**, 392.

(200) (With M. J. Bushell, B. Evans & K. M. Smith) Syntheses and properties of *meso*-methyl porphyrins and chlorins. *Heterocycles* **7**, 67.

(201) (With D. HUDSON, I. MACINTYRE, R. SHARPE, M. SZELKE & G. FINK) The synthesis, assay and conformation of methionine enkephalin. *Molecular endocrinology* (ed. I. MacIntyre & M. Szelke), p. 269. Amsterdam: Elsevier/North-Holland.

(202) 1978 Chairman's opening remarks. Further perspectives in organic chemistry. *Ciba Fdn Symp*. 53 (N.S.), p. 1. Amsterdam: Elsevier/North Holland.

(203) (With I. J. GALPIN, A. G. JACKSON, P. NOBLE & R. RAMAGE) Improved method of gel filtration of protected peptides using Sephadex LH-60. *J. Chromatogr.* **147**, 424.

(204) (With I. J. GALPIN, B. K. HANDA, S. MOORE & R. RAMAGE) Purification of protected peptides by GPC. *Chromatography of synthetic and biological polymers* (ed. R. Epton), vol. 1, p. 331.

(205) (With C. J. DOCKRAY & R. A. GREGORY) *Gastroenterology* **75**, 556.

James Walter McLeod

# JAMES WALTER McLEOD

2 January 1887 — 11 March 1978

Elected F.R.S. 1933

By Sir Graham Wilson, F.R.S. and K. S. Zinnemann

## Family

J. W. McLeod was born in Dumbarton on 2 January 1887. His father, John, an architect, belonged to a family whose occupations ranged through law, medicine, the civil service, industry and commerce, conducted mainly in the south of Scotland. John McLeod had built up a successful practice, and at the time of his marriage in 1884 had just completed the new Glasgow synagogue—a surprising commission for a Presbyterian. He was then aged forty-five and his bride, Lilias Symington McClymont, who was twenty-one years his junior, was the daughter of what was then described as a gentleman farmer in Borgue, Kirkcudbrightshire.

Less than four years later John died of diabetes, leaving his widow with two sons, Norman and James. Norman was to work for many years on irrigation schemes in India, and later to become a technical adviser to the World Bank. Four months after her husband's death, Mrs McLeod bore a third son who was named John, after his father. He was to train as a lawyer and to make his career in banking.

The widow was well provided for. After two or three years she moved to Edinburgh where she sent the two elder boys to George Watson's College. The health of the youngest gave continuous concern, and in 1895 she was advised to take him to Switzerland. The entire family, possessed of no more than the elements of school French, settled in Lausanne. The boys were entered at the Collège Cantonal where they found themselves unable to understand a word. In a surprisingly short time, however, they remedied this defect, and for the rest of his life James Walter spoke French fluently, though with little concession to the accent or intonation of the natives. He was to acquire a similar command of German in the Army of Occupation 25 years later.

When the boys reached Public School age the two eldest were sent as boarders to Mill Hill on the northern outskirts of London, and later to Glasgow University. Their mother returned to Scotland leaving the youngest in Switzerland, where his health gradually improved. In 1914 she moved to London and stayed there till her death in 1952.

## Education and Career

At Glasgow University McLeod began to study medicine in 1903 at the age of 16 and graduated M.B., Ch.B. with commendation in 1908. He excelled in rugby, cricket and athletics. After holding two house appointments he served for a time as ship's surgeon on the India route. In 1909 he was awarded a Coates scholarship, and in 1910 he became a Carnegie scholar. For three years he worked in Professor Robert Muir's Department of Pathology. This was in the heyday of the Department, which supplied professors to most of the universities in England. Under the direction of Robert Muir (later Sir Robert) and of Carl Browning (later F.R.S.), he studied the properties of streptococcal haemolysin. During this period of initiation he received a training in scientific method and objectives that was to serve him all his life.

In 1912 he left Glasgow to take up an appointment as Assistant Lecturer in Pathology at Charing Cross Hospital Medical School in London. When war broke out in 1914 he was gazetted a Temporary Lieutenant in the Royal Army Medical Corps, and later promoted to Captain in charge of the Eighth Mobile Laboratory. In France he was stationed mainly near Amiens. Four times he was mentioned in dispatches, and finally he was awarded the military O.B.E.

On demobilization he joined the Department of Pathology at Leeds University as Lecturer in Bacteriology. In 1922 he was appointed to the newly instituted Brotherton Chair of Bacteriology. In this capacity he worked alongside Professor Matthew John Stewart, who held the Chair of Pathology, until his retirement in 1952. For the last four years of his tenure he succeeded M. J. Stewart as Dean of the Medical Faculty and Chairman of the Board of Medicine.

At the end of this period he, now an Emeritus Professor, and his wife left Leeds and went to live in the lonely Dye Cottage, near Longformacus in the Lammermuirs. On her death in 1953 he left the cottage, but kept it as a weekend home. Moving to Edinburgh he once more became immersed in scientific inquiry. With the support of the Scottish Hospital Endowments Research Trust he joined the Department of Surgery of the University, working there from 1954 to 1963. When his grant expired he found space in the Central Microbiological Laboratories at the Western General Hospital, where he continued his researches till 1973 with assistance from the Royal Society and the Medical Research Council.

McLeod received many honours. He was chosen to be a corresponding member of the Société de Biologie, Paris, in 1928. In 1933 he was elected to the Fellowship of the Royal Society, London. He was made an Honorary Member of the Scottish Society for Experimental Medicine in 1957, and in the same year a Fellow of the Royal Society of Edinburgh; an Honorary Member of the Pathological Society of Great Britain and Ireland in 1961, and an Honorary Fellow of the Royal College of Pathologists in 1970. From 1949 to 1952 he served as President of the Society of General Microbiology. He received the degree of Sc.D. (*hon. causa*) Dublin in 1946 and of LL.D. (*hon. causa*) Glasgow in 1961.

McLeod's first wife, whom he married in 1914, was Jean Christine Garvie, M.A. (Glasgow). According to Sir John McNee, who shared the same laboratory

This photograph of the bronze head of J. W. McLeod by Epstein was taken by the Photographic Section of the Leeds University Audio-Visual Service. The bust itself was commissioned in 1952 on the occasion of Professor McLeod's retirement.

as McLeod at Glasgow, she was a splendid girl of great personality and character, and deeply religious. She came from a Scottish family established at Zyrardów in Poland, and her mother, though Slav in appearance and speaking English with a strong Polish accent, was also of Scottish stock. By Jean he had two sons and five daughters. The second boy died in an accident when only four years old. The eldest daughter, Lilias Richard, M.B., Ch.B., became the third wife of the Earl of Cromartie in 1962. One other daughter qualified in medicine at Dundee, and another trained as a nurse. The son, Thomas McLeod, M.A., C.Eng., F.I.E.E., became a technical expert in Plessey Telecommunications Ltd. In 1956 McLeod married again. His wife, Joyce Anita Shannon, M.B., Ch.B., a general practitioner in Edinburgh, was of great help to him while he was investigating a new method of assessing the action of leucocidins. With her he shared a happy life for over 20 years.

McLeod's last days were clouded by illness. Besides trouble with his hip, which was not altogether relieved by replacement of the joint in 1968, he had an operation for cataract in 1970 and for prostatic enlargement in 1974. By the end of August 1974 he was physically unable to go to the laboratory any longer. His memory failed, and he suffered from delusions, mental confusion and other manifestations of cerebral arteriosclerosis. For the last year of his life he was confined to the geriatric ward of the Royal Victoria Hospital. His death on 11 March 1978 was due to bronchopneumonia.

The bronze bust by Epstein, which was commissioned in 1952 on the occasion of McLeod's retirement from his Leeds post, now stands in the library of the new medical school. Epstein is said to have been doubtful about accepting the commission, but changed his mind once he had seen McLeod's fine head.

## Scientific work

McLeod's scientific career extended over a period of more than 60 years. Broadly speaking it may be divided into five periods:

(1) from 1909 to 1918 he worked in Glasgow, London and France on streptococci and on illnesses occurring in the Army during World War I;

(2) the next ten years were spent at Leeds, mainly on problems of bacterial respiration;

(3) the third period from 1930 to 1940 was devoted to a study of the various types of the diphtheria bacillus and the clinical characters of the disease to which they gave rise;

(4) during and after World War II, up till 1952, when he retired from his professorship at Leeds, his main interest was the rationale of sulphonamide action;

(5) and at Edinburgh from 1952 to 1973, with an intermission of two years, he was occupied chiefly with a study of urinary infections in medical and surgical practice.

### *Streptococci*

Though most of McLeod's work on streptococci was carried out before World War I, he kept on coming back to the subject from time to time; and his contributions to the Medical Research Council's System of Bacteriology on these organisms and on pneumococci were not made till 1929.

As already mentioned, he started with a Coates scholarship in 1909 at Glasgow University in Professor Robert Muir's (later Sir Robert) Department of Pathology and with a Carnegie scholarship in 1910. Under Dr Carl Browning's supervision he studied the properties of the haemolysin produced by pathogenic streptococci. The amount of this he found to be proportional to the extent of growth. The lysin was thermolabile, being destroyed by heat at 50–55 °C in 30 min. With J. W. McNee (later Sir John) he showed that rabbits with little natural antistreptolysin in their blood died of toxaemia after injection with the lysin, displaying both haemoglobinaemia and haemoglobinuria. Less susceptible rabbits survived repeated injections, but suffered from anaemia and hyperplasia of the bone marrow. What was very curious was that, though natural antihaemolysin was present in some degree in the blood of man, the horse, the rabbit and the guinea-pig, even large injections of haemolysin failed to produce antihaemolysin or to increase the natural immunity of the animals. It was therefore not surprising to find that antistreptococcal serum prepared in the horse was useless for the treatment of infected rabbits.

McLeod found that, in addition to the haemolysin, pathogenic streptococci produced a leucocidin. Whether the lytic action on the blood cells and the destructive action on the leucocytes were due to one and the same toxin was not clear.

The virulence of streptococci for man appeared to depend on their activity as toxin producers and on their ability to produce toxin in the blood. Some correspondence was noticed between the capacity of a strain of streptococci to produce haemolysin when grown in fresh human serum and the severity of the lesion from which it was isolated.

When grown on heated blood agar—often referred to as chocolate agar—non-haemolytic streptococci formed colonies surrounded by a yellow-green halo. The reason for this coloration formed a subject of great interest to McLeod. Working with Gordon, he found that these organisms, when grown in media freely exposed to the air and not too rich in catalase, formed hydrogen peroxide, and that the greater the amount of $H_2O_2$ formed the more pronounced was the yellow-green colour of the colonies. From further observations it was concluded that the appearance of colonies of streptococci on blood media probably depended on the interplay of a complex group of bacterial activities, notably haemolysin production, acid production, reducing activities, $H_2O_2$ production, and possibly peptic and tryptic digestion of the corpuscles.

The appellation of viridans to non-haemolytic streptococci had therefore little significance unless the conditions of growth were defined. The greenish colour appeared to be due to an oxidation product of haematin, which itself was formed by the action of heat on the haemoglobin in the blood during preparation of the chocolate agar medium. It may be added that, even now, the exact cause of the greenish coloration is still under dispute.

In classifying streptococci into haemolytic and non-haemolytic groups, McLeod defined lysis as the ability to secrete a filtrable haemolysin when a small quantity of a young culture in 20% serum broth was incubated for $1\frac{1}{2}$ h with 0.5 ml of a 5% suspension of washed ox corpuscles. The non-haemolytic group could be divided into the facultatively anaerobic, including the pneumococcus, and the strictly anaerobic sub-groups.

With Wyon and with Gordon he observed that the growth of *Streptococcus pyogenes*, the typical virulent streptococcus, was inhibited by high concentrations of tryptic digests. This action was apparently due to amino acids, those mainly responsible being glycine, cystine, tryptophan and phenylalanine. This organism was almost devoid of the power to reduce cystine and its compounds, as well as such dyes as neutral red, methylene blue and litmus. The inhibitory effect of amino acids on growth was a subject McLeod later studied in another connection.

### *The years 1914–20*

During World War I McLeod, who was in charge of the Eighth Mobile Laboratory in France, was occupied almost entirely with clinical pathology. He wisely took advantage of such opportunities as came his way to carry out research investigations on the material available. Besides making observations on the cultivation of the typhoid bacillus in a medium containing brilliant green, as recommended by Carl Browning; devising with R. E. Bevan-Brown an apparatus for the withdrawal of blood aseptically from a vein and for sampling the culture medium during incubation; and assessing with A. G. Ritchie the value of the agglutination reaction in the diagnosis of dysentery, he collaborated with a French military captain, P. Ameuille, in a study of the effect of trench warfare on renal function, and ascribed the frequency in British troops of albuminuria to the excess of protein and the lack of fresh vegetables in their diet, which led to a mild degree of scurvy. With D. L. Tate he found that splenic enlargement and a moderate polymorphonuclear leucocytosis were almost constant features of trench fever.

At the end of the war he was joined by A. G. Ritchie and C. A. Dottridge in an attempt to measure the prevalence of Pfeiffer's bacillus, *Haemophilus influenzae*, before, during and after the great influenza pandemic of 1918–19. Ten years or more before the discovery of the viral origin of influenza, the part played by Pfeiffer's bacillus in the causation of this disease was a matter on which the leading bacteriologists of the day were at variance. I (G. S. W.) well remember, as a very junior bacteriologist, a meeting of the Pathological Society of Great Britain and Ireland at Charing Cross Hospital Medical School at which completely divergent views were expressed and the consequent general perplexity that was felt. The contention of those who supported the role of Pfeiffer's bacillus that their opponents had failed to isolate this organism because of their bad technique was manifestly untrue, since the same medium and methods had often been used by the two sets of workers. The difference in the findings was almost certainly due to the variation in time, place and occupation of the frequency of Pfeiffer's bacillus in the upper respiratory tract of man.

A final investigation, carried out with P. Govenlock, and published in 1921, was on a subject that McLeod had not touched on before, namely the production of bactericidins by micro-organisms. In both its subject matter and its technique, it was almost prophetic in anticipating the work on the sulphonamides and penicillin that occupied the bacteriological world twenty years later. They found that many bacteria produced substances inhibiting their own growth and that of other species. They were heat-labile, at 80–85 °C, and needed for their formation a free supply of oxygen. The pneumococcus was studied most thoroughly and was found to produce substances inhibiting the growth of staphylococci and of pneumococci themselves but not that of streptococci, with the exception of *Streptococcus faecalis*. For demonstrating these substances a modification of Eijkman's disk technique was used. It was a long time before these substances, now known as bacteriocines, were studied by other workers and found to be of value in the identification and differentiation of bacteria.

### *Bacterial respiration*

The subject of bacterial respiration fascinated McLeod and kept him busy during the 1920s. Little attention had been paid to the physiology of bacterial growth, and it was not till the end of the twenties that biochemists such as J. H. Quastel, F.R.S., and Marjory Stephenson, F.R.S., at Cambridge took it up seriously. The originality and authoritativeness of McLeod's work were recognized by his being asked by the Medical Research Council to contribute articles on various aspects of the subject for their 'System of bacteriology in relation to medicine' published in 1929–31; and by E. O. Jordan and I. S. Falk in the United States of America on bacterial oxidations and reductions in 'The newer knowledge of bacteriology and immunology' which was published in 1928. In all his work on this subject he made full use of the staff in Emeritus Professor Cohen's adjoining unit of Organic Chemistry. McLeod's interest in bacterial respiration appears to have been first aroused by noting the green discoloration that appeared around colonies of pneumococci grown in heated blood agar (chocolate agar). In collaboration with Gordon, who was a member of his department, he showed that this phenomenon was caused by the production of hydrogen peroxide, and that it was $H_2O_2$ which was responsible for the rapid death of the organisms. $H_2O_2$ could also be demonstrated when pneumococci were grown in a shallow layer of 10% serum broth that had been heated to 65 °C for half an hour to drive off catalase. The substance, thought to be a vitamin, in fresh tissue fluid that promoted the growth of pneumococci was probably catalase, which protected the organisms against the hydrogen peroxide they formed.

Passing on to the study of other organisms they found that lactobacilli also produced $H_2O_2$, as manifested by the green coloration around colonies on chocolate agar, and by the bluish-black coloration on a blood medium containing benzidine (Penfold's technique). The rapid death of vegetative cells of strictly anaerobic bacteria when exposed to air seemed to be explicable by the formation of $H_2O_2$. This supposition was strengthened by observing that a green ring appeared at the upper limit of growth in a deep tube of chocolate agar; that the growth of anaerobes was promoted by catalase; and, in a paper published after his retirement from the Leeds chair, that if the organisms in a liquid culture were centrifuged down, the medium and metabolites in the supernatant fluid removed, and the deposited cells suspended in peroxide-free distilled water and oxygenated, a positive reaction for $H_2O_2$ could nearly always be shown.

From further study it appeared probable that all bacteria in the presence of oxygen formed $H_2O_2$; and on this basis and on that of the formation of catalase they divided bacteria into four groups:

(1) those that were very sensitive to $H_2O_2$ and devoid of catalase, such as the potential producers of peroxide—the anaerobes;
(2) those that were moderately sensitive to $H_2O_2$ and devoid of catalase, such as the peroxide producers—pneumococci, lactobacilli and some streptococci;
(3) those that were moderately sensitive to $H_2O_2$ and devoid of catalase, but that did not produce $H_2O_2$, such as Shiga's bacillus and the haemoglobinophilic group of organisms; and
(4) those that were sensitive in varying degree to $H_2O_2$ but produced catalase—a group that included most aerobes and facultative anaerobes.

The introduction by Clark and Lubbs in the United States of dyes that acted as indicators of the oxidation-reduction potential enabled McLeod to study the reducing action of bacteria, and the relation between this action and the formation of peroxide. Again working with Gordon, he found that all bacteria possessing an active reducing mechanism, i.e. by generating active or atomic hydrogen, and devoid of catalase, produced $H_2O_2$.

In 1928 McLeod and Gordon studied the presence or absence of a thermolabile oxidase-producing system in various bacteria. For demonstrating this they used a 1–1.5% solution of dimethyl-para-phenylene-diamine hydrochloride. When this was poured over a pure culture, oxidase-producing organisms took on a maroon colour within 5 min, deepening to black within half an hour. This reaction distinguished clearly between gonococci, which were positive, and staphylococci and streptococci, which were negative; and also between the oxidase-positive cholera vibrio and the negative colon bacillus. It provided a most valuable means of diagnosis in patients suspected of suffering from gonorrhoea. For this purpose, Ellingworth, McLeod and Gordon found that the tetramethyl compound was superior to the dimethyl. It was oxidized to a substance giving a blue-violet colour that did not turn black but faded away under the influence of reducing enzymes. Its lower toxicity was of special value in enabling colonies of gonococci to be picked off a plate and subcultured before they were killed by the dye.

In his article on bacterial respiration in the Medical Research Council's *System of Bacteriology* in 1930 McLeod brought together many of the observations that he and Gordon had made during the previous eight years, including reducing enzymes, the oxidizing activities of dehydrogenating ferments, and the influence of the gaseous environment in bacterial growth and metabolism. Expanding their previous classification (p. 427) they divided bacteria into two main classes:

*Class 1*

(a) Anaerobic bacteria deficient in catalase, strong reducers, relatively insensitive to potassium thiocyanate (which arrests oxidation processes dependent on the utilization of free oxygen, and paralyses cytochrome by fixing it in the reduced state) and devoid of oxidizing power for substituted phenols;

(b) microaerophilic bacteria, such as the lactobacilli, that are active reducers, and form only traces of $H_2O_2$;

(c) organisms, such as *Streptococcus faecalis*, that are tolerant of oxygen, have a moderate reducing action, and do not form peroxide.

*Class 2*

Bacteria provided with catalase, sensitive to KCN, and incapable of accumulating in cultures detectable traces of peroxide:

(a) bacteria, such as facultative aerobes and anaerobes, that reduce both dyes and nitrates, and lower the redox potential considerably;

(b) bacteria that grow more abundantly aerobically and are rapid oxidase-producers;

(b1) bacteria very sensitive to $H_2O_2$, forming only a small amount of catalase, and reducing nitrates, e.g. vibrios;

(b2) bacteria producing catalase freely, e.g. meningococcus and *Pseudomonas aeruginosa*.

Shiga's bacillus did not fit into any of these categories; though it was sensitive to KCN, it lacked catalase and formed no $H_2O_2$.

Though relating more to metabolism than to respiration, it may be mentioned here that McLeod, working first with Wyon and later with Gordon, found that the growth of some micro-organisms was inhibited by amino acids. He studied the effect of 14 different amino acids on the growth of bacteria in peptone broth. No effect was noted on staphylococci or *Escherichia coli*. The growth of some of the more delicate organisms, however, was inhibited by cystine, glycine, phenylalanine and especially tryptophan, but favoured by taurine, aspartic acid and alanine. The toxic effect appeared to be due to products of deaminization, such as indole, which was found to be more toxic than carbolic acid. Addition of serum to the medium had a protective effect against such toxic products.

With Wheatley and Phelon, McLeod studied in particular the difficulties met with in cultivation of the gonococcus. This organism required carbon, amino acids, and a suitable colloid to protect it against the toxic effect of some of the amino acids present in meat extract, thus enabling it to assimilate them. For this purpose blood heated to 60–100 °C was superior to other colloids. The failure of the gonococcus to grow on ordinary nutrient agar was ascribed to an unduly low ratio of protective colloid to amino nitrogen.

The rapid death of gonococci and meningococci in aerobic cultures was traced, at any rate in part, to the high pH, 8.6–9.0, caused by ammonia and alkaline carbonates that resulted from oxidation of sodium salts of fatty acids in the medium.

One further investigation made during the twenties in collaboration with Sugare was into the bacteriological diagnosis of whooping cough. *Bordetella pertussis* could be isolated from the sputum during the first week of the disease, but less often later. The differential features of the organism from *Haemophilus influenzae* were described, among which the strong catalase effect was stressed. The Medical Research Council's trial on the prevention of whooping cough by vaccination in which he participated before 1951 caused him to take up the subject again. In collaboration with Betty Dawson, Enid Farnworth and D. E. Nicholson, he failed to improve on the original Bordet–Gengou medium for the cultivation of *Bordetella pertussis*. He attributed its excellence to the potato extract it contained, which provided optimal concentrations of the amino acids and peptides required for growth. Many peptones he examined were found to inhibit development of the organism.

## *Diphtheria*

The work that McLeod is best known by and that brought him international fame was that on diphtheria—its bacteriology, epidemiology and diagnosis. It occupied him and his numerous collaborators most of the ten years 1930–40, but after this period he came back to the subject from time to time. During the latter part of the nineteenth century and the first 40 years of the present century diphtheria was a widespread serious disease of childhood causing in 1901 in England and Wales a death rate of about 300 per million inhabitants. It was likewise common in north-west Europe, and during the first 20 or 30 years of the century in the United States and Canada. Its final virtual eradication as the result of active immunization in the forties and fifties was one of the triumphs of preventive medicine, but does not come into our story here.

### *Types of diphtheria bacilli*

McLeod's first paper on this subject was published in 1931 under the authorship of Anderson, Happold, McLeod and Thomson. Incidentally it may be noted that, when working with collaborators, he usually arranged their names in alphabetical order. In this paper he described two main forms, and later on an intermediate form, of diphtheria bacilli, and a new medium on which to distinguish between them and to improve diagnosis. The medium used was the same heated blood agar (chocolate agar) as that on which his studies on bacterial respiration had been conducted, with the exception that the base consisted of meat extract heated not above 75 °C, as recommended by Hedley Wright, instead of the usual 100 °C. To it was added 0.04% potassium tellurite, which turned colonies grey to black by the reducing activity of the growing organisms.

The two main types were designated *gravis* and *mitis* according to the severity of the disease with which they tended to be associated. The type having characters in between these two, and that was met with far less often, was designated *intermedius*. Without going into more detail than is here justified it may be said that, broadly speaking, the bacilli of *gravis* type were usually short, straight, uniformly stained rods having few or no granules; forming low convex pearly grey or greyish-black colonies that assumed in 3–5 days a daisy-head appearance; fermenting starch and glycogen; and being almost invariably virulent for the guinea-pig. Bacilli of the *mitis* type, representing the classical diphtheria bacillus of Löffler, were usually long curved pleomorphic rods with prominent metachromatic granules; forming colonies that varied greatly in size, of a mushroom-grey colour, assuming on further incubation a poached-egg appearance; failing to ferment starch or glycogen; tending to be of lower virulence for the guinea-pig than *gravis* strains, and, when isolated from diphtheria carriers, often non-virulent. *Intermedius* strains, on the whole, resembled *gravis* more closely than *mitis* strains. For distinction he also attached great importance to the three different growth forms in broth—a feature often neglected.

Many observations were made on the relation of the three types of bacilli and the severity of the cases of diphtheria from which they were cultivated. In a paper written in association with Leete and Morrison, McLeod described how in Hull, where the morbidity and mortality of the disease were high, the *gravis* type was responsible for 35 out of 40 toxic deaths and the *intermedius* type for the remaining five. In *gravis* cases the toxaemia ran so rapid a course that serum treatment was often unavailing. *Mitis* cases in Hull were few, and were mild and non-toxic.

Observations, with Anderson, Cooper and Happold, in a series of 500 cases at Leeds confirmed these findings. *Gravis* and *intermedius* strains accounted for nearly all cases of paralysis.

Later observations on over 6000 cases in England and Wales and in Germany occurring during the four years 1931–35, made with a number of collaborators, were reported at a meeting of the Royal Society of Medicine in 1936; the whole subject was reviewed and some of the previous findings were amplified. The *gravis* cases had the highest case-fatality rate and the greatest incidence of paralysis. *Intermedius* cases had nearly as high a case-fatality rate, and an equally high tendency to produce haemorrhagic lesions. *Mitis* strains were more likely than *gravis* or *intermedius* to cause obstructive lesions in the respiratory tract, spreading down to the larynx and lungs; otherwise they were rarely responsible for death. Typical *gravis* strains were so constantly pathogenic to guinea-pigs that virulence tests for confirmatory purpose were deemed superfluous.

In a paper in 1939 with Orr and Hester Woodcock, McLeod gave an account of the morbid anatomy of diphtheria. In *gravis* infections there was much less superficial membrane formation than in *mitis* infections, and less tendency for it to extend into the intrathoracic air passages; the membrane itself, too, was of a looser texture. The tissues of the inflamed parts were penetrated more deeply, and the lymph nodes and surrounding tissue were more often involved. The tonsils in particular were affected, and in some cases were completely replaced by fibrinopurulent and haemorrhagic exudate. Death in *gravis* and *intermedius* infections resulted usually from the action of the diphtheria toxin on the heart and kidneys, and *mitis* infections from respiratory obstruction as the result of membrane formation.

Seven years later McLeod again reviewed the subject. He noted that there was a small proportion of strains of diphtheria bacilli that did not correspond exactly to any of the three types. They were commonest in cases of mild or moderate severity, and were found more often in convalescents and carriers than in severe cases. They had never been observed to become epidemic. *Intermedius* strains caused, as a rule, a slightly lower death rate than *gravis* strains, and disappeared more rapidly in convalescence. This, he thought, might be the reason why they were less likely than *gravis* strains to cause epidemics.

The classification of diphtheria bacilli into three types was misunderstood in the United States. Frobisher, Adams and Kuhns, for example, used the term *minimus* to describe strains from an outbreak at Baltimore in 1944 of greater severity than had previously been experienced. They formed very fine colonies and fermented glucose slowly. When examined by Johnstone and McLeod they were found, for all practical purposes, to be identical with *intermedius* strains. Obviously, Frobisher and his colleagues interpreted the designation *intermedius* as applying to colony size and not to clinical severity. What was far more important was Frobisher's description of virulent strains that fermented saccharose. Saccharose-fermenting strains had always been regarded as belonging to the diphtheroid group of bacilli bearing no relation to the causation of disease. The correctness of Frobisher's observation was confirmed by Johnstone and McLeod, and many years later by Christovão in Brazil on a much larger sample of strains, who found that 28% of 199 virulent strains isolated at São Paulo were saccharolytic.

On the other hand, the fermentation of starch had been defined originally as a property of *gravis* strains associated with virulence. Examining more than 200 starch-fermenting strains from the United Kingdom, West and Central Europe, and the Mediterranean area, McLeod and Robinson found that 5–6% of these proved non-virulent to the guinea-pig, and that 4% of all the typical *gravis* strains were likewise non-virulent. The association, therefore, between starch fermentation and virulence for the guinea-pig was not absolute.

Surveying the epidemiology of diphtheria in north-west Europe and in North America in the period 1920–46, McLeod noted that a high ratio of urban to rural population favoured a continuously high level of diphtheria incidence. Differences in the prevalence of the disease during and after the World War I occurred in different countries and in different towns in the same country. His analysis of the findings established the importance of *gravis* strains in the causation of epidemic diphtheria, and of the ability of *intermedius* strains to cause severe disease. It seemed probable that fluctuations in the occurrence of outbreaks of diphtheria were dependent on the particular type of bacillus that gained access to the population.

Besides the bacteriology and epidemiology of diphtheria, McLeod and his colleagues paid a great deal of attention to the diagnosis of the disease. At a meeting of the Association of Clinical Pathologists in 1935 they recorded that diphtheria bacilli had been isolated from 11% of throat swabs cultured on tellurite medium as against only 3% on Loeffler's medium. In a later communication the results on various media that had been recommended for diagnostic purposes were compared. On the whole, Neill's medium appeared to be the best. They recommended that suspicious colonies on any medium should be picked on to plain heated blood agar for a study of colony formation and of the morphology of the bacilli when stained with alkaline methylene blue. All atypical strains should be tested for virulence. For this purpose they preferred the injection of a quarter to an eighth of the growth on an 18-h Loeffler's slope into the axilla of a guinea-pig to the simultaneous injection of several strains into the skin. A control animal injected with antiserum was unnecessary, provided that the test animal died with a local lesion, pleural effusion and oedema combined with patchy congestion and collapse of the lungs, congestion with or without haemorrhage of the adrenal bodies, and diphtheria bacilli demonstrable in the local lesion.

The article on diphtheria in the 1964 edition of *Encyclopaedia Britannica* covered the whole subject.

During and after World War II McLeod made observations on a miscellany of subjects. With Gordon he described a simple and rapid method of distinguishing *Clostridium oedematiens* (*Cl. novyi*) from other bacteria associated with gas gangrene. Colonies of this organism when left for half an hour exposed to the air became surrounded by green haloes, and when grown on chocolate agar containing benzidine were, again after exposure to the air, coloured black. Both phenomena were due to the formation of hydrogen peroxide. Other clostridia studied showed neither of these phenomena, with the exception of *Clostridium botulinum*, which was slightly positive.

In a report in 1946 with Downie and Robinson on two cases of tetanus, he brought evidence to suggest that dust in the operating theatre was responsible for the infection. In both cases *Clostridium tetani* was cultivated from the dust of the operating theatre floor.

With Czekalowski and Rodican he studied the growth and respiration of *Leptospira icterohaemorrhagiae* in semi-solid media. In deep media, growth occurred in a band a few millimetres below the surface, as Dinger had described. This disk formation was inhibited by a 1/3000 concentration of potassium thiocyanate. The organisms required gaseous oxygen, but were microaerophilic; they lacked catalase, had only slight reducing activity and failed to produce recognizable traces of $H_2O_2$. Witte's peptone was found to be the best for promoting growth, and tryptic digest broth was equally good. The value of laked blood appeared to depend on its catalase content, since the leptospira did not produce this enzyme. The optimal pH for growth was around 7.6.

### *Investigations into the mode of action of sulphonamides*

One of the obligations of the academic staff in McLeod's department was an evening visit to the premises, taken in rotation, between the hours of 8 and

10 p.m. for the reading of tellurite plates inoculated on the previous day; this he found necessary for the early detection of colonies of *C. diphtheriae intermedius* which appear only after 36 h incubation. On these occasions it was quite usual to see the lights switched on in McLeod's room where he sat reading and abstracting English and foreign language medical journals till late at night. One of the subjects of his reading during the 1930s was the antibacterial action of Prontosil and, particularly, after the papers of the Tréfouëls, Fourneau, Nitti and Bovet (1937–38), of sulphanilamide which the French workers had identified as the active part of Prontosil. The mode of action of sulphanilamide occupied McLeod and various collaborators for nine years. On the basis of his earlier work on bacterial respiration he assumed that the *in vivo* action of the sulphonamide compounds was dependent on bacterial oxidation, and that some oxidation derivatives of sulphanilamide, yet to be identified, ought to have much greater bactericidal activity *in vitro* than could be shown for sulphanilamide itself. This line of investigation had been suggested first in the French literature by Mayer, and Mayer and Oechslin in 1938–39, and had been picked up by some American investigators, to be finally chosen by McLeod for intensive research in late 1939 and developed in three papers published in 1939, 1940 and 1942. His efforts in this direction probably resulted in the greatest disappointment in his whole career. In 1944, in two papers, McLeod formally acknowledged the correctness of (a) D. D. Woods's observations on the complete inhibition by *p*-aminobenzoic acid of the antibacterial action of sulphonamides; (b) Paul Fildes's theory, based on D. D. Woods's findings, of *p*-aminobenzene-sulphonamide blocking an unidentified enzyme system that accepts the intermediate breakdown product *p*-aminobenzoic acid as an essential metabolite. He showed in these papers that access of oxygen increased the antibacterial effect of sulphonamides. He regarded the oxidation products of sulphonamides as an essential step in their effective action on bacteria without having been able to explain the relation of his observations to the blocking effect of *p*-aminobenzoic acid on the action of sulphonamides.

During the later stages of these experiments, haemoglobin in the form of laked horse blood had been added to some solid media to serve as a colour indicator for oxidation or reduction. He could not help observing that laked horse blood potentiated sulphonamide action on staphylococci, which did not occur when nutrient agar alone or with addition of laked blood from other species was used. Having followed a wrong line of approach to the mode of action of sulphonamides McLeod now concentrated his efforts on an attempt at explaining the 'potentiating' effect of horse blood on the *in vitro* antibacterial action of sulphonamides, only to be forestalled by Harper and Cawston. In 1945 these authors postulated the presence of unidentified substances in nutrient agar or broth that were inhibitory to the antibacterial action of sulphonamides; and noted the neutralization of this inhibitory effect by laked horse blood. Though not denying the possible truth of the Harper and Cawston hypothesis, he showed in two semisynthetic media known not to contain sulphonamide antagonists that the addition of 2% laked horse blood resulted in greater inhibition of *E. coli* and shigellae by sulphonamides than could be obtained without it. Additionally, a Harper-Cawston broth (laked horse blood filtrate concentrated fivefold *in vacuo* at a temperature below 50 °C) increased the inhibition-diffusion zone of sulphonamides. From these observations McLeod concluded that potentiation of sulphonamide action must play a considerable part in the change brought about by the addition of equine haemoglobin. The closely argued discussion of this report is typical of McLeod's tenacity.

In the context of sulphonamide action a useful paper ought to be mentioned which he published with J. Gordon in 1941 and which he regarded as one of his contributions to the war effort. It had become accepted at that time that the prophylaxis of gas gangrene depended on surgical wound toilet together with the liberal use of sterilized sulphonamide powder in the wound. The prophylactic use of polyvalent or monovalent antitoxin was deprecated officially. In a series of experiments with mice and guinea-pigs McLeod showed that the success of the prophylactic use of sulphonamide injections was limited by the size of the subcutaneous infecting dose of three clostridial species, whereas prophylactic injections of specific antitoxin near the site of infection resulted in survival of from 50 to 100% of the animals. Contrary to the official recommendation to use antitoxin only therapeutically, neither antitoxin nor sulphonamides saved any animal lives when given in established cases of gas gangrene. McLeod and Gordon suggested reversal of the official recommendation, i.e. to use clostridial antitoxin prophylactically and not therapeutically. This report could be criticized for the comparatively small number of animals used, but it must be remembered that wartime imposed severe restrictions on resources and assistance. The advent of penicillin prevented more thorough testing of the conclusions, although the use of clostridial antitoxin near contaminated wound sites should retain its value in conjunction with penicillin and may deserve retesting.

## The Edinburgh period

### *Urinary tract infections*

McLeod's appointment to the Department of Surgery at Edinburgh University was made with a view to entrusting him with the investigation of (a) urinary tract infections arising after urological operations, and (b) of paraplegic patients with an indwelling catheter who were liable to develop similar infections. The problem was not an easy one to solve because of so many variable factors, and the need for the full-time attention of an experienced investigator free from administrative and teaching duties. In a series of seven papers, the result of work carried out between the ages of 67 and 80, McLeod succeeded in defining some of the important sources and pathways of urinary tract infections in these groups of patients and suggesting some methods of preventing or delaying their occurrence. Additionally he devised improved methods for assessing the presence or absence of urinary tract infections in newborns and children.

The most dangerous postoperative infection of the urinary tract is that caused by *Pseudomonas aeruginosa*, which is not a commensal of the external male genitalia. To establish the sources of infection it was necessary to identify individual strains of the species. For this purpose Gould and McLeod (1960) had to devise a method of their own. Their procedures were too technical to be described here. Suffice it to say that two complicated methods had to be used simultaneously for the identification of individual strains isolated.

McLeod then proceeded to apply this method in two urological and one paraplegic hospital ward. Objects of examination were implements and apparatus on wards used in conjunction with patients' urine, dust samples from the floors of wards and the laboratory, the hospital water supplies, catheter lubricants, used blankets, and waste water in ward washbasins and laboratory sinks.

The occasional strain of *Ps. aeruginosa* found in the urine of patients on wards other than urological ones but not at all in that of patients from general practice was different from the three types in urological hospital wards and was usually transient. When the same strain was found more than once, it was in a patient who, as a rule, was confined to bed and had to use urine bottles and bed pans—articles that on urological wards habitually harboured this organism. An almost immediate result at the beginning of the investigation was the finding of *Ps. aeruginosa* in open-necked Winchester bottles collecting the urinary flow from indwelling catheters inserted during prostatectomies. This was a source of infection so obvious to McLeod that, after having isolated the ward strain in only three cases, he could not bring himself, for ethical reasons, to continue this particular aspect of the investigation until he had examined a statistically significant number of cases and controls. He insisted on replacement of open-necked Winchester bottles by a closed, sterilized system installed with aseptic technique. Finally, he came to the conclusion that *Ps. aeruginosa* in urinary infection was not introduced by catheterization, since the micro-organism was not part of the flora of the external male genitalia, did not persist in the dry state, and was, therefore, found only in dust exposed to recent heavy contamination. Its presence resulted from a hospital infection transmitted via urine bottles and bed pans. Sterilizing these, as was general practice, was not enough, as the hands of ward personnel might be infected by handling these implements after they had been used by patients. Urine bottles and bed pans, after proper sterilization, should contain sufficient 2% solution of carbolic acid or 0·2% solution of hibitane to prevent such transmission.

The scope of this investigation was widened subsequently to include micro-organisms other than *Ps. aeruginosa* that were frequently isolated from urinary tract infections. The programme was confined to operations on the bladder and particularly to prostatectomy (1959). First in frequency were coliform infections. Urinary tract infections with *Proteus* species were either present at the onset or occurred rather late in the postoperative period. They were usually afebrile, were associated with chronic urinary dysfunction and with stone formation, which resulted from the alkalinity of the urine and from failure to empty the bladder completely. Infections with *Staphylococcus aureus* and faecal streptococci occurred but rarely. *Ps. aeruginosa* was the only organism responsible for early death, proving fatal in three of the 72 cases studied. The infections it caused were more severe and persistent than those caused by other organisms.

Four years later McLeod found a partial solution to the problem of urinary tract infections with coliform micro-organisms and *Proteus* species. By the introduction of a highly complicated technique he succeeded in keeping three long-term patients free from urinary tract infection for more than 10 weeks in contrast to the average period of 12.5 days.

The last in this group are two reports in the *British Medical Journal* of 1967 published a week before McLeod's eighty-first birthday. Three other authors' names precede his but the design and style of the reports bear McLeod's hallmark. Both papers are concerned with urinary tract infections but this time in newborns and children up to the age of 14. Technical difficulties in the collection of suitable specimens of urine in young subjects presented themselves but, after the examination of normal children and of children suffering from urogenital infection, it proved possible to establish a standard of 10 cells/$mm^3$ combined with a bacterial count of $10^5$/ml in males and $10^6$/ml in females, below which infection was improbable.

*Heat-stable staphylococcal toxin, and a method for measuring leucocidal activity*

Presumably as the result of isolating large numbers of strains of staphylococci in his genito-urinary work, McLeod took up the study of thermostable toxin that many of the coagulase-positive strains of these produce. Death of rabbits injected intravenously with thermostable staphylococcal toxins occurred after 24 h. Only concentrated δ-toxins produced death consistently; heat-labile α-toxins caused death more usually within 5–30 min. Several strains of coagulase-negative staphylococci produced highly heat-resistant haemolysins that were active on human and rabbit red blood cells. These toxins were neither lethal nor antigenic, but were neutralized *in vitro* by normal serum. This curious neutralization distinguished these toxins from Elek and Levy's ε-haemolysin. During the course of this work he noted the presence of considerable quantities of leucocidin in heat-labile (α) toxins, and of smaller quantities in heat-stable (δ) toxins. With his second wife, Joyce, he found that the heat-stable leucocidins acted on leucocytes by producing cell disintegration, whereas heat-labile leucocidins stopped oscillation of the intracellular granules and altered the staining properties of leucocytes. Though Achard and Ramond in 1912 had formed the opinion that granular oscillation was independent of life, McLeod brought evidence to show that this was not so. The microscopic technique used was then applied to his study of the leucocidins that were thought to be present in diphtheria and tetanus toxins. In fact it was found that, in the absence of preservatives, purified specimens of these toxins contained no leucocidins. Leucocidins, therefore, could not be neutralized by commercial diphtheria antitoxin produced with such purified toxin. Yet, in the discussion McLeod expressed the belief that, in severe *gravis* diphtheria, leucodicins did play a part, because of the scarcity of leucocytes in the diphtheritic exudate. Apparently he must have overlooked the fact that in severe *gravis* diphtheria death intervenes too rapidly in cases coming to autopsy for an appreciable number of leucocytes to accumulate.

In this connection, it may be noted that McLeod had always hoped that some special pathogenic property of *C. diphtheria gravis* strains might be found, and was much disappointed when O'Meara's claim for 'substance B' in extracts of strains could not be substantiated by other workers, amongst whom was a member of his own staff. It must be remembered that more than 15 years had elapsed since he had seen the last case of clinical diphtheria. Research on this subject by him and his team had long ceased for lack of material and topical interest. Perhaps one should take care not to go back to a problem that at one time was of the greatest interest to many people unless similar circumstances arose again. There is a lot to be said for Theobald Smith's attitude that one should leave some work to be followed up and completed by others. After all, most advances are made by using work of predecessors as stepping stones. Moreover, posterity will always be the final judge of the value of any original work. And J. W. McLeod was an originator.

Summing up, it may be said that McLeod was a staunch laboratory worker. Though not a particularly able technician, he introduced numerous improvements into bench routine. As Professor Happold writes, there is no 'doubt that his contribution to the development of diagnostic bacteriology was immense'. The reason for this was a combination of thoroughness, patience and determination to do the best, coupled with a wide knowledge of the literature of his subject.

## Personality

I (G. S. W.) first met McLeod in 1912 when, as a prospective student, I was being shown round the Medical School of Charing Cross Hospital by the Dean. McLeod was working at a bench in the pathological laboratory. He was eight years older than I was, and I viewed him with some awe. His massive frame, his rugged features, and the serious, almost visionary, look in his half-closed eyes created in me an indelible impression. To my mind he appeared the prototype of a research scientist. Little did I think at the time that 60 years or so later I should be writing his obituary.

The next time I saw him was after the war when I listened eagerly to the opposing views of the bacteriological pundits of the day on the cause of epidemic influenza. Based on his own observations, McLeod cautiously favoured the aetiological role of Pfeiffer's bacillus. Not till more than ten years later did Smith, Andrewes and Laidlaw show that the disease was primarily due to a filtrable virus. Though this finding has been generally accepted, it must be remembered that all diseases are multifactorial in origin, and that the part played by Pfeiffer's bacillus in paving the way for the entry of the virus, or of complicating the disease it produces is still not fully understood. It would, therefore, be unfair to regard McLeod's views as wrong; they expressed rather only one aspect of the truth as known at the time.

I never had the privilege of working with McLeod, but I met him fairly regularly at the meetings of the Pathological Society, and learnt to admire the enthusiasm with which he approached problems of research. The last time I saw him must have been three or four years before the end. He was walking slowly and painfully with a stick, so differently from the rapid confident stride of his earlier days.

Those who were closer to him than I was were united in regarding him with respect and affection. His outlook on life was dictated by his Presbyterian upbringing and belief. He had a strict code of morals to which he not only conformed himself, but to some extent imposed with kindness on others. His presbyterianism was not that of his eighteenth-century forebears, with the narrow, harsh, inquisitorial bearing depicted, for example, by G. M. Trevelyan. Though he was a disciplinarian, he was humane, understanding, tolerant of the failings of others so long as he thought they were doing their best, putting the welfare of the individual first, just and fair in all his dealings, and the soul of honour and integrity. He was a non-smoker and a life-long abstainer from alcohol. However, he tempered his principles occasionally by consideration for others, and in his later years he learnt to enjoy a cigar. T. S. McLeod writes: 'On one occasion he had found himself in a Danish Park with the wife of a scientist [Madsen] whom he was visiting. To his consternation she produced a picnic basket, poured out a glass of beer and handed it to him. "What was I to do", he wrote [in one of his weekly letters to his family] ? "We had no common language so how could I indicate that I had signed the pledge never to let alcohol pass my lips ? After careful thought I decided that courtesy demanded that I should drink the beer, and I was surprised that the taste was not unpleasant, nor did I feel any sensation of intoxication. But did I act rightly ?" He appeared genuinely relieved to find that there was general support [of his family] for his handling of the dilemma."

His child-like innocence in matters of alcoholic drink showed also in the fact that he could never understand why his wife's trifles did not compare in flavour with those of Mrs M. J. Stewart. When a dinner guest in the Stewarts' house he invariably asked for a second helping of trifle 'particularly from the juice at the bottom of the dish'. His enjoyment was so obvious and the amount of alcohol taken in this way so innocuous that none of those present on these occasions dared ever to tell him of Mrs Stewart's trifle secret.

The McLeod household, though in a big family house, was conducted on very modest lines. Education of the six children took priority over everything else, and economy was strict, as it had to be when he gave away a proportion of his income to the church and to various charities. In 1948 his salary was almost doubled by the receipt of an 'A' distinction award. Of this he did not approve, as he considered that his achievements were due not solely to himself but to a team effort and to the conditions provided at the Medical School. He therefore handed over the annual award to the University, making sure, however, that the University took over the responsibility for settling the extra income tax demand. He practised and enjoyed the Spartan life; and at the Cambridge meetings of the Pathological Society in January would whistle cheerfully as he crossed the snow-covered quadrangle of the College to the common wash houses, clad in no more than pyjamas and a dressing gown. Because of his disapproval of public transport on Sundays he insisted on his family walking to church. T. S. McLeod writes on this aspect of his father: 'He was meticulous in distinguishing essential tasks such as urgent requests from the hospital wards [or the laboratory confirmation of clinical diphtheria] from research and academic work which could be scheduled for week-days . . .. On one occasion he found himself in the laboratory one Sunday morning an hour before the Church service was due to start. With him were the two older of his children, as he seized every opportunity of his children's company. After taking his readings he found there was just time to look at the monkeys. Accustomed as he was to working with mice and guinea-pigs, he was always reluctant to use cats or dogs, and when it was absolutely essential to use monkeys he was visibly upset. He did his best to make it up to them by patting and playing with them. This time he handed one to one of his children who carelessly allowed it to escape, and the next hour was spent in an exciting chase [helped by the animal attendant]. It probably never occurred to him that faced with the choice between an old-time Presbyterian sermon or a monkey chase his children would ensure that the quarry was not caught too soon."

To quote from Sir James Howie, 'Walter, as he was best known to his friends, was a great microbiologist and a great character. As with great characters, remarkable legends as well as verifiable facts accumulated around him.' Both facts and legends were of equal importance in showing how his friends saw him. 'He was in every way a big man, handsome in appearance and generous in spirit', needing Epstein to do justice to so fine and so firm a face. 'Physically, mentally, and morally he was a fit man who enjoyed his strength and used it wisely.' When challenged he could assume a threatening bulldog expression, but equally when telling a humorous story he had an attractive glint in his eyes.

In his youth he was an athlete. In the opinion of Sir John McNee, he might have become one of the great rugby forwards for Scotland. His weight of 14 or 15 stone and his massive frame of solid muscle combined to make him a formidable opponent. Sir Gordon Cox, F.R.S., well remembers a game of football played when McLeod was over 60 years of age. Coming up against him, he said, was like coming up against a stone wall.

Throughout his life he was a great walker, covering long distances at a fast pace. He was also a fast driver of his motor car, causing often no little apprehension in his passengers.

As an elder of the Presbyterian Church he was concerned with parochial activities, and during the whole of his time at Leeds, and later at Edinburgh, he worked with the Boys' Brigade, going to camp with them in the holidays. He gave help to refugees, and was free from colour prejudice.

As an examiner of undergraduates he was fair and generous. According to the late Professor Tulloch, he would ask in the *viva voce* examination quite difficult questions in broad Scottish diction that the English students found difficult to understand. Even hearing was rendered difficult by his habit of closing his eyes and addressing his voice to the ceiling. Fortunately, however, their anxiety was lessened when they realized that he was not only asking difficult questions but was also answering them. On one of these occasions the external examiner said to him that there was nothing to stop a candidate who answered the questions completely satisfactorily from scoring 100 per cent. McLeod decided to test this statement. Writing out a set of model answers to questions in the following examination he had them copied in longhand by his secretary to prevent his handwriting from being recognized and sent them with the other papers to this external examiner. When they came back the comment against his pseudonym was: 'This student is the best of a poor bunch but not really up to honours standard.' T. S. McLeod who contributed this story writes, 'Although the honours that he received gave him genuine pleasure he never forgot this salutary lesson on the fallibility of human judgement.'

His work, which often carried him long hours into the night, was directed particularly towards the welfare of the community. Whether at work or play he was vigorous, persistent and untiring. In his staff he created deep and permanent loyalty; his singleness of mind made him a whole man; and his character was an inspiration to all who knew him.

I (G. S. W.) am greatly indebted to Sir John McNee, Sir James Howie, Sir Gordon Cox, F.R.S., Professor K. E. Cooper, Professor F. C. Happold, and Mr Thomas McLeod and Mrs McLeod for the help they have given me; and in particular to Professor K. S. Zinnemann who has collaborated with me in the preparation of this Memoir.

The photograph reproduced was taken at Leeds, probably about 1950.

## Bibliography

### *Streptococci*

1912 On the haemolysin produced by pathogenic streptococci and on the existence of anti-haemolysin in the sera of normal and immunised animals. *J. Path. Bact.* **16**, 321–350.

1913 (With J. W. McNee) On the anaemia produced by the injection of the haemolysin obtained from streptococci, and on the question of natural and acquired immunity to streptolysin. *J. Path. Bact.* **17**, 524–537.

1914 On the value of antistreptococcal sera. *Lancet* **ii**, 837–842.

1915 Criteria of virulence amongst streptococci, with some remarks on streptococcal leucocidin. *J. Path. Bact.* **19**, 392–416.

1921 Streptococcus classification. *Br. med. J.* **ii**, 791.

1929 (With Hilda A. Channon) On the importance of *thermo-labile* streptococcal toxin, with special reference to its cytolytic effect on leucocytes. *J. Path. Bact.* **32**, 283–291.

The streptococci of the human body. *A system of bacteriology in relation to medicine.* **2**, 30–70.

The pneumococcus: bacterial diagnosis and spread of infection. *Ibid.* **2**, 177–200.

1939 (With N. W. Abdalla) The antigenic properties of streptolysin. *Br. J. exp. Path.* **20**, 245–259.

### *Diphtheria*

1931 (With J. S. Anderson, F. C. Happold & J. G. Thomson) On the existence of two forms of diphtheria bacillus—*B. diphtheriae gravis* and *B. diphtheriae mitis*—and a new medium for their differentiation and for the bacteriological diagnosis of diphtheria. *J. Path. Bact.* **34**, 667–681.

1933 (With J. S. Anderson, K. E. Cooper & F. C. Happold) Starch fermentation by the 'gravis' type of diphtheria. *Lancet* **ii**, 293–295.

1933 (With J. S. ANDERSON, K. E. COOPER & F. C. HAPPOLD) Incidence and correlation with clinical severity of *gravis, mitis,* and intermediate types of diphtheria bacillus in a series of 500 cases at Leeds. *J. Path. Bact.* **36**, 169–182.

(With H. M. LEETE & A. C. MORRISON) Diphtheria in Hull and its relation to bacteriological type. *Lancet* **ii**, 1141–1144.

1935 Recent observations on the bacteriology of diphtheria. *Univ. Leeds med. Soc. Mag.* **5**, no. 2, 26–29.

Bacteriological diagnosis of diphtheria. *Lancet* **ii**, 250.

1936 (With K. E. COOPER, F. C. HAPPOLD, HESTER E. DE C. WOODCOCK, J. S. ANDERSON, W. M. ELLIOT, H. M. LEETE, J. C. SAUNDERS & S. H. WARREN) Review of the observations which have accumulated with regard to the significance of diphtheria types in the last four years (1931–35). *Proc. R. Soc. Med.* **29**, 1029–1054.

1939 (With J. W. ORR & HESTER E. DE C. WOODCOCK) The morbid anatomy of *gravis, intermedius* and *mitis* diphtheria. Observations on a series of 50 *post-mortem* examinations. *J. Path. Bact.* **48**, 99–123.

1940 (With K. E. COOPER, F. C. HAPPOLD, K. I. JOHNSTONE, HESTER E. DE C. WOODCOCK & K. S. ZINNEMANN) Laboratory diagnosis of diphtheria—comparative values of various media. *Lancet* **i**, 865–868.

1943 The types *mitis, intermedius* and *gravis* of *Corynebacterium diphtheriae. Bact. Rev.* **7**, 1–41.

1944 Tipos de cultivo y bacilo diftérico—gravis, mitis e intermedius—y su significado en la epidemiologia de la enfermedad. *Prensa méd. argent.* **31**, 543–554.

1948 (With D. T. ROBINSON) Virulence of gravis strains of *Corynebacterium diphtheriae. Lancet* **i**, 97–100.

1949 (With K. I. JOHNSTONE) Nomenclature of strains of *C. diphtheriae. Publ. Hlth Rep., Wash.* **64**, pt ii, 1181–1187.

1950 A survey of the epidemiology of diphtheria in North-West Europe and North America in the period 1920–1946. *J. Path. Bact.* **62**, 137–156.

1964 Diphtheria. *Encyclopaedia Britannica* **7**, 470–472.

### *Bacterial respiration and metabolism*

1914–15 (With A. R. B. SOGA) A simplified method for the cultivation, in fluid media containing coagulable albumin, of bacteria requiring anaerobic conditions, notably pathogenic spirochaetes. *J. Path. Bact.* **19**, 210–213.

1921 (With G. A. WYON) The supposed importance of vitamins in promoting bacterial growth. *J. Path. Bact.* **24**, 205–210.

1922 (With J. GORDON) On the production of peroxides by pneumococci and other bacteria. *J. Path. Bact.* **25**, 139–140.

(With J. GORDON) Production of hydrogen peroxide by bacteria. *Biochem. J.* **16**, 499–506.

1923 (With G. A. WYON) Preliminary note on inhibition of bacterial growth by amino-acids. *J. Hyg., Camb.* **21**, 376–385.

(With J. GORDON & L. N. PYRAH) Further observations on peroxide formation by bacteria. *J. Path. Bact.* **26**, 127–128.

(With J. GORDON) Catalase production and sensitiveness to hydrogen peroxide amongst bacteria: with a scheme of classification based on these properties. *J. Path. Bact.* **26**, 326–331.

(With J. GORDON) The problem of intolerance of oxygen by anaerobic bacteria. *J. Path. Bact.* **26**, 332–343.

1924 (With J. GORDON) The production of organic compounds of sulphur in bacterial cultures with special reference to glutathione. *Biochem. J.* **18**, 937–940.

1925 (With J. GORDON) The relations between the reducing powers of bacteria and their capacity for forming peroxide. *J. Path. Bact.* **28**, 155–164.

(With J. GORDON) Further indirect evidence that anaerobes tend to produce peroxide in the presence of oxygen. *J. Path. Bact.* **28**, 147–153.

1926 (With J. GORDON) Inhibition of bacterial growth by some amino-acids and its bearing on the use of tryptic digests as culture media. *J. Path. Bact.* **29**, 13–25.

1927 (With BERTHA WHEATLEY & H. V. PHELON) On some of the unexplained difficulties met with in cultivating the gonococcus; the part played by the amino-acids. *Br. J. exp. Path.* **8**, 25–37.

1927 (With H. V. Phelon & G. M. Duthie) The rapid death of the meningococcus and gonococcus in oxygenated cultures; the part played by the development of an unduly alkaline reaction. *J. Path. Bact.* **30**, 133–149.

1928 (With J. Gordon) The practical application of the direct oxidase reaction in bacteriology. *J. Path. Bact.* **31**, 185–190.

Bacterial oxidations and reductions. *The newer knowledge of bacteriology and immunology* (ed. E. O. Jordan & I. S. Falk), pp. 211–217. University of Chicago Press.

1929 (With S. Ellingworth & J. Gordon) Further observations on the oxidation by bacteria of compounds of the para-phenylene diamine series. *J. Path. Bact.* **32**, 173–183.

1930 Variations in the periods of exposure to air and oxygen necessary to kill anaerobic bacteria. *Acta path. microbiol. scand.* **20**, suppl. iii, 255–267.

Bacterial respiration. *A system of bacteriology in relation to medicine.* **1**, 263–291.

1931 Methods of observing the reducing and oxidizing action of bacteria. *Ibid.* **9**, 157–159.

(With P. Fildes) The reduction of dyes; indicators of oxidation-reduction potential. *Ibid.* **9**, 160–162.

Recognition of special oxidizing mechanisms. *Ibid.* **9**, 162–164.

1934 (With J. C. Coates, F. C. Happold, D. P. Priestley & B. Wheatley) Cultivation of the gonococcus as a method in the diagnosis of gonorrhoea with special reference to the oxydase reaction and to the value of air reinforced in its carbon dioxide content. *J. Path. Bact.* **39**, 221–231.

1953 (With R. A. Holman) Observations on Schales' reaction for hydrogen peroxide, with special reference to its use in complex solutions containing sugar and peptone. *Br. J. exp. Path.* **34**, 191–194.

(With J. Gordon & R. A. Holman) Further observations on the production of hydrogen peroxide by anaerobic bacteria. *J. Path. Bact.* **66**, 527–537.

(With J. W. Czekalowski & J. Rodican) The growth and respiration of Leptospira in solid or semi-solid media with special reference to Dinger's phenomenon. *Br. J. exp. Path.* **34**, 588–595.

1954 (With J. W. Czekalowski & J. Rodican) Observations on the nutrition of Leptospira based on the development of Dinger's phenomenon. *J. gen. Microbiol.* **10**, 199–208.

*Sulphonamide action*

1939 Experimental evidence of the value of *p*-aminobenzene sulphonamide and related substances in controlling bacterial infections. *Leeds Univ. med. Soc. Mag.* **9**, 143–149.

1940 (With H. Burton, T. S. McLeod & A. Mayr-Harting) On the relationships between the respiratory activities of bacteria and their sensitiveness to sulphanilamide, *p*-hydroxylamino- and *p*-nitrobenzenesulphonamide. *Br. J. exp. Path.* **21**, 288–302.

1941 (With J. Gordon) Relative value of sulphonamides and antisera in experimental gas gangrene. *Lancet* **i**, 407–409.

1942 (With H. Burton, A. Mayr-Harting & N. Walker) Development of colours from sulphonamides (p-nitrobenzenesulphonamide) under bacterial action and the bearing of such phenomena on the theory of the bacteriostatic and bactericidal activities of the sulphonamides. *J. Path. Bact.* **54**, 407–419.

1944 (With A. Mayr-Harting & N. Walker) The influence of access of free oxygen on the action of antiseptics with special reference to the sulphonamides. *J. Path. Bact.* **56**, 377–389.

(With A. Mayr-Harting & N. Walker) Observations on the bactericidal and bacteriostatic actions of *p*-aminobenzenesulphonamide and *p*-hydroxylaminobenzenesulphonamide, with special reference to their suppression by *p*-aminobenzoic acid. *Br. J. exp. Path.* **25**, 27–37.

1947 (With N. Walker, R. Philip & W. M. Smyth) Observations on the prevention of bacterial growth by sulphonamides, with special reference to the Harper and Cawston effect. *J. Path. Bact.* **59**, 631–645.

*Bacteriological technique*

1912–13 A method for plate culture of anaerobic bacteria. *J. Path. Bact.* **17**, 454–457.

1918 (With R. E. Bevan-Brown) The technique of blood culture. *J. Path. Bact.* **22**, 74–84.

1919 Observations on the cultivation of typhoid and paratyphoid bacilli from the stools with special reference to the brilliant green enrichment method. *J. Hyg., Camb.* **18**, 260–263.

1920 (With A. G. Ritchie) The serum reaction in bacillary dystentery. Observations on agglutination, with special reference to the use of freshly prepared bacillary emulsions. *J. Path. Bact.* **23**, 217–223.

1929 (With H. Sugare) The bacteriological diagnosis of whooping-cough. *Lancet* **ii**, 165–167.

1940 (With J. Gordon) A simple and rapid method of distinguishing *Cl. novyi* (*B. oedematiens*) from other bacteria associated with gas gangrene. *J. Path. Bact.* **50**, 167–168.

1947 Smear and culture diagnosis in gonorrhoea. *Br. J. vener. Dis.* **23**, 59.

1951 (With Betty Dawson, Enid H. Farnworth & D. E. Nicholson) Observations on the value of the Bordet–Gengou medium for the cultivation of *Haemophilus pertussis*. *J. gen. Microbiol.* **5**, 408–415.

*The Edinburgh period*

1958 The hospital urine bottle and bedpan as reservoirs of infection by *Pseudomonas pyocyanea*. *Lancet* **i**, 394–397.

1959 (With Joyce A. McLeod) Oscillation of the intraleucocytic granules as a criterion of survival of the leucocyte and of the potency of cytotoxic agents. *J. Path. Bact.* **77**, 219–230.

Urinary infections associated with operations on the bladder with special reference to prostatectomy. *Br. J. Urol.* **31**, 298–312.

1960 (With J. C. Gould) A study of the use of agglutinating sera and phage lysis in the classification of strains of *Pseudomonas aeruginosa*. *J. Path. Bact.* **79**, 295–311.

1961 (With Joyce A. McLeod) The technique and interpretation of tests for leucocidin with special reference to the value of ethylene diamine tetra-acetic acid (EDTA). *Br. J. exp. Path.* **42**, 171–178.

(With Joyce A. McLeod) The absence of leucotoxic activity in highly purified diphtheria and tetanus toxins (as bearing on the virulence of the bacteria concerned). *Br. J. exp. Path.* **42**, 179–186.

1963 (With J. M. Mason & A. A. Pilley) Prophylactic control of infection of the urinary tract consequent on catheterisation. *Lancet* **i**, 292–295.

Thermostable staphylococcal toxin. *J. Path. Bact.* **86**, 35–53.

(With Margaret M. Taylor) Sterilisation of the skin. The time factor in the action of antiseptics and the possibilities of local application of antibiotics. *Scot. med. J.* **8**, 234–242.

1965 (With J. M. Mason & R. W. K. Neill) Survey of the different urinary infections which develop in the paraplegic and their relative significance. *Paraplegia* **3**, 124–143.

1967 (With H. Braude, J. O. Forfar & J. C. Gould) Cell and bacterial counts in the urine of normal infants and children. *Br. med. J.* iv, 697–701.

(With H. Braude, J. O. Forfar & J. C. Gould) Diagnosis of urinary tract infection in childhood based on examination of paired non-catheter and catheter specimens of urine. *Br. med. J.* iv, 702–705.

*Sundry*

1910 (With J. Cowan & A. R. Paterson) A case of partial heart-block occurring during an attack of acute rheumatism. *Q. Jl Med.* **3**, 115–120.

1914 (With C. Funk) The formation of a peptone from caseinogen by the prolonged action of dilute hydrochloric acid in the cold. *Biochem. J.* **8**, 107–109.

1916 (With P. Ameuille) The effect of trench warfare on renal function. *Lancet* **ii**, 468–472.

(With P. Ameuille) Le fonctionnement rénal chez les troupes en campagne et ses rapports avec les néphrites de guerre. *Bull. Acad. Méd., sér. 3 ième* **76**, 103–106.

1918 (With D. L. Tate) Trench fever: observations on the condition of the spleen and leucocytes. *Lancet* **i**, 603–604.

1918–19 (With D. L. Tate) Observations on the condition of the spleen and leucocytes in 'Trench fever'. *Q. Jl Med.* **12**, 1–13.

1921 (With A. G. Ritchie & C. A. Dottridge) Incidence of infections with Pfeiffer's bacillus before, during and after the 1918 epidemic. *Q. Jl Med.* **14**, 327–338.

(With P. Govenlock) The production of bactericidins by micro-organisms. *Lancet* **i**, 900–903.

1922 Limitations of bacteriology in its application to public health. *Jl R. sanit. Inst.* **42**, 353–356.
1935 (With G. W. WATSON & M. J. STEWART) Fatal case of leptospiral jaundice of obscure origin. *Br. med. J.* **i**, 639–640.
1946 (With D. T. ROBINSON & A. W. DOWNIE) Dust in surgical theatres as a possible source of post-operative tetanus. *Lancet*, **i**, 152–154.
1947 (With J. GORDON, ANNA MAYR-HARTING, J. W. ORR & K. ZINNEMANN) The value of antiseptics as prophylactic applications to recent wounds. *J. Hyg., Camb.* **45**, 297–306.
1949 Penicillin. *Univ. Leeds med. Soc. Mag.* **19**, no. 3, 29–36.
1951 (With S. P. BEDSON, W. C. COCKBURN, E. T. CONYBEARE, R. CRUICKSHANK, A. W. DOWNIE, A. BRADFORD HILL, P. L. KENDRICK, J. KNOWELDEN, H. J. PARISH, A. F. B. STANDFAST, G. S. WILSON & D. G. EVANS). Also with 10 medical officers of health, 11 field workers and 9 other laboratory workers) The prevention of whooping cough by vaccination. A Medical Research Council investigation. *Br. med. J.* **i**, 1464–1472.
(With J. W. CZEKALOWSKI, D. E. DOLBY, K. I. JOHNSTONE & C. J. LATOUCHE) Observations on the destruction of bacteria by a soil amoeba. *J. gen. Microbiol.* **5**, vii.
1954 (With J. W. CZEKALOWSKI) Detailed description of a leptospira obtained in pure culture from the urine in a case of abacterial cystitis. *J. Path. Bact.* **67**, 43–50.

*Obituaries*

1943 (With G. PAYLING WRIGHT & M. J. STEWART) Hedley D. Wright. *J. Path. Bact.* **55**, 113–124.
1956 J. Gordon. *Br. med. J.* **i**, 753.
M. J. Stewart. *Br. med. J.* **ii**, 1179.
M. J. Stewart. *Lancet* **ii**, 1054–1055.
1958 (With K. I. JOHNSTONE & F. S. FOWWEATHER) J. Gordon. *J. Path. Bact.* **75**, 218–225.
J. W. Mackavoy. *Univ. Leeds med. J.* **7**, no. 1, 37.
1968 W. J. Tulloch. *J. Path. Bact.* **95**, 336–348.
1971 Bertha Wheatley. *J. Path. Bact.* **105**, 83–84.

# ROBERT GORDON MENZIES

20 December 1894 — 15 May 1978

Elected F.R.S. 1965

By Sir Frederick White, K.B.E., F.R.S.

## Introduction

Robert Gordon Menzies was born on 20 December 1894 in the country town of Jeparit in the State of Victoria, Australia.

By the brilliance of his intellect he won the scholarships that enabled him to qualify with distinction as a barrister, and to be called to the Victorian Bar. He abandoned the successful professional practice of the law to devote the greater part of his life to a political career, first in his own State, but later in the Parliament of the Commonwealth of Australia. He first became Prime Minister in 1939, four months before Australia joined Britain by declaring war with Germany. Then followed eight years in opposition until Menzies, now leading a new Liberal Party–Country Party coalition, achieved a resounding victory in the election of December 1949. He became Prime Minister and held the leadership of his Party in Parliament for the next sixteen years. Menzies dominated the political scene in Australia in those years. Much has been and will no doubt be written of the major political events and controversies of this period of recovery from the war. The judgement of political and economic analysts will vary widely, but there can be no doubt about Menzies's contribution to education and to science. For 16 years he personally guided the policy of his government to transform the status and magnitude of education throughout Australia, and greatly to enhance the resources devoted to the arts, the humanities and to science. This was indeed a period of intellectual renewal and progress never equalled in Australia's history.

Menzies made a second great contribution to the cultural life of Australia. When he began to attend the Commonwealth Parliament in 1934, only desultory progress had been made in the execution of the plans of the American architect, Walter Burley Griffin, for the building of the national capital of Canberra. Menzies's increasing involvement in the political affairs of the nation inevitably convinced him that 'the new Federal Government and Parliament must be established in an area and city acquired and established for federal purposes'. In the years of his greatest power he created and supported a determined policy that changed tardiness to accelerated action.

These two outstanding achievements will be the main subjects of this memoir.

## YOUTH AND EARLY PROFESSIONAL LIFE

His father, James Menzies, was the son of Scottish crofters who had migrated to Australia in the mid-1850s in the wake of the Victorian gold rush. Through his mother Kate, *née* Sampson, he inherited a link with Cornwall; his grandfather, John Sampson, was a miner from Penzance who came to Ballarat in Victoria to seek his fortune on the gold-fields. Menzies's father was born in Ballarat in August 1862. He went early to work to help support his widowed mother and her family. He became a coach painter and, in the early days of the newly invented H. V. Mackay 'Sunshine' Harvester, is known to have painted the first of these machines made in Ballarat.

The small settlement of Jeparit in the Mallee District of Victoria began about 1870 on the fringe of the developing wheat land, and it was here that James Menzies moved with his wife and their three children to manage a general store recently purchased by his brother-in-law. The railway had not reached this hot dusty village of about 30 buildings and 200 people when the Menzies family arrived late in 1893. In those pioneering days the district was not prosperous, and James Menzies had a serious struggle to support his family.

Robert Gordon, the fourth child, was born on 20 December 1894 not long after the family arrived at Jeparit, and his brother Stanley, the fifth child, was born there later. James and Kate Menzies had little money, but they had all that respect for education and learning so typical of Scots of humble origin of their time. They were determined that their children should achieve the best education of which each was capable. The young Robert Gordon Menzies began his education at the one-teacher, one-room school, where elementary education was provided free by the State. What the school taught him was supplemented by the habit the parents had of reading to their family. Menzies himself recalls 'Henry Drummond for evangelical theology; Jerome K. Jerome for humour; the *Scottish Chiefs* for historical fervour'. He also made good use of the library of the Mechanics Institute, an institution for adult education introduced into Victorian towns from England and Scotland. The only way a clever boy or girl could break out of a rural village through educational achievement was by winning one of the few scholarships awarded by the State, and this became the ambition of the young Menzies. His first scholarship enabled him to attend Grenville College in Ballarat without paying fees. He went to live at his parents' expense with his grandmother in that town. He next won a scholarship which took him to the much larger school, Wesley College in Melbourne, an independent school that the Wesleyan Methodist Church had founded in the nineteenth century in Victoria.

By this time, 1909, his parents had left Jeparit, and moved their home to Melbourne. Robert Gordon Menzies was therefore able to live at home during the whole of the period of his attendance at Wesley College and later at Melbourne University [1]. He graduated in 1916 from the University of Melbourne with first class honours in law; he was awarded the Dwight Prize in Constitutional History (1914), the Sir John Madden Exhibition, the Jessie Leggatt

Scholarship (1915), the Bowen Essay Prize and the Supreme Court Prize (1917) [2]. In 1920 he married Pattie Maie (later Dame Pattie), daughter of the late Senator J. W. Leckie; they had two sons and one daughter.

Menzies was admitted to the Victorian Bar and the High Court of Australia in 1918 and appointed King's Counsel in 1929. After some years of practice as a barrister Menzies entered the Upper House of the Victorian Parliament in 1928 as a Nationalist. In 1929 he resigned from the Upper House and won the seat for Nunawading in the Victorian Legislative Assembly. In 1932 he was Attorney-General, Minister for Railways and Deputy Premier.

When Sir John Latham, after a distinguished political career, was appointed Chief Justice of the High Court in 1934, Menzies stood for and won Latham's vacant and safe seat of Kooyong in the Commonwealth House of Representatives. He held this seat until he retired in 1966. He joined Joseph Lyons who, as Prime Minister, led a United Australia Party government from January 1932 until October 1934, and then a United Australia Party–Country Party coalition until November 1938. Menzies was Attorney-General and Minister for Industry from October 1934 until November 1938. Lyons won the next election but with a much reduced majority. During the next few months dramatic changes occurred. Lyons was unwilling to concede the leadership to Menzies; the latter on 14 March 1939 resigned from his ministerial posts and from the deputy leadership of his party. Lyons died suddenly at Easter 1939; Earle Page led the government for nineteen days and then resigned. Menzies became Prime Minister on 26 April 1939 only four months before the outbreak of the war with Germany. He announced Australia's determination to support Britain by a declaration of war at 9.15 p.m. on 3 September 1939.

His efforts to organize the country for war were frustrated by a lack of confidence in his leadership by his own colleagues. The Labor Party refused his offer to form a national coalition government. When he found in Cabinet that 'There was a strong view that, having regard to our precarious Parliamentary position, my unpopularity with the leading newspapers was a threat to the survival of the Government' he resigned as Prime Minister in August 1941 to allow Arthur Fadden, the leader of the Country Party, to become Prime Minister. Arthur Fadden's government lasted only until 7 October 1941 when he handed in his commission to the Governor-General. John Curtin, assured of the support of the two independent members Arthur Coles and Alexander Wilson, took over the leadership of the Labor Party Government.

In the years that followed, Menzies, with the cooperation of many supporters, succeeded in welding together the political groups throughout the country that held views allied to those of the old United Australia Party. This new grouping, under the banner of a Liberal Party of Australia, and supported by the Country Party, fought and won the elections of December 1949. Thus Menzies became Prime Minister for the second time on 19 December 1949; he remained as the leader of his government until he retired, politically undefeated, from politics on 26 January 1966, aged 71 years.

### The Commonwealth and State Governments

In the nineteenth century and the early decades of the twentieth century the governments of the six States into which the nation was divided founded the institutions which they considered essential for the education of the people and for assisting in the technology necessary for the economic development then important. The purpose of many of these institutions was also to sustain British culture in so far as a government considered it had a responsibility so to do. Each university, founded by an Act of Parliament, was open to all students who could meet the academic standards of matriculation and could afford the fees. Free primary and secondary education was provided by a State Education Department supplemented by schools founded by the churches or by private groups. The State Governments also founded technical schools and agricultural colleges for the special forms of instruction of artisans and farmers. No child in Australia was in theory denied the opportunity of the education that might embrace the highest levels of learning and the professions, but in practice many were no doubt so denied by the financial limitations of their parents or by the remoteness of their homes from the schools and colleges that would have provided for them.

In the closing years of the nineteenth century the people of Australia accepted by referendum a written Constitution for the new Commonwealth of Australia. The Bill giving legal authenticity to the creation of the Commonwealth passed both Houses of the Parliament of Westminster and received the royal assent in July 1900; Queen Victoria signed the proclamation establishing the Commonwealth with effect from 1 January 1901. In discussions of the political activities of the Commonwealth Government in relation to the State Governments, frequent reference is made to the terms of this Constitution; the State Governments retained their sovereign powers inherited originally from the Parliament in Westminster, but agreed to refer certain powers, such for example as the power to legislate in matters of defence, external affairs, navigation, quarantine, immigration, postal and telecommunication services to the Commonwealth Parliament. Other legislative powers of the Commonwealth are difficult to interpret; many Acts of the Parliament have been held by the High Court to be unconstitutional. Frequent attempts by the Commonwealth to achieve greater powers by referendum have been defeated.

The Commonwealth has no legislative power in regard to education except in the Australian Capital Territory and the Northern Territory. In the great reforms Menzies brought about he relied on Section 96 of the Constitution which states in part 'the Parliament may grant financial assistance to any State on such terms and conditions as the Parliament thinks fit'. The exercise of this power calls for political judgement to ensure acceptance by the States of the decisions of the Commonwealth.

### Financial assistance for the State universities

Before World War II there were six universities in Australia and two university colleges. The oldest, the University of Sydney, was founded in 1850 followed by Melbourne in 1853, and the remainder followed as the State Governments saw fit to create universities in each of the capital cities in Australia. Each university was created by a statute of the relevant State Legislature while those founded last century were granted a Royal Charter or Royal Letters Patent. Canberra University College was founded in the very early days of the National Capital and was at that time a small institution preparing students for degrees given by the University of Melbourne. The State universities were financed by State grants, by private endowments or grants, and by fees paid by the students. They all offered courses to matriculated students in the humanities, the arts and the sciences; most provided professional courses in law, medicine and engineering; the Universities of Sydney and Melbourne had courses in agricultural and veterinary science. Great changes occurred in the universities after the outbreak of the war in Europe in 1939 and particularly with the Japanese invasion of the Far East when the direct threat to Australia began to be apparent. Many young men and women who might otherwise have attended the universities enlisted in the fighting services; many members of the staff of the universities either did so also or, if more senior, undertook activities to assist the Government in its war-time efforts.

As the war drew to an end the Labor Government saw the need to cope with the human and economic problems associated with converting the country to a peace-time society, and for the first time began extensively to become involved in education. In particular, the Commonwealth Reconstruction Training Scheme was introduced with the general purpose to provide training or re-training opportunities for those members of the forces whose education had been interrupted by enlistment, and for those who, for a variety of reasons, could also benefit. For some years this scheme injected considerable sums of money into the university budgets.

In 1946 the Labor Government founded the Australian National University in Canberra. In 1949 the New South Wales Government created the University of Technology as the apex, as it were, of the extensive system of technical education institutions of the State Government; this was later renamed the University of New South Wales when its Act was amended in 1958 to allow the teaching of medicine and arts. This broadly was the university situation when Menzies became Prime Minister of the Commonwealth for the second time in December 1949.

Menzies's interest in education at all levels, but particularly at the university level, had been apparent long before he became Prime Minister. His own life and experience had induced this interest. He must early in his career have realized the importance to Australia and to the world of some way of allowing the worthy and intellectual young persons more frequently to achieve the opportunity for higher learning, and for the qualifications for professional life. His personal interests were in the classics and humanities rather than in science and technology, although, as his experience as a politician grew, he came to appreciate the influence of these on national and international affairs. The speech he made in 1939 at the annual commencement of the

Canberra University College entitled *The place of a university in the modern community* reveals the depth of his knowledge of university affairs and his clearly formulated views on the role of the university in society [3]. He was very proud too of having, while Attorney-General in the Victorian Government, introduced the Bill that created the first full-time Vice-Chancellor of his old University of Melbourne.

It was in 1945 in the House of Representatives in Canberra when, as Leader of the Opposition, he expressed his conception of the part that the Commonwealth Government should, and ultimately did, play in the university affairs of the nation. On that occasion he advocated a revised and extended educational system; the need for attention to be directed to secondary, rural, technical and university training; the need for special adult education and the problems of the qualifications, status and remuneration of teachers. He said that these reforms 'may involve substantial Commonwealth financial aid' and advocated the setting up of a qualified commission to advise [4]. This speech was well received by the House and particularly by the Honourable J. J. Dedman, Minister for Post-War Reconstruction, who was responsible on behalf of the Labor Government for the assistance afforded to the universities in the interests of post-war reconstruction.

It was some years however before Menzies was in the position to influence affairs. He was well aware of the difficulties, indeed the crisis, of the Australian universities when he returned to power in 1949. Costs were rising, student numbers being financed by the Commonwealth Reconstruction Training Scheme were falling as ex-service men and women graduated, and thus the universities were losing the benefits of the grants made by the Commonwealth on their behalf. By law the universities were unable to refuse entry to qualified young persons, and could not introduce quotas to limit entry to the different faculties. The salaries of the staff of the university were low compared with comparably qualified persons in the community. In particular the level of research in the universities was extremely low owing mainly to the lack of adequate funds to finance research students, research assistants and the purchase of equipment. Three months after his election success in December 1949, Menzies set up the Commonwealth Committee on the Needs of Universities. This was under the Chairmanship of Professor R. C. Mills, a distinguished economist who was at that time Director of the Commonwealth Office of Education [5]. Menzies asked for and obtained an interim report, and by December 1951 he had passed legislation permitting the Commonwealth to provide money in proportion to that provided by the State Governments. This was the first of a series of the State Grants (Universities) Acts made possible under Section 96 of the Constitution. This was a satisfactory beginning, but Menzies himself considered the sums paltry compared with those given later to support the universities, and for tertiary education in other forms. The sum of $2252 million was provided in 1951 and this increased to $4512 million in 1957; half was provided by the Commonwealth and half by the State Governments.

In the years between 1951 and 1957 when Menzies was again prepared to act, the States had found it impossible to provide adequate finance for the growing demand for tertiary and technical education and even for education at the secondary level. Inevitably in this situation, agitation grew up in all directions. In 1952 the Australian Vice-Chancellors' Committee published a pamphlet titled *A crisis in the finances and development of the Australian universities*, appealing for public attention [6]. The Australian National Research Council, the predecessor of the Australian Academy of Science, organized a symposium in Canberra in 1954 under the chairmanship of the highly respected Chief Justice of the Commonwealth, Sir Owen Dixon, at which the plight of the universities was discussed. The president of the Australian National Research Council, the distinguished anthropologist, Professor A. P. Elkin, wrote to the Prime Minister outlining the plight of the universities and sending the text of a resolution passed at the symposium. However, perhaps the most telling of the appeals came from the late Ian Clunies Ross, at that time Chairman of the C.S.I.R.O. Clunies Ross was a graduate of the University of Sydney and well known in academic and scientific society for his liberal views and for the quality of his public statements. His oration, delivered on the occasion of the Centenary of the University of Sydney on 26 August 1952, was entitled *The responsibility of science and the university in the modern world*. After an inspiring analysis of the role of the university and of science both in Australia and abroad he ended with a discussion of the serious problems of the Australian universities and said:

> 'I would emphasise that action must be taken now. We have not yet experienced the full effects of the scientific age, the age of specialization; indeed it may be said we have scarcely felt its impact if we consider what it will involve ten or twenty years hence. We are living on borrowed capital which is rapidly running out, the capital of an older generation, educated in the tradition of a broader and more liberal scholarship which still exerts a marked influence on the thoughts and attitudes of our day' [7].

Clunies Ross did not rely on this address alone to stimulate action by the Government. He sent a copy of his address to the Chief Justice, Sir Owen Dixon, whom he knew had been the mentor of the Prime Minister at the Bar. He wrote to Mr R. G. Casey, the Minister in Charge of the C.S.I.R.O., to whom he was, as Chairman, formally responsible. He wrote to his close friend Dick Boyer, Chairman of the Australian Broadcasting Commission, to Mr A. M. Campbell, Editor-in-Chief of the *Age* in Melbourne, to Sir Warwick Fairfax, Governing Director of the *Sydney Morning Herald*, and in each case emphasized the importance of his message [8].

In his address he had said that he was fully aware of the constitutional difficulties which, on purely legal grounds, appear to absolve the Commonwealth of responsibility for participation in general university matters. He went on to say that 'good sense and the overriding importance of the issues have found a way round these difficulties and can do so again'. He said 'there could be no more auspicious way in which to mark the centenary of the oldest Australian university than by the setting up by the Commonwealth of a commission of the highest prestige and authority to examine and define the functions, responsibilities and needs of the universities'. In January 1953, Clunies Ross sent a copy of this address to the Prime Minister saying that he would be most grateful if the Prime Minister could find the time to read it. He said also 'there do seem to be, however, so many university issues which will come before your Government in the near future, that I ventured to press the recommendation contained in my oration for setting up of a commission of the greatest prestige and authority to redefine not only the material things but the true purpose and function of the universities'.

Professor Mills had been appointed as Chairman of the Committee of Inquiry into the Universities in 1950 and reported in 1951. However, no action was taken by the Menzies Government, except to continue to pay the grants proposed by Mills, until Menzies appointed the Murray Committee in 1957 [9].

That Menzies did not take action in this period may be attributed to his reluctance to become still further involved with commitments to the State Governments on behalf of the universities. Although Mills had been successful in making recommendations that were acceptable to the universities and to the State Governments, it is nevertheless true that some Vice-Chancellors were very reluctant to accept the idea of a Commonwealth Committee supervising their development, and apprehensive at an intrusion into their autonomy. State Governments have always resented dictation from the Commonwealth, and it is indeed interesting in the years that followed how fully they accepted the Australian Universities Commission as their guide to university development. Menzies might well have been deterred by the financial problems of the early days of his Ministry. When he took office in 1949 the financial state of the economy was uncertain. The price of wool rose to exceptionally high levels in 1950 as a result of American purchases for uniforms of soldiers in the Korean war. The great increase in export income was followed by rapidly rising domestic prices and grave inflation of the currency. The severe increases in taxation introduced in the budget of 1952 were certainly not popular. Menzies won the 1954 elections with a much reduced majority. By 1955 the economy had begun to improve. Almost complete import restrictions and high investment, both from local and overseas sources, induced industrial growth; there was virtually no unemployment in spite of an increasing intake of migrants. The situation in the universities was also changing. Between 1947 and 1955 student numbers at the universities remained nearly constant at about 30 000; although there was a continuing rise in the enrolment of new students between the ages of 17 and 22, the number of returned men and women assisted by the Commonwealth Reconstruction Training Scheme was decreasing. After 1955 a sharp and continual rise in enrolment began; by 1963 the student numbers had more than doubled to 69 000.

The urgings of the Vice-Chancellors, of Clunies Ross, aided by Sir Owen Dixon, and by the Australian National Research Council, and later by the new Academy of Science may have served to keep the plight of the universities in the mind of the Prime Minister. But then, as now, there is not much political capital to be gained by this form of expenditure. It seems highly likely, from what is known of the long term Prime Minister's interests, that he moved as quickly as he could after 1956, when the financial situation of the country seemed to permit it.

### The Murray Committee

In 1956 Menzies decided to act on university affairs. On an official visit to England, he sought the permission of the Chancellor of the Exchequer, Harold Macmillan, to have Sir Keith Murray (now Lord Murray) as chairman of a new committee to investigate the state of the Australian universities. Sir Keith Murray was Chairman of the British University Grants Committee, a man experienced in university affairs and familiar with the long history of the support given to British universities through his committee. Menzies was aiming high and very much in conformity with a suggestion made to him by Ian Clunies Ross and other prominent Australians. As members of this committee he invited Sir Ian Clunies Ross (Chairman of the C.S.I.R.O.), Sir Charles Morris (the Vice-Chancellor of the University of Leeds), Mr A. J. Reid (the Chancellor of the University of Western Australia, a former head of the State Treasury and member of the Commonwealth Grants Commission), and Mr J. C. Richards (an Assistant General Manager of the Broken Hill Proprietary Company). The Committee on Australian Universities, as it was called, was appointed in December 1956 and reported soon afterwards in September 1957. This was very much in conformity with the Prime Minister's wishes, for he now had a sense of urgency in tackling the problem of the universities. In his letter of invitation to the members, he said that the Committee was invited to indicate ways in which the universities might be organized so as to ensure that their long term pattern of development was in the best interests of the nation; in particular to investigate the role of the university in the Australian community; the extension and coordination of university facilities; technological education at the university level; the financial needs of universities over the period and appropriate means of providing for these needs. Clunies Ross and Reid were both very familiar with the Australian university scene; Murray and Morris were experienced in the problems of university finance and academic management. Menzies was thus able to say to the Parliament: 'We are grateful to the Committee for its remarkable speed, thoroughness and grasp of the matters involved in their task.'

The Committee found a sorry scene. They said in their report: 'We had hoped to find the universities adequately staffed and equipped to discharge their existing responsibilities to the student body and to the nation; but this is unfortunately far from the case.' They went on: 'The paramount difficulty facing the universities is the pressure of student numbers, particularly in the first year.' They noted the disturbing aspect of the high failure rate; the general weakness of honours work, postgraduate training and research work, and the lack of accommodation in classrooms, laboratories and libraries. There was almost complete absence of common rooms and student unions, sports facilities, residential colleges and hostels. When they came to make their recommendations, they saw the situation as so serious, that, in addition to the general increases in grants they recommended, they asked for what came to be described as an emergency grant for three years.

The Prime Minister's reaction to this report was immediate and excellent [10]. By 28 November 1957 he was able to make a statement in the House of Representatives giving his views and those of his Government as to what should be done in the future. He first enunciated his attitude to the relationship between the Commonwealth and the States in the matter of education. He said:

> 'It is of course true that under the Australian Constitutional division of powers between the Commonwealth and State, education is in the State field' and later 'we are not promoting any idea that this legislative power over education should, by a Constitutional amendment, be transferred to the Commonwealth. The idea of uniformity can be carried too far. In both primary and secondary education each State, with highly varying conditions of climate and occupational opportunities, is in the best position to judge for itself its own most suitable educational curriculum and organisation.'

The philosophical attitude of the Prime Minister in relation to the task that now faced him of persuading his Government, the Parliament and the people that the Commonwealth should make substantial and increasing grants to the universities is clear from the remarks he made in this speech to the House:

> 'Since this report and the decisions of the Commonwealth Government mark, as I hope and believe, the beginning of a new and brighter chapter in the history of the Australian universities; and as our acceptance of much greater financial responsibility should, if it is not to lend itself to loose generalisation, be clearly related to its own special circumstances, I will take a little time to summarise the particular elements which justify, and seem to us to require, special Commonwealth action.
>
> 'The whole feature of university education is that, upon the basis of a general mental training achieved by the primary and secondary systems, it provides for those willing and able to undergo it, special and higher training. Such training leads to the acquisition of recognised degrees, the attainment of high professional qualifications, the entrance to higher research, particularly but not exclusively in science and technology, and the securing of those immeasurable and civilised benefits which flow, or should flow, from the study of or association with the students of humane

letters. . . . The university must not be narrow or unduly specialist in its outlook. It must teach and encourage the free search for the truth. The search must increasingly extend to, but is not to be confined to, the physical resources of the world or of space. The scientist is of great and growing importance, and what we propose to do will, I believe, enable many more scientists to be trained in proper circumstances and with improved tuition, buildings and equipment.'

Having referred specifically to some of the more important statements by the committee, particularly their estimate that university undergraduate numbers would rise from 36 000 to 70 000 by 1965, and to the unfortunate high failure rate, he then announced the decisions of his Government relating to the recommendations made by the committee. While accepting in principle that there should be a permanent body to advise the Commonwealth Government on matters of university education, he rejected the inclusion of the word 'Grants' in its title, believing that in the Australian context it might indicate a limitation of its function too narrow for his liking. In his speech he used the term 'Australian Universities Committee', but when the time came to form this body the Government adopted the name Australian Universities Commission. He accepted the recommendation that the grant made by the Commonwealth for the years 1958, 1959 and 1960 should be raised to a total of $17.0 million compared with $12.0 million granted in the previous three years. The agreed basis was that every Commonwealth dollar was to be matched by three dollars from State funds plus fees. He also accepted the proposal that the Commonwealth alone should provide an unmatched emergency grant of $9.0 million for these years. He recognized the need to increase university salaries and agreed to provide, on the part of the Commonwealth, $375 000 p.a. for this purpose. He concluded his remarks as follows:

'It is, I think, a happy thing that we should have had the opportunity of reviving our conception of the universities and their work by the presentation and discussion of this brilliant and provocative report.'

### The Australian Universities Commission

In May 1959, only five months after the Prime Minister had stated the Government's decisions, the Australian Universities Commission Act was passed by Parliament. Sir Leslie Martin, F.R.S., Emeritus Professor of the University of Melbourne, was appointed Chairman [11]. Its principal task was to advise the Minister on the financial assistance to be given to the universities, both Commonwealth and State, and the conditions upon which any financial assistance should be granted. These specific functions were qualified by the direction that 'the Commission shall perform its functions with a view to promoting the balanced development of universities so that their resources can be used to the greatest possible advantage to Australia'. Further, the Commission was required to consult with universities and with States in all matters with which it was concerned. Fruitful accord with State governments led to their acceptance to provide $1.85 for every $1.00 from the Commonwealth, and a one-to-one ratio for capital expenditure. This was a remarkable achievement in Commonwealth–State relations.

By the time Menzies retired from Parliament in 1966 the Australian Universities Commission had been very active and its recommendations were, almost without exception, approved by the Commonwealth Government. As a result, a great revolution in university life in Australia occurred. Large sums of money began to be available to the universities. In the 1961–63 triennium, the States Grants Acts provided that the State universities receive from State and Commonwealth Government sources about $149.5 million for operating expenses and in the 1967–69 triennium $355 million. In addition, in the first of those triennia they received $70 million for capital expenditure which rose to $104 million in the latter triennium. For the Australian National University, operating expenditure rose from $19 million to $58 million while capital expenditure rose from $8.5 million to $12 million [12]. These expenditures reached even higher levels in the years after Menzies retired. Student numbers were also increasing; the total of students at all Australian universities in 1963 was 69 000, but by 1969 it had risen to 108 000.

While these figures are impressive, it is the change in the university scene—new buildings, new libraries, new laboratories, larger sites and new universities—that must be reviewed to gain an impression of the impact of this expenditure. The Commonwealth Government and the States agreed that the universities had to be brought up to modern standards, and that the growing demand for university education had to be met.

In Sydney, the University had been built on a site of 52 hectares, selected in 1850, conveniently near the centre of the city. The State Government arranged for the University to acquire an additional area of 18 hectares of adjacent city land on which to erect new buildings principally for the Faculties of Engineering and Architecture. The construction of the new Fisher Library, the Edgeworth David Building for geology, the Carslaw Building for mathematics has, with other changes, transformed this old University to one with modern facilities. The University of Melbourne is conveniently situated near the city centre, and adjacent to its residential colleges, the Royal Melbourne Hospital and other related institutions. The University has, on the limited area of this site, succeeded, by using attractive multi-storey structures, in providing modern facilities for teaching and research for its seven faculties. Worthy of note are the new medical centre, the Howard Florey Laboratories for medical research and the Baillieu Library. The Raymond Priestley Building houses the University's administration. The Universities of Adelaide and Western Australia have each met the challenge of change on the sites selected at their foundation. When Colonel Light, in the mid-nineteenth century, planned the city of Adelaide, he placed the University, the residence of the State Governor and other civic buildings between North Terrace, one of the boudaries of the inner city, and the River Torrens. The traditional design of red brick buildings of this University has been retained for most of the new buildings, but, once again, multi-storey structures have provided a solution. The physics laboratory is named after W. H. Bragg, F.R.S., who went to his first university post in Adelaide in 1886.

The pressure of student numbers has not been quite so great in Western Australia as in the eastern States. The University has been able to accommodate the necessary additions within the admirable site in the suburb of Nedlands along a reach of the Swan River. The beauty of this University has not been seriously affected by the addition of major new buildings. The Universities of Queensland and Tasmania had to meet the challenge of modernity by major moves to new sites. The Queensland Government had, before World War II, agreed to move the University from quite inadequate buildings in the city of Brisbane to an excellent site in the suburb of St Lucia in a bend of the Brisbane River. The main building and the buildings for chemistry, physics, geology and biological sciences were erected at that time in monumental stone. The traditional architecture was not used in building the extensive additions for the University's twelve faculties. The University of Tasmania, the smallest of the original six universities, began in humble circumstances in Hobart. The new university buildings, of modern architectural design, are grouped on a hill-site at Sandy Bay, a Hobart suburb a few kilometres down the Derwent River.

In 1949 the Government of New South Wales decided to meet the growing demand for university education by founding the University of Technology, planned, initially, to provide professional training and research in the technologies and applied science. This plan was liberalized in 1958; the curriculum was extended to include arts and medicine, and the name changed to the University of New South Wales. The site of 38 hectares, in the inner Sydney suburb of Kensington, is crowded, but adequate modern facilities are provided. The University has named the library the Robert Menzies Building. On the coast of New South Wales, both north and south of Sydney, are the cities of the major coal producing areas of the State with associated iron and steel and heavy engineering production. The University of New South Wales acted as a foster parent to the University of Newcastle, which became independent in 1964, and to the University of Wollongong, independent in 1975. The University of Sydney had, from 1938, fostered the growth of the University of New England, which now dates its independence from 1954. This attractive university, situated in the city of Armidale 400 kilometres north of Sydney in elevated pastoral country, teaches not only arts, education, economics and science but specializes in rural science and university teaching by correspondence. By the 1960s it was evident that the potential demand could not be met without another university in the Sydney area. Macquarie University was founded in 1964; it is located on a site of 135 hectares about 18 kilometres north-west of the centre of Sydney. Named after Lachlan Macquarie, Governor of New South Wales from 1810 to 1822, this was one of the first universities to adopt the name of a prominent man as its title. It is now well developed; it had over 8000 students by 1975.

The location of the two new universities for Melbourne took account of the rapid expansion of the domestic, commercial and industrial areas to the north and east of the city and down the Mornington Peninsula between Port Phillip and Western Port Bays. Monash University was founded in 1958 and located about 18 kilometres to the south-east of the city. It is named after General Sir John Monash, an engineer, and distinguished leader in World War I, who developed the large brown coal resources in the State of Victoria. The large multi-storey Robert Menzies School of the Humanities is a conspicuous feature on the landscape. Named after the first Governor of Victoria, La Trobe University, founded in 1964, is about 12.5 kilometres to the north-east of the city. In 1975 these two universities had a total of nearly 20 000 students, 5000 more than Melbourne University.

The name of Mathew Flinders, the navigator of the nineteenth century who charted the coasts of Australia, has been adopted by the second university in South Australia. Beginning as a foster child of the University of Adelaide, the Flinders University of South Australia is situated on an attractive hill-side site at Bedford Park about 11 kilometres from Adelaide. It became independent when opened on 21 May 1966 by Her Majesty Queen Elizabeth The Queen Mother. Following a recent tendency in university organization it had, in 1966, created the Schools of Language and Literature and Social Sciences, Biological Sciences and Physical Sciences. The University of Queensland, in 1961, began to develop a university college about 1000 kilometres to the north of Brisbane, in the tropical coastal city of Townsville. In 1970 it became the James Cook University of North Queensland. In addition to the customary faculties this University has special interests in tropical veterinary science and marine biology. The architects have designed attractive buildings well suited to the tropical climate with heavy summer rainfall. The fifth report of the Australian Universities Commission (1972) states that two new universities will be established, the Griffith University in Brisbane, and the Murdoch University in Perth. Deakin University in Geelong, Victoria, has since been added to bring to nineteen the total of the universities of Australia.

A visit to any Australian university today will reveal a scene incomparably different to that when the Murray Committee made its inspection. Students are now well provided with union buildings and dining facilities; while few universities have room for playing fields on campus, much money has been expended on facilities for sport and recreation. Libraries have been greatly increased; between 1961 and 1970 there was a 99% increase in the number of volumes held by the universities and a 223% increase in library staff. Computers are now commonly used for undergraduate teaching, for higher degree work and research, and computer facilities are as much a normal university facility as the library. Once only one veterinary faculty provided for Australia and New Zealand; now there are four, with James Cook University, in addition, specializing in tropical veterinary science. The expansion of medical teaching in nine universities has been very costly. There is a marked interest today in studies of the cultures and languages of Asia and the Pacific as alternatives to those of Europe and the classics. Earth sciences, behavioural sciences and environmental studies represent changes in academic interest not, of course, confined to Australia.

Menzies, with the help of the Murray Committee and the Universities Commission, initiated a policy of generous university growth; when he retired this forward movement continued but, with the many detailed changes in policy, the story, thereafter, inevitably loses its simplicity. In his memoirs *The measure of the years* [13] Menzies reveals his personal, and indeed emotional, interest in these events. When preparing to present the Murray report to Parliament, he told his Cabinet that he would like it to sit morning, afternoon and evening. He then says: 'The Cabinet, knowing it was an outstanding event in my life, humoured me, and I am still grateful to them.' In the House he referred to 'the novel and sometimes revolutionary features of this historic document'. He reports himself as saying, in presenting the report: 'Mr Speaker, if I may confess it, this is a rather special night in my political career.'

## Research in the universities

Although the professors and lecturers of the six Australian universities of the first three decades of this century had inherited the tradition of original research as an essential complement to teaching, the relative poverty of the universities, the apathy of the governing bodies and the remoteness of Australia from the great centres of progress in science in the old world severely handicapped progress. Nevertheless, the teaching of science was in most faculties at a high level, and there were some centres of exceptional merit. The 1851 Exhibition Science Scholarships offered one of the few opportunities for travel and study abroad; scholars such as T. H. Laby, F.R.S., returned to found distinguished research schools [14]. Edgeworth David, F.R.S., had unique opportunities for original geological research on the continent of Australia, and with Douglas Mawson, F.R.S., explored the Antarctic Continent. In the ranks of the Fellowship of the Royal Society and the Australian Academy of Science are the names of many of those who kept the achievement of original investigation alive.

When World War II began many university staff members sacrificed their personal research ambitions to take part in the national war effort. They experienced the exciting stimulus that almost unlimited money gave to many applied projects such as radar, optical munitions, camouflage, food science and the many aspects of chemistry and metallurgy of war materials. University scientists were not content to return to quite inadequate buildings and facilities, the lack of funds for research assistance and equipment, at a time when student numbers were increasing.

Some attempts had been made in the pre-war years to assist with Commonwealth funds, then a most unusual approach, thought by most Commonwealth politicians to be prohibited by the Constitution. Professor J. P. V. Madsen (later Sir John Madsen), the first Professor of Electrical Engineering in Sydney, avoided this problem by inducing the Council for Scientific and Industrial

Research (the C.S.I.R.) and the Australian Post Office to provide funds which, when distributed by the Radio Research Board, became the means of building up a fine record of ionospheric physics in several universities [15]. An approach to the Treasurer of the Commonwealth, R. G. Casey (later Lord Casey) in 1936 resulted in the sum of $60 000 being made available to the C.S.I.R. for the support of university research. Casey considered that the Constitutional limitation required him to insist that grants be made only to university projects of direct relevance to the C.S.I.R.'s programme. That the C.S.I.R. should tell the universities what research to do was anathema to Sir David Rivett, F.R.S., the Chief Executive Officer of the C.S.I.R.; this was in fact avoided by what can only now be described as skilful maladministration, made all the easier by the casual university administrative methods of those days. The Vice-Chancellors agreed to a proportional allocation to each university and undertook to account for its use to the Commonwealth [16].

After the war a variety of different ways were tried to satisfy the problems of university research finance. The need for trained postgraduate research scientists, both for Government agencies and for industry, and later as university teachers, was now becoming a pressing issue. The amounts of money available were gradually increased, but not to the degree satisfactory to the universities. The demands for modern research equipment were steadily increasing, while, with larger enrolments of higher degree postgraduate students, the universities found it difficult to finance the appointment of well qualified supervisors and technicians. The Commonwealth Committee on the Needs of the Universities, i.e. the Mills Committee, in 1950 recommended to Menzies that the Commonwealth make no special grants for research and that each university finance its research effort out of the total income from the State and Commonwealth grants, both to be increased, and from fees. This became the basis of university finance until 1957, when Menzies began to give effect to the recommendations of the Murray Committee.

By 1961 the universities were receiving money for research from a variety of sources. The Atomic Energy Commission, the C.S.I.R.O. and the National Health and Medical Research Council were each making grants to universities for specific projects. Various agricultural producing industries—wool, wheat and the dairy industry—were providing funds, subsidized by the Commonwealth, to support research by the universities and the C.S.I.R.O. The Commonwealth Bank, through its Rural Credits Development Fund, was helping also. In the United States at this time very large sums of money from the Defence vote were being spent on front line science, and some Australian university people were recipients of grants for special projects. A total of about $4 million from external sources was spent in 1961. About 84% of this was for biological and physical sciences, 10% for technology, while some 6% only was spent on the social sciences and humanities. In the same year the universities expended approximately $10 million on research from their recurrent income; about $8 million went to the natural sciences, $580 000 to technology and engineering, and under $1.4 million to social sciences and the humanities.

The Australian Universities Commission in reporting to Menzies in 1963 stated: 'The Commission believes that national needs demand the allocation of special grants to universities to meet the rising costs of post-graduate training and also to support senior staff in their task of planning and supervising this training.'

This marked the beginning of special arrangements to support university research. In the House on 24 March 1965 Menzies said [17]:

> 'Honourable Members will recall that the second report of the Universities Commission recommended that during the calendar years 1964, 1965 and 1966 the total of $10 million should be provided for the universities to support research activities at the postgraduate level. Of the $10 million half was to be provided by the Commonwealth and half by the States. The Commission had not, at the time of the report, reached a stage where it felt it could make recommendations for the distribution of these funds among universities and therefore confined its recommendation in the first instance to the distribution of $2 million in the year 1964.
>
> 'When introducing the Universities (Financial Assistance) Bill in October 1963, I accepted the recommendation for this initial distribution and said that I hoped the Government would shortly take an opportunity to look at the whole question of Commonwealth involvement in research in Australia. This we have now done. The universities were told, last year, that a further $2 million, or our share of it, would be available in the universities during 1965 for the same purposes as in 1964, and I now announce that our share of another $2 million will be available in 1966, on the same basis as to distribution. After that date, we feel, the Commission should include provision for this form of research grant, bound up as it is with postgraduate teaching, in the general recommendations which it makes for capital and recurrent grants to the universities.
>
> 'Of the $10 million recommended for research activities in the 1964–66 triennium, this would still leave undistributed $2 million of Commonwealth funds and a matching amount from the States.
>
> 'We believe that this sum should be available for particular selected research projects to be carried out by individuals or research teams. We therefore propose to make $2 million available for such particular research projects, and to set up an advisory committee to which we shall refer requests for assistance from such individuals or research teams. We will look to this committee for advice as to the allocations, within the limits of the money available, for such proposals. The committee will receive proposals, in the main, from research workers in universities, although applications from persons working outside universities will not be debarred unless such persons are working for Government authorities. Commonwealth money from this fund will be available on the advice of the committee, subject in each case involving a university, to a matching grant from the State in which the research is to be carried out. As I have said,

> these research grants are not intended for use exclusively in scientific disciplines, nor need the total amount be spent in the 1964/66 triennium.'

The advisory committee promised by Menzies was appointed in 1965 as the Australian Research Grants Committee; its first chairman was Sir Rutherford Robertson, F.R.S. In 1965 it allocated $3.985 million (8% to projects in the humanities and social sciences; 29% in physical sciences; 20% in chemical sciences; 31% in biological sciences—including agricultural, medical and veterinary sciences; 12% in engineering and applied sciences). The total amount allocated was just under $4 million in 1966, the year Menzies retired, but increased gradually to $5.255 million in 1972. Sir Rutherford Robertson, F.R.S., has made the following comment [18]:

> 'When Sir Robert Menzies announced the Australian Research Grants scheme on 24 March, 1965, his Government was meeting the long-felt need for stimulation of high level research in Australia. The detailed arrangements were made by Senator Gorton, the Minister assisting the Prime Minister in matters relating to education and science, and I was entrusted with the task of forming the Australian Research Grants Committee to recommend the projects which should be supported by the grant. For the first time in Australia research workers had the opportunity to obtain finance not merely from the meagre research money available in their universities or research institutions or from that applied to the practical problems of a particular industry. The result was that research in Australian universities, starved for too long, began to flourish and in the first four years of the Committee's existence some 2300 reports on work which it had supported were published.
>
> 'The terms of reference of the Australian Research Grants Committee contained the key phrase "it will base its recommendations on its own assessment of the relative merits of individual proposals". The Committee sought written assessments by leading workers in the same line of research as the applicant and always sought excellence by supporting the most outstanding and the most promising investigators. The result is that Sir Robert's far-sighted scheme has been a lasting success, ensuring not only good research but also provision of opportunities which have aided recruitment of outstanding workers in Australian universities.'

## The Commonwealth Scientific and Industrial Research Organization (C.S.I.R.O.) [19]

Menzies was Prime Minister during the period of the greatest expansion of the activities and facilities the C.S.I.R.O. had ever experienced. He became Prime Minister only a few months after the passing of the Act which changed the Council for Scientific and Industrial Research (C.S.I.R.) into the C.S.I.R.O. and which gave greater managerial responsibility to the governing body, the Executive of three full time scientists and two part time members. The Science and Industry Research Act was formally within the portfolio of the Prime

Minister but, in line with current practice, Mr R. G. Casey, Minister for External Affairs, acted as Minister-in-Charge. Although Casey was a vigorous advocate of all the C.S.I.R.O. activities, it was the Cabinet and thus the Prime Minister who had to approve and provide finance.

The budget of the C.S.I.R.O. rose from $4.0 million in 1948–49 to nearly $41.0 million in 1965–66 in years of low inflation. Many new activities were begun and older programmes took on a new and expanded form. Studies of Australia's coal resources were started for the first time. Research on the nature of keratin, the structure of the wool fibre and its processing soon began to provide the International Wool Secretariat with the data to fight the technical battle with the synthetics. Studies of the healthy sheep and its management were aimed at higher and more efficient wool production. New ideas on suitable beef producing cattle and pasture plants suitable for the tropical north resulted from greatly increased programmes. The unexpected myxomatosis epizootic virtually rid the country of the rabbit plague, and provided unique opportunities for studies of a wild virus disease under field conditions and animal behaviour studies of the rabbit. Quite new ideas, for example on the absolute determination of the ohm, emerged from the National Standards Laboratory. The early post-war researches of J. L. Pawsey, F.R.S., and his colleagues reached a high peak of encouragement when Menzies's Cabinet approved the expenditure of half the cost of the giant radio-telescope inaugurated by the Governor-General, Lord De L'Isle, at Parkes, N.S.W., in August 1961. Menzies approved Casey's initiative to have the government provide the whole of the $500 000 for the phytotron in Canberra; Menzies opened this facility in August 1962. These were the days of high hopes and aspirations, when the attitude, certainly approved by Menzies and Casey, was that new knowledge from front line research would transform the economic and cultural life of Australia. That the scientists of the C.S.I.R.O. were in the forefront of scientific endeavour is testified by elections to the Fellowship of the Academy and Royal Society and by the frequent awards of honours from learned societies and universities.

In 1956 the Science and Industry Research Act provided that two part time members of the Executive of the C.S.I.R.O. were to be chosen for their abilities and knowledge of national affairs. One of these, Mr A. B. Richie, a grazier from the Western District of Victoria, retired from the post in May of that year and the question of his replacement arose. The Minister-in-Charge, R. G. Casey, suggested that we ask the Prime Minister to appoint Mr Arthur Coles then living in retirement in Melbourne. This was an interesting and somewhat surprising suggestion in view of the past association between Coles and the Prime Minister. Arthur Coles had as a young man fought at Gallipoli and in France in World War I and afterwards joined with his brother and uncle in the business enterprise that grew to be one of Australia's largest chain stores of G. J. Coles and Co. Ltd. After two years as Lord Mayor of Melbourne he won the seat of Henty in Victoria as an Independent and entered the House of Representatives in Canberra. With an allegiance to Menzies's

United Australia Party he, and another independent, held the balance of power for the government. Gravely disturbed at the treatment of Menzies by his colleagues he withdrew his support from the United Australia Party and voted with the Opposition to defeat the Fadden government that, for a short time, followed that of Menzies. Coles, an experienced business executive, made a major contribution to the war effort as Chairman of the Rationing Commission. He was also Chairman of the War Damage Commission which compensated civilian citizens in Australia and Papua New Guinea for loss by enemy action. As its Chairman be brought great success to the National Airlines Commission, a Labor government enterprise, which still runs Trans-Australia Airlines.

Arthur Coles (now Sir Arthur) was appointed to the C.S.I.R.O. Executive, on the recommendation of the Prime Minister, by the Governor-General in Council on 26 March 1956. He quickly became an effective colleague; because of his quiet friendly personality and his genuine enthusiasm for the purpose and activities of the C.S.I.R.O. his advice and help were eagerly sought by all ranks. Menzies in appointing Coles made an important contribution to the success of the C.S.I.R.O. of that period. The appointment was continued in 1960 when the size of the Executive was increased; Coles retired on 25 March 1965 after serving for nearly nine years.

Menzies stimulated great interest among scientists by appointing R. G. Casey to the Executive of the C.S.I.R.O. in 1960. This followed immediately on Casey's retirement from politics after serving for ten years as Minister-in-Charge of the C.S.I.R.O. and as Minister for External Affairs. Biographies of both men will certainly reveal the complexity of the personal relationships between them. Judged from the viewpoint of a scientist and former Chairman of the C.S.I.R.O., my impression is that Menzies recognized Casey's interest in and concern for science and his special abilities of leadership in national and international affairs. When Sir Ian Clunies Ross died in July 1959 and my other Executive colleague, Dr Stewart Bastow, went down with his first heart attack shortly afterwards, I was convinced that there were too few full time members of the Executive to maintain the momentum of a large and rapidly growing organization. The Minister-in-Charge, R. G. Casey, agreed with my recommendation that the number of members should be increased by an alteration in the Act [20].

When I saw Menzies to seek his agreement to this change, he told me that Casey (now aged nearly 70 years) wished to retire from Parliament, and asked my view of appointing him a part time member of the new Executive. I warmly welcomed this; Casey had shown keen interest and support of the C.S.I.R.O. during his ten years as Minister-in-Charge; part time members were almost honorary as they were given only a very small emolument; there was likely to be only favourable political reaction. Casey was appointed in March 1960 and served for five years. Menzies then recommended him for a life peerage and, on his advice, Her Majesty The Queen appointed him Governor-General of the Commonwealth.

### The Australian Academy of Science [21]

In 1952 the Fellows of the Royal Society resident in Australia, together with other senior scientists, decided that it would be of benefit to the future of Australian science for there to be an Academy of the highest prestige modelled on the Royal Society of London. The proposal was welcomed by Lord Adrian, and the Royal Society undertook to support an application for a Royal Charter. The proposal was discussed informally with the Prime Minister; Sir Robert Menzies welcomed the concept of the Fellows of the Royal Society as an initial nucleus, together with from ten to twenty other scientists of undoubted eminence in their field. He undertook on behalf of his government to assist in the presentation of a petition to the Privy Council, and to have the Charter prepared in time for it to be presented to the officers of the new Academy during the visit of Her Majesty to Australia. The President, Professor M. L. E. Oliphant, F.R.S., received the Letters Patent from the Queen at Government House, Canberra on 16 February 1954. Menzies laid the foundation stone of the Academy building in Canberra in January 1958. The Commonwealth Government has, since Menzies began, supported the Academy with an annual grant to enable Australian participation in the activities of the International Scientific Unions, and also to aid its general activities in the interests of Australian science.

### The Australian National University

When Menzies became Prime Minister in 1949 the Labor Government had already taken the initiative permitted by the Constitution to found a University within the Australian Capital Territory. Accepting the advice of a distinguished group of Australian academics and public servants, the Prime Minister J. B. Chifley and his Minister for Post-War Reconstruction J. J. Dedman introduced a Bill into the Parliament in Canberra to found a research university distinctly different in academic structure from the Universities in the States. The Australian National University Act 1946–47, assented on 1 August 1946, defined the functions of the University to include the provision of facilities for post-graduate research and study, the education of those persons, suitably qualified, who elected to avail themselves of the opportunities thus provided, and to confer degrees and diplomas. The University was given power to found Research Schools; the Act established the initial structure by providing for Research Schools of Physical Sciences, Social Sciences and Pacific Studies, and a Research School 'in relation to medical science'. The latter, the John Curtin School of Medical Research, gave expression to the interest of the war-time Prime Minister John Curtin who hoped to see the setting up of a national institution devoted to medical research. The Act also stated that 'the University may provide for the incorporation in the University of the Canberra University College', the undergraduate teaching college preparing students for degrees awarded by Melbourne University. The Council appointed the distinguished Australian, Viscount Bruce of Melbourne, F.R.S., as the Chancellor of the University and Professor R. C. Mills as its Deputy

Chairman. Emeritus Professor Sir Douglas Copland was the first Vice-Chancellor.

The University was from the beginning determined to take advantage of the authority of its Act to place great emphasis on research. The first report of the Interim Council stated the principles which were agreed to be of first importance; the establishment of the four research schools, with the duties of the staff being the advancement of knowledge through research, and the training of research workers. But equal emphasis was given to the statement that there should be no undergraduate teaching and no post-graduate vocational training in the Research Schools. The question of incorporation of the Canberra University College was 'deferred' [22]. This must undoubtedly be judged as the right decision at that time; until later events intervened, the University had nearly ten years to perfect the planning of research of the highest international quality. Distinguished scholars were appointed to be the Deans or Directors of the Research Schools. The generous conditions of service and the excellent facilities created attracted research leaders of outstanding merit to this new enterprise. The University began just before a period of exceptional prosperity in Australia; its income, wholly from the Commonwealth budget, it received in grants through the Prime Minister's Department. Menzies thus had ample opportunity to follow the progress of this academically outstanding child of the Federal Government.

The Murray report brought into sharp focus the future planning of university education in the Capital Territory; the Commonwealth was the responsible government and the solution was for Menzies alone to decide. Canberra University College was still, in 1957, housed in temporary buildings but its council and staff wished for a permanent site with adequate buildings and facilities. The staff was highly qualified and enthusiastic, well able to teach more students at the undergraduate and graduate level. It wished to include science in its curriculum and to award its own degrees. The Australian National University had, in its submission to the Murray Committee, emphasized its unique research role, and its wish to 'help to stimulate the work of the State universities by introducing into them fresh points of view, very often before they have been presented to a wider world audience' [23].

The submission included the statement: 'In the event, however, the University has not awarded undergraduate degrees; it has decided after prolonged discussions against the incorporation of the College . . . .' Although the whole of the financial support of the research schools had to be found from his budget, Menzies treated the A.N.U. no less generously than the State universities. Acting on the Murray Committee's recommendation, he provided a grant of \$8.792 million for the years 1958, 1959 and 1960 compared with \$5.608 million for the previous three years. He gave Canberra University College the same 10% increase as the State universities received.

Menzies clearly could not accept the decision of the A.N.U. Council not to incorporate the College. In his public statement in December 1959 [24] he said that Cabinet had devoted much time to the question as to whether the

College should be given full and independent status, or should be 'organically associated with the Australian National University'. His decision was firm—'We have decided in favour of association'. The reasons he gave must be regarded as sensible. Canberra at the time had a population of 50 000 and it would have been difficult to justify the creation of two separate universities. Secondly, if the College was to become a separate university and was not to be a second-rate university, it would have to provide for postgraduate studies with expensive facilities for research. He showed his appreciation of the position in the A.N.U. and his own clarification of his opposing view in the following way: 'We are aware of a view current in the A.N.U. that that body should, to achieve its true position in Australian university life, be related and have duties to all Australian universities and not just to one.' He did not think amalgamation would prevent the achievement of this aspiration. He concluded:

> 'We feel that if the University is to achieve its greatest results, not only in the granting of degrees but in the stimulation of the mind, there will be enormous advantage for students with a bent towards research to have the great advantage of contact with men of great eminence in their own field.'

An amendment to the Act created in 1960 an Australian National University consisting of an Institute of Advanced Studies (the research schools) and a School of General Studies (taking in the College). Both are governed by a single Council with one Vice-Chancellor and a central administration. The new buildings for the Faculties of Arts, Science and Economics were built on the opposite side of the campus from the original Research Schools. The planned separation of the two parts of the University is no longer followed; the newer Research Schools of Biological Science and of Chemistry have chosen to build near the complementary Departments of the Faculty of Science.

The output of meritorious research from both parts of the University testifies to the success of Menzies's policy. On 11 May 1961 the University invited Menzies to lay the foundation stone of the R. G. Menzies Building of the University Library; this building was opened by Her Majesty The Queen. On 13 May 1966 the University conferred on Menzies the degree of Doctor of Laws, *honoris causa.*

### The Anglo-Australian Telescope [25]

The large radio-telescope at Parkes built for the C.S.I.R.O. gave radio-astronomy a new impetus; interest in optical astronomy was likewise stimulated because of the interest in the optical examination of stellar objects, either discovered or examined at radio wavelengths. On 5 April 1965 Sir John Cockcroft, F.R.S., Chancellor of the A.N.U., opened the new Siding Spring Observatory for the telescopes of the University; the original Mt Stromlo Observatory was of declining usefulness owing to the city lights of the rapidly growing Canberra. Australian astronomers were interested in the building of a large telescope in Australia to facilitate joint optical and radio observing, and because a large part of the southern sky contained important stellar objects not visible to northern hemisphere telescopes. British astronomers also had these interests and thus discussions began on the possibility of a joint Anglo-Australian venture.

It was not easy even in that era of comparative affluence to induce governments to provide large sums for exotic scientific projects. Much credit must go to Professor Bart Bok, then Director of the Mt Stromlo Observatory, whose enthusiastic public advocacy undoubtedly commanded the interest of members of Parliament and certainly that of the Prime Minister. Discussions between the Royal Society and the Australian Academy resulted in submissions to the British and Australian Governments advocating the building of a 150 inch telescope for the joint equal use of astronomers from both countries. Menzies had retired by the time the negotiations were concluded and it was his protégé, Senator J. G. Gorton, Minister for Education and Science, who announced on 30 April 1967 that both Governments had agreed. The sequel is now history. The telescope was built and erected on Siding Spring Mountain in N.S.W. and opened by H.R.H. Prince Charles on 16 October 1974. It is an optical telescope of exceptional quality, now in constant use by Australian and British astronomers.

### The Winston Churchill Memorial Trust [26]

'The aim of the Churchill Trust is to give opportunity, by provision of financial support, to enable Australians from all walks of life to undertake overseas study, or an investigative project, of a kind that is not available in Australia.' Menzies, with his life-long attachment to education and learning at all levels of achievement, must have been attracted to the aim of this Trust. He joined a group led by Lord Baillieu to establish the Churchill Trust to honour the memory of his friend, Britain's wartime leader and Prime Minister, Sir Winston Churchill. The group led by Menzies had remarkable success in raising £2 122 654 from the people of Australia within four days of Sir Winston's death in 1965. Sir Robert became the Trust's first National President, and held this position for ten years. In the first twelve years 752 Fellowships were awarded in 54 different categories including awards to persons interested in the land, in art and music, in education, in trades, in the care of the deaf and mentally retarded, in mining and geology, in transport and in medicine. This remarkable tribute to Churchill is indeed worthy of the Trust's first National President.

### Canberra—The National Capital

Before Menzies retired in January 1966 he witnessed in the National Capital the remarkable transformation and growth which he personally inspired and which his government financed. The greater part of the change occurred after his government had formed the National Capital Development Commission 'to undertake and carry out the planning, development and construction of the City of Canberra as the National Capital of the Commonwealth'. Sir John

Overall, the first Commissioner, appointed on 1 March 1958, acknowledges the contribution that Menzies made in the following personal communication [27]:

> 'R. G. Menzies was the first Prime Minister to see the desirability of making it possible for Canberra to be developed from a town of less than 10 000 public servants, to the status of a National Capital of world class. Undoubtedly he was much influenced in the mid-1950s by several factors. He was very familiar with the world scene and was conscious of the importance of the new, developing Capitals, particularly Washington; he had faith in Australians to undertake the specialist task; he had a firm grip on his Cabinet and, because of his popularity in the Australian electorate, he had reason to see himself as Prime Minister for many years to come. Furthermore, unlike most of his Parliamentary colleagues, he liked Canberra as a place to live in. He made his home there for nearly 20 years until his retirement in 1966. He liked the environment, the political atmosphere, the rubbing of minds with the Diplomatic Corps and international visitors, and enjoyed the young city as a cosmopolitan meeting place. Menzies was acutely conscious of the need to weld the six Australian States into the Federal System and realised in this the value of a National Capital of quality, as a proper symbol of national aspirations and national unity. A long depression and two world wars had meant that few incentives or priorities had been given to establishing the new capital. By the mid-1950s, Canberra was very small, perhaps of some 30 000 people. It was a place of very few facilities and consisted of two straggling towns, divided by a flood plain and with no permanent national buildings of any kind. The Parliament House was an interim one and had been erected as a matter of expediency some 30 years previously when the Federal Parliament was moved from Melbourne to the new bush capital. Canberra had little appeal for the Parliamentarians, who in those years reluctantly travelled from far away places and stayed only when Parliament was in session. For them, Canberra consisted of the hotels they stayed in, Parliament House and the airport.
>
> 'By the mid-1950s, Menzies also knew little about the infant capital. However, at this time, his daughter Heather was about to marry a young Australian diplomat and was seeking a house in Canberra. The Prime Minister accordingly took time to look around the areas where people lived and was critical of what he saw. He leaned heavily on the Ministers responsible for this situation and it is worth noting that two Ministers lost their Ministerial appointments over a three year period. The question then was whether Canberra was to remain a national capital in name only or whether it should be developed. Under the influence of Menzies, a Parliamentary Committee of Enquiry was set up to examine the situation and report. It reported in favour of planned development. Subsequently then, in 1958, the National Capital Development Commission was established

as a Statutory Authority with the straight-forward charter "to design, develop and construct Canberra as the National Capital of Australia". R. G. Menzies' important role in all this is illustrated by the fact that he was the politician responsible for the setting up of the Parliamentary Committee in the first place; for the establishment of the National Capital Development Commission and the appointment of the first Commissioner, who was also to serve as Chairman of the National Capital Planning Committee, an advisory panel of leading professional advisors. From 1958 on, Menzies displayed a continuing and lively interest in the development of the Capital until his retirement eight years later.'

Sir John Overall continues:

'The Commission never sought his approval but valued his opinions and made certain he was informed before action proceeded. He occasionally showed displeasure in what had been done. He was a traditionalist in design and did not like developments which departed from British monumentality in architectural forms. Notwithstanding this, he respected those who stuck to their guns as the Commission found it necessary to do on a number of occasions. As a result it was at cross purposes with the Prime Minister from time to time. Shortly after its establishment in 1958, the National Capital Development Commission made it clear to the Government that it considered its task to be fourfold:

1. To complete the establishment of Canberra as the Seat of Government —by providing the facilities necessary for the smooth functioning of the Parliamentary body.
2. To further the development of Canberra as the Administrative Centre —by seeing to a smooth conclusion the Defence transfers already approved, and by providing the necessary physical facilities to permit the early completion of the Commonwealth Public Service personnel transfers from Melbourne.
3. To give Canberra an atmosphere and individuality worthy of the National Capital—by provision of monumental buildings and suitable special features.
4. To further the growth of the National Capital as a place in which to live in comfort and dignity.

The government supported these aims, and actions proceeded in the next decade to put them into effect. Undoubtedly, it was fortunate for the N.C.D.C. that Menzies, as he had foreseen, remained Prime Minister during most of that period, by which time the nation itself had come to accept and take pride in the development of its Capital.'

Sir John concludes:

'Menzies enjoyed public functions, particularly those associated with opening new buildings, and launching new enterprises such as his inauguration of the centrally situated Lake Burley Griffin in 1963. He expected results of quality and if he thought well of what had been done both he and Dame Pattie Menzies could be counted on to officiate with style. He appreciated the opportunity to make the dramatic flourish and to speak in the presence of distinguished audiences. The National Capital Development Commission was in a position to provide many such opportunities. Menzies delighted in these, undoubtedly believing and taking pride in the fact that a worthwhile national endeavour was well under way through the action and initiative which he had envisaged.'

The population of Canberra in 1957 was 40 000; it was estimated to rise to 110 000 by 1975; the suburbs adjacent to the north and south banks of the Molonglo River contained the whole city. No final decision had been taken to build the Lake in the Molonglo Valley. The American War Memorial stood alone on Russell Hill with no major roads in the vicinity. Only the arcades of the Civic shopping centre and the small centres in Manuka and Kingston, built many years before, catered to the needs of the people. This scene was transformed by 1965 [28]. The region of Civic Centre now had a large shopping complex called the Mall, the Law Courts, the head office of the Reserve Bank and the first of the multistorey office buildings forming Hobart Place. The attractive Canberra Theatre complex with two theatres was opened on 24 June 1965. The year before, on 17 October 1964, Menzies had the honour of commemorating the completion of Lake Burley Griffin named after the original designer of Canberra. The Commonwealth Avenue Bridge and traffic interchange spanned the Lake between the Parliamentary Triangle and Civic Centre. Kings Avenue Bridge formed the other arm of Burley Griffin's design; it crosses the Lake to the new headquarters of the Department of Defence opened by H.R.H. Princess Marina on 28 September 1964. The ceremonial Anzac Parade stretching from the Lake shore towards the War Memorial Museum was completed in 1964 in time for the pageantry which marked the fiftieth anniversary of Anzac Day. Many buildings had been added to the Australian National University and to the Canberra Technical College, and several schools had been built. Construction of the monumental building to house the National Library had begun with a target date for completion in December 1967. The new southern suburbs in the Woden Valley west of Red Hill were being designed and built. The Mint, the first major official building in that area, was opened by H.R.H. The Duke of Edinburgh on 20 February 1965. Lake Burley Griffin, crossed by two handsome bridges, wiped out the unattractive valley separating the two halves of the city and brought cohesion to the whole design. The impetus Menzies gave continued for many years after he retired. With a population now of about 200 000, with the growth of the Woden Valley suburbs and the extensive construction of the Belconnen suburbs to the north, Canberra has achieved Menzies's desire for a garden city, excellent to live in, and a city admirably designed for government, education and recreation.

Sir John Overall is right in asserting:

> 'The Nation today has come to take pride and pleasure in Canberra as a modern city of grace and quality. It is visited by millions of Australians every year and the nature of what they see and enjoy in its monumentality, as well as its urban facilities and the integrated system of new towns, is a reflection of the farsightedness of Robert Gordon Menzies and his interest and enthusiasm in clearing the way and making it possible for Australia's young bush capital to be planned, developed and constructed to the status of a National Capital in the world scene.'

About 1960 I, as Chairman of the C.S.I.R.O., was beginning to find great difficulty in keeping the necessary contact with the Minister-in-Charge while our head office was still in Melbourne in the same building that the original Executive Committee of the C.S.I.R. had acquired in 1926. I felt sure that my Executive colleagues and I would, by moving to Canberra, have more opportunity to know personally and maintain contact with the members of the Government, and the senior members of the Public Service who influenced our affairs through their responsibilities for finance and the administration of government policy. I faced two difficulties; to convince some of my colleagues of the wisdom of moving our headquarters to Canberra, and to overcome the delay in making the move if the C.S.I.R.O. had to fall into line according to the programme of transfers of Departments of State to the Capital.

When about 1963 I could not attend the Prime Minister's annual Christmas party, he kindly invited me to his office, where I found only Senator Gorton and the Prime Minister. I seized this informal occasion to ask his opinion of moving our headquarters to Canberra. His response was immediate and enthusiastic; he gave me convincing reasons in favour of moving. I went back to Melbourne, told my colleagues I was moving, and before long took up residence in Canberra in a very temporary office for the Chairman. I traded on the Prime Minister's support to argue the C.S.I.R.O. into a favourable priority for a move of our Melbourne staff, and managed in the end to achieve this mainly through the goodwill towards the C.S.I.R.O. of those senior officers who controlled such things. The new Head Office for the C.S.I.R.O. built in the suburb of Campbell was occupied in January 1971.

## Epilogue

The revolution in university growth and the encouragement given to scientific research did not cease when Menzies retired. He had already enlisted the enthusiastic help of Senator John Gorton, who acted first as Minister assisting the Prime Minister in matters of Education and Science and later as the first Minister for Education and Science. The wide ranging and detailed examination of the Committee on the Future of Tertiary Education in Australia under the chairmanship of Sir Leslie Martin, F.R.S., provided Menzies and later Gorton not only with data but with inspired suggestions for future progress. Although Menzies gave initial approval to its first report the many changes to the structure of tertiary educational institutions throughout the country occurred after he retired. This enterprise deserves the highest commendation of all Australians who are convinced of the need for an effective, wise and well financed policy to foster science and learning [29]. It does not denigrate Menzies's outstanding abilities to say that he had little personal knowledge of science. But he certainly had a deep understanding 'that civilisation in the true sense requires a close and growing attention, not only to science in all its branches, but also to those studies of the mind and spirit of man, of history and literature and mental and moral philosophy, of human relations in society and industry, of international understanding, the relative neglect of which has left a gruesome mark on this century'. It is significant that he chose a physicist as Chairman of the Australian Universities Commission and as leader of the major enquiry into tertiary education.

He regarded the invitation to deliver the Jefferson Memorial Speech in 1963 at the University of Virginia as 'a tremendous honour'. He returned to Virginia in 1966, after his retirement, to give seven lectures with the general title 'Central power in the Australian Commonwealth' [31]. He discussed in detail, and from personal experience at the Bar and in State and Federal politics, the growth in power of the Commonwealth in finance, external affairs, defence and banking. He was personally familiar with how these changes had occurred, mainly through tactics that avoided inducing the voters of Australia to approve of them by the complex formal processes laid down in the Constitution itself.

Menzies spent many years in Canberra; but his life and interests were essentially those of Melbourne where he grew up, was educated and embarked on his legal and political life. On his retirement he became the thirteenth Chancellor of his old University of Melbourne, and remained the head of the University from March 1967 until March 1972. Much earlier in 1942, he had received the first honorary degree of Doctor of Laws of Melbourne University. His responsibility for the revival and growth of university life in Australia was widely acknowledged by the award of honorary degrees in the Universities of Queensland, Adelaide, Tasmania, New South Wales, and the Australian National University and by thirteen universities in Canada, the U.S.A. and Britain, including Oxford and Cambridge. He was Honorary Master of the Bench of Gray's Inn. Many learned institutions, including the Royal College of Surgeons and the Royal Australian College of Physicians, elected him to Honorary Fellowships. His admiration for British institutions and his belief in the significance of the British Commonwealth of Nations is well known. He admired the Royal Family and was stimulated by visits of Her Majesty The Queen to Australia. He commemorated Her Majesty's visit in 1963 by the creation of the Queen Elizabeth II scholarships for mutual exchange of young British and Australian scientists. The ceremonial of the Constable of Dover Castle and Lord Warden of the Cinque Ports appealed to his sense of drama, as indeed did the wearing of academic robes at University functions.

Apart from walking, he claimed no personal participation in any sport; indeed he compared himself to Shakespeare's Falstaff pleading guilty to overweight which limited physical participation. But he had an ardent devotion to two sports, the game of Australian Rules football and cricket, the game so zealously adopted by the countries of what Menzies would have called the British Commonwealth of Nations. Australian Rules is a uniquely Australian development of Rugby dating from the 1850s. The Victorian Football League competitions attract thousands of spectators and dominate conversation and news during the winter season. Menzies showed his affection for the game by his keen following of the Carlton Club for which he had the number one membership badge. His greater devotion was to first class cricket. He said: 'It is occasionally left to people like me to carry with them through life a love and growing understanding of the great game—a feeling in the heart and mind and eye which neither time nor chance can utterly destroy'. He devotes several chapters in his memoirs to cricket for he knew personally most of the outstanding players [30]. He was a Trustee of the Melbourne Cricket Ground, a member of the Marylebone Cricket Club and in 1962 President of the Lords Taverners. In 1951 he induced the Chairman of the Board of Cricket Control to allow him to arrange a one day festival match for the West Indian Team then visiting Austalia. This was played in Canberra against a team he personally selected. This Prime Minister's XI one day match against the visitors became a feature of the tour of a Test team in Australia. The present Prime Minister, the Rt Hon. Malcolm Fraser, and the Australian Cricket Board have agreed that there will be a Sir Robert Menzies Memorial match, played on the Melbourne ground, during every future English tour of Australia. Because of the shortage of time to make these arrangements for the summer of 1978–79 the match between Victoria and England, played on 10 November 1978, was called the 'Sir Robert Menzies Memorial Match'.

He was a delightful companion on those, all too few, occasions when we in the C.S.I.R.O. were privileged to entertain him. At the opening of a building for us he interested as well as amused his audience; knowing our interest in agricultural science he would refer to his life in the Mallee where he learned the problems of the farmer and his reluctance to change.

Robert Gordon Menzies died in Melbourne on 15 May 1978 aged 84 years.

The Sydney *Bulletin*, the traditional commentator on political events, referred to his death, under the caption 'The long innings is over', as 'the most revered figure in Australian politics' [32].

The photograph reproduced was taken in 1966 by the Australian Information Service.

## Honours

1929 King's Counsel
1937 Privy Councillor
1950 Chief Commander, Legion of Merit (U.S.A.)
1951 Companion of Honour
1958 Fellow of the Australian Academy of Science
1963 Knight of the Order of the Thistle
1965 Fellow of the Royal Society of London

1965 Constable of Dover Castle, Lord Warden of the Cinque Ports
1973 Order of the Rising Sun, First Class (Japan)
1976 Knight of the Order of Australia

### Publications of the Rt. Hon. Sir Robert Menzies (a selected list)

1917 *The rule of law during war*. University of Melbourne. (36 pages.)
1941 *To the people of Britain at war from the Prime Minister of Australia*. London: Longmans Green. (95 pages.)
1942 *The forgotten people*. Sydney: Robertson & Mullens. (10 pages.)
1958 *Speech is of time: Selected speeches and writings*. London: Cassell.
1967 *Afternoon light*. Melbourne: Cassell Australia Ltd. (384 pages.)
1968 *Central power in the Australian Commonwealth*. London: Cassell. (198 pages.)
1970 *The measure of the years*. Melbourne: Cassell Australia Ltd. (300 pages.)

A full bibliography of Sir Robert Menzies's numerous writings and addresses on public affairs is available in the Australian National Humanities Library in the National Library of Australia, Canberra.

### References

(1) Sir Robert Menzies, *Afternoon light*, Cassell Australia Ltd, Melbourne, 1967; and Kevin Perkins, *The last of the Queen's men*, Rigby, 1968.
(2) The Registrar, University of Melbourne, personal communication.
(3) R. G. Menzies, *The place of the university in the modern community*, Melbourne University Press, 1939.
(4) *Parliamentary debates, House of Representatives*, vol. 184, pp. 4612–4619, 26 July 1945.
(5) Interim report, *Commonwealth Committee on the Needs of the Universities*, in typescript, 1952.
(6) The Australian Vice-Chancellor's Committee, *Crisis in the finances and development of Australian universities*, Melbourne University Press, 1952.
(7) Ian Clunies Ross, *The responsibility of science and the university in the modern world*, An oration delivered on the occasion of the centenary of the University of Sydney, 26 August 1952.
(8) The C.S.I.R.O. files.
(9) *Report of the Committee on Australian Universities*, September 1957 (the Murray Committee).
(10) *Parliamentary debates, House of Representatives*, vol. 17, pp. 2694–2702, 28 November 1957.
(11) *Australian Universities Commission Act*, 1959 (no. 30). The members of the first Commission were Sir Leslie Martin, F.R.S., F.A.A., Professor N. S. Bayliss, F.A.A., Professor A. D. Trendall, Dr J. Vernon, Sir Kenneth Wills, Secretary David Dexter.
(12) *Reports of the Australian Universities Commission*, First Report 1960, Second Report 1963, Third Report 1966, Fourth Report 1969 and Fifth Report 1972.
(13) Sir Robert Menzies, *The measure of the years*, Cassell Australia Ltd, Melbourne, 1970.
(14) I. W. Wark, 1851 Science research scholarship—Awards to Australians. *Records of the Australian Academy of Science*, vol. 3, no. 3/4, 1977.
(15) F. W. G. White & L. G. H. Huxley, Radio research in Australia 1927–1939. *Records of the Australian Academy of Science*, vol. 3, no. 1, 1975.
(16) The C.S.I.R.O. files.
(17) *Parliamentary debates, House of Representatives*, vol. 45, pp. 267–274, 24 March 1965.
(18) Sir Rutherford Robertson, F.R.S., personal communication.
(19) F. W. G. White, A Personal Account of the Historical Development of the C.S.I.R.O., *Nature, Lond.*, vol. 261, 14 June 1976.
(20) F. W. G. White, Casey of Berwick and Westminster, Baron, *Records of the Australian Academy of Science*, vol. 3, no. 3/4, 1977.
(21) Australian Academy of Science files.
(22) Australian National University, *Report of the Interim Council for the period 1 August 1946 to 31 December 1949*.
(23) Memorandum from the Australian National University, submitted to the Committee on Australian Universities, *The place of the Australian National University in the Australian University system*, June 1957.

(24) Sir Robert Menzies, *University development in Canberra,* public statement, PM no. 50/1959, 17 December 1959.
(25) Australian Academy of Science files.
(26) The Winston Churchill Memorial Trust, *Thirteenth annual report,* 1977.
(27) Sir John Overall, C.B.E., M.C., personal communication (now in the National Library, Canberra).
(28) National Capital Development Commission, *Eighth annual report, July 1954 to June 1956.*
(29) *Report of the Committee on the Future of Tertiary Education in Australia,* vols 1 and 2, 1964, vol. 3, 1965.
(30) Sir Robert Menzies, *Afternoon light,* Cassell Australia Ltd, Melbourne, 1967.
(31) Sir Robert Menzies, *Central power in the Australian Commonwealth.* Cassell, London, 1967.
(32) *The Bulletin,* 30 May 1978.

Gilbert Roberts

# GILBERT ROBERTS

18 February 1899 — 1 January 1978

Elected F.R.S. 1965

By O. A. Kerensky, F.R.S., F.Eng.

## Early days

Gilbert Roberts was born in Hampstead on 18 February 1899. His father, Henry William Roberts, a pharmaceutical chemist, died of tuberculosis when Gilbert was a young child and his mother married again. Gilbert had an elder sister and a half-brother who served in the Merchant Navy, and Gilbert looked after him like a father. Both died before Gilbert.

The Roberts relatives, who originated in Wales but lived in Folkestone, were mostly musicians and artists. Gilbert's grandfather was a musician of some distinction; he composed Victorian dance tunes and, at one time, gave piano lessons to John Ruskin. There were two elderly aunts with whom Gilbert used to stay while on holidays.

His mother sent him to Bromley High School and it was there that he got a glimpse of the theatre; he took a keen interest in school plays. He was a very bright boy, interested in arts and science with a gift for mathematics.

After school he went to Gresham College to study engineering but war had broken out and Roberts was determined to join the Royal Flying Corps. He was under age, but was accepted and, after short training, commissioned as second lieutenant. He was attached to 73 Squadron and sent out to France as an observer —which in those days meant solo-flights in a Moth or as a member of a crew in a bomber.

In 1918 he was shot in the knee while on a bombing raid in a Sopwith Camel; a short time later he was sent back to England. After a spell in hospital he was granted an Army scholarship and in 1919 secured a place in the City & Guilds College of the Imperial College of Science and Technology. Although his service in the Flying Corps was short, one or two of his comrades became his lifelong friends and he wore the R.F.C. tie with pride and affection on all important occasions.

College contemporaries remember him as a serious student, brilliant raconteur and mimic, with strong political views. His recreations were the College Dramatic Society, music, swimming and sailing. Although his wound caused him some pain and discomfort he was a powerful breast-stroke swimmer and a good water-polo player. In the Dramatic Society he met his future wife, Elizabeth Nada Hora, who was a gifted student of mathematics, a keen member of the society and a lover of serious music. Professor A. J. S. Pippard disapproved of Roberts's deviations from work but Roberts could well afford it. Learning came easily to him and he graduated with first class honours B.Sc. in 1922—finishing second in his year. He was a beautifully neat, almost artistic draughtsman.

### With Sir Douglas Fox & Partners

The acute post-war depression had not yet set in and after a short search for a job he joined Sir Douglas Fox & Partners, (later renamed Freeman, Fox & Partners) to work under the late Sir Ralph Freeman on the tender design of the Sydney Harbour Bridge.

The Chief Engineer of New South Wales, Dr J. J. E. Bradfield, had called for 'Design and construct' tenders in 1922, and Dorman Long engaged Sir Douglas Fox & Partners and, in particular, Ralph Freeman, to design the bridge. When they were awarded the contract in 1924 the whole of Freeman's team engaged on the tender design was transferred to Dorman Long & Company's newly formed Bridge Department in London, while Freeman was retained as their consultant in a personal capacity.

### Sydney Harbour Bridge

This was to be the greatest steel arch bridge in the world and Freeman and his team considered every aspect of it from first principles, new materials and new methods of analysis were double-checked and tested whenever possible. Freeman and Roberts consulted Professor Andrew Robertson of Bristol University regarding the testing of some small models of struts in silicon steel which were to be used in the bridge. These tests were later incorporated in Robertson's report on struts. Computers and electric calculating machines had not yet been invented. All calculations were done by hand with logarithm tables and slide rules, and only during later stages with small hand-operated mechanical calculators, the Muldivo limited to only eight figures in the multiplier. Young Roberts's first job was to calculate the secondary stresses in the main arch, treating it as a space frame. Nada was involved in this work with him, helping in the setting up and solution of simultaneous equations with up to eight unknowns, about the practical limit in those days. It took about a week to set up, solve and check back a set of eight equations, even with the aid of the Muldivo. 'Our Bridge is a whopper', Roberts wrote to Nada. Unfortunately, soon after starting work his wounded knee, which had apparently healed up, developed sinusitis and became septic, which necessitated a return to the hospital. He was operated on at the Royal Orthopaedic Hospital. The joint was scraped and the leg bones joined together so that for the rest of his life he had a stiff knee which occasionally troubled him. This state, often an uncomfortable one, was like a challenge and urged him to walk very quickly and to do any steeplejack work which seemed to be necessary. His determined, fast, walk, with the stiff leg swinging outwards (he never used a stick), was well known to his friends and typical of the man, who was always determined to overcome all obstacles at no matter what cost.

However, illness weakened him, especially as it came so soon after his war experience, and he worried about his career with Freeman, for whom he had a genuine admiration. It was then that Nada gave him much support and help.

They were married in 1925. Roberts was sent as an Assistant Engineer on the supervision of construction of a railway shed in Waterloo, Lancs, to gain the outside experience necessary to qualify for Associate Membership of the Institution of Civil Engineers. (He was elected in 1927.)

## With Dorman Long & Company

When Roberts returned to London from Lancashire he automatically joined Dorman Long & Company's Bridge Department and soon became one of their principal designers, working under Frank Freeman (a younger brother of Ralph) and J. F. Pain but with Ralph Freeman retaining special rights to call on his ex staff, of which Roberts was one of the most able members. Pain was a great disciplinarian and an acknowledged leader of his team of some 40 engineers and 60 draughtsmen during the 1924–34 decade. Roberts's position in this team was somewhat unusual. He was of the same age as Pain but about a year behind in experience. By the time he returned from his delayed site experience Pain was in full command of the office but Roberts was given charge of projects, often dealing direct with Dorman Long's top management.

Between 1925 and 1928 the Sydney Harbour Bridge erection calculations were completed but the checking of the final design continued long after the site work had begun. Roberts was in charge of some of the most complex analyses of the main trusses and laterals. The final written-out calculations were completed at about the same time as the bridge (1932).

In 1927/28 Roberts also worked on the erection scheme for the 531 ft (162 m) span steel arch bridge in Newcastle; the site work for which started in August 1925. The erection schemes for the Sydney Harbour and Newcastle Bridges were worked out in minute detail and Roberts contributed much to their success, the Newcastle arch in many ways acted as a prototype for that in Sydney of 1650 ft (503 m) span.

Between 1926 and 1934 he was involved in many other projects, always working with small teams of picked assistants. During these years the Bridge Department trained many young engineers who later spread their influence throughout the construction industry. The contribution made by Pain and Roberts to the training of these engineers was enormous, not only in teaching them how to carry out designs quickly and accurately, and how not to take anything for granted, but also how to stand up to adversity and persevere until an acceptable solution was found.

Among Roberts's colleagues in the Bridge Department besides Pain were W. Storey Wilson, F. A. Partridge, W. E. Hamilton, H. Shirley Smith, F. W. Sully, G. I. B. Gowring, R. S. Read, O. A. Kerensky, R. Pavry, R. A. Foulkes, V. Malcolm, A. G. A. Mackie, K. C. Burden and R. F. Pearson, who all worked together for several years and most of whom remained friends throughout their lives, forming private links between many famous firms.

By 1928 the Roberts had two daughters, Vanna and Gilda, and lived on the meagre salary of a young engineer in a small modest flat in Earls Court. Then, as now, industry under-paid young engineers, expecting them to 'pay for experience'. One of Roberts's unforgettable remarks to young assistants was 'don't pay for experience—try and sell it'. In those hard days Roberts was always well dressed. His suits from Harry Hall were looked after by University Tailors. If asked how he could afford this, he always replied that he could not afford not to. To augment his income he worked as much overtime as was available and did some private tutoring for the professional examinations. However, he and his wife managed to find time and money for the theatre, opera and concerts. There was an occasional men's four for bridge in Pain's lodgings, but Roberts did not become a bridge enthusiast and eventually dropped it altogether. Although his stiff leg was a handicap he continued to swim and play water polo and was the main pivot of the Dorman Long Swimming Club—which for years was reasonably successful in the London Business League competitions.

As the Bridge Department grew into an almost independent enterprise Roberts was always entrusted with new developments. He was responsible for publicizing and giving technical guidance on the use of Krupps's steel piles, which the company rolled under licence.

## High tensile steel

He was involved in the introduction to the structural industry of the new high tensile chrome/copper alloy steel, the 'Chromador' steel. This was the first commercially produced high tensile structural steel in Great Britain. One of its special properties was claimed to be better corrosion resistance and, in this respect, it was a forerunner of the modern corrosion-resistant steels.

Unfortunately, although Chromador steel did corrode more slowly than ordinary carbon/manganese steels, it still required full protection against corrosion to ensure long life, and therefore claims for cheaper protection were not really justified. On the other hand, the economy resulting from the use of higher strength steels was real but not appreciated by the industry and the profession. Nickel and silicon steels had been available for a long time. Nickel steel was well known in the U.S.A., but hardly ever used in Great Britain; silicon steel was used in a big way, for the first time in the Sydney Harbour Bridge. However, both steels were rather expensive 'specials' and were hardly ever used for the general run of medium-sized structures. Relatively cheap Chromador steel altered all this and high tensile structural steel combined with the use of high tensile rivets became a truly competitive material. Much of the credit for this must be given to Roberts, who was put in charge of the work of assessment of the technical advantages of the use of Chromador steels in different types of structures and of its economic benefits. His work showed that there was no doubt about either—a result which is well understood today. Roberts gave many talks and lectures on this subject to the learned societies and in his paper to the Institution of Structural Engineers on 22 March 1934 gave what, in fact, amounted to complete design specification for the use of high tensile steels in structures which later formed the basis of the requirements in the British Standard. Leading designers took part in the discussion of this paper and almost all the problems associated with the use of high tensile steels, some of which are still unresolved, were raised at that meeting. Fatigue, buckling, deflexions, corrosion and costs were discussed. Roberts's enthusiasm for the new material was fully justified, although he was over-optimistic in some of his assertions, particularly concerning resistance of fabricated bridge elements to corrosion and fatigue.

### Arc welding

Roberts's next mission was the introduction of welding into structural engineering—a task that remained with him to the end of his life. He began by learning to weld and very quickly became an expert welder and judge of good welding. No one could fool him during inspection and no detail could escape his trained eye.

### All-welded Billingham bridge

He was a pioneer and innovator in the use of welding from the day in the spring of 1931 when Dorman Long put him in charge of an alternative competitive design for the Billingham Bridge, near Middlesbrough, which was to become the first all-welded bridge in Great Britain. The development of the welding processes for commercial application had began in the late 1920s, and Roberts's job was to assess critically what was known, to develop and test different types of joints and then to design the bridge to suit the successful ones. In his paper to the Institution of Civil Engineers, jointly with P. H. Haldane, on 'Billingham Branch Bridge' delivered on 16 April 1935, the research that preceded the design is fully described.

Series of tests to determine the strengths of side fillets, end fillets and butt welds were carried out first. Then, on the basis of the results of these tests, typical joints were designed and full size models of the principal joints tested to provide information on the best preparation of the parent metal, most suitable welding procedures, and the amount and direction of contraction to be allowed in fabricating the nine main plate girders of the five-span portal frame-type bridge. It was a daring conception at that time, but the design itself was cautiously conservative. The adopted working stresses in fillet welds were smaller than are allowed today and butt welds were reinforced with shaped edge cover plates. A full-scale model test of the stepped joint supporting the suspended spans withstood a static test load $2\frac{1}{2}$ times the working load. After this, to ascertain its resistance to dynamic shock the joint was subjected to blows from a 25 cwt ($1\frac{1}{4}$ t) 'monkey' falling from progressively increasing heights. The breaking blow, the 68th, was delivered from a height of 16 ft (4.9 m). Even so, the final all-welded design of the bridge was 70% lighter than the original riveted one and was built for the same price.

The Billingham Bridge experience enabled Roberts to draft comprehensive rules for the design and making of butt welds, which he gave in a lecture at a symposium on 'The welding of iron and steel' organized by the Iron and Steel Institute and published in their *Proceedings* in 1935.

This pioneering work provided a solid basis for further developments, although naturally not every conclusion derived from it stood the test of time. Roberts's later insistence on shaped edge covers for butt welds was controversial and eventually he agreed with the critics and abandoned their use.

Two years later, in a paper presented to the Institute of Welding, Scottish Branch, in December 1937, on 'The design of welded structures', Roberts dealt with more aspects of welded design and pointed out the advantages of welding. Among other things, he had forecast the use of battle decks (orthotropic plate) which became very popular after World War II.

Roberts applied welding so successfully because he had cultivated a capacity to exercise painstaking care and scientific judgement. He was conscious of the need to learn from and use the allied sciences of chemistry, physics and metallurgy in the control of materials to be welded.

In 1933 Roberts and his family went to live in Westbrook, Margate, for the sake of their daughters' health. Roberts travelled to London daily and seemed to enjoy the long weekends by the sea. In 1934 Dorman Long plunged into a financial crisis and had to transfer the nucleus of the Bridge Department from London to their headquarters in Middlesbrough. Roberts stayed in Margate and continued to promote Chromador steel and welding techniques. This, however, was not sufficient challenge for man of his ability and ambition and in 1936 he secured an appointment as Engineer-in-charge of Development and Construction with Sir William Arrol & Company, Glasgow.

## With Sir William Arrol & Company

The whole family moved to Glasgow. Here full scope was given to Roberts's ingenuity and creative gift. Against some misgivings from the more conservative engineers in the firm, he introduced welding as a basic process in the fabrication of structural steel and designed welded box columns for Braehead Power Station—the first of their kind in Great Britain, but used in almost all major power stations since. Welded plate girders replaced riveted ones. Welded box girders were also introduced into the design of overhead and Goliath travelling cranes, again now used almost universally.

By 1941 when almost the entire industry was switched to war production, Arrol works were in the forefront of welded construction and Roberts was the recognized expert in this field with a reputation for innovation.

In 1943 he became a Director and Chief Engineer of Sir William Arrol, responsible for all design and technical development.

## Welded ships

Early in 1944 the Admiralty placed orders with many firms in England, Scotland and Northern Ireland for the construction of tank landing craft. Arrol was the only firm appointed to proceed with the design and production of all-welded vessels. As eventually developed, each ship consisted of 38 prefabricated units and weighed about 400 tons in all. Stiffened plates were the main element in each unit and most modern methods of welding were introduced. An assembly yard was set up at Alloa, Scotland, with Hubert (now Sir Hubert) Shirley Smith, an old colleague of Roberts from Dorman Long days, in charge.

Roberts was responsible for the design and planning of all the operations, which were entirely novel in British ship-building practice. He was in constant touch with the yard and organized and supervised the training of welders, not only on this but also on other emergency sites. The operation was a great success. From the placing of the first prefabricated unit on the berth to launching took only 14 weeks. The vessels were ready in time for the various landings.

At the same time, Roberts advised on the design and fabrication of the Mulberry Harbour equipment, which involved travelling to North Wales and the south coast of England in the most difficult and trying wartime conditions. This taxed his strength to the limit, but he never complained and appeared on sites after long journeys as if he had just stepped out from a nearby office.

## Industrial design

After the war Arrol returned to its normal work which consisted mainly of design and fabrication of heavy industrial plant and structures. Roberts was deeply involved with W. S. Atkins & Partners in the design and, more especially, fabrication of the exceptionally heavy crane girders for the new steelworks at Margam near Port Talbot in South Wales. The 110 ft (33.6 m) span girders in the melting shop carried 300 t capacity cranes and were the heaviest welded plate girders yet manufactured in the world. They presented many problems in design fabrication and handling.

'Flitch' (transition) plates in Coltuf steel were introduced between the 3 in (7.6 cm) thick flanges and 1 in (2.54 cm) thick web plates to improve welding and to deal with the heavy wheel loads.

Roberts also designed a new type of flap-type dock gate for the Falmouth Docks and invented a rubber joint of an entirely new pattern, which he patented and successfully exploited in other situations.

While with Arrol Roberts continued to improve the art of welding and advocate its use. He gave a series of lectures at the Stow College, Glasgow, in 1942–43 on 'The principles of welded structural design' and many talks to the various branches of the Institute of Welding and to the Iron and Steel Institute. In 1943 his paper on 'Electric welding in shipbuilding' was published by H.M.S.O.

## With Freeman Fox & Partners

In 1945 Freeman Fox & Partners, at the Ministry of Transport's direction, became associated with Mott, Hay & Anderson as consulting engineers for the Severn Bridge Project and the late Sir Ralph Freeman took charge of the design of the superstructure with C. D. Crosthwaite and O. A. Kerensky as his principal assistants (both became Partners later). Early in 1948 the Severn Bridge became an urgent reality and it was decided to establish a joint office which was to be staffed by engineers from the two firms, led by the best available expert designer to be recruited from outside.

The Senior Partners of the two firms, Sir David Anderson and Sir Ralph Freeman, agreed that Gilbert Roberts was the man for the job and Sir Ralph invited Roberts to become a Partner in Freeman Fox and take charge of the newly formed joint office. Roberts agreed with enthusiasm. The prospect of returning to London with all its learned societies, theatrical and musical attractions and of becoming one of the partners in the firm in which he started his engineering career, and which he greatly admired, pleased him and his family enormously but, above all, it was a challenge and a thrill to be involved in the design of the first major suspension bridge outside the U.S.A. His two principal assistants were O. A. Kerensky and Kenneth Anderson, representing the two firms. C. D. Crosthwaite, who had contributed much to the theory of suspension bridges and the early aerodynamic studies, was needed in North Wales to take charge of large hydro-electric projects there.

Anderson, Freeman and Roberts formed a triumvirate which guided the design work and made all the final decisions on the choice of the possible alternative solutions of the many problems that occur during the development of a major engineering project.

### Severn Bridge (first design)

Preliminary geological investigations of the site, and a comprehensive study of the designs and methods of construction used in the major suspension bridges in the United States, had been carried out by the two firms during 1946–48, so that when Roberts took charge of the team the layout of the proposed bridge was already settled and a major aerodynamic investigation was in progress by the Aerodynamic Division of the N.P.L. under the direction of Dr R. A. Frazer, F.R.S., and Mr C. Scruton in collaboration with the engineers and Professor F. R. Farquharson of the University of Seattle, Washington, U.S.A., and of Tacona Bridge fame, who acted as consultant to the joint engineers. Roberts's job was to examine every aspect of the proposed design and to produce the final design for tender purposes.

The work was urgent as it was understood that the Government intended to start construction in 1950–51. For about a year the joint office was working long hours, and Roberts spent many an evening engrossed in discussions with his staff, weighing the pros and cons of the various alternatives and initiating laboratory tests of any new design aspects or new materials and methods of fabrication that were considered to be desirable. Dr E. G. Thomas of the Building Research Station carried out exhaustive tests on a model of an orthotropic plate deck, to be adopted for the first time in a major bridge in Great Britain, while the Road Research Laboratory, under the guidance of W. H. (later Sir William) Glanville, F.R.S., in collaboration with Limmer & Trinidad Limited, conducted full-scale trials of different types of protective treatment and surfacing materials for that deck. Mastic asphalts of different thicknesses and composition and very thin epoxy surfacings were investigated, the final choice being a $1\frac{1}{2}$ in (3.8 cm) thick single layer of stone-filled mastic asphalt laid by hand on the zinc-sprayed plate. The benefits of the composite action of the asphalt with the steel plate were not realized at that time, but are now well understood. The possibility of designing a suspended structure in which full use was made of the deck platform as part of the main stiffening girders, thus achieving optimum efficiency, was very much in Freeman's mind right from the start, but this was always associated with the deep-trussed main girders which were considered to be essential for aerodynamic stability and were invariably used in the United States except for the original Tacoma Bridge. When Roberts joined the team he gave some further thought to the problem; but the urgency of the task, and the fact that this was the first major suspension bridge designed by British engineers demanded caution. Any departure from the orthodox stiffening truss of considerable depth advocated by Mr O. H. Ammann, the Chief Engineer of the Port Authority of New York, designer of the George Washington Bridge, who was consulted by Anderson was not possible at that time. However, the location of the deck itself was controversial. When Roberts joined the firm the deck was located at the level of the neutral axis, i.e. at half-depth of the main trusses, in order to keep the movement of the deck to a minimum. As the design developed, it became clear that the torsional stiffness of the fully braced suspended system was of greater importance than the longitudinal distortions of the deck system. It meant locating the deck above the stiffening trusses and providing top and bottom lateral bracing systems. This solution was adopted, thus creating a latticed box. Final calculations took into account the torsional stiffness of this suspended space frame in calculating deflexions and stresses in the structure, using a method developed by Dr Frazer. The result was a more appropriate distribution of strength in the vertical and horizontal web systems and a significant saving in the weight of the suspended structure compared with one designed by the conventional methods used in all previous suspension bridges.

The second break-through initiated by Roberts was in the design of the main towers, again resulting in substantial economies. Up to that time towers had been designed as struts, fixed at the bottom and free at the top, i.e. with an effective length of twice the height of the tower. The Severn Bridge towers were treated as fixed at the bottom, but with movement at the pinned top end determined and controlled by the elastic behaviour of the main suspension cables. The significance of this is that the tower top is pulled away from the vertical thereby inducing bending stresses, in addition to the direct stresses due to the heavy vertical reaction from the cable (210 000 kN) and the weight of the tower itself. This, in turn, produces further deformation of the tower, but without further deflexion of the top. The behaviour of the tower is nonlinear under this form of loading, but a solution is quickly obtained by successive approximations. Stresses at all sections of the tower, due to different load combinations, were calculated from these first principles—a method based on the limit state philosophy.

## The Dome of Discovery

In 1949 Freeman Fox was appointed by the Festival of Britain 1951 Office as consulting engineers for the buildings of the South Bank Exhibition. The

Dome of Discovery was to be the focal point of the exhibition and the architect, Ralph Tubbs, conceived a sensational building—a circular space of 365 ft (111.5 m) diameter covered by a spherical aluminium sheeted roof spanning the entire area. It fell (as usual) to the engineers to find a structural solution to his idea—the Dome presented a unique opportunity for designing a large space structure in aluminium. Freeman quickly arrived at a brilliant concept for the framework of the Dome and its supports and with Roberts's invaluable help the design was soon developed. The main frame comprised a system of latticed ribs, laid on great circles of the Dome and forming equilateral spherical triangles of about 60 ft (18.3 m) side (plate 1). A fabrication method was suggested by Roberts to ensure the maximum possible amount of shop prefabrication and subassembly. The decision to use aluminium alloy meant that extruded sections of almost any shape could be obtained without appreciable additional cost. The cross-section of the main ribs was triangular, made up of three extruded elements braced together by extruded angle bars. The triangulated framework of the main ribs carried extruded rafters and purlins secured by Lindapters, to which the plain aluminium sheeting was attached by 'pop' rivets, as used in the aircraft industry. All main connections in the ribs and bracing were made with high tensile steel turned and fitted bolts, as corrosion problems could be ignored in a temporary building. Owing to the novelty of the materials, methods of fabrication and uncertainties in design, conservative working stresses were adopted with a factor of $2\frac{1}{4}$ against yield and buckling. The entire design, from first concept to working drawings, specification and invitation to tender, was completed in 3 months.

On 11 March 1950 Sir Ralph Freeman died suddenly of a heart attack. Ralph Freeman junior (later Sir Ralph) became Partner in charge of the entire Exhibition project with Roberts responsible for the final design, fabrication and erection of the Dome. Its novel features were described in his paper to the Institution of Civil Engineers on 3 April 1951.

The Dome of Discovery was the first of its kind, both in size and the subtlety of its structural configuration and details of construction. Professor A. J. S. Pippard described it as probably the most interesting structure designed since the two airships R100 and R101.

When in 1951 the design of the Severn Bridge was nearly completed and ready to go for tender, the Government suddenly decided not to proceed with the project and work on it was more or less abandoned. The joint office was dismantled soon after and Roberts, with Freeman Fox staff, moved to other premises in 110 Victoria Street. With the death of Sir Ralph, Roberts became the Partner in charge of major bridge and special structures projects, with Kerensky as his principal assistant.

## Auckland Harbour Bridge

In May 1951 F.F. & P. had been appointed as consulting engineers to the Auckland Harbour Bridge Authority (formed in March 1951) for the design and supervision of construction of an approximately 3350 ft (1002 m) long bridge

PLATE 1. Dome of Discovery, Festival of Britain, 1951: 365 ft (111 m) diameter aluminium alloy dome supported on a system of intersecting ribs of triangular lattice construction.

PLATE 2. Adomi Bridge, Ghana (formerly Volta Bridge): 805 ft (246 m) span crescent arch. Completed 1957.

across the Waitemata Harbour. in accordance with the Report previously submitted by F.F. & P. to the New Zealand Government. The proposed bridge was to consist of a navigation span of 800 ft (244 m) with two side spans of 580 ft (177 m) and four approach spans on the south side progressively reducing from 407 ft (124.3 m) to 265 ft (81 m). The main truss members were to be in B.S. 548 H.T. steel shop riveted and, at the request of the contractor, site bolted.

In the joints that could be reamed to exact size during shop assembly, high tensile close tolerance bolts were chosen, but for all other connections, 'grip' bolts were specified. These bolts were just coming into use in Germany and the U.S.A. but had not yet been used in any major bridge by the British engineers. As usual, Roberts would not take anything for granted. The grip bolts used up to that time were ordinary high tensile bolts stressed to about 80% of their yield strength and breakages were not uncommon during tightening. Roberts realized at once that such bolts were, by nature, unreliable and also inefficient. Because the cost of drilling holes and fitting up and tightening the bolts was appreciably more than the cost of the bolt itself, increasing the strength of the bolt should be economic, while the consequential reduction in the size of the joints offered further considerable advantages. Roberts designed a waisted bolt, i.e. with the shank diameter equal to the thread root diameter, and had it made of very high tensile steel. Initial tests showed that, when tensioned to beyond the yield stress in the shank, ordinary nuts seized and cracked and the thin washers deformed. Roberts then developed specially shouldered nuts and thick washers made of hardened steel, which proved to be entirely satisfactory. Bolts of $\frac{7}{8}$ in (22 mm) diameter shanks made of 45–55 ton/in$^2$ (700–850 N/mm$^2$) steel were safely tensioned to about 29 ton (290 kN). Joints made with different numbers of bolts were then tested for slip and 'slip coefficients' were determined. Finally, with a factor of 1.7 against slip, the safe design value to resist shear was established. Roberts insisted on the 'turn-of-the-nut' method of tightening bolts because it gave much more determined loads in the shank, than by the torque measuring method and correctly argued that the safety of this procedure was justified by the fact that such bolts could withstand at least two more turns of the nut before breaking. The bolt became known as the 'Roberts' bolt, it was patented jointly by him and the manufacturer to protect the British market but the patent was never enforced. Unfortunately, not being a standard product, these bolts are not normally available in small quantities as a large number of different lengths would have to be stocked. The development of this bolt—a small item in a large structure—was typical of Roberts, who always exercised particular care and scientific judgement in the pursuit of excellence in every minute detail.

A decision was also made to use composite construction in the deck, T-shear connectors welded to the stringers were designed from first principles. The welded mild steel stringers carrying the reinforced concrete deck slab were simply supported so that the top flanges were always in compression and the problem of fatigue could be ignored. This form of construction was well ahead of its time. The B.S. Code of Practice C.P. 117 'Composite construction in bridges' was published only in 1967 and the F.F. & P.'s T-connectors had a place in it.

The shock of Sir Ralph's death and the continuous strain of overwork gradually undermined Roberts's health and in 1954 he was ordered complete rest, away from the office, for several months.

### Design of welded plate girders

Meanwhile work on the development of design and fabrication of welded structures was proceeding and special attention was being paid to plate girders, as the rules in the current British Standards were inadequate and several members of the staff were involved in the production of the new B.S.I. Codes of practice for welded design and welding processes. On his return Roberts took a very active part in the production of B.S. 2642, which deals with the welding of medium high tensile steels to B.S. 968 (first published in 1955).

In 1953 the Ministry of Works organized a Conference on welded structures, at which Roberts and Kerensky gave a paper on 'Plate girder bridges', in which they indicated the lines that a design should follow to achieve real economy, giving many recommended details of construction and advocating orthotropic plate decks and composite construction in steel and concrete, as well as the more general use of high tensile steels. The proceedings of the Conference were published by H.M.S.O. in 1954.

### Volta Bridge (now known as Adomi Bridge)

In 1953 F.F. & P. were asked by Sir William Halcrow & Partners, consulting engineers for the Volta River Project in Ghana, to participate with them in the design of a steel bridge across the Volta River. The conception of this 800 ft (244 m) steel arch and its many new features were almost entirely due to Roberts and are described in a joint paper given to the Institution of Civil Engineers in 1958 by P. A. Scott and Gilbert Roberts. Nothing similar had been built before. All the elements of the suspended deck, consisting of a reinforced concrete slab supported by welded high tensile steel stringers and cross girders, were designed to act compositely, using the type of shear connectors developed for the Auckland Harbour Bridge. The chord members of the two-pinned latticed arch were welded high tensile steel boxes of the smallest practicable size (approximately 2 ft (0.61 m) × 2 ft (0.61 m) fabricated in up to 40 ft (12.2 m) lengths and hermetically sealed on completion. An ingenious innovation was in the design of their joints. The ends of each member were accurately machined, and for the in-service condition when the arch rib was in compression, Roberts relied entirely on the bearing between the machined plate edges, without the usual reinforcement by cover plates and bolts or rivets in shear. However, during the erection of the arch by cantilevering some of the joints would be in tension. Large waisted screwed rods made of heat-treated very high tensile steels were housed in brackets built into corners of the chords; and tensioned against the abutting ends by means of a specially designed hydraulically operated spanner, the prototype of which, together with some other equipment, was made by Mr J. A. K. Hamilton in his small private workshop under Roberts's personal supervision. The total pretensioning of the four rods was in excess of the maximum tensile erection stress across the joint, so that during erection there was only a variation of pressure between the abutting faces, but no movement at the joints. Overall, these connections cost no more than the conventional cover plates, but had the great advantage of maintaining the structure in a truly elastic condition during erection. All field connections of welded web members and laterals were made with high tensile close tolerance bolts (Plate 2).

Yet another innovation was the protective treatment. To avoid an attack on paint by fungus, notorious in some parts of Africa, the entire steelwork was grit-blasted, metal-sprayed in the works with zinc coating 0.0035 in (0.089 mm) thick, shipped to site and left unpainted—a bold decision in 1955—and only possible when, as here, climatic conditions permitted. A certain amount of repair was required because of minor damage in transit.

## Power stations

In 1951 F.F. & P. were appointed as consulting engineers to the Central Electricity Generating Board, for the civil engineering and structural work for Castle Donington Power Station (completed 1959) and in 1954 for High Marnham Power Station (completed 1962). Roberts was responsible for the design of the steelwork with B. P. Wex (now a Partner of F.F. & P.) as his principal assistant. Roberts's experience with Arrol, both in design and in the fabrication of the steelwork for power stations, was fully utilized and it was said by one of the Senior Engineers of C.E.G.B. that the steelwork for these two power stations was the lightest and the most elegant in his experience up to that time. It certainly was very economical.

## 400 ton Goliath crane

Ever since his Arrol days Roberts had been interested in the design of large cranes and in the mid-1950s was pleased to receive a request from Babcock & Wilcox to undertake the design of a giant Goliath crane of 400 t lifting capacity and 250 ft (76 m) span for use by them in the construction of nuclear power stations. They wanted a crane containing the least possible number of separate parts, as easy as possible to erect and dismantle, and weighing not more than 700 t compared with their own estimate of 1200 t for a 'conventional' Goliath of the required capacity. Roberts conceived a structure consisting of latticed legs and a bowstring girder, all with bolted field connections, arranged so that the girder hoisted itself into position using the cranes own winches. Two identical cranes were built in 1957–58 and each was used on two nuclear stations in the United Kingdom before being sent to shipyards in Norway and Spain. F.F. & P. were involved in several other crane designs, but Roberts was particularly proud of this one; as indeed he could well be and the design was duly patented.

## Radio telescopes

In 1956 F.F. & P. faced a new challenge. The firm was commissioned by the Radiophysics Division of the Commonwealth Scientific and Industrial Research Organization (C.S.I.R.O.), of Australia, to study the feasibility of a large steerable radio telescope. This followed on the initial study by Dr (later Sir) Barnes Wallis, who recommended C.S.I.R.O. to invite F.F. & P. to see the project through. This was an entirely new field for all the Partners, and Roberts, who was given charge of the project, began by a study of the problem of providing a light yet rigid dish capable of being steered about horizontal and vertical axes—the so-called Altaz system of mounting. At the same time he appreciated the importance of obtaining a structural concept which provided the right framework for many other disciplines. Many experts were consulted. The conventional equatorial mount was compared with the Altaz one in considerable detail and finally the Altaz mount was recommended with a specific and novel form of control, with a master equatorial mount placed at the centre of motion of the telescope. A reflector dish of 210 ft (64 m) diameter was estimated to be the maximum possible within the funds available, against the client's original requirement of 250 ft (76 m) diameter.

The feasibility report, submitted in September 1957, was approved and in 1958 the firm was appointed to design and supervise the construction of the telescope, to be installed at Parkes, New South Wales. The structure conceived by Roberts and his team, which was led by the late M. H. Jeffery and C. R. Blackwell, was entirely different from that at Jodrell Bank, near Manchester, which was the only comparable instrument in the world at that time. One of the important design features of the Parkes telescope was the central mounting unit containing all the shop-made mechanical parts. This was designed for complete trial assembly in the workshop, where all the precise mechanical fit-ups could be achieved and checked, in a way capable of easy repetition at the site. The work requiring precise initial setting out and fit-up at the site was thus limited to the construction of the steel reflector dish and its surface adjustment. Another important breakthrough was the design of the servo system and master controls. The basic principle of this form of control was propounded by Dr Barnes Wallis in his General Report of September 1955 on the feasibility of large radio telescopes and is described in British Patent Application no. 29248/1955, entitled 'Improvements in telescope mounting', filed by Dr Wallis and Vickers Armstrong (Aircraft Limited). A detailed study of the control system was made by Sir Howard Grubb, Parsons & Company Ltd, and the Control Department of Associated Electrical Industry Ltd.

The 210 ft diameter (64 m) steel paraboloid with wire mesh reflector operated down to 10 cm wavelengths. It would rotate on a machined cast steel track mounted on a 12 m high concrete tower, the total rotating mass exceeding 1000 t. The ingenious design and method of fabrication of the dish and of the assembly of the telescope were conceived by Roberts, again demonstrating his ability to achieve the highest efficiency in the performance of a complex structure.

The telescope was commissioned in October 1961 and was an immediate success. In the same year F.F. & P. were appointed by the National Research Council of Canada to design a 45 m diameter fully steerable telescope to be erected in Algonquin Park, Ontario. The N.R.C. telescope called for even higher reflector accuracy than the C.S.I.R.O. one, with the additional problems of operation and survival in the severe winter climate of Eastern Canada.

This time Roberts made the paraboloid dish out of a stiffened steel plate, which provided extremely high reflector accuracy. To obtain the required rigidity and robustness he decided that the reflector plating should act integrally as part of the structure. It had, however, to be capable of release for adjustment when required. The detailed design by which this was achieved, which involved developing special countersunk bolts for the fastenings and for the attachment to welded stiffeners, was largely his work. The finished structure was really remarkable for the precision of workmanship and quality of performance.

Mounting, drive and control were similar to those of the Parkes telescope. This telescope was completed in 1966 and operates down to 2 cm wavelength.

## Pipe bridges

At about the same time Roberts and Wex had become concerned with the design of a number of high pressure oil and gas pipeline bridges in India and West Pakistan, Six 167.5 m span bridges for Oil India in Assam came first. Then in West Pakistan a crossing of the Sutlej River near Panjanad was called for by Sui Northern Gas Pipelines Ltd. During high flood, bed-scours of around 18 m were liable to occur each year and the 1.5 km wide river could meander over a 6.5 km width. An ingenious and graceful solution was arrived at. The multi-span bridge constructed entirely by field welding was approximately 1830 m long and founded on 27 large diameter bored piles. Gas was transmitted at 7 $N/mm^2$ pressure through the three high tensile steel tubular chords of the triangular space structure. The bridge was very economic and easy to maintain and has functioned well since its completion in 1964.

This was immediately followed by bridges over the Chenab and Jhelum Rivers. These bridges were 475 m and 850 m long and consisted of multi-span continuous cable-stayed girders supporting a 254 mm diameter pipe carrying the high pressure gas. They were completed in 1965 and 1966. The appointment for the next two bridges was made just before Wex was made a Partner. Roberts and he conceived the form they should take, but Wex completed the design. Roberts retired before the site work began. The structures were unstiffened suspension bridges carrying the pipeline across Indus and Kabul Rivers with main spans of 394 and 274 m respectively. Much thought was given by the two designers to achieving complete aerodynamic stability of these very slender structures. The main cable supports the 254 mm pipe from above and, together with two pretensioned inverted catenaries, forms a triangular space structure. The novel construction method for the longer bridge, devised by its designers, involved welding and rigging the entire bridge complete with pipeline on the ground and on a pontoon bridge, then erecting it by jacking—a process which took about two days. The two bridges were completed in 1972.

### Maidenhead Bridge

In 1958 the Ministry of Transport instructed F.F. & P. to proceed with the completion of the Maidenhead Bridge, over the Thames, the construction of which had been started in 1937 but was abandoned in 1940 because of the war.

The firm had been appointed as consulting engineers for this bridge in 1935 and Ralph Freeman had designed a beautiful-looking bridge, utilizing, for the first time in British practice, composite action between the reinforced concrete deck slab and the steel girders. This was to be achieved by bolting the precast reinforced concrete slabs 11 ft (3.35 m) × 11 ft (3.35 m) × 12 in (304 mm) thick to eight main girders which were to be riveted mild steel box girders continuous over the two river piers and tied down at the ends of the short side spans to the abutments. For purely aesthetic reasons the soffit of the 270 ft (82.3 m) river span was made elliptical and the outermost girders were to be welded, the other six being riveted. By 1940 the river works and abutments and piers were completed, the 1600 t of steel partly fabricated at Arrol's works and the huge precast slabs cast and stacked on site.

On restarting the work it became immediately apparent that a very advanced design in the mid 1930s was completely out of date in the late 1950s. Yet any drastic change in the design of the superstructure would involve abortive work and payments. F.F. & P. were determined that an obsolete, uneconomic structure should not be built. The design was completely revised showing big savings in the cost of the superstructure. In the new design concrete deck slab was made $8\frac{1}{2}$ in (216 mm) thick instead of 12 in (304 mm) and the 1600 t of mild steel was replaced by about 600 t of weldable high tensile steel. The riveted box girders becoming welded plate girders. Fortunately, most of the steel at Arrol's works had been used during the war, so only the stack of precast slabs had to be got rid of. All public authorities rightly dislike paying for abortive work, but in this case the advantages of the change were overwhelming and the Ministry of Transport approved it and paid for the new design. The decision to go ahead with the redesign, without previous approval, in anticipation of the result, was typical of the partnership of Roberts and Kerensky, who were jointly involved in this project.

The bridge is fully described by Roberts in his paper to the South London Branch of the Institute of Welding on 8 February 1961. Notch ductile 'Coltuf' high tensile steel had been used in the tension elements of the girders. During discussion of the paper Roberts claimed that he introduced it because its welding qualities were superior to those of ordinary steels to B.S. 968 and not because of his fear of a brittle fracture, but Kerensky and the two senior engineers (M. Field and K. A. Goodearl) were advocating the use of the more expensive steel because of its superior notch ductile properties, as by that time the danger of brittle fractures in welded construction was well known even though the Codes of Practice had not then referred to it.

The 270 ft (82.3 m) span of the all-welded plate girders acting compositely with a reinforced concrete deck slab was at the time of construction the largest of its kind in the world. It is also one of the most beautiful bridges.

## Forth Bridge

In the mid-1950s the Government decided that a bridge across the Firth of Forth with a single span of 3300 ft (1006 m) should take precedence over the Severn Bridge; F.F. & P. were again associated with Mott, Hay & Anderson as consulting engineers to the Forth Road Bridge Board and, as in the case of the Severn Bridge, were responsible for the design of the superstructure. In 1955 the joint office, staffed as before by engineers from both firms, was re-established with Roberts in charge. His principal assistants in the new set-up were W. T. F. Austin and M. Parsons (both now Partners of F.F. & P.) and A. E. Temple and D. W. Smith of Mott Hay & Anderson. The main span of the bridge was only 60 ft (18.3 m) longer than that of the Severn Bridge, but the side spans were appreciably longer. The research and design work done during the years 1945–51 in connection with the Severn Bridge formed the basis for the design of the Forth Bridge, but Roberts reviewed all the previous conclusions and altered some of the details. The final design is described in his paper on 'The design of the Forth Road Bridge' given to the Institution of Civil Engineers in November 1965, for which he was awarded the Institution's highest award—the Telford Gold Medal.

Work on the bridge site started in November 1959 and the bridge was opened to traffic by Her Majesty The Queen on the 4 September 1964. In recognition of his work Roberts was knighted and elected Fellow of the Royal Society in 1965. As soon as the final design of the Forth Bridge was completed, work on the Severn Bridge was resumed, as construction of the latter was to follow that of the Forth.

## The Severn Bridge

This time Roberts was in sole charge of the design of the superstructure, assisted on this occasion by Dr. W. C. Brown (now a Partner of F.F. & P.) and Parsons. Although first-hand experience was gained during the design and construction of the classical Forth Bridge and more or less a repeat of it was expected by everyone, Roberts did not want to do this. Several new ideas had been generated during the interval and he was determined to apply some of them. The most important of these was that of a monolithic aerodynamically stable suspended stiffening girder of shallow depth. In his paper on the design of the Severn Bridge, given to the Institution of Civil Engineers on 15 October 1968, Roberts describes the step-by-step development of this revolutionary concept.

The studies of the behaviour and structure of the wind at the Severn site, initiated in 1947, were completed in 1954 and the more reliable wind data could now be used in aerodynamic tests at the National Physical Laboratory, although turbulence was still not reproducible. With enthusiastic cooperation from C. Scruton and D. E. Walsh of the N.P.L., a large number of sectional models were tested until an ideal shape was found and all the necessary wind-related properties of the proposed structure determined. The new structure was a single aerofoil-shaped box girder only 10 ft (3.05 m) deep. Its streamlined shape reduced the wind drag on the suspended structure to about a quarter of that on the original trussed one. However, aerodynamic tests on the sectional model which accurately represented every detail of the proposed suspended structure indicated that there could be slight aerodynamic movements at wind speeds of about 10–15 knots (18.5–27.8 km/h) with wind inclinations up to about 7.5° to the horizontal, if the damping coefficient of the structure was much less than 0.05.

It was generally accepted that the classical suspended structure consisting of trussed stiffening girders and deck elements with riveted or bolted joints had a damping coefficient of at least 0.05. Roberts and Brown were aware that the damping coefficient of an all-welded suspended box as proposed by them would be appreciably smaller. They therefore began to look for some means of introducing an additional energy-absorbing element and hit on the idea of making use of the hysteresis properties of the wire rope hangers. For this purpose they proposed that the two elements of the hangers be inclined to form a quasi-triangulated system in the vertical plane. Small relative longitudinal movements between the main cable and deck produce a change of stress in the inclined elements of the hangers, the magnitude of the stress depending on the angle between them.

For any given mode of oscillation the longitudinal displacement of any point on the cable relative to the deck can be calculated and from this the stresses induced in the hanger system and, hence, the energy stored in it deduced and expressed as a percentage of the total energy in the structure at the peak of the cycle. Rather surprisingly at that time there were no available data on the absorption of energy by wire ropes subjected to cyclic stresses. Roberts instigated a series of tests on ropes and strands which were carried out by Bruntons (Musselburgh) Ltd and British Ropes Ltd and all the necessary information was obtained for wire ropes of different lay and for bridge strands. Bridge strand wire was selected for the hangers. Finally, a hysteresis value for the individual hangers was estimated and their damping effect on the bridge as a whole obtained by integration. The logarithmic decrement for the first anti-symmetric torsion mode of oscillation, which is the most damaging to suspension bridges, was calculated as 0.052, which compared well with that found in classical riveted trusses. Some additional damping would of course be contributed by the rest of the structure and Roberts was satisfied that a correct solution of the problem had been found. In this the designers were correct as the bridge has shown no tendency to oscillate in any wind speed since it was opened to traffic in September 1966. Roberts patented this form of construction, again to protect the British industry, and again the patent has never been enforced. The other major improvement was that the main towers became single cell box girders instead of multi-cell, resulting in further savings in cost. The very significant reduction in the weight of the suspended structure and of the wind effects on it, with consequential savings in the weight of main cables and towers and, hence, in reactions on the piers and anchorages have greatly increased the range of suspension bridges.

Roberts believed that it was the designer's responsibility to ensure that fabrication and erection require no more than care and common sense on the part of the fabricator and that the fabricator, for his part must be prepared to exercise maximum care in strengthening, flattening, machining and otherwise preparing his material if work in the shop and on site is to go smoothly and economically.

Accordingly, he gave a lot of consideration to the problem of fabrication of large box members. For maximum economy the cost per ton of platework should be comparable to that of lattice girders and therefore shop fabrication on a mass production basis had to be aimed at with a high standard of accuracy for easy site assembly. His experience with welded dock gates and landing craft at Arrol suggested how these problems should be tackled. In the event, the transportable (up to 60 ft (18.3 m) long) panel elements of the boxes were fabricated in the contractors' works in Middlesbrough, Darlington and Glasgow and delivered by road to Chepstow. Complete lengths of boxes weighing up to 130 tons were then assembled on slipways on the banks of the Wye, floated out to the bridge site and lifted into position by specially designed tackle travelling on the main suspension cables. The idea of shop fabrication, followed by assembly into box units near the site of the bridge and floating out, was conceived by Roberts and his team, but the details of the scheme and its execution, including minute planning of every phase, were, of course, carried out by the consortium of contractors, the Associated Bridge Builders Ltd, consisting of Dorman Long, Cleveland Bridge and Arrol.

## The Wye Bridge

The spectacular Severn Bridge somewhat overshadowed the adjacent bridge which carries the M4 Motorway across the Wye and formed part of the same project. Yet this bridge is, in its own class, as remarkable as its big sister. It has a river span of 770 ft (235 m) and two side spans of 285 ft (87 m) flanked by shorter approach spans. The main girders are flat aerofoil-shaped boxes 65 ft (19.8 m) wide on top, 33 ft (10.0 m) wide at the bottom and only 10 ft (3.05 m) deep, similar to those of the Severn Bridge. The total width of the steel battle deck is 100 ft (30.5 m) the areas outside the main girder being supported by 17 ft 6 in (5.33 m) long brackets. The 770 ft (235 m) span is cable-stayed at approximately its one-third points. The slim 96 ft (29.3 m) high towers and the single stays being located in the 13 ft (3.96 m) wide central reservation, separating the two carriageways. The great torsional stiffness of the flat box is thus utilized to the full, while its extreme shallowness gives lateral flexibility which ensures equitable distribution of load to the four main bearings at the piers. When conceived and built, the main span of the Wye bridge was the longest of its kind in the world.

As with the Severn Bridge, the sub-units were fabricated in the shops and delivered to site for assembly into the box units approximately 56 ft (17 m) long and weighing up to 120 t. Floating out was not possible on the Wye River and cantilevered erection from each bank was adopted. To ensure accurate fit at the joints the units were assembled end to end in fully equipped yards adjacent to the bridge. When completed they were winched up side ramps on bogies to the deck level, rolled out to the erection face and there picked up by specially designed erection girders.

Roberts and Brown were again involved in every detail of fabrication, construction and erection of this entirely novel structure. The elegance of the bridge is quite remarkable, although the traffic crossing it is barely aware of its existence.

### Severn Bridge honours

The Severn Bridge was opened by Her Majesty The Queen on 8 September 1966 and became famous in a day; engineers, architects and government officials from all over the world came to see and study it, and many honours were bestowed on Roberts and on the firm.

In 1966 the Court of the Worshipful Company of Carmen awarded Roberts the Viva Shield 'in recognition of his great contribution to the design of large steel suspension bridges . . . and a complete departure from previous methods of combating the hazard of aerodynamic instability in the superstructure of such bridges'.

In the same year the Institution of Structural Engineers gave its Special Award to Freeman Fox & Partners, coupled with the name of Roberts.

In 1967 The Queen's Award to Industry was conferred on the firm 'in recognition of its efficiency as demonstrated by outstanding achievement in technological innovation in suspension bridge design.'

In 1969 Freeman Fox & Partners received the first MacRobert Award 'for an outstanding contribution which, by way of innovation in the fields of engineering or the other physical technologies, or in the application of the physical sciences, has enhanced or will enhance the national prestige and prosperity of the United Kingdom of Great Britain and Northern Ireland'. The award was shared with Rolls Royce for the development by them of the Harrier 'jump jet' concept.

Soon after the opening of the Severn Bridge Roberts was asked by the British Council to do a lecture tour in Japan on 'Developments in bridge engineering'. His lecture covered the development of steel bridges during the last 100 years, from those with eyebar chains, through major girder bridges to modern long-span suspension bridges with steel wire cables; materials employed and methods of fabrication; reasons for the development of welding and the consequential modifications to the properties of steels: and a description of the Severn Bridge and the thinking behind it. The tour was a great success, much enjoyed by his wife and himself.

### The Bosporus Bridge

Other suspension bridges of similar design followed. In 1968 F.F. & P. were appointed as consulting engineers to the General Directorate of Highways of the Republic of Turkey for the Bosporus Bridge project. The knowledge and experience gained in the construction of the Severn Bridge enabled Roberts and his team, again led by Brown and Parsons, to produce an even better bridge, though the basic design was the same.

Bosporus Bridge has a main span of 1074 m, the longest yet completed outside the U.S.A. It carries dual three-lane carriageways and provides the first ever road connection between the European and Asian parts of Turkey. Having reached the age of 70, Roberts retired from the Partnership in 1969, before the construction of the bridge began (in 1970), and Brown and Parsons completed the design and supervised the construction of the bridge with Roberts in the background. However, he and his wife were able to attend the magnificent opening ceremony on 30 October, 1973, at which the President of the Republic cut the tape, while guns and ships saluted the great event of linking the Middle East to Europe by road. Incidentally, the bridge was tested to maximum design capacity, if not beyond, by the solidly packed crowd walking slowly across it.

### Humber bridge

The decision to begin the final design of the Humber Bridge, which with its span of 1410 m would be the longest span in the world, was made in 1971 after Roberts retired. F.F. & P. had been retained as consulting engineers for the bridge since 1926 and Roberts had been involved in its many evolutions throughout that period. Even when he was with Arrol, Freeman often consulted him and employed him to do trial designs for the various alternative schemes. Roberts, in turn, employed Kerensky and other ex-Dormanites to help him with the calculations. The technical break-through for a span of such length, however, came with the success of the Severn Bridge, whereby the estimated price of the Humber Bridge was drastically reduced. Sadly, the genuine estimates made in the late sixties bear little relation to the present cost of the bridge which, owing to financial inflation and productivity deflation, has nearly quadrupled. Roberts was not involved in the final design of the bridge, which was carried out by Wex and Parsons.

### Auckland Harbour Bridge widening

In the late 1960s the four-lane Auckland Harbour Bridge had become inadequate for the amount of traffic using it and Roberts conceived a way of widening it by extending cantilever brackets from the existing piers to support two-lane box girder bridges on both sides of the original one. The box girders were adopted as much for aesthetic reasons as for technical. The 800 ft (220 m) main span girder was one of the largest of its kind at the time of building and certainly the shallowest. From a distance, the lace-like appearance of the old bridge was thus preserved. The widening was completed after Roberts's retirement.

Roberts's designs have a reputation of being light with nothing wasted, but he never took deliberate risks. Shutting one's eyes to something one thought might happen, or overlooking some factor, would be quite inexcusable to him. This, of course, does not mean that he was always right, or that risks unforeseen by him did not sometimes arise. He often said that success or failure of an innovation depended upon the accuracy of the inventor's imagination. Invention to him was 'an extension of experience by imagination' and in one of his lectures he named five of his designs which he considered to be the most imaginative:

Volta Bridge (now Adomi Bridge) in Ghana;
Radio telescope in Australia;
Radio telescope in Canada;
400 t Goliath crane, and
Severn Bridge.

Like most engineers he was well aware that one day a failure, might occur, not so much through mischance as through human error or aberration. There are minor failures, mishaps and even fatal accidents during the work span of most civil engineers, but major tragedies involving heavy loss of human life are relatively rare. Roberts was deeply involved in the tragedies of the Milford Haven and Yarra Bridge collapses. Both were designed and contracts let when he was still in charge.

In the case of Milford Haven, Pembrokeshire (now Dyfed) there was an error, or perhaps a misconception, in the design of the diaphragms over the piers and on 2 June 1970 a span collapsed during cantilever erection. The weakness of the diaphragm was not picked up during the contractually obligatory check by the contractor of the adequacy of all elements of the bridge during erection, i.e. the double-check procedure failed. Legal arguments as to the responsibility followed and lasted over eight years before an out of court settlement was reached but, mercifully the four bereaved families were compensated at once.

The case of the West Gate Bridge crossing the Yarra River in Melbourne, Australia, was quite different. The consulting engineers for the entire scheme were Messrs Maunsell & Partners, who were fully established in Australia.

When it was decided that a steel bridge with a river span of 1100 ft (340 m) was required, Maunsell invited F.F. & P. to help them with its design, which they readily agreed to do, the two firms becoming joint engineers. The first design proposed by Roberts and his team, which for this project was led by Brown, was for a cable-stayed main span with an orthotropic plate deck, as used in F.F. & P.'s previous designs of long span bridges. However, the General Manager of the Bridge Authority had had an unfortunate previous experience with the Kings Bridge in Melbourne, when he was Bridge engineer of the relevant local authority. That bridge was an all-welded structure (shop and site) in Australian high tensile steel. Large cracks developed almost immediately after the opening of the bridge to traffic and the experts decided that the cracks were due to brittle fracture. Fortunately, the bridge could be propped up in time to avoid casualties. Bent on avoiding, as they thought, the danger of similar failures, the Yarra Bridge Authority prohibited site welding and insisted on most stringent welding procedures in the shops. This ruled out the all-welded steel deck surfaced with a thin carpet of mastic asphalt, as had been generally adopted in Great Britain and Western Europe. Roberts, in one of many efforts to satisfy the client, then proposed the use of a lightly stiffened steel plate acting compositely with a reinforced concrete slab, surfaced with asphalt. Except for one large bridge in France (Tancarville suspension bridge) there was no precedent for this form of construction, and even the French example was significantly different. Tests were carried out in England to check the design of the stud-type shear connectors, after which this novel type of deck was adopted.

There was nothing revolutionary in the idea. The composite reinforced concrete slab and steel plate construction is now covered by a British Code of Practice for Composite Construction of Bridges (B.S. 5400, Part 5). However, it was new in 1968 and was viewed with suspicion by many. The problems with this form of construction arise because the lightly stiffened steel plate is liable to be unstable during erection, when acting as the compression flange of the main box girder, before the concrete deck has been poured. In other words, the deck is robust when finished, but sensitive during construction. By the time the bridge was being built Roberts had already retired. The Partner in charge of the supervision on site was the late E. M. Birkett of Maunsell, working in close cooperation with Kerensky, who was Partner in charge in England on behalf of F.F. & P. Inevitably there was duality of control, although F.F. & P. was nominally responsible for the steel superstructure. During the morning of 15 October 1970, for some reason that has never been properly explained, and on somebody's authority that has not been established, the top flange of a simply supported box girder was cut almost in two by removing a number of bolts in the mid-span splice in order to straighten a harmless buckle in the flange plate caused by a previously also unauthorized overloading of the girder by 70 t of kentledge. The girder collapsed, killing 35 men, including the Resident Engineer and the Deputy Resident Engineer, Contractors' Project Manager and one of their junior engineers—almost all the vital witnesses who could have explained the sequence of events and assigned the responsibility for the tragedy. The only surviving engineer involved in the operation was bady injured and, suffering from a loss of memory, was confused about the sequence of events.

The Australian Government appointed a Royal Commission which cross-examined all the surviving people responsible for the design and construction of the bridge. Roberts, who by that time had nothing to do with the administration of the project, was for several long days grilled by the Commission concerning the alleged weakness in the design and failure of communication between London and the site. Not being used to such treatment, Roberts did not make a good witness; he was particularly intolerant to ignorant and irrelevant questions and in the end failed to convince the Commission of the quality of his and Brown's designs.

The mental and physical strain of fighting a losing battle, in a small crowded court with poor ventilation in the middle of an Australian summer, nearly killed Roberts. He suffered a heart attack during the journey home and, on recovery, was ordered complete rest for several months. This tragedy more or less finished his involvement in practical engineering.

He continued to be interested in the work of the firm and of the Royal Society, attending Meetings and serving, as member and chairman, on Sectional Committee 4, which among other things advised on the selection of engineers for election as Fellows. Occasionally he and his wife attended official functions of the learned societies and F.F. & P.'s annual dances, but on the whole they led a quiet life in close touch with their family, particularly enjoying the company of their three grandchildren.

Books were a great standby. Gilbert enjoyed Nada reading aloud to him, particularly Boswell's *Life of Johnson*, but the theatre remained their chief delight and was their main link outside the family. Drama, acting and staging were all of interest and so was the seating in the actual theatre, because seats could be very uncomfortable for a man with a stiff leg. During the last years they derived particular pleasure from going to performances at the Windsor, Richmond and Wimbledon theatres.

Their golden wedding was celebrated in their elder daughter's house in Bournemouth. The grandsons provided a great surprise for their grandparents by arranging a tour of the town in a hired double-decker bus. Great fun was had by all, especially as champagne flowed freely!

## Character

Roberts matured early—no doubt his war experience, academic brilliance and moral courage helped him to develop confidence, assurance and firmness which served him so well throughout his life.

He was dedicated to his work, which needed his gifts of courage, determination, intellect and creative ability. It required confidence as well as courage to make use of his new techniques and, even more so, to follow his own intuitive ideas in creating new forms of structures. A prominent engineer from abroad wrote to Roberts to say that 'the Severn Bridge would collapse under the first fall of snow'. A terrible thing for the designer to read.

There was another quality in his work: the gift of empathy. Perhaps this is akin to inspiration in art. He really felt he lived in the structures he designed and this feeling perhaps gave him more than usual confidence when he gave his opinion that, properly designed, checked and erected, they were safe.

Roberts did not tolerate fools and he despised cowards—moral and physical. He selected his assistants carefully, was demanding and critical of their work, but once accepted he was loyal and protective when anything went wrong, never passing the blame on to weaker shoulders in order to find excuses for himself. However, a few slip-ups would be enough to have the offender removed from his team, if not from the firm. He could be sarcastically cutting to equals but, unless strongly provoked, did not take it out of his subordinates. He would seldom take 'no' for an answer, but his own 'no' was usually final.

Roberts was secretive about his work and in that respect difficult to work with, but his judgement and advice were usually worth listening to.

Strange as it may seem, he was superstitious about the consequences of talking or writing in detail about a project that was not yet finished. He once remarked to a journalist (*The Observer*, 21 July 1968); 'When an Engineer writes a premature paper telling the world how he built it, sure enough a few days later the thing falls down!' A poetical exaggeration but a belief and fear well imprinted on the minds of some of his staff.

He was not a committee man. He would contribute much technically if the subject interested him, but almost nothing at all if it did not. He would never attend for the sake of 'attendance' and therefore had a 'poor' record with the chairmen and secretaries of councils and committees. Although he was an ambitious man, his ambition was to be a top engineer and to be recognized as such, rather than as a president of this or that institution, so he never became one, although he served on the Council of the Institution of Structural Engineers and, for many years, on the Council of the Welding Institute.

Roberts was a devoted family man. Work and physical handicaps left little opportunity for outside interests, but journeys to work sites both at home and abroad were always of interest to him and his wife. For three successive summers they spent a week exploring English sites with the Royal Archaeological Institute, of which his wife was a member. He intensely loved reading a limited range of books, admired good prose and thought Latin was essential to the writing of good English, but had no time for poetry. He read most of Churchill's books and was especially interested in Yeates's *Winged victory*, which recalled his own flying experiences. His own writing was neat and precise and of the highest quality, as can be seen in all the papers and reports presented by him to various learned societies and government departments. He would never tolerate bad grammar or slovenly expressions and often corrected and rewrote letters and reports written by his staff not an unusual necessity in the engineering profession.

His love of classical music, opera and the theatre remained with him from childhood. He was himself, by nature, a good actor with expressive features and a gift for bringing out a brief satirical remark together with devastating mimicry of its victim, but he was basically kind hearted.

Roberts's lifework spans a revolution in structural engineering and he was in the thick of it. He combined his belief in himself and determination in work with personal charm and modesty. To the very end he was unaffected by acclaim. We owe much to Lady Roberts for the devotion and support she gave him throughout his working life.

## Acknowledgments

From the day I joined Dorman Long's Bridge Department in 1927 until the day that Gilbert Roberts died, I was associated with him in work and in other activities, at first as a junior assistant and, for the last 22 years, as a Partner.

Writing this memoir has been a long nostalgic journey into the past, in which I was greatly assisted by his widow, Nada, and by many of his friends and colleagues.

In particular, I am grateful to Dr A. A. Wells, F.R.S., for his appreciation of Roberts's contribution to structural engineering, and to Sir Ralph Freeman and Messrs C. D. Crosthwaite, W. E. Hamilton, F. A. Partridge, C. R. Blackwell, M. Field, M. F. Parsons and B. P. Wex for supplying some of the details of the work in which they were engaged with Roberts, and for their recollections of him.

I must also thank Dr D. Fisher for helping to collect and check the various miscellaneous data, C. E. Butler for assembling the bibliography and my wife for checking the many drafts and re-drafts of this memoir.

The reproduced photograph of Sir Gilbert was taken by G. Argent in 1968.

## Membership of institutions and learned societies

Fellow of the Institution of Civil Engineers
  Member of the Civil Engineering Research Association Committee on Steel Structures
Fellow of the Institution of Structural Engineers:
  Member of Council, 1957–60
  Chairman of *ad hoc* Committee on Aluminium Alloy Structures
Fellow of the Institute of Welding (now the Welding Institute):
  Vice-president, 1958–61
  Member of Council, 1962–68
Fellow American Society of Civil Engineers
Member of the Association of Consulting Engineers

## Honours and awards

Knighted 1965
Fellow Royal Society, 1965
Fellow of Engineering, 1976
Fellow of Imperial College
Fellow of City & Guilds Institute
Manby Premium of I.C.E., 1934
Telford Premium of I.C.E., 1951
Telford Premium of I.C.E., 1959
Trevithick Premium of I.C.E., 1961
Viva Shield by the Court of the Worshipful Company of Carmen, 1966
Special Award of the Institution of Structural Engineers, 1966
Telford Gold Medal of I.C.E., 1967
Royal Medal, Royal Society, 1968
James Watt Gold Medal of I.C.E., 1969
MacRobert Award, 1969
Churchill Gold Medal of the Society of Engineers, 1970

## Bibliography

Papers to the learned societies and printed lectures are given in chronological order. Articles and interviews published in the popular and technical press are not generally listed.

1933/4 (With J. F. Pain) Sydney Harbour Bridge: calculations for the steel superstructure. *Minut. Proc. Instn civ. Engrs* **238**, 256; discussion p. 402; correspondence, p. 437.

1934 A new high tensile steel for structural work. *Struct. Engr* July issue, pp. 314–338.

1934/5 (With W. P. Haldane) Billingham Branch Bridge. *Minut. Proc. Instn civ. Engrs* **240**, 537; discussion, p. 599; correspondence, p. 609.

1935 Design and tests of butt-welded joints. *Iron and steel symposium on the welding of iron and steel*, vol. **1**, pp. 161–171; discussion, pp. 394, 398, 426.

1936 Strength of welded joint in structural steel. *Proc. Cleveland Instn Engrs* 6 January, pp. pp. 51–68.

1939 The design of welded structures. (Institute of Welding, Scottish Branch, 8 December 1937.) *Weld. Ind.* **3**, 435–442.

1943 *Principles of welded structural design*. London: H.M.S.O.

1947 Fabrication of all welded landing craft. *Welder, Lond.* January–March 1946, p. 14 (an appreciation of Sir Gilbert Roberts's work on wartime landing craft).

1950/1 Structural design of the Dome of Discovery: Festival of Britain. *J. Instn civ. Engrs.* **36**, October 1951, suppl. IX–XIX.

1953 (With O. A. Kerensky) Plate girder bridges. *Welding conference 1953*, p. 233, discussion, p. 251. London: H.M.S.O.

1954 (With J. F. BAKER) The bridging of the Severn. *J. Instn Highw. Engrs*, October, **3**, 22–37.

Bridging of Severn. *Surveyor* **113**, 177–181; discussion no. 3236, 13 March, pp. 208–209.

1958 (With P. A. SCOTT) The Volta Bridge. *Proc. Instn civ. Engrs* 9 April, p. 395; discussion, *Proc.* 11 November, p. 366; corrigendum, *Proc.* 10 June, p. 276.

Aluminium structures. *Struct. Engr*, Jubilee issue, July, p. 130.

1958/9 Structural uses of welded high tensile steel. *Jl W. Scotl. Iron Steel Inst.* **66**, 122–130; discussion, pp. 151–186.

1961 (With O. A. KERENSKY) Auckland Harbour Bridge: design. *Proc. Instn civ. Engrs* 18 April, p. 423.

The welded Maidenhead Bridge. *Br. Weld. J.* **8**, 291–309.

1962 Auckland Harbour Bridge: design and construction. Gilbert Roberts. O. A. Kerensky, H. Shirley-Smith, J. F. Pain: Discussion, *Proc. Instn civ. Engrs* 22 May, p. 141.

1964 Men and jobs (interview). *Engng News Rec.* 19 November.

1965 Forth Road Bridge: design. *Proc. Instn civ. Engrs* **32**, November, 333–405; reprinted in *Forth Road Bridge*, pp. 11–83. London: Institution of Civil Engineers (1967).

1966 The Severn Bridge. A new principle of design. International Associations of Bridge and Structural Engineers, Symposium on suspension bridges, Lisbon, November.

Design and construction of the Severn Bridge. Fifth World Meeting International Road Federation, London, September.

1968 Modern developments in design and construction of long span bridges. *Proc. Can. Struct. Eng. conf.*, Toronto, Ontario, The master bridge builder (interview). The *Observer* 21 July. Severn Bridge—design and contract arrangements. *Proc. Instn civ. Engrs* **41**, 1–48; also *Civil Engineering N.Y.* **39**, 68–73.

1969 Evolution of large suspension bridge design. *Aust. civ. Engng* **9**, 26–27, 29, 31.

1970 *Bridges—civil engineering project 70's* 1st ed. London: Instn Civ. Engrs.

T. R. Seshadri

# THIRUVENKATA RAJENDRA SESHADRI

3 February 1900 — 27 September 1975

Elected F.R.S. 1960

By Wilson Baker, F.R.S., and S. Rangaswami

Thiruvenkata Rajendra Seshadri was born on 3 February 1900 in the small town of Kulitalai lying on the bank of the Kaveri, one of the seven sacred rivers of India, and situated in the Tiruchy district of South India. This district formed a part of the Madras Presidency of pre-independent India and is now a part of the state of Tamil Nadu of the Indian Republic. His father, Thiruvengadatha Iyengar, was a teacher in a local school; his mother was Namagiri Ammal, and T. R. Seshadri was the third of five sons who were the only children of the marriage. The family was deeply religious, and this influence was dominant throughout T. R. Seshadri's life, not only in his personal attitudes but also in his complete dedication to his work.

## Education in India

Seshadri's early education was in the local school and then in high school in the town of Srirangam which has one of the holiest temples in India. He then moved to the National College High School in the nearby Tiruchy city, where he was influenced by the high ideals of the deeply patriotic founders of the National School and College. For his collegiate education Seshadri entered the Presidency College in the metropolitan city of Madras in 1917; this was, and still is, one of the three great institutions of higher learning founded by the British soon after the middle of the nineteenth century, the other two being the Presidency College, Calcutta, and the Royal Institute of Science, Bombay. At the Presidency College, Madras, Seshadri became dedicated to chemistry through the influence of a number of inspiring teachers, one of whom, Professor P. A. Narayana Iyer, he always held in the highest esteem. The cost of living in metropolitan cities was relatively very high even in this early part of the century and the merit scholarship that Seshadri received could not quite relieve the financial strains on the family. He therefore had to seek additional help and this he obtained from the Ramakrishna Mission, founded in memory of the great mystic saint of modern renascent India, Sri Ramakrishna Paramahamsa. This non-sectarian and non-denominational institution was based on the cardinal principles of the divinity of man and the importance of a spiritual approach in the lives of individuals and communal relationships. Ramakrishna Missions exist, and carry out these principles, in many important centres in India and other countries; work of a very high order is carried on with emphasis on culture, and the harmonizing of science with the pronouncements of the ancient Indian thinkers, work which finds expression in the running of schools, colleges, students' homes and hospitals. It was one such, the Ramakrishna Mission Students' Home at Madras, that accepted Seshadri as a resident student when he was studying at the Madras Presidency College. The simple living, the discipline and the high thinking that he found in the Students' Home reinforced the traits that had already been formed by his family background and his previous education in distinguished schools, traits that showed themselves during all his life—his dedication to work, eager thirst for knowledge both scientific and spiritual, respect for genuine differences of opinion, a sense of social responsibility, sympathy for the needy and compassion for the weak and absence of the element of self-interest, all of which made him into a very unusual combination of scientist, humanist and spiritualist.

After receiving the honours degree in chemistry of the University of Madras, Seshadri worked in the Ramakrishna Mission for one year, helping in the organization of their newly started Residential High School. Later he worked for three years in the Chemistry Department of the Presidency College, Madras, as a University Research Scholar under the guidance of the late Dr B. B. Dey, Professor of Organic Chemistry. The work was partly on Indian medicinal plants and partly on coumarins and its merit received special recognition from the University of Madras by the awards of the Sir William Wedderburn and the Curzon Prizes.

## Manchester, London, Graz, Edinburgh, 1927–30

In 1927 Seshadri secured an Overseas Technical Scholarship from the University of Madras and this enabled him to proceed to the University of Manchester to work under the Professor of Organic Chemistry, Robert Robinson, whose research school was attracting workers from all over the world. When in the following year Robinson moved to the Chair of Organic Chemistry at University College London, Seshadri accompanied him. Seshadri's Ph.D. thesis, accepted by the University of Manchester, was on the subjects of (1) search for new antimalarials, (2) synthesis of anthocyanins. Seshadri cherished his entry into the Robinson school of research as the most important event in his career, and he would often say that through this he had become a member of the great Perkin family of organic chemists. Seshadri's personal loyalty to Professor Robinson was intense and was reciprocated. In a message for the special commemorative volume on the occasion of Seshadri's 60th birthday in 1960 Robinson wrote as follows:

> 'Even if Professor Seshadri were known to me only as an author of original memoirs in the Chemical Journals, I would be gratified to have this opportunity to add my tribute to his fertility of ideas, his technical skill in execution and his qualities of energetic drive and wise planning. His

original researches have indeed given him world-wide recognition and he is unsurpassed in the experimental survey of the groups of natural products on which he has concentrated his attention. But to me he is no mere name in the literature; I have enjoyed the inestimable privilege of following his development almost from the beginning. His work in my laboratory, especially on the synthesis of anthocyanins, was of the highest calibre and went far to encourage us to pursue the attack in this difficult region of synthesis. It is not appropriate here to recount the outstanding achievements to the credit of Seshadri and his school; that is the purpose for which this volume is dedicated. Suffice it to say that we do homage to a most sincere scientist of unassailable integrity, a brilliant and devoted teacher and a most generous friend.'

After receiving the Ph.D. degree of the University of Manchester and before returning to India, Seshadri worked for brief periods in other important chemical centres in Europe. He spent some months in Graz in Austria learning organic micro-analysis in the laboratory of Professor Fritz Pregl, the father of quantitative organic micro-analysis. This new technique, more than any other introduced at that time and indeed for many years after, made possible much of Seshadri's later work on plant products where frequently only a few milligrams of pure material could be made available for analysis. Seshadri also spent eight months at the University of Edinburgh with Professor George Barger where he worked on the chemistry of retrorsine, and for a shorter period in the laboratory of the Chief Agricultural Analyst to the county of Fife, where he learnt methods of agricultural analysis.

## Madras, Andhra University, the war years, 1930–49

Seshadri returned to India in 1930 at the conclusion of his foreign training. The country was then caught up in the worst economic depression the world has ever seen, and in addition it was rocked by country-wide political agitation in a bid for freedom from colonial rule. Patriotic mass demonstrations which were countered by severe governmental repression were the order of the day. Openings to a career of one's liking were extremely rare for qualified scientists. Discarding other possibilities of employment in more lucrative positions, Seshadri preferred to become a Research Fellow in the University of Madras, and after some months took a government research post in the Agricultural Research Institute at Coimbatore in the Madras State as Soil Analyst. Although this institution offered him the opportunities to get acquainted with different aspects of agricultural science, particularly plant chemistry and plant protection, an opportunity which he valued very much, scope for fundamental work was not enough. Hence when, three years later, an opportunity arose to join a university, Seshadri left government service in the agricultural department and joined the Andhra University at Waltair in South India as Senior Lecturer and Head of the newly opened Chemistry Department. The new department called for a great deal of organizational work; laboratories had to be built and equipped, courses of study had to be framed, and naturally research facilities could not be provided for some considerable time. Nevertheless, within a few years Seshadri had built up a fine department befitting any progressive university. In this task he received the unstinted support of two eminent men who were successively the Vice-Chancellors of the Andhra University, Sir S. Radhakrishnan, who later became President of India, and Sir C. R. Reddy, and Seshadri often expressed his gratitude to these two Vice-Chancellors. It was characteristic of Seshadri that while the laboratories were under construction, he used to rush on a bicycle to the Biochemistry Department of the Andhra Medical College at Visakhapatnam, three miles away, to do his own research, facilities provided generously by Dr V. K. Narayana Menon, Professor and Head of the Department of Biochemistry of the Medical College. In 1934 Seshadri was appointed to a Readership and in 1937 was made Professor of Chemistry at the Andhra University, and his ability and enthusiasm began to attract young research workers to his department. In this same year he was also given the responsibility of looking after the University Department of Chemical Technology when the erstwhile head of the department left. The financial resources of the two departments were extremely small by present day standards, but by prudent and wise husbanding they were stretched to the limit, and served to sustain the activities of a number of research workers. The year 1937 was also that in which Seshadri laid the beginnings of the future Department of Pharmaceutical Sciences of the Andhra University.

Among those who received research training under Seshadri in these early days and who were later appointed to posts of distinction may be mentioned K. Neelakantan (Professor at the Andhra and Annamalai Universities and Sri Venkateswara University), S. Rangaswami (Professor of Pharmaceutical Chemistry at Andhra and later of Chemistry of Natural Products at the University of Delhi), P. S. Rao (Director of the Forest Utilization Laboratory at Bangalore), G. V. L. N. Murthy (Head of Analytical Division of the Tata Iron and Steel Company at Jamshedpur in the State of Bihar), L. R. Row (Professor and Head of the Department of Chemistry, the Andhra University), the late N. V. Subba Rao (Professor of Chemistry at Osmania University, Hyderabad) and V. Baliah (Professor of Chemistry at the Annamalai University and later Vice-Chancellor of the Nagarjuna University, both in South India).

The departments that Seshadri was building up were beginning to take shape when World War II broke out, and supplies of chemicals and apparatus from Europe, on which educational institutions in India had largely to depend, became more and more scarce. In 1941 came the restrictions on lighting as a precaution against air-raids, and laboratory work in the evenings had to be curtailed. Towards the close of the academic year 1941–42, the harbour at Visakhapatnam, about four miles from the University campus, was bombed by Japanese war planes and this necessitated the evacuation of the entire town of Visakhapatnam including Waltair, the site of the University campus. The University buildings were commandeered by the Defence Department and the laboratories so laboriously built up over the years were dismantled and transformed into a military base hospital. All the university teaching departments and administrative offices were moved to a relatively safe inland location, Guntur, about 300 miles south, and accommodated in whatever buildings could be rented and in hastily put up sheds. The practical work of the science departments was accommodated in the science laboratories of two local colleges. This arrangement was indeed a very poor substitute for the facilities left behind at Waltair, and experience of one year at Guntur showed that they were grossly inadequate for chemistry teaching and research, and the chemistry department of the Andhra University was therefore shifted to Madras at the beginning of the academic year 1943–44. The honours classes were squeezed into the Chemistry Department of the Presidency College and the M.Sc. classes and research into the Biochemical Research Laboratories of the University of Madras some distance away. With this change the setback to research experienced by the Chemistry Department during 1942–43 was partly overcome and work began to pick up once more. Even with all the restrictions imposed by the state of war, a remarkably large volume of research work was turned out and several young workers were able to take their doctorate degrees.

## Delhi, an advanced centre of study

The year 1945 saw the formal end of hostilities and all the departments of the Andhra University were ordered back to Waltair so as to begin the academic year 1946–47 there. The Chemistry Department moved into its old buildings, but the laboratories had to be rebuilt since they had been completely dismantled for military use. The task of reconstruction was not easy since there was a shortage of almost everything in the post-war years. The stoppage of scientific supplies from Europe that had begun with the war turned out to be a permanent feature and the sluggishness in the development of a fine chemical industry in India plagued science in that continent for at least a decade after the end of war. The resettlement of Waltair was just completed when Seshadri was invited to accept the headship of the Department of Chemistry at Delhi. The University of Delhi, established formally in 1925, consisted of a group of constituent colleges but had no teaching departments of its own. The early forties saw some growth but it was only after a visionary in the person of Sir Maurice Gwyer, the Chief Justice of India, became its Vice-Chancellor that real progress was made. In 1949 Sir Maurice Gwyer took the major decision that postgraduate teaching and research should be organized in the science departments of the University, and to this end he invited the best men then available in India to take charge of the various departments. Sir Maurice saw Seshadri as the man for chemistry and the invitation to take charge of the Chemistry Department and to build up a worthy school of chemistry was accepted by Seshadri. Unfortunately, this proposed move to Delhi was not welcome in all quarters, and even after he took up the Headship of the laboratories in June 1949, petty opposition continued for some time. These difficulties were, however, faced by Seshadri with characteristic determination and strength of character, and finally orderliness and harmony were established in the department which soon became perhaps the most active centre in the country devoted to the pursuit of knowledge of the chemistry of natural products.

In these endeavours Seshadri received the full support of Sir Maurice Gwyer and of succeeding Vice-Chancellors.

The build-up of the Department of Chemistry was for some time hindered by lack of funds to purchase expensive physico-chemical instruments such as ultra-violet and infrared spectrometers, but Seshadri's work attracted a generous gift for this purpose from the Wheat Loan of the United States, and enabled the work to move abreast of research in the western world. But the best equipment was really the human material. A large number of gifted and highly motivated young men and women rallied round him and to them Seshadri set the pattern not only for chemistry but also for dedication. They forgot the clock and gave up holidays and vacations in order to follow their teacher whose aim was to make his department one of the best centres in the world for natural product chemistry. The laboratories were open from early morning till late at night and Seshadri was always there to advise students when they were in difficulties. It was a common saying that he had no home or social life, he was always in the laboratory. Students staying late were invariably given a lift and taken to their hostels. Sustained work by these competent and dedicated young scientists led to a flow of high quality publications which appeared in Indian scientific journals, in the *Journal of the Chemical Society of London*, in *Tetrahedron Letters* and in *Tetrahedron*. The nineteen-fifties were particularly productive and in 1960 Seshadri was elected to the Fellowship of the Royal Society of London. This was also the year when he reached 60 years of age, and his election was a fitting recognition of two decades of distinguished work.

In 1962 the University Grants Commission of India, a government body charged with the responsibility of regulating and promoting higher education in the country, took a major decision to give official recognition to centres with a record of sustained high quality work by designating them as Advanced Centres of Study. They were given substantial financial assistance to encourage and support men of high quality to undertake research at these centres, both as permanent members and as holders of temporary fellowships. Generous funds were also given for the purchase of expensive equipment and to meet running expenses, and in addition aid was also received from the U.S.A., the U.S.S.R. and the U.K. largely in the form of equipment but also in part to aid the exchange of scientists. The Department of Chemistry of Delhi University was chosen to be the Advanced Centre for the Chemistry of Natural Products and Seshadri was designated as its first Director. It was in connection with the organization of this Advanced Centre that Delhi University invited the Indian author of this memoir to join the Delhi University group. Much has been achieved by the Centre in the field of the chemistry of natural products ever since it came into existence.

## Active retirement at Delhi, 1965–75

In 1965 Seshadri reached the retiring age of 65 and he was thereby relieved of all formal administrative positions and responsibilities, but the University did him the signal honour of making him its first ever Emeritus Professor and continued to provide him with the facilities for research. His standing as the only chemist Fellow of the Royal Society in India led many science funding agencies to entrust him with research projects in which they were interested, for example the Council of Scientific and Industrial Research, the Indian Councils of Medical and Agricultural Research and the Indian National Science Academy. These projects brought many young scholars to work with Seshadri and generous funds for non-recurring and recurring expenses. In addition, other talented young students joined Seshadri's teams with scholarships from the Council of Scientific and Industrial Research. This post-retirement period proved one of the most fruitful in Seshadri's very active life, in spite of a serious heart attack early in 1965 from which he never completely recovered, but his dedication to chemistry was such that he continued to guide and to take active part in research for almost the next ten years.

Seshadri was one of the few who firmly believed that science alone cannot solve all the problems of life and he took keen interest in moral and spiritual education. He, along with Swami Ranganathananda then chief of the Delhi Unit of the Ramakrishna Mission, started the Delhi University Vedanta Samiti, which held regular Sunday morning sittings at which spiritual matters were discussed with the help of ancient spiritual texts of India and explained in terms of modern scientific concepts, and he encouraged all his students to participate in the activities of this group. Seshadri was emphatic that the academic community had a special and unique responsibility to society, but that at the same time academic achievements divorced from ethical, moral and spiritual foundations were not enough. Yet in spite of his endeavours and personal example Seshadri was saddened in the last years of his life by small mindedness and criticism shown by some of those whom he had done so much to help, but he may well have reflected that such disappointments have usually had to be borne by visionaries. Nevertheless, Seshadri's devotion to his students went far beyond guiding them in research at the laboratory bench; he helped them to express themselves lucidly both in writing their theses and in giving accounts of their work before critical audiences, and he helped them to secure suitable posts when they left the University, and even helped them financially whenever the occasion called for it. The admiration and respect in which Seshadri was generally held by his students and by chemists throughout the world was marked by celebrations on his 60th, 65th, 70th and 75th birthdays. Funds were raised to endow medals and prizes at the Universities of Andhra and Delhi, and two important volumes were brought out on Seshadri's 65th and 70th birthdays. The former, *Advancing frontiers in the chemistry of natural products*, contained nineteen reviews contributed by former senior students in their respective special areas; the latter volume, *Some recent developments in the chemistry of natural products*, contained nine articles contributed by Indian chemists unconnected with Seshadri's school and sixteen articles by chemists of other continents.

Almost to the end of Seshadri's life his long and mature experience as a chemist and scientific investigator was sought and utilized by the Government of

India. He served on the Pharmacy Council of India, on the Indian Council of Medical Research, and he held various offices under the Committee for Scientific and Industrial Research including the Regional Research Laboratories at Jammu and Hyderabad. Also under these bodies and of the U.G.C. and the Indian Council of Agricultural Research he was chairman of several Expert Committees. For the wider needs of Government his services were sought and given to the Indian National Committee for Chemistry, to the Ministry of Defence, the Department of Atomic Energy, the Scientific Advisory Committee to the Cabinet and to the Committee of Science and Technology. For some time he was consultant to Unesco.

Seshadri was honoured in many ways by scientific bodies in India. He had been a President of the Indian Chemical Society, Chairman of the North Indian Section of the Royal Institute of Chemistry, a Vice-President of the Indian Academy of Sciences, Bangalore, and President of the Indian National Science Academy and of the Indian Science Congress Association. He had held special lectureships at several Indian Universities, honorary professorships at the Universities of Andhra and Osmania, and received honorary doctorates at the Universities of Andhra, Benares, Delhi and Osmania. He was the recipient of two important medals of the Indian National Science Academy, the Shanti Swarup Bhatnagar Medal and the Meghnad Saha Medal.

After his formal retirement in 1965 Seshadri was given the unusual privilege of continuing his researches as previously with full use of laboratories, adequate funds and authority to act as supervisor of students for higher degrees. He had refused previous offers of more lucrative positions of prestige saying that he wished to remain a university man, active in the laboratory and satisfied if his work enabled him to live simply. For seven years, which proved among the most fruitful of his career, conditions of work and the researches themselves continued smoothly, but in 1972 new regulations of the Delhi University prevented him from receiving any salary or honorarium, any research projects and associated funds, and prevented any graduates from registering with him for a Ph.D. degree. Seshadri was thus reduced to a position without young scholars, research grants or salary, and in spite of his courage and spiritual strength, his health became seriously affected. Further heart trouble afflicted him in 1973 and he died in hospital in September 1975 two days after an operation for a gastric ulcer.

Seshadri's influence on the development of organic chemistry in India can scarcely be over estimated. Many of those who worked with him became leaders of research both in India and elsewhere, among whom may be mentioned Professors V. V. S. Murti, S. K. Mukerjee, A. C. Jain, S. Neelakantan, G. B. V. Subramanian, V. K. Ahluwalia, S. Rangaswami and Dr Varadarajan and Dr K. Aghoramurthy. More than 150 successful candidates for the degree of Ph.D. were trained in Seshadri's laboratories and this has had a pronounced effect on standards of work throughout the country. Seshadri's published work is contained in over 1100 original papers, this remarkably large number arising from his practice of publishing positive results of research almost as soon as they were made, in part to encourage his many collaborators and to help to find suitable posts in industry and teaching. The Bibliography at the end of this memoir lists only some of the more important papers, but a complete Bibliography has been compiled and deposited in the library of the Royal Society.

## Scientific work

The most important contributions of Seshadri and his school have been in the area of the heterocyclic oxygen compounds of plants. They began with the isolation and determination of structure of the flavonoid pigments of Indian plants, both aglycones and glycosides. Methods of methylation were developed to facilitate the degradative study of the aglycones and to gain insight into the structure of the glycosides. In order to synthesize new members having a higher degree of oxygenation, methods had to be evolved for introducing more hydroxyl groups into various positions, and the converse procedure for removal of hydroxyl groups was also worked out. Methods of partial methylation and demethylation were evolved as part of the general strategy. These studies were extended from flavones and flavonols to isoflavones, flavanones, chalkones, aurones, isoflavanones, dihydroflavonols, xanthones and anthraquinones, involving plant materials of numerous families and genera. Methods of total synthesis and interconversions in these areas were also elaborated to include natural compounds containing *C*-methyl and *C*-prenyl groups, furan and chromene rings and combinations of these.

The elusive flavandiols, called proanthocyanidins by Freudenberg and leucoanthocyanidins by Seshadri, and the catechins and tannins received considerable attention by Seshadri, as did also many coumarins, halocoumarins, 3- and 4-phenylcoumarins and related compounds. Other groups of compounds derived from flavonoids or coumarins and characterized by the presence of an additional ring resulting from an oxide bridge connecting the pyrone ring and the side phenyl ring, the biflavonoids and flavanolignans, afforded areas of study. Seshadri became deeply involved with the rational utilization of natural resources such as medicinal, poisonous, dyestuff and insecticidal plants of the country. Intensive work was carried out on *Psoralea corylifolia*, *Pongamia glabra*, species of *Dalbergia*, *Pterocarpus*, *Acacia*, *Morinda*, *Albizzia*, *Gossypium*, *Cassia*, *Citrus* and *Pinus*. Seshadri also made an extensive study of the lichens of India; many of their chemical components were intensively investigated and synthesized. He propounded biogenetic theories on almost all the groups of compounds on which he had worked, and collated Raman, infrared, nuclear magnetic resonance (n.m.r.) and mass spectral data.

In his post-retirement years new areas of investigation covered terpenoids, steroids, alkaloids and saponins. Also with the availability of new techniques requiring very small quantities of products and new spectral methods many plant materials, which had been examined earlier by classical methods, were re-investigated, leading to publications dealing with the minor components of plant materials.

### *Methylation of anthoxanthins and glycosides*

Seshadri's work at the Andhra University during the mid-thirties was concerned with the examination of the flowers of several species of cotton (*Gossypium*) plants (family Malvaceae). The studies were later enlarged to cover other genera of the Malvaceae family, *Hibiscus*, *Tagates* and *Thespasia.* Many individual compounds of the anthoxanthin group were isolated both as free aglycones and as glycosides. The aglycones were studied by classical methods such as alkaline or oxidative degradation, but it was found advantageous to use the methyl ethers, since this enabled easier isolation and recognition of the degradation fragments. Methods of methylation therefore became very important, particularly in the investigation of glycosides. The methylated glycosides, on hydrolysis with acid, yielded the aglycone with all hydroxyls methylated except those which were involved in linkage with sugars. The resulting partial methyl ethers were in turn degraded and the fission products identified, thus enabling the structure of the glycoside to be deduced. A refinement was introduced by ethylating the hydroxyl group or groups liberated on hydrolysis of the methylated glycoside; the resulting mixed ethyl methyl ether of the aglycone could be more satisfactorily studied since the isolation and recognition of its fission products were easier.

Earlier methods using methyl iodide or diazomethane for methylation of anthoxanthins and their glycosides were not entirely satisfactory, and so Seshadri developed the use of dimethyl sulphate and anhydrous potassium carbonate in boiling acetone, by which method complete methylation of all phenolic hydroxyl groups, including the chelated one at the 5-position, could be achieved. For ethylation, ethyl iodide or diethyl sulphate was used along with potassium carbonate. The study of gossypin, the 8-glucoside of gossypetin, provides a good example of the employment of these techniques (192). In subsequent studies it was found that the hydroxyl group at the 7-position of flavonoids was more acidic than the others because of the influence of the carbonyl group of the heterocyclic ring, and hence it could be selectively methylated by suitably adjusting the conditions. Methylation with one molar ratio of dimethyl sulphate and anhydrous sodium bicarbonate led to the clean formation of the 7-methyl ether.

### *Oxidative demethylation and selective demethylation*

Oxidative demethylation in flavonoids, as developed by Seshadri, consists of the formation of a 5,8-quinone by reaction of moderately concentrated nitric acid on the monomethyl or dimethyl (or diethyl) ether of a 5,8-dihydroxy compound (225). The quinone is the same as the product of the 'gossypetone reaction'—the oxidation of 5,8-dihydroxy compounds with *para*-benzoquinone or silver oxide. The method was developed as an elegant synthetic tool for the determination of the structure of many natural substances, e.g. gossypin (192) and the quino-chalkones of *Didymocarpus pedicellata*, and has been extended to substances the structures of which are not otherwise easily accessible, e.g. carthamidin and norkhellin. Selective demethylation of polymethylated flavonoids with anhydrous aluminium chloride proved very useful; its action depends on the reaction medium (250, 416, 481).

### *Nuclear oxidation and reduction*

The development of methods of nuclear oxidation and reduction was a natural corollary to the isolation of a large number of anthoxanthins with varying oxygenation patterns. These were needed to provide synthetic support to structures deduced from degradative studies and also to enable acceptance or rejection of theories of biogenesis of flavonoids and related compounds based initially on speculation. Two methods were used to introduce a hydroxyl group *para* or *ortho* to an existing hydroxyl group in flavonoid precursors (chalkones) and in the flavonoids themselves. Potassium persulphate in alkaline medium was employed to introduce a *para*-hydroxyl group (Elbs persulphate oxidation). Introduction of a hydroxyl in the *ortho* position proceeded in two stages; *ortho*-formylation by heating with hexamine in acetic acid (Duff reaction), or by the Gattermann reaction, was followed by treatment with alkaline hydrogen peroxide (Dakin oxidation). For example, *para*-oxidation at the chalkone stage was applied in the synthesis of the chalkone pedicin and its allies that occur in the leaves of *Didymocarpus pedicellata* and in the quercetagetin group of flavonols. *Para*-oxidation was also employed in the synthesis of 5,7,8-trihydroxy compounds, gossypetin, herbacetin, hibiscetin and wogonin. The rare group of 5,6,8-trihydroxyflavones and flavonols became available by the *para*-oxidation of the 5,6-dihydroxy compounds. Starting from 5,6,7-trihydroxy compounds, the 5,6,7,8-tetrahydroxyflavones and flavonols (176, 201) and methyl ethers thereof, like calycopterin (180, 201) and nobiletin (223, 257) were synthesized. *Para*-oxidation was extended to the nucleus of the phenyl substituent in the synthesis of 6′-hydroxymyricetin (286) and oxyayanin-A (699) and to some flavanones. *Para*-oxidation was also used to convert visnagin (a furanochromone) into the more useful khellin (300).

*Ortho*-oxidation was widely employed in the synthesis of 5,6-dihydroxyflavonols (147) and 6,7-dihydroxyflavonols(152). Some naturally occurring partial methyl ethers like melisimplin, melisimplexin and oxyayanin-B (462) were synthesized by this method. *Ortho*-oxidation was also utilized in the synthesis of the lichen acid diploschistesic acid from lecanoric acid (527). Reference may also be made to Seshadri's syntheses of 6,7,8-trihydroxyflavones (165) and of 5,6,7,8-tetrahydroxyflavonols (168), and to a summary of the results of the earlier years of studies in nuclear oxidation that was published (232, 262). A combination of *para*- and *ortho*-oxidation was employed for preparing fumigatin (a benzoquinone), phthiocol (a naphthaquinone) and aurantiogliocladin (an anthraquinone), among others.

Nuclear reduction was achieved in the laboratory by selective tosylation of the hydroxyl to be reduced and hydrogenolysis of the tosyl ester; the ease of reduction is in the order 7, 5, 3′, 4′. Nuclear reduction was implicated in the biogenesis of several members of the flavonoid group (363, 369, 365). Some flavonols have also been converted into the corresponding flavones by hydrogenolysis of the 3-*O*-tosyl derivative over Raney nickel (742). The bioconversion of mangiferin (1,3,6,7-tetrahydroxyxanthone-2-*C*-glucoside) to euxanthic acid (1,7-dihydroxyxanthone glucuronide) in the cow indicates *in vivo* nuclear reduction. Complete removal of hydroxyl groups was also achieved by this method (370). A combination of nuclear oxidation and reduction was used in the synthesis of polygalaxanthone-B (831).

### *Reduction, hydrogenation and dehydrogenation*

Reduction of flavonoids was studied in detail by Seshadri in connection with the structure and stereochemistry of flavandiols (leucoanthocyanidins) and catechins, employing catalytic reduction and reduction with lithium aluminium hydride and sodium borohydride. These reagents reduce the carbonyl group and saturate the double bond in the pyrone ring. Alkaline sodium dithionite reduces only the double bond; quercetin, for example, gives taxifolin without by-products. Dehydrogenation of flavanones to flavones was standardized, selenium dioxide being found to be the best reagent (466). The use of iodine is less simple. When a flavanone is boiled with iodine and silver acetate in ethanol, the 3-iodo compound or the 3-*O*-acetate is obtained. The former yields the flavone on boiling with pyridine; the latter on heating with alkali or preferably with acid.

### *Anthocyanins, leucoanthocyanidins and quinonoid anhydro-bases*

Part of Seshadri's Ph.D. work under Robert Robinson at Manchester was on the synthesis of anthocyanins. Of the four glucosides of pelargonidin chloride, the 3-glucoside (calistephin) had been synthesized by Robertson and Robinson, and Seshadri synthesized the remaining three. In the fifties an intensive study of anthocyanins in the Delhi University laboratories covered the flowers of many garden plants and trees, forest trees and many edible fruits and agricultural crops. The main work was however with the leucoanthocyanidins and with the quinonoid bases which had eluded precise understanding for decades. These studies are elaborated in the following paragraphs.

Seshadri's work on the anthocyanins, using a wide variety of techniques, is recorded in three papers (364, 426, 588). The leucoanthocyanidins are difficult to isolate and crystallize. The first to be obtained in a crystalline form was melacacidin by King and Bottomley who showed that it was a flavan-3,4-diol with other hydroxyls at the 7,8- and 3′,4′-positions, and it is now known that all leucoanthocyanidins are flavan-3,4-diols. They readily undergo self-condensation to insoluble, amorphous polymers that constitute the non-hydrolysable tannins; the condensation involves the 4-position of one unit and most commonly the 8-position of another. Mild acid treatment can also convert the leucoanthocyanidin into a flavylium salt, involving the elimination of a hydride ion from position 2 of the flavandiol. A convenient method used in the Seshadri laboratories for isolating the leucoanthocyanidins was to extract the plant material with cold acetone (or cold methanol for higher oligomers), remove the solvent in the cold, and precipitate the proanthocyanidins (monomers, dimers, etc.) with light petroleum. The amorphous precipitate, if homogeneous, was crystallized, but was otherwise acetylated or methylated. Boiling the leucoanthocyanidin with dimethyl sulphate and anhydrous potassium carbonate in acetone gave methyl ethers with methylated phenolic groups but free alcoholic groups which can be acetylated. These crystalline products were degraded to recognizable fragments from which the structures of the parent compounds could be inferred. The flavylium salts that result from boiling leucoanthocyanidins with acid were extremely useful in survey work in arriving at the pattern of substitution in the parent diol (544), and quantitative periodate titration gave valuable indication as to whether the substance was a monomer, dimer, trimer or tetramer. By these methods many plant materials, e.g. eucalyptus kino, butea gum, 'Karada' bark, areca nuts and the wood of *Cedrela toona*, were examined and many sources of leucopelargonidin, leucocyanidin and leucodelphinidin were found. Monomeric, dimeric, trimeric and tetrameric procyanidins were isolated (857).

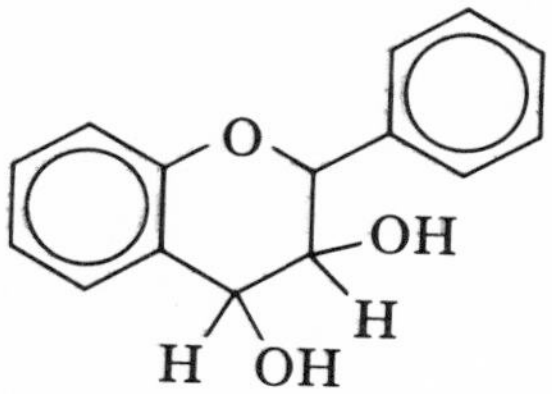

O OH H H OH

Flavan-3,4-diol

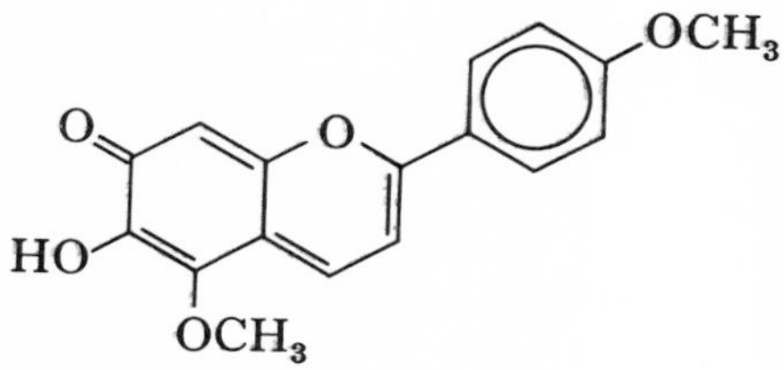

$OCH_3$ O O HO $OCH_3$

Carajurin

The formation of anthocyanidins by reduction of flavonols (Willstätter; Robinson; King and White) was utilized by Seshadri as a convenient route to flavylium salts. Cyanidin chloride was obtained in good yield from (+)-catechin and (−)-*epi*-catechin (479), from taxifolin (dihydroquercetin) by boiling with sodium acetate and acetic anhydride and subsequent treatment with hydrochloric acid (545), and from (−)-*epi*-catechin acetate by oxidation with *N*-bromosuccinimide followed by acid (951). Oxidation of the tetramethyl ether of (−)-*epi*-catechin with dimethylsulphoxide gave cyanidin tetramethyl ether (951). Flavylium salts without a hydroxyl in the 3-position (gesneridin type) were obtained from flavanones and from dibenzoylmethanes by reduction with sodium borohydride followed by boiling with hydrochloric acid (568, 612).

When the pseudo-base of a 7-hydroxyflavylium salt, e.g. 2,7-dihydroxyflav-3 ene, undergoes loss of water involving the hydrogen of the 7-hydroxyl and the hydroxyl at the 2-position, a coloured, conjugated quinone methide results. Two such natural quinonoid anhydro-bases are carajurin and carajurone present in the cosmetic carajura (chica red) prepared from *Bignonia chica*. They are related to scutellarein (5,6,7,4′-tetrahydroxyflavone). The pseudo-base of the corresponding anthocyanidin, scutellareinidin, loses water to yield the red quinone base carajuretin, which can also be obtained by demethylation of the natural substances carajurone which is its 4′-*O*-methyl ether, or carajurin which is its 5,4′-di-*O*-methyl ether. The structure of carajurin proposed by Robinson in

1927 was confirmed by synthesis by Seshadri in 1953. 2,4,5-Trihydroxy-6-methoxybenzaldehyde condensed with 4-methoxyacetophenone and hydrogen chloride to yield a flavylium chloride which when treated with sodium acetate gave the anhydro-base carajurin (348, 367, 388).

### *C-Methylation and C-prenylation*

Many natural *C*-methylated benzopyrones are known and were early studied by Seshadri, and the work was later extended to the *C*-prenylated compounds which may occur in cyclized forms. Extended work on direct *C*-methylation covered flavones, flavonols, chalkones, flavanones (499), isoflavones, xanthones (872) and coumarins, and led to the synthesis of eugenetin, *iso*-eugenetin, *iso*-eugenitol, *pino*-quercetin, angustifolionol and strobochrysin. *C*-prenylation was studied in the late sixties and early seventies. $\gamma,\gamma$-Dimethylallyl bromide gives some *C*-prenyl derivatives when reaction is carried out in the presence of methanolic sodium methoxide (892), but only the *C*-prenyl compound when butyl lithium in benzene is used. 2-Methylbut-3-en-2-ol in the presence of boron trifluoride etherate was also extensively used to achieve *C*-prenylation (924). *C*-Prenylation was successfully achieved with many suitably substituted benzo-$\alpha$-pyrones and benzo-$\gamma$-pyrones (923, 964). The initial *o*-hydroxyprenyl derivatives could be cyclized by acid to yield 2′-isopropyldihydrofurans or 2′,2′-dimethyldihydropyrans; these could be dehydrogenated to the isopropylfurans or dimethylpyrans. With gallacetophenone, prenyl units entered the 5- and 2′-positions leading to the 2,2-dimethyl-3-prenyl-6-acetyl-7,8-dihydroxybenzochroman shown below (1028).

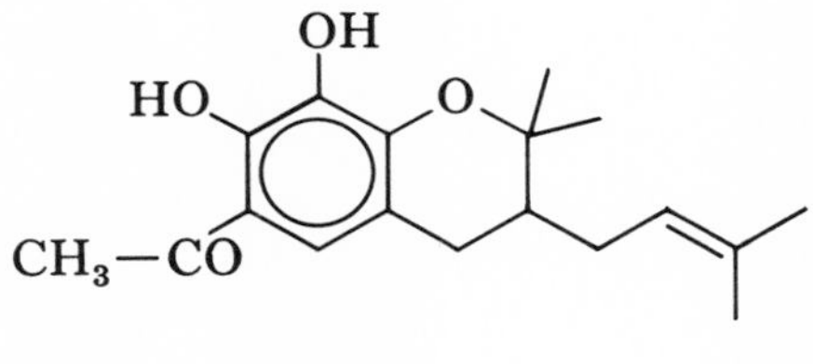

OH
HO O
$CH_3$—CO

### *Studies on the Wesseley–Moser rearrangement*

Seshadri's work added considerably to our knowledge of the rearrangement of 5,8-dihydroxyflavones to the 5,6-isomers and of 5,7,8-trihydroxyflavones to the 5,6,7-isomers (297) which occurs during demethylation of the methyl ethers with hydriodic acid. This is the Wesseley–Moser rearrangement, involving the opening and closing of the pyrone ring. The study led to syntheses of muningin (535) and hinokiflavone (903). A remarkable case of a double Wesseley–Moser rearrangement was observed with *allo*-khellin (7,8-dimethoxy-5,6-2′,3′-furano-2-methylchromone) in which both the chromone and furan rings open when heated with hydriodic acid and cyclize in a different direction; the product was *nor*-isokhellin (5,6-dihydroxy-7,8-2′,3′-furano-2-methylchromone) (1012).

*Furanochromones, chromenochromones, chromenoflavones, etc.*

Furanochromone, chromenoflavone and furanochromenochromone structures are present in many substances having physiological activity. The first substance in this group that came to the attention of Seshadri was karanjin from the seed oil of *Pongamia glabra*, whose structure had been established by Späth as 3-methoxyfurano-(2′,3′-7,8)-flavone. In connection with its synthesis Seshadri developed methods for construction of a furan ring on to chromones, flavones, coumarins, etc., and conversely of an α- or γ-pyrone ring onto a benzofuran. In the case of karanjin itself, 3-methoxy-7-hydroxyflavone-8-aldehyde was converted into the phenoxyacetic ester, and subsequent cyclization, hydrolysis and decarboxylation gave karanjin (289). A similar method was followed for the synthesis of the linear furochromene khellin (the active principle of *Ammi visanaga*), 2-methyl-5,8-dimethoxyfurano-(2′,3′-7,6)-chromone. From 2-methyl-5,7-dihydroxychromone the 7-*O*-acetic ester was prepared, another hydroxyl was introduced into the 8-position by *para*-oxidation, and a formyl group into the 6-position. Cyclization of the 5,8-dimethyl ether with acetic anhydride and sodium acetate was accompanied by decarboxylation and yielded khellin (259).

Another method was to start with the appropriate phenol, prepare its allyl ether, and to subject the ether to thermal migration to get the *o*-allylphenol. Ozonolysis yielded the *o*-hydroxyphenylacetaldehyde which on boiling with polyphosphoric acid cyclized to the simple furan. Ring closure of the hydrobromide of the allyl derivative by boiling with pyridine led to the formation of the α-methyldihydrofuran (497). Dehydrogenation to the α-methylfuran was effected by treatment with *N*-bromosuccinimide in presence of traces of benzoyl peroxide (474). The natural occurrence of α,α-dimethylchromenes led Seshadri to synthesize such compounds by cyclization of phenol-1,1-dimethylpropargyl ethers by heating in boiling dimethylaniline; the angular isomers are the major products.

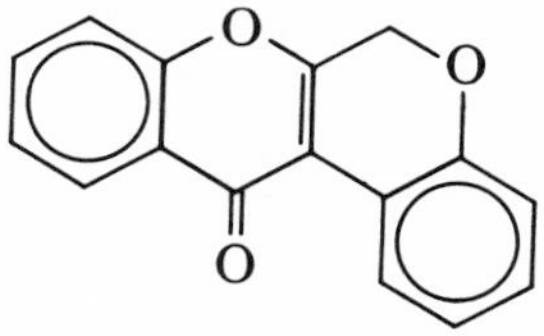

Chromeno-(3′,4′-2,3)-chromone

For synthesizing chromeno-(3′,4′-2,3)-chromones of the rotenoid group, Seshadri adopted a biogenetic approach. The chromeno ring was considered to result from dehydration between the hydroxymethyl group at position 2 and the hydroxyl at position 2′ in a 2-hydroxymethyl-2′-hydroxyisoflavone. A 2′-hydroxyl group was provided in some cases by introduction into the isoflavone by *para*-oxidation. The hydroxymethyl group at the 2-position was made from a 2-methyl group by the action of *N*-bromosuccinimide followed by hydrolysis. Elimination of water between the hydroxymethyl group and the 2′-hydroxyl group was achieved by boiling in acetone solution with anhydrous potassium carbonate, the product being the required chromenochromone (336). In a later procedure a deoxybenzoin with a hydroxyl group in the 2-position of the phenyl ring and a methoxy group in the 2′-position of the benzyl ring was treated with ethoxyacetyl chloride in pyridine giving a 2-ethoxymethyl-2′-methoxyisoflavone. Boiling with hydrobromic acid in acetic acid liberated the two hydroxyl groups enabling subsequent cyclization to the chromenochromone by boiling with acetone and potassium carbonate (418, 497).

### *Studies of some chalkones, flavanones and isoflavanones*

The structures previously assigned to a considerable number of plant products were revised by Seshadri and his co-workers, and the new structures confirmed by synthesis in many cases. Among them the following may be briefly mentioned. Butrin, from *Butea frondosa*, was shown to be the 7,3′-di-*O*-glucoside of the flavanone butin, and isobutrin proved to be the corresponding diglucoside of the related chalkone (91). From the same source palastrin was established as the 3,6-diglucoside of 2-(3,4-dihydroxybenzylidene)-6-hydroxycoumaran-3-one (423). The previous structure of pedicin from *Didymocarpus pedicillata* was in error and was shown by Seshadri to be 2′,5′-dihydroxy-3′,4′,6′-trimethoxychalkone, one of the rather rare derivatives of pentahydroxybenzene. The derived flavanone was isopedicin, 6-hydroxy-5,7,8-trimethoxyflavanone. Oxidation of pedicin to a quinone with benzoquinone or silver oxide followed by partial hydrolysis led to a neat synthesis of the dihydroxymonomethoxyquinochalkone, pedicin (227, 239).

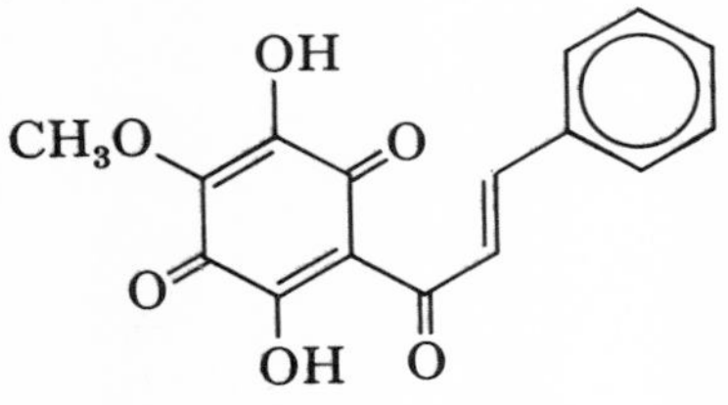

Pedicinin

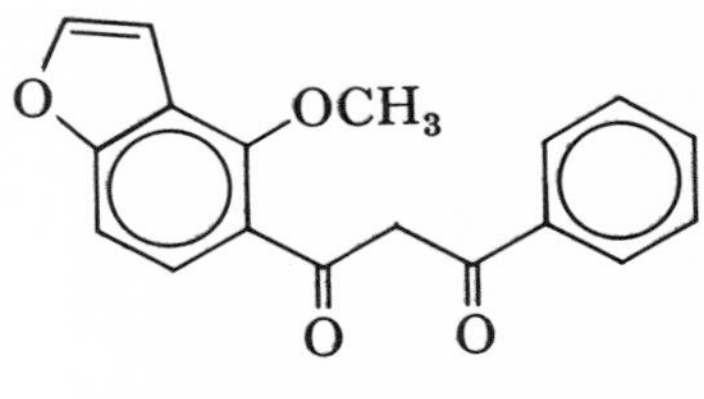

Pongamol

Seshadri provided new methods for the synthesis of carthamidin (5,7,8,4′-tetrahydroxyflavanone) and its isomer isocarthamidin (5,6,7,4′-tetrahydroxyflavanone) isolated from *Carthamus tinctorius* (251). The yellow carthamin was shown to be 4,3′,4′,6′-tetrahydroxy-2′-glucosyloxychalkone, and the red colouring matter carthamone to be the corresponding 3′,6′-quinochalkone with the glucosyloxy group and hydroxyl groups in the same position. The first natural isoflavone was isolated by Seshadri, padmakastein (5,4′-dihydroxy-7-methoxyisoflavanone) from the bark of *Prunus puddum*, together with padmakastin which is its glucoside (302). Padmakastin derivates are dehydrogenated with selenium dioxide to prunetin derivatives and the converse is achieved by hydrogenation in the presence of palladium charcoal (498).

*Constituents of* Pongamia glabra, Psoralen corylifolia *and cotton seed*

The seed oil of *Pongamia glabra* is an important plant in Indian folk medicine; it yields karanjin, proved by Späth to be 3-methoxyfurano-(2′,3′-7,8)-flavone. Later investigations by Seshadri yielded several other components, including canjone (6-methoxyfurano-(2′,3′-7,8)-flavone) (620), pongapin (3-methoxy-3′,4′-methylenedioxyfurano-(2″,3″-7,8)-flavone), and a β-diketone pongamol (1-(2-methoxyfurano-(2′,3′-4,3)-phenyl)-3-phenylpropane-1,3-dione) (410, 432). The roots and the stem bark yielded kanugin (3,7,5′-trimethoxy-3′,4′-methylene-dioxyflavone) (163), 5′-demethoxykanugin (464) and pongachromene a chromenoflavone,3-methoxy-3′,4′-methylenedioxy-6″,6″-dimethylpyrano-(2″,3″-7, 8)-flavone (855). The leaves contain a complex chromenochalkone, glabrachromene (below) (1001). Glabrin is 4,5-dihydroxy-*N*-methylpiperidine-2-carboxylic acid (981).

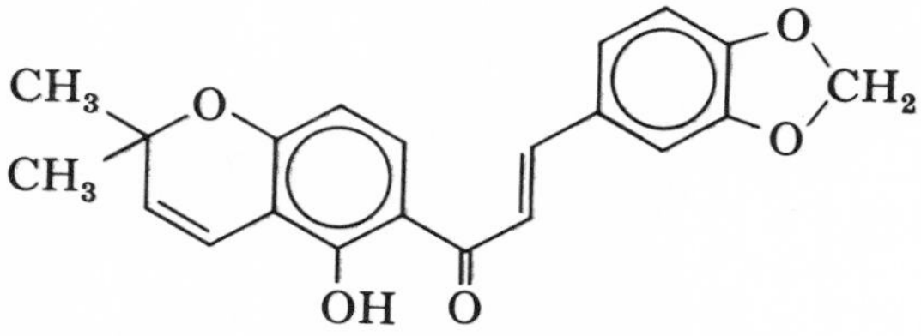

Glabrachromene

*Psoralea corylifolia* seeds constitute a well-known Indian drug. Its active principles, psoralen and isopsoralen (angelicin), were studied in the thirties by Späth and shown to be the linear (7,6) and angular (7,8)-furocoumarin, respectively. Later work by Seshadri led to new methods of synthesis and to the isolation of new substances from the drug. Following a biogenetic pathway, 6-*C*-prenyl- or 6-allyl-7-hydroxycoumarin was ozonized and the resulting 6-acetaldehyde cyclized with polyphosphoric acid to give psoralen. Isopsoralen was similarly synthesized from the 8-allyl-7-hydroxycoumarin (510). New compounds isolated from the drug are bavachin (6-prenyl-7,4′-dihydroxyflavanone) and isobavachin (its 8-prenyl isomer), the chalkone (4,2′,4′-trihydroxy-5′-prenyl-chalkone) corresponding to bavachin, and the analogous isobavachalkone (3′-prenyl compound); all have been synthesized (892, 924, 1008). A new isoflavone, neobavaisoflavone, has been isolated from the seeds and shown to be 3′-prenyl-7,4′-dihydroxyisoflavone (1022).

Gossypol, the yellow colouring matter of cotton seed and its oil, has been studied in the U.S.A., India and the U.S.S.R. Its gross structure was established by Roger Adams as a 2,2′-binaphthyl with hydroxyls at the 1-, 6- and 7-positions, a formyl at 8-, a methyl at 3- and an isopropyl at 5-, in each half of the molecule. Seshadri developed a convenient method for obtaining gossypol by precipitating the sparingly soluble anil and heating it with acetic anhydride whereby gossypol hexa-acetate is obtained (143). Adams had observed that gossypol and its derivatives did not show constant melting point or crystal form. Employing modern methods of separation Seshadri and co-workers isolated hexamethyl ethers and acetates in pure form (1003, 1115) whose n.m.r. spectra showed that in some there were two aldehydic protons, in some only one, and in others none. This is because the hydroxyl and adjacent formyl group can cyclize to form a lactol in one or both rings, and at each lactol carbon atom, two configurations are possible. Hence a total of six methyl ethers and six acetates are theoretically possible. The variation in melting point observed by Adams is ascribed to the presence of different forms of the derivatives, thus giving mixtures.

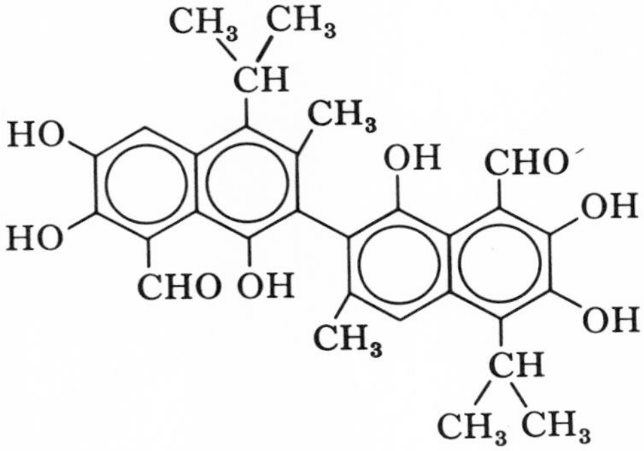

Gossypol

Another important aspect of gossypol chemistry is the optical activity of the parent substance and its derivatives. Much light on this was shed by Seshadri's study of gossypol isolated from another plant of the Malvaceae family, *Thespasia populnea*. The sulphur-yellow flowers of this plant had earlier yielded flavonoids, but a careful re-examination led to the isolation of gossypol which was dextro-rotatory (994), whereas gossypol from the cotton plant is optically inactive, being racemic. The bark and fruits of this plant also contain (+)-gossypol, whose ethers and acetates are also optically active (1116). Adams had envisaged optical activity being the result of lactol formation and also of restricted rotation about the binaphthyl bond caused by steric hindrance. Treatment of (+)-gossypol with 40% alkali caused loss of both formyl groups, giving (+)-*apo*-gossypol, which further lost both isopropyl groups on treatment with concentrated sulphuric acid giving (+)-*desapo*-gossypol. These two degraded gossypols, in which lactol ring formation is impossible, were optically active showing that their activity must arise entirely from asymmetry caused by hindrance to free rotation about the 2,2′ bond. This receives further support from the observation that the bis-aldehydic form of the hexamethyl ether of (+)-gossypol (in which there is no lactolic centre of asymmetry) is also optically active. Work in other laboratories has shown that in gossypol the two naphthalene rings are in fact nearly perpendicular to each other.

*Neoflavonoids*

Seshadri contributed much to our knowledge of derivatives of the 4-phenyl-chromans. Dalbergin, first isolated from the heart-wood of *Dalbergia sissoo*, was shown to be 6-hydroxy-7-methoxy-4-phenylcoumarin (476). Related compounds isolated from *D. sissoo* were the 6,7-dimethoxy-, 6,7-dihydroxy- and 6-methoxy-7-hydroxy-4-phenylcoumarins, and from *Dalbergia latifolia* was isolated the optically active latifolin, 2,4-dimethoxy-5-hydroxyphenyl-2′-hydroxyphenyl-vinylmethane. A closely related compound is dalberginone, α-vinyl-2-benzyl-5-methoxy-1,4-benzoquinone, occurring with the R configuration in *D. latifolia* and with the S configuration in *D. sissoo*. Dalbergichromene, 6-hydroxy-7-methoxy-4-phenyl-3-chromene, was isolated from *D. sissoo* heart-wood (979). A 4-phenylcoumarin obtained from the tropical medicinal tree *Calophylum inophyllum* is ponnalide, a 7-hydroxy-4-phenylcoumarin with an α-methyl-butyroyl side chain at position 8 and a 2′,2′-dimethylchromene ring fused to the 5,6-positions constituting a chromeno-(6′,5′-5,6)-coumarin (991).

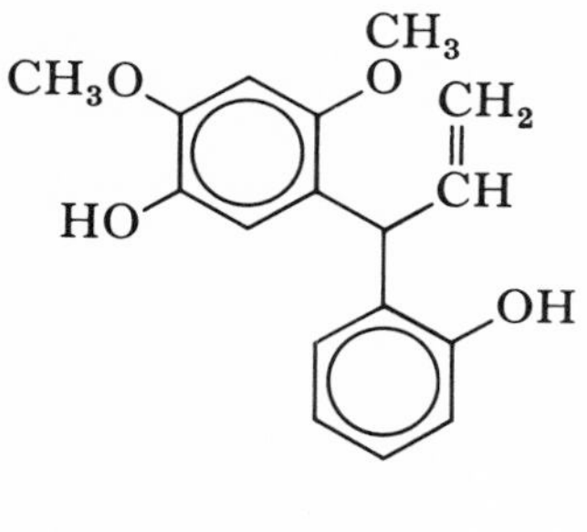

Latifolin

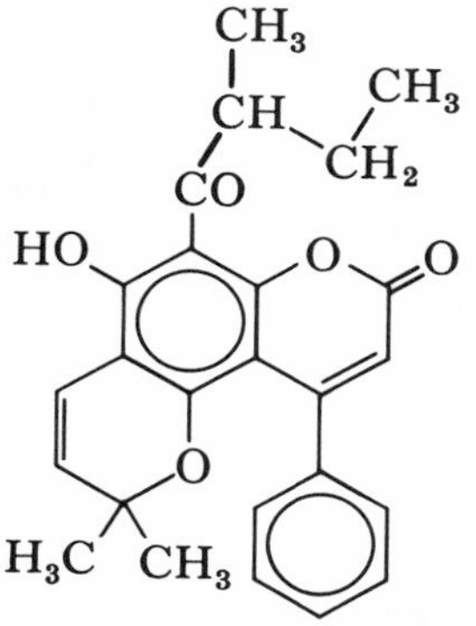

Ponnalide

*Cyanomaclurin and pterocarpin*

An almost classical problem was posed by cyanomaclurin from the Indian jack fruit tree (*Arto-carpus heterophyllus*). It was recognized long ago as a leuco-anthocyanidin derivative by Robinson, who regarded it as a hemiketal. The correct structure was arrived at on the basis of n.m.r. studies independently by Seshadri and by Venkataraman; it is now known to be 4,2′-oxido-3,5,7,4′-tetra-hydroxyflavan. This structure was supported by Seshadri's synthesis of related structures and finally of cyanomaclurin trimethyl ether (728).

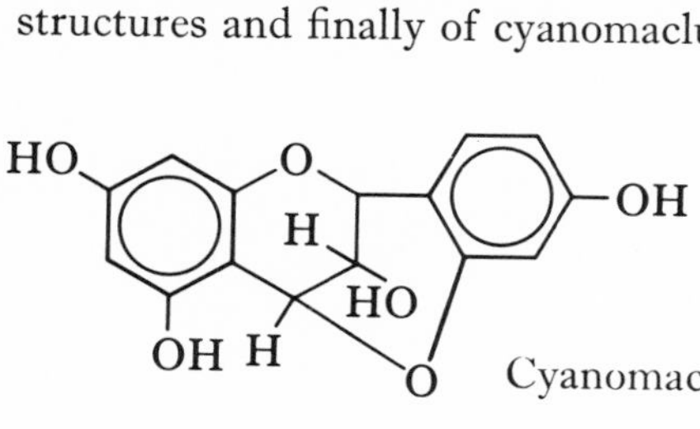

Cyanomaclurin

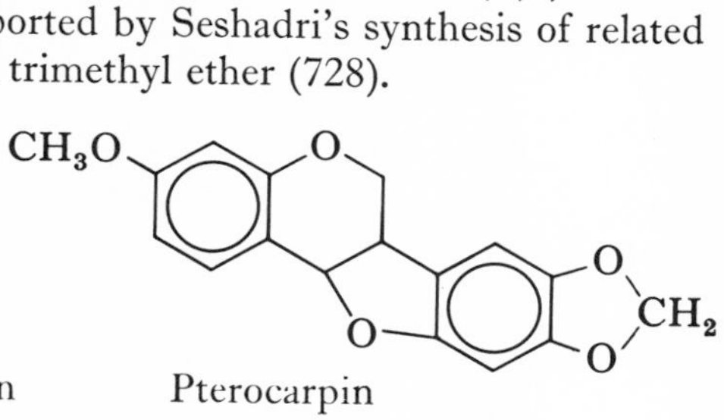

Pterocarpin

The pterocarpans, e.g. pterocarpin, are obtained mostly from the heart-woods of trees, perhaps most importantly *Pterocarpus santalinus*. Their structures have been deduced largely as the result of spectral studies. The first members of this group, pterocarpin and homopterocarpin, were isolated more than a hundred years ago and their structures established in 1940, but their synthesis was not achieved till the 1960s when the necessary precursors, the 2′-hydroxyisoflavones, became available. Treatment with sodium borohydride reduced the carbonyl group and the 2,3 double bond, giving an isoflavan-4-ol, which spontaneously cyclized in presence of acid giving the pterocarpan skeleton. Employing this method a number of variously substituted pterocarpans were synthesized including a racemate of *homo*-pterocarpin (572, 793).

### *Santalin pigments*

The complex red pigment santalin obtained from the heart-wood of the forest tree *Pterocarpus santolinus* was found by Seshadri to be a mixture of two major components, santalin-A and santalin-B. They give the same permethyl ether, and this has been shown by extensive degradative studies to be made up of two linked C9 and C6 units, as shown in the structural formula below. Santalin-A has three methoxy and five hydroxy groups, and santalin-B has four methoxy groups. Ethylation and degradation enabled Seshadri to assign positions to all the methoxyl groups (1066, 1098).

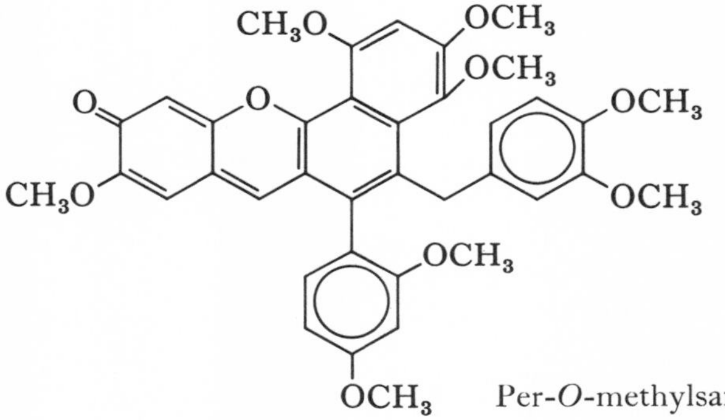

Per-*O*-methylsantolin

### *Flavonolignans and C-glycosides*

The flavonolignans are flavonoids to the phenyl group of which is attached a C9 unit. From the seed hulls of *Hydnocarpus wightiana* Seshadri isolated a new member of the group, hydnocarpin, which was closely studied and shown (1067) to possess the complex structure below; it is a derivative of 1,4-dioxan. The same material also yielded the isomer isohydnocarpin which has a dihydrofuran instead of a dioxan ring (1084). A third flavonolignan isolated from the seed hulls of *H. wightiana* was shown to be a methoxyhydnocarpin (1087).

The first *C*-glycoside to be investigated by the Seshadri school was mangiferin from the mango tree (*Mangifera indica*) and other plants. It was shown (777) to be 2-*C*-β-D-glucopyranosyl-1,3,6,7-tetrahydroxyxanthone, and was synthesized from 1,3,6,7-tetrahydroxyxanthone and tetraacetyl-α-D-glucopyranosyl bromide, the sugar entering the most reactive 2-position (822). Two new *C*-glycosides from

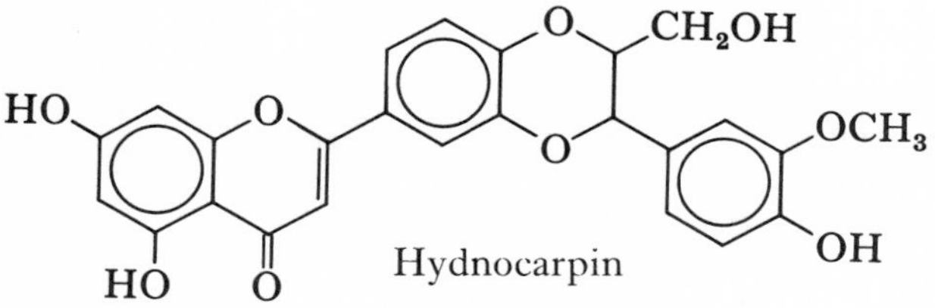

Hydnocarpin

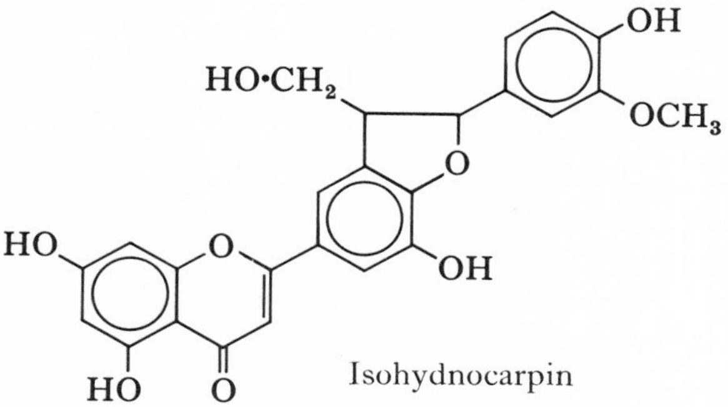

Isohydnocarpin

the leaves of *Parkinsonia aculeata*, parkinsonin-A and -B, proved to be the 8-*C*-glucoside of 5-*O*-methylluteolin and the 8-*C*-glucoside of 5,7-di-*O*-methylluteolin (715). From *Pueraria tuberosa* was isolated the diacetate of puerarin (8-*C*-β-D-glucopyranosyl-4′,7-dihydroxyisoflavone (856). Paniculatin from the bark of *Dalbergia paniculata* was assigned the structure 6,8-di-*C*-glucosylgenistein (932). Volubilin and isovolubilin from the flowers of *Dalbergia volubilis* are 8-*C*- and 6-*C*-L-ribopyranosyl-4′,7-di-*O*-methylgenistein respectively (1096, 1108). From the seeds of *Trigonella corniculata* 6,8-di-*C*-β-glucopyranosyl-4′-*O*-methylapigenin and its monoacetate were obtained and their structures established (986).

### *Chemistry of lichen substances*

Seshadri was a pioneer of lichen studies in India. His investigations began in the thirties at the Andhra University and concerned lichens from South India, Ceylon and some countries of southeast Asia; the survey was extended to lichens of the Himalayas after he moved to Delhi. Several new compounds were discovered, their structures established and syntheses effected in most cases. Montagnetol from *Rocella montagnei* proved to be the erythrityl ester of orsellinic acid (100). It occurs in optically active and inactive forms (109). Erythrin was similarly shown to be the erythrityl ester of the didepside lecanoric acid (112). Montagnetol and erythrin were both synthesized. *Teloschistin* present in *Teloschistes flavicans* was shown by Seshadri to be 4,5-dihydroxy-2-hydroxymethyl-7-methoxyanthraquinone (287) and it was synthesized from the related 2-methyl compound physcion (449). The same lichen also contains the related 2-aldehyde fallacinal and a chlorine-containing depsidone vicanicin (536, 602).

Virensic acid from *Alectoria virens* was shown to be a depsidone acid of which the well-known depside atranorin is the methyl ester (579). *Lepraria citrina*

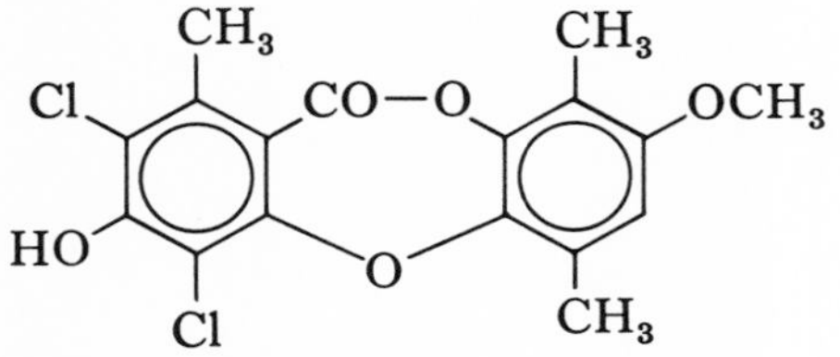

Vicanicin

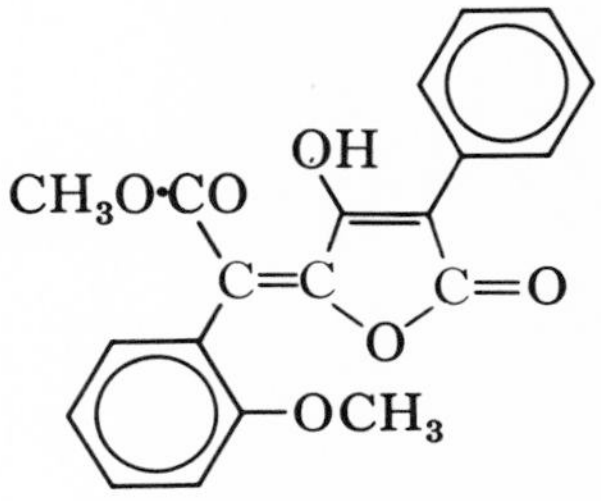

Leprapinic acid

yielded leprapinic acid, a pulvinic and a tetronic acid derivative having the structure shown above (434). It was synthesized by the methanolysis of *o*-methoxypulvinicdilactone (463). Another lichen product, pinastric acid, which had earlier been given an incorrect structure was shown by Seshadri to be methyl-4′-methoxypulvinate (627). Thelephoric acid, an earlier known compound from *Labaria isidosa* and to which an incorrect structure had been assigned, was shown to be the symmetrical terphenyl quinone shown below (538, 563). Pyxiferin from *Pyxine coccifera* was characterized as a tetrahydroxy-monomethyl-2,2′-di-*p*-benzoquinone (677).

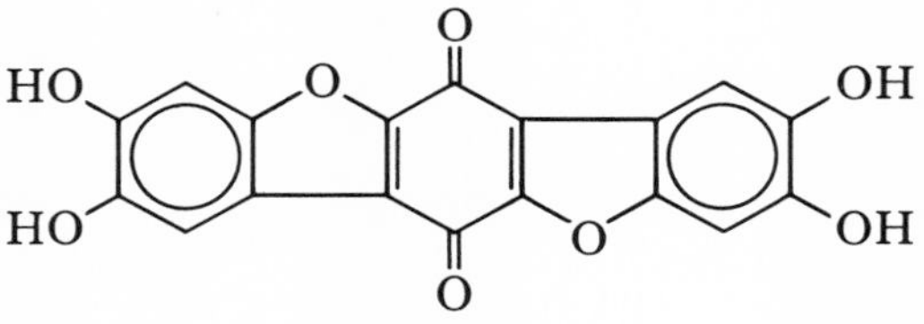

**Thelephoric acid**

The synthesis of di -and tridepsides was simplified by Seshadri and co-workers by the application of condensing agents used in peptide synthesis, namely dicyclohexylcarbodiimide, carbonyldiimidazole and trifluoroacetic anhydride, and in this manner lecanoric acid and evernic acids (582), atranorin (603) and gyrophoric acid (876) were synthesized. Other notable syntheses of lichen compounds are those of thamnolic acid (492), diploschistesic acid (527), diploicin (649), thiophanic acid (838) and lichexanthone (360).

*Theories of biogenesis*

From the foregoing account it will be evident that the exceptionally wide range of Seshadri's work on the isolation and determination of structure of plant products gave him a unique opportunity to consider their inter-relationships and biogenesis. The great volume of evidence on which he could call gave weight to any such suggestions, some of which were corroborated by synthetic work in his own laboratories and by radioactive tracer studies elsewhere. Certainly

Seshadri used the ideas in designing synthetic operations and in quickly arriving at the most probable structures of natural products.

The early speculations regarding anthoxanthins (138) were an extension of Robinson's theory of the parallel origin of the anthoxanthins from a common precursor derived from a C6 and a C9 unit, and involved ideas of sequential evolution by processes of nuclear oxidation, reduction and methylation. Schemes were suggested for the biogenesis of anthocyanins (604), depsides and depsidones (145), xanthones (583), benzoquinones (539), naphthoquinones including binaphthyls like gossypol and perylene quinones (584), anthraquinones (564) and mould metabolites (389). In all these the orsellinic acid C8 unit has been assigned a key role (404). Other groups about whose origins Seshadri speculated are naturally occurring tetronic acid derivatives (541), 3- and 4-phenylchromans and benzophenones (489), stilbenes and phenylisocoumarins (490), the C5 unit in plants (510), pulvinic acid derivatives (468) and mould tropolones (442). Last came the speculations on neoflavonoids (1024) and a revised biogenesis of xanthones in Guttifearae according to which the xanthone arises from a 5-hydroxy-4-phenylcoumarin (999). This may undergo oxidative cyclization between the 5-hydroxyl and 2′-position, followed by ring opening and elimination of C2 and C3 of the coumarin ring.

## Bibliography

The 166 items that follow are selected from the more important papers published by Seshadri and his co-workers. The number given to each paper is that which it bears in the complete Bibliography of Seshadri's 1130 publications that is deposited in the Library of the Royal Society along with 885 similarly numbered offprints. Seshadri's publications cover the period 1926–76; most of the offprints are of papers published between 1941 and 1974.

The following abbreviated titles of some journals are used:

| | |
|---|---|
| *CS* | Current Science |
| *IJC* | Indian Journal of Chemistry |
| *JCS* | Journal of the Chemical Society |
| *JsiR* | Journal of scientific and industrial research |
| *PIAS* | Proceedings of the Indian Academy of Science |
| *T* | Tetrahedron |
| *TL* | Tetrahedron Letters |


(91) 1941 (With P. S. Rao) Constitution of butrin. *PIAS* **14A**, 29.

(100) 1942 (With V. S. Rao) Chemical investigation of Indian lichens. IV. Constitution of montagnetol. *PIAS* **15A**, 18.

(109) (With V. S. Rao) Chemical investigation of Indian lichens. V. Occurrence of active montagnetol in *Roccella montagnei*. *PIAS* **15A**, 429.

(112) (With V. S. Rao) Chemical investigation of Indian lichens. VI. Constitution of erythrin. *PIAS* **16A**, 23.

(138) 1943 (With P. S. Rao) Some aspects of the biogenesis of anthoxanthins. *PIAS* **18A**, 222.

(143) 1944 (With B. Krishnaswamy & K. S. Murty) Chemistry of gossypol. IV. Behaviour of gossypol as an *ortho*-hydroxyaldehyde—formation of α-pyrones and flavylium salts. *PIAS* **19A**, 370.

(145) A theory of biogenesis of lichen depsides and depsidones. *PIAS* **20A**, 1.

(147) (With V. Balaiah & L. R. Row) Synthesis of 5:6-dihydroxy-flavonols. I. *PIAS* **20A**, 274.

(152) 1945 (With L. R. Row) Synthesis of 6:7-dihydroxy-flavonols. I. 6:7:3′:4′-Tetrahydroxy-flavonol. *PIAS* **21A**, 155.

(163) 1946 (With S. Rajagopalan, S. Rangaswami & K. V. Rao) Constitution of kanugin. II. *PIAS* **23A**, 60.

(165) (With V. D. N. Sastri) Synthesis of 6:7:8-hydroxy-flavones. *PIAS* **23A**, 134.

(168) (With V. Venkateswarlu) Synthesis and study of 5:6:7:8-hydroxy-flavonols. I. *PIAS* **23A**, 192.

(176) (With V. V. S. Murti & L. R. Row) Synthesis and study of 5:6:7:8-hydroxy-flavonols. II. A total synthesis. *PIAS* **24A**, 233.

(180) (With V. Venkateswarlu) Synthesis and study of 5:6:7:8-hydroxy-flavonols. IV. A synthesis of calycopterin. *PIAS* **24A**, 349.

(192) 1947 (With K. V. Rao) Constitution of gossypin. II. *PIAS* **25A**, 397.

(201) (With S. Rajagopalan & K. V. Rao) Nuclear oxidation in the flavone series. VI. A new synthesis of calycopteretin and 6:8-dihydroxy-quercetin. *PIAS* **26A**, 18.

(223) 1948 (With V. V. S. Murti) Nuclear oxidation in the flavone series. XI. A new synthesis of nobiletin. *PIAS* **27A**, 217.

(225) (With G. S. K. Rao & K. V. Rao) The formation of quinones by oxidative dealkylation and the effect of methylating agents on them. I. *PIAS* **27A**, 245.

(227) (With K. V. Rao) Nuclear oxidation in flavones and related compounds. XII. Constitution and synthesis of pedicin and its allies. *PIAS* **27A**, 375.

(232) XIII. A discussion of the results. *PIAS* **28A**, 1.

(239) (With G. S. K. Rao & K. V. Rao) Formation of quinones by oxidative dealkylation. II. Constitution of pedicinin. *PIAS* **28A**, 103.

(250) 1949 (With N. Narasimhachari) Synthetic experiments in the benzopyrone series. IX. Partial demethylation of chalkones. A synthesis of sakuranetin. *PIAS* **29A**, 265.

(251) (With N. Narasimhachari & V. D. N. Sastri) X. Synthesis of carthamidin and isocarthamidin. *PIAS* **29A**, 404.

(257) (With V. V. S. Murti) Nuclear oxidation in flavones and related compounds. XXI. Another synthesis of nobiletin. *PIAS* **30A**, 12.

(259) (With V. V. S. Murti) XXIII. A synthesis of kellin. *JsiR* **8B**, 112; *PIAS* **30A**, 107.

(262) XXVI. Phytochemical methods of nuclear oxidation. *PIAS* **30A**, 333.

(286) 1951 (With K. J. Balakrishna & N. P. Rao) Nuclear oxidation in flavones and related compounds. XXXIV. *Para*-oxidation in the side phenyl nucleus—Preparation of 6′-hydroxymyricetin. *PIAS* **33A**, 151.

(287) (With S. Neelakantan, S. Rangaswami & S. S. Subramanian) Chemical investigation of Indian lichens. XI. Constitution of teloschistin—the position of the methoxyl group. *PIAS* **33A**, 142.

(289) (With L. R. Row) Synthetic experiments in the benzopyrone series. XV. Synthesis of karanjin. *PIAS* **33A**, 168.

(291) (With L. R. Row) XVII. Some isoflavono-7:8-furans. *PIAS* **34A**, 187.

(297) 1952 (With D. K. Chakravorty, S. K. Mukerjee & V. V. S. Murti) Nuclear oxidation in flavones and related compounds. XXXV. Isomerization of 5:7:8-hydroxychromones into 5: 6: 7-hydroxychromones. *PIAS* **35A**, 34.

(300) (With S. K. Mukerjee) XXXVIII. A transformation of visnagin to kellin. *PIAS* **35A**, 323.

(302) (With N. Narasimhachari) Components of the bark of *Prunus puddum*. II. Padmakastin and padmakastein. *PIAS* **35A**, 202.

(336) 1953 (With S. Varadarajan) Synthetic experiments in the benzopyrone series. XXXII. A synthesis of 7-hydroxychromeno-(3′:4′-2:3)-chromone. *PIAS* **37A**, 784.

(348) (With Miss L. Ponniah) Nuclear oxidation in flavones and related compounds. XLV. A synthesis of carajuridin chloride and carajurin. *PIAS* **38A**, 77.

(360) (With K. Aghoramurthy) Chemical investigation of Indian lichens. An improved synthesis of lichexanthone. *JsiR* **12B**, 350.

(362) (With Miss B. Puri) Survey of anthoxanthins. III. Paper chromatography of some flavanones and chalkones and their glycosides. Isolation and constitution of isobutrin, a new glycoside of the flowers of *Butea frondosa*. *JsiR* **12B**, 462.

(363) 1953 (With A. C. Jain) Nuclear reduction in the biogenesis of anthoxanthins. *JsiR* **12B**, 503.

(364) (With Miss L. Ponniah) Survey of anthocyanins from Indian sources. I. *JsiR* **12B**, 605.

(365) (With A. C. Jain & O. P. Mittal) A note on nuclear reduction in the biogenesis of xanthones. *JsiR* **12B**, 647.

(367) (With Miss L. Ponniah) Synthesis of isocarajuretin hydrochloride. *PIAS* **38A**, 288.

(369) (With A. C. Jain) Nuclear reduction of anthoxanthins in the side phenyl nucleus. *PIAS* **38A**, 467.

(370) (With A. C. Jain & V. N. Gupta) Nuclear reduction of anthoxanthins. Complete removal of phenolic hydroxyl groups. *PIAS* **38A**, 470.

(388) 1954 (With Miss L. Ponniah) A synthesis of carajurone hydrochloride. *PIAS* **39A**, 45.

(389) (With K. Aghoramurthy) A theory of biosynthesis of some mould products. *JsiR* **13A**, 114.

(404) (With K. Aghoramurthy) The occurrence of C8 unit in natural products. *CS* **23**, 42.

(410) (With S. Narayanaswamy & S. Rangaswami) Chemistry of pongamol. II. *JCS*, p. 1871.

(416) 1955 (With M. L. Dhar & N. Narasimhachari) Synthetic experiments in the benzopyrone series. LIII. Studies in partial demethylation of isoflavone derivatives. *JsiR* **14B**, 73.

(418) (With A. C. Mehta) LVI. A new synthesis of 7-hydroxychromeno-3′:4′-2:3:)-chromone. *PIAS* **42A**, 192.

(423) (With Miss B. Puri) Survey of anthoxanthins. IX. Isolation and constitution of palasitrin. *JCS*, p. 1589.

(426) (With J. N. Sharma) Survey of anthocyanins from Indian sources. II. *JsiR* **14B**, 211.

(432) (With S. K. Mukerjee) Chemistry of pongamol. III. Synthesis. *JCS*, p. 2048.

(434) (With O. P. Mittal) Chemical investigation of Indian lichens. XIX. *Lepraria*—constitution of leprapinic acid. *JCS*, p. 3053.

(439) (With S. K. Mukerjee) Ring isomerism in *C*-methyl-chromones. *Chemy Ind.*, p. 1009.

(442) Biogenesis of mould tropolones. *JsiR* **14B**, 248.

(449) 1956 (With S. Neelakantan & S. S. Subramanian) Chemical investigation of Indian lichens. XX. A new synthesis of teloschistin. *PIAS* **44A**, 42.

(462) (With R. N. Goel & A. C. Jain) Synthesis of oxyayanin-B. *JCS*, p. 1369.

(463) (With O. P. Mittal) Synthesis of leprapinic acid and constitution of pinastric acid. *JCS*, p. 1734.

(464) (With O. P. Mittal) Demethoxykanugin, a new crystalline compound from *Pongamia glabra*. *JCS*, p. 2176.

(466) (With N. R. Bannerjee) Mechanism of selenium dioxide dehydrogenation of flavanones. *CS* **25**, 143.

(468) 1957 (With O. P. Mittal) Occurrence of C9 (forked)-units in polyporic and pulvinic acid derivatives. *CS* **26**, 4.

(474) (With S. S. Chibber, A. K. Ganguli & S. K. Mukerjee) Synthetical experiments in the benzopyrone series. LXV. Synthesis of α-methylkaranjin and related compounds. *PIAS* **46A**, 19.

(476) (With V. K. Ahluwalia) Constitution of dalbergin. II. *JCS*, p. 970.

(479) (With A. K. Ganguli & P. Subramanian) A convenient method of preparation of cyanidin chloride from (+) catechin and (−) epicatechin. *PIAS* **46A**, 25.

(481) (With S. N. Aiyar & I. Dass) Selective demethylation of the 5-methoxyl group in flavanones and synthesis of dihydrowogonin. *PIAS* **46A**, 238.

(489) Biogenesis of naturally occurring 3- and 4-phenylchroman derivatives and benzophenones. *CS* **26**, 239.

(490) Occurrence of C8 units in naturally occurring stilbenes and phenylisocoumarins. *CS* **26**, 310.

(492) (With K. Aghoramurthy & G. B. Venkatasubramanian) Synthesis of dimethylthamnolate and dimethylhypothamnolate. *T* **1**, 310.

(494) 1958 (With R. N. Goel & V. B. Mahesh) Modifications in the iodine oxidation of hydroxyflavones and their methyl ethers. *PIAS* **46A**, 184.

(497) (With P. S. Sarin & J. M. Sehgal) Synthetic experiments in the benzopyrone series. LXVII. Synthesis of α-methyldihydrofuranochromenochromone. *PIAS* **47A**, 292.

(498) (With S. Ramanujam) Components of the bark of *Prunus puddum*. III. Synthesis of padmakastein and its derivatives. *PIAS* **48A**, 175.

(499) (With A. C. Jain & R. N. Goel) Nuclear methylation of chalkones and flavanones. *PIAS* **48A**, 180.

(510) (With R. Aneja & S. K. Mukerjee) A study of the origin and modification of the C5-unit in plant products—new synthesis of angelicin and psoralen. *T* **4,** 256.

(514) 1959 (With T. R. Rajagopalan) Chemical investigation of Indian lichens. XXI. Occurrence of fallacinal in *Teloschistes flavicans*. *PIAS* **49A**, 1.

(527) (With G. B. Venkatasubramanian) A new synthesis of diploschistesic acid. *JCS*, p. 1658.

(535) (With M. L. Dhar) Ring isomeric change in isoflavones: Synthesis of 5:7-dimethoxy-6-hydroxyisoflavone, muningin and 5:7-dihydroxy-6-methoxyisoflavone. *T* **7**, 77.

(536) (With S. Nelakantan & S. S. Subramanian) Chemical investigation of Indian lichens XXVI. Constitution of vicanicin from the lichen *Teloschistes flavicans*. *TL*, p. 1

(538) (With K. Aghoramurthy & K. G. Sarma) The structure of thelephoric acid. *TL*, p. 20

(539) (With S. Neelakantan) Biogenesis of benzoquinones and related substances. *CS* **28**, 351.

(541) (With S. Neelakantan) Biogenesis of naturally occurring tetronic acid derivatives. *CS* **28**, 476.

(544) 1960 (With B. Venkataramani) 3-Hydroxyflavylium salts useful as reference compounds in the study of the leucoanthocyanidins. *JsiR* **19B**, 477.

(545) (With H. G. Krishnamurty & B. Venkataramani) An extraordinary isomeric change of dihydroflavonols. *JsiR* **19B**, 115.

(547) (With R. S. Thakur) The colouring matter of the flowers of *Carthamus tinctorius*. *CS* **29**, 54.

(563) (With K. Aghoramurthy & K. G. Sarma) The structure of thelephoric acid. *TL*, p. 4.

(564) (With S. Neelakantan) Biogenesis of naturally occurring anthraquinone derivatives. *JsiR* **19A**, 71.

(568) 1961 (With H. G. Krishnamurty) Preparation of flavylium salts of the anthocyanidin type. *CS* **30**, 287.

(572) (With K. Aghoramurthy & A. S. Kukla) Synthesis of a racemate of homopterocarpin. *CS* **30**, 218.

(579) (With K. Aghoramurthy & K. G. Sarma) Chemical investigation of Indian lichens. XXIV. The chemical components of *Alectoria virens*—constitution of a new depsidone, virensic acid. *T* **12**, 173.

(582) (With S. Neelakantan & R. Padmasani) A new simplified method of synthesis of depsides. *JsiR* **20B**, 510.

(583) (With S. Neelakantan) Occurrence of C8 units in xanthones. *CS* **30**, 90.

(584) (With S. Neelakantan) Biogenesis of naturally occurring naphthaquinone derivatives. *JsiR* **20A**, 448.

(588) 1962 (With V. Krishnamoorthy) A survey of anthocyanins from Indian sources. III. *JsiR* **21B**, 591.

(602) (With S. Neelakantan & S. S. Subramanian) Chemical investigation of Indian lichens. XXVI. Constitution of vicanicin from the lichen *Teloschistes flavicans*. *T* **18**, 597.

(603) (With S. Neelakantan & R. Padmasani) Synthesis of atranorin. *TL*, p. 287.

(604) Origin of anthocyanins. *J. Indian chem. Soc.* **39**, 221.

(612) 1963 (With H. G. Krishnamurty & V. Krishnamoorthy) Preparation of anthocyanidins and their glycosides from related flavonoids. *Phytochem.* **2**, 47.

(620) 1963 (With R. Aneja & R. N. Khanna) 6-Methoxyfuroflavone, a new component of the seeds of *Pongamia glabra*. *JCS*, p. 163.

(622) (With R. N. Khanna) Pongaglabrone, a new component of the seeds of *Pongamia glabra*: its constitution and synthesis. *T* **19**, 219.

(627) (With S. C. Agarwal) Application of ozonolysis to the study of substituted derivatives of vulpinic acid. *T* **19**, 1965.

(638) 1964 (With S. C. B. Bhrara & A. C. Jain) Some reactions of 2′-benzyloxychalkone epoxides. *CS* **33**, 48; *T* **20**, 1141.

(649) (With S. Neelakantan & R. Padmasani) A note on the synthesis of diploicin methyl ether. *CS* **33**, 365 .

(669) 1965 (With S. C. Bhrara & A. C. Jain) Scope of isoflavone synthesis using 2′-benzyloxychalkone epoxides. *T* **21**, 963.

(677) (With K. Chandrasenan & S. Neelakantan) Naturally occurring dibenzoquinones. *Bull. natn Inst. Sci. India*, no. 28, 92.

(699) (With A. C. Jain & S. K. Mathur) Synthesis of 5,2′,5′-trihydroxy-3,7,4′-trimethoxyflavone and constitution of oxyayanin-A. *IJC* **3**, 418.

(715) 1966 (With V. K. Bhatia & S. R. Gupta) Glycosides of the leaves of *Parkinsonia aculeata*. *T* **22**, 1147.

(728) (With G. D. Bhatia & S. K. Mukerjee) Synthesis of (±)-cyanomaclurin trimethyl ether. *TL*, p. 1717.

(742) (With V. V. S. Murti & P. V. Raman) Removal of 3-hydroxyl group in flavonols to yield flavones. *IJC* **4**, 396.

(753) (With S. K. Manaktala & S. Neelakantan) Synthesis of (±) montagnetol and (±) erythrin. *T* **22**, 2373.

(755) (With K. V. Rao and M. S. Sood) Isolation and constitution of pedicellic acid. *T* **22**, 1495.

(774) 1967 (With V. V. S. Murti & P. V. Raman) Cupressuflavone a new biflavonyl pigment. *T* **23**, 397.

(777) (With V. K. Bhatia & J. D. Ramanathan) Constitution of mangiferin. *T*. **23**, 1363.

(781) (With A. C. Jain & V. K. Rohatgi) A study of the action of alkaline hydrogen peroxide on α-methoxy-chalkones. *IJC* **5**, 68.

(782) (With V. K. Ahuluwalia & G. P. Sachdev) Nuclear allylation of chrysin. *IJC* **5**, 97.

(793) (With V. K. Kalra & A. S. Kukla) Synthesis of new types of pterocarpans. *IJC* **5**, 607.

(822) 1968 (With V. K. Bhatia) Synthesis of mangiferin. *TL*, p. 1741.

(831) (With A. C. Jain & V. K. Khanna) A synthesis of polygalaxanthone-B. *CS* **37**, 493.

(838) (With V. Jayalakshmi & S. Neelakantan) A synthesis of thiophanic acid. *CS* **37**, 196.

(839) (With P. S. Rao) Chemical investigation of Indian lichens. XXIX. Structural studies of retigeradiol. *IJC* **6**, 398.

(855) 1969 (With S. K. Mukerjee & S. C. Sarkar) The structure and synthesis of pongachromene, a new component of *Pongamia glabra*. *T* **25**, 1063.

(856) (With S. P. Bhutani & S. S. Chibber) Components of the roots of *Pueraria tuberosa*. Isolation of a new isoflavone *C*-glycoside (di-*O*-acetylpuerarin). *IJC* **7**, 210.

(857) (With V. Narayanan) Chemical components of *Acer rubrum* wood and bark. Occurrence of procyanidin dimer and trimer. *IJC* **7**, 213.

(872) (With A. C. Jain & V. K. Khanna) Synthesis and study of 2-*C*- and 4-*C*-methylxanthones. *T* **25**, 275.

(876) (With V. Jayalakshmi & S. Neelakantan) A convenient synthesis of lichen tridepsides. *IJC* **7**, 56.

(878) (With G. R. Chopra & A. C. Jain) Isolation and structure of putrolic acid, a new triterpenic seco-acid from the stem bark of *Putranjiva roxburghii*. *CS* **38**, 101.

(892) (With A. C. Jain & Pyare Lal) Nuclear prenylation of 2,methyl-5,7-dihydroxychromone and resacetophenone: Synthesis of peucenin, isopeucenin, isobavachalkone and isobavachin. *IJC* **7**, 1072.

(903) 1970 (With S. NATARAJAN & V. V. S. MURTI) Biflavonoids. VI. Some observations on the structure and synthesis of hinokiflavone. *IJC* **8**, 116.

(905) (With N. R. KRISHNASWAMY & T. N. C. VEDANTHAM) (−)-16α-Hydroxy-kauran-19-oic acid from *Enhydra fluctuans*. *IJC* **8**, 375.

(906) (With G. R. CHOPRA & A. C. JAIN) Structure of putric acid, a new seco-acid from the stem bark of *Putranjiva roxburghii*. *IJC* **8**, 401.

(923) (With A. C. JAIN & PYARE LAL) A study of nuclear prenylation and allylation of isoflavanones and synthesis of 4-methyl ethers of osajin and warangalone. *T* **26**, 1977.

(924) (With A. C. JAIN & PYARE LAL) A study of nuclear prenylation of β-resacetophenone. II. Synthesis of bavachalkone, 4′-*O*-methylbavachalkone and bavachin. *T* **26**, 2631.

(926) (With V. N. AIYAR) Components of *Croton oblongifolius*. III. Constitution of oblongifolic acid. *T* **26**, 5275.

(932) 1971 (With V. NARAYANAN) Paniculatin, a new isoflavone di-*C*-glucoside of *Dalbergia paniculata* bark. *IJC* **9**, 14.

(951) (With R. K. TRIKHA) Convenient methods for the preparation of cyanidin and cyanidin tetramethyl ether. *IJC* **9**, 626.

(960) (With V. N. AIYAR) Chemical components of *Croton oblongifolius*. IV. Constitution of oblongifoliol and deoxyoblongifoliol. *IJC* **9**, 1055.

(962) (With T. SAROJA & S. K. MUKERJEE) Synthesis of iso-obtusafuran and iso-melanoxin methyl ethers from 4-phenylcoumarins. *IJC* **9**, 1316.

(963) (With P. S. SAMPATH KUMAR & V. V. S. MURTI) Synthesis of 2,2-dimethyl-chromenocoumarins. *IJC* **9**, 1319.

(964) (With B. S. BAJWA & PYARE LAL KHANNA) Nuclear prenylation of polyphenols. III. Prenylation of noreugenin, *p*-hydroxyacetophenone and gallacetophenone under acidic conditions. *IJC* **9**, 1322.

(979) (With S. K. MUKERJEE & T. SAROJA) Dalbergichromene, a new neoflavonoid from stem-bark and heartwood of *Dalbergia sissoo*. *T* **27**, 799.

(980) (With M. BANDOPADHYAY & S. B. MALIK) Candicanin, a novel bicoumarinyl derivative from the roots of *Heracleum candicans*. *TL*, p. 4221.

(981) (With P. S. SAMPATH KUMAR & V. V. S. MURTI) Structure of glabrin. *TL*, p. 4451.

(986) 1972 (With A. R. SOOD & I. P. VARSHNEY) Glycoflavones from the seeds of *Trigonella corniculata*: isolation of 6,8-di-*C*-β-D-glucopyranosylacacetin and its monoacetate. *IJC* **10**, 26.

(990) (With N. R. KRISHNASWAMY & T. N. C. VEDANTHAM) The chemistry of enhydrin, a new germacranolide from *Enhydra fluctuans*. *IJC* **10**, 249.

(991) (With V. V. S. MURTI & P. S. SAMPATH KUMAR) Structure of ponnalide. *IJC* **10**, 255.

(994) (With S. C. DATTA & V. V. S. MURTI) Isolation and study of (+)-gossypol from *Thespesia populnea*, *IJC* **10**, 263.

(999) (With S. BHANU, T. SAROJA & S. K. MUKERJEE) Conversion of 4-phenyl-coumarins into xanthones; biogenetic implications. *IJC* **10**, 577.

(1001) (With SULEKHA MAHEY & PUSHPA SHARMA) Structure and synthesis of glabrachromene, a new constituent of *Pongamia glabra*. *IJC* **10**, 585.

(1003) (With S. C. DATTA & V. V. S. MURTI) A study of the derivatives of (±)-gossypol. *IJC* **10**, 691.

(1008) (With B. S. BAJWA & PYARE LAL KHANNA) A new chromenochalcone, bavachromene, from the seeds of *Psoralea corylifolia*. *CS* **41**, 814.

(1011) (With N. CHANDRAMAULI, V. V. S. MURTI & S. NATARAJAN) Structure of cupressuflavone. *IJC* **10**, 1115.

(1012) (With MISS S. RAYCHAUDHURI & S. K. MUKERJEE) A new synthesis of allokhellin and its ring isomeric change. *IJC* **10**, 1125.

(1022) (With B. S. BAJWA & PYARE LAL KHANNA) A new isoflavone, neobava-isoflavone, from the seeds of *Psoralea corylifolia*. *CS* **41**, 882.

(1024) Polyphenols of *Pterocarpus* and *Dalbergia* woods. *Phytochem.* **11**, 881.

(1025) (With V. N. AIYAR) 11-Dehydro (−)-hardwickic acid from *Croton oblongifolius*. *Phytochem.* **11**, 1473.

(1028) 1972 (With B. S. BAJWA & PYARE LAL KHANNA) Nuclear prenylation of polyhydroxy-ketones. V. *TL*, p. 3371.

(1044) 1973 (With V. N. AIYAR, G. R. CHOPRA & A. C. JAIN) Constitution of putrone and putrol. *IJC* **11**, 525.

(1051) (With M. BANDOPADHYAY & S. B. MALIK) Candicopimaric acid, a diterpene acid from the roots of *Heracleum candicans*. *IJC* **11**, 1097.

(1066) (With B. RAVINDRANATH) Structural studies on santalin permethyl ether. *Phytochem.* **12**, 2781.

(1067) (With K. R. RANGANATHAN) A new flavonolignan from *Hydnocarpus wightiana*. *TL*, p. 3481.

(1084) 1974 (With K. R. RANGANATHAN) Constitution of isohydnocarpin isolated from the seed hulls of *Hydnocarpus wightiana*. *IJC* **12**, 888.

(1087) (With K. R. RANGANATHAN) Minor phenolic components of seed hulls of *Hydnocarpus wightiana*: constitution of methoxyhydnocarpin. *IJC* **12**, 993.

(1095) (With N. KUMAR & B. RAVINDRANATH) Terpenoids of *Pterocarpus santalinus* heartwood. *Phytochem.* **13**, 633.

(1096) (With H. CHAWLA & S. S. CHIBBER) Volubilin, a new isoflavone-*C*-glycoside from *Dalbergia volubilis* flowers. *Phytochem.* **13**, 2301.

(1098) (With K. N. GURUDUTT) Constitution of the santalin pigments A and B. *Phytochem.* **13**, 2845.

(1108) 1975 (With H. M. CHAWLA & S. S. CHIBBER) Isovolubilin, a new isoflavone-*C*-rhamnoside from *Dalbergia volubilis* flowers. *IJC* **13**, 444.

(1115) (With N. N. SHARMA) Isolation of the hexamethyl ether of the dilactol form of (±)-gossypol. *IJC* **13**, 865.

(1116) (With N. N. SHARMA) Further study of the three forms of (±)-gossypol hexamethyl ether. *IJC* **13**, 866.

P. A. Sheppard.

# PERCIVAL ALBERT SHEPPARD

12 May 1907—22 December 1977

Elected F.R.S. 1964

By R. C. Sutcliffe, F.R.S., and F. Pasquill, F.R.S.

## Early life and education

Percival Albert Sheppard, Peter to his family and all who knew him well, was a leading academic figure in world meteorology through the 1950s until his death. He was the only son of Albert Edward Sheppard of Box Hill, Wiltshire, who had left school at the age of 12, not of course being exceptional in that, and had become an ornamental and monumental mason. He was a sober-living and serious craftsman who in 1913 or thereabouts set up on his own account, although after initial successes was unable to overcome the difficulties arising in World War I. Accordingly in 1916 he took up munitions work and moved to Bath, seven miles away, so securing better housing and better educational opportunities for his children. Albert Edward had known unemployment and his material resources were limited but he and his wife found enrichment through their church. They were pillars of the United Methodist Chapel, he as superintendent of Sunday School, his wife as organist and choir master, and the family were aware of wider horizons. In Sheppard's words: 'Names like Ruskin, Carlyle, Emerson became familiar.' Home life with two sisters seems to have been happy enough, and the family attachments endured through life, but up to the age of 10 Peter's life at Box Hill had little excitement in modern terms: 'An occasional visit to Bath (seven miles), perhaps including a Mary Pickford film, was a highlight.' He remembered that once when about seven years old he had 'been walked' all the way to Bath and back by his maternal grandmother, 'a great walker for her age'. His education began in the usual way at the local elementary school, Box Hill Church School, was continued in Bath at the Oldfield Council Boys School and then, after his gaining an entrance scholarship in 1918, came his six years at the City of Bath Boys' School. We have no record of his school life until we come to the sixth form where students prepared for the London Intermediate B.Sc. The mid-twenties were lean years for sixth forms and Sheppard was in a class of only four students with a science master who was 'not a particularly inspired teacher and rather easy-going, leaving us to follow our own devices which resulted in our tackling final degree physics experiments from Watson's *Practical Physics*'. The circumstances were evidently no great disadvantage for all four students went on to read physics at Bristol University, Sheppard with a scholarship and presumably the others also. One of them was L. F. Broadway who became Director of Research for E.M.I., another became eminent as Sir Gordon Cox, F.R.S., Secretary of the Agricultural Research Council, a close friend of Peter's for many years. The small sixth forms had other advantages, not least the close contacts with members of the staff and the sense of maturity and responsibility arising from the relationship. Sheppard writes of 'much maturing discussion on literature and life with Latin master (Matthews) and French master (Holden)' and one feels that on entering the university he was already awake intellectually and aesthetically; his sympathy with the *avant-garde* stayed with him always. But the wider interests which he already had as a young man and which were so much part of his character were no distraction from his physics which he took very seriously. Professor A. M. Tyndall, F.R.S., and Professor J. E. Lennard Jones, F.R.S., were, he writes, 'very good teachers'. It was the latter's course in theoretical physics which gave 'confidence in handling mathematics' while Professor Tyndall (with G. C. Grindley) was his guide in experimental work, Sheppard's strong suit. He became president of the students' Physical Society and graduated in 1927 with first class honours.

## The pre-war years

It was two years after graduating, years spent as Student Demonstrator researching on the loading of gaseous ions by polar molecules, that Sheppard got started on his career: in 1929 he accepted a post at Kew Observatory. The appointment was within the Meteorological Office at a time when graduate recruits were few in number and those few for the most part destined to become synoptic meteorologists and weather forecasters to meet the expanding needs of aviation, work which in those days was mostly a matter of empirical skills attained by experience. It is then significant that Sheppard was a rather rare exception who from the beginning was able to apply his knowledge of physics and his laboratory dexterity to the observational problems of Kew Observatory, in particular to studies of atmospheric electrical balance in fine and disturbed weather. In only a short time he found himself preparing for a programme of observations on the same subject in the essentially unpolluted air of the Canadian Arctic, as a member of a small expedition being organized in Britain for the forthcoming International Polar Year. During 1932–33 he was away at Fort Rae on this expedition led by J. M. Stagg (later Director of Services in the Meteorological Office). It was an experience not without its strains in human relations, particularly as the leader, conscientious to a fault, could be a difficult companion, but Sheppard's scientific work gave him a good measure of satisfaction and in later life he was always ready to recall the contribution to atmospheric electricity he made at that time. On arriving back in England to continue his work with the Meteorological Office he was again fortunate, first in a marriage which was to be a sound partnership for life, second in being chosen to join the only research group within the ambit of the Office at that time. This had been set up in 1921 within the Chemical Warfare Experimental Station, a War Office establishment at Porton created to study the problems which had stemmed from the use of poisonous gases in World War I. The associated meteorological group was the result of an initiative by D. Brunt then a Superintendent in the Meteorological Office and later Sir David Brunt, Secretary of the Royal Society 1948–57, and Professor of Meteorology at the Imperial College. As chairman of the Meteorological subcommittee of the Chemical Warfare Committee for more than 20 years Brunt was influential and was able to secure the services over the years of some remarkably able scientists including N. K. Johnson later Sir Nelson, Director of the Meteorological Office, O. G. Sutton, F.R.S., later Sir Graham and successor to Johnson as Director, and several other future F.R.S.'s. To join that group in 1933 with O. G. Sutton as leader was a rare opportunity and Sheppard made the most of it. Sutton was essentially a mathematician and Sheppard with his approach as a physicist combined with real experimental skill was soon a respected member of the team. An account of his contribution to the research of that famous group is given later in this memoir; here we note only that he stayed with them for six years and it was no surprise that in 1939 when Brunt was looking for someone to join his department as Reader at the Imperial College, Sheppard was appointed. Brunt like Sutton was a theoretician who needed the support of an experimentalist but the planned development of the department had to await the end of World War II.

## The war years

Brunt and Sheppard were quickly engaged on the outbreak of war in an intensive programme of training recruits for the Meteorological Office and for military services controlled by that Office, but it was clear that many hundreds of staff of all grades were likely to be required and an elaborate training organization became necessary. Sheppard was then seconded back to the Meteorological Office and spent most of the period at Dunstable, Bedfordshire, the centre of meteorological communications and forecasting for most of the war and for many years afterwards. Curiously enough, placed as he was at the centre of the meteorological service he seemed to show almost no interest in the problems of forecasting, an attitude which was something of a puzzle to those who knew him. Thus, C. H. B. Priestley (later F.R.S.), who was a contemporary of Sheppard's in those war-time Dunstable days, remarks that he 'hardly ever came into the forecast room' and there is no doubt that his shyness of forecasting arose from an innate antipathy for the qualitative arguments and empirical methods employed. The forecaster's exercise of scientific judgement, supremely important though it was for military operations, gave virtually no scope for Sheppard's skills or theoretical insight. He would say in his provocative way that weather forecasting was not 'scientifically respectable'; he always conceived it as his duty to present meteorology as 'atmospheric physics', and as rigorously as he was able. It is only fair to add that C. H. B. Priestley went on to write: 'From that time onwards my image of Peter was that of the most erudite and critical of meteorologists . . . there was always something to be learnt from his judgement and wisdom.' He was soon to find scope for his skills in the technicalities of radiosondes and radar and in the organization for Europe and the Northwest

Atlantic of an expanding network of upper air observing stations including aircraft reconnaissance for which he assumed responsibility. Another of his duties was in connection with the smoke screening of vital targets as a protection from air attack and after European hostilities ended, in 1945, he undertook a special assignment in surveying on behalf of the British authorities the work of certain German scientific institutions. Accompanied by K. L. Calder, then in charge of the meteorological work at Porton, he made official visits of inspection to the Kaiser Wilhelm Institute for Aerodynamical Research, to appraise the wind-tunnel modelling of atmospheric dispersion, and to the Marine Observatory at Greifswald where experiments on naval smoke screens had been made.

## The Imperial College

It was late in 1945 that Sheppard was able to take up his university work once more, to pick up the threads of his personal research and to support Brunt in the teaching and administration of the department. After 1948, when Brunt became Secretary of the Royal Society, Sheppard assumed more and more of the duties and in the expected course of events he succeeded as professor when Brunt retired in 1952. If at the time he seemed something of a lightweight compared with the distinguished Sir David Brunt, F.R.S., he was soon to show his competence and the department continued to flourish. He remained in that post until his retirement in 1974 and as it was the centre of his life's work a brief account of the department is helpful here. It had been established as an effective research and teaching unit on a permanent basis only in 1934 when Brunt was appointed first full-time professor. Before that time Sir Gilbert Walker, F.R.S., and earlier Sir Napier Shaw, F.R.S., had held the chair at the Imperial College, but these were special appointments accommodating those distinguished men retired from the public service: Brunt's arrival in 1934 was a new beginning. It was the only department of meteorology in our universities, indeed the only one in the whole of the British Empire, but it was not thought appropriate to offer a first degree course and from the beginning research work and postgraduate teaching with a small number of students, the majority from overseas, were the objective. But Brunt was soon looking to expansion and Sheppard's appointment as Reader in 1939 gave the department a new look although, as we have seen, little was accomplished until after the war. One of the first postwar students was Henry Charnock now (1978) Professor Charnock, F.R.S., who comments on Sheppard at that time: 'He took meteorology to be a serious and difficult branch of science to be studied in as analytic and rigorous a way as possible. The rather brusque manner in which he communicated his opinion was also typical.' He also comments that 'the course had very little formal teaching and a complete lack of practical training'. These weaknesses were, however, largely corrected after Brunt, taking advantage of the optimism of the post-war years, had obtained laboratories and a workshop and had made some further imaginative appointments. Some of these were from postgraduate students in the department: E. T. Eady who died young but not before securing a permanent place in the history of the subject with some strikingly original contributions to meteorological fluid mechanics; F. H. Ludlum whose novel analyses of clouds and weather systems gained him the personal title of professor; somewhat later R. P. Pearce who became Professor of Meteorology in Reading and H. Charnock, already mentioned, who became Director of the Institute of Oceanographic Sciences as well as F.R.S. and professor in Southampton. Other notable appointments were made from elsewhere: R. S. Scorer who later became Professor of Theoretical Mechanics in the Imperial College, R. M. Goody who was to move on to a chair in Harvard, and B. J. Mason who became Professor of Cloud Physics while in the college, from 1965 Director-General of the Meteorological Office and from 1976 Treasurer of the Royal Society. Together with Sheppard's expertise and Brunt's all-round eminence and reputation as the author of the best textbook of the times, there was a richness of talent and a liveliness of interests which it would not be easy to parallel in any small university department. Sheppard who had much to do with the appointments even before he became professor in 1952 may now be quoted: 'I encouraged my staff to develop research interests over the broad main front of meteorology in spite of incurring a danger of spreading effort too widely. In fact we established world recognition in a very few years in dynamic meteorology and climatology, boundary layer meteorology, cloud physics and atmospheric radiation. I am proud that nine chairs were filled (in physics, mathematics, and physical oceanography as well as meteorology) from members of the staff while I was head of the department.' Naturally there were other students who became distinguished and these were later to be found in many countries. In its time and especially over the years 1950–65 the meteorology at the Imperial College had a world prestige and influence quite remarkable against the background of rapid expansion in effort and advances in knowledge being made elsewhere, especially in America and Russia. They were in a sense the heroic years of meteorology and Sheppard's department played no humble role. It is then all the more uncongenial to recognize that it proved ill adapted to meet the more stringent conditions of university life in the '70s. Most of the staff of the earlier years had found or were finding posts elsewhere and the absence of a degree course in the subject made it difficult to show teaching performance to balance staff numbers in the new climate of 'staff–student ratios' and the like. The chair in meteorology was allowed to lapse on Sheppard's retirement and the department became an 'atmospheric physics group' in the Department of Physics. Opinions have been ventilated on the degree to which Sheppard's policies contributed to the decline of the department which he had done so much to create and it is probably quite fair to say that in spite of the many personal research successes there was a lack of that coherence and leadership in both research and teaching which would have been needed to adapt a university postgraduate department to the changing circumstances.

One factor which certainly distracted Sheppard from the affairs of his department was the heavy demand made upon him by numerous committees, a demand which as the only professor of meteorology in the country he could hardly resist. So we find him from 1949 a member of the Meteorological

Research Committee (the official committee which advises on the research work of the Meteorological Office) and its Chairman from 1958 to 1968, a post he filled with great conscientiousness: he never learnt how to neglect his homework and freewheel through his committee meetings. The appointment carried also a seat on the Meteorological Committee, then chaired by Lord Hurcomb, which advises the Minister on general Meteorological Office policy. Sheppard's C.B.E. of 1963 was a recognition of his public services. In addition he had assisted D.S.I.R. from 1954 to 1956 as a member of the Physics Grants Committee and went on to become a member of the Science Research Council 1966–71, a member of the Astronomy, Space and Radio Board 1965–71 and chairman of the Space Policy and Grants Committee over these same years. Over several years he greatly influenced the work of the Gust Research Committee of the Aeronautical Research Council, being Chairman from 1955 to 1961. The new Natural Environment Research Council also claimed his services from 1966 to 1972 on its Meteorological Research Grants and Training Awards Committee and another particularly heavy commitment was his work for E.S.R.O. (the European Space Research Organization). He served on the E.S.R.O. Council 1965–71, as Vice-chairman 1966–67, on the Bureau 1966–71 and as member of the Scientific and Technical Committee. These were demanding duties requiring much travel to the continent and important as they were it is not surprising that meteorologists were not wholly in sympathy. A view expressed here in Professor Charnock's words was shared by many; 'To me it was regrettable that he spent so much time on Committees of Space Research for I think he could have done more to help meteorology and oceanography at less rarified levels. But his services were much appreciated by the Science Research Council and the European Space Research Organization.' Again we may quote Sir John Mason, Director-General of the Meteorological Office: 'The workload and travelling put a heavy strain on his energies and took him away a great deal from his department . . ..' The uneasiness was general and perhaps he came to share it himself for it was in these vital years that Sheppard's chest began seriously to trouble him and during his last few working years as professor (he retired in 1974) he was carrying on with evident and increasing difficulties.

The foregoing is by no means a complete list of Sheppard's activities, as for many years there was hardly an important appointment made or a policy decision taken relating to meteorology without Sheppard being concerned as committee man, consultant, referee or less formally. He served on the Council of the Royal Society from 1970 to 1972 and the Royal Meteorological Society was always very loyally supported. He was Secretary and edited its *Quarterly Journal* from 1950 to 1953, President 1957–58, and still a member of the Editing Committee carrying a load of refereeing duties at the time of his death. That Society honoured him with its senior award, the Symons Gold Medal, in 1963 and with honorary membership in 1977. He will be remembered in many countries as an influential delegate to several meetings under the auspices of the World Meteorological Organization and as a contributor also to assemblies and committees of the International Association of Meteorology and Atmospheric

Physics of the International Union of Geodesy and Geophysics. In much demand also for lecturing and advisory work in other countries, his many visits included those to Australia, India and Egypt, Western European countries, the U.S.S.R. (he became honorary D.Sc. of Leningrad University in 1969), and of course America, both Canada and the U.S.A. in which countries he was held in high esteem and made several good friends. He must have crossed the Atlantic a score of times and for the year 1963 was Visiting Professor at the University of California, Los Angeles. After his death there was a particularly gratifying occasion on the Island of Anegada where in 1953 Sheppard had been leader of a scientific expedition (the work is referred to in a later paragraph of this memoir). There had been collaboration on the expedition with a U.S. team from Woods Hole Oceanographic Institute and in 1978 on its 25th anniversary a memorial stone was placed in the church engraved 'Professor P. A. Sheppard 1907–1977'. Arrangements were also made for books to be deposited and inscribed 'to the Anegada community library in memory of Professor Sheppard, donated by the US–UK 1953 Weather Expedition'. The initiative for this memorial was mainly American and the information above is taken from an article in the *Bulletin of the American Meteorological Society* by Professor Joanne Simpson, one of the original collaborators.

Sheppard was an able lecturer presenting well prepared material with memorable clarity and was ready if necessary to tackle almost any branch of meteorology (except weather forecasting!). One of the authors of this memoir had the experience of hearing him lecture in Rome to a mainly Italian audience and choosing to do so in French, a language he understood well but which only his great courage allowed him to employ on the platform. Perhaps as a succinct appraisal of Sheppard the professor there is nothing better than another quotation from Sir John Mason: 'He played a very important role, not so much by his leadership in research but as the most widely read and informed meteorologist of his day, whose penetrating criticism, scholarly review articles and lucid lectures were of great value and influence.' But, as we shall now see, his own original research was very considerable.

## Research work

### *The British Polar Year Expedition, 1932–33*

The Polar Year was an international effort organized by the International Polar Year Commission and the British Expedition to Fort Rae, Northwest Canada, was organized by a National Committee with Sir George Simpson, F.R.S., then Director of the Meteorological Office, as secretary. The six-strong team which left for Canada in May 1932 had on it four members of the staff of that Office including the leader, J. M. Stagg, and Sheppard who was one of four 'specialist scientific officers' responsible for a substantial programme of observations in terrestrial magnetism and meteorology, including atmospheric electricity, for which Sheppard had a special responsibility. Suitable instruments were already in use at Kew Observatory where Sheppard had recently taken up his first appointment but some modifications were necessary for the expedition which was to make observations on potential gradient, air–earth current, conductivity, small ion content, rate of production of ionization and numbers of condensation nuclei.

The account which the leader gives in the Royal Society's publication of the work makes engrossing reading for anyone interested in the trials and tribulations of scientific expeditions in difficult terrain and climate. Apart from the inevitable human and domestic problems, there were all sorts of technical challenges, some unexpected, such as the disturbing 'static' produced even by the slow motion of the recording paper of the Benndorf electrograph in the extremely dry conditions, and the stray thermo-e.m.f.s produced by strong temperature gradients in an instrument hut that had to be heated, to mention two of the difficulties resolved by Sheppard.

The programme of observations was carried out, according to plan, for a whole year commencing 1 August 1932. The atmospheric electrical data collected by Sheppard were found, in 'quiet' weather conditions, to display an overall consistent pattern of diurnal and annual variations which were argued plausibly to be essentially a consequence of two basic features—first that the rate of production of atmospheric ions is at a maximum near the ground, second that the upward diffusion of the ions must depend on the atmospheric turbulence and hence on the strength of the wind, which itself possessed characteristic diurnal and annual variations. Also there were some striking variations of potential gradient associated with drifting snow, which appeared to be a consequence of the increase in depth of the drift layer with increase in wind speed. It is interesting that in this excursion into atmospheric electrical work Sheppard found himself already concerned with those problems of boundary layer transport that were to be the major preoccupation of his later research.

### *Wind-profile work at Porton*

In the early 1930s the main research thrust of the meteorology group at the Chemical Defence Establishment, Porton, was directed toward testing and improving the new theory of atmospheric diffusion put forward by O. G. Sutton. A central feature of this theory was the increase of wind speed with height above ground, the precise form of which reflected the widely varying rate of turbulent exchange in the lowest air layers. When Sheppard joined the group (in 1933) studies of the wind profile by A. C. Best had already revealed some puzzling discrepancies in the character of the wind profile at different positions on the Porton ranges, which were well exposed and expected to be essentially uniform as regards the properties of the airflow. These discrepancies stood to be clarified and interpreted in the context of Sutton's diffusion theory and its practical application in the 'concentration-range' tables prepared for the assessment of the effect of poison gas attacks.

Sheppard's contributions over the next few years were to fall mainly in three areas: first the elucidation of the wind-profile anomalies, secondly the development of a greatly improved anemometer with which the necessary wind gradient measurements could be made in a simpler and more reliable fashion both in the on-going research and in the operational applications that were envisaged for the future, and thirdly the intensive theoretical debate that ensued with the object of improving the application and extending the basis of Sutton's theory.

It is relevant to note that some 20 years had yet to elapse before the emergence of the now universally adopted Monin–Obukhov theory of the wind profile and related properties. The logarithmic form of wind profile ($u \propto \ln z$), though known even at this early stage to be the most accurate representation in neutral conditions of flow, was largely neglected in the Porton work at that time, in favour of the obviously less accurate power-law form ($u \propto z^{\alpha}$), for mathematical convenience and because Sutton's theory necessarily led to such a form. From the field studies which Sheppard then undertook it ultimately became clear that over the Porton ranges there was an important effect on the power-law index $\alpha$ arising from variations in the surface roughness, even from a mere difference in the length of grass.

Sheppard's wind profile results were a crucial input to the continuing theoretical debate. By 1937 the theoretical work had been taken over by Sutton's young colleague K. L. Calder, and over a considerable period Sheppard was involved in regular discussions with Calder, providing special physical insights and field experience in support of the mathematical attack. One of us (F. P.), joining the Porton group at this stage, was witness to many of these searching discussions, sometimes it may be said a rather mystified witness in view of the complexities and subtleties under examination. Clarification steadily emerged, obviously due in no small measure to Sheppard's critical appreciation of the physics of the airflow, and the theoretical position was finally set on record after World War II in papers by Calder and Sutton. The essential point is that Sutton's original treatment of vertical transfer predicted remarkably accurate results for an *aerodynamically smooth* surface (notably, for example, in respect of the rate of evaporation from a smooth wet surface). For flow over such a surface Sutton's theory had led correctly to an eddy diffusivity profile determined uniquely by the flow speed and the kinematic viscosity, but most atmospheric flows are *aerodynamically rough*, in which case the kinematic viscosity is irrelevant and the eddy diffusivity is determined (in neutral stratification) by the wind speed and the now-familiar roughness parameter $z_0$. Variations of this parameter had of course been at the root of the wind profile 'anomalies' on the Porton ranges.

Noting that over a 2 : 1 change in height the increase in mean wind speed may be as little as a few parts per cent, it is clear that an adequate specification of the precise form of the wind profile near the ground requires very sensitive anemometers with accurately reproducible calibrations. In Sheppard's early wind profile studies the most suitable instruments available were the vane airmeters commonly used for measurements of low speed flow in ducts and channels. Though adequately sensitive for the natural wind profile measurements these airmeters are somewhat fragile, consisting of a rotor of light aluminium vanes mounted within a cylindrical housing, and need to be handled very carefully as distortion of the vane settings is liable to alter the calibration.

Also the instruments are designed to be used with the rotor axis aligned accurately in the flow direction (within say 10° if the 'yaw' error was to be kept below 1%). In a natural wind, with the direction varying, sometimes over several tens of degrees, this meant that the airmeters had to be mounted on control vanes which held them appropriately pointed into wind, so adding to the cumbersomeness of the field equipment and procedure. The significant results obtained in the the face of these complications were a tribute to the painstaking calibration procedures and skilful handling of delicate field equipment in which Sheppard was a past master.

In view of the foregoing drawbacks of vane airmeters, added to which was their unsuitability in strong winds because of the excessive rotor speeds, there was need for an improved form of wind profile equipment, and to this end Sheppard devoted time and effort to the design and testing of a new form of cup anemometer. This type of anemometer could be expected to have the required robustness to withstand field handling and strong winds and with the cup rotor plane in the horizontal there was no dependence on wind direction and the instrument could accordingly be mounted on a rigid support, instead of on a swinging vane. Cup anemometers did of course already exist, though with quite inadequate sensitivity and response, and the required improvements were achieved only after careful wind tunnel tests to establish the most suitable design as regards cup shape and size, length of cup arm and type of bearings. In the new design the cups were very light, being spun from thin aluminium sheet, and a conical shape was adopted because, in contrast to the conventional hemispherical shape, this gave a closely linear relation between cup speed and wind speed.

The Sheppard anemometer proved to have all the expected advantages over the old vane airmeter system, and although the revolution counter system has since been redesigned and developed in various ways, the basic design has otherwise been retained. Produced commercially, this elegant and reliable portable anemometer has for several decades been an essential component of atmospheric boundary layer studies, and with it countless research workers in that special area of meteorological measurements have had the satisfaction of obtaining useful and significant wind profile data. It is also noteworthy that the semi-conical shape of cup was found to give a more faithful response than the hitherto conventional hemispherical form to rapid fluctuations such as occur in a natural wind, and as a consequence the inevitable over-estimation of the *mean* speed, which could be serious in the hemispherical form, was negligible for most purposes. This feature was established in work which Sheppard carried out in the early 1940s jointly with F. J. Scrase of the Meteorological Office, and led ultimately to a decision to adopt conical cups as standard for Meteorological Office cup anemometers.

### *Turbulence and shearing stress near the surface*

Even during his early years at Porton, when much of his time was taken up by *ad hoc* field studies of the wind profile and by various operational demands such as the assessment of the efficacy of smoke screens in relation to meteorological conditions, Sheppard's thoughts were turning to more basic observational studies, going on from the turbulence investigations of former members of the Porton team, F. J. Scrase and A. C. Best. In 1936, still with the Sutton theory in mind, he made an isolated attempt at measurement of the autocorrelation coefficient $R(t)$ of the fluctuating magnitude of the horizontal wind speed, as a function of time lag $t$, using a hot wire anemometer in conjunction with a cathode ray oscilloscope, in those days an advanced and sophisticated procedure. That the measurements were sound is clear from the consistency of the results with those obtained much later in much more extensive studies, but there were deep complications in the interpretation then in mind, especially in that the correlation coefficient occurring in Sutton's theory refers to a moving particle and not to the fluctuations occurring at a fixed point.

Three years later, just before leaving the Porton team to take up his appointment at Imperial College, Sheppard made the first attempt to measure directly the aerodynamic drag exerted by the natural wind on the Earth's surface. He used an elegantly designed drag plate system in which a circular plate was floated in a shallow bath of oil contained in a large flattish surround shaped so that the oncoming boundary layer flow continued over the test plate with as little interruption as possible. Movement of the floating plate under the action of wind drag on its horizontal surface was restrained by a torsion suspension to which the plate was connected by a short rigid arm, and the very small twisting of the suspension was measured by observing, with a telescope and scale arrangement, the deflexion of a mirror carried on the suspension. To ensure as close similarity as possible of the texture of the metal drag plate and the surrounding ground the apparatus was set up on an existing large area of smooth concrete on the Porton range and the first usable measurements were actually taken by C. H. B. Priestley, who had to take over in the final stages on Sheppard's departure for Imperial College. Substitution of the resulting magnitudes of surface drag in the now familiar logarithmic form of wind profile in neutral flow provided estimates of the von Karman constant, which was of specific interest to the Porton team at that time because it also appeared in the Sutton theory, and the only estimates of that constant hitherto available had come especially from pipe-flow studies. The fact that the estimates of 0.44–0.49 now provided were so close to the then accepted laboratory value of 0.4 was taken with some reserve at the time, partly because the flow conditions were actually unstable, and partly because there was some doubt whether, on grounds of *scale*, the small drag plate could be expected to represent the drag of the surrounding surface in conditions other than neutral. In retrospect there seems no compelling reason for a scale effect of the type envisaged and there is no doubt, to the extent that the drag plate surface *texture* was representative, that Sheppard had made entirely realistic measurements of surface drag and had taken the first step in confirming the magnitude of von Karman's constant in the context of atmospheric boundary layer flow. Since then his eminently successful experimental design has been adapted and modified by others to provide crucial measurements of aerodynamic drag over grassland and over ground carrying low crops.

With the advent of war and his immediate involvement in the training of wartime meteorologists and later in various operational aspects of meteorology (e.g. in the organization of area smoke screens over vital areas) continuation of the foregoing lines of research in his new academic post had to be postponed. Consequently it was not until 1950, on the occasion of the Centenary Meeting of the Royal Meteorological Society, that we find any public reporting of renewed research activity. By then, in conjunction with various research students and colleagues, notably H. Charnock and J. R. D. Francis, he had initiated several projects, including measurements of low level wind and temperature profiles over Lough Neagh in N. Ireland (which was to be a continuing and developing study over two decades with special interest in the drag coefficient and its dependence on wind speed) and of the rapid turbulent fluctuations of temperature and wind speed. The latter activity was extended to fluctuations of humidity in a development with M. K. Elnesr, in which the output of fine-wire thermocouples operated as wet and dry bulbs was fed into an electrical analogue circuit to give the humidity mixing ratio directly. From his early Porton experiences Sheppard had always strongly advocated the need for appropriate fluctuation measurements and for their use in evaluating eddy fluxes directly. His reports on these aspects in 1951 to the first of a series of major international symposia on atmospheric turbulence are particularly revealing of his concern with the relevance of large-scale contributions to fluctuations and eddy flux, both in the physical sense and in the special conceptual problems that were being encountered in the analyses of non-stationary time-series.

The wind profile observations over Lough Neagh were used with the conventional logarithmic form of wind profile to calculate the surface drag ($\tau$), thence the drag coefficient $C_D$ ($\equiv u_*^2/u_{10\,m}^2$, $u_*^2 \equiv \tau/\rho$, $\rho$ being air density), yielding values that were inconclusive on the variation of this property with wind speed, whereas wind tunnel measurements by Francis had indicated an approximately linear increase. This issue was pursued further in a joint study in Australia in 1955 with his former Porton colleague E. L. Deacon, and with E. K. Webb, both then of the C.S.I.R.O. Division of Meteorological Physics headed by C. H. B. Priestley. Here the wind profile measurements were made in Port Phillip Bay, and in Bass Strait a few miles out from Port Phillip heads, with a vertical array of Sheppard-type anemometers mounted on the jib boom and foremast of a 70 ft Fishery Research vessel. To maintain steerage the ship had to be steamed slowly into wind, and the wind speeds relative to the sea surface were obtained by subtracting the ship speed as obtained by timing the passage of simple floats (orange peel!). Much care was taken to evaluate the disturbance of the wind field by the ship's hull and the errors arising from rolling and heaving. The derived drag coefficients, referred as usual to the wind speed at 10 m, provided a tentative indication of a fairly gradual increase with wind speed over the range 4–12 m/s. In general, there has been conflicting evidence and interpretation as regards the existence and precise form of this variation of drag coefficient, and it is noteworthy that more recent work led by Sheppard (with D. T. Tribble and J. R. Garratt), to which we now turn, has confirmed the existence of a significant increase over the water of Lough Neagh.

The latest Lough Neagh work to be reported (1972) used a complete observational system that in the words of the paper was 'the culmination of a development extending over several years'. In its later stages the work owed much to Sheppard's collaborators but it is fair to say that it does represent a considerable fulfilment of his long-cherished aim of providing definitive profile flux properties over a large body of water and it certainly carries the stamp of his meticulous care in the design and instrumenting of boundary layer observations, which are especially difficult over water, and of his capacity for rigorous and imaginative interpretation of the data obtained. The observations were made in westerly winds, for which there was a water fetch of at least 8 km to the site of the instruments just off the eastern shore. Anemometers of Sheppard type with high speed electromechanical counters and dry-bulb and wet-bulb thermocouple elements mounted in naturally ventilated radiation shields were used for the mean profiles. There were also measurements of the fluctuations of the longitudinal wind component, the wind inclination and the temperature, which have been the subject of much subsequent analysis and discussion by Garratt.

In respect of Sheppard's long-standing interest in the behaviour of the drag coefficient it is specially noteworthy that these latest Lough Neagh observations gave an ensemble of over 200 logarithmic profiles which on substitution in the conventional relation led to $C_D$ values displaying a significant increase with increase of wind speed, representable approximately in the simple empirical form

$$10^3 C_D = 0.36 + 0.10 u_{10}, \quad 3\ \text{m/s} < u_{10} < 16\ \text{m/s}.$$

One strange feature, pointed out in the paper, for which no explanation could be found in terms of conceivable systematic errors in the measurements, is that the values of $C_D$ for wind speeds less than 5 m/s are actually less than would be expected from the law for an aerodynamically smooth surface. Interestingly, a point which is not made in the paper, as far as can be judged by eye from the published graphs, the latest Lough Neagh values do not differ systematically from the Australian data obtained from the ship-based wind profiles over the wind speed range 4–7 m/s, though they do fall somewhat lower at higher wind speeds. Also, in considering the extent of generalization provided by the Lough Neagh data on the behaviour of the Monin–Obukhov wind profile function, it is worth emphasizing that these data are for roughness length ($z_0$) values several orders of magnitude less than those representative of land observations. Finally, in Sheppard's discussion of the drag coefficient issue, he is careful to point out that in the overall context of behaviour over the ocean the evidence assembled from all studies still remains inconclusive, so the most he was prepared to conclude in the end was that uncertainties about the behaviour of $C_D$ are being narrowed and that in the meantime his result above represented a simple working relation with some validity. This work marked considerable progress in our knowledge of a basic parameter in air–sea interaction problems.

In this section on turbulent transfer near the surface it is appropriate to refer back to an excursion into the theory of turbulent transfer considered by Sheppard in his 1958 Presidential Address to the Royal Meteorological Society. Here he was concerned with adapting the relations for momentum transfer so as to derive an expression for the surface flux of some other property (such as water vapour) in terms of the difference between the concentrations of that property at the surface and at some reference height. The simplest step was to retain the classical Reynolds analogy in which the eddy diffusivity for the property was taken to be the same as for momentum. Experience had confirmed that such an assumption was essentially correct in neutral conditions when applied not too close to the surface, but the assumption disregards a crucial difference in the mechanism of transfer at a rough surface, by molecular diffusion in the case of a property such as water vapour but by pressure forces in the case of momentum. There had been conflicting views about the inclusion of a molecular diffusion term in the total diffusivity, a procedure then advocated by Sheppard for water vapour with useful results. His insistence on a physically realistic interpretation of the essential difference in the surface transfer of momentum and passive properties has been progressively supported by other workers in subsequent work on the deposition of vapours and gases.

## Wind stress over the sea and momentum transfer through the whole depth of the boundary layer

The inconclusiveness of the early work at Lough Neagh turned the interest of Sheppard and his colleagues to estimating the surface wind stress by the so-called ageostrophic method. Elegant in principle, the method had been first used by L. F. Richardson in 1920 and by one of the present authors (R. C. S.) in 1936 but had never been fully exploited to estimate the wind drag over the sea where few suitable wind observations had been made and where special difficulties arise. It was, then, with the enthusiastic support of his colleagues H. Charnock and J. R. D. Francis that Sheppard planned and in January 1951 carried out a special series of observations over the sea from a base in the Isles of Scilly obtaining by triple theodolites about 100 useful profiles up to some 600 m height. The immediate outcome was, however, to emphasize the complications inherent in the method rather than to obtain values of surface drag. Over the land it is possible by selection of occasions to obtain wind profiles which clearly indicate the boundary layer within which the wind changes quickly with height to attain a comparatively constant wind above. The vertical integral of the ageostrophic wind through the layer, on which the evaluation of drag depends, is then reasonably well defined. With the observations from the Scilly Isles expedition, however, there was a superposed general increase of wind with height (the so-called thermal wind), comparable in magnitude to the effect of drag so that no useful estimate of the drag could be made. Not only was the boundary layer difficult to discern but it was realized that in some cases there was no definite upper limit to the layer over which significant turbulent transfer of momentum might extend in the troposphere. These difficulties led Sheppard and his collaborators to look for situations where the general change of wind component with height in the troposphere would oppose the wind near the surface and impose a level of maximum wind at which, plausibly, the stress would be zero. Such is typically the condition in the Trade Winds and the feasibility of obtaining an estimate of surface stress was confirmed in an analysis (with M. H. Omar, 1952) of routine winds from three small Pacific islands. In pursuit of these ideas an expedition was planned to make special observations in the Trade Wind Zone and was carried out by Sheppard and collaborators in the spring of 1953.

Anegada, in the Virgin Islands, a coral island some 12 km by 3 km with maximum elevation about 10 m above sea level, was chosen. It was small enough and low enough to impose minimum disturbance on the oceanic airflow and yet adequate for the use of intervisible theodolites with sufficiently long baselines. The team spent about a month making a series of nearly 500 balloon soundings and also operating a network of pressure measurements on neighbouring islands with other ancillary observations. A full report with discussion was published in the extensive article in the *Philosophical Transactions.* The period mean winds yielded impressively smooth profiles of the wind components along and normal to the surface wind, the former having a well defined maximum just above 300 m, the latter increasing up to about 900 m and thereafter remaining almost constant. It was still necessary to make various assumptions on the geostrophic wind and its variation with height but reasonably definitive estimates of the surface stress were obtained. For the period mean surface (10 m) wind of just over 5 m/s the drag coefficient was $1.2 \times 10^{-3}$, encouragingly consistent with the value of about $0.9 \times 10^{-3}$ for such a wind speed from both the latest Lough Neagh series and the open sea measurements near Australia.

## The research in retrospect

The highlights of Sheppard's research achievements were the special observations which he designed and carried out, so demonstrating among meteorologists an unusual, even a unique, ability. Beginning early with the Polar Year observations we follow with the improved boundary layer profile observations at Porton, including the original design of the Sheppard cup anemometer, his quite novel drag plate construction giving a direct measure of the drag force of the wind on the ground, his profile measurements over Lough Neagh and his several expeditions to study the boundary layer over the sea as in Australian waters, and, for the whole planetary boundary layer, near the Scilly Isles and in the Trades at Anegada. In each of these undertakings (described in earlier paragraphs) his work was recognized at the time as a significant step forward. It was a time when a growing number of workers were attacking the problems of the Earth's boundary layer, over land and sea, and important theoretical advances were made, particularly in America, Russia and Australia as well as in Britain. On that international scene with the controversy and cooperation which were very much a feature of this subject, Sheppard was a prominent personality and if not himself an originator of mathematical theory his surveys were masterly and his opinion always solicited. And it was not only in boundary layer studies that he had standing. From 1950 onwards his writings show a growing interest in the global circulation of the Earth's atmosphere and the theory of climate which came to be regarded as his second speciality. The problem of global westerly momentum balance attracted his attention and when later in the fifties and sixties international effort was directed to the mathematical modelling of the general circulation Sheppard took a deep interest and had an influential voice. He was particularly proud of the part he played in the launching early in the seventies of a British inter-university group supported by grants from the Natural Environment Research Council which his advocacy was instrumental in securing. The group, with a permanent nucleus of staff and facilities (within the Department of Meteorology of Reading University), brought together research workers from five British universities and other collaborators who in a few years were to make some notable innovations in mathematical modelling of the large scale motions. Sheppard's personal contribution especially in the modelling of the boundary layer and turbulence generally should not be overlooked.

## THE WHOLE MAN

Although Sheppard's vocational interests were all-absorbing and engaged the whole of his creative energies there was nothing pretentious in his stating, in a standard reference work, that his hobby was 'life', for he relaxed with a wide range of interests and made many friends. At some time early in his adult life he had shed the Methodism which meant so much to his parents, and religious rites or dogma found no place in his later philosophy. His wife went along with him in this as in most other respects to the extent that by their choice no ceremony marked their deaths. But he was certainly a man of conscious faith, a faith in the worthwhileness of human life, with an appreciation of man's achievements: a humanist in that sense. He took a simple pleasure in the world around him and became knowledgeable as bird-watcher and botanist, delighting always in the countryside, a splendid companion for a country walk. But he was always fundamentally an intellectual and if he gave to rigorous scientific discovery the pride of place other achievements of imagination and skill were not put far behind: architecture, painting and music came in for much admiration, close study and—characteristically—sweeping judgements. He might have been called opinionated were it not that a lively rejoinder would always bring laughter, his own special hearty variety, to show that this was only his relaxation. As chairman of the Jordans Music Club, a local society near his home but one of wider repute, his love of music was no secret but it is less well known that as early as 1935 he published an article on 'Standards of criticism in art'. A statement in his later years that no year was complete without a visit to Italy was evidence of an affinity long maintained, but if his interests were naturally intellectual there was room for sentiment too. One recalls on an occasion after his retirement when both he and his wife were unwell his remarking 'but we have our friends and in the last analysis nothing matters but friendship'. Perhaps it was his own version of 'God is love' and as much part of his philosophy as his worship of hard core science. Both he and his wife were splendid companions, provocative and argumentative yet appreciative of quality of all kinds, not least of good food with a good bottle. Whether in this country or abroad, for an evening out or a longer holiday together, their company was a delight. With Phyllis deeply interested in people and always ready to support her husband, entertainment at their home near Beaconsfield was enjoyed by many of his colleagues, often from abroad, but their circle of friendship was notably wider than his profession and with much sharing of leisure interests their married life was eminently successful. They had been married on 28 October 1933 in Bath, Somerset. She was Phyllis Blanche, daughter of William Henry Foster (a local preacher and Bath City Councillor) and his wife Blanche (*née* Morrish) both of Paignton, Devon. Their two successful sons were a source of much satisfaction. The elder, Roger, born in 1936, went through agricultural college and flourished in business, something his father never rightly understood, whereas Simon, two years the younger, after graduating in geology in Cambridge, continued on the academic path, and his father lived to see him a petrologist and isotope geophysicist established in the university world. After a life so successful and so zestful their last years can only be described as tragic. With Peter already in poor health Phyllis suffered a serious stroke in May 1973. From then on, in spite of some hard-won improvement permitting even a little conviviality, life was a continuous struggle until she died in March 1976. Peter lived for less than two more years becoming very frail but keeping up with his committees, his interests and his friends to the end.

The writing of this memoir has been assisted by notes left by Professor Sheppard with the Royal Society and by opinions and recollections from his sister Gladys and his two sons. Several professional colleagues have also assisted with advice and the bibliography was kindly provided by the National Meterological Library.

The photograph reproduced was taken by E. G. Jennings in 1973.

## Bibliography

1928 (With A. M. Tyndall & G. C. Grindley) The mobility of ions in air. V. The transformation of positive ions at short ages. *Proc. R. Soc. Lond.* A **121**, 185.

1932 Character of atmospheric ionisation. *Nature, Lond.* **129**, no. 3248.

Some atmospheric electrical instruments for use on the British Polar Year Expedition 1932–33. *J. scient. Instrum.* **9**, 246–250.

1936 Wet and dry bulb hygrometry. *Met. Mag., Lond.* **71**, 85–86.

1937 *British Polar Year Expedition, Fort Rae, N.W. Canada, 1932–33.* Vol. 1, Discussion: Atmospheric Electricity. London: Royal Society.

1939 Atmospheric electricity. *Met. Mag., Lond.* no. 881, **74**, 129–136.

1940 An improved design of cup anemometer. *J. scient. Instrum.* **19**, no. 9, 218–221.

1941 Anemometry: a critical and historical survey. *Proc. phys. Soc.* **53**, 361–390.

1942 A review of recent measurements of atmospheric emissivity in the infra-red. *Q. Jl R. met. Soc.* **68**, 210–213.

1944 (With F. J. Scrase) The errors of cup anemometers in fluctuating winds. *J. scient. Instrum.* **21**, no. 9, 160–161.
1945 An unusual upper air sounding. *Q. Jl R. met. Soc.* **71**, 413–415.
1946 Variations in the field of atmospheric pressure. *Sci. Prog., Lond.* **34**, no. 135, 569–579.
Radio meteorology: influence of the atmosphere on the propagation of ultra-short radio waves. *Nature, Lond.* **157**, 860–862.
The British radio-sonde. *Q. Jl R. met. Soc.* **72**, 169–173.
1947 The aerodynamic drag of the earth's surface and the value of von Karman's constant in the lower atmosphere. *Proc. R. Soc. Lond.* A **188**, 208–222.
The structure and refractive index of the lower atmosphere. *Phys. Soc. and R. met. Soc. Rep.* pp. 37–79.
Radiation in the stratosphere and troposphere. *Sci. Prog., Lond.* no. 137, 87–101.
(With S. Petterssen, C. H. B. Priestley & K. R. Johannessen) An investigation of subsidence in the free atmosphere. *Q. Jl R. met. Soc.* **73**, nos 315–316, 43–64.
The constitution of clouds and the formation of rain. *Sci. Prog., Lond.* **35**, 490–505.
Atmospheric turbulence. *Nature, Lond.* **160**, 859.
1948 Wind structure and atmospheric turbulence. I. *Sci. Prog., Lond.* no. 143, 472–482.
(With A. C. Best & H. G. Booker) Radio meteorology in the United Kingdom 1939–47. *U.G.G.I., Ass. Met. Res. Mem., Oslo*, pp. 66–70.
1949 Wind structure and atmospheric turbulence. II. Theoretical studies. *Sci. Prog., Lond.* no. 145, 68–81.
Large scale vertical motion in the atmosphere. *Q. Jl R. met. Soc.* **75**, no. 324, 185–195.
The exploration of the upper atmosphere. *Sci. Prog., Lond.* no. 147, 487–503.
The physical properties of air with reference to meteorological practice and the air-conditioning engineer. *Trans. Am. Soc. mech. Engrs* **71**, no. 8, 915–919.
1950 Value of some physical functions and constants used in meteorology. Definitions and specifications of water vapour in the atmosphere. *Publication Organisation Météorologique International*, no. 79.
The thunderstorm: a natural dynamo. *Discovery, Lond.* **11**, 385–389, also 402.
The cumulonimbus and thunderstorm. I. *Sci. Prog., Lond.* no. 149, 78–88.
The cumulonimbus and thunderstorm. II. Electrical phenomena. *Sci. Prog., Lond.* no. 151, 487–496.
Atmospheric turbulence. *Br. Sci. News* **3**, 106–109.
1951 The earth's atmosphere. In: *A century of science* (ed. H. Dingle). London: Hutchinson.
(With M. K. Elnesr) On the direct measurement of humidity mixing ratio and its fluctuations. *Q. Jl R. met. Soc.* **77**, 450–453.
Atmospheric turbulence. *Weather, Lond.* **6**, 42–49.
The physics of clouds and their precipitation. *Endeavour.* **10**, 89–94.
The jet stream and related phenomena. *Sci. Prog., Lond.* **39**, 483–495.
1952 The general circulation of the atmosphere. *Sci. Prog., Lond.* **40**, 89–106.
Some deficiencies in current meteorological knowledge in relation to the operation of jet aircraft. *Q. Jl R. met. Soc.* **78**, 455–456.
(With C. H. B. Priestley) Turbulence and transfer processes in the atmosphere. *Q. Jl R. met. Soc.* **78**, 488–529.
(With H. Charnock & J. R. D. Francis) Observations of the westerlies over the sea. *Q. Jl R. met. Soc.* **78**, 563–582.
(With M. H. Omar) The wind stress over the ocean from observations in the Trades. *Q. Jl R. met. Soc.* **78**, 583–589.
Current research at Imperial College, London, on the structure of turbulent flow. In: *Int. Symp. on Atmospheric Turbulence in the Boundary Layer* (ed. E. W. Hewson), *Geophys. Res. Pap.*, no. 19, pp. 155–163.
Current research at Imperial College, London, on the effects of turbulent flow-eddy fluxes. In: *Ibid.*, pp. 345–351.
1953 Turbulence and turbulent transfer processes in the atmosphere. *W.M.O. Commission for Aerology, Toronto 1953, Scient. Pap.*, no. 9.
Meteorological Conference at Toronto. *Nature, Lond.* **172**, 1166–1168.
The vertical transfer of momentum in the atmosphere by turbulence. *U.G.G.I. Ass. Met. Proc. Verb., Bruxelles*, pp. 253–254.
1954 Momentum flux and meridional motion in the general circulation. Proc. of Toronto Meteorological Conference 1953. *Q. Jl R. met. Soc.* (special issue). pp. 103–108.

The vertical transfer of momentum in the general circulation. *Arch. Mét. Géophys. Bioklim.* Série A, **7**, 114–124.

1955 (With H. Charnock & J. R. D. Francis) Medium-scale turbulence in the trade winds (summary). *Q. Jl R. met. Soc.* **81**, 634.

The general circulation of the atmosphere (summary). *Aust. Met. Mag., Melbourne* no. 11, 89–91.

The Department of Meteorology, Imperial College, London (summary). *Ibid.* pp. 91–92.

1956 (With H. Charnock & J. R. D. Francis) An investigation of wind structure in the Trades: Anegada 1953. *Phil. Trans. R. Soc. Lond.* A **249**, 179–234.

The meteorological point of view on observational data in the mesosphere. *Scient. Proc. Int. Ass. Met., Rome, September 1954*, pp. 509–513.

(With E. L. Deacon & E. K. Webb) Wind profiles over the sea and the drag at the sea surface. *Aust. J. Phys.* **9**, no. 4, 511–541.

Airflow over mountains. *Corres. Q. Jl R. met. Soc.* **82**, no. 354, 528–529.

1957 Natural and artificial trace elements in geophysical research. *Nature, Lond.* **179**, 996–997.

Radioactive fallout and the weather. *New Scient.* no. 39, 23–25.

1958 Transfer across the earth's surface and through the air above. (Presidential Address 1958.) *Q. Jl R. met. Soc.* **84**, 205–224.

The general circulation of the atmosphere. *Weather, Lond.* **13**, no. 10, 323–336.

The effect of pollution on radiation in the atmosphere. *Int. J. Air Pollut., Lond.* **1**, 31–43.

1959 Education and research in meteorology in the United Kingdom. (Presidential Address 1959.) *Q. Jl R. met. Soc.* **85**, 187–195.

Dynamics of the upper atmosphere. *J. geophys. Res.* **64**, 2116–2121.

Dispersione di particelle radioattive nell' atmosfera. *Riv. Met. aeronaut., Rome* **19**, no. 3, 3–14.

(Ed. with F. N. Frenkiel) Atmospheric diffusion and air pollution. Proceedings of a symposium held at Oxford, August 24–29, 1958, I.U.T.A.M. and U.G.G.I. *Advances in geophysics*, vol. 6. New York & London: Academic Press.

1960 Meteorology. *Encyclopaedia britannica, Lond.* pp. 277–300.

1962 Properties and processes at the earth's surface in relation to the general circulation of the atmosphere. *Advances in geophysics*, vol. 9, pp. 77–96. New York & London: Academic Press.

1963 The incidence of atmospheric turbulence. In: Atmospheric turbulence in relation to aircraft. *Proc. Symp. held at the Royal Aircraft Establishment, Farnborough, November 1961*, pp. 43–57. London: Ministry of Aviation.

Measurements of wind by 'window' (Chaff) from rocket firings in Australia. *Proc. First Int. Symp. on Rocket and Satellite Meteorology, Washington, D.C. 23–25 April 1963.*

(With K. J. Bignell & F. Saiedy) On the atmospheric infrared continuum. *J. opt. Soc. Am.* **53**, 466–479.

(With J. V. Dave & C. D. Walshaw) Ozone distribution and the continuum from observations in the region of the 1043 $cm^{-1}$ band. *Q. Jl R. met. Soc.* **89**, 307–318.

Atmospheric tracers and the study of the general circulation of the atmosphere. *Rep. Prog. Phys.* **26**, 213–267.

1964 Basic ideas on the general circulation of the atmosphere. Problems in palaeo-climatology. *Proc. NATO Palaeoclimates Conference, University of Newcastle upon Tyne, January 1963* (ed. A. E. M. Nairn), pp. 322–332.

1966 Data requirements for research. *W.M.O.* no. 180, T.P. 90, *Tech. Note* no. 73, pp. 49–52.

1967 Is weather predictable? *Nature, Lond.* **214**, 858.

Global atmospheric research. *Verh. schweiz. naturf. Ges.* pp. 47–72.

1968 Global atmospheric research. *Weather, Lond.* **23**, no. 7, 262–283.

Air–sea interaction studies by the Department of Meteorology, Imperial College, London. *Bull. Am. met. Soc.* **49**, no. 8, 832–834.

1970 The atmospheric boundary layer in relation to large-scale dynamics. In: *The global circulation of the atmosphere*, pp. 91–112. London: R. met. Soc.

1972 (With D. T. Tribble & J. R. Garratt) Studies of turbulence in the surface layer over water (Lough Neagh). I. Instrumentation, programme, profiles. *Q. Jl R. met. Soc.* **98**, 627–641.

# CHRISTOPHER ALWYNE JACK YOUNG

7 March 1912–20 January 1978

Elected F.R.S. 1972

By R. L. Day and A. Spinks, F.R.S.

## Childhood and Schooldays

Alwyne Jack Young, who later adopted the additional name of Christopher, was born in Calne, Wiltshire, on 7 March 1912. Both parents were natives of Wiltshire; his father, Henry George, was a solicitor; his mother was a teacher. As a small boy he attended the Calne preparatory school. He was always a prize-winner there, helped perhaps by an aunt who seems to have taught him some arithmetic before he even started school at five. At the same early age he displayed the force of character that everyone who knew him speaks of, insisting during severe floods in Calne on going to the top of the house to build an ark: on being told that the water could not rise so far he insisted on carrying on, saying that that was just what people would have said to Noah, but they were wrong. His very wide interest in most sports also began at prep. school, perhaps because of his father who had been a runner at the same school, and he did very well at swimming, diving, cricket, rugby, tennis and squash, as well as running. His parents had high educational standards and put him down for Marlborough, but his father unfortunately died shortly thereafter when he was 12; and he went instead to Colston's at Bristol at some financial sacrifice by his mother. He always regretted not going to Marlborough, but was very successful at Colston's, and was always very grateful to his mother for having given him an excellent education in spite of great difficulty. From his father's death when he was 12 he had a feeling of great responsibility to her and his sister and remained devoted to them. On her presentation copy of his book on process control, he wrote: 'With the author's compliments and thanks—"cast thy bread upon the waters: for thou shalt find it after many days (Eccles. XI, 1)".'

In his final year at Colston's his headmaster (Rev. A. R. Millbourn) wrote of his 'natural force of character . . . that led to his appointment as Senior Prefect, in which capacity he showed a really strong sense of loyalty and responsibility, exercising over the whole school a most powerful force for good'. One member of his form remembers him as 'a reserved studious boy, good at games, though not robust; a valuable asset to the school'. Another, K. A. Haddocks, says: 'He had a calm self-confidence which impressed us, and was soon revealing a quiet authority which enabled him to persuade others to conform to his view without using forceful argument.'

He was a very good rugby player, in the 1st XV for each of his last three school years and captain in his final year. He took part in school and house plays, including the name part in *Julius Caesar*. He received the form prize for mathematics and science in each of his three years in the VIth, and was also Head of House and Head of School in the last two. He was awarded the Bardsley–Cann Bat—a prize for sportsmanship. Some of his earliest writing is to be found in his House Notes in the school magazine for 1929: 'Nothing overcomes a team that works or plays as a team and not as a collection of individuals.' This belief never left him.

## University

He went up to St Edmund Hall, Oxford, in 1930, first starting the essential Latin from scratch in the summer vacation under tuition from his sister, three years his junior, and the local curate. He fixed a notice 'Nil desperandum' on his desk and was soon reading Virgil with enjoyment. Financial problems forced him to take mathematical moderations at the end of his first year, when he got a third; he then took a very good second in physics in the final honours school of natural science in June 1933. In October 1933 he was appointed a temporary demonstrator in the Electrical Laboratory of the Department of Physics. J. S. Townsend wrote of him—'has good knowledge of Physics, is personally very agreeable, and readily collaborates with others working in the same establishment'; 'was very successful as a teacher'. His tutor, T. C. Keeley, says that he was a keen and a hard worker with a good general grasp of physics, and a keen and knowledgeable gardener. He was also interested in photography and entomology, and played the piano and sketched very skilfully. Even so, he found time at Oxford for much sport, and obtained his college colours for rugby, playing in the 1933 final against B.N.C. He was also a member of St Edmund's cricket, tennis, hockey and athletics first teams, and treasurer of the J.C.R.

## Early career

His research with Townsend and E. W. B. Gill of Merton was on electric discharges in nitrogen at pressures between atmospheric and 10 cm of mercury, and led to a B.Sc. in 1935, his last degree until Bradford gave him an Honorary D.Tech. in 1969, for he left Oxford to become a temporary master at Radley College in the Easter term of 1934. Just before that he had taught for a month at the Dragon School as a substitute, earning £10.

The Warden of Radley gave him a very warm testimonial and would obviously have welcomed him back. However, his next post as a schoolmaster was to be his last, though he never lost an intense interest in education. He was given a temporary appointment at Cheltenham College in the summer term of 1934, and was appointed to the permanent staff in September 1934, remaining until July 1938. All his Cheltenham references speak very warmly of him—'good physicist', 'good character', 'friendly disposition', 'considerable confidence'. He taught elementary biology, chemistry up to School Certificate, and physics up to both School and Higher School Certificates, and coached in rugby and cricket. He was undoubtedly a very successful schoolmaster, and could have prospered in that career. However, he was restless at Cheltenham, and perhaps in England, since in 1937 he applied for posts as Principal Technical Officer in the Admiralty Technical Pool, and at the Cape of Good Hope Observatory. These applications were unsuccessful but he persisted, and in July 1938 was offered and accepted a post as assistant meteorologist in the Sudan Government Service. His unit helped to develop a forecasting service for Imperial Airways' route from Cairo south through Khartoum to Mombasa. Christopher researched his move to the Sudan with characteristic thoroughness. He concluded that Sudanese surgical services were inadequate and that he ought to have his perfectly healthy appendix removed before he left England. This he did, persisting, again characteristically, through several Harley Street refusals until he finally found a willing surgeon (the father of an Oxford friend).

Christopher always loved travel and greatly enjoyed the voyage to Cairo, and even more that up the Nile to Khartoum. In Khartoum he was often entertained at the Governor's residence, the Palace; his other favourite relaxation was to trek by camel with his Sudanese boy, Osman, carrying full camping equipment with them. On longer trips Christopher and Osman would go as far as the Ethiopian, Ugandan or Kenyan frontiers, trekking usually by way of the Blue Nile, and Christopher's letters to the lady he eventually married, Wendy Henniker-Heaton, show that he particularly enjoyed the river and mountain scenery of this part of Africa. He seems to have been happy there until the outbreak of war led him to apply for jobs of more national use. Considerable difficulty was placed in his way but he continued to apply for transfers to England, including applications for science posts in London. He finally resigned from the Sudanese service in 1940 to volunteer as a pilot in Coastal Command. He was recommended instead to join I.C.I. at Billingham, where the production of iso-octane for the R.A.F. had very high priority.

## Imperial Chemical Industries, Billingham

His earliest significant achievement in I.C.I., in which he spent the rest of his working life, was to remove a bottleneck in iso-octane manufacture by means of an analytical approach. This probably first focused his attention on the necessity for exact measurement, and on mathematical analysis of practical engineering problems, as an essential preliminary to their solution. The availability later of computers, which alone allowed full realization of this aim, and also of full process control, was to be energetically grasped and was an essential factor in his success. Before that, however, he established an I.C.I. reputation as an instrument engineer by work on two other nationally important projects, Fido, a project for the dispersion of fog from airfields, and the Tube Alloys (Atomic Bomb) Project. He later described Fido instrumentation as follows. 'We made several odd instruments for this project, to measure the amount of water in a fog, and naturally we had to have a real fog to test them in. We sat up all night waiting for it, going in search of it, praying for it, just a little patch somewhere within 20 miles. We never caught up with it.' Subsequently, they received a letter from the

Air Ministry congratulating them on arranging the longest fog-free period ever recorded.

His instrument reputation led in 1946 to his being invited by the I.C.I. Technical Director, F. E. Smith (later Sir Ewart Smith, F.R.S.), an exceptionally able and far-sighted executive, to set up a central laboratory to serve I.C.I's long-term needs in the fields of instrumentation and control. Probably no post could have been more appropriate or have pleased him more. He wrote of this later: 'I was fortunate in two respects in 1946. First, I had decided that Instrumentation and Control were going to grow rapidly to a position of great importance; and I knew what had to be done to get them there. Secondly, I was given the opportunity to set up a laboratory to do it.'

Another very important event occurred in 1946, his marriage. He had met his future wife, Wendy Henniker-Heaton, at the home of friends, and since he disliked his christian names, and momentarily confused A. A. Milne with J. M. Barrie, told her that his name was Christopher. Having made this decision he stuck to it through the long wartime correspondence by which their acquaintance grew, and in 1969 actually changed his name by deed poll to Christopher Alwyne Jack Young. His oldest friends continued to call him A. J.; only his family and new friends used Christopher, which he preferred. The liberality with which he and Wendy gave their time and their interest to British and foreign visitors to his laboratory, particularly later at Bozedown, was quite exceptional, and will long be affectionately remembered.

The former Mrs Henniker-Heaton already had two daughters, Jacqueline and Anthea, of whom their new stepfather became extremely fond. When Anthea was very young she could not understand why Christopher was always working, and he told her he was trying to help the Government. Anthea, thinking he said governess, renamed him Mr Bumble, and the girls used this name throughout his life. Since Christopher and Wendy's marriage was childless, these daughters were a great delight to him.

## The Frythe

The Central Instrument Section—later the Central Instrument Research Laboratory—was established first at The Frythe, a former country house in Welwyn, the home also, until 1961, of I.C.I. central research on physics under H. Kolsky, natural products under P. W. Brian, and organometallic catalysis under J. Chatt. Somewhat later, what is now the I.C.I. Central Toxicology Laboratory (then the Industrial Hygiene Research Laboratory) was established at the same site under M. W. Goldblatt. The staff of the five laboratories formed a stimulating scientific community, in which distinguished work was to be done, so much so that three of the five heads ultimately became Fellows of the Royal Society. However, those who were interested in the application of research, as well as research for its own sake, had to suffer a common handicap of a central unit in a strongly decentralized organization with autonomous laboratories—some resistance to external discovery. In these circumstances such qualities as clarity and strength of objective, enthusiasm for it, persuasiveness and evident professional competence were needed to achieve export of useful change. All of these qualities Christopher Young had, though one had to know him well to realize it fully. With help from colleagues in Billingham, Wilton and Cheshire, his influence became very powerful, in spite of superficial appearance, which was of a very reserved man, intensely fastidious and conservative in manner and in style of dress. This could be deceptive on slight acquaintance, but his sharp and original mind soon became evident to colleagues. Some of them found his ideas perhaps ten years ahead of their knowledge, or even comprehension. One of them adds that 'he lived so far ahead of daily life that his hardworking secretary had, more than once, to repay the loan that the King's Cross ticket collector had made him for his fare to Welwyn Garden City'. Another former colleague makes similar points—'If I had to describe him briefly, I would say that his technical background notwithstanding, he had all the marks and attributes of an English country gentleman, with a slightly Edwardian flavour. Travelling with him was a bit like accompanying an English milord on his Grand Tour. Certainly Christopher never made concessions to foreign parts: thus he travelled to the States with a rolled umbrella and a very English hat, and never hesitated to insist on his pink gin whether in New York or Ontario. He was not exactly absent-minded, but did seem a bit accident-prone when it came to losing things. For instance, he managed to lose both his hat and his umbrella on different occasions; he lost his travellers' cheques, so that I had to subsidize him; and he managed once to lose his waistcoat. I found him very outspoken—and very perceptive. I suppose that he did have a typically British reserve at first acquaintance, but he was extremely kind hearted underneath.'

His perception, of the future of his subject and of people, and his kindness, compassion and loyalty to them, particularly if he admired them, were the qualities that allowed him to assemble an outstanding team for the Central Instrument Section, and to lead them outstandingly. This was as true of the shop floor as it was of individualistic scientists. However, his chief interest was in those who interested him; he had no very high opinion of people in general, or much inclination for purely social acquaintance.

The concept that led to the formation of the Central Instrument Section, and of other comparable sections on inspection and engineering standards, was that a central unit should improve the coordination and efficiency of basic work common to many Divisions. Its original remit was: 'A general instrument research and development section should be set up to act as a service to all Divisions, to keep in touch with instrument practice at home and abroad, and hold certain specialized equipment for general use in I.C.I.' (Minute of First Meeting of I.C.I. Committee on Instrumentation, 30.11.45).

Christopher selected the seven original members of the section personally and it is further proof of his perception of people that all of them had very successful careers and that three of them eventually became an I.C.I. General Manager (C. I. Rutherford), the Engineering Director of Metal Box (G. P. Clay) and the Chief Executive of Scottish Agricultural Industries (A. W. Morrison). Another outstanding member of the team, S. T. Lunt, who has kindly provided much material for this memoir records 'that the laboratory was created from a number of empty huts and a disused greenhouse'. He adds that they were all encouraged to use their initiative and ingenuity, and much more was delegated to them than they subsequently experienced elsewhere. Christopher also emphasized that the laboratory should have long-term objectives—he suggested to F. E. Smith that nothing would come from the Laboratory for ten years—and soon produced a much broader approach than the committee had had in mind. In 1948 he defined that approach as the design of process, plant and control equipment as one integrated system to give most profitable performance.

Though expansion of interest thus occurred very early, the Laboratory in its first six years also pursued the development of gas analysers based on ultraviolet and infrared absorption, a thickness meter based on β-absorption, a nylon chip moisture meter, an automatic titrator for continuous recording of boiler water hardness, and test instruments for artificial fibres.

In 1952 Christopher decided that the Laboratory should now leave the development of new instruments to operating units and concentrate on these objectives: '(i) To foster the *analytical approach* and the establishment of the mechanism of a system wherever possible; before designing it, modifying it, adjusting it, or operating it. (ii) To encourage a *quantitative treatment* of problems at all stages of research, development, design and operation. (iii) To introduce the concept of the *mathematical model* to describe any system under consideration. (iv) In the immediate future to eradicate the practice of adding the control equipment as an afterthought to a plant already designed; in the longer term to design the process, plant and control equipment as one unified system.'

In setting out to achieve these objectives Christopher Young and his colleagues soon found that available servo-mechanism theory of World War II could not be applied quantitatively, because the dynamic characteristics of the process and plant to be controlled were not known. They set out to determine those characteristics from theoretical and empirical considerations, making equipment and developing techniques for comparing predictions with responses of actual processes. For example, C. A. J. Y. and C. I. Rutherford (39) developed a technique for analysing the dynamic characteristics of process control loops on an operating production plant by injecting a sinusoidal disturbance into the control valve and recording the consequential, more or less sinusoidal, disturbance of the temperature, pressure etc. being controlled by the loop. After repeating this procedure with sinusoids of three or four periodicities and knowing some of the dynamic characteristics of the process control itself, one could optimize controller settings according to desired criteria. A portable equipment termed 'Portable Pneumatic Analyser' was developed and later helped I.C.I. Divisions with control loop (usually temperature control) difficulties.

Christopher realized that this technique, though imperfect scientifically, provided potentially very valuable insight into the behaviour and design of process control systems. He was equally clear that a much wider range of people than instrument specialists needed this insight, and applied himself with characteristic energy to the presentation of a training course. Plant managers, design engineers and instrument specialists were invited from I.C.I. and also from university departments and instrument manufacturers. His continued enthusiasm for education helped to make these courses very popular, and their demonstration that design for automatic control was feasible as well as desirable was very valuable for many years afterwards.

The early work highlighted the fact that though some commercially available control instruments generated three-term (i.e. proportional plus integral plus derivative) control actions, the effective level of those actions differed from the settings on the calibrated dials because of interactions within the controller itself. He took the initiative of setting up a collaborative programme with instrument manufacturing companies, aimed at characterizing existing controllers and leading to the joint evaluation of proposed new instruments.

Christopher Young, nevertheless, was becoming increasingly concerned by limitations of methodology at this stage of its development, leading to impact mainly on problems of existing processes and instruments, rather than on the desired but difficult prediction of performance of control systems at the plant design stage (2). He highlights this problem in 1950: 'It cannot be long before plants are designed for automatic control and the engineer must know the characteristics he has to incorporate. "Designed for automatic control" in this context does not merely imply that the plants will be designed in the knowledge that they will be automatically controlled. The majority of plants are at present designed in this knowledge—and their design would not be so very different, providing the process could be run without automatic control, if they were to be manually operated. The point is that plants should be, and it is hoped soon will be, designed to take full advantage of the potential benefits of automatic control. Unfortunately, there is not yet available sufficient data on the characteristics of existing plants, as they affect the control problem, to make such design completely possible in detail.' He emphasizes this again in his remarks as Chairman of the Cranfield Control Conference in 1951. 'They also require for useful application a quantitative knowledge of the characteristics of the components of the control loop, which is not yet available in the case of the process control loop for its most important component, i.e. the plant itself.'

This conference (3), the first major international meeting of leading workers on both servo-mechanisms and process control, marks the emergence of C. A. J. Young's international prestige.

In pursuit of these ideas he now set out to recruit chemical engineers and others for an expanded multi-disciplinary approach to research that could have a greater effect at the design stage. He also began to contribute strongly to the development of the subject outside I.C.I. Thus he was a member of the O.E.E.C. mission to the U.S.A. 'Chemical apparatus in the U.S.A.', published in 1952 (5), and published 15 other papers in the next three years (6–20) including one in Sweden (6) and one in the U.S.A. (8). During this same period he had also been working on an authoritative textbook with the purpose 'to help engineers of all kinds to design better control systems' which was published by Longmans in 1955 with the title *An introduction to process control system design*

(15). This book has now run to its fourth impression and been extensively translated into other languages, including Japanese and Russian, but perhaps the most significant fact is that it is still relevant and extensively used as a basic textbook despite the rapid advance of technology.

Mrs Young made an important contribution to the book by getting Christopher to start writing it—a very difficult task. After he had delayed nearly a year she asked him where he would be most comfortable to write easily, and he replied 'in bed'. So on a Saturday morning she settled him there with his college scarf, a blazer, an American wet-weather hat on his head, and a large notepad and several pencils, with encouragement to have several pages written by lunchtime. This was accomplished, and Christopher then wrote the rest voluntarily without much trouble. Christopher dedicated the book to Wendy, and recognized her special contribution by writing on the flyleaf of her copy: 'To my darling Cub, the first copy, with love and gratitude for your help and patience in all things, as exemplified during the writing of this book in a very special way, from Christopher, June 1955.'

Another important aspect of his influence outside I.C.I. during this period was his enthusiastic involvement with the development of the Society of Instrument Technology (S.I.T.). He was its President from 1954 to 1957, and did much to widen its interests from instrumentation to the total design of plant plus control system. The organization of a joint conference with the Institution of Chemical Engineers in October 1955 on 'Automatic control in the process industries' (14) followed in 1956 by a joint conference on 'Plant and process characteristics' at Cambridge illustrates this, and established working links between the two Institutions that have persisted and are still active. This period also led to a strong personal association with Sir Harold Hartley, then President of the Institution of Chemical Engineers, which had a continuing influence on the development of the subject; Sir Harold himself succeeded him as President of the S.I.T. and Christopher was to be the first recipient of the Sir Harold Hartley medal awarded by the then Institute of Measurement and Control for outstanding contribution to the technology.

## Bozedown

In 1956 the aims and size of the research team had outgrown the initial site at The Frythe, and the team was moved to a country house, 'Bozedown', overlooking the Thames at Whitchurch, which Christopher chose rather than a larger but less elegant one at Maidenhead. This concern with quality was a constant characteristic: thus, Professor John Coales has written: 'He was disgusted with anything shoddy and would only countenance the best in anything he did or purchased, the latter almost to the point of extravagance in the eyes of some.'

Christopher built himself a bungalow on the edge of the Laboratory site, appropriately Y-shaped, from which he completely absorbed himself in the work of the Laboratory and where he and Wendy entertained the steady flow of I.C.I. and overseas visitors. The separate site gave him the new responsibility of setting up and controlling workshops, catering, kitchens and gardeners. He insisted on minimizing distinctions between weekly and monthly staff, who shared all facilities, and established common working hours. The loyalty of the weekly staff was an important asset to the Laboratory, for example in the flexibility of approach, speed of response and quality of work from the engineering workshop. It was typical that he was more than willing to involve himself in anyone's personal problem from the gardener to his most senior manager.

This extension of management responsibility coincided with a greatly enlarged research staff (at its peak 170), and he could no longer be closely involved with specific research programmes, but maintained a key strategic role. His management style placed great emphasis on setting ambitious research targets and hence taking risks, and on recruiting outstanding scientists. He was also liable to approach problems in an unorthodox way, as when one morning he invited a group of persistent late-comers into his office for sherry as they arrived for work —apparently very effective. He regarded recruitment as a personal responsibility and spent much time on it: several outstanding recruits were pursued through postgraduate studies in the U.K. and then postdoctoral work in the States.

In order to help the direction of a larger research team with much wider research targets, he took another imaginative step in creating two senior consultant posts in the laboratory. These posts, filled by a chemical engineer and a chemist/economist, were to be purely technical and strategic and uninvolved in the administration of the Laboratory.

In the early years at Bozedown, Christopher directed the Laboratory towards the now well established target of predicting the dynamic behaviour of chemical processes at the design stage. Early work was largely confined to the physical unit operations, for example, distillation (40), heat exchangers (44), evaporators (43) and absorption columns (45). It re-emphasized the difficulty of obtaining good experimental data from full scale plant in order to check theory. At the same time it was becoming increasingly clear that there was the opportunity for a far greater improvement in overall economic performance of processes through changes in operating conditions and perhaps design of the chemical reactors themselves (41). There was also the realization that emerging electronic computer technology would soon make it possible to handle the complex equations involved in mathematically modelling these systems. This led to the development with S. T. Lunt of the concept of the mobile flameproofed measurement caravan containing sophisticated instrumentation that allowed measurements normally only possible in the laboratory to be carried out easily on any operating plant.

The first of these in 1957 (42) was equipped with the latest data-logging equipment capable of recording 50 process variables as electrical (e.g. thermocouples) or pneumatic signals. Christopher set up a small field section at the large Wilton factory to develop this initiative into an important new means of process investigation. This initial caravan was followed later by a second containing high quality infrared and ultraviolet machines not normally found outside the research laboratory, and later still a mobile on-line computer

(Ferranti Argus 100) was provided so that exploratory on-line computer proposals could be assessed without having to justify the large capital expenditure for a permanent installation.

## Computers

By 1956 the electronic computer was becoming a practical reality and Christopher Young quickly saw it as a foundation for his long-term research aims. The first important one was an exploratory project with Elliot-Automation to solve the differential equations describing the I.C.I. ammonia converters. Although successful both as a mathematical exercise and in providing insight into the performance of this chemical reactor, the exercise also demonstrated the difficulty of using digital computers in 1956, with their machine-based, fixed-point programming code. This work led to links with the Electrical Engineering Department at Manchester University where work on development of the Ferranti Mercury computer was taking place, including pioneering work on the high-level language 'Autocode'. The significance of high-level language was starkly demonstrated when a member of the Laboratory was able to define, program and obtain a solution to a meaningful engineering design problem within one day, in contrast to the months required on the earlier project on the ammonia converter.

Christopher was profoundly influenced by this language development, which predated the I.B.M. FORTRAN language by almost two years, and recognized its ability not only to reduce programming time dramatically, but also to allow the scientist or engineer to formulate and solve his own problems. As a result he embarked on an ambitious plan to introduce digital computers into the Laboratory and I.C.I.

A Ferranti Mercury computer was too costly for the Laboratory alone and had to be a central I.C.I. purchase. Getting agreement from fiercely independent I.C.I. Divisions for the Laboratory to run a central computer service required all his powers of persuasion, but the Central Service under his control was established at Wilton in 1958. It included a mixed team of mathematicians, engineers and chemists to work with divisional colleagues in developing new applications, and played a very significant part in helping I.C.I. to establish a coherent program library. The Mercury computer was replaced by an English Electric KDF9 in 1964, and soon afterwards the Company reorganized the Group as part of a new Central Management Services Department, headed first by W. B. M. Duncan, and later by Christopher's former colleague, C. I. Rutherford.

In parallel with these developments a similar program was initiated aimed at exploiting the analogue computer. Christopher again led the Laboratory into a central role in the Company, based on an early instrument from Short & Harland in 1959, followed by a Solartron TR 10 in 1961 and finally the Short & Harland Simlac in 1963. Christopher Young invariably tried to help the British instrument and computer industry, particularly in his later work on on-line computers, though of course the results were not always what he hoped for. The analogue computer soon proved to be less useful than the digital computer but established a special role in simulation of dynamic systems for process control and in chemical kinetics.

Christopher saw clearly that the digital computer must eventually play a major role in process control. For example, in his presidential paper to the joint conference between the Society of Instrument Technology and the Institution of Chemical Engineers in 1955 he says that 'some form of calculating machine or computer will be necessary to receive measurement signals from the plant, to calculate what corrections are required to operating conditions, and to send out signals which will effect the necessary corrections. The electrical computer is well fitted for this role, but a problem exists in making such computers with the necessary reliability. Use of new components and new circuit techniques will certainly be developed to produce the necessary reliability.'

Because of their low reliability the first applications of digital computers in operation of chemical processes both inside and outside I.C.I. were in the 'supervisory mode', that is, the process was still controlled by conventional instruments which were monitored by the computer and used to optimize the process continuously by resetting the objective variable of the individual controllers. In this type of application failure of the digital computer could be tolerated since the process remained under stable control. Christopher was convinced, however, that the major impact of the digital computer on chemical process control would only be realized when the computer system was sufficiently reliable to be entrusted with the basic control task, largely eliminating conventional instruments.

Hence he set the Laboratory the longer term target of highly reliable, direct computer control. Since no commercial computer system was available in the mid-1950s with the necessary reliability and acceptable cost, the Laboratory set out to make its own. The resulting computer, called 'Bedlam', used transistorized logic and magnetic core memories giving 2K of store, and was used to control a small experimental semi-technical scale chemical reactor, in which ethanol was dehydrated to ethylene over a phosphoric acid–coke catalyst that decayed in activity and gave rise to changing temperature profiles in the reactor. By 1960–61 this experimental system had successfully demonstrated the feasibility of achieving reliable direct digital control (d.d.c.).

Thereafter, Christopher became closely involved in the decision by I.C.I.'s Alkali Division to install in 1962 what is believed to be the first on-line process control computer (a Ferranti Argus) in the world to use d.d.c. on an operating full-scale plant.

He was anxious for the Company to maintain this momentum in the development of on-line computer control, which he saw clearly was inhibited by the still relatively high cost of computers. His solution in 1964 was to negotiate personally with the I.C.I. Board for the purchase of six Ferranti Argus computers by the Laboratory on behalf of the Company, and to develop applications jointly with individual Divisions—this again demonstrated his considerable powers of persuasion, described by the then Technical Director, George Whitby, as follows: 'A. J. Y. said to me "I.C.I. will require three or four large data processing computers and I cannot persuade anyone to order now, yet when they finally make up their minds there will be long delays in delivery. I.C.I. must place a bulk order, you are Technical Director and you must sign it!" It was a large sum of money for those days but A. J. Y. produced a comparison of available equipment, recommended what should be bought, and under his pressure I signed the order (no Form A*—but a private nod from Paul Chambers). A. J. Y. then demanded that we secured a position for "on-line" computers with a British maker, so we did that. In a fairly short space of time all these commitments were taken up by the Divisions.' This initiative, and the enthusiastic response of I.C.I. Divisions, allowed I.C.I. to remain among the world's leaders in this field.

One of the most ambitious of the early projects with Divisions went a long way towards realizing one of Christopher's consistent goals—to design the control system as an equal and integral part of the plant itself. This application, in a multi-product dyestuffs plant, was such that the highly integrated process design was only considered feasible and realistic when coupled with its on-line computer control system.

Later in the 1960s it became increasingly apparent that although the cost of the computer itself was decreasing at a rapid rate the cost of installing a total on-line computer system was not, and if anything was rising because of the increasing costs of software and the high cost of interface equipment to connect the computer to the process. Christopher was also concerned by the fact that virtually all computer manufacturers were developing software and interface hardware that were largely incompatible, and by the resulting inefficient handover and rapid obsolescence of systems. This led him to create two new major research initiatives, one aimed at a special high level programming language designed for on-line (i.e. real time) applications RTL (Real Time Language), and the other aimed at a novel system of interface instrumentation MEDIA (Modular Electronic Digital Instrumentation Assemblies). Besides reducing the costs of implementing a complete on-line system both these initiatives shared a further objective, i.e. to be as far as possible 'machine independent' and hence to be free from built-in obsolescence.

RTL needed to differ in several important respects from data processing languages such as Fortran, which are concerned more with high speed control and initiation of actions, and data communication than with numerical calculation. RTL had also to be strongly error-preventing and as far as possible applicable to a wide variety of small computers. The ultimate design of the language RTL/2 to meet these requirements is described by J. G. P. Barnes (52).

Christopher made an attempt to put the RTL work on a wider footing by discussing it with other major user industries, the British computer makers and Government technical departments. Although a limited measure of collaboration was achieved with I.C.L., C.E.G.B. and the British Steel Corporation, the

* The normal I.C.I. documentation for a large purchase.

project remained essentially an I.C.I. development. His unswerving wish to support things British, and in particular the British computer industry, made this a great disappointment to him. It is also worth noting that although this language development had many I.C.I. supporters, particularly among working scientists, it also had many I.C.I. critics who thought it less of I.C.I. than of general world benefit, an argument which again called for all his political skills. During this same period a roughly parallel development was taking place within Government laboratories on a language CORAL for defence applications; although technical exchanges took place the two initiatives were not combined. Both CORAL and RTL were pioneering developments with no realistic equivalents at the time in other countries including U.S.A., and both have been successful, but the international commercial impact of a single U.K. development might have been greater.

The first prototype language RTL/1 was completed in 1970 and was used to program a major I.C.I. on-line system for Terylene polymerization, based on a Ferranti Argus 500, which is still in successful operation.

The final version, RTL/2 was released in 1972 and has since been used to provide the software for nearly 200 I.C.I. computer systems. It has been particularly successful in enabling highly reliable systems to be developed quickly and with modest programming effort. In 1974 RTL/2 was made available commercially and is now in use by some 80 organizations in Europe and further afield. It is also being considered by the B.S.I. as a British Standard.

The general aim of the MEDIA research team (J. R. Halsall *et al.*) (51) was to design a completely digital interface system, using the latest integrated circuit technology based on a small number of basic digital electronic modules, which could be used in varying configurations to interface any measurement and to generate control loop functions. The most novel aspect of the system was a solution to the problems of achieving compatibility with any on-line computer, and freedom from obsolescence as computer speeds increased.

The MEDIA development posed two major problems to Christopher: the need to win and maintain active support for the development and its use within I.C.I. systems, and the need to arrange for an instrument company, preferably British, to take over further development and supply I.C.I. He did much to achieve the first and laid the foundations for the second, although in the event he retired because of ill-health before this was completed. Within I.C.I. both these systems have been used in the great majority of applications over the past few years, and contributed materially to a spectacular increase in the number of on-line computers in plants and laboratories from nil in 1962 to 350 in 1977. Though much of the increase occurred after Christopher's retirement, it all owed much to his efforts.

## PROCESS RESEARCH

The developments that Christopher initiated during the 1950s towards better scientific understanding of chemical plants and processes used computerized mathematical models mainly to predict dynamic and transient behaviour. By

1960 it had become clear to him that this approach must be extended to include the steady-state modelling of both the key unit operations in chemical processes and of the complete process flowsheet. Only in this way could he hope to realize his ultimate aim of designing the process and its control system as a single optimized entity.

This posed a new challenge to develop a major new research initiative in a scientific area where neither Christopher nor the Laboratory was skilled. The team he assembled to pursue this objective, led by R. L. Day and joined later by S. F. Bush, made the theme an important one in the 1960s, and the Laboratory's main task in the 1970s. Although not himself a specialist, his skills of constantly injecting outstanding new recruits both from inside and outside I.C.I., and of insistence on setting ambitious targets created a challenging and motivating environment in which this work flourished.

The initial emphasis was concentrated on the chemical reactor as the single most important unit operation, and at the heart of every chemical process. The traditional approach with few exceptions at the time was empirical, based on experimental extrapolation; chemical kinetics were a rather academic curiosity. Chemical reactors are extremely complex and hence the approach, now standard practice, was firstly to change the experimental aims so as separately to determine the key scientific components of the system (e.g. chemical kinetics, mass and heat transfer, fluid mechanics) and secondly to combine these mathematically by means of a computer-based mathematical model, to predict the behaviour of any particular reactor geometry or set of operating conditions.

As part of this strategy the Laboratory developed novel experimental reactors specifically designed to obtain high quality chemical kinetics under highly defined conditions and where possible free from physical rate constraints. Two of the best known examples, which have been widely used, are (i) the stirred gas–solid reactor (46) and (ii) the jet mixed reactor (49). Both these reactors were deliberately small in size (e.g. 50 ml) in order to achieve well defined operating conditions and at the same time to simplify, cheapen and reduce the time required to obtain kinetic data.

In parallel with this work Christopher took the opportunity to pursue another concept for which he had great personal enthusiasm, the use of the on-line computer in laboratory experiments. The combining of these two highly ambitious aims stretched the skills and resources of the research teams to the limit and is typical of his management style. Both were very successful and at the forefront of developments world-wide, which says much for his personal drive, persuasive charm and motivating skills. The development was based on one of the first Ferranti Argus 400 computers and used a new prototype high-level language developed in the Laboratory (the forerunner of RTL) to allow experimentalists to program the on-line computer directly. This was one of the first successful time-shared systems in the world, running up to six experiments simultaneously (36).

Christopher set up a joint program to apply this new approach to design of a chlorination reactor in I.C.I.'s Mond Division and the successful results were reported in *Proceedings of the Royal Society* in 1969 (50). The reaction is highly exothermic, fast and prone to thermal runaway and instability, and critically dependent on fluid dynamics, mixing and diffusion processes; a combination that made scientific interpretation of results from a conventional experimental reactor virtually impossible. The study led to a fundamentally based mathematical model that successfully predicted the effects of geometry changes, including scaling-up changes in process operating conditions and the start-up and dynamic stability of the reactor, as well as steady-state performance. A later application to the more chemically complex hydrocarbon and naphtha cracking reactions required another important advance (53).

The work on reactors increasingly highlighted the need for mathematical modelling and optimization of the complete process. Early work in 1961 (not published) on *p*-xylene isomerization was an important example where a sensible mathematical model, both of the reactor itself and the total flowsheet, was developed. Here again Christopher set up an initially embarrassingly ambitious project, which nevertheless served to challenge and motivate the team, and led to developments at the forefront of technology. By the mid-1960s this project had developed to the stage where Christopher took the now familiar step of setting up a laboratory team within a Division, Mond Division at Runcorn Heath in this case, in order to involve a practising Division Design and Engineering Department in the development. The prototype 'Flowsheeting' system Network 67 was described in publications in 1968 (47, 48) and led to Flowpack I, the first robust general purpose system to be developed by the Laboratory, and used widely inside I.C.I. and in many universities. This was superseded by Flowpack II which has also been sold to other companies and widely used. These systems have made it possible to examine more alternatives, more thoroughly, in less time. They lead to lower cost and more ideal designs, and can collect together the cumulative experience and advances subsequently made by users. Again, although Christopher retired before Flowpack II achieved this success, the project owed a great deal to his challenging vision, management and support.

## Public Works

Throughout his busy I.C.I. career Christopher Young did his best to ensure the formation of strong British instrument and computer industries, both in the specific ways already referred to and in work for the Society of Instrument Technology, and such bodies as the Instrument and Control Advisory Committees of the Association of British Chemical Manufacturers and the Engineering Equipment Users Association. He chaired the last two from 1954 to 1958 and from 1949 to 1958 respectively. He was a member of the Scientific Instrument Research Association Council from 1953 to 1956, and Chairman of its Control Advisory Committee from 1965 to 1967, and from 1949 to 1959 chaired a B.S.I. committee that established a British standard terminology for control engineers. He also gave much time to education, as a member of the Council of the Battersea Polytechnic from 1956 to 1966, and thereafter of the Council of its successor,

Surrey University. He was also a member of the Instrumentation and Control Engineering Board of the Council for National Academic Awards. He understood, well in advance of its current popularization, the need to interest schoolboys in engineering, and worked hard for this through his membership of the Committee of the Engineering Section of the British Association. He worked also for several government committees and service establishments, including an Interdepartmental Committee on Servomechanisms, the Glazebrook Committee on the role of the N.P.L. in instrumentation, and several committees of the D.S.I.R. and Ministry of Technology. He long hoped to continue working, for education particularly, after retirement, and his appointment as a Fellow of the Royal Society in 1972 gave him a further objective for these future interests, as well as very much pleasure and pride, though unfortunately his health did not allow him to develop them fully. However, he continued to work up to his final, mercifully brief, illness on ideas for a device analogous to a bat's sonar that would help the blind to avoid obstacles. He had always supported the Royal National Institute for the Blind and was for a time on one of its sub-committees.

He was very weak and ill in 1969 when he received a D.Tech. from the University of Bradford, but he had a profound sense of occasion and dignity, and made a great effort to attend the ceremony and was a very dignified figure at it, as he was shortly afterwards when he was presented with the first Sir Harold Hartley medal, receiving it from Sir Harold himself, who said:

> 'It is now my happy privilege and great pleasure first to sing the praises of Dr Christopher Young—still blushing from the laudation at his Honorary degree at Bradford—and then to hand him this medal which he has so richly deserved.
>
> 'The whole of his working life has been dedicated to instrumentation and control; he has a wonderful record of distinguished achievement in those fields. We first met at Billingham many years ago when he was a young physicist and I went to discuss boiler failures. We had a slight argument and I said: "If you are right, I shall have far more failures of locomotive boilers than actually occur". A month later I received a telegram from him, announcing he had been marooned in a train owing to a boiler failure! Fortunately, it was on the North Eastern!
>
> 'Soon after that he rendered me a great service in his work on the instrumentation of two war projects in which I was heavily engaged and in 1946, because of his imaginative approach and the skill with which he had adapted automatic control, data processing, systems engineering to the problems of his great company, Imperial Chemical Industries, they founded a new laboratory, the Central Instrument Research Laboratory, with Christopher at the head. You know what a compliment that was in a company so wedded to a divisional system. There, for the past twenty-two years, Christopher has been the spearhead of development and so many of the developments of his great company stem from him.
>
> 'It was his excellent service with the digital computer at Wilton that led

to the introduction of computers all through the company and, again, it was his first computer-controlled pilot plant that was built on a large scale at Fleetwood and was one of the first computer-controlled plants in the world. It was a great breakthrough.

'I had the good fortune to be President of the Institution of Chemical Engineers during Christopher's brilliant tenure of office as the President of this Institute [of Measurement and Control], or the Society as it then was. We worked together and then he nominated me as his successor and, of course, I had to rely on his advice. So you see, it is not just a coincidence that our two names figure on this medal. It is cause and effect. Without Christopher, mine would certainly not be there.

'It only remains to hand Christopher this medal with our affectionate congratulations, our delight at his gallant recovery, and our pleasure that his wife is here to share in his triumph.'

As Sir Harold implied, Christopher had just undergone a major operation for cancer. He bore considerable discomfort and pain, and full knowledge of the seriousness of his condition, with extraordinary calmness and courage, contemplating death without fear, and studying the latest information about treatments for cancer more to avoid any possible mental impairment than to seek hope.

His illness did not lessen his enthusiasm and interest in his work, but he was unable to command his former superabundant energy. Nevertheless, he was able to bring to fruition a number of the developments which have been referred to above, notably MEDIA and RTL, and was able to see the successful transfer of much control technology into the manufacturing Divisions of I.C.I. It was an immense pleasure to him to see the results and influence of the small group responsible for these discoveries become so much appreciated throughout I.C.I., and indeed widely outside it. However, the toll on his health continued and in 1971 he was content to relinquish the Directorship of the Laboratory and to accept the advisory post of its Technical Director. He still continued to take an active interest in its work and finally retired in March 1973 only a short time before reaching the normal I.C.I. retirement age of 62.

Christopher Young had developed and fostered the Laboratory as a separate corporate institution in I.C.I. and felt strongly that this arrangement, including geographical isolation, was the best to ensure its continued health and value to the Company. It was a source of great regret to him that the decision was finally taken in 1972 to merge the Central Instrument Research Laboratory with the existing Petrochemical and Polymer Laboratory at Runcorn under the new title of the Corporate Laboratory and under a single Director, and to complete the merger by the physical move of his former establishment to Runcorn in 1974. In the event, the ideas stimulated by Christopher Young in his last years at Bozedown have borne fruit in his laboratory's new environment and we hope that he would have been satisfied with the way the work developed after his retirement, though his exceptional ability would no doubt have led to searching criticism.

The authors are very grateful to all those who helped them with details of Mr Young's career, and wish to express their special thanks to Mrs Wendy Young, Mrs J. Hall, and Mr S. L· Lunt.

The photograph reproduced was taken by G. Argent in 1977.

Bibliography

(1) 1949 Modern American instrumentation. *Trans. Soc. Instrum. Technol.** **1** (5), 20–36.

(2) 1950–1951 The automatic control of chemical processes (in 7 parts). *Ind. Chemist* **26,** 147–151, 199–204, 243–249, 343–351, 419–427, **27**, 124–133, 195–203.

(3) 1951 Some reflections on the Cranfield Control Conference. *Instrum. Pract.* **6** (2), 97–101.

(4) 1952 Automatic control in the process industries. *Institute of Physics Fourth Industrial Physics Conf. Brit. J. Appl. Phys.* **3**, 273–277.

(5) Chemical apparatus in the U.S.A. *O.E.E.C. Report,* chap. 3, Standardisation; chap. 5, Instrumentation.

(6) The development of automatic process control. *Trans. Instrum. Meas. Conf., Stockholm* p. 428.

(7) 1953 Instrumentation and productivity. *Ind. Chemist* **29** (8), 339–342.

(8) 1954 ASME and BSI terminologies for process control. *Am. Soc. Mech. Eng.* Paper no. 54–IRD–10.

(9) (With S. T. Lunt) Instrumentation for process control. *J. Inst. Fuel* **27** (1), 39–46.

(10) *Process control* (monograph). Instrument Publishing Co., U.S.A.

(11) Instrument for information. *Process Control* **1** (1), 2–5.

(12) 1955 Research and standardisation in instrument technology. *Soc. Instrum. Technol. Newsl.* September.

(13) Prerequisites of the automatic chemical factory. *Rep. Instn of Production Engineers' Conf. on the 'Automatic Factory'*, pp. 649–676.

(14) Development of modern control technique and the pattern of future development. Conf. on 'Automatic control in the process industries'. *Trans. Instn chem. Engrs* **33**, 223–228.

(15) *An introduction to process control system design.* London: Longmans. (4th impression, 1965.)

(16) Presidential address to Society of Instrument Technology: Future development of automatic process control. *Trans. Soc. Instrum. Technol.* **7** (3), 91–97.

(17) Automation.†

(18) The technical needs of industrial users of instruments with special reference to the role of SIRA. Dept of Scientific and Industrial Research *SIRA* Survey Panel. Confidential paper no. 17.

(19) The trend in instrument development. *Ind. Chemist* **31** (8), 383–384.

(20) Instrumentation at the Wilton 'Terylene' plant. *Ind. Chemist* **31** (9), 449–451.

(21) 1956 The automatic control of chemical processes: trends and economic significance. *Trans. Instrum. Meas. Conf. Stockholm.* (Also, *I.V.A.. Tidskr. Tek.-Vetenskalip* **28**, 289–298, 1957.)

(22) Automatic control in the British process industries. *J. chem. Eng. Jap.* **20** (7), 323–324.

(23) Automatic control in the process industries. *Nature, Lond.* no. 4502, 11 February.

(24) Japanese translation of: *An introduction to process Control System design.*

(25) 1957 Paper presented to O.E.E.C. Conference on Instrumentation in the Process Industries, Paris, June 1957.† (Translated into French and German.)

(26) 1958 Paper read to Gordon Conference, New London. Developments and trends in process control in Europe.

(27) Sampling systems for process measurements: Recommendations to Soc. Instrum. Technol.

* The Society of Instrument Technology has now become the Institute of Measurement and Control.

† Items marked with a dagger have not been published; typescripts are held at the Royal Society library.

(28) Automatic process control. *Financial Times survey of electronics and automation*, 1 December, p. 55.

(29) 1959 (With A. Tustin *et al.*) Automatic control in Soviet industry. Report on a visit to the Soviet Union, May 1959, published by D.S.I.R., September 1959.

(30) 1962 (With I. Gray) Control system design with reference to the use of on-line computers. *Trans. Soc. Instrum. Technol.* **14** (3), 201–214.

(31) 1964 Press conference statement with respect to six control computers.†

(32) 1965 Automation and production in the process industries. British Automation Conf. 1965. *Prod. Engr* **45** (2), 88–101.

(33) 1965 Instrumentation and process control in Great Britain. Conf. of Instrument Society of America, Montreal Section, May 1965. *Instrums Control Syst. J.* **38** (12), 77–82.

(34) Information handling and modern society. Christien Michelsen Annual Memorial Lecture, Bergen, March 1965.†

(35) 1966 (With H. H. Rosenbrock) Real-time on-line digital computers. *Proc. 3rd Congress International Federation of Automatic Control, London*, Paper no. 5, vol. 2, p. 355.

(36) Press conference statement with respect to time-shared computer control system for the automation of laboratory experiments; particularly for determining reaction kinetics.†

(37) 1969 Some recollections by past Presidents. *Meas. & Control* **2** (5), 177–180.

(37a) *Meas. & Control* **2** (6), 225–226.

(38) 1973 The chemical and petrochemical industries. In: A discussion on manufacturing technology in the 1980s. *Phil. Trans. R. Soc. Lond.* A **275**, 329–356.

Other References

(39) 1950 Rutherford, C. I. Practical application of frequency response analysis to automatic process control. *Proc. Instn mech. Engrs* **162**, 334.

(40) 1957 Day, R. L. Dynamic characteristics of the distillation-column reboiler. In: *Conf. on plant and Process Characteristics, 1956*, pp. 29–55. London: Butterworths.

(41) Lunt, S. T. Process development and plant design. *Trans. Soc. Instrum. Technol.* **9** (3), 87.

(42) 1958 Lunt, S. T. Mobile data logger. *Process Control Automn* **5**, 180–183.

(43) 1961 Anderson, J. A., Glasson, L. W. A. & Lees, F. P. Control of single effect concentrating evaporator. *Trans. Soc. Instrum. Technol.* **13** (1), 21.

(44) 1962 Law, W. M. The dynamic response of shell and tube heat exchangers to flow changes. *Neue Tech.* **4** (1), 34.

(45) 1966 Haagensen, A. J. and Lees, F. P. The frequency response of a plate in a glass absorption column. *Chem. Engng Sci.* **21**, 77.

(46) 1968 Brisk, M. L., Day, R. L., Jones, M. & Warren, J. B. Development of a stirred gas–solid reactor for the measurement of catalyst kinetics. *Trans. Instn chem. Engrs* **46** (1), T3.

(47) Andrew, S. M. Computer processing using Network 67: an example. *Trans. Instn chem. Engrs* **46**, T123.

(48) Andrew, S. M. Computer modelling and optimisation in the design of a complete chemical process. In: *Symposium on the Application of Computers to Chemical Engineering Design*. Instn Chem. Engrs.

(49) 1969 Bush, S. F. The design and operation of single-phase jet-stirred reactors for chemical kinetic studies. *Trans. Instn Chem. Engrs* **47** (3), T59.

(50) Bush, S. F. The measurement and prediction of sustained temperature oscillations in a chemical reactor. *Proc. R. Soc. Lond.* A **309**, 1.

(51) 1973 Halsall, J. R., Kirby, I. J. Media: a continuous digital process control system. *ISA Trans.* **12** (3), 281.

(52) 1976 Barnes, J. G. P. *RTL/2 Design and philosophy*. London: Heyden Press.

(53) Bush, S. F. & Dyer, P. The experimental and computational determination of complex chemical kinetics mechanisms. *Proc. R. Soc. Lond.* A **351**, 33.

# CORRIGENDA

*Biographical Memoirs of Fellows of the Royal Society*

Volume 22 (1976)

ERIC KEIGHTLEY RIDEAL

The following should be added to the Bibliography:

1954 (With J. TADAYON) On overturning and anchoring of monolayers.
I. Overturning and transfer. *Proc. R. Soc. Lond.* A **225**, 346.
II. Surface diffusion. *Proc. R. Soc. Lond.* A **225**, 357.

Volume 24 (1978)

FREDERICK CALLAND WILLIAMS

Page 588, 2nd line:
*for* look-follow radar *read* lock-follow radar.

Page 588, footnote:
The correct title of W. Bennett Lewis is 'Distinguished Professor of Science in the Department of Physics', Queen's University, Kingston. (Not Chancellor.)